GAUTAM SINGH

Intelligent Information Agents

Springer
Berlin
Heidelberg
New York
Barcelona
Hong Kong
London
Milan
Paris
Singapore
Tokyo

Matthias Klusch (Ed.)

Intelligent Information Agents

Agent-Based Information Discovery
and Management on the Internet

With 113 Figures and 22 Tables

 Springer

Editor

Matthias Klusch
Computer Science Department
Technical University of Chemnitz
Strasse der Nationen 62
09107 Chemnitz, Germany
E-mail: klusch@informatik.tu-chemnitz.de
WWW: http://www.informatik.tu-chemnitz.de/~klusch

Cataloging-in-Publication data applied for

Die Deutsche Bibliothek – Cip-Einheitsaufnahme

Intelligent information agents: agent based information discovery
and management on the Internet; with tables/ Matthias Klusch
(ed.). – Berlin; Heidelberg; New York; Barcelona; Hong Kong;
London; Milan; Paris; Singapore; Tokyo: Springer, 1999
ISBN 3-540-65112-8

ACM Subject Classification (1998): I.2.11, C.2, H.2-5

ISBN 3-540-65112-8 Springer-Verlag Berlin Heidelberg New York

Typesetting: Camera-ready by the authors
Cover Design: design + production GmbH, Heidelberg
Printed on acid-free paper   SPIN 10696918   06/3142 – 5 4 3 2 1 0

Foreword

We live in a world that is becoming increasing distributed and service-oriented, and this is reflected in the computer systems we design, build, manage and use. We rely on these systems to support our everyday activities through electronic mail, document interchange and other collaboration technologies.

The Internet and World Wide Web [63] allow us to access multimedia data and knowledge located throughout the world. Clearly, these new technologies present enormous opportunities for posting, finding, organizing and sharing vast amounts of information.

Further, electronic commerce is gaining a foothold on the WWW, and presents a vital complement to the normal business activities conducted by corporations and individuals. New paradigms are emerging for e-commerce, both business-to-business e-commerce and entrepreneurial e-commerce, allowing consumers to be linked directly with producers, and thereby bypassing the traditional "middleperson."

In the real world, our service-oriented approach to doing business leads us to delegate both *responsibility* and *authority* for certain negotiations and decisions to our representatives or agents, such as real-estate agents, stock brokers, personal shoppers, secretaries, etc. The major issues confronting consumers of on-line information include access and availability of information resources, confidence in the veracity of the data provided, and an assessment of the trustworthiness of the provider.

If we extend the metaphor to cyberspace, we would like our collection of trusted and reliable agents to represent us in cyberspace in order to:

- search for, acquire, analyze, integrate, and archive data from multiple heterogeneous distributed sources [19, 127, 152, 157, 230, 361, 724],
- inform users when new data of special interest becomes available [602],
- negotiate for, purchase and receive information, goods and services [334, 335],
- explain the relevance, quality and reliability of that information [448, 449], and
- adapt and evolve to changing conditions [164, 227, 303, 333, 364, 571].

Thus, agents will have a role in our evolving information infrastructure, if they can be useful to people, organizations and information systems.

This book addresses the role of intelligent information agents in advanced information systems. In order for agents to cooperate, they must share common objectives, understand each other, communicate their goals and tasks, and be able to share data, information and knowledge. They may also be part of coordinated groups of agents, organized to cooperate in problem solving. There are two specific areas, among others, that can make use of intelligent agents.

Intelligent Integration of Information

The DARPA-sponsored research program on the "Intelligent Integration of Information" (I*3) focused on the acquisition, integration and dissemination of data, information and knowledge. Principal investigators in the I*3 program produced a three-layer Reference Architecture consisting of various types of services, including facilitation and brokerage services, mediation and integration services, and wrapping and data access services.

This three-layer service architecture is amenable to intelligent agents that can support the services offered at each layer [334]. Several chapters in this book address important topics related to I*3, but much work remains to be done in this area.

Electronic Commerce

Many web sites offer "portals" which serve as "ports of entry" into the Internet and World Wide Web. These include such famous sites as Yahoo, Excite, Altavista, and Netscape, to name a few. They offer users Internet services, such as free e-mail, paging services, stock quotes and tailored news (including tailored ads), as well as other web-based services. The goal is to win "brand loyalty" from their subscribers who then read the numerous advertisements, and sometimes visit advertiser web sites to purchase products.

E-commerce is growing rapidly on the web. Electronic commerce today has several components, including: 1) interactive business and financial transactions, 2) electronic cataloguing, 2) electronic order-tracking services, 3) automatic billing and payment services, 4) electronic funds transfer, 5) vendor registration and electronic "brand naming", 6) automatic ordering, contracting and procurement, 7) advertising of products, 8) data mining of consumer information for customer profiling, and 9) customization of advertisements to have more effective impact on prospective customers.

One very important area is business-to-business e-commerce where companies sell their products directly to their corporate customers. For example the Boeing Company allows airlines to order parts from an integrated, authoritative parts catalog. This 24-hour, seven-days-a-week service allows customers anywhere in the world to access the catalog and make purchases. CISCO Systems, a vendor of network routers, estimates that customers will purchase over 5 billion USD via its web site this year.

One phenomenal organization, Amazon.com Books Inc., sells only via the Web, as opposed to its competitors, such as Barnes and Noble, which have retail outlets as well as a web outpost. At Amazon.com customers can post book reviews and authors can post self-conducted interviews. When a reader makes a selection, titles of *related* books are presented. Customers purchase titles which are then ordered from suppliers, thereby reducing inventory.

Here agents can play an important role in profiling user preferences, suggesting related titles, alerting them when specifically requested titles have arrived, and linking them to this shared "knowledge" space. In addition to a comprehensive catalog of holdings, web sites such as Amazon.com inform users as to inventory availability, and delivery times, thereby allowing users to have confidence that the goods will be delivered in a timely fashion. We need to gain a better understanding of the processes that draw users to web sites, their behavior and interactions with the products and services offered, and the way agents can assist both consumers and producers in forming lasting and productive relationships.

It is this last point, *forming lasting and productive relationships*, that seems to be a driver on the web, and this is very much in keeping with the service-oriented approach to building advanced information systems. We see companies forming strategic alliances to better serve their customers by providing ene-to-end services. The most recent example is America Online's purchase of Netscape Corporation, and its forming a strategic alliance with Sun Microsystems, which contributes a large world-wide sales force and the hardware and software to build and manage Web sites.

This book of very topical and relevant contributions will help us to understand the research and practical issues involved in building **Intelligent Information Agents**, and how to transition them from the research labs into the infrastructure of our advanced information systems.

Larry Kerschberg
Professor and Director of
Center for Information Systems Integration and Evolution
George Mason University
Fairfax, Virginia, USA
December 1998

Preface:
Intelligent Information Agents in Cyberspace

Research and development on intelligent information agents is of rapidly increasing importance. In fact, it can be seen as one of the key technologies for the Internet and the World Wide Web. But what are information agents, and what impact will they have on computing early in the next century?

Roughly speaking, information agents are computational software systems that have access to multiple, heterogeneous and geographically distributed information sources. Such agents may assist their users in finding useful, relevant information; in other words, managing and overcoming the difficulties associated with "information overload". Information agents not only have to provide transparent access to many different information sources in the Internet, but also to be able to retrieve, analyze, manipulate, and integrate heterogeneous data and information on demand, preferably in a just-in-time fashion.

In part, there are many approaches and implemented solutions available from advanced databases, knowledge bases, and distributed information systems technology to meet some of these demands. In addition, effective and efficient access to information on the Web has recently become a critical research area. Limitations of search engines and the presence of semi-structured and unstructured information has led to the development of new query languages and data models. But the development of smart information agents in an open, dynamically changing cyberspace is a more tough challenge. It requires strong expertise from several related research areas, such as Artificial Intelligence (AI), Distributed AI, Information Retrieval, Cognitive Sciences, Computer Supported Collaborative Work (CSCW), and Human-Computer Interaction.

Information agents can be classified into the following broad categories:

- *Non-cooperative* or *cooperative* information agents, depending on their ability to cooperate with each other for the execution of their tasks. Several protocols and methods are available for achieving cooperation among autonomous information agents in different scenarios (see Part I of the book), like hierarchical task delegation, simple or complex contracting, and decentralized negotiation.
- *Rational* information agents (see Part II) are utilitarian in an economic sense. They behave and may even collaborate together to increase their own

benefits. One main application domain of such rational agents is automated trading and electronic commerce in the Internet. Examples include the variety of available ShopBots, and systems for agent-mediated auctions on the Web.

– *Adaptive* information agents (see Part III) are able to adapt themselves to changes in networks and information environments. Examples of such agents are learning personal assistants on the Web.
– *Mobile* information agents (see Part IV) are able to travel autonomously through the Internet. Such agents may enable, e.g., dynamic load balancing in large-scale networks, reduction of data transfer among information servers and applications, and migration of small business logic within medium-range corporate intranets on demand.

Figure 0.1 shows this classification as an extension of Franklin and Gaesser's taxonomy of agents in [222].

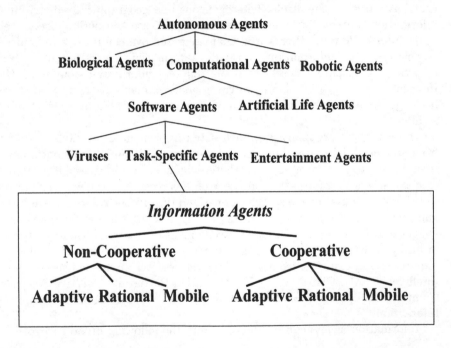

Fig. 0.1. A classification of information agents

Examples for each of the categories of non-cooperative information agents are shown in Fig. 0.2.

References to related literature about and actual links in the Web to these and other information agents can be found throughout the last three parts of the book.

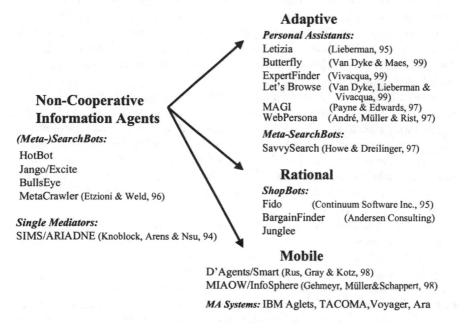

Fig. 0.2. Examples of non-cooperative information agents

Examples for systems of collaborating information agents are presented in detail in the first part (see also [349, 324]). I now briefly discuss the main features, challenges and potential perspectives of intelligent information agents in cyberspace.

Collaboration among Information Agents

The main challenge of collaboration among heterogeneous and autonomous information agents in an open environment is that of mutual understanding. There are already basic frameworks for distributed computing in heterogeneous environments in use [51], like CORBA [692, 144], DCOM [159] and, to a lesser extent, Java RMI. Each of them provides an interface description language and services that allow distributed objects to be defined, located and invoked. They offer mainly high-level services for interconnectivity following the client-server coordination model. The primary benefit of using such frameworks is to encapsulate the heterogeneity of legacy systems and applications within standard, interoperable wrappers. But a common (meta-)knowledge representation and meaningful interaction among agents goes beyond these frameworks.

Additional efforts are required to achieve interoperability among the potentially heterogeneous information agents and systems at all levels in uncertain environments without any global control [500]. Such efforts include the generation and use of ontologies and communication conventions [645, 402, 618, 705, 723], non-proprietary languages for knowledge interchange, and methods for coordinating collaborative work among different agents [292, 293, 496].

Service brokering and matchmaking on the Internet are known techniques to enable collaboration among heterogeneous software agents. Both techniques require in particular a common language for the description and automated processing of advertised and requested capabilities of agents. First steps have been taken in this direction, such as the intelligent use of standardized markup languages, like SGML or XML [742, 650],[1] or suitable agent capability description languages, such as LARKS and its powerful matchmaking process [656, 658].

Another important issue of collaboration that deserves attention is the underlying communication among the agents. A first attempt to arrive at a standardized agent communication language (ACL) emerged from the knowledge sharing project in Stanford and produced the language KQML [204, 205]. Up to now KQML is the only ACL that is implemented and widely used, at least in the academic world. More recently, another effort to come up with a standard ACL has started through the FIPA (Foundation of Intelligent Physical Agents) initiative [206, 207]. Both ACLs base their messages on the theory of speech acts [598], but the outcome is quite different. This is mainly due to the lack of a common consensus on the semantics of the performatives of these ACLs [134].

Collaboration among information agents may also follow some sort of social obligations from given or emerging joint intentions [84, 600, 311, 268], delegation of tasks and responsibilities, or team plans [394, 662, 344]. Related questions concern the modeling of agent roles in different application domains and scenarios, how to analyze relationships among roles, and what types of conversation are needed to achieve agreements among agents to adopt goals for each other in a distributed collaborative environment (see, e.g., [114, 663, 244, 622, 621, 715, 69]).

The complex social interactions involved in human negotiation, cooperation, and teamwork are among the most difficult to adopt by software agents. Research into modeling such interactions and the strategies they entail, how to design rules and semantics for conversations based on the semantics of

---

[1] XML is mainly used to describe the semantics of the content of Web pages. This enables agents to automatically scan these pages, and to find relevant information. It is assumed that provided meta-information (via XML tags) is consistently maintained and interpreted across boundaries.

speech acts, negotiation protocols, auctions, and so on, continues. It is inspired especially by related work from CSCW and cognitive and social sciences [110, 155, 172, 459, 457]. A rough classification of types of cooperation in multi-agent systems is discussed, for example, in [176].

Adaptive in Changing Environments

Modern information environments are mainly open and might change rapidly over time. Thus, the agents have to deal with uncertain, incomplete and vague information in an efficient, reliable way such that they are able to make intelligent decisions on the fly [164].[2]

One approach to achieving more flexible behavior in single information agents or teams of collaborating agents in an open environment is to enable them for gradual adaptation. This means that an agent may cope with any kind of dynamic change, such as change in usable bandwidth or location and content of information sources in the Internet. In addition, if an agent is used as a personal assistant, it is particularly important that it anticipate the user's needs and preferences as quickly and conveniently as possible. In order to achieve this goal, different techniques for user profiling, reputation, and recommendation are used.

Research and development on learning personal assistants or intelligent interface agents on the Web has become very popular, and this will probably continue for the next few years. However, only a few systems of collaborating information agents currently show adaptive behavior (see, e.g., Chapters 13, 14). Strictly speaking, not much is known about the relation between single and multi-agent adaptation, and vice versa. First steps are being taken to investigate how collaborative information agents may learn to coordinate their actions and task execution in different domains (see, e.g., [420, 654, 535, 534, 747] and Chapter 11).

The development of adaptive collaborating information agents remains the main challenge in the areas of multi-agent systems, machine learning [443], and cooperative information systems [509]. Regarding this, the future question will be how an information agent behaves ingeniously, rather than what it looks like.

Interaction with Information Agents

Any progress towards a flexible, more convenient human-agent interaction (HAI) could help to increase the human user's acceptance of information agents for doing his or her everyday business on the Web. Such an interac-

---

[2] Efficient information discovery appears to be a real challenge regarding, e.g., a comprehensive search in the huge indexable Web with its estimated more than 320 million pages [371].

tion includes, e.g., an effective multimedia representation of available information as well as individually sensitive, multi-dimensional navigation within
cyberspace. This relies in particular upon precise information about possibly
different user communities, domains of discourse, tasks and context. Notably,
the impact of virtual user communities in cyberspace and their use of information agents to social interaction and psychological well-being in real life
still remains to be investigated.

Advanced forms of user's guidance through potentially shared virtual information spaces might be realized by, e.g., techniques from Virtual Reality using synthetic characters like animated creatures or believable avatars
[184, 41, 13]. In addition, the development of highly interactive interfaces
may include automated speech and motion recognition such as used for affective computing [527, 679]. Improved interaction among human users and
information agents is also due to the rise of multimedia pushed to a new level
by, e.g., more powerful 3D graphics acceleration and display hardware, significant increase of mass storage capacity, ultra-high performance connections
among sites in the Internet(-2) and standards for multimedia integration on
the Web, like SMIL [634].

HAI and its application to information agents still appears to be un-
charted territory, though some promising steps have been taken in this direction recently [382]. This includes in particular the research efforts in intelligent information interfaces carried out, for example, by projects in the
European I3Net initiative started in 1997 [302].

Agent-Based Trading on the Internet

Electronic commerce on the Internet is steadily growing.[3] The use of simple ShopBots and virtual bookstores on the Web has already become very
popular in the past five years. But more sophisticated agent-based trading
continues to be a key challenge for economists, computer scientists, and business managers alike. It might reshape the way we think about economic
systems and business processes in an increasingly networked world.[4] In open
cyberspace, information agents are paid and have to pay for any services they
provide to their customers. Even network bandwidth has recently become a
traded commodity online [113].

Methods for flexible multilateral contracting, decentralized utility-based
negotiation, and dynamic supply chain management are main components
in the design of rational information agents [714, 559, 240, 711, 455, 582,
209, 712, 583, 242]. Many research efforts are under way in that direction

---

[3] According to the recent Forrester report, worldwide 3.2 trillion USD e-commerce
sales are expected by 2003.

[4] Electronic commerce on the Web might indeed happen without "intelligen" agents
if agent technology fails to be injected into currently emerging Internet-mediated
transaction standards and systems [525].

such as the development of methods for utilitarian coalition formation among autonomous agents [336, 611, 749, 347, 141], agent-mediated auctions, and agent-based marketplaces (see, e.g., Chapters 6, 7, 8). At marketplaces and auctions in the Internet multiple information agents from different providers may meet each other to exchange relevant data for their customers, and to negotiate individual sums as charges for service provision. Even if this appears to be somewhat exotic, it might become a common practice on the Web soon. In fact, online auctions on the Web such as OnSale Exchange [487], FairMarket [199], or AuctionWeb/Ebay [29] have recently started to become popular.

In addition, any emerging consensus on an accounting and pricing structure, such as flat-rate, capacity-based, or usage-sensitive pricing [423], is as important as effective trust and security mechanisms to facilitate e-commerce transactions in a digital economy. In particular, trust must be built up gradually, involving only manageable risks for customers and vendors. This can be achieved without the use of trusted third parties and goes beyond any cryptographic protocol [540, 543].

The situation becomes even more complex when we recall that customers as well as vendors, their products, services, and quality may change rapidly over time. There is still no known satisfactory method which agents may use to react to such changes in an appropriate way.

However, unbridled and unauthorized access to Web users' profiles might be harmful. It could result, e.g., in receiving annoying spam mail, and may even cause criminal acts against users in real life, such as credit card frauds. There is obviously a need for common standards for protocols and methods for secure transactions and privacy of communication. Some of these standards are already in use or on the way, like those for secure electronic transactions (SET), secure sockets layer (SSL3), open profiling (OPS), and the platform for privacy preferences project (P3P) of the Web Consortium [607, 491, 521].

Mobility and Issues of Security

A potential feature of information agents which has recently started to attract great interest is mobility. A mobile agent is programmed to be able to travel autonomously in the Internet from one site to another for the execution of its tasks or queries on different servers. Such agents may reduce network bandwidth usage, and achieve more flexible and efficient information discovery under certain circumstances.

Although there is an ongoing discussion about what characterizes a mobile and intelligent agent, how mobility can be achieved on heterogeneous platforms, and what the payoff from applying mobile agent technology in different application domains will be, it is certainly not science fiction anymore [690, 721, 567], even if for some people it may still sound a bit like that.

In contrast, efforts towards a standardization of mobile agent technology are being made by the Object Management Group (OMG [485, 480]) as well as by FIPA.

In any case, mobility relies basically on appropriate run-time environments allowing different agents to do their work on different servers. Some main related issues concern the assignment of server resources to visiting agents, code persistence, recovery from failures, and platform-independent development of mobile agents [526].

Moreover, in open networks, security problems and the costs of potential solutions might outweigh the benefits of mobility. The question of security goes in both directions (see also Chapter 18 and [252]): How can database servers be protected from malicious actions of mobile agents, and, conversely, how can an information agent, packed with private data and information, be protected from servers and other agents while traveling through cyberspace?

The main application area of mobile agent technology is currently the area of telecommunications [530, 704] where it is being used as a part of the decentralized service architecture of next-generation networks such as TINA [358]. In only a few years, some systems of mobile information agents might be able to operate on heterogeneous and wireless connected hand-held devices as well as wearable intelligent computers [671, 520].

But mobile agent applications are still mainly governed by emotion and misunderstanding, rather than objective decisions. Risks and challenges pointed out in many past discussions about harmful software viruses threatening the Internet come into the mind of users, server administrators and business managers.[5] Thus, there won't be any widespread use of mobile agents for several years until mature standards for their development and security in the Internet have been set up and widely accepted.

A Brief Outlook

Today, there are enough available pieces of different technologies to put things together. In fact, a number of systems of information agents have already been developed in the academic area over the past few years. They just have to wait to make it into the real world of Internet users broadly.

However, since information agent technology emerges across disciplines, it is even bound to encounter some inertia. This is mainly due to problems in adopting and transferring knowledge among different research areas. I believe

---

[5] According to a recent survey by the American Computer Security Institute and the FBI, the average corporate network is attacked by hackers 12 to 15 times each year. And in some companies, up to 98% of attacks go undetected. Even in security-conscious government agencies, more than 70% of the test hacks the Defense Information Systems Agency in Washington, DC, conducted went undetected [174].

that fielded systems of collaborating information agents might show up in cyberspace within the next decade.

The currently most promising application areas of information agents are, among others, distributed Web-based collaborative work, information discovery in heterogenous information sources and intelligent data mangement in the Internet or corporate intranets.

As mentioned before, further research is needed on how interoperability among different information systems and agents can be achieved at all levels. Equally important are approaches for effective interaction with users as well as distributed information retrieval and fusion in sources with semi-structured or multimedia data. In addition, distributed object and component technology is a keystone for the software development of intelligent information agents in scalable corporate information networks.

Making sense of the mass of data and (mis)information that fills the Web is a major AI-hard problem. Notably, none of the known limitations of AI [697] has impeded the development of more or less "intelligent" software agents in a variety of real-world applications, nor will it be in future [215]. Rather, the question is when and to what extent such kinds of agents are used on the Web. And finally, of course, the future of the Web itself, as it is actually governed by the W3C [233] as a kind of moral authority, strongly affects the development of information agents for a broad range of Web-based applications in cyberspace.

This book covers the whole thematic range of intelligent information agents. It has four parts, each of them focusing on a theme of particular relevance in the research area of information agents. These are collaboration, rationality and electronic commerce, adaptivity, mobility and issues of security in the Internet. Each part consists of a short coherent introduction and contributions from leading researchers and experts in the field. I hope that the book will be helpful for researchers, professionals, lecturers, and interested students as well, and that it may inspire some beneficial interdisciplinary research and development of intelligent information agents.

Acknowledgements

First, I would like to thank the authors for their preparation of outstanding contributions, and all people who very carefully reviewed drafts of several parts of this book. Last but not least, I am indebted to Alfred Hofmann and Antje Endemann from Springer-Verlag for their kind assistance and technical support during the whole book project.

Pittsburgh, December 1998   *Matthias Klusch*

Table of Contents

Part I

Cooperative Information Systems and Agents

Introduction

The rapidly accelerating rate of change in today's information-based business environments coupled with increased global competition, makes corporations face new challenges in bringing their products and services to the market. Modern enterprises in medicine, manufacturing, banking, education, environmental management and so on are increasingly dependent on the continuous flow of information for virtually every aspect of their operations. This results in an increasing demand for streamlining of operations, and an efficient, unified access to information resources that are distributed throughout a local or worldwide network. Information agent technology is one of the key technologies for this purpose.

Although the low-level infrastructure has been developed to support interoperability between heterogeneous databases and application programs, this is not sufficient when dealing with higher-level object organizations such as vertical business object frameworks and workflows. Existing multidatabases or federated database systems do not even support any kind of active information discovery. This creates the need for an advanced middleware infrastructure based on the inclusion of "intelligent" software agents, that support higher levels of cooperation and provide the required services.

One idea to build such an infrastructure is to enhance the functionality of stand-alone database or legacy systems by appropriate information agents. This led to the paradigm of so-called *cooperative information systems* (CIS) originated from Papazoglou, Laufmann and Sellis in 1992 [507]. An information agent of a CIS is expected to be smart enough to

- shield the local system it is assigned to from any unauthorized access,
- cooperate on demand with other agents for task or query execution,
- reason about its own and other agents' capabilities, and the environment, and
- actively search for relevant information on behalf of his users.

In the following, we use the notion of a CIS in a weaker sense in that different kinds of collaborating information agents are allowed. Furthermore, we do not assume any exclusive one-to-one assignment of agents to local information sources.

One key challenge of a CIS is to balance the autonomy of databases and legacy systems with the potential payoff of leveraging them by the use of

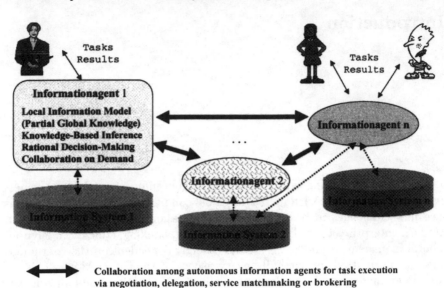

Collaboration among autonomous information agents for task execution
via negotiation, delegation, service matchmaking or brokering

Fig. I.1. Macrostructure of a cooperative information system (CIS)

information agents to perform collaborative work. On the other hand, information agents should collaborate without losing an individually significant degree of autonomy in planning and task execution.

As mentioned in the preface, collaborating information agents can be further classified in terms of their mobility, adaptiveness, or rationality in an economic sense. Some examples for each category are given in Fig. I.2.

What are the main research issues and challenges of collaborating information agents and systems? First of all, information agents in a CIS have to mutually understand each other when they are supposed to perform any kind of meaningful collaborative action. For this purpose methods, tools and languages for knowledge representation and sharing have been developed. Most prominent are common ontologies [257, 489, 746] and agent communication languages (ACL) such as KQML or FIPA ACL[6] [205, 134, 207].

Information agents have to deal with the problem of retrieving and integrating data from heterogeneous sources. In particular, the agents have to be able to resolve semantic conflicts among objects in different information sources, like databases, file systems, or knowledge-base systems. This problem is treated, for example, in the advanced multidatabase research area for years. A comprehensive overview of proposed solutions is given, e.g., in [579]. Most of them rely on, e.g., the use of common or appropriate domain ontologies, thesauri, partial gobal or summary schemata, and meta-data repositories, as

---

[6] Although most ACLs base their messages on the theory of speech acts [598] there still is a lack of consensus on the semantics of the performatives.

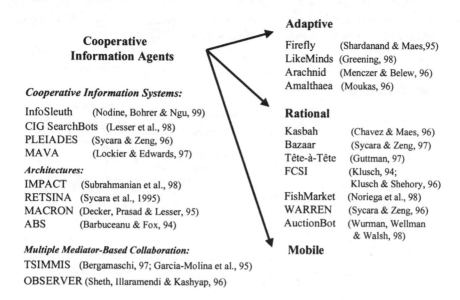

**Cooperative
Information Agents**

Cooperative Information Systems:

InfoSleuth (Nodine, Bohrer & Ngu, 99)
CIG SearchBots (Lesser et al., 98)
PLEIADES (Sycara & Zeng, 96)
MAVA (Lockier & Edwards, 97)
Architectures:
IMPACT (Subrahmanian et al., 98)
RETSINA (Sycara et al., 1995)
MACRON (Decker, Prasad & Lesser, 95)
ABS (Barbuceanu & Fox, 94)

Multiple Mediator-Based Collaboration:
TSIMMIS (Bergamaschi, 97; Garcia-Molina et al., 95)
OBSERVER (Sheth, Illaramendi & Kashyap, 96)

Adaptive

Firefly (Shardanand & Maes,95)
LikeMinds (Greening, 98)
Arachnid (Menczer & Belew, 96)
Amalthaea (Moukas, 96)

Rational

Kasbah (Chavez & Maes, 96)
Bazaar (Sycara & Zeng, 97)
Tête-à-Tête (Guttman, 97)
FCSI (Klusch, 94;
Klusch & Shehory, 96)
FishMarket (Noriega et al., 98)
WARREN (Sycara & Zeng, 96)
AuctionBot (Wurman, Wellman
& Walsh, 98)

Mobile

Fig. I.2. Some examples of cooperative information systems and agents

well as on methods for distributed knowledge discovery [328, 500, 496, 618]. Automated ontology-based interoperation among different intelligent software agents is an inherent issue for research and development of cooperative information systems [645, 402, 705, 723][7].

Main techniques to enable collaboration among heterogeneous information agents in a CIS include *service brokering* and *matchmaking* via middle agents [165, 658, 656, 214, 360]. We differentiate among three types of agents:

1. Provider agents provide their capabilities, e.g., information search services, retail electronic commerce for special products, etc., to their users and other agents.
2. Requester agents consume informations and services offered by provider agents in the system. Requests for any provider agent capabilities have to be sent to a middle agent.
3. Middle agents, i.e., matchmaker or broker agents, mediate among requesters and providers for some mutually beneficial collaboration. Each provider must first register itself with one (or multiple) middle agent. Provider agents advertise their capabilities (advertisements) by sending some appropriate messages describing the kind of service they offer.

---

[7] However, the underlying ontological mismatch problem can be solved in principle only by support from relevant human users and administrators.

Requests and advertisements of agents are specified in a common agent capability description language such as LARKS [658, 656].

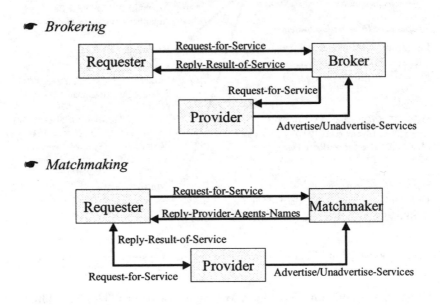

☞ *Brokering*

☞ *Matchmaking*

Fig. I.3. Service brokering and matchmaking in a CIS

Every request a matchmaker or broker receives will be matched with its actual set of advertisements. If the match is successful a matchmaker agent returns a ranked set of appropriate provider agents and the relevant advertisements to the requester. In contrast to a broker agent, a matchmaker does not deal with the task of contacting the relevant providers, transmitting the service request to the service provider and communicating the results to the requester. This avoids data transmission bottlenecks, but it might increase the amount of interaction among agents.

A variety of approaches for coordination strategies, planning and decentralized negotiation protocols for different multi-agent environments exist [670, 479, 564]. Only a few approaches deal with multiple distributed broker or matchmaker agents [314]. Recent work investigate the benefits of learning to choose an appropriate coordination strategy by a single agent in a multi-agent system [534].

On a lower level, frameworks for *distributed computing in heterogeneous environments* are available such as DCOM [159] or CORBA [692, 144]. Each of these frameworks provides an interface description language and services that allow distributed objects to be defined, located and invoked. For example, CORBA enhances traditional RPC-based client/server architectures by allowing relatively transparent distribution of service functionality. However, any meaningful knowledge-based interaction among agents towards intelligent information retrieval and integration goes far beyond these frameworks.

As mentioned in the preface, collaboration among information agents may also follow some sort of social obligations from given or emerging joint intentions [84, 600, 311, 268], delegation of tasks and responsibilities, or team plans [394, 662, 344]. Research into modeling cooperative behavior and entailed strategies continues; related works are inspired in particular from research in CSCW, cognitive and social sciences [110, 155, 621, 622, 459, 457]. Possible types of cooperation in multi-agent systems are discussed, e.g., in [176].

Many past efforts towards an intelligent agent-based integration of information rely on the concept of a *mediator agent* introduced by Wiederhold in 1992 [722, 725]. The main purpose of such an agent is to enable intelligent interoperability among heterogeneous sources. A mediator agent is supported by a set of so-called wrapper agents each of them providing access to a local information source, extracting content from that source and perform appropriate data conversion. In addition, a mediator in a CIS may collaborate with other information agents such as broker or matchmaker agents, ontology agents, and several user interface agents [292, 293]. The mediator

- translates between individual, domain ontologies using a common ontology (maintained by an ontology agent),
- decomposes and executes complex queries on distributed relevant sources with the help of a matchmaker agent, and
- finally composes the partial responses obtained from multiple information sources.

Several mediators, one for each domain of application, may be coordinated by a *facilitator agent*. The perspective of the DARPA I3 (Intelligent Integration of Information) project [153] is to allow federations among such facilitators on demand. However, most implemented mediator-based systems, such as SIMS/ARIADNE [350, 352], ABS [38, 39], InfoSleuth [469] and to some extent TSIMMIS [677, 230, 272], consider scenarios with one central mediator agent collaborating with multiple wrapper agents. The issue of ontology-based collaboration among multiple mediators or facilitators, like in OBSERVER [617] or InfoSleuth II [471, 470], is absent. The same goes for multi-brokering among different agent communities [314]. A centralized, single mediator-based system can hardly be seen as a CIS where multiple heterogeneous and autonomous information agents may collaborate.

The following five chapters provide an overview of cooperative information systems and agents from different perspectives, and report on ongoing, significant research and development in this area (see also [349, 324]).

The Contributions

In Chapter 1, *Michael Papazoglou* and *Willem-Jan van den Heuvel* present a middleware infrastructure which comprises distributed computing facilities and information agents. This middleware supports the development of a CIS in any enterprise framework.

The authors argue that CIS services and applications will be assembled on demand from a montage of legacy applications and other internetworked information sources. These sources have been encapsulated as object components and combined with business objects. Thus, technological advancements can be achieved by leveraging distributed object management technology, and advancing it by more sophisticated software components: intelligent information agents. As mentioned before, such agents are implemented on top of collections of already existing information systems.

Much previous work on information agents has concentrated on the lower-level aspects of information systems, such as connectivity and data access. However, newer, general, and reusable approaches and architectures are now emerging. In Chapter 2, *Michael Huhns* and *Munindar Singh* consider some particular, recent advances in applying multi-agent systems to the area of information systems. These advances take the form of applying various high-level social abstractions for specifying and building agents and multi-agent systems. The applications include manufacturing, electronic commerce, and logistics.

Extraction and fusion of information from multiple, heterogeneous sources of textual data is a challenging research topic not only in the multidatabase area. Any solution of this problem will have an immediate impact on the development of information agents. In particular, meaningful collaboration among agents and the integration of information without using contextual information and founded semantics is almost impossible [500]. The next three chapters present approaches which aim to overcome these problems.

In Chapter 3, *Sonia Bergamaschi* and *Domenico Beneventano* present two ongoing projects towards an intelligent integration of information. They adopt a structural and semantic approach, TSIMMIS (The Stanford IBM Manager of Multiple Information Sources) and MOMIS (Mediator environment for Multiple Information Sources), respectively. Both projects focus on mediator-based information systems.

The authors describe the architecture of a wrapper and how to generate a mediator agent in TSIMMIS. Wrapper agents in TSIMMIS extract informations from a textual source and convert local data into a common data model; the mediator is an integration and refinement tool of data provided by the wrapper agents.

In the second project, MOMIS, a conceptual schema for each source is provided, adopting a common standard model and language. The MOMIS approach uses a description logic (or concept language) for knowledge representation to obtain a semi-automatic generation of a common thesaurus. Clustering techniques are used to build a "unified schema", i.e., a unified view of the data to be used for query processing in distributed, heterogeneous and autonomous databases by a mediator.

Another issue of collaboration among heterogeneous information agents is the management of information in the context of user-specified tasks. Many current systems of information agents lack the ability to get such contextual information or simply use it to automate information filtering.

The RETSINA (Re-Usable Task-Structured Information Agents Architecture) project at Carnegie Mellon University aims to develop a reusable multi-agent software infrastructure that allows heterogeneous agents on the Internet to collaborate with each other to manage information in the context of user-specified tasks. In Chapter 4, *Katia Sycara* provides a brief overview of the RETSINA system architecture and then focuses on its capability for in-context information management. The RETSINA architecture as well as several of its applications in different domains, like portfolio management and office work, is implemented in Java supporting the reuse of agent program code.

In Chapter 5, *Aris Ouksel* presents the SCOPES (Semantic Coordinator Over Parallel Exploration of information Spaces) approach for an intelligent integration of information sources in an open environment. In SCOPES, semantics are seen as a matter of continuing negotiation and evolution in the presence of inconsistent, uncertain and incomplete information.

SCOPES aims to support collaboration among heterogeneous and autonomous structured and semi-structured information sources on the Web. Then, the concepts developed therein are extended to handle multimedia objects, and temporal, spatial and causal relationships. SCOPES is able to leverage knowledge learned in previous interactions and to incrementally improve performance as the number of interactions increases. Particularly interesting in this approach is the use of the Dempster-Shafer theory of evidence to resolve semantic conflicts and to discover dependencies among objects in different database schemas.

1. From Business Processes to Cooperative Information Systems: An Information Agents Perspective

Michael P. Papazoglou and Willem-Jan van den Heuvel

InfoLab, Tilburg University,
PO Box 90153, Tilburg, The Netherlands,
E-Mail: {M.P.Papazoglou,wjheuvel}@kub.nl

1.1 Introduction

Modern enterprises are increasingly dependent on the continuous flow of information for virtually every aspect of their operations. This dependency on critical business information has instigated an increasing demand for globalization, streamlining of operations, and more importantly in a request for unified access to information resources that are distributed throughout a local or worldwide network. In this marketplace, enterprises must look for strategic advantages through computing infrastructures that are engineered for flexibility. It is thus not surprising that nowadays the fastest growing segment of corporate computing is in the area of open, distributed client-server applications. This increasingly decentralized and communication-focused business climate requires new kinds of applications that can be rapidly deployed and used throughout the business organization and outside the enterprise by its partners, suppliers and customers. Innovative companies with good partner relationships are beginning to share sales data, customer buying patterns and future plans with their suppliers and partners. This type of information collaboration requires new computing paradigms that deliver information services that are integrated, open in nature and global in their scope [460], [664].

In order to successfully deploy enterprise-wide client/server solutions and increase collaboration between enterprises and their partners, two major challenges must be addressed:

- Redefinition of company tasks in holistic or *process-oriented terms* that result in innovative process-integrated business solutions. Corporate structures must be shaped around business processes and entire process chains that cross functional or organizational boundaries should be engineered and modeled in such a way that enterprises can integrate all their critical business activities and respond to changes in the market more effectively.
- Deployment of a more sophisticated *middleware infrastructure* that supports company-wide and cross company distributed information processing activities. This infrastructure should naturally promote interoperation between web-enabled applications and a large number of interconnected

legacy information systems, and satisfy a request, irrespectively whether the business logic lies in the legacy system or in an Internet-enabled workflow transaction.

The combination of business process definitions with an advanced middleware infrastructure have the potential to make possible a real acceleration of productivity improvement for inter-networked organizations and will enable new forms of business and work. We briefly highlight aspects of these two critical challenges below, while their integration into an enterprise framework is the concern of this chapter.

To remain competitive in a global market businesses are aligning themselves with other companies and suppliers. This growth in inter-company exchange of information strives to support the comprehensive exploitation of distinctive competencies without leakage at organizational boundaries. Hence, it requires the effective integration of business routines and processes not only internally but also across organizations. This novel approach cuts square through the traditional organization since it requires a shift from functionally organized enterprises (vertical organization) to process-centered businesses (horizontal organization) [308]. Accordingly, it demands new forms of flexible, modular business processes that can be easily adapted to the individual needs of the customers and become more responsive to changes in the market [156, 270].

To meet the architectural requirements of modern organizations, and get better reuse from software, distributed object programming is the preferred solution. Coupled with powerful networks, distributed object computing can create a new class of enterprise application that is flexible, powerful, and relatively easy to maintain and upgrade. Although distributed object technology provides the means for distributed communication and messaging, it does not provide yet appropriate support for higher-level (semantically-oriented) business constructs, e.g., business processes and workflows. Recently, there has been a lot of interest in extending distributed object frameworks such as CORBA with business objects (Business Object Facility (BOF) as proposed by the OMG [101]). Business objects can be the key building block in the re-engineered company as they can realize domain business processes and default business logic that can be used to start building applications in these domains. Furthermore, domain specific models can be designed as business frameworks so they can be easily extended and modified, e.g., SAP and IBM's San Francisco business objects. These can be deployed for integrated enterprise-wide applications that can be easily built upon distributed broker architectures such as CORBA.

Currently, distributed object technology, e.g., DCOM, CORBA and distributed Java, provide interface description languages and services that allow distributed objects to be defined, located and invoked. The primary benefit of using them is to encapsulate the heterogeneity of legacy systems and applications within standard, interoperable wrappers. To allow such components to effectively interconnect high-level business objects, business process and workflow applications with low-level legacy wrapper objects, in a way that respects business semantics, new technologies need to be developed. Another major challenge is to permit continuous enhancement and evolution of current massive investments in information sources and systems. In summary, this infrastructure must support the migration of large numbers of independent multi-vendor databases, knowledge bases, and application software into dynamic and highly connected (evolvable) components running over distributed information networks. All these are challenges for the next generation of information systems. We call such systems *Cooperative Information Systems*.

The remainder of this chapter is organized as follows. In the next section, we introduce the (conceptual) enterprise framework. This framework provides in a layered, object-oriented model of the organization. In Section 3, we introduce critical enterprise elements such as business objects, business processes and policies, and workflows. Subsequently, we discuss integration of legacy systems and business processes and present a methodology for linking business and legacy objects. Section 4 discusses the improved middleware infrastructure comprising distributed computing facilities and information agents to support the high-level constructs required for the enterprise framework. Finally Section 5, presents our conclusions.

1.2 The Enterprise Framework

In this section, we present the enterprise framework, or conceptual architecture, that can be used to structure a *particular vertical* business domain. A vertical business domain, or a tower, represents one specific type of businesses such as automotive, health care, financial services, chemical and pharmaceutical, telecommunications and so on. Vertical domains (or business domain orientation [91]) concern the tailoring of business services with respect to application domain requirements and standards to meet the unique requirements of the domain as well as application interoperability. Vertical domain-orientation involves not only just standards within a particular domain (e.g., sales logistics) but also across multiple-domains, since value-added chains are usually not confined to a single domain. For example, sales logistics involves order handling, shipping, contracting, billing, customer consignment, stock handling and so on.

The architecture that we present in this chapter, is based on similar enterprise architectures that can be found elsewhere in literature: [538], [1], [626], [147] and [591]. The architecture is stratified and inherently object-oriented: higher layers inherit and specialize characteristics and behavior from the lower-layer(s).

The enterprise framework can provide an ideal base for the effective encapsulation of business practices, policies, and tactics in modular high-level components. This leads to the design, testing, and deployment of new networked applications in less time and considerably less effort than traditional development methods.

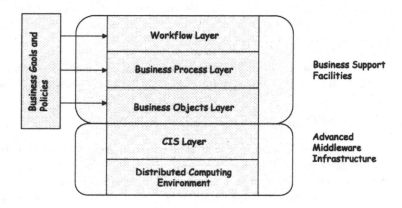

Fig. 1.1. The Enterprise Framework

It is convenient to view an enterprise framework as comprising two dimensions corresponding to the critical factors that we addressed in Section 1.1, namely business support facilities and middleware infrastructure (see figure 1.1). Each of these comprises in its turn a number of layers.

The business support facilities comprise the following three layers:

– The workflow layer.
– The business processes layer.
– The business objects layer.

The middleware infrastructure comprises the following two layers:

– The cooperative information systems layer.
– The distributed object infrastructure and services layer.

1.3 The Business Support Facilities

Before we discuss the layers comprising the business support facilities, we will give definitions of some of the key concepts used in this section.

Business object: A business object is defined as the representation an entity that is active in a business domain. It includes the business name and definition including attributes, behavior, relationships, business rules, policies and constraints [183].

Business process: A set of one or more linked activities which collectively realize a business objective according to organization constraints and policies within the context of an organizational structure defining functional
roles (authorization/responsibilities) and relationships.

Workflow: The automation of a business process, during which information
or tasks are passed from one participant (or process) to another for action,
according to set of procedural rules.

We will start our description of the business support facilities by outlining
the characteristics of its most elementary component, the business objects.

1.3.1 Business Objects

Business objects provide a natural way for describing application-independent
concepts such as product, order, fiscal calendar, customer, payment and the
like. The business objects play a central role in capturing the semantics of
actual business entities and processes, in a way that is understandable by
the business [414], [91]. Business objects are still objects with object-oriented
characteristics such as encapsulation, polymorphism, inheritance, etc [626].
Business-critical distributed object technology is used to assemble systems
where objects are located across a variety of physical platforms and environments, and where business-critical levels of data manageability and integrity
is ensured.

Business objects (BOs) can be conceptual, i.e., analysis/design objects,
as well as implementation objects, e.g., implemented in Java. The conceptual, or model business objects can be used as a core concept in enterprise
models. These are models that can be used to model the business processes,
recourses, people, goals, policies and constraints within an enterprise. Examples of enterprise (reference) models can be found in: [591], [147], [190].
Such enterprise models are constructed during the strategic modeling phase
of the software life-cycle [247] which takes place before the analysis phase.
The implementation business objects, that are based on the design BOs, are
independent, language neutral and persistent objects that require a software
infrastructure to run [626]. Ideally, there is a one to one mapping between
the conceptual business objects and the implementation business objects.
However, distributed runtime applications have additional requirements like
utility objects and a separation of concerns, e.g. the Model-View framework
which handles the interactions between model and view objects [183].

Business objects communicate with each other at a semantic level and
encapsulate the meta-data and business rules associated with the specific
business entity they describe. Such business rules are related to the manner that organizational objectives are modeled. By defining applications in
terms of business objects, enterprise-wide definitions and behaviors can be
enforced for all applications. Obtaining agreements between enterprises on
business object definitions is necessary to enable networked, e.g., electronic

commerce applications, such as the connection of one enterprise's ordering to another enterprise's delivery of goods and service processes. For these types of applications appropriate names and descriptions of products in a particular (vertical) market are generated by means of a standard ontology [508]. The semantic definition of the meaning of each trade element or product is then stored in a concept dictionary.

The Business Object Domain Task Force (BODTF) of the OMG has proposed a standardization initiative for Common Business Objects (CBOs) [101] that addresses some of the issues mentioned above. CBOs standardize the semantics of business objects in a particular business domain or a specific region [101]. Until now the BODTF has only provided syntax to describe the interface of a business object in an uniform manner by means of a Component Definition Language (CDL). However, truly semantic standards for domain-specific CBOs are also needed.

1.3.2 Business Processes

A business process is the definition of a set of interrelated activities that collectively accomplish a specific business objective, possibly, according to a a set of pre-specified policies. The purpose of this layer is to provide *generic business processes*. These provide a set of basic building blocks for an application in a specific business domain, e.g., procurement management, general ledger, etc. These building blocks can be specialized and extended to capture domain or application specific processes which are realized at the workflow layer. Business processes can be conceptual as well as implementation, e.g., Java, objects. Examples of implementation business processes can be found in the San Francisco framework [1].

Typical examples of generic business processes common to multiple applications, include retail (shopping, order fulfillment, and shipping), business-to-business (procurement, order entry, inventory and supply chain management, and logistics) functions. These can be specialized to cater for the needs of different kinds of applications. The core business processes are identified by looking at various application implementations in the domain and identifying those processes that are needed by most of the applications in that domain, e.g., San Francisco general ledger. Understanding and streamlining business processes is crucial in successful workflow implementations that follow.

Business processes are initiated by events that trigger activities in the organization [56], [147]. These events can be internal (e.g., rules) or external (e.g., customer requests). The business processes are initiated on the basis of an incoming event (e.g., a customer request), and result in an outgoing event (e.g., the notification that a product is ordered). Business processes operate on business objects, i.e., they change their states. Business processes are conceptual in nature and usually comprise three elements: an *activity*, a *transition* and *decisions* [183]. Every business process consists of one or more activities. Activities can follow each other, therefore a transition occurs when one activity finishes and hands control over to another activity. A transition may depend on a decision that has associated conditions.

We can identify three types of business processes: operational business processes, recourse processes and management processes. Operational business processes are the only kind of business processes that are related to the primary business value-added chains, e.g., to optimally manage merchandise flow and operating costs in order to improve customer service and profitability. The recourse processes are non-core activities that support the operational and management processes. Lastly, the management processes consist of controlling and planning activities. These three types generally will be mixed to implement a certain business workflow. The separation between operational processes and management (control and coordination) is essential to workflow systems that we discuss in the next subsection. The workflow has to be managed in such a way that the operational processes minimize the consumption of available resources, e.g., parallel synchronized services between distributed workflows [506].

1.3.3 Workflows

The workflow layer provides the means for developing inter-business, or networked, applications which interconnect and manage communication among disparate business applications and put the business processes in motion. For instance, workflows provide the opportunity to automate business processes and provide continuity between a customer requiring service, and the production of these services. Another distinguishing feature of a *distributed workflow* is assigning activities to actors according to the state of each process in progress and moving the process forward from one activity to the next. Workflow applications rely on an extensive foundation of reusable components, viz. the core business processes, that form the basis for building new applications. Workflow-enabled business processes track transactions across, department, company and enterprise boundaries. This type of distributed workflow layer provides the sequence of business activities, arrangement for the delivery of work to the appropriate inter-organizational resources, tracking of the status of business activities, coordination of the flow of information of (inter and intra-) organizational activities and the possibility to decide among alternative execution paths [506].

The workflow layer allows users to develop control scripts to manage the execution of sequences of operations that relate to particular business objects and processes. The workflow service lets you model distributed (networked) applications to match a certain business procedure. Workflow activities invoke existing applications, e.g., legacy objects, and connect those with newly developed applications. Several of the workflow activities have a transactional nature which requires long running interactions. A transactional workflow uses distributed system services, particularly transaction monitor services in conjunction with a business rules-based control script that brokers requests to drive large-scale compound transaction processing applications. It allows a user request to weave multiple application programs, views of data, and interact with numerous business objects and services.

The workflow layer typically provides the user-interface that manages the communication sessions between a human client and one or more of the distributed applications and remote database servers across many different platforms and organizations. Web browsers provide a natural facility for interfacing to applications and distributed data.

1.3.4 Representing Business Policies

It is important that business objects and business processes, in a business, application are designed so as to include elements of the business mission of an organization. The business mission is abstract and oriented towards the environment in which the organization operates. The business mission describes, for example, the product-market combination in which the business will be active, the market share the organization tries to gain, and so on. The business mission can be made concrete in business strategies described in terms of critical success factors. These quantifiable factors can, on their turn, be used as a starting point for the business goals [56]. In the end, the business goals must be satisfied by the business activities in the form of constraints or rules, also collectively referred to as *business policies.* Business policies can be used to define various implementations of the same business process, e.g., policies for credit or order management. The business policies must be defined in coherence with the business goals. Figure 1.2 illustrates how the organization structure, business processes and policies can be mapped to the enterprise framework depicted in figure 1.1. In summary, the combination of the business activities and their constraints, the business policies/rules, defines the business processes and operating constraints of the organization.

Business policies impact all levels of the enterprise framework ranging from company wide policies that impact the workflow level, to the object specific policies that constrain the business object level. At the lowest level, business policies can have an effect on the way in which the methods of a business objects are implemented. The policies can place certain constraints on these methods. An example of a policy at the business object level is a discount-policy for a customer business object. For example: a special "10%" discount of the "Discount-Policy" class may be invoked for regular customers of a manufacturing firm. Policies can be implemented in two ways. Either by hard-coding the policy in the business object or by extending the behavior of a business object by a policy object construct that defines the policy constraints. The first approach is rigid and does not cater for evolution of business policies. Changes in business operations need only be reflected in the business rules (policy object) and not throughout an entire application.

Business policies can also be defined at the business process, or business task level. In this case, the business policies prescribe the behavior of all

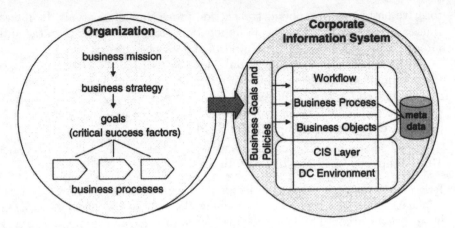

Fig. 1.2. Mapping of organizational structure and activities into information systems.

business objects in the business process. More specifically, the business policy defines constraints on the interaction pattern between the business objects. Such policies can again be implemented by means of a business process policy object that can be easily adapted to changing process requirements, e.g., changed government legislation. An example of a business policies that applies to the process level is a stock-order policy (just-in-time) for the order process business object. The order business policy could be concerned with ordering products at particular sides/plants, at specific times, with specific quantities.

Lastly, at the business workflow level, the policies can be used to describe the constraints of relations between the various business tasks. For example: one order-handling management workflow policy could be that regular customers only have to make use of the "check order details" and "deliver" business processes, whereas new customers first need a "solid credit check".

1.3.5 The Enterprise Application Domain Framework

In recent years a lot of activities have concentrated on what constitutes a good design practice [217]. From these studies it became evident that there are significant groups of capabilities that are common within a particular application domain. These capabilities support the core business processes performed by any business within this domain. Such consideration gave rise to the concept of an *enterprise application framework* [228, 217]. An enterprise application framework is a set of classes representing business entities that capture a reusable design for a specific type of core business problem and cooperate to implement it. In other words, a framework is a complete generic application that users can customize or extend to address particular needs. A framework captures the design decisions that are common to its application domain, e.g., financial services. Frameworks are important elements that allow the development of networked applications as they provide standard business objects that can be used across applications (in a vertical domain). They also emphasize that the range of semantic protocols that must exist to support forms of information systems cooperation must generally be based on a unified design approach, together with consistent standards [414].

Frameworks emphasize providing reusable design guidance, rather than code reuse, for developing large-scale systems. The reusability of design itself has a significant effect on the overall development cost of a system, far more than the reuse of individual software components. Frameworks are quite different from class libraries as they include dynamic aspects which are totally missing from class libraries. Frameworks embody business processes, architectural elements of a particular business domain model and include application flow and business logic built in this model. Frameworks can also be used on the system level. For example, the Taligent Application Environment [661] provides application-level frameworks for text and graphics editing, and support frameworks for networking, device drivers, file system and I/O support. In this way we can develop, for instance, an accounting application based on the combination of tested standard frameworks such as an accounting specific framework, a user-interface and a persistent object storage framework. The use of frameworks is becoming increasingly common and influential. For example, higher-level business frameworks are at this moment being developed in the San Francisco project at IBM [1].

1.3.6 Change Management

To remain competitive organizations must be able to move fast and quickly adapt to change. Such changes must be mapped to the business object level and related to already existing enterprise models. Organizations are subject to many changes, for example on the basis of external stimuli like changing tax regulations. One can distinguish between four types of change [149]: technology changes, product and service changes, structure and system changes and people changes. Of particular interest are structure and system changes since they relate to changes with concern business policies, structure and information systems in an organization.

In the enterprise framework described herein, we take the classical organizational view that business changes are initiated by changes to business goals. We can identify various degrees of specificity of the enterprise goals, starting at the highest level of abstraction, the strategic goals to the most specific operational goals [398]. The strategic business goals describe the long-term goals of an organization. The strategic goals are translated in tactical goals, that define the business processes, recourses and organizational structure. Since the enterprise framework described in figure 1.1 focuses on the business processes in the organization, it is only natural to link the organizational goals to business processes and their business rules (policies) (see figure 1.2).

Various approaches towards linking the organizational goals to business activities have been identified in the literature. Two of these approaches, most relevant to the work described in the chapter, are outlined below.

- The Enterprise Knowledge Development (EKD) approach represents an organization as a set of cooperating business processes that satisfy business goals [331], [397]. The business processes are defined in terms of involved actors, that can play certain roles to execute activities on objects according to well-defined rules. The business goals are decomposed in more specific, operational goals and linked to the roles. For example the role "Credit Handler" could be linked to the business process "Credit Application".
- The i*-framework [744], [745] perceives organizations as cooperating agents. The agents in an organization are dependent on each other in order to fulfill the organizational goals. Yu distinguishes between four types of dependencies: goal dependencies, task dependencies, recourse dependencies and soft goal dependencies.

These approaches can be used to map the enterprise model (the left circle in figure 1.2) to the corporate information system model (the right circle). Constructs in both domains are isomorphic: business concepts that are identified in the organizational domain have the same characteristics and behavior as in the systems domain. Changes in the business goals will percolate down to the lower levels of the enterprise architecture, and, the corporate information system architecture, since the business goals are linked to the business processes (workflows).

When developing a framework for change management we distinguish between three types of changes: *active* change management (planned change), *reactive* change management (unplanned change), and *pro-active* change (making the system responsive to reactive change) [434]. With active change management the current model of reality is compared with the model of new reality, then the differences are identified and implemented into a new business model which encompasses the current business model, see figure 1.3.

Reactive changes consist of reverse engineering the changed reality (in terms of a business model), and re-implementing, if necessary, the supporting systems. With reactive changes systems are changed directly without resorting to any new business model. With active changes new business models and system implementations can be introduced in a piecemeal and controlled manner, while with reactive change these happen in a rather ad-hoc manner. It is generally accepted that the systems in the business should be pro-active: they should be capable of coping with unplanned changes [434]. In Section 1.3.8 we describe a pro-active approach to change management based on componentization and the reuse of business functions from legacy systems.

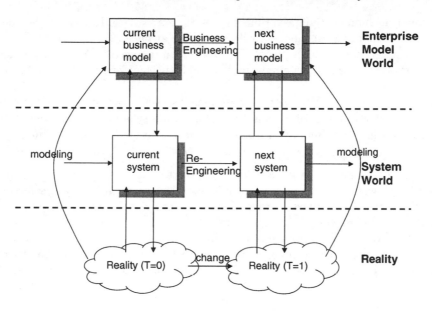

Fig. 1.3. The Relation between the Enterprise and System Domain

1.3.7 Business Support Facilities and Legacy Systems

In an enterprise framework there is a pressing demand to integrate business-driven processes with legacy perspectives, processes and applications. Legacy systems are systems that are critical for the day-to-day functioning of an organization, they normally comprise monolithic applications that consist of millions of lines of code in older programming languages (e.g., COBOL), are technically obsolete with a poor performance and hard to adapt and maintain [681].

We can identify various types of legacy systems, ranging from highly decomposable legacy systems to monolithic (non-decomposable) systems [92], [681]. The highly decomposable systems can be decomposed in user interface components, application components and database components. However, it is not likely that most of the legacy systems will meet these requirements. Various ways to deal with legacy systems are discussed in the literature [92], [681], [632]:

– Ignore. This strategy should be followed in case the legacy system has a low business value and a low technical condition [632], for example if the legacy system is non-decomposable.
– Rebuild from scratch. This strategy has two variants: the chicken little and the cold turkey option. In case of the chicken little approach, the organization gradually migrates from the legacy environment to the target environment. The communication between the legacy and target environ-

ment is channeled via a various (types of) gateway(s). In case of the cold turkey approach, the system will be replace at once.

- Selectively integrate in place. This option can be used if one wants to use (part of) the legacy system in current and future implementations by access in place.
- Data warehouse. Yet another approach to tackle the legacy problem is by the development of a "shadow" information systems that can generate frequently asked (mainly statistical) information for reporting to management.

The approach that we describe in the next section is based on the third strategy selective access-integration in place since we integrate a only selective portions of legacy programs and databases with new business components, and not with the entire legacy system.

The most useful approach to combining business objects with legacy systems is by applying wrapping techniques to legacy systems and treat them as legacy objects. The advantages of this technique are briefly described in Section 1.4.1.

1.3.8 A Methodology for Binding Business Application Objects to Legacy Systems

Enterprises need flexible, modular business processes that can easily be configured to meet the demands of business and technology changes. As already explained in preceding sections, when developing applications based on business objects and processes it is important to address two factors: (a) requirements for change so that business information systems can evolve over time, and (b) the linking of business objects with legacy information systems. The common aim of these two requirements is the integration of new, and existing (legacy), business components with a running application. In both cases there is a need for the added business components to interoperate seamlessly with components present in the current execution environment. This should happen without the risk of disrupting the application or business process it models, thus, facilitating the graceful, incremental, evolution of complex systems.

One important characteristic of business object technology, that contributes to the critical challenge described above, is the explicit separation of interface and implementation of a class. Business objects technology takes this concept a step further by supporting *interface evolution* in a way that allows the interfaces of classes to evolve without necessarily affecting the clients of the modified class. This is enabled by minimizing the coupling between business components. Client and server classes are not explicitly bound to each other, rather messages are trapped at run-time by a semantic data object that enforces the binding at the level of parameter passing semantics [183]. The key aspect of this mechanism is that messages are *self-defining* as the message name is maintained in the request, and the parameter names are defined in the semantic data object that is also passed in the request. This mechanism is greatly facilitated by the use of a Component Definition Language (CDL) which defines a component's contractual interfaces with potential clients. In the following we will restrict ourselves to describing a methodology for combining business objects with legacy systems. The same approach can be employed for coping with changes to existing business objects.

Most of the approaches to integrate legacy systems with modern applications are designed around the idea that data residing in a variety of legacy database systems and applications represents a collection of entities that describe various parts of the operations of a business. Moreover, they assume that by objectifying (wrapping) and combining these entities in a coherent manner with legacy functionality, legacy systems can be readily used in place. In this way it is expected that the complexities surrounding the modern usage of legacy data and applications can be effectively reduced. However, these approaches do not take into account the evolutionary nature of business and the continual changes of business processes and policies. Although part of the functionality of a legacy system can be readily used many of its business processes and policies may have changed with the passage of time. A critical challenge is therefore to identify the reusable and modifiable portions (functionality and data) of a legacy system and combine them with modern business objects in a piecemeal and consistent manner. These ideas point to a methodology that facilitates pro-active change management of business objects that can easily retrofitted to accommodate selective functionality from legacy information systems.

The *BALES* (binding Business Application objects to LEgacy Systems) methodology that we are developing has as its main objective to link parameterizable business objects with legacy objects. Legacy objects serve as conceptual repositories of extracted (wrapped) legacy data and functionality. These objects are, just like business objects, described by means of their interfaces rather then their implementation. Business objects in the BALES methodology are configured so that part of their implementation is supplied by legacy objects. This means that their interfaces are parameterizable (or self-describing) to allow these objects to evolve by accommodating upgrades or adjustments in their structure and behavior. In the following we highlight some of the aspects of this methodology.

The BALES methodology borrows ideas from the object-oriented application development literature based on *use cases* [307], [308] and *task scripts* [247]. BALES combines ideas from business process re-engineering [270], [156] with concepts from the area of enterprise modeling [591], [744]. Moreover, BALES also borrows ideas from more contemporary approaches in the field of Enterprise Recourse Planning (ERP) package development, e.g., the San Francisco-project of IBM. The BALES-method combines three phases:

1. Forward engineering the business;
2. Backward engineering the legacy systems;
3. Mapping the backward and forward engineered models to each other.

We use a simple example to illustrate the BALES mapping methodology. The vertical domain that has been chosen consists of a simplified ordering process, that is presently developed by synthesizing business objects and a set of legacy systems, see figure 1.4. The upper part of the figure, shows

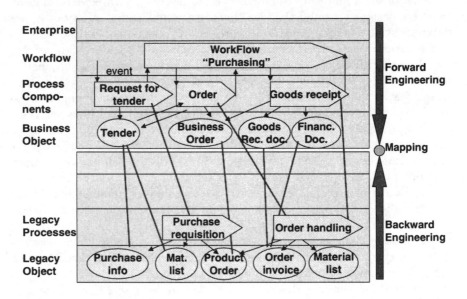

Fig. 1.4. The BALES methodology.

the results of the forward engineering of the business domain (phase 1) in terms of the enterprise architecture that we represented in Section 2. The forward engineering activity results in interface descriptions of the business objects and processes. The lower part of the picture, represents the reverse engineering part.

In the second phase of the BALES-methodology, we reverse engineer the legacy components and processes and decide which parts can be reused. Subsequently, data and functionality are pulled together and wrapped in legacy objects. The binding phase occurs where the two arrows in figure 1.4 meet. This phase indicates that business objects like "tender" and "business order" are partly implemented by means of the legacy objects "purchase information" and "material source", and "product order", respectively. Hence, the interfaces of the business objects such as "tender" are defined by linking them to the interfaces of the legacy objects "purchase information" and "material list" and to any auxiliary objects that are needed to adjust the structure and behavior of the legacy objects.

To formally describe the interfaces of business and legacy objects we use a variant of CDL that has been developed by the BODTF of the OMG [154]. CDL is declarative specification language (a superset of OMG IDL) that is used to describe composite behavior of communities of related business objects. A specification in CDL defines business object interfaces, structural relationships between business objects, collective behavior of communities of business objects and temporal dependencies [154]. An object defined using CDL can be implemented using any (legacy) programming language as long as there exists a CDL mapping for that language. In the following we give an example of an CDL-definition for the "business_order" business process object in figure 1.4.

```
#include metamodel.cdl
module Workflow_purchasing {
model Process_order {

// forward references
entity Tender;
entity Business_order;

// DEFINITION OF THE BUSINESS_ORDER ENTITY

 [keys={orderID}] entity Business_order {
 relationship ordered_for Many Product inverse ordered_by;

 attribute int orderNr;
 [required] attribute String productName, supplierName,
                     supplierAddress, supplierLocation;

 // Do state transition for placing an order
  apply StateTransition order_being_placed {
    trigger = place_order;
    source = input; // set state to input
    target = placed; // set state to placed
 };

 // Require that the customer has credit when the order is placed
  apply invariant Check_credit {
    trigger = placed;
    guard = (order_total < ordered_for.credit_available);
 };

process Order {
 relationship the_notification References Shipping_Notification;
 attribute int quantity;

  // import manage_order from LO
  this -> Order_handling.Order_processing.Product_order.
       Manage_Order;
```

```
      // add to it the following invariant (business policy)
      apply Invariant Check_Stock {
        trigger = Order.placed;
        guard = quantity < ordered_products.Stock_level;
      }
    }; // end process Business_order

  }; //end business_order entity

}; // end process_order model

// Model descriptions for other business_processes/-objects
.............
.............

}; // end workflow_module
```

The CDL specification for the business object "Business_Order" includes a reference to the legacy object "Product_Order". This is achieved by parameterizing the process "Order" in the business object with the legacy process "Manage_Order". Note that the business process "Order" includes an additional invariant "Check_stock" which is applied to its legacy counterpart.

The interface of the legacy component is also described below in CDL for reasons of completeness. Here we assume that the legacy objects have been created by applying the process of reverse engineering to legacy systems and by combining and objectifying appropriate legacy data and functionality.

```
#include metamodel.cdl
module Order_handling {
 model Order_processing {

 // forward references
 entity Product_order;
 entity Order_invoice;

 // DEFINITION OF THE PRODUCT_ORDER ENTITY

  [keys={orderID}] entity Product_order  {
  relationship ordered_for Many Product inverse ordered_by;
  relationship invoiced_by_for Many Invoice inverse refers_to;

  attribute int orderNr;
  [required] attribute String product_name, supplierfirstName,
  supplierLastName, supplierAddress, supplierLocation,
  supplierTelephone;


   process Manage_Order {
     relationship the_product_order References Product_order;
     relationship the_order_invoice References Order_invoice;
```

```
    relationship the_material_source_list References Material list;

    state ordering{input, placed, check_invoice, reject_order}

  }; // end process manage_order

}; // end product_order entity

// Model descriptions for other legacy processes/-objects
.............

}; // end module
```

Although the above example is very simplistic it indicates the usefulness
of the BALES approach. To facilitate the parameterization and eventual mapping of business objects with legacy objects functionality we may extend CDL
with some querying facilities based, for example, on some form of a logical
formalism like an object variant of Telos [456].

The BALES methodology can also be used to combine standard ERP
packages like SAP R/3 [147] or San Francisco [1] with legacy and other business objects. These result in business objects which have no legacy components. ERP objects arc also represented using CDL.

1.4 The Advanced Middleware Infrastructure

In this section we describe the advanced middleware infrastructure starting
from its most elementary part, the distributed system services layer.

1.4.1 Distributed System Services Layer

This layer sits above the network and communication protocol layers, and
comprises a host of critical middleware communications, program-to-program,
and data management services. These facilities are realized through distributed objects. Distributed objects form a natural model for the distributed
computing infrastructure by providing a reliable communications/messaging
infrastructure. Distributed objects address the heterogeneous aspects of the
distributed computing infrastructure because the messages that are sent to
distribute objects depend on their interfaces and not on their internal structure. In addition, distributed objects can also accommodate autonomy characteristics as they may change independently and transparently, provided
that their interfaces are maintained. These characteristics allow objects to
be used in the development of new component systems in the enterprise
framework (openness) as well as to encapsulate access to legacy systems; two
key aspects of a distributed infrastructure in support of business objects.

Distributed application development and interoperability considerations have been taken into account by OMG's CORBA, whose mission is to define interfaces for interoperable software using distributed object technology. CORBA's distributed object approach enables diverse types of implementations to interoperate at the same level, hiding idiosynchracies and supporting component reuse. This interoperability is accomplished through well-defined interface specifications at the application level. CORBA's Object Request Broker (ORB) functions as a communications infrastructure, transparently relaying object requests across distributed heterogeneous environments. CORBA currently provides many services including naming, security, persistence and so on. Moreover, CORBA 2.0 defines a backbone protocol specified to allow interoperability among different ORB implementations. The Internet Inter-ORB Protocol (IIOP) specifies a series of messages for communication between ORBs and maps them to TCP/IP services. These facilities can form a natural framework to support the distributed computing infrastructure. However, there two additional important facilities that need to be provided by the distributed computing infrastructure, namely: wrapping and transaction monitor facilities.

Object wrapping is the practice of implementing a software architecture given pre-existing heterogeneous components. Object wrapping allows mixing legacy systems with newly developed applications by providing access to the legacy systems. The wrapper specifies services that can be invoked on legacy objects by completely hiding implementation details. It provides external applications a clean legacy API that supports a host of abstract services irrespective of the complexity of internal representations of the legacy systems. The legacy API is the software access path to the legacy implementations' supported functions. The advantage of this approach is that it promotes conceptual simplicity and language transparency. This technological advancement can be achieved by harnessing the emerging distributed object management technology and by appropriately compartmentalizing existing software and applications. For example, a simple layer of software mapping the legacy APIs to, for example, CORBA IDL, provides for broader system interoperation and distribution of legacy system services through CORBA. Encapsulation is used to partition and componentize legacy systems. Each component can be objectified separately, and then the system can be re-integrated using object-based messaging. The benefits of this approach is that each component can be reused, and system upgrades can happen incrementally.

An area of growing interest for the distributed computing infrastructure is the integration of ORBs with Distributed Transaction Processing (DTP) monitors such for example Encina and Tuxedo. DTPs are important to enterprise-wide and cross-enterprise applications in which a business procedure may be broken into a set of processes, each of which may consist of several business events. Events can consist of one or more transactions that can span a variety of interconnected database resource managers. DTPs provide an open environment that supports a variety of client applications, databases, legacy systems, networks and communications options. DTPs provide both an API for development of transaction applications and a facility for more efficient execution. Monitors can support large numbers of users requesting concurrent access to transaction programs and services, e.g., database, security, workflow; balance local and distributed loads to optimize performance; and efficiently synchronize data updates to multiple databases during transaction using standard protocols [12]. DTPs create a logical ensemble of interactions ensuring that the business transaction is secure and reliable, and is completed with integrity. They are also able to run nested transactions that can span many resources while allowing failures to be trapped and retried using an alternative method which still allows the main transaction to succeed.

1.4.2 Cooperative Information System Layer

Business objects are used to design systems that mimic the business processes they support. In the real world, business events are seldom isolated to a single business object. Instead, they typically involve groups of interacting objects. To mimic their real-world counterparts, business objects must be able to communicate with each other at the semantic level. Although the distributed computing infrastructure offers the fundamentals of low-level interopability, e.g., distributed message passing, concurrency, binding, naming, and so on, issues like semantic interoperability, exchange of knowledge, formation of ontology based collections of information systems, reflection and introspection facilities are lacking from the distributed systems services layer. Such advanced facilities would enormously ease the development of business objects and workflow applications through the deployment of mission-critical information systems from reusable software components. These systems interoperate seamlessly at a semantic level with modern running applications.

Distributed workflow applications (see Section 1.3.3) track business transactions across unit, company and enterprise boundaries, thus, they must possess the ability to assemble information services on demand from a montage of networked legacy applications and information sources comprising business objects and possibly ERP package applications. In Section 1.3.8 we described a methodology to compose business objects out of existing legacy systems and explained that legacy objects are objectified legacy data and functionality. It has to be understood that these legacy objects can be synthesized out of a large number of related heterogeneous legacy systems after discovering the appropriate information sources; applying syntactic/semantic-reconciliation and translation between diverse data representations; solving ontological mismatch problems; aligning functionality and rectifying data inconsistencies; and partially integrating the data and functionality. A promising approach to this problem is to compose business objects and enact workflows by providing an execution environment realized by means of an organized collection of cooperating information agents [507], [351]. A networked system that comprises a large number of information agents, each having a particular narrow area of specialization, e.g., tender, order handling, goods processing, etc, that work cooperatively to solve a complex problem in a vertical domain is called a Cooperative Information System (CIS).

In each vertical domain tackled by a CIS network, there is:

- *distribution of data:* purchase information, product order information and invoices.
- *distribution of control:* each individual business process is responsible for performing a set of tasks, e.g., order processing or goods shipping.
- *distribution of expertise:* a business process's knowledge, e.g., order handling, is quite different from that of another, e.g., request for tender.
- *spatial distribution of resources:* a legacy information system may be responsible for providing information and functionality about purchase requisitions while a remote ERP package may provide financial or accounting activity services.

In situations like these information agents provide a natural way of executing workflow scenarios involving business objects and their interactions. A CIS network posses the capability of breaking apart a complex workflow enabled application, comprising business processes and objects, to the level of specialized information agents. Subsequently, the information agents plan for the efficient fulfillment of parts of the application, using a montage of legacy and current generation systems information sources, e.g., modern databases and ERP packages, through coordinated interaction and exchange of information. Information agents make certain that the cooperating application components (legacy and business objects) understand the format of the application that they are sharing and the rules governing its exchange. To accomplish a complex task, an information agent uses an incremental processing style, which might include recruiting other agents in the process of task execution in a dynamic and opportunistic way. This agent capability assumes that an information agent can invoke the functionality of other such agents, see figure 1.5. The information sources underlying a CIS network are referred to as its *component information systems*.

CIS computing is concerned with combining appropriately information agents (both humans and computers) working cooperatively over space and time to solve a variety of complex problems in medicine, engineering, finance, banking, commercial enterprises and so on by providing the semantic support infrastructure for high-level elements such as business objects, business processes and workflows. In this new computing paradigm, the classical client/server model is extended to a more dynamic and versatile architecture. Individual information agents support users in effectively performing complicated tasks – e.g., medical diagnosis, engineering design, banking decision making – efficiently using the most appropriate information and computing resources (be they processing, knowledge and/or data) available in large computer networks. Moreover, they will be in a position to dynamically change their role in the client/server relationship: at times they may function as recipients of information services, from other application-supporting agents, and at other times they will serve as providers.

1.4.3 Characteristics of CIS

The following list outlines some of the most important dimensions of functionality and behavior that we expect CIS to provide us with.

1. A CIS exhibits a flat structure of its component information systems where sources of responsibility alternate depending on where the posed problem originates from. Loosely speaking we can think of this approach as being opportunistic. This should be contrasted with tightly coupled database topologies where there is a single logical source of authority, viz. the global manager.
2. Component systems in a CIS can be used in unanticipated combinations which are determined by the nature of the problem addressed.

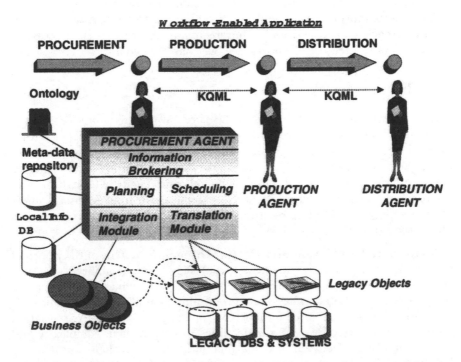

Fig. 1.5. Connecting Workflows and processes and business objects to information agents.

3. A CIS comprises a large collection of pre-existing component information systems with each having its own domain of expertise, problem solving capabilities, structure and terminology. These need to be brought to a level of lateral understanding (both structurally as well as semantically) in order to be able interact, coordinate their activities and achieve cooperation in a pairwise manner.

4. CIS are highly dynamic environments. They address a set of problems that are beyond the capabilities and expertise of individual component information systems and which require the synergy of a collection of component information systems to be solved. In these environments, information agents should know about their capabilities and should exchange knowledge and information with other such systems to achieve cooperation. This should be contrasted with the static approaches taken by federated or multi-database systems which address a fixed set of problems.

5. CIS have an unprecedented impact on all aspects of a modern organization and will have particular influence on how cooperative business modeling should be conducted in distributed organizations. It is necessary to have an understanding of the organizational environment, its goals and policies, so that the resulting systems will work effectively together with human agents to achieve a common objective. Therefore new modeling tools and methodologies are required to address the problems of change management and requirements engineering in the context of large distributed organizations, see Sections 1.2 and 1.3.

1.4.4 Information Agents

Information agent in a CIS are "coarse" in that they comprise a number of modular pieces of software that combines several competencies. Each information agent is essentially another information source, however, it draws on already existing information repositories and applications and combines them with organizational and business model components. Through the CIS approach, inter-networked information systems move from a passive information supplying role to more pro-active and agile systems that can reason about their functionality and competence.

Information Translation and Partial Integration. One of the principal characteristics of information agents is that they have the ability to act as a translation agent by homogenizing heterogeneous legacy information systems (e.g., older generation databases and programming applications) and provide an abstraction of these in the form of a wrapped legacy objects. A translation module provides data presentation facilities to reduce client complexity and conversion of data between incompatible data representations, formats and languages. The translation/wrapper module of an information agent provides the appropriate interface code (and translation facilities) which allows an existing information source to conform to the conventions of an organization. Standard ontologies provide the basis for rectifying terminology mismatches. Mismatches can be dealt with by means of a common ontology and translators that provide mappings to the terms used in the interfaces of the related BOs.

Once diverse representations originating from heterogeneous information systems have been homogenized the following step is to selectively integrate semantically interrelated legacy data into cohesive legacy objects. These legacy objects are then combined with business objects in the enterprise framework. These virtual objects provide the connections to underlying legacy data and functionality. Thus the integration module is another important module of an information agent which provides consolidated access to distributed data and services by aggregating various types of data and functions, see figure 1.5.

The translation and integration modules provide the core support facilities for building new workflow-based applications by mapping services into a collection of host distributed information systems and applications.

Information Brokering. Another important characteristic of an information agent is the ability to act as an information broker in order to discover the appropriate information sources and support services (i.e., wrapper enabled services) in order to fulfill an organizational requirement or a user's needs. Information brokers in a CIS provide facilities such as locating other information agents that are required to solve a common problem, e.g., sales and distribution processing, by name (white pages), by capabilities (yellow pages), content-based routing or problem decomposition. To achieve this purpose an agent must have a model of its own domain of expertise, the *agent expertise model*, and a model of the other agents that can provide relevant information the agent *awareness model* [313]. These two models constitute the knowledge model of an agent and are used to determine how to process a request that comes for example from an integration module.

Each agent is specialized to single area of expertise and provides access to the available information sources in that domain. This results in the formations of clusters (or groups) of information sources around domains of expertise handled by their respective information agents, see figure 1.5. The expertise model does not need to contain a complete description of the other agents capabilities, but rather only those portions which may directly relevant when handling a request that can not be serviced locally. This approach provides conceptual simplicity, enhances scalability and makes interactions in a large collection of information sources become tractable.

Currently there is widespread interest in using ontologies as a basis for modeling an agent's expertise model [723], [436], [328]. An ontology can be defined as a linguistic representation of a conceptualization of some domain of knowledge. This ontology consists of abstract descriptions of classes of objects in a vertical domain, relationships between these classes, terminology descriptions and other domain specific information and establishes a common vocabulary for interacting with an information agent and its underlying information sources. The information sources in the network describe both their contents and their relationship in accordance with an ontology [509]. Hence an ontology can be viewed as some form of a knowledge representation scheme.

Both expertise and awareness models may be expressed in some concept representation language such as Loom [422], or KL-ONE [83] and be formalized by using concept lattices [727] (a formal method based on a set-theoretical model for concepts and conceptual hierarchies). An example of the use of concept oriented languages for building ontologies can be found in [328].

Self-Representation Abilities. As already explained, one of the most challenging problems to be addressed by cooperative information systems is the development of a methodology that opens up the general process of constructing and managing objects based on dispersed and pre-existing networked information sources. Activities such as object integration, message forking to multiple object subcomponents, scheduling, locking and transaction management are until now totally hidden and performed in an ad hoc manner depending on the application demands. What is needed is the ability to work with abstractions that express naturally and directly system aspects and then combine these into a final meaningful implementation.

Such ideas can benefit tremendously from techniques found in reflection and meta-object protocols. The concepts behind meta-object protocols may be usefully transferred to cooperating systems. Core cooperative tasks, carried out in an ad-hoc manner up to now, can be performed using meta-level facilities. These can be used to separate implementation, e.g., issues relating to distribution of control and resources, from domain representation concerns and to reveal the former in a modifiable and natural way [182]. Therefore, information agents may provide a general coordination and policy framework for application construction and management of legacy and business objects, one that allows particular construction and management policies to be developed and applied in a controlled manner. This results in self-describing, dynamic and reconfigurable agents that facilitate the composition (specification and implementation) of large-scale distributed applications, by drawing upon (and possibly specializing) the functionality of already existing information sources.

Agent Communication Languages and Protocols. In order to perform their tasks effectively, information agents depend heavily on expressive communication with other agents, not only to perform requests, but also to propagate their information capabilities. Moreover, since an information agent is an autonomous entity, it must negotiate with other agents to gain access to other sources and capabilities. The process of negotiation can be stateful and may consist of a "conversation sequence", where multiple messages are exchanged according to some prescribed protocol.

To enable the expressive communication and negotiation required, a number of research efforts have concentrated on knowledge sharing techniques [513]. To organize communications between agents a language that contains brokering performatives can be particularly useful. For example, the Knowledge Query and Manipulation Language (KQML) [204] can be used to allow information agents to assert interests in information services, advertise their own services, and explicitly delegate tasks or requests for assistance from other agents. KQML's brokering performatives provide the basic message types that can be combined to implement a variety of agent communication protocols. This type of language can be used for both communication and negotiation purposes and provides the basis for developing a variety of inter-agent communications protocols that enable information agents to collectively cooperate in sharing information.

Scripting Facilities. Rather than relying on a monolithic application, cooperative information systems will consist of a suite of cooperating business objects (see Section 2). These objects can be linked together via scripts written in a scripting language which is needed to describe and execute arbitrary tasks. This makes it possible to design new kind of collaborative, viz. workflow-enabled, applications that can be controlled through scripts and semantic events. Semantic events provide a form of messaging that business objects can use to dynamically request services and information from each other.

Scripting is a critical element for allowing developers to automate the interaction of several business object applications to contribute to the accomplishment of a particular common task. Scripting technology is essential for agents, workflows, and cooperative (long-lived) transactions. Scripting languages provide added flexibility as they use late binding mechanisms and can, thus, attach scripts dynamically to component business objects. Accordingly, they provide the means for creating ad-hoc (dynamic) collaborations between business components and processes which is the very essence of cooperative applications.

1.5 Concluding Remarks

Cross-enterprise business-critical applications are networked applications developed due to an increasing demand for globalization, streamlining of operations, and more importantly due to a request for unified access to distributed information resources. Most of the networked applications that are being developed presently are based on distributed object concepts. These applications combine two very powerful concepts to deliver business value: object orientation and distributed systems. This chapter has claimed that although the low-level infrastructure has been developed to support interoperability between disparate pre-existing databases and application programs, this is not sufficient when dealing with higher-level object organizations such as vertical business object frameworks and workflows. The combination of such high-level components creates the need for an infrastructure which provides a necessary foundation for the inclusion of "intelligent" software modules that support higher levels of cooperation.

We argued that cooperative information system services and applications will be assembled on demand from a montage of legacy applications and other internetworked information sources that have been encapsulated as object components and combined with business objects. Thus technological advancements can be achieved by leveraging distributed object management technology and advance it by developing more sophisticated software attachments, viz. the information agents, implemented on top of collections of already existing information systems. This new technology combine a variety of functions required for supporting workflow enactments comprising interacting business objects and processes in modern enterprise frameworks, while also catering for evolution in response to market changes.

2. Social Abstractions for Information Agents

Munindar P. Singh[1] and Michael N. Huhns[2]

[1] Department of Computer Science, North Carolina State University,
Raleigh, NC 27695-7534, USA.
E-Mail: singh@ncsu.edu
[2] Department of Electrical and Computer Engineering, University of
South Carolina, Columbia, SC 29208, USA.
E-Mail: huhns@sc.edu

2.1 Introduction

Most of the modern applications of computing technology arise in large-scale, open, information-rich environments. Open environments are distinguished by fact of having a number of networked and interrelated, but heterogeneous, information resources. The applications include ubiquitous information access, electronic commerce, virtual enterprises, logistics, and sensor integration, to name but a few. These applications differ from conventional database applications not only in the nature and variety of information they involve, but also in including a significant component that is beyond the information system. An information system must inevitably perform its immediate duties: create, store, transform, use, and dispose of information. However, as the above applications suggest, there is a large world outside the realm of pure information where reside physical and economic objects and organizational processes that manipulate them.

Early work on information-rich environments naturally enough focused on infrastructural issues, but as those issues have come to be resolved, attention is increasing on the high-level aspects more naturally addressed in an agent context. We define *information agents* as the agents that exist and act in such environments. We show that this definition is more general than typically studied, and we show how systems of multiple information agents can be specified and built from the social level.

Even with information agents, previous work has focused on some of the simpler aspects of distributed computing and databases. Many of the features that make agents a worthwhile metaphor for computer science have not been deeply investigated yet. These features include the sociability of agents, which is the theme of this chapter. We describe some social abstractions for agents that are centered around the notion of social commitments. Social commitments have garnered much attention in the literature on theoretical aspects of multiagent systems. In this chapter, we show how commitments can be part of a practical architecture for information-rich environments, and can be applied to a range of interesting problems. To give a flavor for the social abstractions in information access, we discuss a reconstruction of the

MINDS system, one of the first adaptive multiagent systems applied to the problem of building a referral network for cooperative information access. To show how the social abstractions fit even more directly into information update, we discuss two examples on electronic commerce and virtual enterprises, which were prototyped, albeit in a rather simple manner, using the above abstractions.

Organization

Section 2.2 introduces the key themes in information-rich environments and motivates a notion of coherence-preserving information agents. Section 2.3 describes social abstractions centered around the notion of social commitments. Section 2.4 discusses the problem of interoperation in cooperative information systems and shows how commitments may be used to specify the requirements for interoperation. Section 2.5 applies these notions to applications in referral networks, electronic commerce, and virtual enterprises. Section 2.6 concludes with a discussion of future directions.

2.2 Key Concepts

In order to discuss social abstractions for information agents, we first discuss information-rich environments and then some important aspects of information agents in which our approach differs from more conventional approaches.

2.2.1 Information-Rich Environments

Information-rich environments have been around for a long time. We previously defined them in broad terms as environments consisting of a large number and variety of distributed and heterogeneous information sources [294]. The associated applications are varied. They include the purely informational ones, such as database access, information malls, workflow management, electronic commerce, and virtual enterprises. They also include the information component of physical applications, such as distributed sensing, manufacturing, transportation, energy distribution, and telecommunications. Information-rich environments have the following properties. They

- Span boundaries of ownership and control, that is, they inherently have an interenterprise scope
- Include components of various designs and construction, that is, they are heterogeneous
- Comprise information resources that can be added or removed in a loosely structured manner
- Lack global control of the accuracy of the contents of those resources
- Incorporate intricate interdependencies among their components.

Information-rich environments may often involve a significant physical or social component. However, they are amenable to specialized multiagent systems, termed *Cooperative Information Systems (CISs)*, which are multiagent systems with organizational and database abstractions geared to open environments (see also Section 1.4). A typical CIS, as shown in Figure 2.1, includes an environment consisting of a variety of information resources, coupled with some kind of a semantic directory or ontology for the domain of interest. Some of these are described in Section 2.4. The semantic directory contains descriptive information about the resources, including any constraints that apply to their joint behaviors. Each component of the environment, as well as its human user(s), is modeled as associated with an agent. The agents capture and enforce the requirements of their associated parties. The agents interact with one another appropriately, and help achieve the robustness and flexibility that is necessary for effective operation.

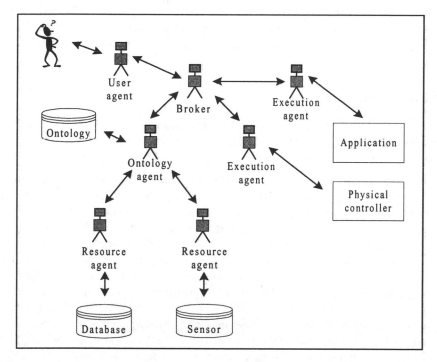

Fig. 2.1. A schematic view of a Cooperative Information System

Information access involves finding, retrieving, and fusing information from a number of heterogeneous sources. At the level of abstraction that concerns CIS, we are not concerned with network connectivity or the formatting variations of data access languages. Rather, our concern is with the meaning of the information stored. It is possible, and indeed common, that when different databases store information on related topics, each provides a different model of it. The databases might use different terms, for example, *employee* or *staff*, to refer to the same concept. Worse still, they might use the same term to have different meanings. For example, one database may use *employee* to mean anyone currently on the payroll, whereas another may use *employee* to mean anyone currently receiving benefits. The former will include assigned contractors; the latter will include retirees. Consequently, merging information meaningfully is nontrivial. The problem is exacerbated by advances in communication infrastructures and increases in competitive pressures, because different companies or divisions of a large company, which previously proceeded independently of one another, are now expected to have some linkage with each other.

The linkages can be thought of as semantic mappings between the application (which consumes or produces information) and the various databases. If the application somehow knows that *employee* from one database has a certain meaning, it can insert appropriate tests to eliminate the records it does not need. Clearly, this approach would be a nightmare to maintain: the slightest changes in a database would require modifying all the applications that consume its results!

2.2.2 Information Agents

Approaches based on agents and multiagent systems are natural for information-rich environments [296], but there are three major definitional matters that come up that must be resolved.

– The first is the quite routine issue of the definition of agents. Numerous definitions of agents are known in the literature [222, 294, 524]. Indeed, the only agreement seems to be that there is a range of definitions! Some of the important properties of agents include autonomy, adaptability, and interactiveness, but exceptions reveal that an agent need not have these properties. However, we believe that agents *must* be capable of interacting with other agents at the social or communicative level [291, 294]. We distinguish social or communicative interactions from incidental interactions that agents might have as a consequence of existing and functioning in a shared environment [295]. Independently, Wegner has also argued that interaction is a key extension beyond traditional computer science [703].[1]
– The second is the less contentious matter of the definition of information agents. Information agents are loosely defined as agents who help find information. In most work, agents play the role primarily of accessing resources and retrieving information from them. However, a better view of information agents is as agents who manage information. This view is not entirely

---

[1] As a practical instantiation of these requirements, an agent, when queried appropriately, should be able to state its name, date of creation, type (and its version), and the identity of its instantiator (or the equivalent).

inconsistent with current work. However, it is an important enough distinction and therefore emphasized here. There are two main reasons why the ability of agents to make updates is significant:

- The agents are applied in settings where the information they gather is fed into a larger process in the enterprise or virtual enterprise in which it functions. This information flow happens, for example, in the case of applications that involve commerce among the various participants or the construction of artifacts, such as in configuring mechanical parts.
- The agents must maintain knowledge about each other in order to coordinate successfully and to assist or compete with others as appropriate. Consequently, even if the agents only retrieve information that the user directly cares about, they may perform updates on their internal data structures. These "hidden" updates are extremely important for the effective and efficient performance of desired tasks. Their presence, however, changes the true model of the information access from mere retrieval to management.
- Applications in information-rich environments belie an important and common assumption of traditional information environments. Traditional environments are centered around databases (treated here not as arbitrary collections of data, but rather those that are built and accessed using a database management system (DBMS) [185]). Databases, through the transaction concept, are designed to ensure that the stored data remains consistent despite any number of concurrent users and despite any kinds of application failures [249]. Consistency is, of course, a desirable property and is essential in applications such as those involving banking.

However, there is an implied assumption in the traditional work, which is that consistency is essential for all applications. It turns out that this assumption is readily falsified in information-rich environments for the following reasons:

- The mutual consistency of autonomous information sources would usually be an unrealistic expectation. When information is to be accessed from several independent sources, the most we can hope for in general is that all of the sources and the partial results generated from them be relevant to the information request. Ideally, a smart information agent may be able to synthesize the partial results into a reasonable argument that supports or refutes some claim.
- When the information is gathered in a multiagent system whose member agents maintain knowledge about each other, the choice of the agents with which an agent interacts is often not governed by their mutual consistency, but by the expected structure or suitability of the combination of the resulting answers.
- When the information gatherers are part of a larger process, there may be additional organizational requirements. For example, if the agents are updating information sources, they might wish to coordinate these updates.

More importantly, if the information sources are not updated by the agents but change anyway—due to other factors—the agents might still benefit from informing each other of those changes. For instance, an agent in electronic commerce may notify the agents of potential customers of the change in price or unexpected delays in availability.

For the above reasons, we argue that a more applicable theme in open environments is *coherence*. This is not to suggest that consistency is undesirable. For example, in electronic commerce, orders should still be billed consistently. However, in cases of failures in the underlying information or exceptions arising due to unexpected events in the physical environment, the loss of consistency can be rendered harmless if coherence is preserved. This situation corresponds to human organizations, which manage to survive and function well despite inconsistencies, because they have procedures for recovering from a variety of inconsistencies. Consequently, consistency, while still useful, has a much reduced role in the kinds of applications that are the most important in open environments.

2.3 Social Abstractions

We hinted above that the notion of process in information-rich environments is richer and more flexible than in conventional settings. Indeed, traditional abstractions such as database transactions are notoriously unsuited for representing and managing flexible processes. Accordingly, we have been pursuing a research program termed *Interaction-Oriented Programming (IOP)* to develop and study primitives for the specification of systems of agents and constraints on their behavior. These primitives include societies, the roles agents may play in them, what capabilities and commitments the roles require and what authorities they grant. Agents can autonomously instantiate abstract societies by adopting roles in them. The creation, operation, and dissolution of societies are achieved by agents acting autonomously, but satisfying their commitments. A commitment can be canceled, provided the agent then satisfies the metacommitments applying to its cancelation.

The representations for IOP must support several functionalities, which typically exist informally, and are either effected by humans in some unprincipled way, are hard-coded in applications, or are buried in operating procedures and manuals. Information typically exists in data stores, or in the environment, or with interacting entities. Existing approaches do not model the interactive aspects of the above. The IOP contribution is that it (a) enhances and formalizes ideas from different disciplines (especially, databases, distributed computing, and distributed artificial intelligence); (b) separates these ideas out in an explicit conceptual metamodel to use as a basis for programming and for programming methodologies; and (c) develops schedulers and other infrastructure to program with those ideas.

The notion of commitments may be familiar from databases. However, in databases, commitments correspond to a value being declared and are identified with the successful termination of a transaction. When a transaction terminates successfully, it commits, but it is not around any longer to modify its commitments. Thus, the commitments are rigid and irrevocable. If the data value committed by one transaction must be modified, a separate, logically independent transaction must be executed to commit the modified value. Traditional commitments presuppose that different computations are fully isolated and that locks can be held long enough that the atomicity of distributed computations can be assured. Thus programmers are pretty much on their own when they wish to go beyond the scope of a single, brief transactions. Because of the above reasons, traditional commitments—although suitable for traditional data processing—are highly undesirable for modern applications, such as electronic commerce and virtual enterprises, where autonomous entities must carry out prolonged interactions with one another [629].

Fundamentally, commitments reflect an inherent tension between predictability and flexibility. By having commitments, agents become easier to deal with. Also, the desired commitments serve as a sort of requirement on the construction of the agents who meet those commitments. However, commitments reduce the options available to an agent. With the above motivation, we propose an alternative characterization of commitments that is better suited to agents and multiagent systems. In our formulation, the commitments are directed to specific parties in a specific context. Thus, an agent might not offer the same commitments to every other agent. The context is the multiagent system within which the given agents interact. An agent or multiagent system with jurisdiction over some resources and agents is called a *sphere of commitment (SoCom)*. Briefly, a commitment $C(x, y, p, G)$ simply relates a debtor x, a creditor y, a context G, and a condition p. The *debtor* refers to the agent who makes a commitment, and the *creditor* to the agent who receives the commitment. Commitments are formed in a *context*, which is given by the enclosing SoCom (or, ultimately, by society at large). The condition is what is being committed to.

To emphasize that the above conception of commitments is flexible, we define the following six key operations on commitments.

O1. *Create* instantiates a commitment. It is typically performed as a consequence of an agent adopting a role or by exercising a social policy (explained below).

O2. *Discharge* satisfies the commitment. It is performed by the debtor concurrently with the actions that lead to the given condition being satisfied.

O3. *Cancel* revokes the commitment. It can be performed by the debtor.

O4. *Release* essentially eliminates the commitment. This operation is distinguished from both *discharge* and *cancel*, because *release* does not mean success or failure of the given commitment, although it lets the debtor off the hook. The *release* action may be performed by the context or the creditor of the given commitment.

O5. *Delegate* shifts the role of debtor to another agent within the same context, and can be performed by the new debtor or the context.

O6. *Assign* transfers a commitment to another creditor within the same context, and can be performed by the present creditor or the context.

Importantly, the above operations enable commitments to be manipulated quite flexibly. In particular, the *cancel* operation deviates from the very notion of irrevocable commitments. But if commitments can be canceled, how do we make sure that they are still commitments? The obvious idea is to ensure commitments cannot be arbitrarily canceled (or otherwise manipulated). In our approach, we define additional constraints on the above operations as *social policies*. Policies are conditional expressions involving commitments and operations on commitments. Policies have a modeling significance, which is that they can add uniformity to how operations are executed. They have a computational significance in that they can be known to the participants from the start, that is, when they sign up to play a particular role in a multiagent system. Indeed, agents can commit to social policies just as to other expressions; in this case, the agents' commitments are higher order, and are termed *metacommitments*. An example metacommitment is $cancel(x, \mathsf{C}(x, y, p, G)) \Rightarrow create(x, \mathsf{C}(x, y, q, G))$, which means that x can cancel his commitment for p if instead he adopts a commitment for q (for suitable p and q). Although we shall not get into the formalism in this expository paper, the above expression gives a flavor for the kinds of requirements that a designer may impose upon a multiagent system being designed.

2.4 Commitments for Interoperation

A number of architectures for cooperative information systems, which can be thought of simply as multiagent systems in information-rich environments, have been proposed. These architectures not only allow a cooperative information system to be constructed and managed, but also can be seen as paradigms for achieving interoperation. Despite small variations, these architectures are converging to a more or less "standard" pattern. This pattern is based on the idea of mediators, as proposed by Wiederhold [725].

A mediator is a simplified agent that acts on behalf of a set of information resources or applications. The basic idea is that the mediator is responsible for mapping the resources or applications to the rest of the world. Mediators thus shield the different components of the system from each other. To construct mediators effectively requires some common representation or *ontology* describing the meanings of the resources and applications they connect [514]. It is a sign of their maturity that cooperative information systems are beginning to evolve a standard set of agent types. These are identified in Figure 2.1.

- *User agents*, which contain mechanisms to select an ontology; support a variety of interchangeable user interfaces, such as query forms, graphical query tools, menu-driven query builders, and query languages; support a variety of interchangeable result browsers and visualization tools; maintain models of other agents; and, provide access to other information resources, such as data analysis tools, workflows, and concept learning tools.
- *Broker agents* implement a "yellow pages" and "white pages" directory service for locating appropriate agents with appropriate capabilities. Brokers manage a namespace service, and may have the ability to store and forward messages, and locate message recipients. Broker agents also function as communication aides, by managing communications among the various agents, databases, and application programs in the environment.
- *Resource agents* come in a variety of common types, depending on which resource they are representing, and provide a variety of capabilities. Wrappers implement common communication protocols and translate into and from local access languages. For example, a local data-manipulation language might be SQL for relational databases or OSQL for object-oriented databases. Database agents manage specific information resources. Data analysis agents apply machine learning techniques to form logical concepts from data or use statistical techniques to perform data mining. Resource agents apply the mappings that relate each information resource to a common context to perform a translation of message semantics. At most n sets of mappings and n resource agents are needed for interoperation among n resources and applications, as opposed to $n(n-1)$ mappings that would be needed for direct pairwise interactions among n resources without agents.
- *Execution agents*, which might be implemented as rule-based knowledge systems, for example, in CLIPS, are employed to supervise query execution; operate as script-based agents to support scenario-based analyses; execute workflows, which might extend over the web and might be expressed in a format such as the one specified by the Workflow Management Coalition [740].
- *Mediators* are specialized execution agents. With help from brokers, mediators determine which resources might have relevant information for the query at hand; decompose queries to be handled by multiple agents; combine the partial responses obtained from multiple resources; and translate between ontologies.
- *Ontology agents* are essential for interoperation. They provide a common context as a semantic grounding, which agents can then use to relate their individual terminologies; provide (remote) access to multiple ontologies; and manage the distributed evolution and growth of ontologies.

The resultant architecture of standard agent types renders development and deployment of CISs much easier, and essentially raises the abstraction level at which CISs can be described. Most agent-based information systems incorporate one or more agents of the above types. This standard architecture described above and any of its variants help resolve some important issues in the design of multiagent systems. These issues are

- Deciding the main functionalities that could be provided as part of the routine infrastructure on which domain-specific and application-specific solutions may be readily built; the functionalities would ideally be available in reusable toolkits, but do not necessarily have to be.
- Determining how each agent may interface with other agents, such as how an agent may register with or unregister from a broker.
- Determining the normal control flow in an application.

The standard architecture and its constituent agent types have some useful properties. Mediators generalize naturally from the traditional client-server architecture used in database-centric information systems. Brokers and directories can provide useful services in helping find agents with specified names or supported capabilities. There is also a semantic aspect to effective interoperation. The above architecture addresses that aspect through the notion of ontologies and ontology agents. An ontology can provide a shared basis for the exchange of information among agents, and can thus help reduce or eliminate the effects of terminological discrepancies.

However, there is yet another aspect of interoperation, which may be termed *pragmatic*. This aspect involves how the agents interact with each other, and goes beyond the exchange and comprehension of the terms used in the individual messages. The pragmatic aspect deals with the high-level protocols governing how the agents should interact. It has a normative force to it, and requires that the agents behave felicitously. In other words, the pragmatic aspect is what deals with the coherence requirements of the cooperative information system being designed.

Having a separate specification of the coherence requirements can be easily accomplished by specifying an abstract multiagent system in terms of the roles required for instantiating that multiagent system. For each role, we can specify the coherent behaviors in terms of the commitments entered into and satisfied by any agent playing the role under different circumstances. This specification serves two important purposes.

- The clear specification of coherence requirements is an important step in the design of a system, and corresponds roughly to the capturing of the important use-cases [218] in traditional software engineering [537].
- The coherence requirements can be used as a touchstone for evaluating agents contributed by different vendors. Any agent that is touted as being able to play a role in a certain abstract system must be able to satisfy the coherence requirements for the system as those requirements reflect on the given role. A (more or less) objective test for suitability and compliance with requirements is the key to true interoperation in open settings, where

we would expect the agents to be contributed by independent vendors and to belong to different people or commercial interests. A multiagent system can thus be incrementally modified while executing as long as the agents being added met the coherence requirements.

Our prototype system applies commitments as follows. Initially, abstract SoComs are defined in terms of their *roles*. Each role is associated with the capabilities it requires, the commitments it engenders, and the authorities it creates. The capabilities are the tasks the agent can do, the commitments are what the agent must do, and the authorities are what the agent may do. The commitments associated with a role are metacommitments, which reduce to base-level commitments when the agents are acting according to the role.

At some point, possibly during execution, an agent may decide to enter into a SoCom as a particular role or roles. To do so, the agent would have to cause the SoCom to be instantiated from the abstract specification. To adopt a role, the agent must have the necessary capabilities, and accept the associated commitments. In doing so, he also obtains the authorities to properly play the role. The agent must then behave according to the commitments. Agents can join a SoCom when configured by humans or during execution: such flexibility at run-time requires publishing the definition of the abstract SoCom.

2.5 Applications

We begin with a reconstruction of the MINDS system as a referral network with social abstractions. Then, we consider an example in two parts. The first deals with electronic commerce; the second adds aspects of virtual enterprises [309]. The commitments are designed based on their corresponding roles in human society.

2.5.1 Referral Networks

The ready online availability of information often leads to the problem of judging its quality and relevance. For the above reason, it is often preferable to ask someone who knows than to attempt to collect and assimilate the information all by oneself. Informally, people try to remember which of their acquaintances is familiar with and can give reliable information about a certain class of topics. There is, naturally enough, much interest in building agent-based referral networks as well [330].

One of the earliest projects that constructed referral networks of agents was the Multiple Intelligent Node Documents Servers (MINDS) project [297]. We briefly review this project next, and then reconstruct its referral components using the social abstractions introduced here above. MINDS is also an instance of how updates may happen in a retrieval-only system.

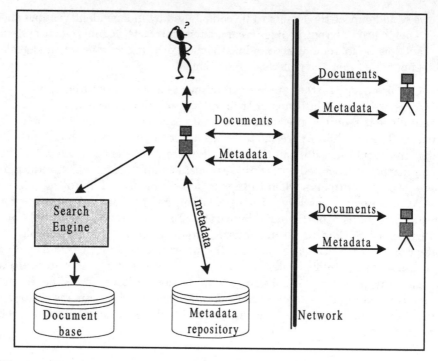

Fig. 2.2. The architecture of MINDS

MINDS is a distributed collection of agents for efficiently managing and retrieving documents in a networked environment. Figure 2.2 shows each agent managing documents and metadata about them, dealing with a user, and communicating with other agents. To better assist their users, the agents learn about the users' preferences and the distribution of the documents.

The agents share both knowledge and tasks to cooperate in retrieving documents for users. The agents essentially learn who to ask about what kinds of documents. This enables them to farm out queries to other likely agents and fuse the results locally. To enable this, some of the heuristics used include (1) consider locally produced documents more relevant provided they match and (2) when a query is answered successfully by a remote agent, both agents strengthen their confidence in each other. The metacommitments entailed by participation in MINDS are interesting:

– an agent will respond to a query if it has matching documents
– if an agent receiving a query does not have matching documents, but knows of an agent who answered a similar query, it will forward the new query to it
– if an agent receiving a query does not have matching documents, but knows of an agent who was asking a similar query, it will return the name of the agent.

The above metacommitments help make MINDS a self-initializing system in that a newly introduced can acquire models of the other agents and become an active participant. However, when social abstractions are used, a wider range of social behavior can be naturally specified. For example, an agent might proactively notify others when it changes its view of the relevance of a document.

2.5.2 Electronic Commerce

For a simple electronic commerce setting, we define an abstract SoCom for buy-sell deals. The SoCom server includes this abstract SoCom. One role is *buyer* whose capabilities include asking for a price quote and placing an order. The other role is *seller* whose capabilities include responding to price quotes and accepting orders based on checking the inventory locally. The *buyer*'s metacommitments include paying the quoted price for anything he orders. The *seller*'s commitments include (a) giving price quotes in response to requests and (b) fulfilling orders that he has accepted.

Suppose two agents, *customer* and *vendor*, wish to engage in a trade. They find the above abstract SoCom, and decide to join it as *buyer* and *seller*, respectively. The SoCom server instantiates the appropriate deal for them after confirming their capabilities. The *customer* can now check the price of a valve with a diameter of 21mm. Upon receipt of the query from the *customer*, the *vendor*—based on its role as *seller*—offers an appropriate answer, and the process proceeds straightforwardly from there onwards.

2.5.3 Virtual Enterprises

Now we consider more general situations where one or more agents may form a virtual enterprise. For simplicity, we assume that teams have a distinguished agent who handles their external interactions. We refer to this agent as the VE. In the first situation, there are two agents with authority over the Valvano and Hoosier databases. These agents have similar capabilities to the *seller* described above. They form a VE, which can adopt the role of *seller*. The *buyer* behaves as before and expects the *seller* to behave according to the buy-sell deal. However, the *seller* is implemented differently, with commitments among its members, which we do not elaborate here. The metacommitments of the VE include the following.

- The VE will give price quotes to anyone who requests them.
- The VE will refund the purchase price if an order with matching valves and hoses cannot be fulfilled. There are still no refunds if an order for matching valves and hoses can be fulfilled.
- If the VE cannot fulfill an order, it will try to find an alternative order that will satisfy the *customer*'s requirements.

In particular, even if the original vendors would not take refunds individually. Thus, a customer might be saddled with valves for which matching hoses could not be found. However, when dealing with the VE, a customer can get a refund in those situations. Thus certain kinds of exceptions are naturally handled by this organizational structure.

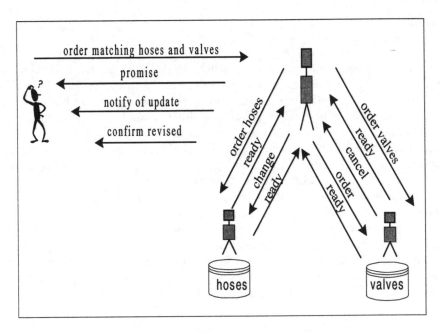

Fig. 2.3. Commitment-based virtual enterprises

Suppose an order for matching valves and hoses is successfully placed. It turns out later that the valve manufacturer discontinued the model that was ordered, but recommends a substitute. The substitute valve fits different diameter hoses than the original choice. The VE knows that the original order could be satisfied using the new valve and a different set of hoses. The VE can process this replacement itself and, based on its prior commitment, not charge the customer any extra. The customer does not need to know of the internal exchanges among the members of the VE SoCom. This scenario is illustrated in Figure 2.3.

In this situation, where the VE detects a problem in the supply of valves for which an order has been placed, the VE automatically meets its commitments by revising the order and notifying the customer. The discontinuation of a valve after an order for it was accepted exemplifies a kind of failure that arises after an original interaction had ended. Traditional approaches would be inapplicable in such a situation.

2.6 Conclusions and Future Work

Although multiagent systems have been known for a number of years and practical applications of them are spreading, building good multiagent systems remains somewhat of a black art. These problems also hold in information-rich environments. Prevailing techniques do not support the fundamental properties that make MAS attractive, either because they are suited to conventional, consistency-based settings or because they ignore special properties of the underlying systems, resulting in completely *ad hoc* modes of construction.

Engineering in general must be based on good science, albeit with the availability of tools and methodologies that facilitate the application of the scientific ideas. The engineering of cooperative information systems is no different. Work on social abstractions has been proceeding for a while, although it was mostly centered around a rather small community of researchers. The expansion of information-rich environments has attracted a larger body of researchers to the study of social abstractions. For the above reason, progress has accelerated. Although we do not claim that the approach described here is ready for commercial use, its uses for research prototypes have been promising.

We described interaction-oriented programming, and outlined some conceptual modeling issues in it. IOP offers some benefits over previous approaches for building multiagent systems. In the spirit of conceptual modeling, IOP focuses on higher-level concepts than the underlying implementations. These concepts provide a superior starting point to the traditional approaches. Fundamentally, conceptual modeling is as good as the methodologies that we may use to build conceptual models. Accordingly, we have been considering methodologies that may be applicable to IOP. In the above, we gave a sampler of some of our preliminary results. These methodologies are presently being applied by hand, although there is some work afoot to build tools to assist in their application.

The idea of using the social abstractions to specify the coherence requirements in a system is a valuable one. On the one hand, it can be used to ensure that the agents can be constructed more easily to yield the complex varieties of behavior that are often desired. On the other hand, it can be used as a basis for specifying standard or quasi-standard cooperative information systems for which independent developers and vendors could supply the member agents.

There are some important directions for future research. Of special interest is the development of richer metamodels to capture the realistic ways in which a set of computations may be considered coherent. Developing good metamodels requires empirically identifying the "best practices" in key application domains, encapsulating them as reusable patterns, and incorporating them in metamodels. Typical application areas would be contracting among autonomous entities, accounting, and other enterprise functions.

There is a strong need for an intuitive formal semantics. We have made some progress along the development of such a semantics [630]. A related theme is compositionality, which we applied in combining individual models for electronic commerce and virtual enterprises. However, a full formal treatment of specification and verification that would allow dynamic composition of models remains to be made; for more traditional temporal logics approaches, such results are now becoming available [189]. In related research, we have begun developing algorithms for temporal, causal reasoning, which can be used to analyze and design commitment protocols for high-level interaction among autonomous agents. We have also begun to develop techniques for social learning among agent communities.

Lastly, the problem of *social learning* is extremely important. Agents that function as part of a community can learn not only from their own actions, but also from other members of the community. For example, imagine a logistical deployment. A conventional deployment is centrally managed, and suffers from an inability to handle exceptions properly. A multiagent approach would obviously be more flexible and would allow each item being moved to optimize its route based on information that is most relevant to its specific situation. However, we need a method through which the agents can learn from each other, for example, about what routes to take and what modes of conveyance to use.

We envisage two kinds of learning to take place. Class-level learning would adapt the general algorithms or strategies pursued by intelligent agents for different kinds of materiel. This would benefit agents instantiated later and could be performed at the agent "factories." Instance-level learning would adapt the tactics used by a particular agent responsible for a particular physical item. The latter would not only benefit instantiated agents but with the right metacommitments would also benefit others in similar situations.

Acknowledgments

A previous version of this chapter was presented at the Second International Workshop on Cooperative Information Agents (CIA-98), held in 1998. Michael Huhns was supported by the Defense Advanced Research Projects Agency. Munindar Singh was supported by the NCSU College of Engineering, the National Science Foundation under grants IIS-9529179 and IIS-9624425 (Career Award), and IBM corporation. We have benefited from discussions with Manny Aparicio and Anuj Jain. Anuj also prototyped the virtual enterprises example.

3. Integration of Information from Multiple Sources of Textual Data

Sonia Bergamaschi[1,2] and Domenico Beneventano[1]

[1] Dipartimento di Scienze dell'Ingegneria Universitá di Modena, Italy.
   E-Mail: sbergamaschi@deis.unibo.it
[2] CSITE - CNR, Universitá di Bologna, Italy.
   E-Mail: sonia@dsi.unimo.it

3.1 Introduction

The number of information sources in the Internet is exponentially increasing. As a consequence, for a given query, the set of potentially interesting sites is very high but only very few sites are really relevant. Furthermore, information is highly heterogeneous both in its structure and in its origin. In particular, not only data types are heterogeneous (textual data, images, sounds, etc.), but even the representation of a single data type can differ.

Even in the restricted domain of textual data, the problem of *organizing* data (often a huge amount) coming from multiple heterogeneous sources in *easily accessible structures*, in order to provide *true information*, is a challenging research topic for different research communities: database, artificial intelligence, information retrieval. Let us individuate two increasing complexity scenarios:

1. *known sources* – the sources of heterogeneous textual data are known;
2. *unknown sources* – the sources of *relevant* heterogeneous textual data must be individuated.

The first scenario is being, at present, widely investigated in the database area, involving many research topics and application areas: decision support systems (DSS), integration of heterogeneous databases, datawarehouse. Decision makers need information from multiple heterogeneous sources (including databases, file systems, knowledge bases, digital libraries, information retrieval systems, and electronic mail systems), but are usually unable to get and fuse them in a timely fashion due to the difficulties of accessing the different systems and to consistently integrate them. Significant contributions about the integration of well-structured conventional databases exist (e.g. [5, 42, 262, 342, 389, 668]). Many projects have adopted *Object Oriented* (OO) data models to facilitate integration [5, 105, 505] and, recently, systems for the integration of sources with minimal structure have appeared [223, 503, 620]. Furthermore, the DARPA Intelligent Integration of Information (I^3) research program is devoted to this problem. However, as a consequence of the rapid development of prototype implementations in this area, the initial outcome of this program appears to have been to produce a new set of systems. While they can perform certain advanced information integration tasks, they cannot easily communicate with each other. With a view to understanding and solving this problem, a workshop was held on this topic at the University of Maryland in April, 1996 [98, 724].

The second, most complex scenario, is associated with the so-called *information discovery* problem. This problem arised mainly due to the *Internet* explosion. In this scenario we have, first, to face the problem of individuating among a huge amount of sources of heterogeneous textual data a *possibly low amount* of *relevant* sources and, then, to face, if necessary, the problem of scenario 1. Research efforts devoted to face this problem come from different research areas: information retrieval, artificial intelligence, database. This scenario is out of the scope of this chapter as the amount of approaches and systems very recently proposed is as large as to require a paper on its own.

In this chapter we will discuss problems and solutions of the extraction/integration of information from multiple sources, highly heterogeneous, of textual data and of their integration in order to provide *true information*. Main problems to be faced in integrating information coming from distributed sources are related to structural and implementation heterogeneity (including differences in hardware platforms, DBMS, data models and data languages), and to the lack of a common ontology, which leads to semantic heterogeneity. Semantic heterogeneity occurs when different names are employed to represent the same information or when different modeling constructs are used to represent the same piece of information in different sources [342]. Some approaches have been recently proposed in the literature for the extraction and integration of conventional structured databases [90] and semi-structured data [99, 111] taking into account semantic heterogeneity. Data integration architectures are usually based on *mediators* [722], where knowledge about data of multiple sources is combined to provide a global view of the underlying data. Two fundamental approaches have emerged in the literature: *structural* [230, 566] and *semantic* [18, 57, 90].

There are many projects following the "structural approach" [64, 88, 158]. This approach can be characterized as follows (considering TSIMMIS [461] as a target system):

– a *self-describing model* where each data item has an associated descriptive label and *without a strong typing system*;
– semantic information is effectively encoded in rules that do the integration.

Let us introduce some fundamental arguments in favour of the "structural approach":

1. the flexibility, generality and conciseness of a self-describing model makes the "structural approach" a good candidate for the integration of widely heterogeneous and semistructured information sources;

2. a form of first-order logic languages that allow the declarative specification of a *mediator* is provided; a mediator specification is a set of rules which defines the mediator view of the data and the set of functions that are invoked to translate objects from one format to another.
3. the schema-less nature of modelled objects is particularly useful when a client does not know in advance the labels or structure of the objects of a source.
   - In traditional data models, a client must be aware of the schema in order to pose a query. With this approach, a client can discover the structure of the information as queries are posed.
   - A conventional OO language breaks down in such a case, unless one defines an object class for every possible type of irregular object.

Many other projects follow a "semantic approach" [17, 18, 105, 298, 271, 566]. This approach can be characterized as follows:

- for each source, meta-data, i.e. conceptual schema, must be available;
- semantic information is encoded in the schema;
- a common data model as the basis for describing sharable information must be available;
- partial or total schema unification is performed.

Let us introduce some fundamental arguments in favour of a "semantic approach" adopting conventional OO data models:

1. the schema nature of conventional OO models together with classification aggregation and generalization primitives allows us to organize extensional knowledge and to give a high level abstraction view of information;
2. the adoption of a schema permits us to check consistency of instances with respect to their descriptions, and thus to preserve the "quality" of data;
3. semantic information encoded into a schema permits us to efficiently extract information, i.e., to perform query optimization;
4. a relevant effort has been devoted to develop OO standards: CORBA [485, 481, 638] for object exchanging among heterogeneous systems; ODMG93 for object oriented databases [112];

One of the most promising lines of research in this environment is the *virtual approach* [300]. It was first proposed in multidatabase models in the early 80s [389, 668]. More recently, systems have been developed based on the use of description logics [17, 377] such as CLASSIC [76]. All of the virtual approaches are based on a model of query decomposition, sending subqueries to source databases, and merging the answers that come back. Recent systems based on description logics are focused primarily on conjunctive queries (i.e., expressible using select, project and join), and have more the flavor of the *Open World Assumption* - the answer provided through an integrated view will hold a subset of the complete answer that is implied by the underlying databases. For the schema, a "top-down" approach is used: in essence a global schema encompassing all relevant information is created, and data held in the source databases is expressed as views over this global schema [680]. See [17, 376, 378, 680] for some of the algorithms used in this approach.

In order to show and discuss the "structural approach", one of the most interesting projects, TSIMMIS, is presented. Then, a virtual description logics based approach, the MOMIS project, is introduced.

The outline of the chapter is the following. Section 3.2 is devoted to present the TSIMMIS system[1] and Section 3.3 is devoted to present the MOMIS project. Section 3.2 begins with an overview of the TSIMMIS project, including the *OEM* data model and the *MSL* language adopted in the project. Subsection 3.2.2 describes the architecture of a TSIMMIS *wrapper*, i.e., an extractor of informations from a textual source which converts data into the *OEM* data model. Subsection 3.2.3 describes the TSIMMIS approach for generating a *mediators*, i.e., an integration and refinement tool of data coming from wrappers.

Section 3.3 begins with an overview of the MOMIS project. Subsection 3.3.1 presents the MOMIS architecture, the ODL_{I^3} language and the overall approach. Subsection 3.3.2 and Subsection 3.3.3 present the generation of the mediator global schema and the Global Schema Builder, respectively. In Subsection 3.3.4 an overview of description logics formalism and related inference techniques plus the obd system are presented. Subsections 3.3.5 shows the role of ODB-TOOLS in the MOMIS project. Section 3.4 presents some final remarks.

Remarks all over the chapter fix relevant choices which lead to the design of an I^3 systems as MOMIS.

3.2 The TSIMMIS Project

Let us introduce the problems and the solutions recently proposed within scenario 1, by describing one of the most interesting projects: the **TSIMMIS** (**The Stanford- IBM Manager of Multiple Information Sources**) Data Integration Project, under development at the Department of Computer Science - University of Stanford (biblio references: http://db.stanford.edu). TSIMMIS is a joint project between Stanford and the IBM Almaden Research Center whose goal is the development of tools that facilitate the rapid integration of heterogeneous textual sources that may include both structured and unstructured data [461].

The TSIMMIS data-integration system provides integrated access via an architecture that is common in many other projects: *wrappers/translators*

---

[1] This section is a resume taken from papers of the TSIMMIS project. The contribution of the authors of this chapter is restricted to the remarks.

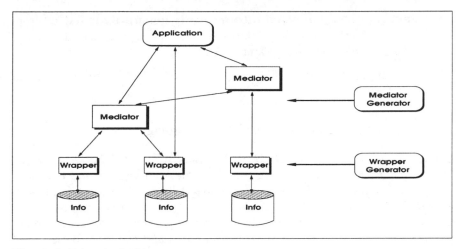

Fig. 3.1. Tsimmis Architecture

[105, 221, 505] convert data into a common model; *Mediators* combine, integrate or refine the data from the wrappers. The wrappers also provide a common query language for extracting information. Applications can access data directly through wrappers but they can also go through *mediators* [503, 505, 722].

In Figure 3.1, the TSIMMIS architecture is shown: above each source is a *translator (wrapper)* that logically converts the underlying data objects to a common information model; above the translators lie the *mediators*. The translator converts queries over information in the common model into requests that the source can execute and data extracted from the source into the common model. The common model is the *OEM (Object Exchange Model)*, a *tagged* model allowing simple nesting of objects. Furthermore, two query languages, *OEM-QL* and *MSL (Mediator Specification Language)*, for requesting *OEM* objects have been developed. *OEM-QL* is an SQL-like language, extended to deal with labels and object nesting and *MSL* is a high level language that allows the declarative specification of mediators. The possible bottlenecks of the above architecture are:

– an ad-hoc translator[2] must be developed for any information source;
– implementing a mediator can be complicated and time-consuming.

Thus, important goals of the project (and of any other project with the same aim) are:

1. **to provide a translator generator** that can generate an *OEM* translator based on a description of the conversion that needs to take place for queries received and results returned (see *wrapper/generator* box in Figure 3.1);

---

[2] translator and wrapper are synonymous in TSIMMIS.

2. **to automatically or semi-automatically generate mediators** from high level descriptions of the information processing they need to do (see *mediator/generator* box in Figure 3.1).

The solutions proposed in TSIMMIS for the above goals are described in Section 3.2.2 and 3.2.3.

3.2.1 The OEM Model and the MSL Language

Let us briefly introduce the *OEM* model [505]. It is a *self-describing model* [416] where each data item has an associated descriptive label and *without a strong typing system. OEM* is much simpler than conventional OO models: supports only *object nesting* and *object identity*, while other features, such as classes, methods and inheritance are not supported directly. An object description in *OEM* with a top-level object (ob1) and five sub-objects (sub1 to sub5) has the format:

```
<ob1:   person,   set,         {sub1,sub2,sub3,sub4,sub5}>
        <sub1:    last_name,    str,    'Smith'>
        <sub2:    first_name,   str,    'John'>
        <sub3:    role,         str,    'faculty'>
        <sub4:    department,   str,    'cs'>
        <sub5:    telephone,    str,    '32435465'>
```

Each *OEM* object has the following structure: an object-id, a label, a type, a value. A label is a variable-length string describing what the object represents.

Remark 1. *A relevant feature of* OEM *is that objects sharing the same label do not follow a unique schema: for example an other object with the same label 'person' could have different sub-objects. This feature make the integration of data coming from heterogeneous sources with different schemas easier than in conventional OO data models.*

Let us briefly introduce the *MSL* language [503] (a more detailed description is given in Section 3.2.3). *MSL* is a first-order logic language that allows the declarative specification of mediators; an *MSL* specification is a set of rules which define the mediator view of the data and a set of functions that are invoked to translate objects from one format to another. Each rule consists of a *head* and a *tail* separated by the symbol :-. The tail describes the pattern of the objects to be fetched from the source, while the head defines the pattern of the top-level integrated object supported by the mediator.

3.2.2 The TSIMMIS Wrapper Generator

TSIMMIS includes a toolkit, say *OEM Support Libraries*, to quickly implement wrappers, mediators and end-user interfaces. These libraries contain procedures that implement the exchange of *OEM* objects and queries between

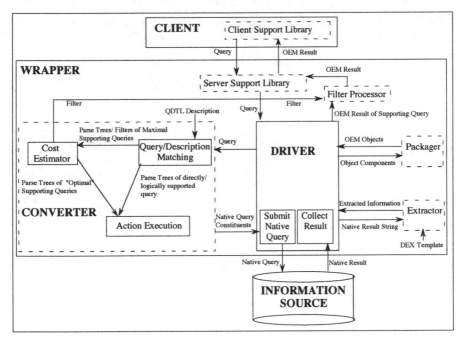

Fig. 3.2. TSIMMIS wrapper

a server (either a translator or a mediator) and a client (either a mediator, an application or an interactive end-user) and procedures to translate queries into a suitable format.

The architecture of wrappers generated by using the toolkit is shown in Figure 3.2:

- the white rectangles are available in the toolkit: *CONVERTER*, *CLS (Client Support Library)*, *SSL (Server Support Library)*, *Filter Processor*, *Packager*, *Extractor*;
- The *CONVERTER* is the wrapper component which translates a query expressed in the *MSL* language into a sequence of operations executable by the information source. The translation is performed by using descriptions expressed in *QDTL (Query Description and Translation Language)*;
- *QDTL description* for the *CONVERTER* and *DEX template* for the *Extractor* must be specified;
- An architecture component, say the *DRIVER*, must be completely developed from scratch, for each wrapper, as it depends on the information source.

CONVERTER and QDTL. To illustrate the *CONVERTER* functionalities and the *QDTL* syntax[3], let us refer to a university professors and

---

[3] A full description of the *CONVERTER* and of *QDTL* is in [504].

students WHOIS information source. Let us suppose that this source allows only very simple retrieve operations, for example, the following:

1. retrieve persons with a given last_name: `>lookup -ln 'ss'`
2. retrieve persons with a given last_name and first_name: `>lookup -ln 'ss' -fn 'ff'`
3. retrieve all the records of the source : `>lookup`

The above operations are mapped into *QDTL* descriptions in order to enable the *CONVERTER* to decompose a *MSL* query into subqueries executable by the source. A *QDTL* description is composed by a set of templates with associated actions. The query templates for the three operations (no actions are specified for the moment) are:

```
D1: (QT1.1) Query ::= *O :- <O person {< last_name $LN>}>
    (QT1.2) Query ::= *O :- <O person {< last_name $LN>
                                       <first_name $FN>}>
    (QT1.3) Query ::= *O :- <O person V>
```

Each query template is described after the : : = symbol and is a parameterized query. Identifiers preceded by the $ symbol represent the corresponding constants of an input *MSL* query. The variables in capital letters (V) correspond to variables of an input *MSL* query.

The *CONVERTER* includes an algorithm able to exploit each template to describe much more queries than the ones that could be executed directly using the template. The class of supported queries is the following:

— *Directly supported queries*: queries with a syntax analogous to the template;
— *Logical supported queries*: A query q is logically supported by a template t if q is *logically equivalent* to a query q' directly supported by t[4] or if it is subsumed by a query q' directly supported by t;
— *Indirectly supported queries*: a query q is indirectly supported by a template t if q can be decomposed in a query q' directly supported by t and a *filter* that is applied on the results of q'.

Let us consider as an example the query:

```
(Q6) *Q :- <Q person {<last_name 'Smith'> <role 'student'>}>
```

Q6 is not logically supported by any of the D1 templates, but the *CONVERTER* is able to detect that Q6 is subsumed by the query Q7 which is directly supported:

```
(Q7) *Q :- <Q person {<last_name 'Smith'>}>
```

Q7 contains all the information necessary to determine Q6 answer set; to obtain Q6 answer set a filter, i.e. a new MSL query: `*O :- <O person {<role 'student'>}>` is generated which, applied to Q7 answer set, gives Q6 result. Let us observe that, in general, for a given query q we can have more than

---

[4] Two queries are logically equivalent if they give the same answer set in the same context.

one query able to support it. For example query Q6, besides Q7, is supported by the following Q8 query:

$$\text{(Q8)} \quad \texttt{O*} \; \texttt{:-} \; \texttt{<O person V>}$$

which, in its turn, subsumes Q7.

Remark 2. *The* CONVERTER *should consider all the possible subsuming supporting queries in order to select the most efficient one. The lowest subsuming supporting query could be a good candidate.*

Actions in *QDTL* templates express the query in a format executable by the source. In the described Converter actions are expressed in the C language. Let us refer to *D1* description to show some actions:

```
D2: (QT2.1) Query ::= *O :- <O person {<last_name $LN>}>
    (AC2.1)          {printf (lookup_query, 'lookup -ln %s',$LN);}
    (QT2.2) Query ::= *O :- <O person {<last_name $LN>
                                       <first_name $FN>}>
    (AC2.2)          {printf (lookup_query, 'lookup -ln %s -fn %s ',
                                       $LN,$FN);}
```

Extractor, DEX Templates, and Filter Processor. A query result is often expressed in a unstructured format. The *Extractor* component uses the *DEX* templates to analyze and structure data received from the sources. *DEX* templates contain the description of the data received from a source and information about the fields to be extracted. After the extraction of the information needed from the source output, they are converted by the *Packager* into a set of *OEM* objects. Then, this set of objects is filtered in the *Filter Processor*. The filter to be applied to the set of objects is a *MSL* query built by the *Converter* during the translation activity of the input query into executable commands. The *Filter Processor* applies this query to the set of retrieved objects and sends the subset thus obtained to the *Client*.

3.2.3 The TSIMMIS Mediator Generator

The **MedMaker** system [503] is the *TSIMMIS* component developed for declaratively specifying mediators. It is targeted for integration of sources with unstructured or semi-structured data and/or sources with changing schemas. **MedMaker** provides the high level language *MSL* that allows the declarative specification of mediators.

At run time, when the mediator receives a request for information, the *Mediator Specification Interpreter (MSI)* collects and integrates the necessary information from the sources, according to the specification. The process is analogous to expanding a view against a conventional relational database and *MSL* can be seen as a view definition language that is targeted to the *OEM* data model and the functionality needed for integrating heterogeneous sources.

<&e1,	employee,	set,	{&f1,&l1,&t1, &rep1}>
	<&f1,	first_name,	string, 'Joe'>
	<&l1,	last_name,	string, 'Chung'>
	<&t1,	title,	string, 'professor'>
	<&rep1,	reports_to,	string, 'John Hennessy'>
<&e2,	employee,	set,	{&f2,&l2,&t2}>
	<&f2,	first_name,	string, 'John'>
	<&l2,	last_name,	string, 'Hennessy'>
	<&t2,	title,	string, 'chairman'>
............etc.			
<&s3,	student,	set,	{&f3,&l3,&y3}>
	<&f3,	first_name,	string, 'Pierre'>
	<&l3,	last_name,	string, 'Huyn'>
	<&y3,	year,	integer, 3>

Table 3.1. CS objects in OEM

The Mediator Specification Language MSL: An Example. Let us introduce an example to illustrate *MSL*. We have two input sources: a relational database with two tables:

```
employee(first_name,last_name,title,report_to)
student(first_name,last_name,year)
```

and a university system 'WHOIS' with information on students and professors. For the first source, a wrapper called 'CS' exports the information (some of which is shown in Table 3.1), as *OEM* objects; the second source uses a wrapper called 'WHOIS' (some objects are shown in Table 3.2).

<&p1,	person,	set,	{&n1, &d1, &rel1, &elem1}>
	<&n1,	name,	string, 'Joe Chung'>
	<&d1,	dept,	string, 'cs'>
	<&rel1,	relation,	string, 'employee'>
	<&elem1,	e_mail,	string, 'chung@cs'>
............etc.			

Table 3.2. WHOIS objects in OEM

Let us suppose that a mediator, called 'MED' with objects integrating all the information about a person, say 'Chung', of the department 'CS', coming from the two wrappers has to be developed. Given the objects of Table 3.1 and 3.2, **MED** must be able to combine them to obtain the object of Table 3.3.

Let us introduce the rules of Table 3.4, expressed in MSL, which define the mediator 'MED'.

```
<&cp1,   cs_person,   set,        {&mn1, &mrel1, &t1, &rep1, &elm1}>
    <&mn1,     name,        string,   'Joe Chung'>
    <&mrel1,   relation,    string,   'employee'>
    <&t1,      title,       string,   'professor'>
    <&rep1,    reports_to,  string,   'John Hennesy'>
    <&elem1,   e_mail,      string,   'chung@cs'>
```

Table 3.3. An object exported by **'MED'**

```
(MS1) Rules:
<cs_person {<name N> <rel R> Rest1 Rest2}>
        :-   <person {<name N> <dept 'cs'> <relation R> | Rest1}>
             @whois
             AND decomp(N, LN, FN)
             AND <R {<first_name FN> <last_name LN> | Rest2}>@cs
External:
decomp(string,string,string)(bound,free,free) impl by name_to_lnfn
decomp(string,string,string)(free,bound,bound) impl by lnfn_to_name.
```

Table 3.4. Rules of **'MED'**

Remark 3. *The "creation process" of a mediator object is a pattern match-ing process: first the objects extracted by the wrapper satisfying the tail are collected and their components are linked to the variables, then the bindings are used to create objects expressed in the head.*

With reference to the example, we want to search the objects of the sources **'CS'** and **'WHOIS'** which links to the tail expressed in rule 'MS1' (i e. top-level person object of **'WHOIS'** with sub-object name, dept='cs' and relation; top-level person object of 'cs' with FN and LN obtained from the corresponding N of whois (&e1 satisfies the model).

The decomp function executes the string transformations in order to ob-tain first_name and last_name of a person. When the objects satisfying the tail pattern have been obtained, the rule head is used to build the virtual object which is the union of data coming from the wrappers (&cp1 is the result of the union of &p1 e &e1).

MSL has other querying functionalities to facilitate integration of hetero-geneous sources: expressing only variables in the value fields it is possible to obtain information about the structure of an information source (e.g. after a schema changing). MSL allows 'wildcard' to search objects at any nest-ing level without specifying the whole path as it would be necessary with conventional OO languages.

Architecture and Implementation of MSI. The Mediator Specification Interpreter *(MSI)* is the component of **MedMaker** which processes a query on the basis of the rules expressed with *MSL*. It is composed of three modules: *VE&AO (View Expander* and *Algebraic Optimizer); cost-based optimizer; datamerge engine. VE&AO* reads a query and, on the basis of the *MSL* specification, discovers what objects have to be obtained from a source and determines the conditions that the obtained objects must satisfy; gives a result called *logical datamerge program* which is passed to the second module *cost-based optimizer.* The optimizer develops an access plan to retrieve and combine objects, i.e. , what requests to submit to the sources; the order of request submissions; how to combine the results to obtain the requested objects. The access plan is passed to the third component, *datamerge engine,* which executes it and gives the results. Let us consider an example of the *MSI* query processing.

Suppose that a client wantet to retrieve information about 'Joe Chung'; the query expressed in *MSL* is the following:

> (Q1) JC :- JC :< cs_person {<name 'Joe Chung'>}> @MED

The object pattern in the tail of the query Q1 is matched against the structure of the objects held in *MED.*

View Expansion. Having as input the query Q1 and the *MSL* rules, *VE&AO* substitutes the query tail with the pattern of the objects in the sources, obtaining the datamerge rule R2:

```
(R2) <cs_person {<name 'Joe Chung'> <rel R> Rest1 Rest2}>
             :- <person {<name 'Joe Chung'> <dept 'cs'>
                      <relation R> | Rest1}>@whois
             AND decomp( 'Joe Chung', LN, FN)
             AND <R {<first_name FN> <last_name LN> |
                  Rest2 }>@cs.
```

The rule obtained in this way has a head representing the query and a tail, obtained from *MS1* rule, indicating how to select the objects from the wrappers.

Execution plan - when the *MSI* knows what objects have to be fetched from the sources, the *cost-based optimizer* builds the *physical datamerge program,* that specifies what query should be sent to the sources. A possible efficient plan to process query Q1 is the following:

1. Bindings for variables R and Rest1 are obtained from the source by **'WHOIS'** execution of the following query:

   ```
   <bind_for_whois {<bind_for_r R> < bind_for_Rest1 Rest1>}>
             :- <person {<name 'Joe Chung'> < dept 'cs' >
                  < relation R> | Rest1 }>@whois
   ```

2. Bindings for variables LN and FN are obtained from one of the two decomp functions: decomp (name_to_lnfn)
3. Each bind of R is combined with a value obtained at step 2, and the query is submitted to **CS** to obtain the values of the variable Rest2.

4. the objects satisfying the head of rule R2 can be generated (e.g. &cp1 should be an object built following these steps)[503].

3.3 The MOMIS Project

The goal of the MOMIS (Mediator envirOnment for Multiple Information Sources) project[5] [58] is to provide an *integrated access* to information sources, allowing a user to pose a single query and to receive a single unified answer. The approach follows the *semantic* paradigm, in that conceptual schemata of an involved source are considered, and a common data model (ODM_{I^3}) and language (ODL_{I^3}) are adopted to describe sharable information. ODM_{I^3} and ODL_{I^3} are defined as a subset of the corresponding ODMG-93 [112] ODM and ODL. A Description Logics olcd (*Object Language with Complements and Descriptive cycles*) constraints [60, 52, 53]) is used as a kernel language and ODB-TOOLS as the supporting system [54]. An overview of description logics formalism, inference techniques and of ODB-TOOLS are presented in Subsection 3.3.4.

With references to the classification of integration systems proposed by Hull [300], MOMIS is in the category of "read-only views", i.e. systems whose task it is to support an integrated, read-only, view of data that resides in multiple databases. The most similar projects are the GARLIC and SIMS project. The GARLIC project [105, 566] builds up on a complex wrapper architecture to describe the local sources with an OO language (GDL), and on the definition of Garlic Complex Objects to manually unify the local sources to define a global schema.

The SIMS project [17, 18] proposes to create a global schema definition exploiting the use of description logics (i.e. the LOOM language) for describing information sources. The use of a global schema allows both GARLIC and SIMS projects to support all possible user queries on the schema instead of a predefined subset of them.

Information integration in MOMIS is based on schemata and is performed through an *extraction and analysis* process followed by a *unification* process. The extraction and analysis process is devoted to deriving a Common Thesaurus of *terminological relationships*, based on ODL_{I^3} schemata descriptions, and to the construction of clusters (by means of clustering techniques) of ODL_{I^3} classes, describing similar information in different schemata. The unification process builds an integrated global schema for the analyzed sources by integrating ODL_{I^3} classes in a given cluster.

The use of the olcd description logics together with hierarchical clustering techniques are the original contributions of the approach to enhance a semi-automated integration process. Description logics allows us to interactively

---

[5] developed in collaboration between the Università di Modena and the Università di Milano. Papers of the MOMIS project are available at: http://www.sparc20.dsi.unimo.it/publications.html.

set-up the Thesaurus by deriving explicit terminological relationships from ODL_{I^3} schemata descriptions and by inferring new relationships out of the explicit ones. Moreover, optimization of the queries against the global schema is possible using description logics.

Clustering techniques allow the automated identification of ODL_{I^3} classes in different source schemata that are semantically related and thus candidates to be unified in the global schema.

3.3.1 Overview, Architecture, and ODL_{I^3} Language

In Fig. 3.3 the architecture of the MOMIS system is shown. With respect to the literature, this can be considered as an example of the powerful I^3 system [98] and follows the TSIMMIS architecture [461]. Above each source lies a *wrapper* responsible for translating the structure of the data source into the common ODL_{I^3} language. In a similar way, the *wrapper* performs a translation of the query from the OQL_{I^3} language to a local request to be executed by a single source. Above the *wrapper* there is a *mediator*, a software module that combines, integrates, and refines ODL_{I^3} schemata received from the *wrappers*. In addition, the mediator generates the OQL_{I^3} queries for the *wrappers*, starting from the query request formulated with respect to the global schema. The mediator module is obtained by coupling a "semantic approach", based on a description logics component, i.e. ODB-TOOLS Engine, and an extraction and analysis component, i.e., Schema Analyzer and Classifier ARTEMIS, developed at the University of Milan [108, 109], together with a minimal ODL_{I^3} interface.

In order to easily communicate source descriptions between wrappers and mediator engines, we introduced a data description language, called ODL_{I^3}.

According to the recommendations of [98], and to the diffusion of the object data model (and its standard ODMG-93), ODL_{I^3} is very close to the ODL language and adds features to support requirements of our intelligent information integration system. ODL_{I^3} is a source independent language used by the mediator to manage the system in a common way (we suppose to deal with different source types, such as relational databases, object-oriented databases, files)[6]. The main extension, w.r.t. ODL, is the capability of expressing two kinds of rules: *if then* rules, expressing in a declarative way integrity constraints intra and inter sources, and *mapping* rules between sources. It will be the wrapper task to translate the data description language of any particular source into ODL_{I^3} description, and to add information needed by the mediator, such as the source name and type.

The MOMIS approach to intelligent schema integration is articulated in the following phases:

---

[6] The syntax of the language is included in [58].

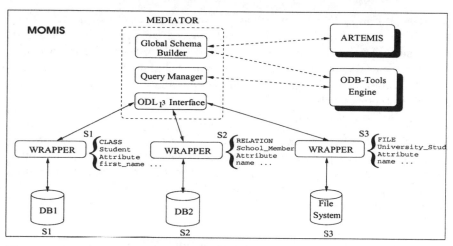

Fig. 3.3. Architecture of the MOMIS I^3 system

1. *Generation of a Common Thesaurus.*

   The objective of this step is the construction of a Common Thesaurus of *terminological relationships* for schema classes belonging to different source ODL$_{I^3}$ schemata.

   The following kinds of terminological relationships are specified: SYN (Synonym-of), defined between two terms t_i and t_j, with $t_i \neq t_j$, that are considered synonyms, i.e., that can be interchangeably used in every considered source, without changes in meaning; BT (Broader Terms), or hypernymy, defined between two terms t_i and t_j such as t_i has a broader, more general meaning than t_j; RT (Related Terms), or positive association, defined between two terms t_i and t_j that are generally used together in the same context.

   Terminological relationships are derived in a semi-automatic way, by analyzing the structure and context of classes in the schema, by using ODB-TOOLS and the description logics techniques.

2. *Affinity analysis of ODL$_{I^3}$ classes.*

   Terminological relationships in the Thesaurus are used to evaluate the level of *affinity* between classes' intra and inter sources. The concept of affinity is introduced to formalize the kind of relationships that can occur between classes from the integration point of view. The affinity of two classes is established by means of affinity coefficients based on class names and attributes [108, 109].

3. *Clustering ODL$_{I^3}$ classes .*

   Classes with affinity in different sources are grouped together in clusters using hierarchical clustering techniques. The goal is to identify the classes that have to be integrated since describing the same or semantically related information.

4. *Generation of the mediator global schema.*
   Unification of affinity clusters leads to the construction of the global schema of the mediator. A class is defined for each cluster, which is representative of all clusters' classes and is characterized by the union of their attributes. The global schema for the analyzed sources is composed of all these new classes, derived from clusters, and is the basis for posing queries against the sources.

Each phase of the integration process is described in detail in [58, 59]. Once the mediator global schema has been constructed, it can be exploited by the users for posing queries. The information on the global schema is used by the *Query Manager* module of MOMIS for query reformulation and for semantic optimization using ODB-TOOLS, as discussed in [58].

3.3.2 Generation of the Mediator Global Schema

In this section we present the process which leads to the definition of the mediator global schema, that is the mediator view of data stored in local sources.

University source (S_1)

```
Research_Staff(first_name,last_name,relation,
email,dept_code,section_code)
School_Member(first_name,last_name,faculty,year)
Department(dept_name,dept_code,budget,dept_area)
Section(section_name,section_code,length,room_code)
Room(room_code,seats_number,notes)
```

Computer_Science source (S_2)

```
CS_Person(name)
Professor:CS_Person(title,belongs_to:Division,rank)
Student:CS_Person(year,takes:set⟨Course⟩,rank)
Division(description,address:Location,fund,
sector,employee_nr)
Location(city,street,number,county)
Course(course_name,taught_by:Professor)
```

Tax_Position source (S_3)

```
University_Student(name,student_code,faculty_name,
tax_fee)
```

Table 3.5. Example with three source schemata

Running Example. First, we introduce an example used in this section to explain the approach (see Table 3.5). We consider three different sources. The first source is a relational database, University (S_1), containing information about the staff and the students of a given university. The second source Computer_Science (S_2) contains information about people belonging to the computer science department of the same university, and is an object-oriented database. A third source is also available, Tax_Position (S_3), derived from the registrar's office. It consists of a file system, storing information about student's tax_fees. For the complete source descriptions see [58]. The generation of Common Thesaurus, the Affinity analysis and the Clustering techniques applied to our example give rise to the cluster tree shown in Fig. 3.4, which classifies classes into groups at different levels of affinity.

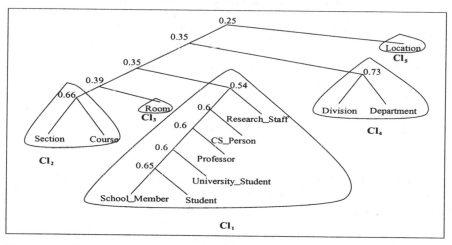

Fig. 3.4. Affinity tree of S_1, S_2, and S_3

Starting from the affinity tree produced with clustering, we define, for each cluster in the tree, a global class *global_class$_i$* representative of the classes contained in the cluster (i.e., a class providing the unified view of all the classes of the cluster). The generation of the *global_class$_i$* is interactive with the designer. Let Cl_i be a cluster in the affinity tree. First, the Global Schema Builder component of MOMIS associates to the *global_class$_i$* a set of global attributes, corresponding to the union of the attributes of the classes belonging to Cl_i, (the attributes with affinity are unified into a unique global attribute in *global_class$_i$*). The attribute unification process is performed automatically for the names of attributes with affinity, according to the following rules:

– for attributes that have name affinity due to SYN relationships, only one term is selected and assigned to the corresponding global attribute in *global_class$_i$*;

```
interface University_Person
(extent Research_Staffers, School_Members, CS_Persons
       Professors, Students, University_Students
 key    name)
{ attribute string name
   mapping_rule  (University.Research_Staff.first_name and
                  University.Research_Staff.last_name),
                 (University.School_Member.first_name and
                  University.School_Member.last_name),
                  Computer_Science.CS_Person.name,
                  Computer_Science.CS_Person.last_name),
                  Computer_Science.Professor.name,
                  Computer_Science.Professor.last_name),
                  Computer_Science.Student.name,
                  Computer_Science.Student.last_name),
                  Tax_Position.University_Student.name;
  attribute string rank
   mapping_rule  University.Research_Staff = 'Professor',
                 University.School_Member = 'Student',
   ... }
```

Table 3.6. Example of global class specification in ODL$_{I^3}$

- for attributes that have name affinity due to BT and NT relationships, a name which is a broader term for all of them is selected and assigned to the corresponding global attribute in *global_class$_i$*.

For example, the output of this attribute unification process for cluster Cl_1 of Fig. 3.4, is the following set of global attributes:

$Cl_1 =$ (name, rank, title, dept_code, year,
         takes, relation, email, student_code,
         tax_fee, section_code, faculty)

In general, additional information has to be provided by the designer to complete the global class definition, thus a global class *global_class$_i$* including specification of attribute mappings and default values represented in the form of *rules* must be specified in ODL$_{I^3}$. An example of ODL$_{I^3}$ specification for the global class University_Person is shown in Table 3.6. As we can see from this figure, for each attribute, in addition to its declaration, mapping rules are defined, specifying both information on how to map the attribute on the corresponding attributes of the associated cluster and on possible default/null values defined for it on cluster classes. For example, for the global attribute name, the mapping rule specifies the attributes that have to be considered in each class of the cluster Cl_1. In this case, an *and* correspondence is defined for name for the class University.Research_Staff (we use dot notation for specifying the source of a given class belonging to the cluster). A mapping rule is defined for the global attribute rank to specify the value

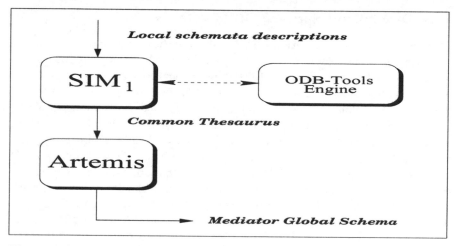

Fig. 3.5. Global Schema Builder

to be associated with rank for the instances of University.Research_Staff and University.School_Member.

The global schema of the mediator is composed of the global classes defined for all the clusters of the affinity tree.

3.3.3 Implementation of MOMIS: The Global Schema Builder

In this section, a brief description of the Global Schema Builder module is given, to outline the state of implementation of the MOMIS project. The Global Schema Builder processes the local schemata descriptions, received from the information sources, to obtain the Mediator Global Schema, that will be the base for the user's queries. It is composed by the following components (shown in Fig. 3.5):

1. **SIM_1**(Schemata Integrator Module, first version): it reads the local schemata descriptions, expressed in the ODL_{I^3} language, to derive the Common Thesaurus. In particular, a set of terminological relationships is stored in the thesaurus, by interacting with the user and by using description logics (supported by ODB-TOOLS) to express the logical links existing intra and inter sources;

2. **Artemis**: starting from the relationships of the Common Thesaurus, Affinity Coefficients are computed between all the pairs of local classes to be integrated, to evaluate their level of similarity. Similar classes are grouped together using *clustering techniques*: every generated cluster will correspond to a mediator global class [108][7].

---

[7] This component has been developed at the University of Milano.

3.3.4 Description Logics and ODB-Tools

Description Logics languages - DLs[8], derived from the KL-ONE model [83, 738], have been proposed in the 80's in the Artificial Intelligence research area. DLs are fragments of first order logic: they enable *concepts* to be expressed, that can be viewed as logical formulas built using unary and binary predicates, and contain one free variable (to be filled with instances of the concept). They bear similarities with Complex object data models (*CODMs*), recently proposed in the database area [2, 3, 4, 27, 60, 372, 373]. CODMs are concerned with only the structural aspects of object-oriented data models proposed for Object-Oriented Databases (*OODB*) [25, 112, 341] and represent well-known notions such as types, complex values, classes, objects with identity and inheritance. DLs too are concerned with only structural aspects; concepts roughly correspond to database classes and are organized in inheritance taxonomies. An additional feature of DLs with respect to CODMs is that concepts are differentiated in *primitive* and *defined*: a primitive concept description represents necessary conditions (thus corresponding to the usual database class semantics); a defined concept description represents necessary and sufficient conditions (thus corresponding to the semantics of a database view or a query).

Remark 4. *By exploiting defined concepts semantics of DLs, and, given a type as set semantics to concept descriptions, it is possible to provide reasoning techniques : to compute* subsumption *relations among concepts (i.e. "isa" relationships implied by concepts descriptions) and to detect* incoherent *(i.e. always empty) concepts.*

The research on DLs has provided reasoning techniques to determine incoherence and subsumption of concepts and has assessed the complexity of these inferences for a variety of *acyclic*, i.e. not allowing recursive descriptions, DLs (see e.g.[175]).

DLs reasoning techniques are profitable for database design activities, as will be briefly argued in the following. In fact, if we map a database schema including only classes (no views) into one of the DLs supported by a system, we are able to automatically detect incoherent classes. A more active role can be performed with the introduction of views.

Remark 5. *By means of DLs reasoning techniques, a view, can be automatically* classified *(i.e., its right place in an already existing taxonomy can be found) by determining the set of its most specific subsumer views (subsumers) and the set of its most generalized specialization views (subsumees).*

Thus, besides a passive consistency check, *minimality* of the schema with respect to inheritance can easily be computed. In [61] well-known conceptual data models have been mapped in a suitable DL and polynomial subsumption and coherence algorithms are given.

---

[8] *DLs are also known as Concept Languages or Terminological Logics.*

The expressiveness of CODMs gave rise to new problems for this mapping, as many of their features were not supported by implemented DLs. For instance, most of the CODMs introduce a clear cut distinction between values and objects with identity and, thus, between object classes and value types. This distinction was not present in DLs. Further, CODMs often support additional type constructors, such as set and sequence. Mostly important, CODMs support the representation and management of *cyclic classes*, i.e., classes which directly or indirectly refer to themselves, are allowed.

A description logics (odl = *Object Description Logics*)[9] overcoming the above problems, and a theoretical framework for CODM database design based on subsumption computation and coherence detection has been proposed in [60].

Remark 6. *The* odl *description logics represents the structural part of OODB data models (and of the standard data model ODM of ODMG93 [112]) and incorporates: value-types, complex values, classes, objects with identity, and inheritance.*

The main extension of odl, with respect to CODMs, is the capability of expressing *base* and *virtual* classes. Base classes correspond to ordinary classes used in database systems and virtual classes (corresponding to defined concepts semantics). Cyclic classes (base and virtual) are allowed and a *greatest-fixedpoint* semantics [462] has been adopted to uniquely assign an interpretation to cyclic virtual classes.

Furthermore the interpretation of tuples in odl implies an *open world semantics for tuple* types similar to the one adopted by Cardelli [103] and in analogy with all DLs.

For instance, if we have the following assignments of values to objects:

$$
\delta : \begin{cases}
o_1 & \mapsto [\text{a: } "xyz", \text{b: } 5] \\
o_2 & \mapsto \langle true, false \rangle \\
& \vdots \\
o_{128} & \mapsto \{o_1, o_2\} \\
& \vdots
\end{cases}
$$

Adopting an *open world semantics for tuple*, it follows that[10]

$$
o_1 \in \mathcal{I}\Big[\triangle[\text{a: String}]\Big], \qquad o_1 \in \mathcal{I}\Big[\triangle[\text{a: String}, \text{b : Int}]\Big],
$$
$$
o_2 \in \mathcal{I}[\triangle\langle \text{Bool} \rangle], \qquad o_{128} \in \mathcal{I}[\{\triangle \top_C\}].
$$

Remark 7. *The adoption of an open world semantics for tuple types in* odl *permits an alternative formulation of the OEM capability to express semi-structured objects (see Remark 1): objects of a class share a common minimal structure, but can have further additional and different properties.*

---

[9] not to be confused with the homonymous ODL language of ODMG93 [112].

[10] $\triangle$ is an object constructor operator; $\top_C$ is the top class containing any domain object.

Remark 8. *Coherence checking and subsumption computation are effective for query optimization. A query has the semantics of a virtual class, as it expresses a set of necessary and sufficient conditions. If we restrict the query language to the subset of queries expressible with the schema description language we can perform incoherence detection and subsumption computation for queries.*

The choice of restricting the query language in order to have DDL=DML has been made in the some works on query optimization based on acyclic DLs such as CANDIDE [44], CLASSIC [76], BACK [401] and [95].

Remark 9. *Coherence checking and subsumption computation can be classified as* semantic query optimization *techniques [117, 343, 614], as they perform a transformation of a query into a semantically equivalent one, that minimizes query execution costs.*

- if the query is detected as incoherent a null answer can immediately be returned without accessing the database;
- if the query is coherent, it can be temporarily classified in the schema with respect to views. As a result, either an *equivalent* view or the set of *immediate subsumers* and *immediate subsumees* is returned. In the former case, the answer set is simply the set of all objects that are instances of the view equivalent to the query; in the latter case, the union of the sets of instances of immediate subsumee views are included in the answer set and only objects that are instances of the immediate subsumer view, but not instances of the immediate subsumee views, have to be checked against the query condition.

Usually, in a database environment, query languages are more expressive than schema description languages. This holds for Relational Databases and, more recently, for OODB, see for example the proposed standard *OQL* language [112].

Remark 10. *In the context of extraction and integration of textual heterogeneous data sources, provided that a highly expressive OO schema description language is available, we can adopt as query language the same language. The choice of a simple query language (a significative restriction of OQL) has been also recently made at the I^3 workshop on mediators language standards [98].*

A system, called ODB-TOOLS, implementing algorithms for incoherence detection and subsumption computation has been developed at the Dipartimento di Scienze dell'Ingegneria of the University of Modena[11]. ODB-TOOLS includes an extension of odl, called olcd, allowing the expression of *quantified path types* and *integrity constraints* rules (IC rules). The former extension has been introduced to deal easily and powerfully with nested structures. Paths,

---

[11] ODB-TOOLS is available on Internet at the following address: (http://sparc20.dsi.unimo.it/).

which are essentially sequences of attributes, represent the central ingredient of OODB query languages to navigate through the aggregation hierarchies of classes and types of a schema. In particular, *quantified* paths to navigate through set types are provided. The allowed quantifications are existential and universal and they can appear more than once in the same path. IC rules, expressed as *if then* rules, whose antecedent and consequent are `olcd` *virtual* types, allow the declarative formulation of a relevant set of integrity constraints [53, 54].

Following the key idea of *semantics expansion* of a type in [53] integrity constraints can be used to optimize queries. The semantics expansion of a query is obtained by iterating the following transformations: if a query *implies* the antecedent of an integrity rule then the consequent of that rule can be intersected with the query; subsumption computation is used to compute logical implication. In this way new "isa" relationships can be found and it is possible *to move the query down* in a schema hierarchy.

Remark 11. *By using a description logics including if then integrity rules it is possible to perform semantic query optimization with respect to usual OODB schemata including only base classes.*

ODB-TOOLS is composed of two modules: ODB-DESIGNER [37] and ODB-QOPTIMIZER. ODB-DESIGNER is an active tool which provides an ODL (ODMG93) standard interface and supports the design of an OODB schema preserving coherence and minimality with respect to inheritance. It implements the theoretical framework of [60]. ODB-QOPTIMIZER performs semantic optimization of OODB queries [53]; it provides an OQL (ODMG93) standard interface.

3.3.5 On the Role of ODB-TOOLS in the MOMIS System

The key idea at the basis of the MOMIS project was that starting from a system based on description logics as ODB-TOOLS, following the "semantic approach" and some interesting features of TSIMMIS, it is easy to develop a powerful mediator of an I^3 system. In fact:

1. the standard ODM-ODMG model and ODL-ODMG language can adopted both for sources and mediators;
2. the ODL language is extended to represent rules in analogy with *MSL*;
3. the ODL language is extended to represent QDTL;
4. a *minimal core language* which is a restriction of the OQL-ODMG language such that it will accept queries for relational databases is adopted;
5. `olcd` is extended to support QDTL translation.

A mediator can be generated with the above system by introducing the following knowledge:

− describe the schemata of the sources to be integrated and the mediator schema in the ODL-ODMG language;

- describe query templates in the *minimal core language*;
- describe the mediator rules in ODL_{I^3}.

Having ODB-TOOLS available, the knowledge expressed in the standard languages above is automatically translated into `olcd` classes and virtual classes and the the `olcd` incoherence detection and subsumption algorithms can be exploited in the following way:

- to perform data integration by exploiting mediator rules;
- to execute a query by determining the most efficient one among the supported subsuming queries.

Two final remarks: as observed in Remark 7, the adoption of an open world semantics overcomes the problems of conventional OO data models mentioned above; for sources supporting OODBMS or RDBMS, query templates are not necessary and ODB-DESIGNER can be used as a powerful query optimizer for OQL queries.

3.4 Discussion and Final Remarks

In this chapter, we have presented two approaches to schema integration of heterogeneous information sources. The first one, the "structural approach", has been illustrated by means of the TSIMMIS system. The second one, the "semantic approach", has been presented by means of the MOMIS system. It is based on a description logics component (ODB-TOOLS) and a cluster generator module (ARTEMIS) together with an ODL_{I^3} interface module. In this way, generation of the global schema for the mediator is a semi-automated process.

It is the authors' opinion that *the schema-less* assumption of the structural approach leads to two major drawbacks w.r.t. the semantic approach:

- inefficient retrieval of data to be integrated;
- incapability to answer not–predefined queries.

On the contrary, the use of a schema permits the support of every possible user query on the schema instead of a predefined subset of them. For this reason, they strongly believe that the semantic approach is more promising.

The authors are conscious that, due to lack of space, the above presentation is incomplete with respect to many topics. Among the more relevant, let us mention:

- query decomposition and optimization;
- object fusion in mediator system;
- integration of semi–structured data.

On the other hand, the authors think that the contents of the chapter includes topics sufficiently investigated by the research community whereas other topics, such as those mentioned above, need more research efforts.

Acknowledgements

This research has been partially funded by the MURST 40% 97 Italian Project: 'INTERDATA'.

We would like to thank S. Castano and S.De Capitani di Vimercati of the Università di Milano who developed the ARTEMIS component of the MOMIS system, and S. Montanari and M.Vincini of the Università di Modena who contributed to the project and development of the Global Schema Builder.

A special thanks to the students of the "Laurea in Ingegneria Informatica" of the Università di Modena contributing to the software development of the MOMIS project.

4. In-Context Information Management through Adaptive Collaboration of Intelligent Agents*

Katia Sycara

The Robotics Institute, Carnegie Mellon University, Pittsburgh,
PA 15213, USA.
E-Mail: katia@cs.cmu.edu

Summary.

Although the number and availability of electronic information sources are increasing, current information technology requires manual manipulation and user-specification of all details. Once accessed, information must be filtered in the context of the user's task. Current systems lack the ability to get contextual information or use it to automate filtering. At Carnegie Mellon University, we have been engaged in the RETSINA project, which aims to develop a reusable multiagent software infrastructure that allows heterogeneous agents on the Internet, possibly developed by different designers, to collaborate with each other to manage information in the context of user-specified tasks. In this chapter, we will provide a brief overview of the whole system and then focus on its capability for in-context information management.

4.1 Introduction

The Web is full of information resources. This abundance of information holds great potential for being brought to bear at the right time on decision making tasks. Current practice in automated finding and filtering of information from the Web, however, is far from helping accomplish this goal. The context of the task for which the information is needed remains in the user's head; moreover, the user must spend much time manually searching for relevant information. Task context is currently expressed only through keywords that are manually submitted to search engines. Keywords are a very impoverished expression of task context making it difficult for the user to accurately express requirements for information relevant to the task under consideration. Currently, there are no formal languages that allow representation of task context to guide information retrieval. Search engines don't adapt their search strategies according to different users. Moreover, the problem is exacerbated because the information sources have high "noise", i.e. most of the pages are irrelevant to the interests of a particular user. Research on intelligent software agents is under way to address these issues. Intelligent agents are programs

---

* This research has been supported in part by DARPA contract F30602-98-2-0138, and by ONR Grant N00014-96-1222.

that act on behalf of their human users to perform laborious information-gathering tasks [655] and they are one of the "hot" topics in Information Systems R&D at the moment. The last ten years have seen a marked interest in agent-oriented technology, spanning applications as diverse as information retrieval, user interface design and network management.

We have been developing the RETSINA multiagent infrastructure to aid users in decision making and information management (information gathering, filtering, integration) tasks [655]. Users can delegate tasks to RETSINA agents who coordinate with each other to fulfill the delegated tasks. The RETSINA multiagent infrastructure provides a reusable framework for structuring agents that operate in an open Information environment (e.g. the Internet), where they form adaptive teams on demand in order to solve decision making and information management tasks delegated by users. RETSINA agents provide capabilities for in-context information gathering and filtering at different levels of automation and sophistication.

The simplest model of task context for information retrieval is expressed by a set of user-supplied keywords. In current practice, these keywords are supplied by the user to search engines that return a set of documents that are indexed by the provided keywords. Unfortunately, when this simple keyword-based context is used, current search engines return far too many documents to be useful. Meta search engines (e.g. MetaCrawler) try to improve the situation by taking the intersection of documents returned by each engine using a given set of keywords. Document intersection increases search relevance somewhat but does not solve the problem by any means. Besides these two very simple in-context information retrieval strategies, RETSINA agents provide more sophisticated ways to define the task context for information retrieval. We briefly mention these mechanisms in the rest of this introduction and present them in more detail in the rest of this chapter.

Instead of a user trying for each task to use ad hoc keywords for information retrieval, a more robust sense of context can be established by automatically supplying refinement keywords that can constrain the search, thus hopefully increasing the relevance of the returned information. RETSINA agents use two methods to automatically supply refinement keywords to establish such a context: using the trigger pair model and document similarity assessment based on relevance feedback.

An even more reliable information context that RETSINA agents provide can be established as an agent monitors user's actions and learns and tracks user interests as the user executes manual information searches. Then the learned user profile can serve as the information context. This type of context has the advantage that it has been learned from repeated information search trials and by utilizing user feedback. It still suffers from the fact that the task for which the information gathering was being performed is still implicit in the user's head.

RETSINA supports explicit task and goal representation and delegation to agents. A user can specify goals to be solved for. Agents form teams on demand to cooperatively form task-based plans to fulfill the delegated goals. The planning takes place in an open information environment where information sources, agents or communication links can change, appear or disappear dynamically. Hence information access and monitoring is an integral part of the planning process. Thus, the context of information gathering is the current task that an agent is planning for on the user's behalf. We present the computational mechanisms that allow an agent or a set of agents to cooperatively plan to fulfill user-delegated goals and tasks. In addition, we provide tools that allow a user to specify and delegate tasks to RETSINA agents. This is accomplished through two main tools, the Task Editor and the Agent Editor. The Task Editor allows explicit representation of tasks in hierarchical task networks. Task networks represent plan skeletons and are stored in an Editor task library. Through interactions with the user, task networks can be retrieved and instantiated or combined with newly provided task fragments to represent new tasks. Once the task networks for a new agent have been specified, the Agent Editor instantiates the new agent automatically.

Providing an explicit computational formalism to express task context is extremely important since it (a) guides information searches so that only relevant task related information is returned, and (b) saves the user great amounts of manual effort.

The paper is organized as follows. Section 11.2 presents an overview of the RETSINA infrastructure. Section 4.2.1 presents the basic architecture of a RETSINA agent that, as is discussed in subsequent sections, supports the explicit task context representation. Section 4.3 presents the methods that an interface RETSINA agent uses for automatically supplying keywords to refine user-supplied information management context. User interests and information profile could be a more reliable context for information gathering and filtering. Implemented methods for learning and keeping track of multiple user interests are presented in Section 4.4. Section 4.5 presents how RETSINA agents represent task context explicitly and how the context is utilized in collaborative information gathering tasks to support user goals. Finally, we conclude with a summary of the chapter and future work.

4.2 Brief Overview of RETSINA

Our work on the computational framework of intelligent agents has been motivated by a number of considerations.

– *Distributed information sources:* Information sources available on-line are inherently distributed.
– *Sharability:* Typically, user applications need to access several services or resources in an asynchronous manner in support of a variety of tasks. It

is desirable that the architecture support sharability of agent capabilities and retrieved information.

- *Complexity hiding:* Often information retrieval in support of a task involves quite complex coordination of many different agents. To avoid overloading users with a confusing array of different agents and agent interfaces, it is necessary to develop an architecture that hides the underlying distributed problem solving complexity. Complexity hiding, while alleviating cognitive overload, should not come at the price of making agents' expertise opaque. To alleviate the agent opacity problem, we have committed to explicit knowledge representation of agent behaviors, and explanation capabilities.
- *Modularity and Reusability:* One of the basic ideas behind our distributed agent-based approach is that agents should be kept simple for ease of maintenance, initialization and customization. Another facet of reusability is that it should be relatively straightforward to incorporate access to pre-existing information services.
- *Flexibility:* Intelligent agents should be able to interact in new configurations "on-demand", depending on the requirements of a particular decision making task. This includes the capability to migrate to other platforms to take advantage of locally accessible resources.
- *Robustness:* When information and control is distributed, the system should be able to degrade gracefully even when some of the agents, the information sources or the communication links are out of service temporarily.

Our framework explicitly admits the notion that agents are part of multi-agent systems. This has the implication that agent coordination is not an afterthought but part of our system and agent architectural commitments. Such multi-agent systems can compartmentalize specialized task knowledge, organize themselves to avoid processing bottlenecks, and can be built expressly to deal with dynamic changes in the agent environment.

Our distributed agent-based architecture has three types of agents (see Figure 4.1): *interface* agents, *task* agents and *information* agents. This is a simplification of the possible types of agent categories both for purposes of exposition and purposes of determining in a principled manner particular agent reusable behaviors that can serve as agent software building blocks. These three broad agent categories share common architectural components (Section 4.2.1) but have different sets of agent behaviors. The behaviors in each class of agent are reusable.

Interface agents interact with the user receiving user specifications and delivering results. They acquire, model and utilize user preferences to guide system coordination in support of the user's tasks. For example, an agent that filters electronic mail according to its user's preferences is an interface agent. The main functions of an interface agent include: (1) collecting relevant information from the user to initiate a task, (2) presenting relevant information including results and explanations, (3) asking the user for additional information during problem solving, and (4) asking for user confirmation, when necessary. Interacting only through a relevant interface agent for a task hides the underlying distributed information gathering and problem solving complexity. For example, in our WARREN system[657] for financial portfolio management, more than 10 agents are involved. However, the user interacts directly only with the portfolio management interface agent.

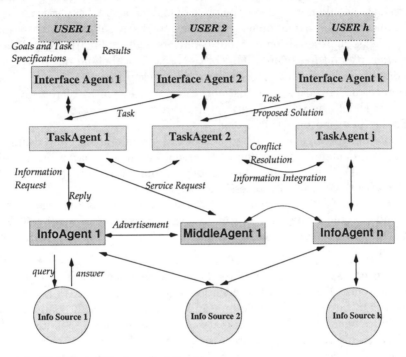

Fig. 4.1. Distributed System Architecture

Task agents support decision making by formulating problem solving plans and carrying them out through querying and exchanging information with other software agents. Task agents have knowledge of the task domain, and which other task agents or information agents are relevant to performing various parts of the task. In addition, task agents have strategies for resolving conflicts and fusing information retrieved by information agents. For example, an agent that makes stock buy or sell recommendations is a task agent. A task agent (1) receives user delegated task specifications from an interface agent, (2) interprets the specifications and extracts problem solving goals, (3) forms plans to satisfy these goals, (4) identifies information seeking sub-goals that are present in its plans, (5) decomposes the plans and coordinates with appropriate task agents or information agents for plan execution, monitoring and results composition. This type of intelligent agent differs from traditional AI systems since information-seeking and communication during problem solving is an inherently built-in part of the system. This enables it to deal with open world environments (new information from the environment is incorporated during the agent's problem solving). Planning and execution are interleaved since retrieved information may change the planner's view of the outside world or alter the planner's inner belief system.

The main function of an information agent is to process intelligently and efficiently information retrieval and information monitoring requests. These requests come externally from other agents; the information used to fulfill these requests comes from arbitrary external information sources. Typically, a single information agent will serve the information needs of many humans or machine agents. An information agent is quite different from a typical WWW service that provides data to multiple users. Besides the obvious interface differences, an information agent can reason about the way it will handle external requests and the order in which it will carry them out.

In order to allow agents to find others in an open environment such as the Internet, we have developed a set of agents, called *middle agents*. Middle agents receive advertisements of agent capabilities and store these advertisements in an internal data base. When an agent (a requester or consumer agent) would like to find a service provider agent that possesses certain desired capabilities, it sends a request to a middle agent. The middle agent matches the request to its data base of received advertisements to determine whether an agent whose capabilities math the request is known. We have identified different types of middle agents (e.g. matchmakers, brokers) and have reported experimental results that show different performance tradeoffs of these agents [165]. In addition, we have developed the language LARKS (Language for Advertisement and Request for Knowledge Sharing)[656].

The presence of the middle agents in the RETSINA framework allows adaptive agent organization. The high level goals and tasks imparted by the user form the context within which agents can adaptively (with the help of middle agents) form teams/coalitions so that this collaboration will fulfill the goals and tasks. This adaptive collaboration is also supported by the internal architecture of RETSINA agents (see Section 4.2.1). Overall system robustness is also facilitated through the use of middle agents. Agents can have replicated capabilities. For example in the Warren financial portfolio management application[657], there are different information agents that can find stock quotes from the Web (e.g. Security APL, Gault). If a particular service provider disappears, a requester agent can find another one with same/similar capabilities by interrogating appropriate middle agents.

When an agent is created, it advertises itself to some entity such as a matchmaker or broker [238, 203, 360, 163]. This advertisement, expressed in terms of an agent's information base schema (Section 4.5.4), specifies the information services that the agent is making available, the associated ontology(ies) and any associated query limitations. This advertisement acts as a commitment by the agent to respond to appropriate requests in the future. In general, the process of matchmaking allows one agent with some objective to learn the name of another agent that could take on that objective. In addition, an agent has a shutdown and an initialization process. At startup, the agent executes the initialization process which bootstraps the agent by giving it initial goals, i.e. to poll for messages from other agents and to advertise itself with a matchmaker or broker. The shutdown process is executed when the agent either chooses to terminate or receives an error signal. The shutdown process sends messages from the terminating agent to any current customers and the matchmaker or broker informing them of service interruption.

The agents in our system communicate using KQML [203]. Our focus on long-term behaviors, such as periodic queries and database monitoring, has required us to extend the language with performative parameters to allow the specification of deadlines, task frequencies, and other temporal behavioral constraints. Coordination of information agents is accomplished by placing them in an organizational context that provides implicit commitments: each agent takes on an organizational role that specifies certain long-term commitments to certain classes of actions. Thus, these simpler agents can work effectively with one another as well as with more complex agents, such as task agents, that reason about commitments explicitly to produce coordinated behavior [166].

4.2.1 Overview of Single Agent Architecture

Currently the RETSINA framework provides an abstract basic agent architecture consisting of and integrating reusable modules, as depicted in Figure 4.2, and a concrete implementation of each module. Each agent consists of multithreaded Java code, and each module of an agent operates asynchronously. This enables the agent to be responsive to changing requirements and events. Each RETSINA agent consists of the following reusable modules:

- *communication and coordination* module that accepts and interprets messages from other agents, and sends replies.
- *planner* module that produces a plan that satisfies the agent's goals and tasks.
- *scheduler* module that schedules plan actions.
- *execution monitoring* module that initiates and monitors action execution.

The modules use well defined interfaces to interact with data structures that are used for keeping process information and for control purposes. In addition, each agent has the following knowledge components:

- *a set of domain independent and domain dependent plan fragments (Task Schemas)* indexed by goals. These plan fragments are retrieved and incrementally instantiated according to the current input parameters.

- *Belief Database* that contains facts, constraints and other knowledge reflecting the agent's current model of the environment and the state of execution.
- *Schedule* that depicts the sequence of actions that have been scheduled for execution.

We have provided an implementation of each of these modules and the associated data structures. Since we characterize agents from the structural point of view we are not committed to particular implementations of the planner, scheduler or any other module. The interfaces between the modules and the control flow paths are well defined. Different modules for planning or scheduling, for example can be "plugged-in" as long as they provide specific interface functionality. For a more extensive description of the agent architecture, see [655]. Depending on the agent type, there could be additional modules present. For example, information agents contain in addition, a local information database.

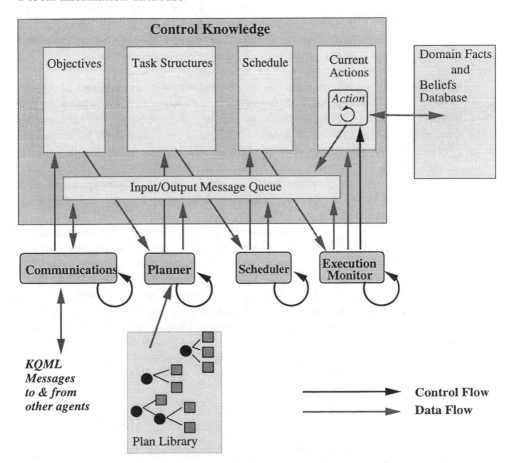

Fig. 4.2. The RETSINA Basic Agent Architecture

4.3 Automated Information Context Refinement by an Interface Agent

Sin gle keywords are usually ambiguous, or too general. Moreover, they can occur in vast quantities of documents, thus making the search return hundreds of hits, most of which are irrelevant to the intended user query. The single keywords are not a very useful context for information retrieval. Giving additional keywords can refine the context and constrain the search providing considerable improvement in the retrieval results. Good refinement words must have meanings that help disambiguate or make more specific the original search word. For example, the word "stock" has more than 10 definition in the WordNet[1] including "the capital raised by a corporation through the issue of shares entitling holders to partial ownership", "gun-stock", "inventory", "stock certificate", etc. Providing the refinement words that correspond to each one of those meanings, would help a search engine, for example, to prune out documents where the word is used with any of its other meanings. There are three ways to expand the query: manual query expansion, semi-manual query expansion, and automatic query expansion [273]. No matter which method is used, the key point is to get the best refinement words. In manual query expansion, although the user knows the intended meaning of the keyword she is using, she may not be able to provide the best refinement words. "Best" here means refinement words that most frequently co-occur with the word in its intended meaning in large number of documents. In other words, one of the characteristics of good refinement words is that they be domain specific. In this section we present methods for automatically finding appropriate keywords to constrain and refine search for relevant documents. These methods are: (a) using trigger pairs for automated keyword expansion, and (b) relevance feedback. The methods have been implemented in WebMate[2], an interface agent in the RETSINA system.

WebMate is composed of a stand-alone proxy that can monitor a user's actions to provide information for learning and search refinement, and an applet controller that interacts with a user. The stand-alone proxy is an HTTP proxy that sits between a user's web browser and the World-Wide Web. All HTTP transactions pass through WebMate which can monitor a user's browsing and searching activities and learn from them. The applet controller is the interface between the user and the stand-alone proxy. Through it, the user can express his interests when he browses and provide relevance feedback when he searches. In addition, through the applet controller, the user receives intelligent help from WebMate.

---

[1] http://www.cogsci.princeton.edu/~wn/
[2] Work on WebMate is joint with Liren Chen.

4.3.1 Automatic Keyword Refinement

WebMate uses the Trigger Pairs model to automatically generate refinement words. The Trigger Pairs Model [563, 235] is as follows:. If a word S is significantly correlated with another word T, then (S, T) is considered a "trigger pair", with S being the trigger and T the triggered word. When S occurs in the document, it triggers T, causing its probability estimate to change. That is, when we see the word S appearing at some point in a text, we expect the word T to appear somewhere after S with some confidence[3]. The mutual information (MI) that considers the word order is a measure of the correlation and used to extract trigger pairs from large corpus. The mutual information is given by the following formula:

$$\mathcal{MI}(s,t) = \mathcal{P}(s,t) \log \frac{\mathcal{P}(s,t)}{\mathcal{P}(s)\mathcal{P}(t)}$$

By experimenting with language corpora of varying domain specificity, we found that trigger pairs are domain specific. For example, the triggers to "Stock" in news and media domain (Broadcast News Corpus, 140M words) are {company, bond, buy, business, bank, dow, earning, composite, cent, analyst, big, chrysler, investor, cash, average, economy, close, capital, chip, ...}. However, in business and Economic (Wall Street Journal Corpus, 1M words) the triggers are {share, investor, index, exchange, price, dow, market, buy, point, jone, trade, trader, average, cent, industrial, gain, shareholder, company, board, ...}

The trigger pair method can provide several candidate refinement keywords. An additional question is, how many and which ones to use under any given circumstances. For a search with only one keyword, the top several triggers to the keyword are used to expand the search. But for a search with more than 2 keywords, the choice becomes more complicated. Let us assume that the keywords are $K_1, K_2, \ldots, K_m$, and the expected number of refinement words is N. We use an algorithm that involves finding the trigger pairs of all keywords with the highest mutual information and take subsets of their intersections. The detailed algorithm is reported in [122].

Besides allowing automated selection of refinement keywords to constrain search, this method also provides disambiguation information for ambiguous query words. We present in some deail a typical example of how our refinement method indeed helps improve retrieval results. Suppose the user is interested in documents where the word "stock" appears in its financial meaning. Inputting simply the keyword "stock" to Lycos and Altavista returns the following results.

---

[3] In the Trigger Pairs Model, (S, T) is different from (T, S), so the Trigger Pairs Model is different from the method of using co-occurrence of two words that is generally used in other keywords expansion experiments[273]

From Lycos:

1) YOSEMITE STOCK PHOTOS, ROCK CLIMBING, Daniela Masetti PHOTOS
2) YOSEMITE STOCK PHOTOS, ROCK CLIMBING PHOTOS
3) YOSEMITE STOCK PHOTOS, FISHING PHOTO
*4) Stock information Java Applet
5) STOCK GRAPHICS & PHOTOS
*6) American Stock Transfer & Trust Home Page
*7) STOCK CHARTS
*8) GROWTH STOCK ADVISOR FULL DISCLAIMER
*9) Stock information Java Applet
10) Ocean Stock

Only 5 hits are relevant to the financial meaning of "stock" in the top 10. From Altavista:

1. E. coli Genetic Stock Center
2. Michael Paras Photography: Photographs, Photography, stock photos,stock photo
*3. iGOLF Features - Stocks & Industry - Stock Report: Tuesday,September 5, 1995
4. Cedar Stock Resort Trinity Center Marina
*5. Stock 4 Art: HOME PAGE!
6. NET INFO - Luc Sala - Myster - stock footage
*7. The Official Vancouver Stock Exchange
*8. Stock Club
*9. NIAGARA MOHAWK DECLARES PREFERRED STOCK DIVIDEND
*10. The Italian Stock Exchange

There are 6 hits that are relevant to the financial meaning of the "stock" in the top 10. At this point, although the user may not be satisfied with the returned search results, it is difficult for him/her to figure out what words should be used to refine the search. So the trigger pairs can be used to expand the current search. The triggers to "stock" are {share, investor, index, exchange, price, dow, market, buy, point, jone, trade, trader, average, cent, industrial, gain, shareholder, company, board, ... }. If we use the first word "share" in the ranked triggers list to expand the keyword "stock" and send {stock share} to the above two search engines, all the top 10 hits returned are relevant to the financial meaning of "stock". We can see that these results are better than before. We can also refine the search "stock share" if the results are still not satisfactory. The intersection of the triggers sets of "stock" and "share" can be used for such search refinement.

4.3.2 Relevance Feedback

One of the most important ways in which current information retrieval technology supports refining searches is relevance feedback. Relevance feedback is a process where users identify relevant documents in an initial list of retrieved documents, and the system then creates a new query based on those sample relevant documents [235]. The idea is that since the newly formed query is based on documents that are similar to the desired relevant documents, the returned documents will indeed be similar. The central problems in relevance feedback are selecting "features" (words, phrases) from relevant documents and calculating weights for these features in the context of a new query [577].

Given a relevant page, WebMate first looks for the keywords (assume K_i is one of the keywords) and context of the keywords. The context is composed of the words that come before or after the given keyword. For example, the 5-context of the keyword K_i is $\dots W_{-5}W_{-4}W_{-3}W_{-2}W_{-1}K_iW_1W_2W_3W_4W_5 \dots$. For each keyword $K_{(i)}$, the system then extracts the chunks of 5 words $W_{-5}W_{-4}W_{-3}W_{-2}W_{-1}$ before K_i and the chunks of 5 words $W_1W_2W_3W_4W_5$ after K_i until all the keywords in the query are processed. Then, a bag of chunks are collected and passed to the processes of deleting the stop words and calculating the frequency. After that, the top several frequent words are used to expand the current search keywords.

For example, the following text is part of the overview of our Intelligent Agents project at CMU[4]. Suppose a user gives this text as a relevance feedback to the search keywords "intelligent agent".

> Intelligent Software Agents
> The voluminous and readily available information on the Internet has given rise to exploration of Intelligent Agent technology for accessing, filtering, evaluating and integrating information.
> In contrast to most current research that has investigated single-agent approaches, we are developing a collection of multiple agents that team up on demand—depending on the user, task, and situation—to access, filter and integrate information in support of user tasks. We are investigating techniques for developing distributed adaptive collections of information agents that coordinate to retrieve, filter and fuse information relevant to the user, task and situation, as well as anticipate user's information needs.
> Approach is based on:
> adaptable user and task models
> flexible organizational structuring
> a reusable agent architecture
> Underlying Technology
> Our intra-agent architecture and inter-agent organization is based on the RETSINA multiagent reusable infrastructure that we are developing.

Using our method, the refinement words extracted from the text are {software, structure, reusable, architecture, technology, organizational, network, schedule, research, rise}. Most of the refinement words reflect the characteristic of the project well. But, if instead of using the context method, we considered the whole content of the page when calculating the frequency, then the expanding words would be {software, information, task, area, application, technology, user, current, develop, underlying}. Obviously, the context of the search keywords can reflect the relevance better than the whole content of the web page. Subsequently, we used the top 5 words {software structure

---

[4] The URL of our project is: http//www.cs.cmu.edu/~softagents.

reusable architecture technology} to expand the search "intelligent agent". Of the top 10 results returned by Lycos, 7 were relevant to the query.

4.4 Learning of Information Retrieval Context

The automatically learned and continuously updated user profile can possibly serve as a more reliable indicator of information retrieval context than user-supplied keywords. There are several machine learning approaches that can be used to learn a user profile, such as Bayesian classifier, Nearest Neighbor, PEBLS, Decision Trees, TF-IDF, Neural Nets [515, 502]. In order for a particular technique to be effective, it should match the characteristics of the task and the user.

The filtering task for our agent involves judging whether an article is relevant or irrelevant to the user based on the user profile, in an environment where the prior probability of encountering a relevant document is very low compared to the probability of encountering an irrelevant document. In such an environment, it would be very frustrating and time consuming for a user to interact with an agent that starts with no knowledge but must obtain a set of positive and negative examples from user feedback. When a user browses, he does not want to evaluate all web pages that might contain potentially interesting information. To reduce user evaluation burden, WebMate collects only examples that are interesting to the user (only positive training examples). This kind of interaction presents potential problems since the documents that a user might label as "I like It" might fall into many distinct domains (e.g fishing, computer science, soccer). Those subclasses correspond to the different interests a user has. There have been two methods to address the problem of multiple user interests. The first is to keep a single user profile where the keywords might come from different domains but are "averaged'. This method has the disadvantage that averaging the vectors from the different documents might decrease too much the weights of words that are important for only a few of the interest categories. The second method is to ask the user to explicitly provide labels for the sub-categories of interest. Instead, WebMate learns the categories automatically.

WebMate utilizes the TF-IDF method [578] with multiple vectors representation. We have developed an algorithm for *multi TF-IDF* vector learning that we summarize here. For more details, see [122]. Let N be the assumed number of user interests. For each of the first N documents that the user marks "I like it", extract the TF-IDF vector and place it in a different "interest profile bucket". For each subsequent document, calculate the cosine similarity between every two TF-IDF vectors (including the vectors already in the profile and the new vector) so that the old vectors and the new vector can be placed in the appropriate "interests profile bucket". This algorithm is run whenever a user marks a document as "I like it". Thus, the user profile is incrementally, unobtrusively and continuously updated.

After a profile has been learned, it can be used for document filtering and anticipating user information requests. In particular, we have used the continuously updated user profile to compile a personal newspaper [36, 213, 545] and conducted informal experiments to determine the effectiveness of the method. In our experiments, the system monitors 14 news sites that contain articles about high technology including LAN time news[5], Media Central [6], PC magazine online [7], etc. Experimental results show that the average accuracy (relevance rate) that the recommended news is relevant to our interests is between 50% and 60% in the top 10 news articles . Generally the system will spide more than 500 pieces of news each day. In the whole recommended news, the average accuracy is about 30%. But if the news are randomly chosen from 500 pieces of news in which we assume there are 100 interesting news to us (this is based on our observation that for a typical news site such as LinkExchange, there are about 10 out of 50 pieces of news that are interesting to us in any given day), the default accuracy in the whole news is about 20%. So a 50% to 60% accuracy, achieved by WebMate, represents a two to three-fold accuracy increase.

4.5 Explicit Context Representation in Task Schemas

If agents have an explicit representation of the user's task that they can computationally reason about, then they could use this task representation as the information gathering and filtering context. Making use of this context would support the user's decision making more effectively. One way to explicitly specify the task context is to simply give an agent a set of goals it should fulfill. This assumes that the agent has the capability of producing plans to satisfy the goals. In addition, simply specifying high level goals might result in ambiguity and misunderstandings.

A more detailed specification includes, in addition to goals, a set of skeletal plan fragments that can be composed and instantiated to fulfill the given goals. In RETSINA, a task and its subtasks along with other useful computational parameters are represented using the formalism of Hierarchical Task Networks (HTNs)[728]. An HTN has nodes that denote abstract tasks, links between parent and children nodes that denote subtask relationships, and links between sibling nodes that denote precedence orderings. Leaf nodes represent *actions* that can be scheduled and executed. A task is *reduced* by instantiating a set of subtasks. Planning using a HTN formalism takes as input the agent's current set of goals, the current set of task structures, and a library of task reduction schemas. A task reduction schema presents a way of carrying out a task by specifying a set of sub-tasks/actions. In addition,

---

[5] http://www.lantimes.com/
[6] http://www.mediacentral.com/Magazines/MediaDaily/Archive
[7] http://www8.zdnet.com/pcmag/

Task Reduction schemas specify preconditions and postconditions for task reductions, and different types of constraints (state, temporal and resource constraints). These prescribe task interdependencies and dictate static control flow. In addition to these static relations, there are also runtime relations describing the information flow between subtasks. That is, the reduction may specify that the result of one sub-task (e.g. deciding the name of an agent) be provided as an input to another sub-task (e.g. sending a message). Runtime information flow is expressed by *provisions* whose variables are bound during runtime reflecting information coming in from the environment (e.g. sensors) or supplied by other agents.

Actions may require that certain information be provided before they can be executed, and may also produce information upon execution. Action execution produces an *outcome* to indicate different results of action execution (e.g. completion, different types of failures) and a *result* that expresses particular information about a returned outcome. The outcome is one of a finite set of predefined symbols. The results can be any arbitrary piece of information returned by the code object that implements the action. An example will make clear the intended difference between outcomes and results. Consider the action of retrieving a web page. The outcomes of such an action might be OK or ERROR, depending on whether the action succeeds on fetching the page or not. If the outcome is OK, the result of the action would be the web page itself. If the outcome is an ERROR, the result might be some description of the error. Such outcomes of one subtask reduction can be propagated at runtime to match provisions of another subtask. For example, the act of sending a KQML messages requires the name of the recipient and the content of the message, while the act of deciding to whom to send some message would produce the name of an agent. If the value(s) of the outcome(s) matches the value(s) of the provision, and if all the required inputs have been supplied, then the action is *enabled* and can be scheduled for execution. Final action selection, sequencing, and timing are left up to the agent's local scheduler.

These mechanisms support the representation and efficient execution of plans *with periodic actions, externally triggered actions and loops* [728]. Task schemas and alternative task reductions are blueprints for representing agent requirements, specification information and processing structure. This representation enables an agent to understand its requirements and reason about how its behavior can satisfy the requirements.

A task typically has alternative task reductions, that is alternative execution paths that can satisfy it depending on the parameters of the current situation. Thus, even simple tasks such as answering a query may result in very different sequences of actions (asking a middle agent, using an already known agent, using a cached previous answer).

4.5.1 Agent Advertisement Behavior

An agent behavior is a particular approach to accomplishing a goal. Behavior instances are represented by a task instance, a set of sub-tasks or primitive action instances, and the information-flow relationships between them. An agent's task reduction schemas are retrieved and incrementally instantiated by its planner module to provide task structures that are subsequently scheduled and executed. The execution of the resulting task structures composes the agent's behaviors. Thus, the specification of a particular set of task reduction schemas defines a class of behaviors which will be shared by all agents which have those schemas in their libraries. For example, since the behavior of advertising its capabilities is shared by all RETSINA agents, each agent contains the same task structures and standard reductions for this behavior, shown in Figure 4.3.

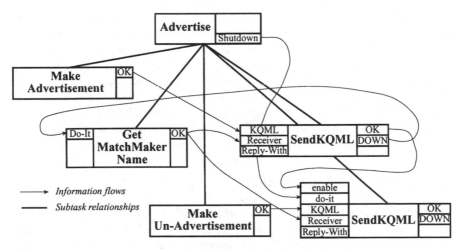

Fig. 4.3. The standard task reduction for the "advertise" task.

The three actions "Make Advertisement", "Get Matchmaker Name", and the topmost instance of "SendKQML" are involved in sending the advertising message. Both "Get Matchmaker Name" and this instance of "SendKQML" are periodic. All three tasks have an initial deadline of "as soon as possible". "Make Advertisement" constructs the KQML advertisement message content (using the agent's local infobase schema plus execution information gathered and persistently stored from previous invocations) and provides it to Send-KQML. In our current implementation, the typical first reduction for "Get Matchmaker Name" is to use a predefined name. [8] The matchmaker name is supplied as the RECEIVER of the KQML message, and the REPLY-WITH

---

[8] In our system, the matchmaker is the only agent with a known name. The default matchmaker name can be changed by a Unix environment variable, thus our

field is supplied by the planner at task-reduction time. If no matchmaker currently exists or some other network error occurs, the SendKQML signals a "DOWN" outcome, which provides a new signal to Get Matchmaker name, and the two tasks are rescheduled (they are periodic) and rerun.

The two action instances "Make Un-Advertisement" and the second, lower right SendKQML instance comprise the *shutdown* actions for this task. A task is shutdown whenever:

1. The planner removes the current reduction (because, for instance, it has failed). This would not typically happen for advertisement, but does for other tasks.
2. The agent itself intentionally (via a "Termination" action) or unintentionally (unrecoverable error/signal) goes off-line.

Shutdown actions are placed on both the regular and a special shutdown scheduling queue. Both actions are non-periodic and have a deadline of "only execute if there's nothing better to do". Actions on the shutdown queue are architecturally guaranteed to execute at least once, so in particular, the "Make Un-Advertisement" action will either execute during normal processing when the agent would otherwise be idle, or during shutdown if the agent never had any spare time. The SendKQML that actually passes the advertisement retraction on to the matchmaker has two extra enablement conditions: first, that the initial advertisement actually completed without error, and second that the task is being shutdown. This basic advertising behavior is shared (reused) for all information agents (simple and multi-source).

4.5.2 Forms of Task Delegation

To facilitate the interactive specification of task structures and task reductions by human agent designers, we have implemented the Task Editor and the Agent Editor. The Task Editor provides a library of task schemas and task reduction schemas that are indexed by the goals they accomplish and can be automatically retrieved. A user may specify new schemas, and/or new reductions needed to define the behaviors of a new agent. The Task Editor possesses a Graphical User Interface that shows graphically the tasks and task reductions. In addition, it has facilities for checking the consistency of specifications. When a user is finished with specifying the tasks and reductions for a new agent, the Agent Editor is invoked. The Agent Editor automatically composes the specified task and reductions and instantiates the new agent. We are currently designing tools to increase the user-friendliness of the Task Editor so that it can be used as a task delegation mechanism by end users.

A task/sub-task schema includes notation as to whether the agent itself is capable of reducing the task schema and executing the leaf actions, or the

---

group can have agents working in multiple logical agent namespaces even though they share a small set of physical processors.

agent must delegate this to another agent[9] that has the requisite capabilities. If, during planning, an agent finds out that it should delegate particular task reductions or actions to other agents, it automatically generates a message to be routed to the appropriate middle agent [10] requesting agents that have the capability required by the current (sub)-task reduction. In this way, task delegation among agents is dynamic, and takes into account the openness of the environment. Alternatively, for reasons of efficiency, an agent may have cached the names and locations of agents with whom it has collaborated in the past. In this case, the agent does not need to send requests to middle agents.

Since arrival of goals, planning and execution are on-going and interleaved, the planning process modifies the current set of task structures—by removing tasks, further reducing existing tasks, or instantiating new tasks—to account for any changes to the agent's goals. The flexible representation and incremental instantiation of task schemas and task reduction schemas and the presence of middle agents act synergistically to allow adaptive interleaving of information management (e.g. information gathering, filtering and integration) and execution in the context of the tasks that are being planned for. For example, at any time, any agent in the system might be unavailable or might go off-line. The agent's task reductions and execution monitoring ability handle these situations so that such failures are dealt with smoothly. If alternate agents are available, they will be contacted and the subproblem restarted. If no alternate agent is available, the agent will replan. Such replanning may result in choosing alternative task reductions that may require a different set of service provider agents.

In the next section, we take a more detailed look at how information agents are specified and how they operate.

4.5.3 Functional Overview of Information Agents

Typically, a single information agent will serve the information needs of many other agents (humans or intelligent software agents). An information agent can reason about the way it will handle external requests and adapt to different environmental events. Moreover, information agents not only perform information gathering in response to queries but also can carry out long-term interactions that involve *monitoring* the Infosphere for particular conditions, as well as information updating. The RETSINA agents communicate through message passing using the KQML [203] communication language.

In particular, we will focus on the behaviors of *basic information agents* that encapsulate a single (or very closely coupled) information source; we will also briefly discuss how these can be extended into a class of *multi-source information agents*. Each class of information agents has a fixed set

---

[9] This operationalizes the *intent-to* and *intent-that* predicates of [259].
[10] In the current implementation of RETSINA, such middle agents are matchmakers.

of behaviors. When a new information agent is created/instantiated the programmer does *not* choose or program behaviors, instead he/she specifies a domain-level data model and a domain-specific access method. This greatly simplifies the process of creating new information agents and facilitates agent interactions.

The dominant domain level behaviors of an information agent are: retrieving information from external information sources in response to one shot queries (e.g. "retrieve the current price of IBM stock"); requests for periodic information (e.g. "give me the price of IBM every 30 minutes"); monitoring external information sources for the occurrence of given information patterns, called change-monitoring requests, (e.g. "notify me when IBM's price increases by 10% over $80"). Information originates from external sources. Because an information agent does not have control over these external information sources, it must extract, possibly integrate, and store relevant pieces of information in a database local to the agent. The agent's information processing mechanisms then process the information in the local database to service information requests received from other agents or human users. Other simple behaviors that are used by all information agents include advertising their capabilities, managing and rebuilding the local database when necessary, and checking for KQML messages from other agents.

An information agent has three conceptual functional parts: the agent's *current activity information,* the agent's *local infobase,* and the *problem-solving library* that includes site-specific external interface code. The current activity information supports agent communication and planning. It keeps track of which customer has registered for which kind of information service, and with what reply deadline. It supports scheduling of the tasks necessary to fulfill an information request and monitoring of the execution of a current action. The information agent's knowledge about its current activities and responsibilities is also important because it is crucial to the agent's ability to reflect, introspect and adapt its behavior (e.g., by self-cloning or politely refusing requests [613]).

Since information agents share the basic agent architecture of a RETSINA agent, they too have a library of task schemas and task reduction schemas. These task structures allow information agents to plan about how to execute information requests. The agent's problem-solving part contains the planner's task reduction library and some site-specific interface code. Task reductions, indexed by the goals they achieve, are retrieved from the library and instantiated. The primitive actions in the instantiated reductions are then scheduled and executed. The way that an information agent accesses external information sources and creates local infobase records from them in response to a requesting agent(s) query(ies) is called the *external interface* and is the only non-reusable portion of an information agent's knowledge structures. However, the bulk of an information agent's knowledge about possible problem-solving activities—behaviors—is reusable, i.e. domain independent and fixed for the particular class of information agent. This includes the behaviors of advertising, listening for messages, and accepting, recording, running, and responding to queries.

4.5.4 Local Information Agent Infobase

In an information agent, retrieval of external data is separate from query processing. This allows for a domain-independent specification of an information agent in terms of the abstract schema of its local infobase. The information agent's local infobase contains records that have been retrieved from external information sources in relation to one or more queries. This local infobase is important because it allows the information agent to become more than just a fancy wrapper. The agent's local infobase is defined in terms of an *ontology*, a set of *attributes*, a *language*, and a *schema*. The infobase ontology links concept-names to their data types and domain-specific meaning (and must match on any incoming KQML message). Infobase attributes are meta-information stored about a field in a record. By default, information agents will keep track of two attributes: timestamp and previous value. The timestamp indicates when the field value in the record was last updated. Note that when a local agent infobase is formed from information gathered from multiple external information sources, the timestamps on every field in a record may be different. The previous value is the value the field had before the last infobase update. The database *query language* specifies a pre-determined format for the KQML :CONTENT slot. The "simple-query" query language is a set of predicate clauses on field values and attributes, joined with an implicit "AND".

The local infobase is constructed from a data definition language description. This description also serves as a way to describe the services a particular information agent offers to other agents. Since agent advertisement is done through the local infobase schema, the infobase allows all information agents to present an internally consistent, domain-independent interface to other agents that specifies the capabilities of the agent, or alternatively, the services provided by the agent. In addition, the local infobase allows an information agent to potentially tie together multiple external information sources, and also provides three performance enhancements. First, multiple related queries can be grouped to limit access to the external information source and free up processing bandwidth. Second, the local infobase acts to buffer the requesting agents from unexpected problems with the external information sources. Third, the local infobase provides attribute enhancements, such as storing historical data for each record field. This type of caching is not without tradeoffs; it uses more memory, and one must be careful to not introduce inconsistencies between the external source and the cache. A recent discussion of some of these tradeoffs in the context of higher-level multi-source information agent caching can be found in [17].

4.5.5 Examples of Information Queries

An information agent's external goals, i.e. answering a one-shot query, setting up periodic queries and monitoring information changes are communicated to it in KQML messages originating from other agents. The query is expressed in the :CONTENT slot of the message. The communication module receives and parses messages, extracts the information goals and passes them to its planner module. Since an information agent does not have control over an external information source, it executes the query on the cached information in its local infobase. An example of a one-shot query, "give me the most recent GH record" is:

```
(query security-apl :CLAUSES (eq $symbol "GH") :OUTPUT :ALL)
```

An example of a monitoring query, "tell me whenever Oracle reaches a new 52-week high price" is:

```
(query security-apl
  :CLAUSES
  (eq $symbol "ORCL")
  (> $52-week-high (previous-value $52-week-high))
  :OUTPUT :ALL)
```

For a different information domain, such as news articles, a new ontology must be specified, but the local infobase specification and the underlying infobase manipulation functions are reusable. As an example of a new infobase specification, we present the Dow Jones news feed that provides unstructured text information.

```
(DATABASE dow-jones-news
  :ONTOLOGY news
  :ATTRIBUTES nil
  :QUERY-LANGUAGE simple-query
  :SCHEMA
  (newsgroups :SELECTABLE :RANGE "dow-jones.*")
  (message-id :PKEY)
  (subject)
  (date :RANGE (> (- *today* 5days)))
  (body))
```

Below, we give an example of a monitoring query KQML message (including sender and receiver agents) for every article on IBM earnings from the dow jones news.

```
(monitor
  :SENDER barney
  :RECEIVER news-agent
  :LANGUAGE simple-query
  :ONTOLOGY news
  :REPLY-WITH ibm-query-2
  :NOTIFICATION-DEADLINE (30 minutes)
```

```
:CONTENT (query news
         :CLAUSES
         (=~ $newsgroups "dow-jones.indust.earnings-projections")
         (=~ subject "IBM")
         :OUTPUT :ALL))
```

Creating an instance of a totally new information agent for an information source in any domain requires only that the agent be provided with a infobase schema definition as described above, and a site-specific function for querying new external information source(s). Everything else is shared and reused between information agent instances (and thus improvements and new functionality are shared as well).

4.6 Conclusion and Future Research

As the Web is used my increasing numbers of users for different tasks, there is a need for information query management (e.g. retrieval, filtering, integration) to take into consideration the user's current task. Such in-context information retrieval can increase relevance of retrieved information. Currently, the task is in the user's head, therefore information management is through user searching and browsing. Search engines have notoriously low accuracy in finding directly relevant task information. We have presented different techniques implemented in the RETSINA multiagent infrastructure for in-context information retrieval. Task context can be implicitly defined through a list of keywords directly supplied by the user, or augmented automatically through provision of refinement keywords by an agent. A more robust form of information retrieval and filtering context consists of the user interests that can be automatically learned and tracked over time. Explicitly representing task context in computational forms and allowing agents to reason about it, originate and delegate information requests to others is the most advanced way of taking task context into consideration. In RETSINA, the representational vehicle is task structures in Hierarchical Task Networks. We have presented how the task structures can be used to represent task context and agent behaviors, and how information retrieval and filtering requests are accomplished though adaptive collaboration of agents. In future work we plan to rigorously evaluate these different techniques.

5. A Framework for a Scalable Agent Architecture of Cooperating Heterogeneous Knowledge Sources

Aris M. Ouksel

The University of Illinois at Chicago, Dept. of Information and Decision
Sciences, Chicago, IL 60607, USA.
E-Mail: aris@uic.edu

Summary.

Interoperability amongst heterogeneous information sources continues to
pose enormous challenges to the database, AI and other communities.
While significant progress has been achieved in system, syntactic, and
structural/schematic interoperability, comprehensive solutions to
semantic interoperability remain elusive. We present and motivate the
conceptual framework underlying SCOPES (Semiotic/Semantic
Coordination of Parallel Exploration Spaces), a scalable agent
architecture designed to support interoperable, autonomous and
heterogeneous knowledge sources. It is posited that the traditional
approach to semantics is insufficient to account for a variety of
misinterpretations in a realistic social world. Agents are viewed as
existing in a social world (of beliefs, expectations, commitments, etc)
constrained by pragmatics (intentions, communication, etc) and with
particular semantics (meanings, propositions, validity, etc) and syntactics
(formal structures, language, data, deduction, etc). We then concentrate
on semantic interoperability and how this is handled in SCOPES.
Semantic reconciliation is viewed as a non-monotonic query-dependent
that requires flexible interpretation of query context, and as a mechanism
to coordinate knowledge elicitation while constructing the query context.
We elaborate on the specific concepts needed to build this context, and
briefly discuss the SCOPES' algorithm for context construction.

5.1 Introduction and Objectives

The Internet continues to gain in popularity, as a means of communication
for organizations and individuals alike, at an explosive rate. Access to relevant
and accurate information is becoming increasingly complex in an environment
characterized by large numbers of diverse autonomous and dynamic information
sources. Underscoring this complexity is the evolving semantic, pragmatic, and
structural heterogeneity of these probably cross-disciplinary, multicultural and
rich-media knowledge sources. These problems are exacerbated by the rapid

changes in technology, in the economy, and their implications on the nature of work and collaboration, that mandate flexible and dynamic organization structures — such as virtual organizations (or adhocracies) — and the concomitant requirement to flexibly interpret the available knowledge in light of new market contingencies and the variety of intra- and cross-disciplinary forms of collaboration scientific or otherwise.

In this environment, agents (humans through computer-mediated communication and artificial surrogates for knowledge and/or service customers) are connected together through knowledge networks (who shares what information with whom) and interaction networks (who communicates with whom). The networks change over time as agents interact and learn, and pragmatic constraints and the semantic and syntactic contexts of the interaction affect this change. While the presentation in this chapter is limited to the SCOPES' framework and semantic interoperability issues, SCOPES (Semantic/Semiotic Coordination Over Parallel Exploration Spaces) [458,496] is a scalable agent architecture, designed to investigate larger fundamental questions such as:

- What is the appropriate conceptual framework needed to design architectures for agents engaged in realistic "social" interactions?,
- How can agents' autonomy be preserved, while providing capabilities for handling and managing heterogeneity, and for achieving interoperability amongst knowledge sites with (possibly) incomplete, uncertain, and multimedia information sources?
- What is the nature of an agent's memory? Specifically, how does an agent learn from complex interactions and augment this memory? How does this memory enable emergence of communities?
- How does domain specific knowledge impact interaction? What conceptual constructs are necessary to capture this knowledge?
- How can this understanding be formalized, modeled and implemented? What features will ensure scalability of the architecture?

To address these questions, SCOPES emphasizes computer-mediated conversation (using a multi-layered approach to the design of higher abstraction protocols for argumentative discourse) between agents. Interaction is wholly peer to peer, consisting of connections among individual agents, entered into and terminated at will, with no recourse to any central management facility. Organization structure of agents may not necessarily be fixed in advance, they may be dynamic states emerging from the patterns of interaction; culture, language, discipline and the nature of tasks form natural boundaries, which within SCOPES are overcome through negotiation. An important feature of SCOPES is that it provides for monitoring an agent's contextual interactions and for knowledge discovery through these interactions. This feature is essential to understanding the emergence of communities within the interaction and knowledge networks. Organizations are viewed as stable, overlapping, and nested patterns of actions and knowledge rather than as fixed structures of responsibility, communication, and control.

The scope of this work is best summed up by Munindar Singh[1]: "Pieces of the above work have been studied by others and the investigators in this proposal, albeit fragmentarily, in areas as diverse as distributed computing (DC), databases (DB), distributed artificial intelligence (DAI)", sociology (S), behavioral economics and game theory (GT), linguistics (L), and philosophy (P). "The DC and DB work focuses on narrower problems such as synchronization, and eschews high-level concepts such as social commitments" or complex asynchronous negotiations on evolving semantics and pragmatics. Our challenge in SCOPES is to enhance and synthesize several of the above ideas into a rigorous framework to investigate significant social questions about interaction and knowledge networks, and yet be flexible to allow the development of a practical system. The SCOPES architecture is a significant step towards this challenge.

In Section 2, the conceptual framework underlying the design of SCOPES is presented. We review in Section 3 several approaches to semantic interoperability show their limitations and motivate our own. In Section 4 we describe semantic interoperability in SCOPES [496], and discuss several extensions. Finally, in Section 5, we conclude with a brief discussion on on-going research to extend SCOPES.

5.2 A Conceptual Framework for SCOPES

SCOPES was originally designed, and is currently partially implemented [493], to support semantic interoperability and to investigate dynamic semantics amongst autonomous and heterogeneous information sources.   Semantic interoperability   requires   reconciling   a   variety   of   context-dependent incompatibilities, generally called semantic conflicts. SCOPES supports mechanisms to coordinate knowledge elicitation in constructing the "context" within which meaningful interaction can occur. Semantics, however, is only the first step, albeit fundamental, to understanding complex interactions between agents in a social world. Additional constructs are necessary.

Current theories are inadequate for supporting the dynamic integration of autonomous and heterogeneous information sources with possibly evolving and incompatible internal semantics [280]. These theories also ignore several other aspects of heterogeneity, particularly, pragmatics. The type of system flexibility required cannot occur without intelligent, and query-directed and partial integration of information sources in an open architecture, which views semantics as a matter of continuous negotiation and evolution in an environment of uncertain and incomplete information, and which preserves the autonomy of the information sources. High performance can only be achieved by leveraging

---

[1] Munindar Singh, "Panel on Cooperative Multiagent Systems", Anupam Joshi, 1997 International Conf. On Cooperative Information Systems, Kiawah Island, South Carolina, other panelists: Aris M. Ouksel, Amit Sheth.

relevant knowledge learned over time, as interaction increases, to constrain subsequent coordination and search.

The tendency in the literature and in practice is to propose intelligent agents [739], mediators [623,723] or ontologies [257] to take care of the problems of semantic heterogeneity without clearly specifying, and ircumscribing the capabilities of the underlying abstraction mechanisms. As a result, ad-hoc systems have been proposed with limited generality and flexibility, where rigid assumptions are made on interagent semantics and pragmatics and commensurability of knowledge. In the next section, we review the most promising approaches in the case of heterogeneous and autonomous structured and semi-structured information sources, and illustrated these limitations [494,495]. Clearly, without powerful abstraction mechanisms it is unlikely that general solutions can be devised to deal with the complexity of heterogeneous semantics. Further, without an implementation model a practical system cannot be built. These are the issues we addressed in SCOPES.

A Semiotics Framework for Constructing Interaction Context

The semantic approach adopted in SCOPES to construct context, while pertinent in many problems in heterogeneous information sources, is insufficient to account for a variety of misinterpretations in a realistic social environment. Context is commonly conceived to be <u>constructed</u> partly on the basis of mutually accepted propositions (beliefs). These mutual beliefs (MBs) are expected to bear on establishing shared ontologies and contribute to delineating emerging communities of interest on the Web. Before any domain-specific collaboration between communities of interest can occur, they must identify themselves to each other; mutual belief is expected to be an important diagnostic for defining communities of interest.   While the metaphor of <u>constructing</u> a context appropriately connotes activity [732], we supplement that with another metaphor connoting an even more dynamic development: agents <u>negotiate</u> contexts. Negotiation recognizes that contexts dynamically evolve as agents learn more about each other and as interests broaden or become more focused. The current SCOPES implementation reflects this fundamental concept within the semantic approach. Negotiation of context in a query-based framework is expected to favor solutions to problems of identification of domains for collaboration.   One important question in a query-based program is how to structure queries for efficient construction of domains of mutual interest by way of cooperative negotiation.   Another issue concerns the presuppositions of negotiation and the conditions that must be established to reasonably expect favorable outcomes.   To what extent can mutual belief bear the entire burden of constructing or negotiating context? Other pragmatic elements beside (MB) are expected to play a prominent role in establishing appropriate contexts for specific investigations. Clearly, pragmatic parameters such as domain specification (among others) will need to be determined if ambiguities are to be avoided or resolved. Related issues pertain to alternative approaches in pragmatic theory in which (MB) plays a prominent role, principally that of P.Grice [254] (Cooperative Principle and Maxims) and that of

D. Sperber and D. Wilson [641] (Relevance Theory). These theories, which depend on and also augment (MB), introduce fundamental concepts of communicative cooperation and relevance necessary for understanding communication and inference. At the same time they offer to afford simplifications of semantic theory. SCOPES promises to offer a useful framework in terms of which these concepts can be systematically investigated and developed.

The construction of context involves several abstraction layers other than semantics. These layers are best captured within a semiotics framework. Peirce [519] founded semiotics as a formal theory of sign. It consists of three distinct layers: syntax, semantics, and pragmatics. The social layer is added to provide a more comprehensive picture of the issues to examine in social interaction and knowledge networks [621]. According to Andersen [10], the semiotics approach to computing emphasizes the importance of integrating computers in social reality. The resulting framework is shown in Figure 1.

SOCIAL WORLD - beliefs, expectations, commitments, contracts, law, culture, …
PRAGMATICS – intentions, communication, conversations, negotiations,…
SEMANTICS – meanings, propositions, validity, truth, signification, denotations, …
SYNTACTICS - formal structure, language, logic, data, records, deduction, software,file, …

Figure 1. Open Systems Framework for Social Interaction

The semiotics framework provides an extensive blueprint to guide our research in interaction and knowledge networks. It allows a modular extension of SCOPES as our understanding of the issues within this framework deepens. The architecture of a SCOPES agent is illustrated in the Figure 2 below. The *knowledge acquisition and dialogue layer* handles conversations with outside agents and acquires information relevant to the query, such as anchors, possibly utilizing available ontologies and mediators. It includes the negotiated policies and constraints established with remote sources. It is also responsible for answering requests from other SCOPES agents in the network. The *knowledge wrapper layer* services requests from other SCOPES agents on the network about the local knowledge source (book, database, a human agent, etc…) in an agreed upon format. More details are given in [493]. The context negotiation layer will be discussed in the next section.

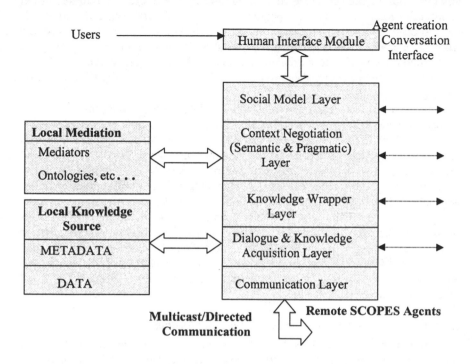

Figure 2. Architecture of a SCOPES agent

Mechanisms for Context Construction

We identified, motivated, and partially implemented[2] [493] four mechanisms essential to context construction. Below we discuss the four mechanisms for context construction:

Designing Rules of Interaction

This is not a standardization of semantics as in ontologies [499]. Rather, an agreement on the format of messages and the data types communicated without

---

[2] Availability of off-the-shelf software tools for the development of multi-agent architectures simplified our task. Specifically, we are using JAFMAS --a Java-based framework for multi-agent system design [5]; JESS -- a Java-based Expert System Shell, developed at Sandia Labs [51], it is a clone of the popular expert system shell CLIPS developed at NASA [51]; JATMS -- a Java-based Assumption Truth Maintenance System, which we are currently customizing and re-implementing in our lab from the original Lisp-based implementation [59] to Java; and finally, RMI (Remote Method Invocation) -- this an API (Application Program Interface) standard for building distributed Java systems. RMI will be used to facilitate the communication and coordination of agents that are internal and external to SCOPES.

any infraction on the substance being communicated. We referred to these rules of communication as Semantic Cooperation Protocols (SCPs) [623]. These protocols need to be extended to the other layers of the framework. The concept is inspired from the Conversation Architecture proposed by Winograd and Flores [730] and is in some aspects akin to a domain-independent Knowledge Interchange Format (KIF) [340]. Incidentally, these rules may allow interacting parties to agree on ontologies.

In a virtual organization setting, rules of interaction provide means for the parties to reach agreement on norms, i.e., the general patterns of behavior of the agents involved in the system. Responsibilities are defined, using deontic concepts related to obligations, permissions and prohibitions. We referred to this type of dialogue as policy, procedure and strategy handshakes [496]. In our approach, we want the rules to permit the parties to convey their beliefs, desires, and intentions akin to those defined in the well-known BDI (Beliefs/Desires/Intentions) model [542]. This is especially important in collaboration. The challenge in SCOPES is to identify the type of messages between agents (information, coordination or control), according to the beliefs/desires/ intentions of the sender. Doxastic and deontic logic [282,284] may be one way of modeling BDI. Our research in this area is aimed at analyzing the properties satisfied by various BDI-logics [542] and their computational tractability.

Reengineering the Pragmatics, Semantics, and Syntactics

Interoperability involves two phases: discovery of the relationships or mappings between cooperating parties, and then integration. It is the discovery phase that makes cooperation extremely complex. Discovery involves eliciting pragmatics, semantics, and syntactics knowledge from another information source to support assumptions about context mappings. Two parties can only communicate if their respective spaces of possible interpretations generate overlapping contexts. The practical success of this approach depends on the efficiency with which the search for the existence or non-existence of an overlap is done.

Discovery and data mining in SCOPES are incremental and refinement processes and require integrating various sources of evidence in a consistent manner. Mediators and ontologies [243,257,723] play an important role in this phase, but are limited. Discovery is dependent on who the requester is. To paraphrase an old adage, "Interpretation lies in the mind of the beholder". Within this paradigm, interpretation cannot be anticipated. Mediators and ontologies are therefore only partial solutions, as they make strong assumptions on the commensurability of knowledge [499]. Our view is that semantic knowledge elicitation must be query-directed. A priori interpretation is only possible if the query has been encountered previously wholly or partially under the same conditions.

Handling Approximation

Reasoning about context mappings occurs under incomplete and uncertain information. The extent to which one information source is integrated with another can only be done partially, as dictated by the needs to answer an information request; otherwise it will be difficult to achieve flexible and dynamic interpretation of the content of information sources. Further total integration, besides being impractical [245], violates the autonomy property on the Web by standardizing the set of interpretations. As a result, a complete semantic description of another information source may not be available, i.e., the space of evidence necessary to support a specific mapping is not known.

Uncertainty is caused by the absence of a measure over the evidence set needed to assert a mapping between contexts, and the unavailability of a priori conditional probabilities. In addition, research on conceptual structures [640] does not in many cases provide precise criteria as to when two concepts can be declared to be equivalent. Thus, in the discovery process, mappings are merely plausible [516]. A context constructed under these conditions is simply an approximation of the context that may be required to answer a query. A system designed to solve the semantic conflict problem is necessarily incremental and iterative. This component requires additional research into probabilistic context algebra, context optimization for ranked outputs, and object server support for complex dynamic context indexing that are used for subsequent retrievals.

Coming to Agreements

The focus here is on distributed systems whose components have disparate interests. The issue here is not the details of how to package the information on the network; it is not even in the higher-level issue of how agents communicate with one another. Rather, once we assume the agents can communicate knowledge information and understand one another, how do they come to agreements? This question synthesizes ideas from artificial intelligence (e.g., the concept of a reasoning, rational computer) with the tools of game theory (e.g., the study of rational behavior in an encounter between self-interested agents) [564]. Using rules of dialogue as described above, and representations for policy and strategy constraints, the interlocutors engage in negotiations to reach policy and strategy agreements.

5.3 Current State of Knowledge in Semantic Interoperability

Traditional Multidatabase Approaches

Semantic interoperability amongst heterogeneous information sources (HIS) requires data integration, which generally means the standardization of data definitions and structures through the use of a *conceptual* (or a *global*) *schema* across a collection of data sources. The conceptual schema specifies field and record definitions, structures, and rules for updating data values [389]. Using various *mappings* and *transformations*, source data is converted into a semantically equivalent, compatible form. Rules for performing these mappings in a HIS environment typically exist as a separate layer above the component databases [243,389].

The problem with the conceptual schema approach [496,494,615] is that: (a) it is extremely difficult to create and maintain; (b) its emphasis is on the resolution of schematic heterogeneity with little or no consideration to the reconciliation of semantic heterogeneity; (c) it assumes global coherence and commensurability of knowledge. That is, the various underlying explications of data are not captured in the conceptual schema thus resulting in Astatic" or "a priori" interpretations. Further, the resources required for the development of common coding systems and data definitions to form an effective, integrated system are enormous. Extensive changes in the component database schemas would necessitate further major modifications to the applications software that access and manipulate data stored in the component databases. It has been argued that attempts towards *total integration* may not be possible, due to the complexity and size of the underlying network of information systems [243], or that they may fail because in certain organizational contexts, total integration does not provide sufficient benefits to offset their cost [245]. Besides violating the autonomy, this approach is not justifiable economically since it increases short-term costs for long-term benefits that are at best uncertain.

An alternative to total integration is the *multidatabase language* approach (or *Federated Database* approach) [389,615]. This approach provides relief from some of the problems of creating a global schema by proposing a multidatabase language to facilitate semantic interoperability. This language shifts most of the hardship of data integration to the users by assuming that users know the information of interest. A particular database may chose to export parts of its schema and import schema portions from remote databases. For example the language provides users easy access to schema contents, such as attribute and entity names, attribute values etc, of all participating information sources in the network. It is the responsibility of the users to determine the semantics of the data items in each information source in the network.

Despite the presence of a multidatabase language, it is unreasonable to expect users to be familiar with the meaning of all existing *concepts/terms in* every information system across the network. While the traditional data integration approaches might be appealing for a small number of strongly interconnected databases they are clearly not scalable. As a result, semantic interoperability requires more flexible and scalable solutions.

Advanced Multidatabase Approaches

Researchers and practitioners have responded to the challenge of semantic interoperability by proposing a variety of advanced semantic reconciliation approaches to overcome the problems inherent in the traditional data integration approaches. We classify these techniques into five categories namely:

(a) **Information Retrieval** based techniques for structured data, for example Concept Hierarchy Model (CHM) [746], and Summary Schema Model (SSM) [90];

(b) **Shared Ontology** based techniques, for example Semantic Proximity [327], Context Interchange Network (COIN)[243], Dynamic Classification Ontologies (DCO)[323] and Knowledge Sharing Ontology [272,617];

(c) **Neural Networks** based techniques, for example Semantic Integration using Neural Nets (SemInt);

(d) **Mediator** based techniques, for example TSIMMIS [272] (see also Chapter 3); and

(e) **Software Agents** based approaches [739], for example Softbot, Internet Learning Agent (ILA) [194], Info- Agent [151], and MACRON [160], information matchmaking [360,656,658], information brokering using context logic [547].

Note that this list is by no means exhaustive, but it is fairly representative of the various advanced multidatabase approaches to semantic interoperability. For example, information retrieval systems [578] and common sense knowledge base systems [299] and others [347,17,734,746] are not discussed. Most distributed information retrieval systems are designed to work in homogeneous environment. There has been some work to extend schemes to a network of heterogeneous information retrieval systems. These extensions did not deal with the problem of semantic reconciliation. The semantic reconciliation techniques in a), b) and c) are only applicable to HIS environments containing *structured* component information sources, whereas those in d), e) and f) are also used for semi-structured. In the following, we assess the role advanced reconciliation approaches play in overcoming the challenges of semantic interoperability among HIS.

Assessment of Approaches for Structured Information Sources

Structured information sources comprises those in which a logical data model, such as the relational data model, object oriented data model, network data model, the hierarchical data model, or the object exchange model is used. In [494,495], we investigated several advanced reconciliation techniques for structured information sources, and found them to exhibit serious limitations in overcoming the challenges of semantic interoperability amongst autonomous, dynamic and heterogeneous information sources: a) failure to dynamically identify and classify all cases of semantic conflicts; b) failure to support flexible query-dependent interpretation of semantic conflicts; and c) failure in supporting discovery and reconciliation of semantic conflicts in an environment of incomplete and uncertain semantic knowledge.

Despite these drawbacks, the advanced semantic reconciliation techniques are useful in that they provide initial linguistic links between schema terms between cooperating HIS. We refer to these semantic links as **anchors**. Anchors are used in SCOPES as points of departure for the exploration search for a context. For example, if the two terms are attributes in their respective information sources, their corresponding domains or objects will be the next entities compared.

Assessment of Approaches for Semi-structured Information Sources

Semi-structured information sources are those in which the data representation is *not* based on a logical data modeling approach. Examples of semi-structured data are most Web-based documents, newspapers, books, magazine articles. The lack of structure in information sources increases the difficulty to resolve semantic conflicts. Many researchers (see [539]) have suggested that semi-structured information sources must be converted into a structured format before the resolution of semantic conflicts is tackled. Two general approaches have been proposed to facilitate this conversion: (1) *Wrappers*, such as the ones used in TSIMMIS, extract information from semi-structured Web-based information sources and convert it to a structured format; (2) *Software Agents,* such as *ShopBot* and *Internet Learning Agent* (ILA) [194], automatically learn the descriptions of Web based documents, and extract information from these sources in a structured format. While the extraction of structured information from semi-structured sources is not the focus of our research, SCOPES takes advantage of approaches such as those proposed in [539] to gain access to a structured view of semi-structured information sources, which in turn greatly simplifies the semantic reconciliation process.

Software Agents Based Data Integration Approaches

Effectiveness of Software Agents Based Data Integration Approaches

A semantic reconciliation approach based on software agents architecture is effective for several reasons: Software agents exhibit concurrency which is extremely useful when the search space is extremely large, as in the case of a large HIS environment. Instead of residing at a centralized location, agents can reside at the information source and perform distributed coordinated retrieval. The latter narrows the search space and returns a small yet more relevant subset of data to the user. Moreover semantic reconciliation is a knowledge intensive process, and may require the well coordinated interaction of several independent knowledge sources, such as thesauri, ontologies, database schemas, data dictionaries, advanced reconciliation techniques, etc. To provide support for this coordination, the software agents' paradigm can be utilized to design *Multi-Agent Systems* (MAS). The MAS are as a " loosely coupled network of problem solvers (or agents) that work together to solve problems that are beyond their individual capabilities" [119]. The MAS framework explicitly addresses the following issues: 1) *Communication:* how to enable agents to communicate? What communication protocols to use? 2) *Interaction:* What language should agents use to interact with each other and combine their efforts? 3) *Coherence and*

Coordination: How to ensure that agent's coordinate with each other to bring about a coherent solution to the problem they are trying to solve?

Many researchers [327,496,596,615] have emphasized that a successful semantic reconciliation system must support features such as *autonomy, flexibility, transparency, semantic communication independence, modularity, method extensibility* and *scalability*. All these features can be supported by software agents based systems architecture [739]. In SCOPES, we adopt a weak notion of "coherence" to preserve autonomy of information sources and to enhance scalability.

Evaluation of Agents-Based Approaches

Most of the work on software agent systems has concentrated on improving information discovery methods on the web and adopt them for cooperative agent configurations. The protocols of the web provide purely keyword based index services and look up collections of documents. Most software agent approaches employ some form of knowledge representation to enable more sophisticated representation of information sources and inferencing abilities. A few of the most notable include MetaCrawler, Internet Softbot[194], InfoAgent[151], MACRON [160] information matchmaking [360], and information brokering using context logic [547]. Our analysis of these systems reveals that they suffer from the same shortcomings as approaches for structured information sources.

The MetaCrawler forwards the users query to several commercial search engines such as Lycos, Altavista, Yahoo, etc. MetaCrawler=s semantic reconciliation capabilities are limited by the capabilities of keyword based matches returned by the search engines. For example MetaCrawler examines only those results that are provided by other search engines, and ranks the resulting documents according to its own document-to-query matching algorithm. MetaCrawler does not exhibit sufficient capabilities to either identify all possible types of semantic conflicts, or to provide a flexible query dependent semantic interpretation. Further details regarding the MetaCrawler can be found in [194].

The Softbot utilizes the *ftp, telnet, mail, netfind* and other file manipulation commands for discovery of structured web-based information. For example, if asked to find the phone number of a faculty-member at a university, the Softbot would initiate the *netfind* command to find this information. Softbot is sophisticated in that it utilizes relevance feedback to refine its search criteria. For example if there are more than one faculty members with the same name at the university, the Softbot may ask the user to provide additional information, such as the faculty members department, to help refine the search. Since the Softbot is presently limited to intelligent usage of file manipulation commands, it is only capable of handling relatively simple queries. The Softbot=s main focus is information gathering as compared to the identification and reconciliation of semantic conflicts among HIS.

Matchmaking [360,656,658] is an automated process whereby information providers and consumers are cooperating assisted by an intelligent facilitator utilizing a knowledge-sharing infrastructure. Matchmaking depends on messaging and content language and allows information providers and consumers to continuously issue and retract advertisements and requests, so that information does not become stale. Again, this system does not provide sophisticated mechanism to resolve semantic conflicts.

Info Agent [151] *and MACRON* [160] rely on a *shared ontology* approach for interpreting a user's query and for locating relevant information sources in a network. A *shared ontology* is a Adescription of concepts and the relationships that can exist for an agent or a community of agents" [257]. The ontology specifies a vocabulary that is used to provide mutual understanding among its users as they adopt it to describe and interpret the information shared among them [257,489].

Information brokering   [360] is a tool-kit for information broker development based on the Ontolingua system [257]. Ontolingua is an integrated tool system for developing domain-specific ontologies in the Knowledge Exchange Format (KIF) and for translating the resulting ontologies into application-oriented representation languages. Their information brokers maintain declarative, logic-based, object-oriented models of their domain of expertise and the domain of expertise of their underlying resources.

Despite the information gathering capabilities of Info Agent, MACRON, and Information brokering, our investigation [499] shows that ontology-based semantic reconciliation suffers from drawbacks similar to those of the global schema approach, because: a) It is neither practical nor theoretically possible to develop and maintain an ontology that strictly adheres to the design criteria of ontologies (clarity, coherence, extensibility, minimal encoding bias, ontological commitment) [257], particularly in an environment of autonomous, dynamic and heterogeneous information sources; b) It does not identify and classify semantic conflicts accurately; c) It cannot handle query-directed reconciliation, which requires multiple interpretations of semantic conflicts; d) It does not provide a coordination mechanism to discover metadata knowledge for semantic reconciliation, and to ensure consistency across all the mappings relevant to a query. Despite the obvious advantages of using the software agent paradigm, none of the present agent-based systems effectively addresses the problem of semantic reconciliation among HIS as we specified it in the introduction.

5.4 Semantic Interoperability in SCOPES

In [498,499,496], our investigation concluded that semantic reconciliation amongst cooperating heterogeneous information sources required the existence of a classification of semantic conflicts and a coordination mechanism to support:

(a) query-directed dynamic elicitation of semantic knowledge and partial integration;
(b) discovery and reconciliation of conflicts in environment of incomplete and uncertain semantic knowledge; and
(c) coexistence and management of multiple plausible interpretations (or contexts) during reconciliation.

SCOPES [496] is a novel architecture that satisfies these requirements. It integrates automatic and semi-automatic techniques to assist a human integrator in the semantic reconciliation process. Below we briefly describe the fundamental concepts underlying the SCOPES design and the architecture.

Classification of Semantic Conflicts

Without loss of generality the semantic reconciliation process assumes the existence of an object-oriented schema describing structured or semi-structured information sources. Our classification of semantic conflicts [458] classifies conflicts along three dimensions namely, *naming, abstraction*, and *levels of heterogeneity*. The Inter-Schema Correspondence Assertion (ISCA) which represents the semantic relationship between two elements of different databases has the general form:

Assert [naming, abstraction, heterogeneity]

Where *naming* (*abstraction*) stands for a naming (abstraction) function between an element x in the local database and an element y in either the local or the remote database; heterogeneity indicates the structural schema description of x and y in their respective databases. This classification combines the dimensions of semantic conflicts with a structural description, thereby facilitating the process of operational integration.

Abstraction

	Class	Generalization	Aggregation	Function
Synonym	(1) S/D	(2) S/D	(3) S/D	(4) S/D
Homonym	(5) S/D	(6) D	(7) D	(8) D
Unrelated	(9) S/D	(10) D	(11) S/D	(12) S/D

Along the dimension of naming, the relationships between two elements x and y can be categorized as *synonyms*, denoted *syn(x,y)*, which are terms having similar meaning; *homonyms*, denoted *hom(x,y)*, which are similar terms representing different concepts; and *unrelated* , denoted *unrel(x,y)* which are not related along the dimension of naming, however these could be related in some other way such as functional relationships. Along the dimension of abstraction, the relationships between two elements x and y can be categorized as *class* relationship, denoted *class(x,y)* ; *generalization / specialization* relationship, *gen(x,y)*; *aggregation* relationships, denoted *agg(x,y)*; and relationships due to *computed or derived functions,* denoted *function-name(x,y).*

The level of heterogeneity dimension includes the *object* level, the *attribute* level and the *instance* level of the database schema. Semantic conflicts due to naming and abstraction can occur at any of these levels within the same or two different databases. Thus this level provides us with a structural mapping between two corresponding elements from different databases. This dimension requires a pair of values, one for each element *x* and *y*, as represented in its corresponding schema. Each value is denoted either *att(x,O,DB)*, where *x* is the element considered in the assertion, *O* the object to which it is attribute, *DB* the database in which it appears; or *obj(x,DB)*, where *x* is an object in *DB*; *inst(x,O,DB)*, where *x* is an instance of object *O* in *DB*.

The most important advantage of this classification is the partitioning of semantic conflicts into 12 disjoint classes based on the dimensions of naming and abstraction. Some of these classes are transient because they are valid only in the dynamic reconciliation environment (indicated by a "D" entry in the table), where they represent semantic conflicts which are classified in the presence of incomplete semantic knowledge, whereas the other classes are valid in both the static and the dynamic reconciliation environment (a "S/D" entry in the table). These disjoint classes are described in the table above and in more details in [494], where it is shown that the classification captures all semantic conflicts discussed in the literature on heterogeneous conceptual schemas.

Context-Driven Reconciliation and Management of Multiple Contexts

Integration in SCOPES incrementally discovers and assembles the knowledge from a remote information source to answer a specific query posed locally. We refer to the knowledge gathered in this fashion as **context**, and the integrator's approach as *context driven reconciliation*. Reconciliation is thus a *partial dynamic integration,* which offers the flexibility of query-dependent interpretation. In contrast, *total* (or static) *integration* as pursued in the global schema approach and in many advanced reconciliation approaches imposes a priori interpretation.

The classification allows us to formally define **context** as a consistent set of ISCAs necessary to answer a specific query [496]. *A satisficing context* is one that is sufficient, not-necessarily complete, to answer a specific query. ISCAs are asserted on the basis of evidence that is gathered from a variety of knowledge sources. This evidence is in general not deterministic. Thus multiple plausible ISCAs for any two elements may co-exist, leading eventually to multiple plausible contexts for the same query. The probability in any context being considered by SCOPES may be revised as additional supporting or contradictory evidence is uncovered. SCOPES utilizes an Assumption Based Truth Maintenance System (ATMS) [168] for the management of multiple plausible contexts. The ATMS is essentially a collection of data structures and procedures used for accomplishing probability revision. SCOPES also utilizes a modification of the Dempster-Schafer theory of evidence [516], which is derived from Bayesian inference theory, in conjunction with the ATMS to model the likelihood of each ISCAs and thereby of each context.

Salient Features of the Dempster-Shafer (DS) Theory of Belief:

Given two elements from two different databases, there are 12 possible interschema correspondence assertions (ISCAs) based on the two dimensions of naming and abstraction. Let this set of assertions be Ω. There are 2^{12} possible subsets of Ω represented by the power set $P(\Omega)$. To represent an uncertain context, for example the context representing a mapping between terms, say ASS#$\cong$ from a database DB1 and AID$\cong$ from DB2, with respect to a query Q, we use the DS theory to assign portions of belief committed to the subsets of Ω. The DS theory of belief is formulated in terms of a function **m: $P(\Omega)$ | [0,1] st: m(ϕ) = 0 and $3_{A\phi\Omega}$ m(A) = 1**

The function **m** is referred to as a *mass function* or a *basic probability assignment*; Every subset of the environment which has a mass value greater than 0 is called a focal element. Assume that while investigating a possible mapping between terms ASS#$\cong$ from DB1 and AID$\cong$ from DB2, evidence **E** provides support for the following assertions:

> A1:Assert[syn(SS#,ID), class(SS#,ID), (att(SS#,Faculty,DB1), att(ID, Employee,DB2)]
> A2:Assert[syn(SS#,ID), gen(SS#,ID), (att(SS#,Faculty,DB1), att(ID, Employee,DB2)]
> A3:Assert[syn(SS#,ID), agg(SS#,ID), (att(SS#,Faculty,DB1), att(ID, Employee,DB2)]

Let a mass function assign a value of 0.4 to the set {A1,A2}and 0.4 to the set {A3}. These assignments may be based on general rules from conceptual structures, expert knowledge, thesauri or some other knowledge sources. The left over mass value is assigned to the larger set Ω (m (Ω) = 0.2) denoting that there may be additional conditions beyond evidence E which are true with some degrees of belief.

Definition (Evidence Set): Let Ω be the domain of values for a set of interschema correspondence assertions. Evidence set is a collection of subsets of Ω associated with mass function assignments. For example in the above case $ES_1 = [\{A1, A2\}^{0.4}, \{A3\}^{0.4}, \Omega^{0.2}]$ is an evidence set.

Definition (Belief Function): A belief function, denoted by *Bel*, corresponding to a specific mass function m, assigns to every subset A of Ω the sum of beliefs committed exactly to every subset of A by m, i.e. *Bel*(A) = $3_{X\phi A}$ m(X) . For example, *Bel*{A1, A2 A3} =m[{A1}]+ m[{A2}] +m[{A3}]+ m[{A1, A2}] +m[{A1, A3}] +m[{A3, A2}] +m[{A1, A2, A3}] =0 + 0 +0.4 +0.4 +0 +0+0 = 0.8

The above belief function is a measure of the minimum degree of support in favor of the set of assertions {A1, A2, A3}. An important observation must be noted here concerning the DS theory. Consider the assertion set {A1, A2, A3} using a pure bayesian approach. The probability P (A1, A2, A3) = 0, since these assertions contradict each other. Assertions A1, A2, A3 can coexist only with respect to uncertain evidence.

Definition (Plausibility Function): A plausibility function, denoted by *Pls*, corresponding to a specific mass function m, determines the maximum belief that can be possibly contributed to a subset of A, i.e.

$$Pls = 1 - Bel (A^c)$$

where A^c is the complement of A in Ω, and is equivalent to (Ω - A). The plausibility function is defined to indicate the degree to which the evidence set fails to refute a subset A. For example, $Pls(\{A1, A2, A3\}) = 1 - Bel(\{A1, A2, A3\}^c) = 1-0=1$

The plausibility function denotes the maximum degree to which the assertion set {A1, A2, A3} cannot be disproved and hence is plausible. We can observe that by definition, Bel(A) # Pls (A) . Their difference Pls(A) - Bel(A) denotes the degree to which the evidence set is uncertain whether to support A or A^c.

Combining Evidence Sets: There may exist multiple evidence sets supporting different mass function assignments on a domain of values. Given two mass functions m_1 and m_2 from two evidence sets ES_1 and ES_2 respectively, we can use the Dempster=s rule of combination to combine them. The combined mass denoted by $m_1\rho\ m_2$ is defined as: $m_1\rho\ m_2\ (Z) = 3_{Z=X1Y}\ m_1(X) \cdot m_2(Y)$. For example consider the availability of evidence ES_2 which supports the following set of assertions:

> **A1: Assert[syn(SS#,ID), class(SS#,ID), (att(SS#,Faculty,DB1), att(ID,Employee,DB2))]**
> **A3: Assert[syn(SS#,ID), agg(SS#,ID), (att(SS#,Faculty,DB1), att(ID,Employee,DB2))]**
> **A4: Assert[syn(SS#,ID), function(SS#,ID), (att(SS#,Faculty,DB1), att(ID,Employee,DB2))]**

For clarity of expression let the mass function m corresponding to ES_1 above be denoted as m_1. The mass function corresponding to ES_2 is denoted by m_2 and assigns values 0.3 to the set {A3, A4}, and 0.6 to the set {A1}. The remainder of the mass value is assigned to the larger set Ω (m (Ω) = 0.1). Hence ES_2 = $[\{A3,A4\}^{0.3}, \{A1\}^{0.6}, \Omega^{0.1}]$. Table 1 shows how these two pieces of evidence can be combined in the DS theory to further refine the context.

	$m_2[\{A1\}] = 0.6$	$m_2[\{A3,4\}] = 0.3$	$m_2[(\Omega)] = 0.1$
$m_1[\{A1,A2\}] = 0.4$	$\{A1\}0.24$	$\{\phi\}\ 0.12$	$\{A1,A2\}\ 0.04$
$m_1[\{A3\}] = 0.4$	$\{\phi\}\ 0.24$	$\{A3\}\ 0.12$	$\{A3\}\ 0.04$
$m_1[(\Omega)] = 0.2$	$\{A1\}\ 0.12$	$\{A3,\ A4\}0.06$	$\Omega\ 0.02$

The values in the internal boxes are the result of the combination of evidence sets ES_1 and ES_2. Since by definition $m_1\rho\ m_2\ (\phi)$ should be equal to zero, we need to normalize the internal values in the above table by using the following general formula:

$$m_1\rho\ m_2\ (Z) = [3_{Z=X1Y}m_1(X) \cdot m_2(Y)] / (1-k) \text{ where } k = 3_{X1Y=\phi}\ m_1(X) \cdot m_2(Y)$$

For the example in table, $k = 0.12+0.24=0.36$ and $1-k=0.64$, the values in the boxes should be modified as follows: $m_1\rho\ m_2\ (\{A1\}) = (0.24+0.12)/0.64 =0.56$; $m_1\rho\ m_2\ (\{A1,A2\})= 0.04/0.64 = 0.0625$; $m_1\rho m_2\ (\{A3\})= (0.12+0.04)/0.64 =0.25$, $m_1\rho m_2\ (\{A4,A5\})= 0.06/0.64 = 0.093$; $m_1\rho m_2\ (\Omega)= 0.02/0.64 = 0.031$; $m_1\rho m_2\ (\phi)= 0$.

The above description is sufficient to illustrate the use of the Dempster-Shafer inference to semantic inference. The primary computational burden of this procedure lies in determining the normalization constant of Dempster's rule. This normalizer requires a summation over all pairwise combinations of support values. It has complexity of $O\ (n**2)$, where n is the number of assertions.

Why the D-S and the ATMS Approaches (Briefly)

The utility of probability theory for modeling reasoning with uncertainty is limited by the lack of sufficient data to accurately estimate the prior and conditional probabilities required to use Bayes= rule. The D-S theory sidesteps the requirement for this data. It accepts an incomplete probabilistic model without prior or conditional probabilities. Given the incompleteness of the model, the D-S theory does not answer arbitrary probabilistic questions. Rather than estimating the probability of a hypothesis, it uses belief intervals to estimate how close the evidence is to determining the truth of a hypothesis. When used to model sources of evidence that are not independent, it can yield misleading and counterintuitive results. The fact that the classification decomposes semantic conflicts into disjoint classes helps significantly in the process of avoiding errors. It is important to note that a non-monotonic approach in accumulating assertions have provisions for retracting assertions and the D-S approach can be used together with a non-monotonic approach.

The use of the D-S approach requires an inference engine to deduce belief functions. We use an Assumption-Truth Maintenance System (ATMS) to provide a symbolic mechanism for identifying the set of assumptions needed to assemble the desired proofs, so when we assign probabilities of these assumptions, the system can be used as a symbolic engine for computing degrees of belief sought by the D-S theory. The second important use of the truth maintenance system is to handle the effect of retracting assumptions when they are invalidated by the evidence and to keep track of the multiple plausible sets of assertions which can coexist in the absence of complete knowledge. Truth maintenance systems arose as a way of providing the ability to do dependency backtracking when assumptions or assertions are retracted because they are contradicted by the current knowledge, and so to support nonmonotonic reasoning. Nonmonotonic reasoning is an approach in which axioms and/or rules of inference are extended to make it possible to reason with incomplete information.

Currently we are modifying the Dempster-Shafer inference process to deal with two known deficiencies in this theory; namely, the case of disappearing uncertainty even in the face of conflict, and the temporal-recency effect which favors more recent events over distant events on the evidential calculation. Basically, we are adapting a method called certainty factors to Dempster-Shafer to allow us to perform consistent inference.

Inference

In SCOPES evidence to support assertions may be obtained using a number of knowledge sources including ontologies [257,435] lexicons, reconciliation techniques, general or domain specific knowledge repositories, metadata specifications, general rules derived from conceptual structures. The strength of this evidence is determined by its source. In SCOPES the reconciliation techniques and knowledge sources are coordinated using the following simple interface template:

r: If C(p) Then consequent. [$p.q$]

where the antecedent of the rule **C** is defined recursively in BNF (Backus - Naur Form) as follows:

C::=E *Assertion *Assumption *E and C *Assertion and C *Assumption and C

In addition, C may include quantified variables over the domains of variables. Clearly AC$\cong$ can be an extremely complex typed predicate logic expression constructed from either a directly elicited piece of evidence AE$\cong$, available knowledge, a reasonable assumption, or a combination thereof. In the above template "consequent" is a disjunction of assertions about two objects O1 and O2, p represents the degree of belief in all the assertions in AC$\cong$, and q is the degree of belief in rule r if $p = 1$.

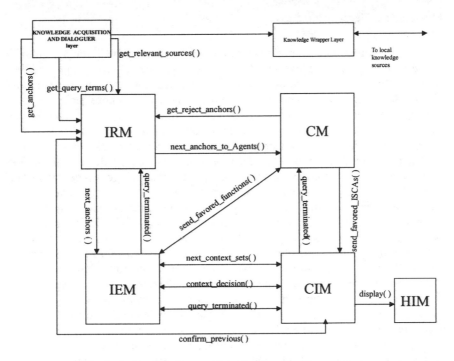

Figure 3. Module interactions in Context Negotiation

In case, there are many rules that derive the consequent of rule *r*, the D-S theory provides a feature called *parallel reduction* to derive the degree of belief in the consequent. However all the matching rules need not be activated at the same time. We are currently devising strategies to select from among all the relevant rules. This type of rule is referred to as "premise" in the D-S theory. Below we illustrate a few examples of this type of rule. These rules are general, and thus independent of any specific domain or information source.

Note: Obj(O,t) denotes that Object O is represented by term t; term(t,O) denotes that t is the term corresponding to object O; dom(O) denotes the domain of object O; key(t,O) denotes that t is the term corresponding to the key of object O: Note that the probability 1 will be distributed over the terms of consequent. In the absence of any other information, the distribution will be uniform.

r1: **IF** syn (t, t=) ϖ Obj(O,t) ϖ Obj(O=,t=) **THEN** syn (O,O=) ω gen(O,O=)
    ω agg(O,O=) [1.0]
r2: **IF** syn (O,O=) ϖ key(t, O) ϖ key(t=,O=) **THEN** syn (t,t=) [1.0]
r3: **IF** gen(O,O=) where term(t,O) ϖ term(t=,O)**THEN** gen(t,t=) [1.0]
r5: **IF** dom(O)   dom(O=) ϖ hom(t,t') ϖ Obj(O,t) ϖ Obj(O',t') **THEN**
    hom(O, O=) [1.0]
r6: **IF** ∀ v1⊐ dom(O), ∃ v2⊐ dom(O=) (syn (v1, v2)) **THEN** syn(O,O=) [1.0]

The Context Negotiation Layer

The four mechanisms described in the Section 2 overlap all internal modules which comprise the context negotiation layer of one SCOPES agent. These include an *information resource module*, whose main function is to ascertain what information sources are relevant; a *classification module*, whose main role is to classify semantic conflicts based on a classification scheme we designed [458] and on a variety of existing semantic reconciliation tools; *inference engine module*, whose role is to infer probabilistic semantic relationships based on new information provided by the classification agent, and on a rule base developed from knowledge of conceptual structures [640], and also to trigger additional search for evidence to continue reconciliation; a *context indexing module*, whose main role is to maintain a context index whose elements are plausible contexts generated through the knowledge elicited during the reconciliation process; a *human interface module*, whose role is to provide mechanisms for human intervention into the semantic reconciliation process. SCOPES provides the flexibility for human intervention when ambiguity can no longer be resolved automatically or performance is not tolerable or deliberate decisions are necessary to interject new facts, through a *Human Interface Component*, whose role is to allow a human user to intervene directly in the reconciliation process, or to simply utilize the *dialogue and knowledge acquisition component* to access the network.

A major concern in designing SCOPES is how to achieve *scalability* while preserving *autonomy* of information sources. Both these properties dictated against the use of network-wide global directory such as in the case of the Carnot project that uses the Cyc common-sense knowledge base as an extensive global context and federating mechanism [299,734]. They also dictated against global schema, multidatabase approaches [389] and advanced data integration approaches which mainly focus on sharing distributed meta-information and not on information discovery. We have also discarded several agent-based information retrieval systems [151,194] because they do not meet the requirements established in SCOPES. The SCOPES layered architecture, and particularly the encapsulation of the context negotiation layer permits scalability.

Another goal is to analyze improvements in query processing performance as interaction with relevant information sources increases. SCOPES includes an indexing mechanism that dynamically incorporates knowledge learnt over in past interactions into a *context index*. Comparison between contexts is based on subsumption [497]. The set of contexts forms a lattice structure. The elements of the index are the filters of the lattice. This context index is utilized to incrementally improve performance by reducing the need to construct the context for every request. The context index behaves in a fashion similar to materialized views, at the semantic level. The architecture of the negotiation layer provides several opportunities for parallel computation both internally to the site from where a request originates, i.e., use of cooperating multiple semantic reconciliation techniques, and pruning of the search space for a context, and externally to the site, i.e., simultaneous requests to multiple cooperating sites. To improve efficiency, we have also designed several heuristics to prune the search space based on theory of conceptual structures, and on domain-specific knowledge. A detailed discussion of these issues is beyond the scope of this presentation.

A context index is a trace of all an agent's interactions and shared knowledge. As indicated above, it forms a lattice structure under a containment relation. Mining interactions to determine who communicated with whom and what knowledge is shared, and what ties evolved from the interactions, partitions the community of users into groups. It is clear, for example, that filters in the lattice represent very closely-knit communities.

Algorithm: Context Construction

1. Initialization: Search for semantically relevant sources, first in CIM (for previously accessed sources
2. Mapping query terms: Search in IRM for next highest (in similarity) non-rejected anchors in remote sources
3. Schema propagation: Use local schema relationships to generate additional mappings to remote sources
4. ISCAs inference: Use inference rules in IEM to generate new ISCAs, or complete current ISCAs
5. Derivation: Mine current ISCAs for additional evidence
6. Repeat steps 4 and 5 until no derivation
7. Context merging: integrate ISCAs between schematically related objects
8. Repeat steps 2 to 7 until all query terms are processed

5.5 Conclusion and Extensions to SCOPES Currently Being Investigated

Rich Media Objects, Temporal, Spatial, and Causal Relationships

One goal of this project is to significantly advance our understanding of semantic conflicts involving complex objects and relationships. The discovery and representation of semantic conflicts requires the capability to classify these conflicts. Our current version of classification [458] deals solely with text-based semantic conflicts. We propose to extend this classification to handle multimedia objects. Many objects in a scientific database for example will be difficult to compare semantically. Images, digitized outputs of experiments, graphs, and video clips are all examples of data types where it is extremely difficult to define semantic comparison operators. In many cases, these objects will be part of composite objects or will be referred to by other objects. A semantic comparison model for multimedia objects goes beyond simple syntactic comparisons; it would require eliciting knowledge from related objects. Our preliminary results reveal that our original classification and context-based comparisons may require only modest changes to handle multimedia objects, given an object-oriented model for these objects.

With recent advances in database theory and practice, many information systems include *temporal* and/or *spatial* dimensions. For example, four different types of databases have been identified with respect to time. These include rollback databases, transaction time databases, and temporal databases. Data captured within systems such as geographic information systems (GIS), satellite based information systems, image processing, and image retrieval systems are all examples of spatial data. The temporal and spatial dimensions can be significant sources of semantic conflicts and multiple interpretations. Therefore, accurate processing across heterogeneous and autonomous information sources cannot occur without fixing interpretations in context along these dimensions.

Use of Domain-Specific Knowledge, Search, and Reasoning Capabilities

Most of this research in this section is being done in collaboration with Larry Henschen [278]. The ISCA notation and the three-dimensional semantic conflict classification scheme provide a rich formalism for classifying general kinds of semantic relationships. The SCOPES architecture provides for easy integration of the kind of domain-specific knowledge necessary to dynamically discover and resolve semantic issues in query processing. To see why the use of such knowledge must be dynamic, i.e. query-dependent, consider an example heterogeneous biomedical knowledge system composed of a network of hospitals and biomedical research institutes. Suppose there is a knowledge base at a cancer institute, where the patients there have already been diagnosed with cancer. A query from another node in the network about liver diseases could be answered without even accessing the cancer institute knowledge base because there is an implicit assumption that all the liver diseases there are cancer; also, a query could be blocked if it asked about a specific liver disorder that was not cancer. On the other hand, suppose a doctor at the cancer institute asks a question about liver diseases. There are three possibilities -- i) the doctor is interested only in cancer of the liver, ii) the doctor really does want to find about other liver diseases, perhaps to find ones with similar symptoms, and iii) the doctor is not even aware that the cancer institute knowledge base makes this implicit assumption. The SCOPES classification system will be augmented to allow for this kind of query-dependent, domain-specific knowledge.

Another important and unique feature of the SCOPES system is that it provides for the discovery and formation of virtual communities of users, that is groups of users who have common interests. Of course, the most interesting ones will be those formed on the basis of domain-specific features, such as users from a variety of knowledge sites who ask questions about cancer or about the liver or about cancer of the liver. Again, SCOPES provides the basic framework for this, and we are developing techniques for using domain-specific knowledge in this process.

The incorporation of domain-specific knowledge into the SCOPES system leads to several major research questions. First, a suitable representation formalism needs to be developed which allows for both the general kind of semantic classification expressed by the ISCAs of SCOPES and the domain-specific kind of knowledge cited in the previous paragraphs. The basic language of the present SCOPES system represents general classification mechanisms, like SYN, CLASS and AGG. To represent domain-specific semantic conflict, information will require at least a set of new predicates and will most likely require the use of domain-specific symbols. The development of a new set of general predicates that can classify a large subset of the domain-specific kind of knowledge is one major research effort. A related research effort is to develop a smooth interface between general classification of domain-specific knowledge and knowledge expressed in the domain-specific language. This representation may take the form of ordinary first-order deductive rules, a combination of that with object-oriented representation or even something totally new.

Next, the appropriate extensions to the basic reasoning methods of SCOPES need to be developed to account for the combination of general classification and domain-specific knowledge. There are two phases in which reasoning is required. First, reasoning is required during the negotiation process between knowledge sites when their semantic relationships are being determined; second, reasoning is required when users ask queries. In both cases the style of reasoning will be heavily dependent on the presence of both kinds of knowledge, general classification and domain- and query-specific. One major research issue is how to combine standard, logic-based reasoning in general rule systems with the Dempster-Shaefer methods for reasoning about evidence during the negotiation phases between knowledge sites. A second major research issue is how to efficiently combine general and domain-specific reasoning to determine contexts when a query is asked. Reasoning schemes in standard and non-standard logical calculi may be required.

A third major research focus will be on domain-specific and implicit knowledge discovery. The techniques currently known for discovering general, non-domain-specific classification knowledge may not be sufficient for the discovery of domain-specific and implicit knowledge. In particular, new methods will be needed to help uncover implicit assumptions in knowledge sources when the schemas may have no specific reference to the assumptions, as in the example mentioned earlier. Eliciting such knowledge will require the application of global, general knowledge about the domain to the individual local schemas. A major part of this research will be to determine just how much of it can be fully automated.

Similar remarks apply to a fourth major research focus, namely query processing. The user asking a query from within a local knowledge base will certainly not be aware of implicit domain knowledge in other knowledge sites and may not even be aware of them in his/her own knowledge base. Reformulating a query for processing in remote sites must go well beyond the standard transformations in other heterogeneous systems. In some cases, the system should be able to automatically generate the appropriate transformations, based perhaps even on past history for the user or knowledge gained through contexts and/or membership in one or more virtual communities. In other cases, however, it will be impossible for the system to make choices about whether or not the user should be made aware of special differences in the semantics of the remote knowledge and, if so, how to guide the user towards the query the user really wants answered. In such cases, it appears necessary to initiate a dialogue with the user. How to represent, store and use the knowledge necessary for the system to make such decisions and to engage in a user dialogue will form a major part of the research. In particular, we plan to study how contexts and the notion of virtual community, augmented with domain knowledge, can play a role in helping the system either automatically transform queries or working with the user.

Finally, in any knowledge-based system it is important to both believe in the answers returned by the system and to trust that the system has found all the information relevant to the query. That is, the reasoning processes should be both sound and complete. This is complicated in the presence of uncertainty, and uncertainty is a major feature of the SCOPES approach to negotiations about semantics between collaborating knowledge sources. Some work on reasoning in the presence of conflicting knowledge has been done in the past but is not completely applicable to the kinds of semantic conflict handled in the SCOPES system [496]. Indeed, the notions of soundness and completeness have to be redefined because of the use of Dempster-Shaefer analysis in SCOPES for accepting and using evidence about semantic conflict. What does an answer mean to a query in a system with negotiated agreements on semantic conflict and domain-specific and implicit knowledge in the various knowledge bases? To what extent the notions of soundness and completeness are relevant and how our new inference mechanisms meet these properties?

Part II

Rational Information Agents and Electronic Commerce

Introduction

It is evident that cyberspace will become more and more commercialized in near future[1]. Reasonably, trading information agents have to be equiped with sophisticated methods for making economically rational decisions [666, 80]. A personalized rational information agent may make purchases for his customer up to a preauthorized limit, filter information and solicitation from vendors, dynamically trades commodities and components within business-to-business digital markets, and increase the level of trust in his actions gradually over time. Most current tools for developing agents for electronic commerce (EC) in the Web fall into the categories conversational interfaces and profiling, collaborative filtering, comparison-shopping, and agent-based marketplaces [304, 264].

Conversational interfaces and profiling characterize a style of user-agent interaction which aims towards an individual and efficient information gathering. Collecting appropriate information about the likes and dislikes of a customer to tailor products and services is the core of any success of trading information agents and privacy concerns as well. Examples for conversational interfaces are NetSage Sage [465] and Extempo Imp [196].

One main benefit of trading based on user profiling is that the vendor may gain customer loyalty in case the agent-mediated deals were mutually successful. It is unlikely that the customer who has invested time and effort in supplying a significant amount of more or less private information to a vendor will repeat that effort to another vendor site. On the other hand, the customer's personal agent won't be tempted to lose the credit it gained from its customer for a perfect deal by changing to new vendor sites or agents frequently.

Collaborative information filtering (see also Part III) essentially automates the process of "word of mouth" in a given user community. The main purpose and application is to enable agents to anticipate the individual needs of a user in the context of other users. In addition, trust among user and

---

[1] According to the recent Forrester report, 3.2 trillion USD e-commerce sales are expected worldwide by 2003. As one example, currently the highest earning Web site in the UK in terms of advertisement revenue is the site of the newspaper *The Financial Times*, bringing in more than 1.7 million USD in the six months up to August 1998. The site has 1.2 million registered users spread across 230 countries [305].

agents is even easier to gain, since it is very difficult to manipulate the recommendations an agent makes using collaborative filtering. Popular systems of trading information agents in the Web using this technique include Firefly [208], LikeMinds [253], GroupLens [548], and WiseWire [731].

Comparison-shopping technologies let information agents compare the prices and features of products from different vendors. The agents select the best combination of price and feature for potential purchases of their users. The main underlying assumptions are that

- all relevant vendors' Web sites are accessible for agents,
- the contents can be automatically scanned and understood by agents,
- the user is willing to browse through any of the recommended Web sites displayed by his agent, and to purchase without checking other criteria, like speed of shipping and reputation, corporate policy, reported reliability and friendliness of rated vendors.

Many ShopBots[2] do currently provide comparison shopping on the Web, like Junglee/Yahoo! [321], Jango/Excite [310], Fido [201], or compare.net [138]. The first and most prominent ShopBot, BargainFinder [40] from Andersen Consulting, is no longer available in the Web mainly due to insufficient profitability for the vendors. An interesting question is whether ShopBots may compete with the enormously successful virtual bookstores, like amazon.com and barnesandnoble.com, in the near future.

Many negotiation and trading mechanisms rely on auction-based protocols, multi-attribute utility theory, decision theory, dynamic supply chain management, and variations of the contract net protocol (see, e.g., [714, 559, 240, 711, 455, 582, 209, 712, 583, 242]). Particularly interesting are virtual agent-based marketplaces and methods for utilitarian coalition formation among rational information agents.

Virtual, agent-based marketplaces provide locations where multiple information agents from different users and providers may meet each other to negotiate and exchange relevant data and information. Negotiation may concern, e.g., the amount of charges for provided services as well as the kind of services or goods itself. Actually, there are several agent-based marketplaces and retail commerce auctions available in the Web such as Persuader [651], Kasbah [326], OnSale Exchange [487], AuctionBot [713], FairMarket [199] and FishMarket [211, 474].

Coalition formation [322, 611, 347] enables utilitarian collaboration among rational information agents. Agents may negotiate and form coalitions to increase their individual benefit, or the benefit of the system itself. Most methods to form agent coalitions rely on principles from cooperative game theory, economics and operations research. The main issues addressed by coalition formation are

---

[2] Simple information agents used for shopping in the Web only are also called ShopBots.

- regulations and protocols for formation and maintenance of stable coalitions,
- variety of potential strategies of the agents,
- dynamics of coalition formation due to utilized regulations and strategies,
- agents' attitudes to collaborative work, such as benevolence, selfishness or bounded rationality, and the
- applicability of the approach in theory and specific domains in real life.

Although grounded techniques for utilitarian coalition formation and automated negotiation among self-interested agents are known [611, 336, 564, 337, 588, 347, 338, 589], no multi-agent system for EC in the Web using one of these techniques is yet available. A recent application of methods for coalition formation among rational information agents is in the power transmission planning domain [141].

As mentioned in the preface, any emerging consensus on an accounting and pricing structure [423] is as important as effective methods for fraud detection, trust and security to facilitate e-commerce transactions [607, 491, 521]. Trust should be built up gradually, involving only manageable risks for both, customers and vendors [540, 543]. In addition, there is a need to develop methods which enable agents to react to rapid changes in products and services provided by different vendors in an appropriate way. No fielded system of rational information agents capable of a sophisticated, complex utilitarian decision-making and providing an advanced, comfortable human-agent interaction is yet available in the Internet. This might change rapidly if information agent technology may be injected into emerging Internet-mediated transaction standards and systems [525].

The Contributions

In Chapter 6, *Robert Guttman*, *Alex Moukas* and *Pattie Maes* survey current approaches for agent-mediated electronic commerce. The role of each approach is described in the context of a consumer buying behavior model. This model augments traditional marketing models with concepts from software agents research to accommodate the growing (non-traditional) electronic markets. The authors discuss the variety of AI technologies that support agent mediation, present recent work done in that area at the MIT Media Laboratory, and conclude with future directions of agent-mediated electronic commerce research.

In the following four chapters, different approaches for negotiation and collaboration among rational information agents are proposed.

First, in Chapter 7, *Pablo Noriega* and *Carles Sierra* present a framework for describing agent-mediated auctions, and show how heterogenous trading agents can participate in such auctions in a way that is trustworthy. The framework is based on two general notions, that of an agent-mediated institution, and that of an agent institutor which are applicable to auctions but also to other forms of agent-mediated interactions. Both proposals are grounded in a kind of dialogical stance by which agents are thought of as intelligent entities that engage in dialogue under some explicitly shared conventions. The approach is illustrated by means of the well-known traditional fish market auctions as one of the standard commodities-trading institutions.

In an open information economy, buyers and sellers of information goods and services attempt to reach mutually beneficial agreements to allocate goods and services to tasks. If buyers or sellers can reason strategically about others' buying and selling behaviors, then they can sometimes extract additional profit, at the cost of sometimes degrading the overall system performance. *Edmund Durfee, Jose Vidal, Sun Park, Tracy Mullen, Peter Weinstein,* and *Aaron Armstrong* survey a set of techniques for performing, and restraining, strategic reasoning in the service market society of the Digital Library of the University of Michigan in Chapter 8.

As mentioned above, for rational information agents it might be beneficial to form teams or coalitions. In this case some problems emerge regarding the representation and execution of joint actions. To rectify these problems, several models for distributed collaborative planning have been proposed.

In Chapter 9, *Meirav Hadad* and *Sarit Kraus* present such a model, called the SharedPlan model. Unlike other models, it avoids the notion of irreducible joint intentions and addresses the need for agents to commit to their joint activity. The model also deals with agents having only partial knowledge of the way in which to perform an action. The authors designed and implemented a collaborative multi-agent system based on the formalization of the SharedPlan model. In particular, the system efficiently supports the cooperative processes of buying and selling goods such as in agent-based trading and electronic commerce on the Web.

Finally, in Chapter 10, an approach for electronic commerce motivated by supply chain applications is proposed by *Dajun Zeng* and *Katia Sycara*. Two important performance measures of a supply chain are cost and lead-time. These two issues are addressed in the proposed model in an unified fashion for a variety of supply chain activities, such as outsourcing, supplier selection, production capacity, and inventory positioning. The main research focus of this chapter is to structure supply chains dynamically and flexibly such that goods and services can be delivered by the agents at the right time in a cost-effective manner.

6. Agents as Mediators in Electronic Commerce

Robert Guttman, Alexandros Moukas, and Pattie Maes

Software Agents Group, MIT Media Laboratory, Cambridge, MA 02139, USA.
E-Mail: {guttman,moux,pattie}@media.mit.edu

6.1 Introduction

Software agents are programs to which one can delegate (aspects of) a task. They differ from "traditional" software in that they are personalized, continuously running and semi-autonomous. These qualities make agents useful for a wide variety of information and process management tasks [406]. It should come as no surprise that these same qualities are particularly useful for the information-rich and process-rich environment of electronic commerce.

Electronic commerce encompasses a broad range of issues including security, trust, reputation, law, payment mechanisms, advertising, ontologies, online catalogs, intermediaries, multimedia shopping experiences, and back-office management. Agent technologies can be applied to any of these areas where a personalized, continuously running semi-autonomous behavior is desirable. However, certain characteristics will determine to what extent agent technologies are appropriate. For example, how much time or money could be saved if a certain process was partially automated (e.g., comparing products from multiple merchants)? How easy is it to express your preferences for the task (e.g., shopping for a gift)? What are the risks of an agent making a sub- optimal transaction decision (e.g., making stock market buying and selling decisions or buying a car)? What is the potential for missed opportunities? Generally, the more time and money that can be saved through automation, the easier it is to express preferences, and the lesser the risks of making sub-optimal transaction decisions, the more appropriate it is to employ agent technologies in electronic commerce.

Software agents will play an increasing variety of roles as mediators in electronic commerce. This paper explores these roles, their supporting technologies, and how they relate to electronic commerce in its three main forms: business-to-business, business-to-consumer, and consumer-to-consumer transactions (with an emphasis on the latter two).

6.2 Roles of Agents as Mediators in Electronic Commerce

It is useful to explore the roles of agents as mediators in electronic commerce in the context of a common model. The model we present stems from traditional Marketing Consumer Buying Behavior (CBB) research and comprises the actions and decisions involved in buying and using goods and services. However, we augment traditional CBB models with concepts from Software Agents research to accommodate the growing (non-traditional) electronic markets.

Although CBB research covers many areas, it is important to recognize its limitations upfront. First, CBB research focuses on the retail market although many of its concepts pertain to business-to-business and consumer-to-consumer markets as well [276,570]. Also, as mentioned earlier, electronic commerce covers a broad range of issues, some of which are beyond the scope of a CBB model (e.g., back-office management and other merchant issues). Nevertheless, the CBB model is a powerful tool to help us understand the roles of agents as mediators in electronic commerce.

6.2.1   Consumer Buying Behavior Model

There are several models that attempt to capture Consumer Buying Behavior -- e.g., the Nicosia model [468], the Howard-Sheth model [285], the Engel-Blackwell model [188], the Bettman information-processing model [67], and the Andreasen model [15]. Although different, these models all share a similar list of six fundamental stages guiding consumer buying behavior. These six stages also elucidate where agent technologies apply to the consumer shopping experience and allow us to more formally categorize existing agent-mediated electronic commerce systems [666]:

1. *Need Identification*

    This stage characterizes the awareness of the consumer's needs. Within this stage, the consumer can be stimulated through product information. This stage is called *Problem Recognition* in the Engel-Blackwell model [188].

2. *Product Brokering*

    This stage comprises the retrieval of information to help determine *what* to buy. This emcompasses the evaluation of product alternatives based on consumer-provided criteria. The result of this stage is the "evoked set" of products.

3.   Merchant Brokering

This stage combines the "evoked set" from the previous stage with merchant-specific information to help determine *who* to buy from. This includes the evaluation of merchant alternatives based on consumer-provided criteria (e.g., price, warranty, availability, delivery time, reputation, etc.). The Nicosia model merges both brokering stages into one *Search Evaluation* stage [468]. The Engel-Blackwell model disects these two stages orthogonally into an *Information Search* stage and an *Evaluation of Alternatives* stage [188].

4.   Negotiation

This stage is about *how* to determine the terms of the transaction. Negotiation varies in duration and complexity depending on the market. In traditional retail markets, prices and other aspects of the transaction are often fixed leaving no room for negotiation. In other markets (e.g., stocks, automobile, fine art, local markets, etc.), the negotiation of price or other aspects of the deal are integral to product and merchant brokering. Traditional CBB models do not identify this stage explicitly, but the conclusion of the Negotiation stage is comparable to the *Choice* or *Decision* stage found in other models [468,188].

5.   Purchase and Delivery

The purchase and delivery of a product can either signal the termination of the negotiation stage or occur sometime afterwards (in either order). In some cases, the available payment (e.g., cash only) or delivery options can influence product and merchant brokering.

6.   Product Service and Evaluation

This stage involves product service, customer service, and an evaluation of the satisfaction of the overall buying experience and decision. The nature of this stage (and others) depends upon for whom the product was purchased.

As with most models, these stages represent an approximation and simplification of complex behaviors. As noted, CBB stages often overlap and migration from one to another is sometimes non-linear and iterative. From this CBB perspective, we can identify the roles of agents as mediators in electronic commerce. The personalized, continuously running autonomous nature of agents make them well suited for mediating those consumer behaviors involving information filtering and retrieval, personalized evaluations, complex coordinations, and time-based interactions. Specifically, these roles correspond (most notably) to the *Product Brokering*, *Merchant Brokering*, and *Negotiation* stages of the Consumer Buying Behavior model.Table 6.1 lists the six CBB stages and shows where several existing agent systems fall in this space. The rest of this section expounds the three agent-centric stages of the CBB model.

6.2.1.1   Product Brokering

The *Product Brokering* stage of the CBB model is where consumers determine *what* to buy. This occurs after a need has been identified (i.e., in the *Need Identification* stage) and is achieved through a critical evaluation of retrieved product information. Table 6.1 shows several agent systems that assist consumers in deciding which products best fit his/her personal criteria: PersonaLogic, Firefly, and Tete-a-Tete.

	Persona Logic	Firefly	Bargain Finder	Jango	Kasbah	Auction Bot	T@T
1. need identification							
2. product brokering	X	X					X
3. merchant brokering				X	X		X
4. negotiation					X	X	X
5. payment & delivery							
6. service & evaluation							

Table 6.1 : Roles and Examples of Agents as Mediators in Electronic Commerce. Notes: In the need identification stage, only a few primitive event-alerting tools (e.g., gift shops that track birthdays) help anticipate consumer needs and provide paths into the subsequent CBB stages. However, systems like Firefly can alert a consumer and provide product recommendations when consumers with similar interests purchase a specific product. The payment & delivery and service & evaluation stages usually include feedback about two distinct elements of the shopping process: product brokering and merchant brokering. Traditionally, customer remarks are accessible (and used)

by either the marketing staff of manufacturers or the customer satisfaction staff of merchants. However, agent-based distributed trust and reputation mechanisms (like Kasbah's Better Business Bureau) enable customers to share and combine their experiences and use merchant and product reputations as additional aspects of brokering and negotiation.

PersonaLogic [522], seen in Figure 6.1, is a tool that enables consumers to narrow down the products that best meet their needs by guiding them through a large product feature space. The system filters out unwanted products within a given domain by allowing shoppers to specify constraints on a product's features. A constraint satisfaction problem (CSP) engine then returns an ordered list of only those products that satisfy all of the hard constraints. PersonaLogic is marketed as a service that merchants offer to their customers that enables them to select the best product from the merchant's catalog.

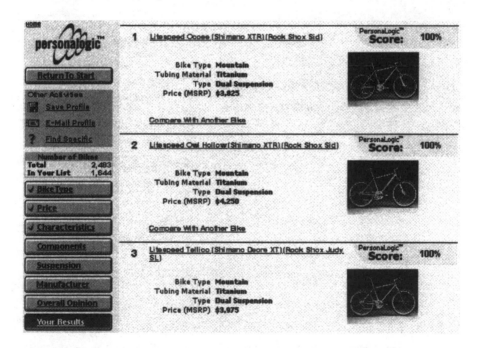

Fig. 6.1. PersonaLogic orders product results by how well they satify the shopper's preferences

Like PersonaLogic, **Firefly** [208,610, see also Chapter 12, Section 12.6.1], Figure 6.2, helps consumers find products. However, instead of filtering products based on features, Firefly recommends products via a "word of mouth" recommendation mechanism called automated collaborative filtering (ACF). ACF first compares a shopper's product ratings with those of other shoppers. After identifying the shopper's "nearest neighbors" (i.e., users with similar tastes), ACF recommends products that they rated highly but which the shopper may not yet have rated -- potentially resulting in serendipitous finds. Essentially, Firefly uses the opinions of like-minded people to offer recommendations. The system is currently used to recommend commodity products such as music and books.

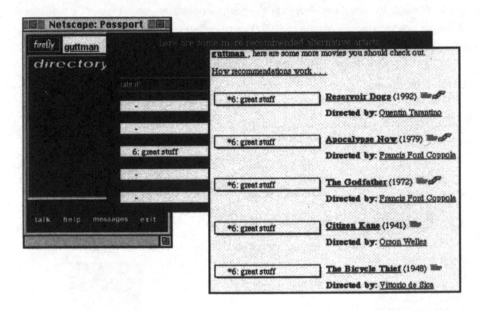

Fig. 6.2. Firefly recommends simple products based on opinions of like-minded people

6.2.1.2   Merchant Brokering

Whereas the *Product Brokering* stage compares product alternatives, the *Merchant Brokering* stage compares merchant alternatives.

Andersen Consulting's **BargainFinder**, seen in Figure6.3 was the first shopping agent for price comparisons [40]. Given a specific product, BargainFinder would request its price from each of nine different merchant Web sites using the same HTTP request as a web browser. Although a limited proof-of-concept system, BargainFinder offered valuable insights into the issues involved in price comparison in the online world. For example, a third of the online CD merchants accessed by BargainFinder blocked all price requests from BargainFinder. This was because merchants inherently do not want to compete on price alone. Value added services that merchants offered on their web site were being bypassed by BargainFinder and therefore not considered in the consumer's buying decision. However, it was also the case that Andersen Consulting received requests from an equal number of little-known merchants who wanted to be included in BargainFinder's price comparison. In short, companies competing on price wanted to be included, the others didn't.

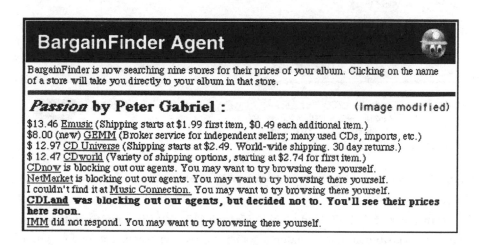

Fig. 6.3.   BargainFinder is the original price comparison shopping agent

Jango [310,177] can be viewed as an advanced BargainFinder (Figure 6.4). Jango "solves" the merchant blocking issue by having the product requests originate from each consumer's web browser instead of from a central site as in BargainFinder. This way, requests to merchants from a Jango-augmented web browser appear as requests from "real" customers. This kind of "aggressive interoperability" makes it convenient for consumers to shop for commodity products but does not leave merchants with many options. If merchants provide online catalogs, they can be accessed by agents whether merchants want them to or not.

Jango's modus operandi is quite simple: once a shopper has identified a specific product, Jango can simultaneously query merchant sites (from a list maintained by NetBot, Inc.) for its availability, price, and related information. These results allow a consumer to compare merchant offerings on price. Jango does not, however, help consumers identify which product(s) to purchase nor does it provide merchant comparison tools (e.g., a reputation mechanism) once merchants have been found. Jango also does not provide an avenue for merchants to offer customer loyalty incentives nor other value added services.

Shopping Results				
Hitachi	VISIONBOOK PLUS PENT-200 MMX 2.1GB 32MB 12.1 DSCAN 20X 56K W95	BUYCOMP.COM	$1799.00	Buy!
Toshiba	SATELLITE 310CDS PENT-200 MMX 2.0GB 32MB 12.1 DSCAN 16X	BUYCOMP.COM	$1829.95	Buy!
Compaq	Presario 1220 Portable Media GX 200MMX 2.1GB/ 32MB Sync 12.1HPA 20X	ComputerESP	$1950.00	Buy!

Fig. 6.4.   Jango returns a list of product offerings differentiated by price

In Figure 6.5, MIT Media Lab's **Kasbah** [121,326] is a multiagent system for consumer-to-consumer electronic commerce. A user wanting to buy or sell a good creates an agent, gives it some strategic direction, and sends it off into a centralized agent marketplace. Kasbah agents pro-actively seek out potential buyers or sellers and negotiate with them on their owner's behalf. Each agent's

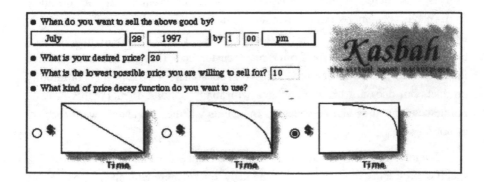

Fig. 6.5.   Kasbah is one of the first online agent systems for negotiating consumer products

goal is to make the "best deal" possible, subject to a set of user-specified constraints, such as a desired price, a highest (or lowest) acceptable price, and a date to complete the transaction by. The latest version of Kasbah incorporates a distributed trust and reputation mechanism called the Better Business Bureau. Upon the completion of a transaction, both parties are able to rate how well the other party managed his/her half of the deal (e.g., accuracy of product condition, completion of transaction, etc.). Agents can then use these ratings to determine if they are willing to negotiate with agents whose owners fall below a user-specified reputation threshold.

6.2.1.3 Negotiation

Negotiation is the process of determining the price or other terms of a transaction. Examples of where we see negotiation used in commerce include stock markets (e.g., NYSE and NASDAQ), fine art auction houses (e.g., Sotheby's and Christie's), flower auctions (e.g., Aalsmeer, Holland), and various ad-hoc haggling (e.g., automobile dealerships and commission-based electronics stores).

The benefit of dynamically negotiating a price for a product instead of fixing it is that it relieves the merchant from needing to determine the value of the good a priori. Rather, this burden is pushed into the marketplace itself. A result of this is that limited resources are allocated fairly -- i.e., to those who value them most. However, there are impediments to using negotiation. In the physical world, certain types of auctions require that all parties be geographically co-located, for example, in auction houses. Also, negotiating may be too complicated or frustrating for the average consumer. For instance, this sentiment inspired Saturn automobile dealerships to switch from price negotiation to fixed-price. Finally, some negotiation protocols occur over an extended period of time which does not cater to impatient or time-constrained consumers. In general, real-world negotiations accrue transaction costs that may be too high for either consumers or merchants.

Fortunately, many of these impediments disappear in the digital world. For example, OnSale [486] and eBay's AuctionWeb [29] are two popular web sites that sell retail and second-hand products using a choice of auction protocols. Unlike auction houses, these sites do not require that parties be geographically co-located (only virtually co- located). However, these sites still require that consumers manage their own negotiation strategies over an extended period of time. This is where agent technologies come in.

Table 6.1 shows several agent systems that assist the customer in negotiating the terms of a transaction: AuctionBot, Kasbah, and Tete-a-Tete.

AuctionBot [28], seen in Figure 6.6 is a classified ad Internet auction server at the University of Michigan. ActionBot users can create new auctions to sell products by choosing from a selection of auction types and then specifying parameters for that auction (e.g., auction time, reserved price, etc.). Once the auction is created, the seller's negotiation is completely automated by the system as defined by the auctioneer protocols and parameters of the selected auction.

Fig. 6.6.   AuctionBot offers many auction protocol permutations

As in OnSale Exchange [487], AuctionBot buyers can place bids for second-hand products according to the protocols of a given auction. What makes AuctionBot different, however, is that it provides an application programmable interface (API) for users to create their own software agents to autonomously compete in the AuctionBot marketplace. Such an API provides a semantically sound interface to the marketplace unlike the "wrapper" technologies discussed in Sections 3.1 and 3.4. However, as with the Fishmarket Project [559,211], it is left to the users to encode their own bidding strategies. This may be one reason why here does not appear to be much activity at the AuctionBot site.1 Fishmarket is not currently being used as a real-world system, but has hosted tournaments to compare opponents' hand-crafted bidding strategies [212] along the lines of Axelrod's prisoner's dilemna tournaments [31].

Kasbah, as described earlier, is a Web-based multiagent classified ad system where users create buying agents and selling agents to help transact products. These agents automate much of the *Merchant Brokering* and *Negotiation* CBB stages for both buyers and sellers. Negotiation in Kasbah is straightforward. After buying agents and selling agents are matched, the only valid action in the negotiation protocol is for buying agents to offer a bid to sellers with no restrictions on time or price. Selling agents respond with either a binding "yes" or "no".

Given this protocol, Kasbah provides buyers with one of three negotiation strategies: anxious, cool-headed, and frugal -- corresponding to a linear, quadratic, or exponential function respectively for increasing its bid for a product over time. The simplicity of these negotiation strategies makes it easy for users to understand what their agents are doing in the marketplace. This was important for user acceptance as observed in a recent Media Lab experiment [121]. A larger Kasbah experiment is now underway at MIT allowing students to transact books, music, and Magic Cards [326].

Tete-a-Tete [263, see also Chapter 6, Section 12.7.1] provides a unique negotiation approach to retail sales. Unlike most other negotiation systems which negotiate only over price, Tete-a-Tete negotiates across multiple terms of a transaction -- e.g., warranty length and options, shipping time and cost, service contract, return policy, quantity, accessories/bundles, credit/loan options, payment options, and other merchant value add (see Figure 6.7).

Like Kasbah, this negotiation takes the form of multi-agent, bilateral bargaining but not using simple raise or decay functions as in Kasbah. Instead, Tete-a-Tete's shopping agents use the evaluation constraints captured during the *Product Brokering* and *Merchant Brokering* stages as dimensions of a multi-attribute utility function (discussed in Section 3.3). This utility function is used by agent a shopping to negotiate an optimal deal with a complementary sales agent.

---

1   In the past week, there have been only two active, public auctions. There could be private auctions, however.

In essence, Tete-a-Tete integrates all three of the *Product Brokering*, *Merchant Brokering*, and *Negotiation* CBB stages.

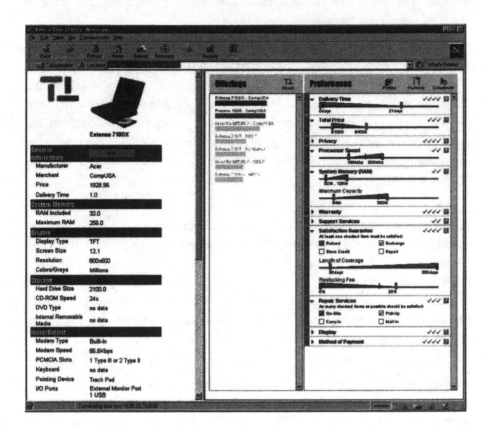

Fig. 6.7.   Tete-a-Tete's shopping interface

6.3 Agent Technologies for Electronic Commerce

Most of the technologies supporting today's agent-mediated electronic commerce systems stem either directly or indirectly from Artificial Intelligence (AI) research. From the notion of software agency [440,279] and cognitive models [268,466,93] to extracting meaning from ambiguous Web pages [93], from planning trips to Hawaii [388,709] to learning users' music preferences [610,208], from negotiating delivery contracts [582,564,379] to deciding on which car to buy [242,332], AI technologies will continue to provide software agents with increased know-how to successfully mediate electronic commerce transactions.

In this section, we review several AI technologies that support the systems described in Section 2, discuss user interface challenges, then focus on issues and technologies concerning the next-generation agent-mediated electronic commerce infrastructure.

6.3.1 Recommender Systems

The majority of product recommender systems are developed using content-based, collaborative-based or constrained-based filtering methods as their underlying technology.

In *content-based filtering* [572,48,450,383] the system processes information from various sources and tries to extract useful elements about its content. The techniques used in content-based filtering can vary greatly in complexity. Keyword-based search is one of the simplest techniques that involves matching different combinations of keywords (sometimes in boolean form). A more advanced form of filtering is the one based on extracting semantic information of the documents' contents. This can be achieved by using techniques like associative networks of keywords in a sentence or pricelist, or directed graphs of words that form sentences.

Systems like BargainFinder and Jango try to collect information (like product descriptions, prices, reviews, etc) from many different Web information sources. These sources were intended to be read by humans and their content is rendered and presented accordingly (i.e., in HTML). Different sources have different input (cgi-scipts, java applets) and presentation methods so recommender systems have to adjust their interaction methods depending on the Web site. Since there is no standard way to access and define merchant offerings, it was proposed that the recommender systems employ *"wrappers"*, which would transform the information from Web sites into a common (but proprietary) format. Different systems followed different approaches to create wrappers. In BargainFinder, the Internet locations of online CD stores and the methods to access them (i.e., searching for a product and get its price) were hand-coded by Andersen Consulting programmers. This method worked well at the beginning but was very hard to scale since it involved maintenance of the warpper for each site whenever it changed its access methods or catalog presentation format (even slightly). Jango automatically creates wrappers for new sites by generalizing from example query responses to online merchant databases. This technique is not perfect, but boasts a nearly 50% success rate in navigating random Internet resources [362].

Firefly uses a collaborative filtering technology [610,368,545] to recommend products to consumers. Systems using collaborative techniques use feedback and ratings from different consumers to filter out irrelevant information. These systems do not attempt to analyze or "understand" the features or the descriptions of the products. Rather, they use the ranking of the consumers to create a "likability" index for each document. This index is not global, but is computed for each user on the fly by using other users with similar interests. Documents that are liked by like-minded people will have a priority over documents that are disliked.

Like content-based approaches, constraint-based techniques use features of items to determine their relevance. However, unlike some feature-based techniques which access data in their native formats, constraint-based techniques require that the problem and solution space be formulated in terms of variables, domains, and constraints. Once formulated in this way, however, a number of general purpose (and powerful) *constraint satisfaction problem* (CSP) techniques can be employed to find a solution [672].

Finite-domain CSPs are one type sof CSP and are composed of three main parts: a finite set of *variables*, each of which is associated with a finite *domain*, and a set of *constraints* that define relationships among variables and restricts the values that the variables can simultaneously take. The task of a CSP engine is to assign a value to each variable while satisfying all of the constraints. A variation of these "hard" constraints is the ability to also define "soft" constraints (of varied importance) which need not be satisfied. The number, scope, and nature of the variables, domains, and constraints will determine how constrained the problem is and, for a given CSP engine, how quickly a solution (if any) will be found [358].

Many problems can be formulated as a CSP from manfucaturing scheduling to planning problems to machine vision. In PersonaLogic, CSP techniques are used in the *Product Brokering* CBB stage to evaluate product alternatives. Given a set of constraints on product features, PersonaLogic filters products that don't meet the given hard constraints and prioritizes the remaining products using the given soft constraints.

CSP techniques are core to Tete-a-Tete and are used to assist shoppers in the *Product Brokering*, *Merchant Brokering*, and *Negotiation* CBB stages. This is achieved by consumers providing product constraints (as in PersonaLogic) as well as merchant constraints such as price, delivery time, warranty, etc. These hard and soft constraints are used to filter and prioritize products and merchants as well as construct a utility function that is used to negotiate with the merchants. This negotiation takes the form of a distributed CSP [135].

6.3.2 User Interface Approaches

Traditional shopping experiences can be quite diverse depending on the needs of the consumer. For instance, sometimes are just browsing without a specific intention to buy, sometimes the shopper intends to buy but is unfamiliar with the features of the specific product category (e.g., "I just need a camcorder whose tapes are compatible with my VCR."), othertimes the shopper intends to buy and has a deep understanding of the product category (e.g., "I need a S-VHS camcorder with x16 optical zoom.") Moreover, the electronic catalog interface that most of the systems use looks like a glorified pricelist and consumers feel lost because they cannot associate a set of products with a physical location (like in a supermarket or department store experience). Solutions like 3D VRML shopping malls have been developed but they haven't lived up to their expectations because navigation in a 3D world with a 2D interface feels awkward.

Another traditional shopping experience that consumers report to be missing in electronic transactions is the lack of any kind of immediate positive feedback and personalization of the consumer's needs by an experienced salesperson. Some companies like Extempo [196] offer avatars, semi-animated graphical characters that interact in natural language with the consumer and feature a longer-term consistent "personality" that "remembers" each consumer, his or her shopping habits, etc. Anthropomorphising agents attempts to make consumers feel closer to the agents and facilitate the building of trust relationships [597]. However, as of today, it is still a very controversial solution and none of the claims of anthropomorphising agents have been proven [717].

The issue of trust is very important in any agent system, especially when money is involved. A crucial issue in developing trust in an agent system is the ability of the agent to exhibit somewhat predictable behavior and to provide some sort of explanation for its actions. For instance, a consumer can follow the decision process of a constraint satisfaction system like PersonaLogic much easier than that of a collaborative filtering system like Firefly which bases its recommendations on "invisible" clusters of like-minded people.

In regards to complexity and predictability of behaviors, preliminary experiments with the Kasbah system showed that consumers preferred simple, predictable agents with pre-determined negotiation strategies over "smarter" agents that continuously adapted their behavior depending on an analysis of the marketplace. It is safe to assert that, as with any other software system, agents that facilitate electronic commerce can benefit greatly from a well-designed and tested user interfaces.

6.3.3   Negotiation Mechanisms

Negotiation is a form of decision-making where two or more parties jointly (often competitively) search a space of possible solutions with the goal of reaching a consensus [564]. Economics and game theory describe such an interaction in terms of protocols and strategies. The protocols of a negotiation comprise the rules (i.e., the valid actions) of the game. An example of a simple negotiation protocol is the non-discriminatory Dutch auction where the only legal bidding action is an open outcry of "mine!" (or comparable) as an auctioneer decrements the price of the good.

For a given protocol, a player (e.g., a bidder) may elect to use a rational strategy (i.e., a plan of action) to maximize his or her "utility function". A utility function is a model of a player's preferences and knowledge (e.g., motivation, valuation, risk, information asymmetry, etc.) that can be executed by a given strategy for a given protocol. Oftentimes, a utility function only reflects a player's self-interest. In other cases, it encompasses desirable social welfare or global performance goals such as system-wide equilibria [717,586].

Whereas economics research often focuses on these (partial and general) equilibrium aspects of market-based negotiation, game theory research tends to focus on the nature of the protocols and optimal (self-interested) strategies for a variety of negotiation protocols [564]. A key idea from both of these research areas is that the specification of the protocol will have substantial, rippling effects on the nature of the overall system [564]. In other words, protocol design in the CBB *Negotiation* stage of agent- mediated electronic commerce should be considered carefully.

In this regard, there are two general approaches to consider when designing negotiation (or bargaining) protocols: distributive negotiation and integrative negotiation [379]. *Distributive negotiation* focuses on how each self-interested party can acquire the largest piece of the available "pie". This type of negotiation is inherent to all zero-sum, single-resource marketplaces. Examples of systems that employ this type of negotiation are AuctionBot, Kasbah, and all other price-based negotiations where as the price changes, either buyers or sellers are better off, but never both.

Integrative negotiation focuses on all of the terms of a transaction and the parties involved try to enlarge the available "pie" rather than simply attempt to acquire certain pieces of it. The benefit of this approach over the distributive negotiation approach is that it's possible to find new points in the solution space that benefit both buyers and sellers. Examples of systems that employ this type of negotiation are Persuader [651] from Carnegie Mellon University which finds it roots in distributed artificial intelligence (DAI), decision theory and multi-attribute utility theory and Tete-a-Tete [263] which takes a distributed constraint satisfaction approach to multi-attribute negotiation.

Another approach to negotiation from DAI research is the *Contract Net* [635]. The original Contract Net was a distributed problem solving system designed for opportunistic, adaptive task allocation with agents announcing tasks, placing bids, and awarding contracts [545]. Limitations of the original Contract Net Protocol (CNP) have been addressed in more recent work by Sandholm and Lesser [582,587]. Related work includes Malone, et al.'s Enterprise system which allocates computer tasks using negotiation mechanisms [413] and protocols for automated coalition formation among agents [749,611,588,336]. These latter protocols allow self-interested agents to cooperate on tasks (e.g., leverage economies of scale) without a priori relationships among their owners.

6.3.4   Infrastructure, Languages, Protocols

As discussed, there are already many agent-mediated electronic commerce systems, each roughly focused on only one or two CBB stages (see Table 6.1). Ideally, we would be able to mix and match systems playing in complementary stages to provide a full consumer shopping experience. Unfortunately, these systems were not designed to interoperate in this way and linking these disparate systems together would require a good deal of work.

In fact, several of the systems discussed (e.g., BargainFinder and Jango), require proprietary "wrapper" techniques to "scrape" Web pages for product and merchant content. This is because web pages are currently written in HTML (hypertext markup language) which is a data *format* language. In contrast, XML (extensible markup language) is a data *content* meta-language allowing for the semantic tagging of data [78,650,742]. Microsoft and Netscape have each promised support for XML with style sheets in their respective web browsers to help replace HTML with XML as the language of the Web.

However, XML is not a panacea for inter-business interoperability. Even with tagged data, tags need to be semantically consistent across merchant boundaries at least for the full value chain of a given industry. CommerceNet and member organizations are working towards such common ontologies [68]. However, it's still an open question how transactional terms should be universally defined and who should manage their evolution.

Related agent-based languages and protocols include KIF (Knowledge Interchange Format) [340], KQML (Knowledge Query Manipulation Language) [203,205], and Ontolingua [256], an ontology sharing protocol. These were designed so heterogenous agents and systems could describe knowledge and communicate it meaningfully in order to interoperate. In electronic commerce, this knowledge would include the definitions and semantics of consumer profiles, merchants, goods, services, value add, and negotiation protocols (among others).

In the business-to-business world exists EDI (Electronic Data Interchange). EDI is a set of ANSI and U.N. standard protocols for inter-business transactions [72,536]. EDI facilitates large-scale, repetitive, pre-arranged transactions between businesses in specific industries with each industry adapting the EDI protocol to its specific needs. Standard EDI transactions are performed through expensive, proprietary Value-Added Networks (VAN). Although a pioneering protocol for inter-business electronic commerce, EDI has several dissadvantages: it is ambiguous, expensive to implement and maintain, and it is focused on large scale business-to-business transactions leaving small and medium-sized enterprises (SME) without a business-to-business transaction protocol standard. This forces business relationships to be established a priori and provides a disincentive to dynamically explore more lucrative deals. This is counter to the trend towards leaner, more agile companies.

Other electronic commerce protocol proposals that agents may need to "speak" include Internet-based EDI (EDIINT) [179], XML/EDI (a grassroots effort) [415], Open Buying on the Internet (OBI) [490] for high-volume, low-dollar business-to-business purchases, as well as a host of niche protocols such as Open Financial Exchange (OFX) [484] for financial transactions, Secure Electronic Transactions (SET) [607] for credit card transactions, and Open Profiling Standard (OPS) [491] and Personal Privacy Preferences Project (P3P)

[521] for defining privacy options for consumer profile data -- to name only a few.

In addition to document and protocol standards, there is a need for electronic commerce component standards for objects and agents. There are several competing technologies in this space including the Object Management Group's CORBA/IIOP (Common Object Request Broker Architecture/Internet Inter-ORB Protocol) [692,144], Microsoft's COM and DCOM [562], and Sun's Java and RMI (Remote Method Invocation) [643,557] as well as several mobile agent platforms such as ObjectSpace's Voyager [695], Mitsubishi's Concordia [139], General Magic's Odyssey [483], and IBM's Aglets [301] -- several of which have been proposed for OMG's Mobile Agent Facility (MAF) [480]. Requirements for open, heterogenous component-based commerce systems include backward-compatibility to "legacy" systems, fault-tolerance, efficient performance, extensibility, scalability, security, some concurrency control, and some registry mechanisms to tie all of the pieces together. Many of these issues are core to multi-agent systems research, distributed database research, distributed systems research, and group communications research.

6.4   AmEC at the MIT Media Laboratory

In addition to our Kasbah and Tete-a-Tete systems described above, and the Reputations system described in detail in Chapter 13 in this book, we have been actively working on two additional projects: the first is about knowledge brokering and the ability to find experts at a given field. The second investigates how the currently disjoined virtual and real marketplaces can be brought together using PDA-like systems with positioning, communication and computational capabilities.

6.4.1   Knowledge Brokering and Expert Finder

These projects investigate how software agent technology can be used to facilitate knowledge brokering and "just-in-time-consulting". Imagine a person trying to acquire expertise about a particular problem being able to get assistance in real time: we propose an infrastructure which allows that person to - without much effort - locate an expert who is available to help the expertise-seeker remotely at that moment in time. Specifically, we are building an "electronic market for expertise" by creating agents that can match up expertise-seekers and experts and make deals for an on-the-fly consulting relationship.

To participate in this knowledge marketplace, a person can create selling agents that know what expertise that person has and when that person is available to help someone else (and possibly how much he charges). Someone in need for consulting can create a buying agent that knows what kind of expertise that person needs and by when (in the next 3 minutes, in the next 3 days, etc.). The buying agent may also have information on how to compare different people offering the expertise (criteria such as: price charged, reputation of the expert, level of expertise, availability, etc.). The market automatically matches up these different buying and selling agents. Once a match has been made, other media are used to implement the tutoring relationship (email, phone, as well as richer communication media).

For instance, a doctor while examining a patient with a rare disease might want an additional expert's opinion for that disease in the next ten minutes (while the patient is still there). The doctor's agents would search for other doctors that can be of assistance in that case and based on a series of parameters (doctor reputation, availability, cost, expertise etc.) decide with which ones to begin negotiations with, conduct the negotiations along a set of different attributes (for instance, if the consultant doctor is in the middle of a meeting, the consulting fee would be higher), conclude them in real time and place a phone call to the consulting doctor.

Our first approach to knowledge brokering is the Expert Finder [693, see also Chapter 12, Section 12.6.3]. The system's first domain is that of knowledge about software applications: it is normal to find oneself "lost" in an application, not knowing how to get something done and unable to find it in the on-line help systems (when they exist), especially when one is new to the application. In these cases, the easiest way out is to ask someone who also uses this software, but has more experience with it (an expert). The present Expert Finder watches what programs are being used and makes that information available to the other Expert Finder agents. Each user's level of expertise is determined by a person's software usage pattern. When help is needed using some software package, the user can query the agent, and it will find an expert to help with the chosen application. One of the most important brokering dimensions in this knowledge market is that of reputation. The next section describes our efforts to provide a robust, distributed mechanism for handling reputation.

6.4.2   Shopping on the Run

Our goal is to create an electronic market for goods and services, which would be accessed by mobile devices as well as from the desktop. Let us describe the functionality of the system by providing a few scenarios of consumers equipped with a PDA-like device with communication and positioning abilities:

• *Walking near a bookstore*: As a consumer is walking in Boston's Newbury street, the shopping agent in her PDA is looking for deals from nearby merchants. Her profile information shows that she is interested in buying a Pablo Neruda book. The shopping agent starts negotiating with a couple of near-by bookstores for the book and closes a preliminary deal. At the same time, it checks the prices at different on-line merchants: the book is $2 cheaper (including shipping and handling), but the agent takes into consideration her preference for visiting bookstores, closes the deal and notifies her.

• *Driving down a highway*: A couple is driving down the highway and they are interested in a nice seafood restaurant in New Jersey that serves fresh catfish and can accommodate them in the next fifteen minutes. Again, the shopping agent contacts local restaurants and restaurant recommendation guides in order to best accommodate the request.

• *An expert is nearby*: A travel-lover is departing for the Aegean island of Myconos in a few of days and would like to talk with some sort of expert in the night-life and accomodations options on the island. He is willing to spend $20 to talk for a few minutes with an expert in Myconos if there was one in the vicinity in order to get some advice.

The system provides just-in-time brokering for products, services, information and knowledge in a localized fashion. It can locate local merchants by using geography as a self-organizing merchant directory (without the need of a centralized yellow pages-like structure.) It can subsequently search and negotiate about products of interest to the consumer and receive information and locality-based services from content providers. In terms of equipment and infrastructure some sort of computational device (PDA-like or integrated to a mobile telephone,) with communication (multi-hop network, cellular service, two-way paging, etc.) and positioning capabilities (GPS, cellular telephone localization) is required. In our implementation we are borrowing elements from almost all the projects mentioned in this paper. We are currently testing the validity of the physical topology brokering, mobility and communication aspects of the architecture using a real-time simulator (described in detail in the CarTalk and Trafficopter [452] projects.)

6.5   Conclusion and Future Directions

The first-generation agent-mediated electronic commerce systems are already creating new markets (e.g., low-cost consumer-to-consumer) and beginning to reduce transaction costs in a variety of business models. However, we still have a long way to go before software agents transform how businesses conduct business. This change will occur as Software Agent technology matures to better manage ambiguous content, personalized preferences, complex goals, changing environments, and disconnected parties, but more importantly, as standards are adopted to succinctly and universally define goods and services, consumer and merchant profiles, value added services, secure payment mechanisms, inter-business electronic forms, etc. During this next- generation of agent-mediated electronic commerce, agents will streamline business-to- business transactions, reducing transaction costs at every stage of the supply chain. At some critical threshold, new types of transactions will emerge in the form of dynamic relationships among previously unknown parties. At the speed of bits, agents will strategically form and reform coalitions to bid on contracts and leverage economies of scale -- in essence, creating dynamic business partnerships that exist only as long as necessary. It is in this third-generation of agent-mediated electronic commerce where virtual and non-virtual companies will be at their most agile and marketplaces will approach perfect efficiency.

7. Auctions and Multi-agent Systems

Pablo Noriega* and Carles Sierra

Institut d'Investigacio en Intelligencia Artificial, CSIC-Spanish Scientific
Research Council, Campus UAB, 08193 Bellaterra, Barcelona, Catalonia, Spain.
E-Mail: {pablo,sierra}@iiia.csic.es

Summary.
   In an auction house, buyers and sellers coordinate so as to exchange
goods following a highly structured and apparently simple procedure.
These coordination conventions have evolved through the years, and are
currently used in commercial institutions for exchanging diverse goods
and services. In this chapter we take as an instance a traditional auction
house, the *Llotja* (a fish market) of Blanes, and we discuss how a virtual
and adaptable electronic fish market can be derived from it. In this virtual
institution the mediating functions are performed by autonomous agents,
and customers or vendors can be either individuals or software agents.
We also show how the underlying notions can be applied to define other
institutions where the participants can be software agents.

7.1 Introduction

According to some economists (for instance, Cassady [107] or Wolfstetter
[735]), auctions are price-fixing mechanisms in which negotiation is subject
to a very strict coordination process. Buyers and vendors take part in this
process, but the exchange is done through a mediator —the auctioneer—
who presents the goods to exchange and makes (or receives) offers for such
goods following a pre-established *bidding convention* which determines the
sequence of offers as well as the way to decide the winner and the price to
be paid by the winner. For instance, in the traditional Spanish fish markets
a so-called "downward bidding" convention is followed. In it, the auctioneer
typically signals a fish crate, declares an initial price, and starts singing a
fast sequence of descending prices until a buyer says 'mine', thus indicating
his/her acceptance of the last price sung.

   Other economists (such as Smith [637] or McAfee and McMillan[421]),
however, refer to auction houses as *institutions* [478] and are careful to point
out that, in addition to the bidding conventions, other equally relevant conventions and elements are used in an auction house to achieve a proper
co-ordination of buyers and sellers: conventions for the registration of participants and goods, conventions on guarantees and payment, commissions,
starting prices, etc..

   The approach adopted in this chapter is closer to the latter view of an auction, although we imbue this view with elements from artificial intelligence.

---

* On leave from the Laboratorio Nacional de Informática Avanzada, (LANIA),
  Xalapa,Ver. México

An auction house is viewed as an *institution* where three types of conventions are defined and enforced:

1. **Ontologic and Communicational Conventions** in which all the elements which form an auction and the meaning of the illocutions exchanged are clarified.
2. **Social Conventions** which regulate the interactions among participants in an auction while they are taking part in it.
3. **Individual Behaviour Rules** to which the participants in an auction are subject and which establish the commitments, obligations and rights which concern them.

Through these conventions, an auction house imposes objective conditions which concern:

- The availability, presentation and delivery of goods,
- the admission requirements for buyers and sellers,
- the behaviour rules for participants in an auction, and
- the fulfilment of public commitments acquired by participants in an auction.

By imposing such conventions, the institution articulates the interactions between buyers and sellers establishing and warranting that negotiations and transactions are carried out in a fair and transparent manner.

Furthermore, in this chapter we are concerned not with traditional auction houses, but with a sort of *virtual institution* that serves the same purpose. A traditional auction house and its virtual institution counterpart are essentially the same, but for two key differences. On the one hand, whereas the place where auctions are carried out in a traditional institution is a physical place, the virtual auction is carried out in a *virtual* location. On the other hand, participants in a traditional auctions are usually called *agents*, but in contrast we allow agents taking part in a virtual institution to be not only humans but also software agents[1]. Consequently, this virtual institution could be understood (in an abstract sense) as a *multi-agent system model*, or more specifically, as its *computational realization in the Internet*.

Considering the computational realization of an institution in which agents take part allows focusing attention on an obvious, though not trivial, aspect of this realization: *agents interact exclusively through message exchange*. These messages can be built with illocutions in a formal language, and thus, the interaction between agents in a virtual institution becomes an

---

[1] Note that we distinguish between *auction house* (an institution which carries out auctions), and *auction* (the *process* of goods exchange subject to the conventions of an auction house or to an *instance* of that process). We also distinguish *bidding conventions* (those to regulate only the negotiation *rounds* of an auction) and the *auction* conventions (which regulate other sections or scenes in addition to rounds). In this article we will only refer to *sale* auctions (or "round off"), but everything said can also be applied to *purchase* auctions (or "procurement").

illocution exchange. We call this observation the *strong dialogical stance* and it means supposing that the multi-agent system which models the institution is a *dialogical system* (in the sense it is understood by Hamblin [269][2]). In practice, this means saying that any commitment which could be admitted as a *valid commitment* in a virtual auction house will correspond with a message which was uttered by a participant and received by another (or another group of participants) during the auction, according to the rules established by the institution. Formally speaking, as far as we are concerned, an "agent" will be "an entity capable of establishing commitments" and every commitment adopted in a virtual institution will correspond either to a pre-condition or a post-condition of an illocution exchanged by agents according to the institution's rules of interaction.

In this chapter we will show how a traditional auction house can inspire a virtual institution which adapts its traditional coordination conventions to the current conditions of electronic commerce. We will first concentrate (in Section 7.2) on the social conventions for the virtual institution and later on the individual rules of behaviour to which participants are subject; we will see the commitments these dialogical exchanges lead to and discuss some classical variants of this protocol. Later, in Section 7.3, we will indicate how it is possible to formalize these ideas in a *virtual institution*, and we will mention the computational realization of the Fishmarket. Finally, in Section 7.4 and 7.5 we will mention how these specific examples can be generalized to build other virtual institutions inhabited by agents that mediate, and interact with other participants which can be either humans or software agents.

Note that our approach is mainly descriptive, and that we will not mention any of the predictive aspects. Nevertheless, these are very frequent in auction literature, so much in the one called by economists *Mechanism design* as in the auction literature of the A.I. community that usually includes them in the *Market-based Programming*. In Mechanism Design, the objective is, essentially, to identify these coordination conventions (certainly auctions, but also double auctions, stock markets and, in general, different types of structured negotiation) which warrant certain optimality conditions or "balances"; or exploring the consequences of adopting alternative conventions —in those balances— under suppositions on the rationality of participants, the offering of goods or the participants expectancies (cf. Mas-Colell *et al.* [419] or Varian [685], for more theoretical approaches; Paarsch [277] for the experimental ones). In Market-based Programming, on the contrary, techniques and results of the Economic Theory are used to resolve programming problems in which the market metaphor is happily evoking (cf. Wellman [710] and Clearwater [131]); for instance, the task assigning (through auction) between a network's processors (Smith and Davis [636], Mullen and Wellman [454]) or the partitionable data base storing (Schwartz and Kraus [595]); or the identification

---

[2] See Noriega [474, Ch.4] for a detailed discussion on this point and the corresponding references.

of problems in which a certain auction type cannot be applied (Sandholm [584]) and, particularly, those which directly concern the software agent's coordination (e.g. Sandholm and Lesser [589]).

Even though analytic modelling is feasible in the Fishmarket framework (as indicated in [476] and in [560]) our approach is more related to proposals such as *Magnet* [678, 136], *Kasbah* [120] and *Bazaar* [266]. In these proposals the creation of virtual markets in which participants may rely on software agents for some purchase/selling activities is examined. Our approach is also related to the recent proposals of the *AuctionBot* project[28] which involves an "auction server" which allows the activation of on-line auctions, whose conventions can be very flexibly specified and in which it would even be possible to participate with self-made software agents. The content of this chapter reformulates some of our research group's previous papers, in particular [474] and is an adequate introduction to more recent works such as [476].

7.2 The Fishmarket

In the sections below we will show how it is possible to build a virtual institution, the Fishmarket, which corresponds to a given traditional fish auction in a small fishermen's village.

7.2.1 Scenes and Performative Structure

The fish market ('Llotja') which currently exists in Blanes (Girona), may be understood as an institution in which a series of scenes involving agents with clearly defined roles or behaviour patterns are *performed*. In Blanes there are five basic scenes, each of which has a characteristic *location* and is coordinated by a member of the Llotja staff. The seller admitter (**sa**) is in charge of the reception of products from sellers in the corresponding zone (**RR**), while the buyer manager (**bm**) is in charge of updating the buyer's credits and delivering the goods to the delivery room (**DR**), etc. (See Figure 7.1).

Each scene in the Llotja is subject to a strict *protocol* that the staff member must comply with and uniformly enforce upon all external agents. For instance, the central scene of an auction —the bidding round proper— is carried out in the "auction room", is controlled by the auctioneer and, in the case of the Fishmarket, follows the protocol depicted in Figure 7.2[3].

---

[3] Nodes stand for the states (of the commitments) of the participants, the squares stand for scenes. Arcs are labelled by illocutions (which are abbreviated in the diagram due to space limitations, but they appear complete in Table 7.1) and the arrows signal origin. Note that every illocution has the structure $\iota(\alpha, \Gamma : \varphi; \tau)$ where ι is an illocutionary particle, α is the agent uttering the illocution; Γ is the set of listeners; φ is the propositional content of the illocution (the message) and τ the moment in which the illocution is produced (which we will consistently omit in this chapter).

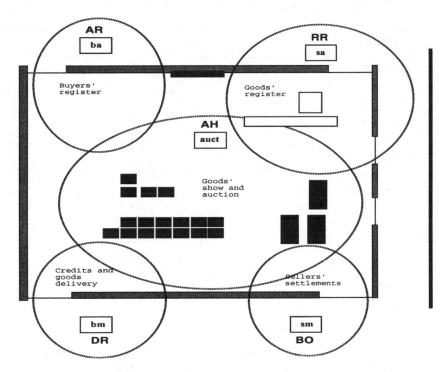

Fig. 7.1. Scenes in the Blanes Llotja.

$$offer(auct, all : tosell(g, p))$$
$$assert(b, auct : bid)$$
$$request(auct, bm : creditstatus(b, p_t))$$
$$assert(bm, auct : valid(b))$$
$$assert(bm, auct : fined(b, fine))$$
$$request(bm, auct : expel(b))$$
$$declare(auct, all \cup \{bm\} : sold(g, b, p, t_\omega))$$
$$declare(auct, \{b, bm, ba\} : expelled(b))$$
$$command(auct, b, outto(DR))$$
$$declare(auct, all : expelled(b))$$
$$declare(auct, b : fined(b, \kappa))$$
$$declare(auct, all : invalidbid)$$
$$declare(auct, all : collision(g, \bar{b}, p))$$
$$declare(auct, all : tiebreak(\bar{b}, b))$$
$$declare(auct, all : endoflot)$$
$$request(b, auct : exitto(DR))$$
$$request(s, auct : exitto(BO))$$

Table 7.1. Illocutions used in an upward bidding round in the Fishmarket.

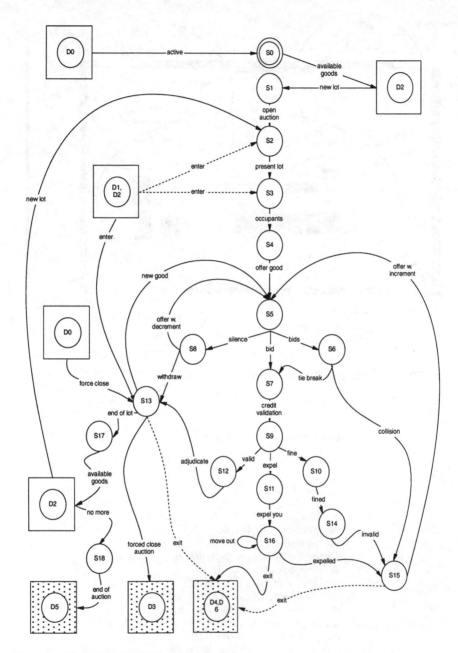

Fig. 7.2. Fishmarket bidding rounds.

This protocol reflects the actual peculiarities of the Blanes auctions, but it has been adapted to the fact that in Fishmarket the participants can be computer programs executed in a remote location. Thus, for instance, the basic bidding convention of the fish market is that the first *valid* offer is the one to win the round[4]. It is acceptable for instance, that buyers and sellers attend the auction, enter and exit the market at will but whereas in Blanes buyer and seller traffic is constant and free, in Fishmarket the (virtual) room is "closed" while the round is in process (to guarantee equity). Another subtle and illustrative difference may be seen in the way collisions are managed in the Fishmarket. In Blanes, in the event of two buyer's offers coinciding at a given price a "tie" is declared and the good is reauctioned at an increased price. However, in the Fishmarket the number of consecutive ties between two or more buyers must be limited somehow, since there may exist a real possibility that two or more software agents maybe implementing the same heuristics (and thus could cause an infinite sequence of collisions). In a real fish market, participants seldom coincide more than once, and the auctioneer acts discrectionally to break any anomalous tie. In the Fishmarket, repeated ties are broken by a random selection of a winner.

Although in any given auction the basic scenes are enacted over and over, these scenes are *articulated* in a systematic way: there are temporal and causal relationships between scenes which must be preserved for an auction to be performed and to be *legitimate*. The *buyers*, on the one hand, bid for the fish they want to buy, but they have to register as buyers previously and establish an adequate credit line which should be renewed when it is about to be exhausted (or completely exhausted). When a fish crate is bought, buyers should collect it, pay for it and take it with them. *Sellers* register their goods in the auction and collect the benefit when the goods are sold.

This articulation of scenes will be called the "Performative Structure" of an auction. Figure 7.3 is a schematic and simplified version of the Fishmarket, where each box corresponds to a scene whose diagram will be similar to the one for the bidding rounds.

Since in an institution each interaction is linked to an illocution (see Section 7.1), these diagrams allow to describe simply all the admissible interactions in the auction house. It is clear that these schemata indicate the illocution sequences which are exchanged by agents participating in each scene, but they are not enough to determine what really happens when an illocution is made, or the conditions which must prevail in the market for a certain illocution to be expressed by an agent. For this reason we require two additional elements: the market *commitments* and the *individual rules of behaviour*[5].

---

[4] An offer is valid if the bidder has enough credit to pay for that bid. If this condition is not fulfilled, infractors are fined or expelled, and the good is auctioned again at a price a percentage higher than the invalid offer.

[5] There are other notational conventions to express these diagrams' content: coloured Petri nets, Script languages, π-calculus, etc. Some of them may de-

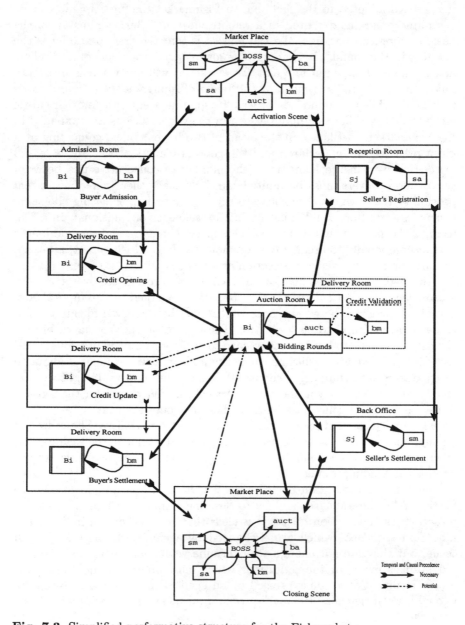

Fig. 7.3. Simplified performative structure for the Fishmarket.

7.2.2 Commitments

In classical pragmatics terminology (e.g. Austin [30] or Searle [599]) illocutions "change the world" or "denote changes in the world" by establishing or modifying the *commitments* or *obligations* which are shared between participants.

The "world" for an auction house is anything which concerns auctions performed in that auction house[6]. Consequently, commitments established in an auction house are related to the exchange of auctioned goods, their features and the exchange conditions (that is, the registered good in the auction, who is its current owner, whether it has a reservation price, how much credit a certain buyer has, if he/she has to be fined, etc.). These commitments, whose satisfaction the institution is in charge of warranting, are established and modified exclusively through illocutions that *the institution considers acceptable* (because they attain to the institution's conventions) and thus we will call them "market commitments".

In the Fishmarket, as in most auction houses, market commitments are viewed as *terms* of a formal language —which can be interpreted as a database (distributed and with different views for each participant)— and can be specified around three main information structures: the auction's *catalogue* (which dynamically stores information related to the goods auctioned), *each seller's account* (which registers the most relevant aspects of that vendor, as its identification, the income and commissions applied) and *each buyer's account* (which includes data referring to his/her credit and the purchases made)[7].

The catalogue may be defined as follows:

Definition 1 (Auction Catalogue). Be $G = \{g_m\}_{m \in M}$ a set of good identifiers, T a time model, and be B and S, respectively, the buyers and the vendors of an auction. Then, CAT, the **auction's catalogue** is the set $CAT : G \times \widehat{G} \times S \times (B \cup \{\perp, \pm\}) \times I\!R^4 \times T^2 \times 2^{T \times INCI}$, whose dimensions' meaning are defined on Table 2.

Where:

- $\widehat{G} = \{\hat{g}_k\}_{k \in K}$ is the set of types of good.
- $\perp, \pm$ denote that the good *was not sold* or was *withdrawn*.
- INCI an *incident* list (collisions, ties, fines, expellings).

Commitments referring to the catalogue are established, modified, and published according to the indications on Table 3. Other market commitments are described in a similar fashion.

---

note, in the very formalism, the protocol and some market commitments, as well as conventions regarding individuals.

[6] It is the "Dialogical Framework" (cf. Section 7.3.1).

[7] There are other complementary structures with an operative or implementational character (collision count, virtual space occupants, etc.).

$$
\begin{array}{lll}
CAT_1 = & g \in G & \text{(the \emph{catalogue number} of g)} \\
CAT_2 = & \hat{g} \in \widehat{G} & \text{(the \emph{good type} of g)} \\
CAT_3 = & seller(g) \in S & \text{(the \emph{seller} of g)} \\
CAT_4 = & buyer(g) \in B \cup \{\perp, \pm\} & \text{(the \emph{buyer} of g, if it exists)} \\
CAT_5 = & p_{rsv}(g) \in \mathbb{R} & \text{(\emph{reservation} price of g)} \\
CAT_6 = & p_0(g) \in \mathbb{R} & \text{(\emph{initial} price for g)} \\
CAT_7 = & p_t(g) \in \mathbb{R} & \text{(\emph{price} in t time)} \\
CAT_8 = & p_\omega(g) \in \mathbb{R} & \text{(\emph{final price})} \\
CAT_9 = & t_0(g) \in T & \text{(\emph{registering} time)} \\
CAT_{10} = & t_\omega(g) \in T & \text{(\emph{sale} time)} \\
CAT_{11} = & incdt_t(g) = \{\langle t;i \rangle : t \in T \wedge i \in INCI\} & \text{(\emph{incidents} with g)}
\end{array}
$$

Table 7.2. The Fishmarket catalogue

7.2.3 Individual Behaviour Rules

This way of describing social conventions, however, is not very explicit. If one wishes to make sure that all agents taking part in an auction follow "the rules of the game", it would be convenient to state these rules in a way that is easy to communicate to external agents and its observance easy to check (by internal agents, or by some other external agent). One could then unambiguously define, for each illocution, its *generation* and *interpretation* conditions. That is, which are the *conditions which must prevail* in the market commitments for the participant which utters them, and which are the *effects* that such illocution should have on the market commitments of those participants hearing it.

For instance, for an auctioneer (**auct**) to offer a good, such good should be the first unsold good in the catalogue. And if a buyer accepts an offer, the buyer manager (**bm**) is *required* to change that buyer's account, to fine him/her if he/she is insolvent or to expel him/her; if the good is assigned, the institution will cease to have this good in store and will be *compelled* to deliver it to the buyer, and to reflect in the catalogue the state of the good, it's final price and it's buyer.

Let us look for instance at four rules (Table 7.4) which specify the auctioneer and buyer manager's expected behaviour in the assignment of a good and the choice of the next good in the catalogue (that is, from state S12 and to the states S17 and S5 in Figure 7.2).

The process is the following: when the buyers' manager (**bm**) declares a valid buyer's (**b**) credit (i.e. the potential buyer is solvent), the auctioneer (**auct**) will update the information corresponding to such good in the catalogue as well as the unsold goods list and his/her own unsettled tasks before declaring the good assigned. This reasoning is represented by Rule 1.

When the good is assigned, the auctioneer will attempt to auction another good. If there are still unsold goods, it will choose the first on the list, but

CAT_i	Content	Definer	When	Known
CAT_1	g (id)	sa	newlot	All
CAT_2	$\hat{g}$ (type)	s,sa	register	auct
CAT_3	$seller(g)$	s,sa	register	auct
CAT_4	$buyer(g)$	auct	cr-val/re-dec.	bm
CAT_5	$p_{rsv}(g)$	s,sa	register	auct
CAT_6	$p_0(g)$	s,sa	register	auct
CAT_7	$p_t(g)$	auct	newgood/rebid	All
CAT_8	$p_\omega(g)$	auct	cr-val/re-dec.	bm
CAT_9	$t_0(g)$	sa	register	auct
CAT_{10}	$t_\omega(g)$	auct	cr-val/re-dec.	bm
CAT_{11}	$incdt(g)$	auct	coll/cr.val	All

CAT_i	Content	Definer	When	Known by all
CAT_1	g (id)	sa	present(lot)	-
CAT_2	$\hat{g}$ (type)	s,sa	newlot	present(lot)
CAT_3	$seller(g)$	s,sa	newlot	present(lot)
CAT_4	$buyer(g)$	auct	credit-val.	adj./w.
CAT_5	$p_{rsv}(g)$	s,sa	newlot	withdrawn
CAT_6	$p_0(g)$	s,sa	newlot	new-good
CAT_7	$p_t(g)$	auct	offer	-
CAT_8	$p_\omega(g)$	auct	credit-val.	adj./w.
CAT_9	$t_0(g)$	sa	newlot	present(lot)
CAT_{10}	$t_\omega(g)$	auct	credit-val.	adj./w.
CAT_{11}	$incdt(g)$	auct	tie/rebid	-

Table 7.3. Market Information about Goods in the Fishmarket

before offering it (with the appropriate initial value) the auctioneer will have to update its commitments (Rule 2).

If the auctioneer has got no more goods to sell, it must ask the sellers' admitter (**sa**) for a new lot to auction (Rule 3)[8].

Meanwhile (Rule 4), when the buyers' manager (**bm**) is informed of a good being assigned, he/she proceeds to updating the market income ($ahincome$) and the corresponding buyer's account ($BA(b)$)[9]. The sellers' manager (**sm**) reacts analogously by changing the seller's account and charging the corresponding commission.

In general, rules are stated for each participant type, in each scene and for each illocution that the type of participant can utter or receive; as it was seen in the previous case, there can be more than one rule for each illocution. This enumeration of rules is based on two methodological reasons: The first, which

---

[8] These Fishmarket rules use terms such as: SG and UG (sold and unsold goods list, respectively), $Pend_{auct}$ (auctioneer's pending tasks), $bundle(b)$ (the "shopping basket" for b), Δ_{rounds} (the waiting time between rounds), etc. It can also include instructions such as $WAIT$ and $REST$ which refer to the computational realization of the corresponding operations.

[9] Whose credit ($credit(b)$) reflects the cost of the purchase, since the credit manager should have changed it before declaring the bid valid.

Rule 1. (adjudicate$_{auct}$)
$IF \quad assert(bm, auct : valid(b), t)$
$THEN \ credit_{t_{now}}(b) :=$
$\qquad credit_t(b) - p_t(g)$
$AND \quad buyer(g) := b$
$AND \quad bundle(b) := bundle(b) \cup \{g\}$
$AND \quad t_\omega(g) := t$
$AND \quad SG := APPEND(SG; g)$
$AND \quad UG := REST(UG)$
$AND \quad Pend_{auct} := UG$
$AND \quad declare(auct, all :$
$\qquad sold(g, buyer(g), p_\omega(g),$
$\qquad t_\omega(g)); t_{now})$

Rule 2. (newgood$_{auct}$)
$IF \quad declare(auct, all :$
$\qquad sold(g, buyer(g), p_\omega(g),$
$\qquad t_\omega(g)); t)$
$AND \quad UG \neq \emptyset$
$THEN \ g := FIRST(UG)$
$AND \quad p(g) := p_0(g)$
$AND \quad WAIT(t_{now} \geq t + \Delta_{rounds})$
$AND \quad offer(auct, all :$
$\qquad tosell(g, p(g)); t_{now})$

Rule 3. (newgood$'_{auct}$)
$IF \quad declare(auct, all :$
$\qquad sold(g, buyer(g), p_\omega(g),$
$\qquad t_\omega(g)); t)$
$AND \quad UG = \emptyset$
$THEN \ request(auct, sa : moregoods;$
$\qquad t_{now})$

Rule 4. (adjudicate$_{bm}$)
$IF \quad declare(auct, all :$
$\qquad sold(g, buyer(g), p_\omega(g)); t)$
$THEN \ ahincome := ahincome+$
$\qquad (\Pi_{spremium} \times p_\omega(g))$
$AND \quad BA(b) := APPEND(BA(b);$
$\qquad \langle t; purchase : b, g, p_\omega(g);$
$\qquad credit(b) \rangle)$

Table 7.4. Adjudication rules in the Fishmarket

we have already mentioned, is due to the need of making these conventions explicit and more intelligible for users or external observers. The second is to facilitate the definition and update of the institution's conventions. This second methodological reason is expanded on in the section below.

7.2.4 Convention Variants

It should be evident that the individual behaviour rules must correspond with the scene protocols. However, such correspondance is not always easy to achieve. The art is in the choice and analysis of illocutions and it's interrelation with the diagrams. To illustrate this point let us look at a very important variant of the Fishmarket: *closed bid* auctions. In this convention there is a single bidding round where the ones to bid submit their offers which are known to the rest of the bidders (hence the name) and the highest bid wins. Figures 7.4 represents the closed bid protocol (CBP) which here includes a few additional illocutions to deal with offer validation and the limiting case when no bids are received[10]. It should be no surprise that the

---

[10] A correction suggested by simple comparison with the Fishmarket bidding protocol.

illocutions on this diagram are almost identical to the ones on Table 1, with the exception that in the Fishmarket the buyer only *accepts* the auctioneer's offers including a price, whereas here, it is the bidder whom proposes the price he/she is ready to pay in the bid[11]. The credit validation request is also slightly more complex since the auctioneer communicates the credit manager a (sorted) list of bids which satisfy the auction house's requirements, so that either the highest valid one be returned, or none in case there is not. These considerations produce the following illocutions:

$$offer(auct, all : tosell(g))$$
$$assert(b, auct : bid(b, p))$$
$$declare(auct, bm : selected(\{bid(b_i, p_i)\}))$$
$$request(auct, bm : creditstatus(\{bid(b_i, j)\}))$$
$$assert(bm, auct : valid(b, p))$$
$$declare(auct, all \cup \{bm\} : sold(g, b, p, t_\omega))$$
$$assert(bm, auct : invalid)$$
$$declare(auct, all \cup \{sm\} : withdrawn(g, t_\omega))$$
$$declare(auct, all : endoflot)$$

From these illocutions some individual rules should be stated for all participants. This is a trivial task since market commitments can be represented by the same information structures from Fishmarket even though a new *selected* operator should be added and the *creditstatus* extended so as to be able to cope with the new offer selection processes (in the Fishmarket the only offer received was selected or a tie was broken selecting randomly one of the bids).

Let us suppose that we have finished this tedious process and we have the new upward-bidding protocol and its corresponding rules, conveniently debugged and correctly described. Then, we can *immediately* generate a new Fishmarket variant: *Vickrey* bidding ([687]). This is also a closed bidding process, in which the winner is also the highest bidder, but he/she pays only the amount of the second highest bid. In order to represent this new bidding convention, assuming the previously represented closed bid convention, one then only need to change the *selected* operator (and the corresponding auctioneer rule); the rest remains the same[12]. The *selected* operator is the key in this flexibility. In fact, most of the upward-bidding conventions in *public procurement* are variants of the *closed bid* biddings, and can be represented through simple modifications in the selection operator which can be defined in general as a function associating the bidder to the amount it should pay if the good was assigned to him/her. That is why *parametrizing* it would be convenient, in such a way that the same protocol, the same individual rules, the same illocutions and the same operators could be used for any of its vari-

---

[11] Additionally, we do not take expellings and fines into account.

[12] In the definition of *selected* the only offer case must have been solved, whereas in the case of zero offer reception, this had to be resolved in the definition of *creditstatus* —since it was introduced for the *closed envelope* convention.

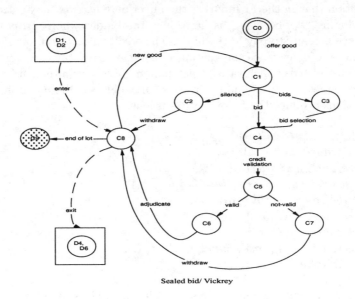

Sealed bid/ Vickrey

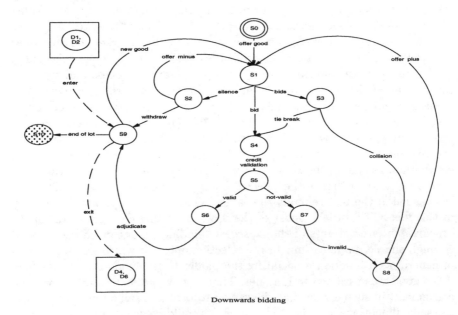

Downwards bidding

Fig. 7.4. Classic diagrams for two bidding protocols.

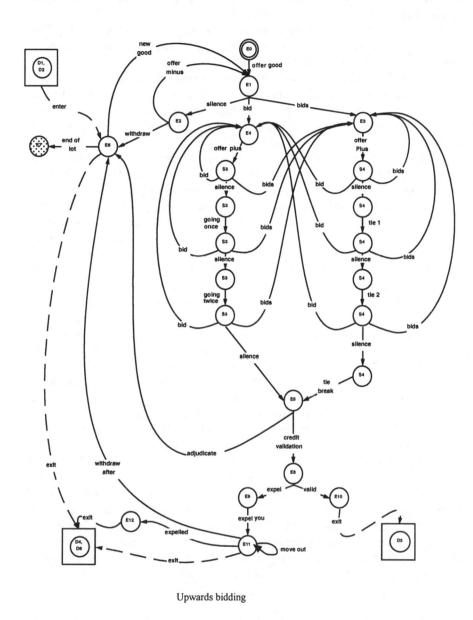

Upwards bidding

Fig. 7.5. Classic diagram for the upwards bidding protocol.

ants, and it were only necessary to make these operator's parameters explicit
to use it in a given licitation convention.

Let us now compare, without entering details, the upward-bidding Fishmarket diagram with the *upward-bidding* (or "*English*" bidding, bottom of
Figure 7.5). It is clear that the resemblances are less evident here than in
the centre of the diagrams, inspite of superficial similarities. But considering the complete Fishmarket performative structure and substituted in the
bidding rounds scene, the current bidding protocol for the *upward-bidding*
protocol, we would almost immediately obtain an auction house very similar
to Sotheby's.

The steps from the *closed bid* auction to *Vickrey* and to a generic conventions of the *public procurement* became trivial. In fact, the step from the
Fishmarket bidding to the closed envelope was simple since we aimed at
changing only the upward-bidding protocol and two operators. Fishmarket's
transformation for *upward-biding* is not so easy, but its description and depu-
ration would follow processes very similar to the ones followed by the first
transformations, since the elements that must undergo modification can be
directly made explicit. It would be worthwhile obtaining a way of characteriz-
ing those elements of an *auction convention* which could be **systematically
varied** and produce alternative conventions —without requiring substantial
modification s either in the operators, in the rules or in the protocols.

Having so much simple diagrams and the corresponding rules sets in a
relatively simple notation to represent interactions, allows for the description
these potential variants in a reasonably simple way. It is in commitments,
and the way in which the operators which manipulate them work, where
practical diffiulties lie. These difficulties can be greatly avoided through the
use of sufficiently general operators (which, when parametrized, are equally
useful for the different variants) and the information structures which are
appropriate for these forseeable operator variations.

The truly difficult problem to face is that rules and protocols must be
executable. That is, if an auction house adopted them and buyers and sellers
met at auction houses to exchange a set of goods, then exchange must adhere to these conventions (if enough resources and interest existed). For this
reason it is necessary to show that a given description based on diagrams, information structures and rules are correct. That is, coherent in the handling
of commitments and *feasible in pragmatic terms*. To discuss this difficulties,
we will try to formalize some aspects of the Fishmarket.

7.3 Towards a Formal Model

At the beginning of this chapter we stated that in order to characterize a
virtual institution three types of convention were necessary: The ontologic,
social, and the individual behavioural conventions. We have devoted most

of the chapter to the later two. We shall now concentrate on the ontologic conventions so as to approach some formal elements of the other conventions.

7.3.1 Dialogical Framework

In previous examples goods, participants, roles and locations, instants and time intervals, incidents, actions, prices and many other elements were parts of illocutions, rules and commitments. To establish (either operationally or formally) the individual and social conventions which constitute the Fishmarket *deontology* (or of any other auction) we need a rich *ontology* and have the appropriate communication and specification languages for these norms. A common reference framework for all participants in an auction is required which will enable them to communicate (and understand each other) inside the auction house. Since we have decided to understand some virtual institutions as multi-agent systems in which all participants interact *dialoguing* —through an illocution exchange— we will call this common reference framework for all participants *Dialogical Framework*.

The components of such *Dialogical Framework* for the Fishmarket, DF_{FM}, are the following:

1. **Agents**$_{FM}$ a set of identifiers (which could be used to denote specific agents),
2. **Rol**$_{FM}$ = {**boss, auct, sa, sm, ba, bm**} $\cup$ {**s, b**} (the agent types taking part in a Fishmarket auction)
3. SR_{FM} = {$\langle$**boss**, $x\rangle$: $x \in$ **Rol**$_{FM}$ \ **boss**} (Authority relationships in the Fishmarket: the *market boss* has authority over all participants in an auction)
4. **Loc**$_{FM}$ = {AH, RR, AR, DR, BO, M} (the virtual locations)
5. L_{FM} the "object language" {$\Delta_{bid}, \Pi_{spremium}, \ldots, CAT, \ldots bid, tosell, endoflot, credit, ahincome, \ldots$})
6. CL_{FM} (a communication language, with formulae of type $\iota(\alpha, \Gamma :$ $\varphi; \tau)$, with $\alpha \in$ **Rol**$_{FM}$, $\Gamma \subseteq$ **Rol**$_{FM}$, $\varphi \in L_{FM}$ and $\iota \in I_{FM}$ = {$assert, request, deny, accept, declare, command$}),
7. ML_{FM} the corresponding metalanguage to define behaviour rules (including other languages).
8. T a time model (e.g. discrete, acyclic and forward branching).

Adopting a nominalist attitude, we may assert that the Fishmarket is formed by all the *entities* which we have to refer to inorder to establish the "rules of the game" of that auction house. Recall that such game rules were described by the "Performative Structure" —formed by scenes, their protocols and commitments— and the "individual rules of behaviour" to which each participant is subject when taking part in a scene. We will now introduce some more elements for the purpose of referential clarity.

7.3.2 Fishmarket's Deontology

We have seen before that there are six virtual locations in the Fishmarket (**AH,RR,AR,DR,BO,M**) and that there is always a staff member who is in charge of supervising the scenes taking place there (**auct,sa,ba,bm,sm** and **boss**, respectively). In some virtual spaces more than one scene may be performed (for instance, in **DR** credits are opened, closed and updated and in **M** the market is activated and closed).

We have also seen that in each scene there is a protocol in which all the permissible illocutions for those scenes by the participants are indicated according to their roles. We also mentioned that certain structures keep each other a (temporal and causal) precedential structure. Given these elements we define the "Performative Structure" (PS_{FM}) of the Fishmarket as:

- The scene sets: $\Sigma_{FM} = \delta_0, \ldots \delta_8$ whose interdependence is given in Figure 3, and in which an interaction diagram with its corresponding illocutions corresponds to each box (as the one in Figure 2 —with Table 1— corresponds to scene D_4 of auction Rounds).

For each participant and each scene we associate to each illocution in that scene the individual behaviour rules which may affect that participant in the given scene (either the producer or receiver of that utterance).

That is, if ρ is a role in $\mathbf{Rol}_{FM}$ and δ a scene in Σ_{FM}, then $BR(\rho, \delta)$ will be the individual behaviour rules of the participant performing a ρ role in the scenes δ. $BR(\rho, \delta)$ is formed in the following way:

- For all illocutions $\iota(\alpha, \Gamma : \varphi; \tau)$ of the scene δ such that $\rho \in \{\alpha\} \cup \Gamma$, at least one rule R exists such that:
  - If $\rho = \alpha$, then $\iota(\alpha, \Gamma : \varphi; \tau)$ is in the antecedent of R, and
  - If $\rho \in \Gamma$, then $\iota(\alpha, \Gamma : \varphi; \tau)$ is in the consequent of R

From these role and scene rules we may define the Fishmarket individual behaviour rules as $BR_{FM} = \{BR(\rho, \delta) : \rho \in \mathbf{Rol}_{FM}, \delta \in \Sigma_{FM}\}$.

With the *dialogical framework*, the *performative structure* and the *individual behaviour rules* we define an *institution*. In fact, we have already "formalized" an *auction house FM* which corresponds to the Fishmarket:

$$FM = \langle DF_{FM}, PS_{FM}, BR_{FM} \rangle$$

7.3.3 Models and Implementation

In order to formalize this Dialogical framework and interpret the Performative structure of the Fishmarket and it's behaviour rules, we must rely on a given semantics and pragmatics.

The semantics may be relatively standard (using the obvious intuitions of the meanings of the elements in the dialogical framework and translating them to a formal structure which interprets them in terms of market commitments). The pragmatics has to account for how an institution permit an auction which respect it's conventions.

Let us suppose that A is an auction, characterized by the auctioned goods G, the participating agents A and the status of the market along time (that is, a finite sequence of states which indicate how the goods possesion, the resources, the incidents evolve, since the situation before the auction, E_0, until the auction finishes E_ω. And be FM an auction house.

We want to build an FM *institution* which allows for the *performance* of the auction A, in such a way that one can go from E_0 to E_ω through a dialogical process in which involves the agents faithfully following the FM conventions.

Notion 1. An auction $A = \langle A, G, \langle E_0 \ldots E_\omega \rangle \rangle$ is **performed** in an auction house FM, $FM \models A$, if E_0 becomes E_ω through a dialogical process involving A and G which satisfy the auction conventions of the FM institution.

There are various options to formalize FM. One of them consists in adopting a convention similar to Model Theory (e.g VanLinder and Dignum [172] or Dialogical extensions to Singh [627] or Vandervecken's [601] proposals). Another possibility is formal specification; for instance, one based in Dynamic Logics (as the one proposed in our articles [475] and [474, Ch.10]) or closer to implementation, one based in π-calculus ([501]). But one may also directly use a *computational realization as a multi-agent system*, as our virtual lodge FM96.5 ([559]).

While the first options have an analytic and formal interest (which, amongst other things, may provide with formal predictive results), the last has normative and evidently practical advantages.

Space does not allow us to enter into details, but we must mention that in FM96.5, the abstract version of the Fishmarket that we have discussed here is reproduced with remarkable faithfulness and a fair, lively and reliable more than reasonable for the performance of on-line auctions through a "reliable" web[13].

The interest of this development does not only lie on its virtual institution character. From the methodological point of view, it also provides some teachings. The most obvious are the advantages of dialogically describing the auction house (with the consequent economy in the definition of the agents, their interactions and ostensible behaviour), the anthropomorphizing of the intermediate agents (and consequently the ease to produce variants and adaptations from the original model) and to be able to achieve, from the performance (but not only formal) point of view, that human and external agents

---

[13] That is, a Web (such as the internet) in which it is guaranteed that messages are not lost and that their broadcasting sequence is preserved (even though neither homogeneous answer times or synchronization are guaranteed).

become *indistinguishable* [14]. In fact, FM96.5 has now an additional layer of computational developments which make it an auditable auction house, as well as making it a most flexible and robust testing ground for variants of the Fishmarket (FM97.6) (see [476]).

7.4 Institutions

The notion of virtual institution we have presented here to describe and formalize the Fishmarket is very general. In a similar way to the one used for the Fishmarket it is possible to describe the scenes and behaviour rules of other multi-agent systems in which the interactions must adhere to a more or less precise protocol; and from there, building its computational version.

For instance, in order to reproduce an auction house as Sotheby's, in which the main differences lie on the upward-bidding conventions, changing the upward-bidding and downward-bidding diagrams in Figures 7.5 and 7.4 in the corresponding part of Figure 7.2 (and varying the corresponding individual rules) would be sufficient, but the surface performative structure and the rest of the scenes would be unaltered. In the same line, generalizing $FM = \langle DF_{FM}, PS_{FM}, BR_{FM} \rangle$ for an auction house generally means only pointing out which fragments of each of these three components are preserved and made explicit in the change of diagrams and rules.

In addition to auctions, it is also possible to define in similar terms less structured interaction convention types. For instance, the open negotiation described in [624] may reflect a dialogical framework simpler than the Fishmarket (since it includes only a scene and no mediating agents) but whose language is more elaborate (in L (*Deals*) are mentioned, in CL requests, offers, threats and other arguments, and ML includes elements as the one denoting each agent's preferences, reification functions, etc). In the case of the argumentative negotiation, the performative structure includes only a scene which diagram joins the Open Negotiation Protocol and the individual rules corresponding to the rules which make this interaction sequence clear and the minimum common components for the generation and interpretation of illocutions.

In all these cases, an *agent-mediated institution* is defined as a collection of participating agents (in principle software agents) in which the theoretical components are specified around the three mentioned structures: dialogical framework, performative structure and individual behaviour rules. The implementation of such a multi-agent system corresponding to these institutions may be achieved the same way as FM96.5 and FM97.6. Indeed, current developments allow the implementation of simple variants of the Fishmarket (as the Vickrey auctions and the public licitations).

---

[14] Which is achieved through a careful analysis of the implementational aspects of the protocols of the scenes and the invention of *institutor* devices which restrict the behaviour of external agents to the institution conventions strictly.

Following the same methodological criteria used in the development of FM96.5, more robust flexible and checkable multi-agent systems may be built, as FM97.6.

With such an approach, we have adopted the formalization of the "Cohabited Mixed Reality Information Spaces" project; real-virtual spaces where human agents use automatic personal assistants to perform some joint actions, such as arranging meetings during a fair [528]. In this project we use the notion of *agent-mediated institution* to represent not an auction house or a market, but a fair or congress space and characterize the typical scenes in these events in which a person may benefit from the help of a computerised personal assistant to explore that space, identify interesting action opportunities and even coordinate some of them. Again, the dialogic approach makes not only the identification and implementation of interaction protocols' formal framework mentioned above easier, but also the implementation of the *institutional environment*, the multi-agent system and the specific agents, which allow performing a virtual institution.

Also as part of the SMASH project [633] we have started using the idea of *Agent-Based Institutions* to represent the "medical protocols" of care and attenti on towards patients. The aim of that project is to endow the different participants in a hospital (patients, physicians, nurses, managers) with artificial assistants which allow them to follow the steps of a "medical protocol" and identify omission of expected protocol steps, take note of changes, give notice to the one in charge, adjust the protocol or carry out corrective measures. For this reason, the institutions on roles, scenes, protocol and rules mentioned around the Fishmarket are used again.

7.5 Closing Remarks

This research and development exercise may be justified on three different grounds: from the point of view of general Artificial Intelligence, from the most specific of multi-agent systems, and from the approach of optics related to electronic commerce.

1. *For Artificial Intelligence* at least two considerations can be pointed out which are relevant. On the one hand, the analysis and modelling of a particular auction house, and of institutions based on agents in general is a interdisciplinary problem. Distributed computation, pragmatic linguistics, mathematical economy, negotiation and metaphysics are only but a few problems which Artificial Intelligence may provide relevant methodological and technical solution.(cf. e.g., [405, 599, 627, 356, 170]). The other consideration is during auction modelling, where three identification lines which are fundamental to this modelling were identified, and may be of interest to other fields of AI: the *Situated Reasoning* characteristic of Dialogic Systems ([544, 269, 699, 473]) or Computational

Dialectics ([684, 533, 399]); the *Agent-Based Institution Design*; and the *reliability* condition to which all interactions in a virtual institution are subject to.

2. *For multi-agent systems*, the agent-mediated auctions in which software agents may take part, or software agents such as buyers and sellers may perform a function, have a special appeal for at least the following reasons:

   - They constitute a *non-trivial problem*. The challenge is that the information present in an auction is not only abundant and contains a great uncertainty, but also constantly changing and, in the typical auctions (such as the Fishmarket), it changes very quickly. For this reason the development of agents which can successfully develop in such an environment is very difficult, and requires making use of a great amount of proposals and developments on automated reasoning.
   - They are, on the other hand, a domain in which *competitive evaluation* is possible: one which is objective and direct in the development of participants (and of the own institutions) due to the very competitive nature of an auction. This is an element which is used to build test platforms such as FM97.6, which can be applied to the evaluation of auctions and a very wide number of agent-based institutions.
   - The most significant reason is that auctions are a *conveniently scalable* problem inside a general program of investigation in multi-agent systems. Such scalability is possible due to the fact that the *social* features, which are present in this form of coordination, are very simple and alien to the *individual* factors implicit in decisional processes. That is why it is possible to easily separate both factors and using auctions as a testing ground for the development or experimentation of architectures, heuristics, and strategies which, when applied to agents taking part in an auction, may also be relevant for other means of coordination (as the crossing of intentions in a stock market or open negotiation and bargaining).

3. Finally, from the perspective of *Electronic Commerce*, we must point out three additional aspects:

   - Electronic exchanges through the Internet (cf. [683, 425, 482]), and particularly the sudden success of on-line auctions, has considerable potential and relevance. This trend emphasises a need for scientific and technologic considerations for opportunities in developing trading institutions for automated negotiation or mediation through software agents.
   - The opportunity of developing agents which take part such institutions. Solving the difficulties (either ergonomic, rule-related, operative or ability-related) with an intensive and generalised use in commerce will result in patents.

– Finally, the interest derived from the development (and design) of *new commerce practices* as a result of the aforementioned mentioned developments. But, in addition to that, the need of instituting *other practices* (and the consequent technological instruments) which are reliable, checkable and possibly subject to some kind of certification and independent audit. Such practices and technologies must build a *reliable, safe* and *profitable* electronic commerce.

Acknowledgements:

This work has been possible thanks to financial supports from a number of sources including: SMASH Project, (CICYT TIC96-1038-C04001); COMRIS project (ESPRIT LTR 25500-COMRIS); CONACYT (México) (Ref.69068-7245). We also want to acknowledge the support provided by the members of the Fishermen Guild in Blanes, specially to Xavier Márquez and Josep Llauradó.

8. Strategic Reasoning and Adaptation in an Information Economy

Edmund H. Durfee, Tracy Mullen, Sunju Park,
José M. Vidal, and Peter Weinstein

AI Laboratory, EECS Department, University of Michigan
1101 Beal Avenue, Ann Arbor, MI 48109-2110, USA.
E-Mail: {durfee, mullen, boxenju, jmvidal, peterw}@umich.edu

Summary.

One of our goals when building the University of Michigan Digital Library (UMDL) has been to prototype an architecture that can continually reconfigure itself as users, contents, and services come and go. We have worked toward this goal by developing a multi-agent information economy, where agents buy and sell information goods and services from each other using our commerce and communication protocols. We refer to the services and protocols offered by this economic infrastructure as the Service Market Society (SMS). Within the SMS, agents are able to find, work with, and even try to outsmart each other, as each agent attempts to accomplish the tasks for which it was created. When we open the door to decentralized decision-making among self-interested agents, there is a risk that the system will degenerate into chaos. In this chapter, we describe the protocols, services, and agent abilities embedded in the SMS infrastructure that combat such chaos while permitting flexibility, extensibility, and scalability of the system.

8.1 Introduction

A library serves a community of users by making available information content and services that are valued by that community. In a digital library, the information content and services are electronically available, and the user communities are no longer geographically defined. Realizing a digital library therefore includes difficulties in digitizing contents, computerizing services, and networking together users, services and contents. A tremendous amount of work has gone into all of these areas, and while many challenges remain, increasing numbers of digital libraries with interoperating components are appearing.

But even as these difficulties are being overcome, the result can well be an overwhelming tangle of possible information sources without the structure and selectivity that renders a library navigable. In other words, if the administration of a traditional library is challenging, the administration of a digital library can border on impossible due to the magnitude of content and services available, the rate of change in what is available, the size of a user population that is not bounded by physical proximity, and the evolving nature of that population.

The focus of this paper is on meeting this challenge. That is, in this paper we take for granted a rich network of interoperating information providers, consumers, and services. We also assume that it is impractical to marshal all of the information sources and services to address every information need for every user. Choices must be made, such that services are applied where they are expected to yield the most benefit. Traditionally, these choices are made by administrators who: identify, characterize, register, and track a user community; seek out and include the content that will benefit that community; and provide the most valuable services for tasks such as organizing, searching, abstracting, and disseminating the content.

Because we see the pace of library evolution increasing in the digital age, we instead embrace an alternative approach where we want to move as much of the administrative overhead into the digital infrastructure as possible. Rather than requiring frequent and costly intervention by human librarians, the library should evolve guided by the policies that humans embed within the infrastructure. The infrastructure should encourage:

- **Flexibility**: It should be able to embody a wide variety of policies to realize different flavors of information economies (public libraries, corporate libraries, university libraries, personal libraries,...)
- **Extensibility**: Providers and consumers of information goods and services should have incentives to join the information economy and be able to find their counterparts.
- **Scalability**: As the plethora of users, goods, and services grows, the underlying, computerized administration of the library should not bog down.
- **Robustness**: The infrastructure should support resistance against any agent manipulating the system to its own benefit and at the expense of other agents.

Toward this end, the University of Michigan Digital Library (UMDL) is structured as a collection of agents that can buy and sell services from each other using our commerce and communications infrastructure. To many, the concept of commerce in a library is heresy, and conjures images of library patrons having to pay as they go. Before continuing, therefore, let us briefly dispel this misunderstanding. Treating a library as an information economy provides us with a well-studied framework for making decentralized decisions about the allocation of the limited information goods and services that are available. Poor allocation decisions can lead to users receiving poor service, or none at all! Yet, users need not necessarily be aware of the underlying economic decisions being made, just as they are generally shielded from the decisions library administrators must make as they weigh the pros and cons of subscribing to a particular monograph series versus hiring another reference librarian. Thus, in many cases, users will be unaware of the underlying infrastructure, though if it is working well they will reap the benefits.

Indeed, our initial agent infrastructure forms the core of the UMDL system that has been deployed to several schools in southeastern Michigan, where it is used by hundreds of students daily. For the most part, the services used by the students have been selected and added to the deployed UMDL system by project members, and with only hundreds of students performing similar tasks, issues of flexibility, scale, extensibility, and robustness have not yet been stressed. This has allowed our research efforts to begin developing answers to these issues and experimenting with our answers before they have become critical to the wider deployment of the system. In this chapter, we outline the definition and design of the infrastructure for the UMDL information economy, and the kinds of agents that exist in it, that allow decentralized (scalable) ongoing configuration of an extensible set of users and services. We refer to the services/protocols offered by this infrastructure as the Service Market Society (SMS).

The SMS requires the integration of numerous agent technologies for knowledge exchange, commerce, learning, and modeling. Some of our earlier publications [180] have already explained the general agent architecture of the UMDL, along with the agents' communication system. In this paper we concentrate on how agents reason about and interact with each other, and how this in turn can lead to structural adaptation on the part of the entire system. We describe our prototype SMS in which a changing population of agents can find each other, enlist each other's aid (for a price), decide on the terms of an interaction, and learn to differentiate among providers. Furthermore, due to the decisions that the agents make, the structure of the economy can evolve to increase the chances of better interactions in the future.

We use our prototype to demonstrate how these technologies contribute to providing a flexible, extensible, scalable, and robust digital library. The agents and services we describe, unless otherwise noted, are implemented within the UMDL, but to avoid disrupting the use of the deployed system the experimental SMS agents are ignored by agents that are supporting the UMDL educational mission. As the kinks are worked out of experimental agents, therefore, deploying them has been trivial: an agent stops describing itself to the UMDL as experimental, and thus is available to the deployed system. Recently, for example, instances of many of the agents described in this paper (including auction agents, the auction manager, and the price monitor) have become part of the UMDL system used by the schools.

We start with an overview of the SMS (Section 8.2), and its component technologies: the UMDL ontology (Section 8.3) and the auctions (Section 8.4). These technologies support research allocation issues (such as limited library resources that must be shared fairly among patrons) and commerce issues (such as encouraging outside parties to supply services). We illustrate the former with a simple example of balancing load based on supply and demand (Section 8.5). We then turn to the latter issue of whether our infrastructure encourages extensibility by looking at the impact of adding profit-seeking agents that reason about other agents into the mix (Section 8.6). Once agents can attempt to overcharge for services, and return services that therefore are not valued as highly, agents that buy these services can over time learn which providers to prefer buying from (Section 8.7). Demand might outstrip supply, leading to the need for additional service providers, as the system adapts to the changing needs of users (Section 8.8). What has been learned about what providers to avoid can also be institutionalized by partitioning service providers into different markets depending on how they are perceived. We conclude with a summary of how our work addresses the needs of flexibility, extensibility, scalability, and robustness (Section 8.9).

As the reader will surmise, the SMS brings together several related threads of work, and this paper attempts to summarize these pieces and how they fit together. The work addresses only one (high-level) facet of the digital library enterprise, concentrating on describing, finding, allocating, and evaluating services, and is as yet incomplete even for this aspect of digital libraries.[1] Yet, we hope to convince the reader of the promise of this approach for meeting some of the long-term challenges in managing large-scale, open, rapidly-evolving digital libraries.

8.1.1 Other Digital Library Infrastructures

There is a tremendous amount of work going on on many facets of digital libraries; entire conferences and journals are devoted to the topic, and surveying all of the excellent work in the field is beyond the scope of this paper. Here, we will only mention a few projects that directly address aspects of digital library infrastructures. The InfoBus [561] system extends the current Internet protocols with a suite of higher-level information management protocols. This work concentrates on the details of the communication protocols which are, in fact, quite similar to those used in the UMDL[2]. They have even implemented some commerce interfaces [338]. However, in contrast to the work in this paper, they do not address the higher-level problem of agents finding each other (i.e. finding the services they want) and effectively taking part in the economy. The Alexandria Project [225] also addresses the issue of communication between users, collections, and mediators, but it does not use an economic framework for making resource allocation decisions.

---

[1] For example, the current SMS does not address issues of privacy, security, and even payment. In the description of "buying and selling" in SMS that follows, our current simple model assumes that buyers and sellers are each keeping track of their "balances" and honestly incrementing (decrementing) as services are sold (bought). We have attempted to make our system compatible with the various payment mechanisms being developed elsewhere.

[2] Both projects use the ILU CORBA implementation. Some degree of interoperability between the two projects has been achieved.

8.2 The Service Market Society

The UMDL SMS implements a multi-agent information economy where agents buy and sell services from each other. Agents can be added to or removed from the system at any time. Instead of having to rely solely on internally designed agents, the UMDL SMS is designed to attract outside agents to provide new services. These agents in turn are motivated by the long-term profit they might accrue by participating in the system.[3]

The raw resources of a digital library consist of collections of information, where a collection might be a database of journal articles or it might be a collection of related web pages. Collection Interface Agents (CIAs) provide access and search services for these collections. Various middlemen, or *mediator* agents (such as QPAs, see below), transform the raw information resources into finished products or services which the end-user desires. Each user, or library patron, has a User Interface Agent (UIA) which interacts with the UMDL on his or her behalf to acquire these services. Finally, within the system are *facilitator* agents (such as the Registry, SCA, auctions, etc. as described below) which facilitate the process of agents classifying, locating, and connecting agents to provide more comprehensive services.

Figure 8.1 shows a simple scenario which we will be using throughout this paper. In this scenario, users want to find sources of information for various topics (e.g. history, science or mathematics) and various audience levels (e.g. middle school, high school, or professional). Query Planning Agents (QPAs) [688], act as middlemen, accepting queries from users and returning collections related to those queries. Initially, the user sends a query, via a web-based Java interface, to the UIA. The UIA must then find an agent that can service this query. In order to allow agents to find the services they need, we have implemented an ontology of services. Every agent must be able to describe the services it wishes to buy or sell using terms from the UMDL ontology.

The User Interface Agent (UIA) describes its needs to the Service Classifier Agent (SCA) and is told the appropriate service label. The UIA asks the Auction Manager Agent (AMA) for an auction where the service is sold, and goes to that auction. The Auction matches the UIA with an agent providing the service (in this case, a QPA, which returns the name of a Collection Interface Agent (CIA)). The SMS supports any number of UIA, CIA, QPA, and Auction agents.

In order to join the UMDL, every agent must register its unique agent-id with the Registry. An agent can then advertise by sending[4] its service description to the Service Classifier Agent, as shown by the dotted lines, and receiv-

---

[3] While designed to encourage third-party agent/service development, to date the third-party services in the UMDL have been introduced by the project team. Bootstrapping the process to the point where third-parties have sufficient incentive to join is, not surprisingly, hard!

[4] Agent communications use KQML primitives implemented using CORBA objects, see [180] for details.

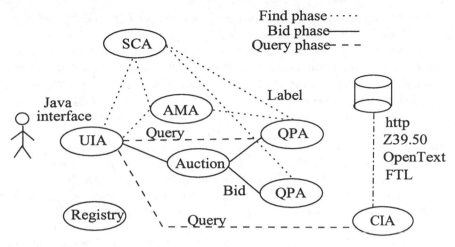

Fig. 8.1. The UMDL Service Market Society

ing a service-label. The SCA automatically classifies the advertised service descriptions into a subsumption-based taxonomy. This organization enables the SCA to match requests for services to "semantically close" descriptions, to recommend the most appropriate services out of those that are currently available. We encourage agents to describe their needs with as much detail as possible. The SCA can then recommend the available services with the least general subsuming descriptions.

Once an agent has acquired the appropriate service-label from the SCA, and is ready to buy/sell that service, it sends the desired label to the Auction Manager Agent (AMA) (as shown by dotted lines). The AMA queries the SCA to determine the appropriate auction—since an auction is essentially just another kind of service. The AMA then returns to the agent a list of auctions which sell matching services. The agent then sends buy or sell bids to a particular Auction agent (solid lines). UMDL *auctions* operate by collecting offers from participating agents and determining agreements consistent with those offers and the rules of the auction, matching individual buyers and sellers.

In our scenario, UIAs want to buy query planning services while QPAs want to sell this service. Once a match is found for the UIA, it will send its query to the matching QPA. The QPA returns the appropriate CIAs and the UIA then forwards its query to them. The CIAs can translate UMDL queries to a variety of protocols (e.g. http, Z39.50, FTL, etc.) and return the appropriate documents.

The sequence of events for an example service provider (QPA) and consumer (UIA) is summarized in figure 8.2.[5] The principal foci of this paper are on the decisions by providers/consumers and by the auction manager agent. Because the agents in our system are free to return services of differing qualities and to disagree on the subjective quality of a given service, we would expect that service-providing/consuming agents might try to take advantage of each other by manipulating their buy/sell offers or the qualities (and hence production costs) of the services rendered. An agent attempting to manipulate the system in this way is said to be doing *strategic reasoning,* typically based either on broader knowledge about the economy or on learned experience. In this chapter, we investigate how the addition of these strategic agents changes the dynamics of the UMDL SMS. We find that strategic agents increase the robustness of the system. We also find that the SMS market works to minimize the amount of strategic thinking that the agents can gainfully engage in, but does not completely eliminate the need for having some agents with strategic abilities, even if these abilities are not always used.

The decisions of the auction manager agent can affect the dynamics of the SMS as well. Specifically, the auction manager agent can monitor various features of the auctions, such as price fluctuations and the participants' satisfaction, and change the climate of the economy either by triggering a change in the population of buyers/sellers or by changing the configuration of auctions that bring buyers and sellers together. In this chapter, we investigate both of these forms of adaptation.

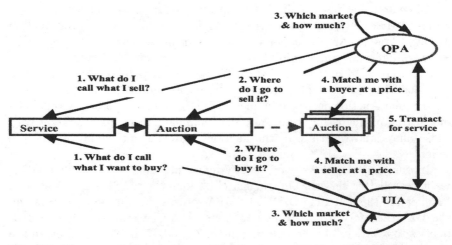

Fig. 8.2. The steps that a service provider (such as a QPA) and a service consumer (such as a UIA) go through in the SMS.

---

[5] Actually, in the implemented system, the SCA actually directly returns to the UIA the names of available auctions, rolling together the first 2 steps of the sequence shown into a single step.

Before turning to issues in strategic reasoning and adaptation, however, we first describe in slightly more detail the other components of the SMS—the Service Classifier (and its ontology) and the Auctions.

8.3 The UMDL Ontology

We use ontologies to encode declarative descriptions of complex agent services. Declarative descriptions are required to establish a space of services independent of the implementation of the current set of agents.

Representing complexity in a digital library, and any other "real-world" domain, demands expressiveness that is substantially more powerful than that of relational databases. Services have many descriptive dimensions (attributes), may be partially described at any level of granularity (with any combination of dimensions), and may be viewed from many perspectives (accessed by different sequences of attribute values). For example, an agent might seek a service to recommend a collection of articles on volcanoes, for high-school audiences, to be contracted for via auction. Alternatively, the agent might seek an auction that sells a service to recommend collections. (In Figure 8.3, follow links either from "recommend-dlcollection" at the top, or "auction" at the bottom of the figure). In an ontology, both perspectives can be represented simultaneously, and retrieval supports queries on any level of granularity. Declarative formalisms with less expressiveness than ontologies, such as relational databases, force a commitment to particular levels of granularity and particular perspectives.

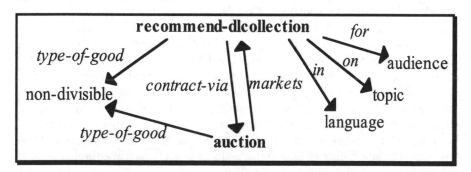

Fig. 8.3. Multi-dimensional, multi-perspective complexity

To promote reuse, the UMDL ontology is divided into nested modules (each of which is itself called an ontology) [705]. The most general includes library content and services that we consider to be part of a "generic" digital library. The second module adds concepts specific to the UMDL implementation, such as auctions. The third module describes agent services. We call this last ontology "dynamic" because agents define new service concepts at run-time. In contrast, "static" ontologies are either fixed, or are changed slowly over time by committees of persons.

8.3.1 The Service Classifier Agent

In the current SMS, UIAs, QPAs and Auction agents use the same SCA, and thus subscribe to the same ontologies. Figure 8.4 illustrates these agents' interactions with the SCA. Agents are in ovals, ontologies in rectangles, and the arrows connecting agents represent messages, paraphrased in natural language. These messages are expressed in Loom, a description logic in the KL-ONE family [422]. To communicate with the SCA, agents use terminology from the nested ontologies. The messages are shown with font styles that correspond to the ontology labels (plain, italics, and upper-case), to highlight the source of their terminology.

Figure 8.4 shows a typical agent interaction with the SCA. Messages are numbered chronologically. The QPA advertises its service (message 1a in Figure 8.4). Its label is classified in the Agent Services ontology, and can thus be used as part of further definitions. Next, the QPA asks for an auction to sell its service (message 2a). If an appropriate auction is not already active, the AMA classifies the services of auctioning the QPA's service (2b), starts a new auction, and responds to the QPA's request (2d). Subsequently, the UIA finds an auction to buy appropriate query planning by referring to terms from the ontologies, and searching for the most specific service concept that subsumes its request (3a).

Figure 8.4 illustrates the ability of the SCA to construct new terminology from existing terms at runtime.[6] Concepts in the SCA's dynamic ontology hide knowledge, just as words chunk meaning in natural language. Auctions sell some service, but they don't need to know anything about that service. The AMA asks the SCA for a service label for an auction, using the QPA's service label, but it does not know anything about that service. The SCA classifies the auction service using characteristics inferred from the QPA's service label. Thus, the SCA can respond to the UIA's request for an auction, which is phrased in terms from the static ontologies, rather than phrased in terms of the label which the AMA used to define the auction service. This appropriate hiding of knowledge reduces overall system complexity, and increases reusability and maintainability.

---

[6] Note that by "new terminology" we mean new, meaningful combinations of the core terms in the ontology. There are a huge number of ways that the core terms in the ontology can be composed into descriptions, only a small number of which will be meaningful. New terms are those that are dynamically created because they are useful. If the primitive terms in the nested ontologies cannot express a concept in any combination, then the static "UMDL" and "Digital Libraries" ontologies must be extended; we assume that at this level the growth of the ontologies requires human intervention.

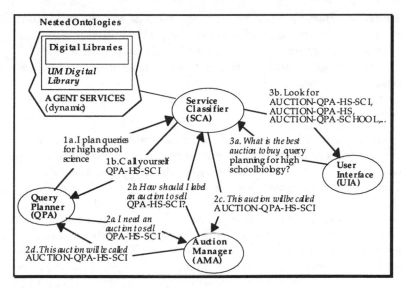

Fig. 8.4. Agent interaction with the SCA in the SMS

The most dramatic contribution of the SCA to the SMS derives from its declarative description of services, and its ability to rank available services given a target and search strategy. For example, when a new QPA provides a service that better meets a UIA's needs, this fact is captured by the service description. The UIAs can then automatically switch to buying services from the new QPA.

8.4 The UMDL Auctions

Since the UMDL cannot know at design-time what services will be available in the future or what the best negotiation mechanisms are for any given situation, its languages and protocols have been designed for flexibility and extensibility. In the case of negotiation mechanisms, UMDL uses a generalized auction specification to allow goods and services to be offered under a wide variety of terms [455].

While generalized auctions are not the only possible kinds of negotiation mechanisms, they offer many advantages. They provide a structured, yet flexible market infrastructure promoting automated negotiation due to the following characteristics:

1. **Mediated** (vs. Unmediated): Buyers do not have to separately find and contact every seller; a useful property in a large-scale and dynamic environment. Information about current status can be easily and uniformly disseminated.

2. **Price** (vs. Barter): Price summarizes much of the relevant information about scarcity and value of resources. It provides agents with a common currency for trading across different goods as well as a store of value for trading across different time periods. Thus, price can minimize and simplify communication between agents.

3. **Formal** (vs. Informal): Standardized offers simplify communication between agents.

Auction specifications consist of parameters which can be tuned to reflect the type of good being sold, timing requirements, or mechanism properties desired. For example, a query planning service might be sold differently depending on how it is bundled (e.g., per-query, subscription), its characteristics (topic, audience, timeliness), its terms (redistribute, read-only), or to whom it is sold (individual, library, group). We can capture information about the different auction rules and protocols in a compact, reusable manner by using parameterized auction descriptions. An auction's attributes include how often it clears, its price determination rules (e.g., first price, second price), the allowed number of buyers and sellers, as well as what information is publically available. Different kinds of auctions will have advantages and disadvantages for different types of information goods and services in various contexts.

Although evaluating tradeoffs between desirable properties of different auction types is important, the role of the UMDL is not to require that a particular auction be used in a given circumstance, but rather to provide an open framework whereby the use of these market facilitator agents is supported. To automate the creation and management of auctions as much as possible, we use the Auction Manager Agent (AMA). We shall turn to more advanced features of the AMA shortly (Section 8.8.2); for the time being assume that the AMA is capable of receiving a service label from a buyer/seller, and (perhaps with the help of the SCA), returning the names of one or more auctions where that service could potentially be bought/sold.

8.5 Simple Market Scenario - Price Takers

Let us set the stage for our description of techniques for strategic reasoning and adaptation in the SMS information economy by first considering a very simple market scenario that requires neither, and yet allows dynamic load balancing among service providers. This initial scenario uses the same agents and services as shown in Figure 8.1 and assumes that the QPAs have been designed within UMDL to behave competitively. Competitive agents take prices as given– ignoring any market power they might possess, thereby eliminating the need to reason strategically about other agents' bidding behavior. Since the service provider in this scenario is the library itself, which wants only to cover its costs and not make a profit, designing the agents to be competitive both simplifies the agent design and auction choice.

Simple competitive providers of the same service can use a price mechanism to distribute service loads among themselves. Specifically, consider the case where we want to balance the service load between several high-school science QPAs running on separate machines. Each QPA provides the same service, in this case, *exactly* the same service since each one is just a spawned copy of the same code. We have simplified this scenario in a number of ways, assuming that all sites provide free access, and all queries are the same.

In designing the QPAs, we assume they are competitive, and bid their marginal costs, namely what it would cost them to provide another unit of their product. This pricing policy directly reflects the cost to the system of using the input resources to provide this service. QPAs use computational and network resources to produce query planning service. Since these resources get congested as the load on a machine or network gets heavier, the marginal cost of adding another query will increase with the number of queries currently being processed. We modeled this technology in the QPAs using a quadratic cost function:

$$\text{Cost(query)} = A * \text{load}^2 + B * \text{load}$$
$$\text{Marginal Cost(query)} = 2 * A * \text{load} + B$$

Each additional query the QPA processes is priced at its marginal cost. Note that this cost function does not represent any real computer load model, but it does capture the basic notion of using a congested resource. The parameters A and B can be set to reflect relative differences between QPA technologies. For example, a QPA with $A, B = 1$ could be thought of as running on a faster machine than a QPA with $A, B = 2$.

All sellers (QPAs) make offers based on their current marginal cost. Buyers (UIAs) are assumed to want to purchase the query planning service immediately upon bidding. Query planning services are traded in an auction which matches the current lowest price seller with an incoming buyer, as long as the buyer's bid is above that price. Note that because of the way the agents have been designed, we know that this auction is incentive compatible for buyers, i.e., their best bidding strategy is to bid their true value for query planning services. This is because the QPAs, who would normally have an incentive to try and strategize about bid amounts, have been engineered to be competitive[7]. Once a transaction occurs between a given seller and buyer, both offers are removed from the standing offer list. The QPA recomputes its marginal cost based on having an additional query to process and submits a new, higher, sell offer to the auction.

To see how this results in query load balancing, let's consider what happens where there are two QPAs, (QPA-1 and QPA-2). Given the same initial query load, the sell offers for each agent will be the same, and the first buyer will be matched up arbitrarily with one of them, say QPA-1. At this point,

---

[7] If the QPAs had not been engineered, a better solution would have been to use a second price auction.

the query load for QPA-1 will rise, causing its marginal cost to rise, and it will submit a new offer at a higher price than before. The next incoming buyer will be matched with the current lowest price seller, QPA-2. QPA-2 now makes its new higher sell offer to reflect its increased load. Assuming that QPA-1 and QPA-2's previous queries are still being processed, both agents are again offering query planning service at the same, although higher, price. If one of QPA-1's queries finishes, then it sends in a new lower offer, and will be matched up to the next incoming buyer. Given a steady load of user queries, this system appears to settle down to an equilibrium price, although we have not done any formal analysis of these results. Notice that the dynamic addition or deletion of an agent does not affect the long-term running of the load balancing mechanism. For example, if any one of the agents were to die, it would only affect the queries that they were processing at that time. Future query planning requests would be matched with the remaining QPAs still participating in the auction. Similarly, spawning a new QPA means that it can start making offers to the query planning auction immediately.

Similar situations where this mechanism would be useful are in the provision of basic library services, which outside agents may not be interested in supplying. By making the agents competitive, UMDL can assure that the system costs are accounted for, that users get a low price, and agent designs are kept simple. Another example is distributing the access load to collections for which the library has a site license. Even though the site license may allow unlimited access, there are still associated network and compute costs, and for popular collections we may want to create mirror sites and distribute the load across them. A consistently high price of access may indicate when a given collection should be mirrored.

The point in the preceding is that the SMS economic foundation provides a flexible means for making decentralized resource allocation decisions. When we consider specifically the problem of load balancing, there are clearly many other load-balancing algorithms that have been developed in fields such as distributed computing and operations research. For many problems, such as when the available resources are fixed, the task needs well-defined, the performance criteria are globally determined, and the control centralized, alternative algorithms can provide optimal or near-optimal (within well-defined bounds) allocations. What we have illustrated in our work is that the economic principles of supply and demand provides an alternative load balancing mechanism which appears to be particularly useful in domains where resources come and go, tasks may have uncertain resource requirements, the participants can have different performance criteria (the costs and values they ascribe to activities and outcomes can differ), and the control is decentralized. More work remains in determining exactly the circumstances in which an approach like ours will outperform more traditional "command and control" methods.

8.5.1 Conclusions from Simple Market Scenario

We showed how UMDL agents which use system resources to provide query planning services to library users can use competitive bidding to distribute system load efficiently. The task of choosing an auction mechanism is vastly simplified when dealing with competitive sellers, especially for issues such as how to achieve incentive compatibility (having bidders bid their true evaluation, so that resources can be allocated efficiently) or deciding what kinds of information the auction should release (clearing price, bid quotes, bids) and how that affects agent behavior and system properties. In this case, sellers are designed to bid what it costs the system to provide the service. The auction used was a type of double auction, where each buyer's bid is cleared immediately and is priced at the lowest seller's price. Thus, library users can bid their true value for the service and be assured that, as long as their value for the service is greater than the cost to the system to provide it, they will acquire the service at system cost. Neither buyer nor seller agents need any information when bidding about other agents or even, in this simplified scenario, auction prices.

8.6 Strategic Agents

In the preceding, we saw how agents that bid their costs, which reflect their respective loads, can use markets to balance load. Of course, in many real economic settings, a service provider does not only want to recoup its costs, but also to turn a profit. In fact, the provider wants to maximize its expected profit: it wants to charge as much as it can while still having a good chance of finding a buyer willing to pay the price! In setting its price, therefore, an agent could reason strategically, using what it knows about the other current or pending buyers and sellers to set a price that is expected to reap the greatest profit.

For example, if an agent has knowledge about an expected increase in the number of buyers/sellers, it should be able to use this knowledge to its advantage. Also, if an agent is the only seller of a service then it should be able to take advantage of its monopoly, while if the buyers find that a seller's prices are too high for the service it sells, they should be able to avoid buying from him. Agents should, in sum, be strategic. One drawback of this, however, is the possibility that agents will spend all their time thinking strategically rather than carrying out their domain tasks. Fortunately, as we soon show, our economy discourages agents from engaging in ever-increasing amounts of strategic thinking.

8.6.1 A Strategy Based on Stochastic Modeling (p-Strategy)

We have developed an agent's bidding strategy based on stochastic modeling (called p-strategy) for the UMDL SMS, the details of which are given in [510].

The main idea behind the p-strategy is to capture the factors which influence the expected utility for the agent, using Markov chains. For instance, a seller is likely to raise its offer price when there are many buyers or when it expects more buyers to come. The number of buyers and sellers at the auction, the arrival rates of future buyers and sellers, and the distribution of buy and sell prices are among the identified factors. The p-strategy is able to take those factors into account in its stochastic model.

In our previous research [510], we have shown that an agent possessing the p-strategy has an advantage over agents that do not possess it when they compete in multi-agent auctions. Given that the p-strategy is effective in the UMDL auction, nothing prohibits any self-interested agent from adopting the p-strategy. We expect many p-strategy agents to coexist in the UMDL, and thus are interested in the collective behavior of such agents. In what follows, we briefly summarize our observations which are more completely detailed elsewhere [511].

8.6.2 Experimental Results

In our experiments, the p-strategy agents have models of how the auctions in the SMS evolve as buyers and sellers enter and are (sometimes) matched. Thus, these experiments should be considered illustrative of performance for the current SMS economic framework; under different assumptions about, for example, auction parameterizations, different observations might hold. But for the SMS, we are interested in the effects of p-strategy agents on the efficiency. We measure the efficiency of the system in two ways. First, we measure the efficiency of allocation, by comparing a p-strategy agent's absolute and relative performance. Second, we measure the efficiency of the market, using the total profit generated.

Session	Description	Bidding strategy						
		S-1	S-2	S-3	S-4	S-5	S-6	S-7
(1)	All competitive	C	C	C	C	C	C	C
(2)	1 p-strategy	C	C	C	C	C	C	P
(3)	2 p-strategy	C	C	C	C	C	P	P
(4)	3 p-strategy	C	C	C	C	P	P	P
(5)	5 p-strategy	C	C	P	P	P	P	P
(6)	All p-strategy	P	P	P	P	P	P	P

Fig. 8.5. Experiment setting. C: Competitive. P: p-strategy agents. S-X: Seller X

Figure 8.5 shows the six experimental settings with 7 buyers and 7 sellers. The buyers bid their true valuations, while the sellers bid their sell prices depending on their strategies. In Session 1, all seven sellers are type C (Competitive) and bid their true costs. From Session 2 through Session 6, we introduce more type P (p-strategy) agents into the auction.

A p-strategy agent has an upper hand over other-strategy agents, but this may not hold in the presence of other p-strategy agents. To test this we compare the profits of Seller 7 (p-strategy agent) across Sessions 2 to 6. As shown in Figure 8.6, the marginal profit of the p-strategy (smart) agent decreases as the number of p-strategy agents increases.

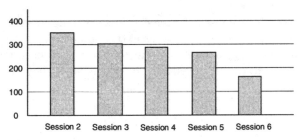

Fig. 8.6. The profit of the p-strategy agent (seller 7)

By replacing Seller 1 with a fixed-markup agent (who bids its cost plus some fixed markup), we also measure the relative performance of the fixed-markup agent (Seller 1) and the p-strategy agent (Seller 7). In Figure 8.7, we find that the simpler strategy agent (fixed markup agent) generally gets less profit than the p-strategy agent, but the difference decreases with the increase of p-strategy agents. That is, the disadvantage of being less smart decreases as the number of smart agents increases.

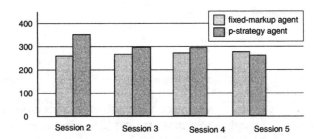

Fig. 8.7. The profit comparison between the fixed-markup agent and the p-strategy agent

This result indicates that an agent may want to switch between using p-strategy and using a simpler strategy depending on what the other agents are doing. By dynamically switching to a simpler strategy, an agent can achieve a similar profit (to that of using the p-strategy) while exerting less effort on computing bids.[8]

We measure the market efficiency using the total profit generated from the buyers and sellers (see Figure 8.8). The total profit eventually decreases with more p-strategy agents, as the market becomes inefficient due to strategic misrepresentation of p-strategy agents (and therefore missed opportunities of matches). Note that the total profit does not decrease as sharply as one might expect (it in fact increases slightly up to Session 4) due to the inefficiency of the UMDL auction mechanism.

We conjecture that having strategic sellers poses interesting tradeoffs between strategic inefficiency and surplus extraction. By misrepresenting their true costs, the p-strategy agents miss out on possible transactions. By anticipating the future arrival of buyers, on the other hand, they are able to seize more surplus.

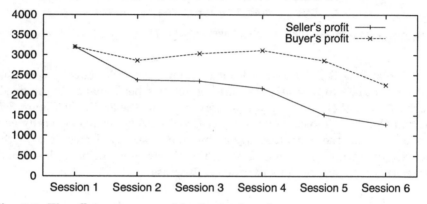

Fig. 8.8. The efficiency measured by the total profit

8.6.3 Conclusions from Experiments with Strategic Agents

Although a self-interested agent in the UMDL has the capability of strategic reasoning, our experiments show that strategic thinking is not always beneficial. As previously shown, the advantage of being smart decreases with the arrival of equally smart agents.

---

[8] While the chances are that the computational effort in computing bids is small compared to the costs of providing the service, it is still important to consider this cost. Specifically, because the UMDL auctions match buyers and sellers as bids are received, higher-cost bidding strategies can delay the submission of bids such that an agent consistently arrives at the auction "too late." The overhead is worthwhile, however, if the agent makes up for missed opportunities by extracting more profit in the cases where it does succeed in making a match.

We expect the UMDL is likely to evolve to a point where some agents are being strategic some of the time. An agent may want to switch between being strategic and not depending on the behavior of other agents: if enough other agents behave strategically, and agent can achieve additional profit even if it stays non-strategic.

Finally, the market efficiency of the UMDL will not decrease as sharply as one might expect. The profit-seeking behavior of self-interested agents will keep the UMDL agent population mixed with some strategic and some non-strategic agents. Thus, even though the market efficiency decreases with the increase in the number of strategic agents, the UMDL will not suffer the market inefficiency in the worst case.

8.7 Learning Agents

In this section, we continue to use the scenario from Figure 8.1, and emphasize how individual agents can learn to adapt to each other and overall market forces. To this end, we give sellers the freedom to return services of any quality. The only thing that will prevent them from consistently returning low quality (hence low cost) services is the buyers ability to learn to avoid sellers that overcharge for their services. To increase the information available for learning, we also allow the auctions to reveal all information (i.e. bids) they have to all interested agents. The agents are free to ignore any of this added information. By learning from this information, agents can avoid miscreant agents, and the performance of the information economy thus will not be compromised (or at least not for long) by such agents.

Learning in a Market System. While the UMDL ontology provides a way for agents to characterize the services they sell, there is no guarantee that all the goods sold at an auction for service x are indeed instances of service x. Agents could intentionally misrepresent their services. More frequently, agents might not entirely agree on precisely what constitutes service x. Indeed, subjective preferences might mean that some agents are quite satisfied with service x from a particular provider, while other agents are dissatisfied with that same provider's service. For example, while all agents might agree that QPA1 does sell service x, one agent might think that QPA1's service is faster, better, or more thorough than the same service x as provided by QPA2. This being the agent's subjective opinion, it is unlikely to be in agreement with all the other agents, but the agent might still be willing to pay more for service x from QPA1 than from QPA2.

Learning provides a means for agents to discriminate between services (or providers of services) when they have found sufficient grounds to make the discrimination useful. By learning, an agent can avoid being disappointed in its interactions by learning which agents to not interact with. If agents can learn from others' interactions (by observing others' experiences or sharing their experiences), they can as a society quickly ostracize rogue agents. Indeed, some agents might provide "recommendation services" by sampling and rating agents, and sharing (perhaps for a price) what they have learned with other agents. When agents learn, therefore, they increase the robustness of the system by partitioning away (what they see as) faulty agents.

In essence, learning provides a way for agents to develop expectations about others, and exploit these expectations to their mutual benefit. We can consider this as a rudimentary form of *trust* among agents. For a market-system to work well, an agent needs to be able to trust that its partners' view of good x is the same as its view of x. Similarly, an agent that uses recommender agents needs to trust their recommendations. This trust can be acquired by repeated iterations with the agents in question. Once the trust is acquired the learning is no longer needed, that is, until the trust is broken. This is why we argue that agents need the *ability* to learn, even if this ability is not always exercised.

Lastly, we propose that learning agents are not only useful, they are inevitable. In a society of selfish agents, we can expect that the designers will use every technology available to enhance the profits of their agents. Learning is one such technique. By implementing learning agents ourselves, we can determine how much of an advantage they will have and how they will affect the system.

Experimental Results. To demonstrate the viability of the SMS with learning agents and under real-world heavy usage conditions, we ran several tests on the scenario shown in Figure 8.1. We implemented UIAs that periodically (every 16 seconds) buy a query from some QPA using the protocol described earlier. We also used one Auction, AMA, and SCA, along with several UIAs and QPAs. All the agents were deployed in machines all over our network. The UIAs kept track of how long it took for the QPA's reply to arrive and used this value in their learning. In general, the UIAs preferred fast and cheap service, and they were willing to pay more for faster service. A QPA's only preference was to increase its immediate profit, i.e. place its bid in order to maximize its expected profit (remember that failing to get a sale means the QPA gets zero profit).

We gave the agents different learning abilities (see [689]). 0-level agents used reinforcement learning on the prices/values received. 1-level agents actually tried to model the other agents as 0-level agents. That is, they remembered what other agents had bid in the past and made probabilistic predictions based on the assumption that they will behave in the future as they behaved in the recent past. The 1-level agents then took actions based on these predictions.

0-level agents. For our first test we used 0-level UIAs and QPAs. They all began with no knowledge about what prices to bid or accept. UIAs quickly learned that they can expect to get higher value if they pick lower prices, while QPAs learned what price they can charge that will maximize their expected profit. As predicted by economic theory, this price was their marginal cost, i.e. the lowest price they can charge without losing money. This equilibrium was reached even while all the agents acted purely selfishly.

However, this equilibrium is not completely stable. Network and machine delays, along with the agents' occasional explorative actions[9], add noise to the system preventing the price from staying fixed at the marginal cost.

Even with only 0-level agents (i.e. no 1-level agents) we can see how the system behaves in a robust manner. Figure 8.9 shows the clearing price for an auction which starts with only one seller QPA. This QPA quickly "realizes" that it has a monopoly and starts to raise its prices. A second QPA is then added (as marked by the first vertical line), and we can see how its addition makes the price drop, but eventually it gets overloaded and the price rises again. A third QPA is added (at the second vertical line), affecting the price, and more QPAs are added at regular intervals (one at each vertical line).[10] The equilibrium price gets fairly close to the QPAs' marginal cost of 0. Towards the end the QPAs start to leave the system so the price starts to rise accordingly. This type of experiment gives us confidence that the agents will behave in a reasonable way even under boundary conditions, e.g. when a lot of the agents die, or when new services are added. If the agents were to determine their bid prices based on a fixed utility function, we might expect to find periodic or chaotic behavior [283], which we wish to avoid.

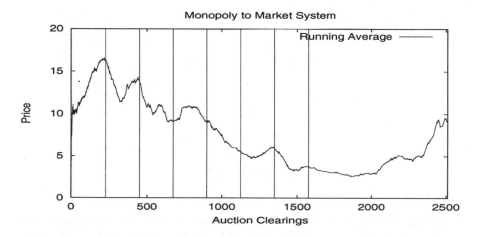

Fig. 8.9. Clearing price for successive auctions

---

[9] The agents were set to take a random action with probability of .05. This keeps them from converging on a local maxima.

[10] Note that these QPAs are *not* added because of some price bounds as with the Price Monitor Agent (Section 8.5 but rather are simply added at fixed intervals.

1-level agents. 1-level QPAs take advantage of price fluctuations by keeping models of the QPAs and UIAs and using these to make better predictions as to what they should bid. The 1-level models, while computationally expensive, allow QPAs to track the individual agents more closely, thereby identifying when a UIA is willing to pay more than the going rate. Previous research has shown that the advantages of 1-level models can be correlated to the price volatility (see [689]).

However, this strategic thinking is only successful against 0-level UIAs. When we tested the 1-level QPAs against the 1-level UIAs, as seen in Figure 8.10, we found the QPA's performance on par with other similar 0-level QPAs. In fact, the sellers that made more were the ones that could answer the query faster, not the 1-level seller. In other experiments we also found that 1-level sellers' extra profit is reduced as other 0-level sellers become 1-level. In both cases, the 1-level sellers incentive to be 1-level (instead of 0-level) disappears with increased competition.

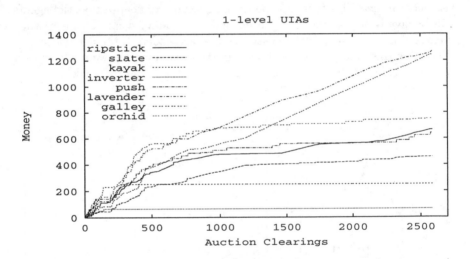

Fig. 8.10. Total revenue accrued by seller QPAs

Conclusions from Learning Experiments. The results on learning deeper agent models show that the UMDL SMS benefits from the existence of agents that have the *ability* to keep deeper models and look out for their best interests, even if they *do not always use this ability*. Agents are encouraged to model others because this can bring them higher profit. However, there is a computational cost associated with modeling, and a decreasing return for the agent as other agents also start to build models. This means that that the SMS will likely evolve to a point where some agents build models, some of the time, in the same manner as we expect some agents to use p-strategy some of the time. Moreover, it is possible that the agents that learn can trigger adaptation at a more systemic level, such that the society of agents as a whole benefits from the learning of a few agents.

8.8 System-Wide Adaptation

So far, we have focussed on system-wide dynamics that support load balancing, and how strategic reasoning and learning can be used by agents to make better individual decisions and to make the overall system more robust to agents that misrepresent themselves. While the effects of strategic reasoning and agent adaptation have an impact on system-wide performance, the results of agent reasoning and learning have so far not been explicitly reflected in the structure of the economy. Specifically, individual agents are reacting to imbalances in supply and demand and to learned preferences among alternative service providers, but more effective system-wide performance could result if the imbalances and preferences could trigger adaptation on the part of the overall SMS, either in terms of changing the population of agents or the structure of the market space. It is these kinds of adaptation that we next describe.

8.8.1 Price Monitor Agent

In a large-scale, dynamic system, information about the current status of the system can serve as feedback to different kinds of control mechanisms. In this section, we describe a simple monitor agent, called a Price Monitor Agent (PMA), which collects information about an auction's prices over time and uses that information to decide whether to spawn more service providers. Thus, the PMA adapts the population of service providers to balance system-wide supply and demand.

In our scenario, the PMA monitors the price of query planning services. The price in this auction reflects the load on the QPAs— a consistently high price means that the QPAs are heavily loaded. One way to reduce the load is to replicate QPAs (assuming that there are other less heavily loaded machines on the network). When the load is reduced, the price should come down.

The PMA is initially set with a given minimum and maximum price bounds, although they can be changed later. When the price exceeds the upper bound, i.e., the load on each QPA is getting high, it spawns additional QPAs. This effectively distributes the load from future queries.[11] When the

---

[11] In fact, there is nothing to prevent a QPA from itself attempting to find another QPA to service a query. That is, an overloaded QPA, which has been awarded a query because it is the least overloaded of all the QPAs, might periodically check the auction and attempt to pass off one or more of its assigned queries. Thus, new QPAs can in principle reduce the current load, although in our current implementation the QPAs do not do this.

price goes below the lower bound, i.e., the QPAs load has fallen, the PMA has a choice of either removing or just inactivating one of the extra QPA, depending on whether it expects the load to increase again in the near term. The effect of this behavior is to keep the load across QPAs (and therefore the response time to users) within specified bounds even though the user demand is dynamic.

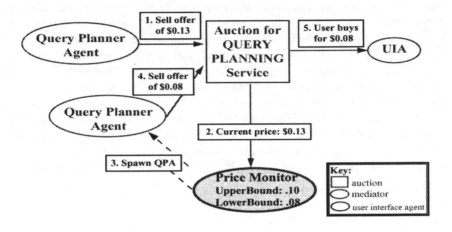

Fig. 8.11. Price Monitoring Scenario

Figure 8.11 shows an overview of how the PMA operates. Below is a description of what is occurring at each step:

1. A heavily loaded QPA sells its services for $0.13.
2. The PMA checks the current price at the Auction.
3. Since the price is above it's upper bound ($0.10), the PMA spawns another QPA.
4. The new QPA sells its services for $0.08.
5. The user is matched with the lowest priced (least loaded) QPA.
6. (not shown) When/if the price goes below $0.08, the PMA inactivates one or more of its spawned QPAs.

In our experiments, the PMA, given reasonable bounds for the prices and activity of the agents, was successfully able to keep the price within the given price bounds. However when the price bounds were too tight or the activity on the system was too dynamic, the PMA would oscillate. For example, if too many agents get added, the price may fall too low, causing too many agents to get removed, which causes the price to go too high, and so forth. Providing the monitoring agent with knowledge about usage patterns, or having it collect statistics about usage, is one way to address this problem.

Finally, let us briefly address the question about where to set the upper price bound. Since price reflects load, which in turn reflects response time, we might determine the maximum desired response time and from that compute the maximum price. However, if this is done for all potentially replicable services, then we risk overtaxing the available computational and network resources with too many copies of too many agents. Ultimately, any policy for replication needs to determine whether the resources that will be devoted to a new agent could be more usefully applied elsewhere. While right now the PMA simply uses user-specified bounds (and indeed, only replicates QPAs so that there isn't any competition between requests for spawning different agent types), ultimately the resources available for replicated agents should themselves be auctioned off, such that PMAs for different classes of agents will compete for the resources and those resources will be allocated based on the same economic principles as other UMDL services.

8.8.2 Auction Configuration

The second form of system-wide adaptation mentioned above concerns the configuration of auctions in the system. Designing a good auction configuration is a difficult task. Each auction should be large enough to bring together all of the relevant parties, otherwise desirable transactions might be missed. But increasing the size of an auction could come at the cost of mixing similar but not identical services together, and the differences in services could matter to agents that are subjectively evaluating them.

Identifying the proper set of auctions that strike a suitable balance is thus difficult, and might need to be an ongoing task since the distinctions between services that truly matter are known only by the agents (not by the system designer ahead of time), and those distinctions can change as the concerns of each agent change and the population of agents as a whole evolves. Thus, the space of auctions should evolve to "fit" the dynamic preferences of the agents.

In our current SMS system, the Auction Manager Agent (AMA) evolves the space of auctions in very simple ways. The AMA creates new auctions at the request of one or more agents who have identified situations where one auction mixes agents that should be separated. In this way, the space of auctions can grow based on learned distinctions. The space of auctions will shrink because the AMA eliminates auctions that go unused for a sufficient period of time.[12]

Let us consider an example run of SMS that illustrates how the space of auctions grows to reflect agent preferences. The example follows the same basic scenario we have used. In this case (Figure 8.12), the UIA has gone to

---

[12] Actually, in the current implementation, such auctions simply remove themselves, but the AMA must be aware of this fact so as to update its representation of the space of auctions.

the QPA-Auction numerous times, and has been matched with each of the four QPAs several times. By evaluating its subjective preferences, it determines that there are two of the QPAs that it would prefer being matched to consistently. Thus, it would prefer to participate in an auction that included those two QPAs and that excluded the other two. It sends this request to the AMA.

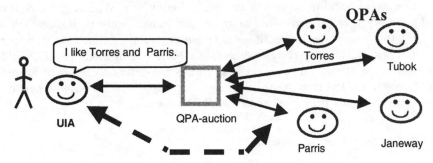

Fig. 8.12. Learning Preferences Among Agents

The AMA in turn consults with the SCA. In examining the space of service descriptions, the SCA can find an appropriate "least-common-subsuming" concept. As a simplified example, consider the subset of the service description space and relations shown in Figure 8.13, where our simplifications give the description space a hierarchical structure to make the subsumption rela-

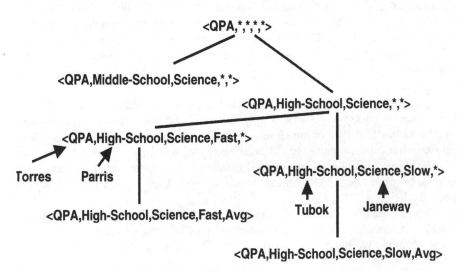

Fig. 8.13. Using the Ontology to Find Useful Agent Subclasses

tions more easily seen. Given where the descriptions of the QPAs fit in, the SCA recognizes that more detailed classifications can differentiate between the preferred and disliked QPAs. That is, when the QPA-auction was set up, the SCA and AMA lumped the different types of QPA together, since larger auctions are generally better given that it was not clear that the differences between the types of QPAs would matter to the other agents. Given the feedback that the differences do matter, a more specific auction is created.

Finally, the UIA now has the opportunity to participate in either the more general auction or the more specific auction it had requested. Initially, it will experiment with both, to determine which gives it the best price/performance combination (Figure 8.14). Note that, because the more specific auction has fewer participants and thus less supply, prices might rise significantly, driving the UIA back to the less specific auction. Ultimately, if buyers move to particular auctions and thus leave other auctions unused, those auctions will be deleted.

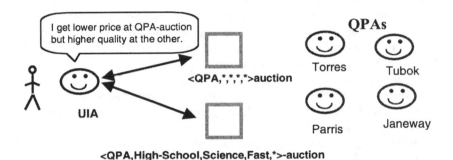

<QPA,High-School,Science,Fast,*>-auction

Fig. 8.14. Tradeoffs Between Participating in Alternative Auctions

This simple, implemented example illustrates the opportunities for having the space of auctions in the information economy adapt to the changing needs of the agents, which are themselves adapting based on their interactions with each other. Clearly, much more work needs to be done. The mechanisms currently do not support the composition of two separate auctions that could safely be combined. The decisions about when to create new auctions should be based on better measures of expected societal impact than simply a request by a single agent. The costs of creating and maintaining auctions should be reflected in the decisions as well, to prevent a proliferation of auctions. All of these issues (and more) remain open for future investigation.

8.9 Conclusion

We have given a condensed overview of the UMDL SMS and the agents, protocols, and languages that it encompasses. Through this description, we hope that we have conveyed how our SMS infrastructure supports our desiderata:

- **Flexibility**: In our SMS work, we have already explored several policies for designing an information economy, ranging from a more "public" flavor where agents that are assumed truthful and interested in providing services for the lowest possible price, to a more commercial flavor where agents might misrepresent themselves and will try to maximize their individual profits.
- **Extensibility**: We have described how agents with new services (as described by composing new descriptions in the shared ontology) can join the UMDL, and why they would have incentive to join. We have also shown how the space of auctions can evolve as variations of services come and go and preferences over them change.
- **Scalability**: We have described how decentralized resource allocation decisions are made through the market mechanisms coupled with agent reasoning methods for computing bids, and how services in high demand can be replicated. Note that, typically, new agents bring their own resources into the system with them; thus, when agent developers have incentive to introduce their agents, they are also introducing resources for managing the larger system (at a minimum, their agents have to decide for themselves on bids to make).
- **Robustness:** We have illustrated how the system can still perform well despite the potentially conflicting desires of the participating agents and the possibility of misrepresentation in the system.

Collectively, the mechanisms we have described can automate much of the administration of a digital library, including organizing information and services using ontological relationships, selecting, evaluating, and remembering useful services using machine learning, and deciding how to allocate (finite) resources to meet the evolving demands of a user community.

These results were achieved via the merging of different technologies which include: ontology design, market oriented design, and nested agent modeling and learning. The agents and protocols that we have described have all been implemented and integrated into the UMDL SMS. Some of these, such as the auctions and the Price Monitor Agent, are also used by agents in the deployed UMDL system. For example, these agents can automatically spawn more QPAs during high demand periods by the students using UMDL simultaneously from many schools.[13] Thus, our SMS "information economy" model is already being used by UMDL patrons; while they are unaware of

---

[13] Because QPAs are not currently a bottleneck given that students pose new questions fairly slowly relative to the processing time needed by a QPA, we have not seen much need for spawning new QPAs. However, when we take the log files

the economic foundations of the system, those foundations are already being used in a rudimentary way to improve the system performance for the users.

Of course, given the specific needs of the current UMDL user community, and the rights we currently have over the UMDL content, other possible means for controlling resources and providing services would work for the UMDL. Specifically, we could develop management algorithms tailored specifically to the UMDL. While it could be the case that, for the short term, such an alternative might be more effective, we are not convinced of its long-term viability when the system is truly open, dynamic, and large. While much remains to be done within the SMS strategy for addressing these long-term issues (many open issues have been raised throughout this paper), we believe that the SMS has already demonstrated promise in being able to meet the needs of the open, evolving, information economy of the future.

Acknowledgments. The rest of the members of the UMDL SMS group all contributed to its design and development. They are: Anil Arora, Bill Birmingham, Eric Glover, Dan Kiskis, Anisoara Nica, and Bill Walsh. This chapter is a revised and extended version of a paper that appeared in the Proceedings of the Second International Workshop on Cooperative Information Agents (CIA'98). This work was supported, in part, by the NSF/DARPA/NASA Digital Library Initiative under grant CERA IRI-9411287.

---

collected over several weeks at the schools, and simulate having 40 classrooms with 15 workstations each using UMDL over a one-hour period, the load triggers the creation of two more QPAs via the mechanisms we have described.

9. SharedPlans in Electronic Commerce

Merav Hadad[1] and Sarit Kraus[1,2]

[1] Department of Mathematics and Computer Science Bar-Ilan University,
52900 Ramat-Gan, Israel.
E-Mail: hadad@cs.biu.ac.il
[2] Institute for Advanced Computer Studies, University of Maryland, College Park,
MD 20742, USA.
E-Mail: sarit@cs.biu.ac.il

9.1 Introduction

Rational agents often need to work together [356]. There are jobs that can
not be done by one agent, because no one individual has sufficient competence, resources or information to solve the entire problem alone. In other
situations, agents that work in the same environment may benefit from cooperation. A joint action by a team does not consist merely of simultaneous
and coordinated individual actions to act together. A team must be aware
of and concerned with the status of the group effort as a whole. To rectify
this problem, it was proposed that agents should have a well-grounded and
explicit model of cooperative problem solving on which their behavior can be
based. Several such models have been proposed [375, 344, 311, 259].

In recent years, many researchers as well as commercial companies have
attempted to create intelligent, agent-based markets or retail outlets on the
Web (see Section 9.3.2). However, these systems have not had the anticipated impact on the methods commerce implemented on the Web. Tsvetovatyy and Gini [678] claim that a main cause of this shortfall is the lack of
automated purchasing and agent cooperation algorithms. They developed a
general framework for automated agents that buy and sell on the Web, but
have not developed cooperative capabilities for these agents.

In our work, we designed a system based on the SharedPlans model of
Grosz and Kraus [259], and we have developed a collaborative multi-agent
system for buying and selling items such as clothes[1]. In our Web-based buying and selling environment, SharedPlans may be formed between agents
belonging to the same enterprise to work together to maximize their enterprise's benefits and also among agents that are self-motivated and interested
in collaboration because it may maximize their individual benefits. For example, suppose a buyer of one enterprise would like to buy an item from a
seller of another enterprise. Even though each agent tries to maximize its
enterprise's benefits and they have certain conflicting interests they have the
same joint goal of the transaction taking place. In particular, a seller wishes

---

[1] Other implementations of a collaborative multi agent systems that are based on
the SharedPlan model in other domains were presented in [394, 512, 662].

to have a noncompetitive relationship with its buyers. Today's sellers desire highly cooperative, long-term relationships with their buyers to maximize customer satisfaction and to increase their long-term benefits [216, 265].

When an automated seller interacts with a human buyer using Shared-Plans is beneficial to both sides. The seller can, for example, work it with the buyer to identify an item which is relevant to his/her needs by maintaining the intentional context of their interaction. For instance, the intentional context for buying a CD to listen to a specific song is different from that of buying a CD since the user admires the singer or likes the music style of the CD. In the last case, if the CD is not available, the automated seller may offer another CD of the same style. In the second case, it may offer a different CD of the same singer, and in the first case suggests a different CD which includes the same song (possibly by a different singer).

In order to increase their benefits in the Electronic Commerce environment the agents need to plan their activities. For example, planning may be needed when a buyer of some enterprise detects a missing good in its stock. Thus, the buyer must form an individual plan to obtain the missing good (e.g. she may decide whether to buy or to produce the missing good and which resources to use, given her choice). The forming plan may be only partial. For example, she may have decided to purchase the missing good, but has not yet chosen the supplier from which to buy it. In addition the buyer must take into consideration several constraints, for instance, in order to perform the purchase she must have enough money.

Since the Electronic Commerce environment is a dynamic environment, the agents must take into account the dynamic nature of plans. In this environment plans are developed over time. For example, frequently a buyer is able to state only her general needs, i.e., she is not able to characterize the exact details of the item she would like to buy. The seller can assist the buyer in defining her needs, using his information about available items and their properties. By providing such information the seller and the buyer develop a plan for the purchase over time. That is, the agents in this environment begin with partial plans and extend them until they become complete plans. In addition, in this environment, an agent's beliefs may be faulty or the world may change. For instance, a buyer and a seller may agree upon the date of the payment for a selected item. As this date approaches, the buyer may realize that she is unable to pay for the item as originally planned. Thus, while the agent is planning or is acting on the basis of a partial plan, partial plans may have to be revised. To address these needs, the SharedPlan formalization [259] provides for both individual and collaborative plans to be partial. Thus, using the SharedPlan formalization enables us to develop agents which are able to act in the dynamic Electronic Commerce environment where they are uncertain concerning their own actions and have incomplete information about the other agents and the environment.

Since this chapter focuses on the planning formalism of SharedPlan, we summarize the SharedPlan model's definitions in Section 9.2. In Section 9.3 we present the electronic commerce domain which we use in the implementation, explain why using SharedPlan is beneficial in the Electronic Commerce domain and compare our approach with others. In Section 9.4 we present a general system for implementing the SharePlan model, and demonstrate its usage in electronic commerce scenarios. Finally, in Section 9.5 we review the contributions of this chapter.

9.2 The SharedPlan Model

When agents form teams, new problems emerge regarding the representation and execution of joint actions. To rectify these problems it was proposed that the agents use a model of collaborative planning. The SharedPlan model [259] has been proposed to support the design and construction of collaborative computer systems, including systems that are able to collaborate with one another [311], systems that support groups of people working together, and collaborative systems for human-computer communication [394, 550].

The SharedPlan formalization [259, 258] provides mental-state specifications of both *SharedPlans* and *individual plans*. SharedPlans are constructed by groups of collaborating agents and include subsidiary SharedPlans [394] formed by subgroups as well as subsidiary individual plans formed by individual participants in the group activity.

The SharedPlan of a set of agents depends upon the individual plans of its members. For an agent G to have an individual full plan for an act α, it must satisfy four requirements: (1) G must know how to perform α; i.e., it must have the constituents of the act α, (2) G must believe that it can perform the subacts (i.e, α's constituents) (3) G must intend to perform the subacts, (4) G must have a subsidiary (individual) plan for each of the subacts which are not basic actions[2].

SharedPlans differ from individual plans in requiring that the set of agents have *mutual belief* of these requirements. In addition, because SharedPlans are multi-agent plans, the subsidiary plans of a SharedPlan may be either individual or shared, depending upon whether they are formed by a single agent within the group or by a subgroup. The full group of agents must mutually believe that the agent or the subgroup of each subact has a plan for the subact. However, only the performing agent(s) itself needs to hold specific beliefs about the details of that plan.

This section discusses the SharedPlan formalism as defined in [259]. Because the formal plan definitions are complex, in the following section we will

---

[2] We assume that a basic level action is an action which does not involve more than one agent, which must be performed in one sequence and which there is only one way to perform it.

provide an informal example that motivates the definitions presented in this section. We will refer to this example throughout the chapter.

9.2.1 A Collaborative Trade Scenario

The scenario that is considered includes two enterprises. Each enterprise has two intelligent agents, a buyer and a seller. The job of the buyer agent is to obtain the missing goods from the stock of its enterprise. The job of the seller agent is to sell the enterprise's goods to the other enterprise through the enterprise's buyer agent.

The example that is used exemplifies situations in which, the buyer agent of the first enterprise has an individual plan to maintain the stock. Particularly, we will consider the collaborative planning that arises when the individual agent, the buyer of one enterprise, detects a missing good in its stock. We will denote this agent by Buyer1[3]. In her individual planning to obtain the missing good, she discovers that a SharedPlan is required. Figure 9.1 illustrates the subactions which are needed for a "maintain the stock" action.[4] Suppose, Buyer1 finds out that the seller of the second enterprise can help her to complete her planning to maintain the stock. We will denote this agent Seller2. We assume initially that Buyer1 and Seller2 agents agreed to jointly perform the common action "transact". They have identified a recipe for doing the action "transact", i.e., they have figured out the relatively high level description of how to do the action, but they have not yet worked out the lower-level details. For instance, they may not have decided how to do some of the subactions in the recipe or who will do them. The subactions of the action "transact" is portrayed in Figure 9.1. Suppose they decided that:

1. Seller2 will do the subaction find-the-item, e.g, will check if he has such an item in the catalog of his enterprise.
2. Buyer1 will do the verification, e.g, Buyer1 will check that Seller2 finds the exact item which she intends to obtain.
3. Seller2 will check if he has the item in stock, and determine the date that he can supply the item.
4. Buyer1 and Seller2 will decide together about the method of payment (e.g., how Buyer1 will pay for the item) and the price of the item.
5. Buyer1 will execute the payment.
6. One of the agents will deliver the item. We assume initially that they did not decide who will do the delivery.

---

[3] In the example, we will take the initiator of the joint action to be a female and the other participant to be a male, thus affording the use of the pronouns "she" and "he" in analyzing the example.

[4] Note that in the recipe for the single-agent action "maintain the stock" there is a multi-agent action "transact". Thus, performing "maintain the stock" requires cooperation with other agents.

Thus, Buyer1 and Seller2 must each form individual plans, Buyer1 forms plans for "verification", and "execution-payment"; Seller2 forms plans for "find-the-item", and "determine-date-supply". They do not need to know the complete details of each other's individual plans, but they need to prevent conflicts between these plans. For example, if it is decided that Seller2 will perform the subaction "execution-delivery" and it is decided that he will put the item in Buyer1's home at a specific time, Buyer1 cannot leave her home at that specific time in order to arrange the "execution-payment" subaction. Thus, as they develop their individual plans, choosing how to do actions and what resources to use, they must consider potential conflicts with each other and communicate if they detect a possible problem. In addition, Buyer1 and Seller2 together must form a shared, collaborative plan for the "determine-price-and-payment". The particular details of how they will do this must be mutually decided upon by an agreement of both of them. In forming their plans, Buyer1 and Seller2 may interleave planning and acting; hence, at any stage of their activity, their plans may be only partial. For example, Buyer1 decides to "borrow-money" for "execution-payment", but has not yet chosen a recipe for doing so. Alternatively, she may have chosen the recipe, but not yet decided how she will do some of the subtasks.

Two types of agents:
   Seller: sells goods.
   Buyer: obtains missing goods.
Single-agent-Action:
  Maintain the stock:
     – determine-the-missing-items.
     – transact.
Multi-agent action:
  Transact:
     – find-the-item.
     – verification.
     – determine-date-supply.
     – determine-price-and-payment.
     – execution-payment.
     – execution-delivery.

Fig. 9.1. Maintain-the-stock Action Example.

9.2.2 Definitions and Notation of the Model

Actions in the model are abstract complex entities that have associated with various properties such as action type, agent, time of performance, and other objects involved in performing the action. Following Pollack [531], the model uses the terms "recipe" and "plan" to distinguish between knowing how to do an action and having a plan to do the action. When agents have a SharedPlan to do a group action, they have certain individual and mutual beliefs about how the action and its constituent subactions are to be implemented. The term *recipe* [531, 395] is used to refer to a specification of a set of actions, which is denoted by β_i $(1 \le i \le n)$, the doing of which under appropriate *recipe-constraints*, denoted by ρ_j $(1 \le j \le m)$, constitutes performance of α.[5] The meta-language symbol R_α is used in the model to denote a particular recipe for α.

Recipes may include actions at different levels of abstraction and the parameters of an action may be partially specified in a recipe either in the library or in a partial plan. Thus, a recipe may include variables which are not instantiated (e.g., for the agent or time of an action) and constraints on these variables. However, for agents to have a complete plan, the parameters must be fully specified in a manner appropriate to the act-type.

The subsidiary actions β_i in the recipe for action α, may be either single-agent or multi-agent actions; all basic-level actions are single-agent actions. Likewise, a single agent "determine-price-and-payment" carried out only by Seller2 (e.g., Seller2 determines the price and payment by himself) is a different type of action from multiple agents "determine price and payment" together, (e.g., Seller2 and Buyer1 determine the price and payment together).

The intended actions that play a role in individual and collaborative plans are always planned and performed in some context. Various operators, functions, and predicates on actions as well as the plans that are formed for performing them need to refer to this context. The model represents two constituents of the context parameter. The first, Θ_α, includes a "constraints" component that encodes constraints on the performance of α. For example, Seller2's individual plan to "determine date supply" has the constraint of being done before a certain time or the constraint of not determining this date after a particular time. The second, IC_α, includes a representation of the intentional context in which an agent G is doing α. For example, if α is being done as part of doing some higher-level action $\mathcal{A}$, i.e., α is part of the recipe adopted in the plan to do $\mathcal{A}$, then IC_α encodes this fact.

Notation	Meaning	Comments
α	action	Also: $\beta_i, \beta_r, \beta_k, \delta, \gamma$
IC_α	intentional context of α	
R_α	recipe for α	Also, R_β
G	agent	
GR	group	
Θ_α	constraints of α	Also, ρ_j

Table 9.1. Summary of notation used for special variables and constants.

---

[5] The indices i and j are distinct; for simplicity of exposition, we omit the range specifications in the remainder of this document.

Grosz and Kraus' plan definitions employ four different intention opera-tors: **Int.To** and **Int.Th** represent intentions that have been adopted by an agent; **Pot.Int.To** and **Pot.Int.Th** are variations of the first two that are used to represent *potential* intentions.

Int.To and Pot.Int.To are used to represent an agent's *intentions to* do some action; Int.Th and Pot.Int.Th are used to represent an agent's *intention that* some proposition hold. The commonality between intending-to and intending-that is that both commit an agent not to adopt conflicting inten-tions [715] and constrain replanning in case of failure [84]. The significant distinction between them is not in the types of objects each relates, but in their connection to planning and in their different presumptions about an agent's ability to act within the boundaries of the intention.

An Int.To commits an agent to means-ends reasoning [84] and, at some point, to acting. In contrast, an Int.Th does not directly engender such behav-ior. Int.Th's form the basis for meshing subplans, helping one's collaborator, and coordinating status updates [85, 600, 375], all of which play an important role in SharedPlans; any of these functions may lead to the adoption of an Int.To and thus indirectly to planning and performing actions. In addition, an agent can only adopt an intention-to toward an action for which it is the agent.

The model distinguishes between five different types of plans: **FIP** for *full individual plans*; **PIP** for *partial individual plans*; **FSP** for *full SharedPlans*; **PSP** for *partial SharedPlans*; and **SP** for SharedPlans of indefinite complete-ness. When PIP or FIP exist for an agent, that agent has the collection of intentions and beliefs specified in the meta-predicate definition in [259].

The SharedPlan meta-predicate representing that a group of agents GR has a collaborative plan to jointly perform some action α. The meta-predicate FSP is used to represent the situation in which a group of agents has com-pletely determined the recipe by which they are going to do some group activity, and members of the group have adopted intentions-to toward all of the basic-level actions in the recipe as well as intentions-that toward the actions of the group and its other members.

Partial SharedPlans, like their counterpart partial individual plans, differ from complete ones in four ways: (1) the agents may have only a partial recipe for doing the action; (2) they may have only partial individual plans or partial SharedPlans for doing some of the subsidiary actions in the recipe; (3) they may have only partial individual plans or partial SharedPlans for doing some of the contracting actions; and, (4) there may be some subactions about which the group has not deliberated and for which there is as yet no agent (individual or subgroup) selected to perform the subaction.

9.2.3 Complex Actions for Planning and Cultivating Process

In the SharedPlan formalization, means-ends reasoning is represented by the complex planning action **Elaborate_Individual** and the group plan-

Type	Notation	Meaning
Modal Operators	Int.To	intend-to
	Int.Th	intend-that
	Pot.Int.To	potential intention-to
	Pot.Int.Th	potential intention-that
	Bel	belief
	MB	Mutual belief
	Do	performance of action
Meta-Predicates (Plans)	FIP	full individual plan
	PIP	partial individual plan
	SP	SharedPlan
	FSP	full SharedPlan
	PSP	partial SharedPlan
Act-types for Planning Actions	Select_Rec	agent selects/extends recipe
	Select_Rec_GR	agt. group selects/ext. recipe
	Select_Agent	agt. group selects member f. action
	Select_Subgroup	agt. group selects subgroup f. action
	Elaborate_Individual	agent extends partial plan
	Cultivate	cultivate an intention-that
	Elaborate_Group	agt. group ext. partial SharedPlan
	Select_Rec_GR_Member	planning action f. Select_Rec_GR
	Select_Agent_Member	planning action f. Select_Agent
	Select_Subgroup_Member	planning action f. Select_Subgroup
	Elaborate_Group_Member	planning action f. Elaborate_Group
	Reconcile	reconcile new intention with old ones
Processes	CULTIVATE	process f. *Cultivate*
	ELABORATE_GROUP_MEMBER	process f. Elaborate_Group_Member
	SELECT_AGENT_MEMBER	process f. Select_Agent_Member
	SELECT_SUBGROUP_MEMBER	process f. Select_Subgroup_Member
	SELECT_REC_GR_MEMBER	process f. Select_Rec_GR_Member
	RECONCILE	process f. Reconcile

Table 9.2. Summary of notations.

ning activity is represented by the complex action **Elaborate_Group**. In order to develop mechanisms for expanding partial plans to more complete ones, Grosz and Kraus provide the complex planning actions **Select_Rec** and **Select_Rec_GR** which refer respectively to the act-types for the complex planning actions that agents perform individually or collectively to identify ways to perform (domain) actions. A basic claim of the SharedPlans formalization is that collaborative activity is rooted in the individual mental actions and domain actions of individual agents. This constraint holds of complex group planning actions as in domain actions. Thus, Elaborate_Group and Select_Rec_Group comprise individual planning actions of the group members. We use the complex actions **Elaborate_Group_Member** and **Select_Rec_GR_Member** to represent these individual actions, respectively. In addition, the SharedPlan formalization includes complex planning actions, **Select_Agent_Member** and **Select_Subgrp_Member**, for determining which agent(s) will do the constituent actions of the chosen recipe.

In multi-agent activities, participants not only do means-ends reasoning about their own actions, they also reason about how to coordinate with and support the actions of others in the group. These activities require plan-based reasoning that ensues from the participants' attitudes of intentions-that toward the actions of others and of the group as a whole. To handle this aspect of the dynamics of SharedPlan the complex planning action, **Cultivate** was introduced [260]. In particular, SharedPlans are motivated by intentions-that and thus Cultivate plays a central role in the architecture.

To assist the reader, Table 9.1 provides a summary of the notation used in the formalizations in this chapter. Table 9.2 lists the various operators and predicates used in the formal definition and provides an informal description of their meaning.

9.3 The Benefits of Using SharedPlans in Electronic Commerce

As we mentioned, the environment which we consider includes several enterprises, each with several kinds of goods which it sells to users or to other enterprises. Each enterprise has intelligent seller and buyer agents. The job of the seller agents is to sell the enterprise's goods to users or to other enterprises through their buyer agents. The job of a buyer agent is to obtain from other enterprises the goods that are missing from the stock of its enterprise. This environment requires complex SharedPlans of groups of more than two agents including both people and automated agents. However, for simplicity our current implementation considers an environment, in which each enterprise includes only one seller and one buyer (see Figure 9.2).

Agents that belong to the same enterprise can form SharedPlans to work together toward the shared goal of maximizing the benefits for their joint enterprise. SharedPlans also provide a beneficial framework for communication processes between different enterprises. Even though each agent has its own goals and in respect to certain issues (e.g. the price of the item) their interests may conflict, they have the same shared goal that the purchase will be carried out. The seller of one enterprise would like to sell an item to the buyer of another or to a user, and the buyer or the user would like to buy the item. Forming a SharedPlan may increase the benefits of both agents.

9.3.1 Means for Collaboration

As has been discussed above, SharedPlans in our environment may be formed between agents belonging to the same enterprise who try to maximize their enterprise's benefits and also among agents that are self-motivated and interested in collaboration because it may maximize their individual benefits. To

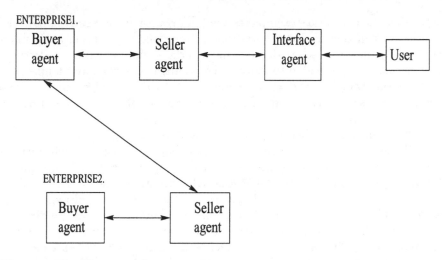

Fig. 9.2. The Electronic Commerce scenario

provide the basis for more collaborative interactions, our system will include capabilities for helpful behavior and the avoidance of conflicting intentions. The importance of such capabilities in this environment and the way the SharedPlans formalization supports it are illustrated below.

The definitions of partial and full SharedPlans require each of the participating agents to intend-that the group action α be performed. Furthermore, the group must mutually believe that all members have such intentions-that the action be performed. In addition to explicitly representing each group member's commitment to the group's performance of α, this clause in the definition captures three key characteristics of collaboration: (1) agents avoiding the adoption of intentions that conflict with their doing α; (2) agents forming intentions to help each other in the performance of α; and (3) agents adopting intentions to communicate about their plan for doing α and its execution. The importance of these key characteristics in the Electronic Commerce domain, are illustrated by the following examples: In the first example, the buyer and seller agents engaged in collaborative activity must reconcile intentions and avoid conflicts among them. In particular, buyer and seller agents that work for the same enterprise will avoid taking resources from one another. For example, if a seller agent needs the company's largest truck to deliver some goods to a primary customer, then the buyer agent—wanting the seller agent to succeed—will not intend-to use this truck at the same time. The second characteristic may be illustrated by the following example. Frequently, a buyer will be able to state only his general needs. He will not be able to characterize the exact details of the item he would like to buy. The seller can assist the buyer in defining his needs, using her information about available items and their properties. By providing such information the seller can help making the purchase take place which is a shared goal of both buyer and seller. The next example exemplifies the importance of the third characteristic. As part of their recipe negotiation, a buyer and a seller will agree upon the supply date of a selected good. As this date approaches, the seller may realize she will be unable to deliver the product as originally planned. To address this problem, the seller communicates with the buyer, and to keep the collaboration active works with the seller to identify a new date or means of delivery.

The definitions of SharedPlans also stipulate that each participant have intentions-that toward the ability of other agents to carry out their parts of the group action, i.e., doing the constituent actions β_i required for doing α (according to the recipe they have adopted); intentions-that relate to ability are required both for individual-agent subactions and for multi-agent subactions. These intentions-that ensure that the subsidiary plans (individual and group) for doing the subsidiary actions are compatible. For example, the plan for the "transact" action which is discussed in Section 9.2 includes Seller2's intention that [Int.Th] Buyer1 'be able to' do "verification", and "execution-payment", and Buyer1's intention that [Int.Th] Seller2 'be able to' "find-the-item" and "determine-date-supply". The Buyer1 and Seller2's intention that [Int.Th] provide the basis for more collaborative interactions between Buyer1 and Seller2 as described below.

Several axioms for the operator Int.Th are needed to support the roles of intending-that in ensuring that agents avoid conflict, assist each other, and provide status information when necessary. The formalization [260] have specified a set of conflict avoidance axioms that constrain an agents' adoption of intentions (both intentions-to and intentions-that) so that they do not simultaneously hold conflicting intentions. In addition, the formalization has developed a set of axioms to encode situations in which intending-that would lead agents to consider engaging in helpful behavior. We do not describe these axioms here for space limitations, but instead we discuss them informally.

One of these axioms states that if an agent has an intention-that toward some proposition that it believes is not currently true and the agent believes it is able to do some act γ that will bring about the proposition's holding, then the agent will consider doing γ. In particular it will adopt a potential intention to do γ, leading to deliberation about adopting an intention to do it, and, barring conflicts, lead to this becoming a full-fledged intention. This situation may be illustrated with the maintain-the-stock example. Suppose Buyer1 and Seller2 are doing the "transact" action together and Seller2 believes that Buyer1 will *not be able* to execute the payment and furthermore believes that he can take some action to remove the roadblock to his being able to do so (e.g., delaying the payment date of the good), then Seller2 will adopt a potential intention to do that action.

A second axiom provides for more indirect helpful behavior. This covers the case in which Buyer1 has an intention-to "transact" several goods until a specific date, but there are no such goods in the stock of Seller2's enterprise. Therefore, the buyer of Seller2's enterprise, Buyer2, will adopt potential intention-to "transact" in order to buy goods until this date. The axiom states that if an agent has an intention-that toward some proposition that it believes does not currently hold and the agent believes it is able to do some act δ that will enable another agent (or group of agents) to do an action γ that will bring about the proposition's holding, then the agent will adopt a potential intention to do δ.

A third axiom provides a basis for helpful behavior specifically in the SharedPlan context, i.e., for helping a collaborative partner. For example, if Seller2 needs to deliver some goods to Buyer1, and the buyer that belongs to Seller2's enterprise (we denote this buyer as Buyer2) needs to deliver some goods from the city of Buyer1's enterprise. Seller2 might offer to deliver these goods to Buyer1. The situation this axiom covers is one in which Buyer2 believes that the overall cost to him of the maintain-the-enterprise will be less if he does this delivery than otherwise.

As we mentioned, our environment includes both human and automated agents. Most of the current trader agents [659, 177, 594], which help users with all aspects of online shopping, do not keep track either of what the user is trying to acquire or of the dialogue context. As a result, trader agents do little to support user-agent collaboration on a transaction. Most of the work of keeping track of the context of their communication is thus left to the user. Those trader agents that do maintain some kind of history of what the user has done record a linear history list of the user's commands to the system. They do not represent the intentional structure of the dialogue nor track intentional state. As a result, they can not take the advantage of the structure of the user's work, and hence grow linearly with it. For example, the intentional context of buying a book for a present is different from the intentional context of buying a book for learning for an exam as well as buying a book for learning in the classroom. In the first case, if the book is not in the stock, the agent may suggest alternative books in the same price. But, in the second case the alternative option is suggesting a book with similar subjects. In the last case, since the user must have the specific book which he had indicated, the only alternative option is to inform the user of the date that this book will be in stock.

To provide the basis for more collaborative trader agents, we enable the users to communicate with the seller agents when SharedPlans are used for providing the collaborative task context. Our seller agents take an active role and can, for example, work with the users to identify a product which is relevant to their needs. Again, for space limitation we cannot demonstrate the efficacy of the human seller's collaboration.

9.3.2 Comparison with Alternative Implementation of the Electronic Commerce Domain

In this section, we compare our multi-agent system, for buying and selling, to alternative works which have created intelligent agent-based markets or retail outlets.

Takahanshi et al. [659] introduce an information tool called DION that collects shop and service information. This tool consists of several agents. One of them supports the user when creating queries. The other agents search and locate information, fetch the information and organize the search result. Their approach uses telephone-dictionary information as a well-organized index. However, their tool helps users find items to buy, and does not try to automate the process of buying and selling as we do.

Doorenbos et al. [177] design, implement, and analyze shopping agents that can help users with all aspects of online shopping. Their initial focus has been the design, construction, and evaluation of a scalable comparison shopping agent called ShopBot. Like DION, the ShopBot does not include any automated processes of buying and selling, and it focuses on extraction of information.

Schrooten [594] in his work presents an example of a pilot application concerned with the production of electronic consumer catalogs and their delivery to customers through the Internet. The technology behind the application is based on software agents. Schrooten's work illustrates new opportunities for electronic commerce and discusses the contributions of an agent-based approach, but he does not illustrate any cooperation model which we believe is necessary for the development of beneficial agents for electronic-commerce.

Chavez et al. [120] designed the Kabash system. Kasbah is a Web-based multi agent classified ad system where users create buying agents and selling agents to help transact goods. A user who wants to buy or sell goods creates an agent, gives it strategic direction, and sends it off into a centralized agent marketplace. Kasbah agents pro-actively seek out potential buyers or sellers and negotiate with them on behalf of their owners. Their work is focused on negotiation "strategies". That is, unlike our system, the buyer and seller agents in the Kasbah system do not include any planning capabilities or collaboration capabilities which are based on a cooperation model.

Another system is the Michigan Internet AuctionBot [741], which is an online auction server. When a user would like to sell an item it put it for sale through the AuctionBot. The user chooses a type for his auction from a selection of auction types and specifies its parameters (e.g., clearing times, permitted, etc.). AuctionBot manages the auction according to the user's specifications. As the Kasbah system the AuctionBot is only focused on negotiation skills (e.g., auctioning skills).

Klaus et al. [210] in their paper advocate the use of intelligent agents as a useful metaphor and as a software engineering methodology for the design and operation of virtual enterprises. They focus on how agents can support the cooperative process of setting up virtual enterprises through the Internet by performing tasks such as presentation, information retrieval and extraction, and the participation in auctions in electronic markets. In their paper they only offer a perspective of the high potential of agent-based technology, by presenting the main objectives of the research project AVE (Agent in Virtual Enterprises). The agents in AVE are designed according to the INTERRAP agent model. These agents include three layers. One of these layers is the cooperative planning layer (CPL) which extends the planning functionality of an agent to joint plans, i.e., plans by and/or for multiple agents that allows conflict resolution and cooperation. This cooperation is based on a general negotiation model. In our implementation, the cooperation is based on the SharedPlan model. Thus, our implementation includes more methods for achieving cooperation.

Albayrak et al. [7] present the REkos project (intelligent agents for realization of electronic market services). The REkos project consists of creating and realizing tools for the implementation of cooperating complex services. Their architecture includes management module processes. During the execution, the management module accesses the knowledge base. In doing this the agent is controlled by its intentions and goals. The management module includes several components. One of the components is the cooperation manager, which supervises the execution of the cooperation protocols and scripts, in which the agent is involved. Another module that REkos architecture includes is the intentionality module. In the intentionality module, goals and intentions of the agent are represented. Although REkos architecture includes a cooperation manager, this cooperation manager refers to the communication between the agents. That is, REkos architecture does not consist of SharedPlans which plays a central role in the cooperation of our implementation. As a result, REkos architecture does not provide, for example, capabilities for helpful behavior and avoidance of conflicting intentions.

9.4 The General SharedPlan System

In this section, we describe a general system for the implementation of a multi-agent collaborative system that is based on the SharedPlans formalization which is discussed in Section 9.2. We demonstrate the behaviour of the system using a specific implementation of agents that sell and buy in an electronic-commerce environment. The system was implemented using Alegro Common-Lisp running on a Solaris Workstation.

In order to enable the agents to act in a realistic environment we provide each agent in the system with the ability to plan several actions simultaneously. Each agent in our system is able to plan in parallel several actions, $(\alpha_1, \ldots, \alpha_n)$, where its plan for each such action may be only partial (see Figure 9.3). For example, the agent can begin to perform several "transact" actions with several different enterprises, negotiate the price and then select the best bid. We first describe the data structures of the system, and then discuss the system's processes. The system demonstrates the ability to use the general architecture of collaborative agents based on the theory.

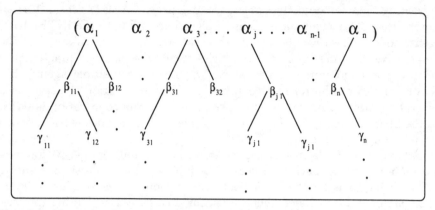

Fig. 9.3. Example of several actions which agent G plans simultaneously. While G detects that it is not able to continue working on the plan of action α_j, G can continue working on the plan for another action, α_i ($i \neq j$), until it will be able to continue working on α_j's plan. $\beta_{j,k}$ are the subactions of R_{α_j} and $\gamma_{j,l}$ are the subactions of $R_{\beta_{j,l}}$.

9.4.1 The Information and Data Structures of the Agent

To help explain the necessity of information and data structures which are given in this section we will examine a scenario based on the example which is presented in Section 9.2. Suppose that Buyer1 and Seller2 from the "transact" action example (see Figure 9.1), have agreed on the supply date of the selected good, T_{supply}, and they agreed that Seller2 will do the delivery and Buyer1 will execute the payment when she will get the good. Thus, Buyer1 has intention to [Int.To] do the "execution-payment" subaction at T_{supply}, intention that [Int.That] Seller2 will do "execution-delivery" subaction at T_{supply}, a belief that she will be able to do so, and an individual plan for doing so; likewise, Seller2 has an intention to [Int.To] "execution-delivery" at T_{supply}, an intention that [Int.That] Buyer1 will do the "execution-payment" subaction at T_{supply}, a belief he can do it, and an individual plan for doing so. We also assume that Buyer1 and Seller2 do not have enough knowledge in order to continue working on their plan for the "transact" action, until the supply date, T_{supply}, will be reached. Thus, Buyer1 and Seller2 do not do anything with respect to their SharedPlan of "transact" in the time interval $(T_{present}, T_{supply})$, while $T_{present}$ denotes the present time. Suppose that another buyer of another enterprise, Buyer3, also wants to buy an item from the enterprise of Seller2. Seller2 can begin a new "transact" action with Buyer3.

When Seller2 begins this new "transact", action he has to maintain his intention to "execution-delivery" at T_{supply}, and his intention that [Int.That] Buyer1 will do "execution-payment" subaction at T_{supply} in the context of his SharedPlan with Buyer1. Seller2 cannot adopt new intentions that are conflicting with the intentions that he currently has (unless he reconciles the intentions and decides to discard the old one). He also has to remember to continue working on his joint plan with Buyer1 for the "transact" action at T_{supply}, and he has to continue this planning from the point where he had stopped coordinating his planning with Buyer1. Thus, the agent needs structures which will help him to "remember" what he did not finish with respect to the "transact" action, and structures for maintaining its intentions and the planning actions, and a method for enabling him to perform the "execution-delivery" subaction at T_{supply}. At the time T_{supply} Seller2 has to perform the "execution-delivery" but he also has to remember to continue its planning for the new "transact" action it has begun.

Suppose that Buyer1 and Seller2 decided together that Buyer1 would pay cash to Seller2 at T_{supply} when performing "execution-payment," but that Buyer1 did not succeed to get enough cash by that date. Because Buyer1 knows that Seller2 expects to get the cash at T_{supply} she has to communicate to Seller2 and inform him about the problem and together they can change their plan. However, in some situations they may discard the SharedPlans and cancel the transaction. In order to re-plan the subaction "execution-payment", the agent needs to save all the relevant information which will help her to return to the "execution-payment"'s planning.

To allow such complex multi-agent partial planning, each agent uses structures and data which are discussed briefly below. In particular, each agent in the system applies three major modules: (1) Domain module; (2) Planning module; and (3) Communication module. The **domain module** contains the information which is known by the agent about its specific domain as beliefs of the agent, domain actions and the recipes library. The **planning module** contains structures which are used by the agent while it plans its actions. This module consists of: (a) domain actions: $(\alpha_1, \ldots, \alpha_n)$ that the agent plan in parallel; (b) the agenda which includes all the types of the intentions which have been adopted by the agent; (c) a schedule and a queue: the schedule contains basic domain actions and the queue contains all the processes that the agent needs to activate; and (d) the context which refers to the intentional context, IC, in the formalism. The agent associates such context with the following objects: with each intention in the agenda, with each basic-level domain action in the schedule and with each planning action in the queue. The **communication module** handles the communication processes which are different from the other processes in the system.

9.4.2 Actions and Recipes

Actions, in the model (see Section 9.2), have been described as abstractions with some properties such as action type, agents, time and other objects involved in performing the action, likewise, constraints. This approach works equally well for *action types*. That is, the action types include the same properties of actions. But, they also include the information as to whether the action is basic, as well as action preconditions, effects and results.

A *recipe* has been described as a specification of a set of action-types and constraints. The recipe's set of actions may be at different levels of abstraction. It also has been noted in the model that a recipe may include variables and constraints on these variables. The following sections describe the structures of an action type and a recipe as has been used in our system.

Action Type Structure. As observed above, the action includes an action type as one of its properties. In our system, the action types are also associated with various properties, but unlike actions the action types in the system are abstract. For example, the action-type "transact" is an abstract entity which represents a general activity of buying an item. When agents act to execute purchase, then this actual activity is referred to as the "action transact". In general, an action type structure consists of: (1) name of the action; (2) parameters of the action; (3) some constraints; (4) the action consequences; (5) action level; and (6) result variables.

```
(setq transact (make-action-type
  :name 'transact
  :agents '(A1 A2)
  :time 't1
  :params '(item-description)
  :param-constraints 'nil
  :time-constraints '()
  :agent-constraints '(
      (not (eq (?enterprise ?A1) (?enterprise ?A2)))
      (member ?A1 ?capability-sell)
      (member ?A2 ?capability-buy))
  :preconditions '()
  :results '(
      (increase-present-amount ?item-description ?A1)
      (increase-money ?A2))
  :effects '(
      (decrease-money ?A1)
      (decrease-present-amount ?item-description ?A2))
  :basicp 'nil
  :result-var '() ))
```

Fig. 9.4. Action Type Example.

In Figure 9.4 the action type structure of "transact" is presented. The variables and functions are prefixed by ?; we use this prefix to refer to the values of the instantiated variables and the values are returned by functions. The action's name slot contains the name of the action-type (e.g., "transact"). The action type structure includes three types of parameters' names: the first type are agents, the second is the time of the action, and the third type includes all the other parameters' names that are involved in performing the action. The action-type's constraints may be of two types: One type, can restrict the actions' agent, actions' parameters, and the actions' time, i.e., the *param-constraints*, *time-constraints*, and *agent-constraints* fields in Figure 9.4 respectively. The second constraints type, is applicability constraints, which restrict the applicability of the action, i.e., the *precondition* field. The action consequences also may be of two types: The first type is its result, i.e., the 'intended' consequences of the action, e.g., in the "transact" example the intended result of the buyer is to increase the amount of the products in the stock. The second type is side effects: in this aspect the agent does not intend the consequences, e.g., in the "transact" example, the agent has to pay for the product, as such she loses money. The action level is a 'boolean' value that defines whether the action is basic or complex. Sometimes, the values of the action parameters can be identified by other subactions. For example, in order to do "execution-the-payment" the agents have to identify the price of the item, but the price of the item is the value that is returned by the action "determine-price-and-payment". The result-var field consists of the names of the parameters which will contain the values to be returned to the agents that perform this action type after the performance of this action type.

Recipe Structure. In our system, recipes are associated with action-types. An agent may know several recipes for the same action type, but for each action the action type is unique. Figure 9.5 presents a recipe for the the multi-agent action "transact". In general, a recipe structure consists of: (1) unique identifier; (2) a set of subactions; (3) result variables; (4) constraints; (5) new parameters; (6) the recipe consequences (see, for example, Figure 9.5).

The *applic-constraints* field refers to the applicable constraints. Performing the subactions of the recipe under the appropriate constraints may cause changes in the domain as well as in the agents mental states. The recipe *consequences* describe those changes. In the "transact" example, if the buyer using the 'I do the delivery' recipe for the execution delivery subaction, it has the consequence of making his car occupied, and using the 'hire carrier' recipe has the consequence of spending money.

9.4.3 Getting from Individual Plan to SharedPlan

There are several situations in which a recipe for a single-agent action includes multi-agent subactions, as in the "maintain-the-stock" example (which is discussed in Section 9.2.1). Thus, while an individual agent detects that she cannot complete her individual plan alone, she can join other agents and form a SharedPlan. The agent which detects the need for a SharedPlan becomes

```
(make-recipe
  :action-type transact
  :name 'transact1
  :applic-constraints '(?catalog-number (? 1))
  :subactions '(
     0. (find-the-item ?A1 (? 1) ?t1 (?the-item))
     1. (verification ?A2 (? the-item) ?t2 (?verify))
     2. (determine-date-supply ?A1 (? the-item) ?t4 (? date))
     3. (determine-price-and-payment ?A1 (? the-item) ?t5 (?price ?payment))
     4. (execution-payment ?A1 (?price ?payment) ?t6)
     5. (execution-delivery ?A2 (?date) ?t7))
  :new-params '(the-item verify date price payment)
  :param-constraints '()
  :time-constraints '(
     (≤ (end-time ?t1) (start-time ?t2))
     (≤ (end-time ?t2) (start-time ?t3))
     (≤ (end-time ?t5) (start-time ?t6))
     (≤ (end-time ?t4) (start-time ?t7)))
  :agent-constraints '(
     (member ?A1 ?capability-sell)
     (member ?A2 ?capability-buy))
  :consequences '()
  :result-var '() )
```

Fig. 9.5. Multi-agent Recipe Example.

the organizer. Being the organizer does not yield any privileges in deciding on recipes, roles etc.

The roles of the organizer are to: (1) identify other community members who will be willing to participant in the SharedPlan and send them a message that SharedPlan is required; (2) determine a unique name for the common action; and (3) determine the "common-recipe-tree-path". The "common-recipe-tree-path" of a subaction includes all the actions leading to the need for the given action from the first time that any other agent or the organizer in the system began to plan this action. For example, if in an agent's plan δ is a subaction in a recipe R_β for β and β is a subaction in a recipe R_α for doing α and α is the highest level action, then the "common-recipe-tree-path" of δ is (α, β, δ). The "common-recipe-tree-path" is used by the agents, as unique identifiers in the messages that are exchanged between them and in order to uniquely identify the parameters of the actions.

9.4.4 The Processes in the System

The Grosz and Kraus' model (see Section 9.2.3) has demonstrated the need for planning actions, and offered a sketch of some of these actions. Although all the necessary planning actions have been defined, the detailed design of each of them is not obvious. In this section, we specify the system's processes which are consistent with the theory.

The Controller Process. Figure 9.6 shows the main constituent steps of the controller process of agent G. It is comprised of three major constituents:

1. Check for messages, and allocate any newly received messages to the relevant processes.
2. Check the schedule. If it is time to run a process associated with a domain action, do so.
3. Choose α_i from the actions-list which consists the domain actions, $(\alpha_1, \ldots, \alpha_n)$, that G plans in parallel (see Figure 9.3) and then check the queue of α_i. If possible, run the next process in queue(α_i). The processes of the queue are associated with planning actions.

Assumption:
Agent G is currently working on action $\alpha_j \in (\alpha_1, \ldots, \alpha_n)$.
We denote the agenda of the action α_j by *agenda(α_j)*. agenda(α_j) includes all the types of the intentions which have been adopted by G in order to perform the action α_j. We denote the queue of α_j by queue(α_j). queue(α_j) contains all the processes that G needs to activate in order to perform the action α_j.

CONTROLLER-LOOP:

```
1     Check for arriving messages; send each message to its relevant process;
2     While time of first action in schedule is greater or equal to the current time do:
3          execute the corresponding action;
4     If agenda(αj) is not empty, then:
5          If queue(αj) is not empty then:
6               Choose an item from queue(αj) to establish;
7          Else, the queue(αj) is empty and
               the time of the first action on the schedule has not arrived yet then:
8               If the actions-list includes other actions then:
9                    abandon αj, select another action αi (i ≠ j) from actions-list;
10    Else, if G believes that her plan to do action αj is complete, then:
11         delete αj from the actions-list;
12         If actions-list includes other actions then:
13              abandon αj, select another action αi (i ≠ j) from actions-list;
14         Else, the actions-list is empty then:
15              Wait, until a new message will arrive;
16    Start the Controller-Loop again;
```

Fig. 9.6. Pseudo code for the Controller Process.

We will discuss each of the above tasks of the controller in the following: As the first step in Figure 9.6, the controller process handles the inter-agent communication. Messages are exchanged between the planning process of a sender agent, and those of the recipient. The need to send a message usually arises during the execution of a joint planning process, and thus messages are sent out by the planning processes themselves. Making sure that it reaches the right process is a non-trivial task. The decision on what the relevant process is for each message received, making this process aware of the message, is the controller's job.

A process is associated with each of the actions the agent has committed to (that is, with each of the actions for which it has adopted either an Int.To or Int.Th). A process is initiated when its Int.To (or the Int.Th) is created, and spends the lifespan of the Int.To (resp. Int.Th) either running or waiting. However, there is a difference in the way basic level domain actions and the way complex domain actions are handled: a basic domain action is associated with a process 'make-basic-action' and is maintained in the schedule. A complex domain action is associated with a Select-Rec planning action and is kept in a queue with the other planning actions[6]. All the scheduling is handled by the controller process: The controller loops:

1. Check the schedule and if the time of the earliest 'make-basic-action' process in the schedule has arrived the controller initiates this process. In particular, if the specific time of the earliest basic domain action has not arrived the agent can continue its planning.
2. Check the queue and if the queue contains any process, the controller takes out the first process from the queue and initiates this process in order to continue the planning of the agent.

Processes for Planning. In order to develop mechanisms for expanding partial plans to more complete ones, the model provides complex planning actions. In our system, each planning action is implemented via a process. Each process is associated with either Int.To or with Int.That. Below we describe the processes in our system and demonstrate the usage of these processes in the Electronic-Commerce environment. For limited space reasons and since the processes are complex, we will briefly describe a selected subset of them[7].

Processes That Are Associated with Int.To. Since our Electronic-Commerce is a dynamic environment, our system requires a mechanism for efficiency backtracking and modularity. Thus, the elaborating process, which is used in our system for extending partial plans to complete ones, initiates several processes (see Figure 9.7) such as a process for selecting recipes which identifies ways to perform (domain) actions.

   Elaborate-Individual: this process is needed when an intention to perform a single agent action α exists but, the plan for that action is incomplete. Elaborate-Indiv is responsible for the completion and the construction

---

[6] The processes in the queue that are associated with complex actions are handled differently from the processes in the schedule that are associated with basic-level actions: First, the processes in the schedule are scheduled for a specific time and are ordered by an increasing order of the performance time, while planning processes are kept in a queue according to their arrival time. Second, while there is a separate sub-queue for each action in the actions-list, there is only one schedule for all the actions.

[7] The other complex processes of the system are described in [267].

of the plan for α. For example, in order to perform the single agent action "maintain-the-stock", Buyer1 initiates an Elaborate-Indiv process for "maintain-the-stock".

Select-Recipe-Individual: the main responsibilities of the Select-Recipe-Individual process include: (a) selection of an applicable recipe; (b) for each single agent subaction in the recipe being used, ensure that an attempt will be made to execute it by initiating an Elaborate-Indiv process for this subaction; (c) for each multi agent subaction in the recipe being used, ensure that an attempt will be made to execute it by forming an intention-that the proposition "Initiate-SP" of that subaction will hold. For instance, in the "maintain-the-stock" example Buyer1 forms an intention-that the proposition "Initiate-SP(transact)" will hold in order to perform the multi-agent subaction "transact".

Processes That Are Associated with Shared Plans. In this section we describe the complex processes **Elaborate_Group** and **Select_Rec_GR** which play a role in expanding partial SharedPlans to complete ones.

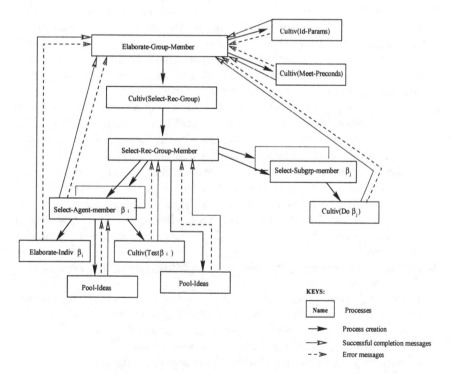

Fig. 9.7. Elaborate-Group-Member and Select-Rec-Group-Member

Elaborate-Group-Member: A basic claim of the SharedPlans formalization is that collaborative activity is rooted in the individual mental actions and domain actions of individual agents. This constraint holds of complex group planning actions as well as of domain actions. Thus, Elaborate-Group (see 9.4.4) comprises individual planning actions of the group members. We use the process Elaborate-Group-Member to represent these individual actions. Elaborate-Group-Member processes are the multi-agent counterparts of Elaborate-Indv processes. That is, they are responsible for building up plans for multi-agent actions. The Elaborate-Group-Member process must perform each of the following tasks:

1. *Make sure that α's parameters have been identified by initiating a cultivate process to identify parameters* (see Section 9.4.4). For example, the parameter which has to be defined in the multi agent subaction "transact" which is included in the recipe of "maintain-the-stock" example, are the products that Buyer1 intends to buy. In this case, the parameter is identified by the cultivate process of Buyer1 and is given by Buyer1 to Seller2, but there may be situations in which the group members jointly identify it.

2. *Verify that all the preconditions of α have been met by initiating cultivate process for meeting the preconditions* (see Section 9.4.4). For example, the precondition for doing the "determine-price-and-payment" subaction is that Buyer1 knows exactly what she wants to buy. In this case, Buyer1 checks if the precondition is satisfied and only then they can perform "determine-price-and-payment" subaction.

3. *Reconcile the potential intention that the group perform α with the intentions already held.* Reconciling a potential intention involves making sure that no conflicting intentions are already being held, and then replacing the potential intention-that with an intention-that. If there is an existing conflicting intention, a decision should be made whether to keep the old intention, or to discard it and to adopt the new one [492]. The Reconcile-int-that is the major locus for agents to assist one another. For example, in our domain, the buyer and seller agents that work for the same enterprise will avoid conflicts in resource use (and hence conflicting intentions).

4. *Initiate a process to select and setup a recipe for α, this process is described below.*

5. *Inform the parent process of its success or failure, as needed.* For example, in "maintain-the-stock" action, if the multi agent action "transact" fails, then the job of the Elaborate-Group-Member process of each participant is to inform its parent, the Cultivate process of the failure. This will lead to backtracking or to cancelation of the action performance.

6. *Deal with failure and success messages sent by other processes* (mostly its children).

7. *Inform the collaborating agents of its success or failure, as needed.*

8. *Deal with failure and success messages sent by other agents.* For example, in the "transact" action when Seller2 finishes the execution of "find-the-item," the Elaborate-Group-Member process of Seller2 will send a message to Elaborate-Group-Member process of Buyer1, informing Buyer1 if the execution of "find-the-item" has succeeded or failed.

Figure 9.7 presents briefly the relationships and the communication between the processes associated with a SharedPlan. For space limitation reasons, we only discussed the Select-Rec-Group-Member process (see [267] for a detailed description and examples of the system.)

Select-Rec-Group-Member: The group recipe selection process will cause individual agents to invoke the Select-Rec-Group-Member process. Select-Rec-Group-Member processes are the multi-agent counterparts of Select-Rec process. That is, they are responsible for the selection and initiation of the recipes for multi-agent actions. The main responsibilities of the Select-Rec-Group-Member process include:

1. Selection of an applicable recipe.

   The selection of an applicable recipe is more complicated than the individual case because of the need to coordinate with other agents to reach agreement. For example, in the multi agent action "determine-price-and-payment", although Buyer1 and Seller2 have the common general goal that the transaction will succeed, the interest of the buyer is that the price will be low while the interest of the seller is to agree upon a high price. In this case the agents may use negotiation in order to solve the conflict [357].

   Thus, to select the applicable recipe the following steps are executed:

   a) Each agent selects applicable recipes from its library that it prefers to use. Then, it sends these recipes to the other participants of the action.

   b) Each participant collects the proposed recipes.

   c) The agents applied an agreed upon decision making process (currently they randomly choose one, but negotiation or voting can be applied)[8].

2. For each single-agent domain subaction in the recipe being used, ensure that attempts will be made to select an agent that will execute it, by initiating a Select-Agent-member process which is responsible for the selection of the agent which will perform the single-agent subaction. In the "transact" example, although it is clear which agent will execute the subactions "find-the-item" "verification" and "execution-the-payment", it is not clear who, for example, will execute the "determine-date-supply" or "execution-delivery". This will be done through the Select-Rec-Group-Member processes of Buyer1 and Seller2.

---

[8] A more complex decision-making scenario, is one in which no single agent has a complete recipe. The agents work together to combine pieces of recipes that they discover individually.

3. For each multiple-agent domain subaction of the recipe being used, ensure that an attempt will be made to select the subgroup which will perform the subaction, by initiating a Select-Subgrp-member process which is responsible for the selection of the agents which will perform a multi-agent subaction.
4. Inform the parent process, Elaborate-Group-Member, of success or failure, as required.

Figure 9.7 illustrates how these tasks are performed by creation of processes, and the communication between these processes.

Processes That Are Associated with Int.That.

Cultivate: The intentional attitude, intending-that, was introduced into the SharedPlan formalization to account for the commitment participants in a group activity make to one another's actions and to their joint activity. Intentions-that, like intentions-to, serves both to constrain the intentions an agent adopts and to affect (indirectly) its plan-based reasoning. In particular, the Cultivate process is the general process which is active whenever an agent has an intention-that. The Cultivate process determines the actions that an agent might take as a result of having an intention-that toward a proposition, i.e., creates potential-intentions to do them, as a result of having an intention-that toward a proposition. The following section describes briefly some of the propositions associated with the cultivate in the context of SharedPlans.

1. **Id-params:** The role of the cultivate process, which is associated with an Int.Th the proposition Id-Params(α) holds, is to ensure that the agent will identify the parameters of the act it performs. In order to verify this, the cultivate process, first, checks if the agent already knows the parameters. If the agent knows the parameters, then the cultivate process checks if the agent plans to identify these parameters[9]. If the agent does not have a plan for identifying these parameters the cultivate process initiates the Id-Params process. For instance, in the "transact" example the parameter that has to be identified in the single agent action "execution-the-payment" is the price of the item. In this case the parameter is identified when Buyer1 and Seller2 perform the multi-agent subaction "determine-price-and-payment", i.e., in this situation the group members jointly identify the parameter.
2. **Meet-Preconds:** The role of the cultivate process which is associated with an intention-that Meet-Preconds is to make sure that the preconditions will be satisfied. If the cultivate process reveals preconditions that are not satisfied, it activates the Meet-Preconds process. For instance,

---

[9] As described in [267] in several cases the parameters may be identified by other subactions

suppose that the precondition for the subaction "execution-delivery" is "the product existing in Seller2's enterprise" and suppose that it is decided that Buyer1 will perform the subaction "execution-delivery". In this case, although the action is performed by Buyer1 it is the role of the cultivate process of seller2 to make sure that the precondition of "execution-delivery" is satisfied. If Seller2 finds out that the preconditions cannot be satisfied he will update Buyer1.

3. **Initiate-SP:** When an individual agent detects that she cannot complete her plan for an action α alone, she can join other agents to form a SharedPlan by forming intention-that the proposition Initiate-SP will hold. The role of the cultivate process, which is associated with an Int.Th the proposition Initiate-SP(α), is to initiate the cultivate process which is associated with Do (this process is described below). For example, if Buyer1 detects that she cannot complete her plan for "maintain-the-stock" alone, then she joins Seller2 to form a SharedPlan.

4. **Do:** The intention-that toward the proposition Do in the formalism describes the intention of the agents to begin to do an action α together. The roles of the cultivate process which is associated with such an intention-that are:

   a) Establish that all the group members of the multi-agent action α hold the intention-that for doing α, and establish a mutual belief among the members of the group that each one will be a participant in the group doing α. That is, each agent in the group has to send a message informing its commitment to join in α performance. In addition a similar commitment message must be received from all the group members. This is done by the Establish-MB process that is described in [267]. For example, in the "transact" action this cultivate process of Buyer1 sends a commitment message that she joins the "transact" action to Seller2 and Seller2 and waits for a similar message from Seller2. Seller2 sends a commitment message that he joins the "transact" action to Buyer1 and waits for a commitment from Buyer1. Then, Buyer1 and Seller2 can hold the intention-that for doing the "transact" and establish a mutual belief that each of them is committed to the group performance of "transact".

   b) In order to form a SharedPlan (for doing α) group members must form a full SharedPlan to do the Elaborate-Group action. The cultivate process which is associated with the proposition Do also initiates the agent's adoption of an intention-that the group will undertake this planning activity. Since the collaborative activity is rooted in the individual mental actions the cultivate process which is associated with an intention-that Elaborate-Group, will cause individual agents to activate an Elaborate-Group-Member process; that is, the participants must each have their own internal process to complete the partial shared plan.

Figure 9.8 presents the creation of these processes and communication between them.

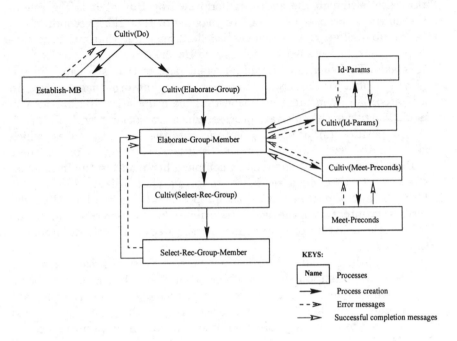

Fig. 9.8. Cultivate Do

Our SharedPlan system for buying and selling items which consists of the above planning processes provides automated purchasing and agent cooperation algorithms. Thus, in contrary to other agent-based markets or retail outlets on the Web (see Section 9.3.2), which focus on either extraction of information or negotiation "strategies", our system supports cooperative interactions of buying and selling goods. Using the SharedPlan formalization enables us to develop agents which are able to act in the dynamic Electronic Commerce environment where they are uncertain concerning their own actions and have incomplete information about the other agents and the environment.

9.5 Conclusion

In this chapter we focused on two major issues. First, we demonstrated the efficacy of collaboration in the Electronic Commerce environment and compared our implementation with other implementations for this environment.

In this environment SharedPlans may be formed between agents belonging to the same enterprise to work together to maximize their enterprise's benefits and also among agents that are self-motivated and interested in collaboration because it may maximize their individual benefits.

Second, we have designed and implemented a collaborative multi-agent system based on SharedPlan formalization for selling and buying goods such as clothes and furniture on the Web. The Web-based buying and selling system requires complex SharedPlans of groups of more than two agents including both people and automated agents. Our Web-based buying and selling system demonstrates the usefulness of models of collaboration for multi-agent systems and tests the formalization.

Acknowledgement:

This research was supported in part by the National Science Foundation grant number IIS9724937.

10. Dynamic Supply Chain Structuring for Electronic Commerce Among Agents

Daniel Dajun Zeng and Katia Sycara

Graduate School of Industrial Administration, The Robotics Institute,
Carnegie Mellon University, Pittsburgh, PA 15213, USA.
E-Mail: katia@cs.cmu.edu, dz25@andrew.cmu.edu

Summary.

Electronic commerce and the vast amounts of real-time information available through means of EDI and the Internet are reshaping the way enterprises conduct business. A new computational infrastructure and models are needed for a business to gain a competitive edge through effective use of this information base. One of the key issues in competing in the electronic marketplace is product/service differentiation. Currently there are no computational models for multi-issue decision making in electronic commerce.

We develop a model of interorganizational electronic commerce that explores various new choices and opportunities that the electronic marketplace offers. The particular motivating applications of our work are supply chain management. Two major performance measures of supply chain activities are cost and leadtime. In our model, we explicitly address these two issues in a unified fashion for a variety of supply chain activities, such as outsourcing, supplier selection, production capacity, transportation mode selection, and inventory positioning. We model different business entities as autonomous software agents interconnected via the Internet. The main research focus of our efforts is how to coordinate software agents in supply chains dynamically and flexibly such that goods and services can be delivered at the right time in a cost-effective manner.

The supply chain structure is modeled by an AND/OR network. We develop an efficient algorithm for software agents in supply chains to evaluate the alternatives that offer different leadtime and cost parameters. We have coupled this model with operational level decision making such as stochastic inventory management. Experimental results show that our model results in significant improvement in solution quality as compared to traditional models.

10.1 Introduction

Current networking technology and the ready availability of vast amounts of real-time data and information on the Internet-based Infosphere bring to business decision makers more abundant and accurate information. Many online businesses specialize in delivering electronic catalog services and performing other intermediary functions such as business/product yellowpage and matchmaking. Emerging computing paradigms such as Internet-based software agents are also making locating and accessing information increasingly easier.

Electronic commerce is reshaping both consumer market and interorganizational business. How to compete in the electronic marketplace effectively poses significant challenges to practitioners and researchers. In this chapter, we focus on interorganizational electronic commerce in the context of supply chain management. Researchers and practitioners have observed that the nature of competition in electronic commerce does not resemble undifferentiated Bertrand competition. This suggests that price alone is not the only decision criterion. Other decision criteria related with product/service differentiation need to be considered. Two of the prominent performance measures of a supply chain are cost and leadtime. By leadtime, we mean the amount of time that elapses from the instant that an order (or service request) is placed until it arrives. By cost, we mean the sum of the costs of all activities required to satisfy the order (or deliver the service). Some examples of these supply chain activities and decisions are:

- **Supplier selection**. Procurement management is playing an increasingly important role nowadays with the globalization of manufacturing and advances in network information infrastructure. There usually exists a rich set of suppliers offering raw materials of varying quality, cost, and delivery leadtime. Decisions regarding supplier selection have to be made after a careful evaluation of the impact of raw material cost and delivery time responsiveness on the supply chain as a whole.
- **Subcontracting**. In manufacturing, managers face "make or buy" decisions, i.e., the choice between making components/products in house or subcontracting them to outside sources. When making in house is not an option or is clearly suboptimal, management has to select the appropriate subcontractors from a pool of potential subcontractors that offer different levels of service under different prices. These decisions are critical in today's highly competitive and dynamic business environment.
- **Transportation mode selection**. Typically, multiple transportation modes are available to supply chain managers, offering a wide range of cost/time options. Decisions regarding which mode is best suited for the current order are dependent on how urgently the order needs to be filled, how expensive these modes are, and where this transportation activity is located in the supply chain network.
- **Assembly/subassembly**. Assembly/subassembly operations cannot start until all the components/subcomponents/raw materials required become available. Production managers need to make sure that all these materials are accessible for use at the right place and the right time.
- **Production rate decision**. Production rate decisions correspond with the choice between using faster, more expensive, high-capacity production facilities versus slower but cheaper facilities. To evaluate the tradeoffs between these options is not trivial considering all the upstream and downstream activities in the supply chain.

In this chapter, we present a model of interorganizational electronic commerce that explicitly addresses the time and cost issues in a unified fashion. We model different business entities as autonomous software agents interconnected via the Internet. These agents act on behalf of their human users/organizations in order to perform laborious information gathering tasks, such as locating and accessing information from various on-line information sources, filter away irrelevant or unwanted information, and provide decision support. Section 10.1.1 discusses some of the related literature. Section 10.2 presents a brief description of our supply chain model, called LCT (Leadtime-Cost-Tradeoff). The LCT model needs to be integrated with other operational level decision making models such as inventory management to enable intelligent agents to make the full range of supply chain decisions. Section 10.3 presents how to integrate LCT into the EOQ model where the demand rate is assumed to be constant. We present in Section 10.4 our model and analysis of stochastic inventory management given the leadtime/cost choices. Experimental results show that our model results in significant improvement in solution quality as compared to traditional models. Computing optimal policies for the resulting model proves to be computationally difficult. Section 10.5 presents a computational study of making inventory decisions that take advantage of leadtime/cost options. We conclude the chapter in Section 10.6 by summarizing the results and pointing out other extensions to our agent-based multi-issue supply chain model.

10.1.1 Related Literature

Effective use of the Internet by individual users, organizations, or decision support machine systems has been hampered by some dominant characteristics of the Infosphere. Information available from the net is unorganized, multi-modal, and distributed on server sites all over the world. The availability, type and reliability of information services are constantly changing. In addition, information is ambiguous and possibly erroneous due to the dynamic nature of the information sources and potential information updating and maintenance problems. The notion of Intelligent Software Agents (e.g., [739, 653]) has been proposed to address this challenge. In the following, we model a supply chain as a multi-agent system where different business entities interact with one another through intelligent software agents that act on their behalf. In general, multi-agent systems can compartmentalize specialized task knowledge, organize themselves to avoid processing bottlenecks, and can be built expressly to deal with dynamic changes in the agent and information-source landscape. In addition, multiple intelligent agents are ideally suited to the predominant characteristics of the so-called Infosphere or Cyberspace (and in particular supply chain management), such as the heterogeneity of the information sources, the diversity of information gathering and decision support tasks that the gathered information supports, and the presence of multiple users/organizations with related information and decision aiding needs.

In order for autonomous software agents to make sensible decisions in any nontrivial domain such as supply chain management, they need to have access to domain-specific decision making models and related computational mechanisms[392]. We briefly survey some of these models in literature that are most relevant to multi-issue (time and cost) supply chain management.

The first models that consider the possibility of purchasing shorter lead-times at a premium cost appeared in [96] and [226], among others. The main objective of these papers is to find the optimal ordering policy that mini-mizes ordering, holding and penalty costs when subject to random demand. Structural results regarding the optimal replenishment policy were estab-lished when there are only two options and the leadtimes of the two options differ by one time unit (in periodic review situations).

Kaplan in [325] analyzed optimal policies for a dynamic inventory problem when the leadtime is a discrete random variable with known distribution. Assuming that outstanding orders do not cross in time, Kaplan derived the structure of optimal policies which is shown to be similar to those obtained with deterministic leadtimes. Although [325] is not concerned with different leadtime options, it gives a good survey for the technical difficulties that we also encountered.

Song and others in [639] studied the impact of stochastic *leadtimes* on the optimal inventory decisions and the optimal cost in a base-stock inven-tory model. The focus there is to evaluate the impact of the variability of leadtimes but not to derive an inventory policy which makes use of the avail-ability of multiple leadtime/cost options. In [370] Lau and Zhao considered the order splitting between two suppliers that offer different leadtime with uncertainty. The authors assumed a constant splitting ratio among two sup-pliers and developed computational methods to compute the optimal ratio, ordering quantities and reordering point in a continuous review inventory set-ting. Several papers (e.g., [49]) deal with situations where leadtimes is one of the decision variables. Their assumption is that by paying "leadtime crashing cost" leadtime reduction can be achieved. The goal of these papers is to find the single best leadtime option under single sourcing.

10.2 The LCT Supply Chain Model

We have developed a supply chain model, called LCT, based on an AND/OR network representation[287]. This model is capable of capturing a variety of supply chain activities and decisions.

In LCT, a supply chain is modeled as a directed acyclic graph with paral-lel arcs. The model follows an activity-on-arc representation where each arc corresponds to a particular supply chain activity (production, transporta-tion, subcontracting, etc.). Note that each activity/arc has two performance measures: leadtime and cost. In this supply chain network, nodes represent completion of activities and may be used to establish precedent constraints among activities. The graph is directed towards one particular "root node". The root node corresponds to the retailer of the product that the supply chain produces. End customers interact with the root node only. We define two types of nodes that each specifies conditions for satisfying prior activities: *conjunction* and *disjunction* nodes. Conjunction nodes or AND nodes are nodes for which *all* the activities that correspond to the incoming arcs must be accomplished before the outgoing activities can begin; whereas disjunction nodes or OR nodes requires that *at least one* of the incoming activities must be finished before the outgoing activities can begin.

Based on LCT we have developed efficient computation methods to identify the entire efficient frontier between leadtime and cost in supply chains. This efficient frontier at the "root node", i.e., the retailer point, compactly represents all the undominated, feasible combinations of supply chain activities. By a feasible combination of supply chain activities, we mean the set of activities that guarantee the availability of goods or services at the root node. We say a combination dominates the other when the former offers cheaper cost and shorter leadtime than the latter. Given the efficient frontier coupled with the market demand profile and pricing strategy at the root node, management can converge on the optimal tradeoff point specifying a particular supply chain configuration.

One of the limitations of LCT is that the model doesn't explicitly consider inventory. Without inventory, the solution concept based on the leadtime cost efficient frontier applies to "one-shot" scenarios in which single period demand is considered at the root node (e.g., make-to-order). If demand for the end product is repetitive, holding inventory at one or more places in the supply chain clearly has the potential of improving the performance of the whole system. The rest of the chapter focuses on integrating LCT with inventory management—out first step to extend LCT to address multi-period demand.

In the following, we assume that inventory can be held only at the root node[1]. In other words, we are concerned with integrating one stage inventory management within the context of LCT. Since we only add the inventory capacity at the root node, the entire efficient frontier between leadtime and cost in the supply chain network remains the same. We are interested in ways through which the end product retailer can take advantage of the availability of multiple options with varying leadtime and cost parameters. Despite the restrictive assumption made in this model as to the inventory location, this model captures the fundamental characteristics of a variety of supply chain management situations. For instance, the model is readily applicable for retailers who may get goods/services from various manufacturers that quote

---

[1] The extension of LCT which allows inventory at arbitrary nodes in the supply chain network is beyond the scope of this chapter.

different unit price and delivery leadtime. In another example, a manufacturing firm is structuring its international sourcing base. Suppose that this firm adopts a make-to-stock policy. Our model can be applied to make sourcing decisions based on the current inventory stock level.

10.3 LCT in Inventory Models with Constant Demand Rates

In this section, we demonstrate how the LCT model can be integrated into inventory models that assume constant demand rates.

Let l denote the leadtime, $UP(l)$ the cheapest unit ordering cost for goods for which the order fulfillment takes at most l. The leadtime cost efficient frontier computed in LCT takes the form of the function $UP(l)$. When the leadtime measure can be properly discretized (e.g., in units of days), $UP(l)$ is a step function:

$$UP(l) = c_i \quad \text{if } i \leq l < i+1 \quad \text{for } i = 0, 1, \ldots, M$$

where M is the maximum leadtime from all possible alternatives and c_i is the minimum unit ordering cost if the target leadtime is expected to be strictly less than $i+1$. Without loss of generality, we assume that c_i is nonincreasing with respect to i.

Let $SK(l)$ denote the setup cost associated with selecting the cheapest supply chain configuration that achieves leadtime l.

$$SK(l) = K_i \quad \text{if } i \leq l < i+1 \quad \text{for } i = 0, 1, \ldots, M$$

The total ordering cost $TC(x, l)$ for x units of product with the leadtime requirement l is given by

$$TC(x, l) = K_i + c_i x \quad \text{if } i \leq l < i+1 \quad \text{for } i = 0, 1, \ldots, M$$

We follow the standard assumptions of the EOQ inventory model: The demand rate λ is constant; no stockout or backlogging is allowed. Consider the following situation which is a special case of our model. There is only one alternative available that offers leadtime k, setup cost K, and unit ordering price c. The optimal ordering policy in this case is well known. It follows the (Q, R) policy, where Q is the standard EOQ quantity, R is the reorder point which is equal to $k\lambda$. (We assume $k \leq Q/\lambda$ for simplicity.)

Let's consider the general case where more than one alternatives are available. We only consider the cycle inventory which is the amount of inventory physically on hand at any point in time. The optimal ordering policy involves using the alternative with leadtime i^* which is defined as follows:

$$\lambda c_{i^*} + \sqrt{2K_{i^*} \lambda h} \equiv \min_i (\lambda c_i + \sqrt{2K_i \lambda h})$$

This implies a single sourcing policy will be optimal. Search for i^* can be easily done by enumerating all available modes. It is clear that when K_i is nonincreasing with respect to i, the least expensive alternative that also offers the longest leadtime is always the mode of choice. After the alternative i^* has been chosen, the classical (Q, R) policy can be used to determine the order amount and reorder point. Obviously, other extensions such as finite production capacity can be done in the same fashion without causing additional technical problems.

10.4 LCT in Periodic Review Stochastic Inventory Model

In the previous section, we show that integrating LCT with inventory models with constant demand rates can be easily done. When we consider inventory management with uncertain demand, however, the situation changes dramatically. In this section, we first present a formal formulation of the problem and then proves some formal properties. We demonstrate the technical difficulties of finding optimal policies and motivate our computational work (presented in Section 10.5) in finding effective suboptimal policies.

We study an N-period stochastic inventory problem in which there are m different ordering options. These options represent different leadtime and cost tradeoffs which can be computed using the LCT model given the network topology of a supply chain and time/cost information for the supply chain activities. We ignore the setup cost in this study[2].

We use the following notation in our study. Most of the notation follows the standard one used in N-period single-stage stochastic inventory modeling:

$N =$ the number of periods in the planning horizon

$m =$ the number of delivery/production options. We assume that $m < N$.

$\lambda_i =$ the leadtime associated with option i, $i = 1, 2, \ldots, m$. We assume that these leadtimes are deterministic. Without loss of generality, we assume that $\lambda_i < \lambda_j$ when $i < j$.

$\tau =$ the maximum leadtime from all possible options. $\tau = \lambda_m$

$c_i =$ the unit ordering cost with option i, $i = 1, 2, \ldots, m$. We assume that $c_i > c_j$ when $i < j$[3].

$t =$ the demand for the item during each period. We assume that the demand is stationary.

$e(x^+) =$ the salvage value of having $x^+ = max(x, 0)$ units of inventory on hand at the end of the period N. We assume $e(x^+)$ is convex.

$\alpha =$ the one-period discount factor

---

[2] It is not entirely arbitrary since electronic commerce contributes to the setup cost reduction.

[3] This is not a restriction. See the discussion in Section 10.4.3

$x_1 =$ the current stock level

$x_2, x_3, \ldots, x_\tau =$ the outstanding orders such that x_2 is due at the start of the next period, x_3 is to be delivered two periods hence, etc.

$z_i =$ the amount of goods to be ordered at the start of the present period using option i, $i = 1, 2, \ldots, m$. These are the inventory decision variables.

$L(x) =$ the expected operational costs during the period, exclusive of ordering costs, w.r.t. the stock on hand at the beginning of the period:

$$L(x) = \begin{cases} \int_0^x h(x-t)f(t)dt + \int_x^\infty p(t-x)f(t)dt & x > 0, \\ \int_0^\infty p(t-x)f(t)dt & x \le 0 \end{cases} \tag{10.1}$$

We assume that the holding cost $h(\cdot)$ and penalty cost $p(\cdot)$ are nondecreasing and convex. The unfulfilled ordered are backlogged. Since integration preserves the convexity, the convexity of $L(x)$ is easily seen.

$C_n(x_1, x_2, \cdots, x_\tau) =$ the minimum expected cost following an optimal policy, given that only n future periods are to be taken into account, where $(x_1, x_2, \ldots, x_\tau)$ represents all the information about the current stock level as well as the amounts of goods whose orders have been submitted and are to be delivered during the following $\tau - 1$ periods.

To simplify the notation, we also use the following vector-based representations:

$\underline{x}$: the row vector of $(x_1, x_2, \ldots, x_\tau)$

$\underline{z}$: the row vector of $(z_1, z_2, \ldots, z_m)$

The functional equation for $C_n(\cdot)$ is easily seen to be

$$C_n(x_1, x_2, \ldots, x_\tau) = \min_{z_i \ge 0, \text{for } 1 \le i \le m} \left\{ \sum_{i=1}^m c_i z_i + L(x + y_0) + \right. \tag{10.2}$$

$$\left. \alpha \int_0^\infty C_{n-1}(x_1 + y_0 - t + x_2, x_2 + y_1, \cdots, x_\tau + y_{\tau-1}, y_\tau) f(t) dt \right\} \tag{10.3}$$

where, y_i is defined as follows:

$$y_i = \begin{cases} z_{\lambda_j} & \text{if } i = \lambda_j, \\ 0 & \text{otherwise} \end{cases} \tag{10.4}$$

Under these assumptions, we can prove the convexity of the value function.

Theorem 10.4.1. $C_n(\underline{x})$ is convex.

Proof.. We prove Theorem 10.4.1 by induction. Given the cost structure of the salvage value,

$$C_0(\underline{x}) = p(x_1^-) + e(x_1^+) \tag{10.5}$$

$C_0(\underline{x})$ is convex.

By induction on C_{n-1}, we will prove that C_n is also convex. We first introduce some auxiliary vectors to simplify the notation. Define

$$g(\underline{x}, \underline{z}, t) \equiv C_{n-1}(A \begin{bmatrix} \underline{x} \\ \underline{z} \\ t \end{bmatrix}) \tag{10.6}$$

where A is a $\tau \times (\tau + m + 1)$ matrix. Each element of A, A_{ij}, is given as follows:

$$A_{ij} = \begin{cases} 1 & \text{if } i = 1 \text{ and } j = 1, \\ -1 & \text{if } i = 1 \text{ and } j = \tau + m + 1, \\ 1 & \text{if } j = i + 1 \text{ for all } i \in [1, \tau - 1], \\ 1 & \text{if } \lambda_j = i \text{ for all } j \in [\tau + 1, \tau + m], \\ 0 & \text{otherwise} \end{cases} \tag{10.7}$$

It can be easily verified that the functional equation (10.2/10.3) can be rewritten as:

$$C_n(\underline{x}) = \min_{\underline{z}} \left\{ \sum_{i=1}^m c_i z_i + L(x + y_0) \quad + \alpha \int_0^\infty g(\underline{x}, \underline{z}, t) f(t) dt \right\} \tag{10.8}$$

Given that C_{n-1} is convex and that A is a full-rank linear transformation, $g(\underline{x}, \underline{z}, t)$ is convex due to [558] Theorem 5.7 Part A.

Define

$$q(\underline{x}, \underline{z}) = \int_0^\infty f(t) g(\underline{x}, \underline{z}, t) dt \tag{10.9}$$

We know that $q(\underline{x}, \underline{z})$ is convex since $f(t) \geq 0$ due to [24].

Since the operating cost L is convex, and q is convex, we conclude that the summation $\sum_{i=1}^m c_i z_i + L(x + y_0) + q(\underline{x}, \underline{z})$ is convex. Due to [558] Theorem 5.7 Part B, we know that C_n is convex.

10.4.1 Optimal Inventory Control Policy

Karlin and Scarf in [23] studied inventory models in the presence of a time lag. Their models can be viewed as a special case of ours since they assumed that there is only one leadtime option available. Based on the convexity of the objective function, they proved that the optimal policy follows an order-up-to policy. Simply put in our notation, if $m = 1$, $z_1^* = (S - (x_1 + x_2 + \dots + x_{\lambda_1}))^+$, S being the order-up-to level to be determined. Fukuda in [226] extended this result to deal with 2-mode cases. Again, based on the convexity of the objective function, he proved that the optimal control policy is very similar to an order-up-to policy except for an additional stock level up to which it is desired to order using the quicker and more expensive option. The intuition is that to use quicker option to handle large, unexpected demand while the steady portion of the demand flow is handled by the slower and less expensive option. In both cases, the optimal inventory policies are not difficult to compute.

One might think that the similar intuition may be extended to the general m option case by having m order-up-to levels for each leadtime option. Unfortunately, this is not the case. By solving a very simple 2-mode ($\lambda_1 = 0, \lambda_2 = 2$) problem, we found that no simple order-up-to or order-up-to like structures exists. The complexity of the problem is coming from the fact that although the convexity of the objective function holds, the optimal controls are functions of all the x_i for $i = 1, 2, \ldots, \tau$ rather than functions of $\sum_{i=1}^{\tau} x_i$.

Using the value iteration approaches in dynamic programming, we can compute the optimal control policies regardless of whether they follow the order-up-to structure or not. However, these value iterations approaches are almost impossible to scale up since the size of state space itself is exponential with respect to the maximum leadtime. For practical purposes, we need to find other more efficient algorithms.

The same technical difficulties have been identified in different inventory management and dynamic programming settings. (e.g.,[325]). In order to get analytically appealing results, the standard way of avoiding these difficulties in inventory management is to assume that at any certain moment, there is only one outstanding order. This is clearly not our option, since what we are interested is precisely using multiple options at the same time.

To address these computational issues, we have developed several suboptimal polices that are easy to compute. In Section 10.5, we reported these policies and an experimental evaluation of their performances. To illustrate the significance of making use of multiple leadtime options, in Section 10.4.2 we use a numerical example to demonstrate that using multiple leadtime options can result in significant improvement in solution quality. As a side result, we establish in Section 10.4.3 a simple dominance relationship among leadtime options that can be used to eliminate certain options from consideration without compromising the solution quality. Admittedly, this dominance relationship does not help in worse case scenarios where no leadtime options are dominated by others. It could, however, save some computation by throwing out the dominated options.

10.4.2 An Numerical Example: The Value of Having Multiple Leadtime Options

In this section, we use a numerical example to demonstrate that having multiple leadtime options can result in significant improvement as compared to having one (Karlin and Scarf's model) or two leadtime options where the leadtime difference is 1 time unit (Fukuda's model).

Consider the following scenario. We assume that one period demand is discretely distributed according to the following probability mass function:

d	0	1	2	3	4
$p(d)$	0.2	0.2	0.2	0.2	0.2

To construct a comparison baseline, we first start off with using one lead-time option only. We are interested in minimizing the infinite horizon average cost per stage since we want to explore the average performance of the system in steady states. Suppose that the unit holding cost $h = 1.00$ and the penalty cost $p = 30.00$. When there is only one leadtime option available, say, one with the ordering cost $c_1 = 15$ and the delivery leadtime $\lambda_1 = 0$ (instantaneous delivery), we know that the order-up-to policy is optimal. We compute the optimal order-up-to levels and find that the average cost per stage is 33.62. In effect, based on Karlin and Scarf's theorem[23], we can computer the optimal order-up-to level and the average cost for any (one) option with a positive delivery leadtime. Using 33.62 as the target cost, we are interested in the ordering cost of other leadtime options that lead to the same 33.62 average cost. The isocost curve is given in Figure 10.1. The x-axis represents the delivery leadtime. The y-axis represents the ordering price required to achieve the target cost.

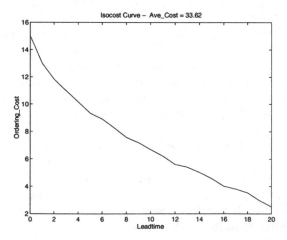

Fig. 10.1. An Isocost Curve

For simplicity, let us consider the first three points on this isocost curve. If we can use only one option, we are indifferent among option 1 (leadtime 0; ordering cost 15.00), option 2 (leadtime 1; ordering cost 13.01), or option 3 (leadtime 2; ordering cost 11.84). Suppose that now we have two options—Option 1 and Option 2—available at the same time. How should we take advantage of this additional choice? Recall that this is exactly what Fukuda's model addresses (see Section 10.4.1). We compute the optimal control and find the average cost decreases from 33.62 to 30.46. Using option 2 and option 3 results in a average cost of 30.55, computed similarly.

How about using these three options together? Since the size of the problem is very small, we can afford to enumerate all the states in the state space and compute the optimal control for each state. We use a linear program coded in AMPL to compute the minimal steady state average cost. The result is 27.18. Percentage wise, it represents a 19.16% decrease in operating cost from 33.62 (using one option only), which is quite significant.

This example reinforces our intuitive notion that by dynamically combining these multiple leadtime options contingent on the current inventory position and outstanding orders, the system can achieve lower cost. Due to the complex interactions between these leadtime options, we could not find an analytically elegant solution. Nevertheless, this model presents an abstraction of realistic supply chain management scenarios and could potentially offer significant benefits. This has motivated our work in developing computational methods to construct suboptimal yet effective policies, reported in Section 10.5.

10.4.3 A Simple Dominance Relationship

As we discussed in Section 10.4.1, considering all leadtime options poses serious computational challenges. In this section, we establish a simple dominance relationship which, when applicable, helps reduce computational efforts by excluding certain options—the dominated ones—without compromising the solution quality.

The intuition behind this dominance relationship is quite obvious: for any option i, if there is another option j that offers either quicker delivery under same ordering cost, or offers lower price while ensuring same delivery, or offers both lower price and quicker delivery, option i will never be used in the optimal controls and therefore can be ignored. In this case, we say i is dominated by j. The following lemma formalizes this notion.

Lemma 10.4.1. *An option i with leadtime λ_i and ordering cost c_i is dominated by another option j with leadtime λ_j and ordering cost c_j when $c_i \geq c_j$ and $\lambda_i \geq \lambda_j$. There always exist an optimal control policy which does not use option i.*

The proof is straightforward. Consider the set of all the control policies that use option i, denoted by ω_i. For each control $u_i \in \omega_i$, substitute option j for option i as follows: if $\lambda_i = \lambda_j$, simply use option j whenever i is used. If $\lambda_i > \lambda_j$, use option j whenever i is used but delay the orderings by $\lambda_i - \lambda_j$. It is clear that the resulted control policy after substitution costs equal to or less than the original control policy u_i that uses option i. Since this is true for any arbitrary u_i, the lemma immediately follows.

10.5 Computing Inventory Policies with Multiple Leadtime Options

For computational purposes, we assume that demand is a discrete random variable. For problems that have small maximum leadtime from all options (say, the maximum leadtime $\tau < 4$) and do not require fine-granularity demand discretization, the optimal policy can be found either by policy iteration through linear programming or value iteration through dynamic programming [65]. Both linear programming and dynamic programming require the explicit storage of the state space. Since the size of the state space grows exponentially with the maximum leadtime, neither linear programming nor dynamic programming can be used to solve large-sized problems (say, with more than 5 options). To give an example how quickly the size of the state space becomes unmanageable, consider the following scenario: Suppose that we have 5 leadtime options whose delivery leadtimes are 1, 2, 3, 4, 5, respectively. Furthermore, suppose that one-period demand is a discrete random variable that takes on values from zero up to 20. The minimum number of the states required by value iteration using dynamic programming is in the order of magnitude of 10^{74}. To maintain such a large state space and compute optimal control for each and every state repeatedly till the value function converges is not practical. Neither can policy iteration handle computation of this size.

In this section, we propose three suboptimal control policies that are easier to compute than the optimal policies. The performance of these policies is evaluated via simulation.

10.5.1 The Dynamic Switching Policy

By the dynamic switching policy, we mean the policy that uses only one leadtime option at each ordering point but does not require the same option to be used at different ordering points. This type of policy has a nature mapping in practice: "do not split orders between suppliers at each ordering point; but switch among suppliers in different time periods if needed". Using our notation, this means:

$$\sum_{i=1}^{m} z_i = z_j \quad \text{for some } j: 1 \leq j \leq m \tag{10.10}$$

In order to search for the optimal policies within the set of dynamic switching policies, we still need to explicitly represent the state space and therefore we are limited to solving small-sized problem instances. However,

---

[4] We do not consider the complications at the boundaries of the state space when we compute this minimum number of states required. In practice, larger state space is necessary to ensure that value iteration returns reliable results.

to compute the optimal controls (how much to order using which option) for each state for the dynamic switching policy is much easier as compared to finding the true optimal controls for each state in general due to the fact that choices are much limited. In addition to its favorable computational properties, we are interested in dynamic switching polices because of its managerial implications.

10.5.2 The Echelon Order-up-to Policy

It is clear that we cannot afford to explicitly carry around the state space in order to solve large-sized problems. One way of avoiding representing the state space is to apply the idea of *parameterize the control policies*. We consider a class of controls that can be characterized by a small number of parameters. Based on these parameters, we can easily deduce the corresponding control for any given arbitrary state. For instance, consider an one-option inventory model (See Section 10.4.1), an order-up-to policy is characterized by one parameter order-up-to level S. Given any state x (the current inventory position), the control (order amount) is $(S - x)^+$. This way, the original problem of finding optimal control policies is transformed into finding the best parameters S^* that minimizes the overall system cost. Note that in this case, we do not need to explicitly record and visit each state in the state space.

Note that for our general m-option inventory problems, the order-up-to policy or its variants have been proved nonoptimal. The simplicity of the order-up-to policy and its wide acceptance in practice, however, have rendered itself as a good candidate suboptimal policy in which we are interested. In our study, we consider the following policy fashioned after the order-up-to policy.

$$z_i = (S_i - \sum_{j=1}^{\lambda_i} x_j - \sum_{j=1}^{i-1} z_j)^+ \quad \text{for } i = 1, \ldots, m \tag{10.11}$$

We call this the "echelon order-up-to policy" due to the similarity between this policy and the policies developed in multi-echelon inventory research [129]. Intuitively, we can imagine that for each leadtime option, there is an "order-up-to" level that guarantees that the sum of future arrivals and committed orders using quicker options reaches a predetermined level. The rationale behind this is similar to that behind Fukuda's policy for two adjacent (in terms of leadtimes) options. As long as we have enough inventory on hand and on order, we use slow options. The costly quick options are used to handle situations where shortage occurs.

10.5.3 The Separating Planes Policy

As we will report in Section 10.5.4, although the echelon order-up-to policy is easy to compute and can be used to solve large-sized problems, the resulting solution quality measured by the average per stage cost is not entirely satisfactory. To achieve lower and closer-to-optimal costs, we develop the following policy which can be viewed as a generalization of the echelon order-up-to policy.

$$z_i = (\beta_i - \sum_{j=1}^{\tau} \alpha_{ij} x_j)^+ \quad \text{for } i = 1, \ldots, m \qquad (10.12)$$

Recall that when we follow an echelon order-up-to policy, we weigh all the x_j and z_j equally. We analyzed a number of the optimal policies (for small-sized problems) produced by policy iteration or value iteration and observed that equally weighing x_j and z_j clearly violates optimality. In the meantime, to a large extent, the points in the high-dimensional space of $(x_1, x_2, \ldots, x_m, z_j)$ for $j = 1, 2, \ldots, m$ can be separated by hyperplanes. These hyperplanes are not necessarily in parallel. This motivates the development of the separating plane policy. This policy, like the echelon order-up-to policy, does not require explicit representation of the state space and therefore can be used in solving large-sized problem instances. The separating plane policy involves more parameters than the echelon order-up-to policy and therefore are more computationally intensive. Using the separating plane policy, however, results in lower average per state system cost, as demonstrated in Section 10.5.4.

10.5.4 Experimental Comparisons

To evaluate the effectiveness of the proposed control policies, we performed the following experiments. We generated 396 problem instances by varying the number of leadtime options available, demand profiles and cost parameters summarized below:

– **Leadtime options:** we considered the following groups of leadtime options: two leadtime options with leadtimes 0 and 2; three leadtime options with leadtimes 0, 1, and 2; three leadtime options with leadtimes 1, 2, and 3. Different combinations of the unit ordering costs for these options are tested[5]. The cost values tested are shown in the following table:

leadtime	ordering costs tested
0	10, 9, 8
1	8, 7, 6
2	6, 5, 4
3	4, 3

– **Demand distributions:** we considered the following two groups of discrete demand distributions. The first group includes discretized truncated

---

[5] Not all combinations are tested.

normals with negative mass moved to zero and upper-tail mass moved to 10. The mean of these distributions was set to 5 and the following standard deviations were tested: .5, 1, 2, 5, 10. The second group is consisted of 10 distributions with one period demand t taking on values from 0 to 3. The tested probability mass functions are given in the following table.

	\multicolumn{4}{c}{probability mass function}			
	$p(t = 0)$	$p(t = 1)$	$p(t = 2)$	$p(t = 3)$
1	0.25	0.25	0.25	0.25
2	0.8	0.05	0.05	0.1
3	0.1	0.05	0.05	0.8
4	0.1	0.8	0.05	0.05
5	0.05	0.05	0.8	0.1
6	0.4	0.35	0.05	0.2

– **Cost parameters**: the holding cost per period is always set to 1. We tested two values of the penalty cost per period: 15 and 30.

We developed the simulation testbed in the C programming language. All experiments were performed on a Sun Ultra-1 machine. Table 10.1 represents the summarized results. Results of the policies are stated as percentage excess over the optimal cost which was obtained using value iterations. Table 10.2 records the average amount of time in CPU minutes that it took to compute the policies for one problem instance. Little attempt was made to make the coding efficient, so these time figures should be viewed with caution.

Leadtime Options	Dynamic Switching	Echelon Order-up-to	Separating Plane
2 modes (0, 2)	15.3	11.6	5.4
3 modes (0, 1, 2)	16.2	12.2	6.2
3 modes (1, 2, 3)	18.7	12.1	6.3

Table 10.1. Average Performance of Policies Considered (% Error)

Leadtime Options	Optimal Policy	Dynamic Switching	Echelon Order-up-to	Separating Plane
2 modes (0, 2)	12.2	0.3	0.9	1.9
3 modes (0, 1, 2)	12.4	0.3	4.8	11.4
3 modes (1, 2, 3)	200.0	3.2	4.9	12.8

Table 10.2. Average CPU time of Computing Policies Considered (in minutes)

From these experimental findings, we make the following observations: the dynamic switching policy is easy to compute (for small-sized problems) but the solution quality measured by the average per stage cost is not satisfactory (16.2% above the optimal cost on grand average). The echelon order-up-to policy takes a moderate computational effort to compute and yields reasonable results (11.9% above the optimal). The separating plane policy takes relatively intensive computational efforts to compute but yields very good results (5.8% above the optimal cost).

We have also conducted experiments for problem instances of larger size (maximum leadtimes ranging from 4 to 6) using the echelon order-up-to and the separating plane policies. For these problems, optimal policies are not known since neither value iteration nor policy iteration can be applied because of the size of the problem. In addition, the dynamic switching policy cannot be used due to the size of the state space. Initial experimental results suggest that the echelon order-up-to and the separating plane policies are capable of handling large-sized problems and the separating place policy outperforms the echelon order-up-to policy by roughly the same percentage which we observed for the small-sized problems. Further investigation is needed to determine how effective these policies are, possibly through establishing lower bounds on the average cost.

10.6 Concluding Remarks

Interorganizational electronic commerce is reshaping the way enterprises conduct business. In this chapter, we present a model of supply chain that explicitly addresses time and cost issues. We have coupled this model with inventory management and performed a computational study to find effective control policies. These models and computational mechanisms are essential for software agents to take advantage of abundant choices that come with the increasingly accessible worldwide information infrastructure, and to gain competitive edge in highly dynamic business environments.

We conclude this chapter by presenting some of the extensions to our agent-based supply chain model.

Other performance measures of supply chains such as product quality, service levels, etc., are not addressed in our current model. We plan to enrich our model to address these additional measures.

Our current model assumes that cost/leadtime information associated with each supply chain activity is known and deterministic. In practice, more often than not uncertainty will arise, especially in leadtime. Models that deal with the stochastic leadtime is highly desirable. We have proved that finding stochastic leadtime/cost efficient frontier is intractable if using the first order stochastic dominance alone. We are currently working on identifying other stochastic dominance relationships (possibly of the heuristic nature) that cut down computation.

In this chapter, we discussed how to integrate inventory decisions into the LCT model. We assumed that inventory is held at the root of the supply chain. We are currently working on integrating LCT with multi-echelon production/inventory models. Current multi-echelon inventory literature typically is not concerned with leadtime issues. To evaluate the impact of leadtime options in a multi-echelon setting is significant. The main research issues are: how to measure and evaluate the overall performance of such a complex supply chain, how to make inventory positioning decisions, how to compute efficiently multi-echelon inventory policies with leadtime options, etc.

Part III

Adaptive Information Agents

Introduction

Regarding the research and development of agent-based applications for the World Wide Web, learning personal assistants have become fashionable in the past four years. In general, an adaptive information agent is able to cope with any kind of dynamic change in an open information environment in which it has to execute its tasks. This might concern for example the location and content of data sources as well as user profiles and relevancy of delivered information.

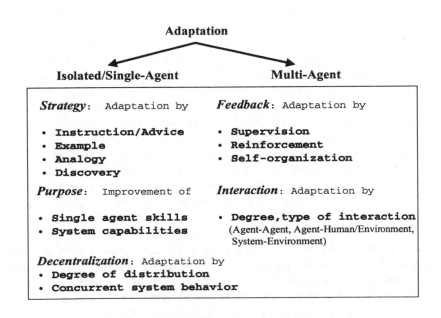

Fig. III.1. Categories of single and multi-agent learning

Adaptation of an agent to the environment can be done in an isolated way or in collaboration with other agents by using methods for single or multi-agent learning, respectively (see, e.g., [606, 246, 162, 164]). Learning among multiple agents may be collective, i.e., the agents adapt themselves in order to improve the benefits of the system. But system adaptation can even emerge without any collaboration when individual learning of one agent affects that of other agents in a beneficial way. An agent may exhibit adaptivity relative to a variety of internal reasoning processes concerning communication, coordination, planning, scheduling and task execution monitoring [652]. All approaches and systems for single or multi-agent adaptation may be evaluated by different criteria as shown in the figure above (see [707] for a detailed discussion). These criteria concern the

- applied strategy such as learning by example, analogy, or discovery,
- kind of feedback and guidance for the agents by means of reinforcement, supervised or unsupervised learning,
- type of interaction among agents, human users and the multi-agent system in the environment,
- purpose of learning as to improve the skills of a single agent or the whole system,
- distribution of data and concurrent computations for adaptivity in the multi-agent system.

Single adaptive information agents do not collaborate with other agents. Examples are almost all personal assistants and adaptive interface agents currently deployed on the Web such as WebMate [122], Butterfly [181], TrIAS [43], InfoAgent [151] and Letizia [383] (see also Chapter 12). The main purpose of such agents is to search for relevant information by anticipation of information needs and preferences of registered users. The adaptive search should be done as quickly and conveniently for the user as possible. In order to achieve this goal, different techniques for user profiling, reputation and recommendation have been invented. Most of them rely on observing the user's online activities and preferences as well as his credit assignments to the agent. Popular methods used by adaptive information agents include, e.g., heuristic breadth-first search in the Web [383, 386], reinforcement learning [387, 315], and efficient methods for knowledge discovery in databases [354] and information retrieval [261].

For systems of collaborating adaptive information agents, one of the most effective recommendation techniques is so-called collaborative filtering [208, 548, 682]. It is a powerful method for leveraging the information contained in user profiles. A document or product advertised on a vendor's site in the Web is recommended by the agent to his user if it has been recommended by other users who share similar likes and dislikes with the user.

This is in contrast to more traditional content-based information filtering [575, 572]. Alternative approaches for collaborative information filtering use, e.g., concepts and techniques from evolutionary programming and genetic algorithms (see for example Chapters 13, 14).

Adaptive information agents may also provide the user with a comfortable, advanced form of human-agent interaction (HAI). That includes,

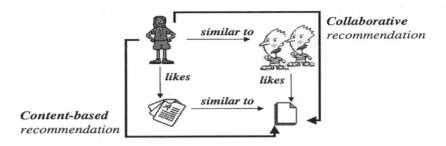

Fig. III.2. Collaborative information filtering

e.g., an effective multimedia representation of available information, learning of individual interaction styles and multi-dimensional navigation within cyberspace[6]. Such forms of interaction may be realized by synthetic characters, like animated creatures or lifelike, believable avatars [184, 41, 13], or utilization of techniques for affective computing [527, 679]. The success of HAI in practice also relies, for example, on more powerful 3D graphics acceleration and display hardware, significant increase of mass storage capacity, and ultra-high performance connections among sites in the Internet(-2) or corporate intranets as well as on standards for multimedia integration on the Web, like SMIL [634]. In general, HAI and its application to information agents appears to be of increasing interest in past few years. This includes in particular research efforts in intelligent information interfaces [302].

Most popular application domain of adaptive single and multi-agent systems is currently electronic commerce and information gathering in the Web. Equally important domains are manufacturing [86], digital libraries (see, e.g., Chapter 8), logistics, and telecommunication networks. Open questions and challenging research issues are among others:

- Mechanisms for learning successful negotiation and coordination strategies in a multi-agent system [420, 654, 535, 534, 747].
- When is adaptation of single agents harmful or beneficial for the system they are involved in [654, 669]?
- How can collaborative behavior among multiple adaptive information agents effectively evolve [20, 622, 97, 31]?
- Which methods for knowledge discovery, representation and maintenance are most appropriate for an information agent in an open environment?

A detailed overview of the relatively new research area of adaptation in multi-agent systems is given, e.g., in [706, 707]. The following contributions report on recent advances in the field of adaptive information agents.

---

[6] This relies in particular upon precise information about possibly different user communities, domains of discourse, tasks and context.

The Contributions

In Chapter 11, *Sandip Sen, Anish Biswas*, and *Sumit Ghosh* present a number
of very interesting approaches by which information agents can adapt to select information sources that satisfy performance requirements. The authors
interpret performance in terms both of the quality of information provided by
the sources and of the response time to process information requests. In the
chapter a couple of approaches are presented by which self-motivated agents
can learn to choose lightly loaded resources. The resultant load balancing
effect results in increasing throughput for the entire system as well as faster
response times for individual agents. In addition, an expected utility maximization approach to selecting information sources that are likely to deliver
better quality information to different classes of queries is presented.

There are only a few implementations of collaborating and adaptive information agents available; the next two chapters describe some of the most
interesting ones in more detail.

Alexandros Moukas and *Pattie Maes* present two different systems,
Amalthaea and Histos. Amalthaea is an evolving, market-like multi-agent
ecosystem for personalized filtering, discovery and monitoring of sites in the
Web. Like in distributed, adaptive knowledge bases [432], the approach uses
methods and notions from evolutionary computing and genetic algorithms
such as cross-over and fitness. Two different categories of agents are introduced in the system: filtering agents that model and monitor the interests of
the user and discovery agents that model the information sources. Agents that
are useful to the user or other agents may reproduce while low-performing
agents are destroyed by the system. The authors present results from various
experiments with different system configurations, and varying ratios of user
interests. Finally issues like fine-tuning of the system and how to achieve
equilibria in the ecosystem are discussed.

Transitive recommender systems generate recommendations of products
and documents in the Web from the connected paths of ratings of human
users themselves. This is in contrast to collaborative filtering where the recommendations are produced from the direct ratings of preferences. The authors describe such a recommender system, called Histos, and its basic reputation mechanism for highly connected online communities, and report some
experimental results.

Filippo Menczer presents another implemented approach of how to apply
machine learning methods for the construction of ecologies of adaptive information agents. These agents, called InfoSpiders, search online for relevant
informations by traversing links in the Web. As with Amalthaea, the idea of
InfoSpiders is to complement existing SearchBots in the Web with respect to
two of their main difficulties: scaling and personalization. The static character
of an index database as a basis for any search engine cannot keep up with the
rapid dynamics of the growing and changing Web. In addition, the general

character of the index building process cannot exploit the different profiles and needs of different users. SearchBots in the Web provide global starting points, and based on statistical features of the search space InfoSpiders can use topological features to guide their subsequent search. The author illustrates through a case study how InfoSpiders can be used to achieve scalability.

11. Adaptive Choice of Information Sources

Sandip Sen, Anish Biswas, and Sumit Ghosh

Department of Mathematical & Computer Sciences, University of Tulsa,
600 South College Avenue, Tulsa, OK 74104-3189, USA.
E-Mail: sandip@kolkata.mcs.utulsa.edu

Summary.
We present a number of learning approaches by which agents can adapt to select information sources that satisfy performance requirements. Performance can be interpreted both in terms of the quality of information provided by the sources, as well as the response time to process information requests. We first present a couple of approaches by which self-motivated agents can learn to choose lightly-loaded resources. The resultant load balancing effect results in increasing throughput for the entire system as well as faster response times for individual agents. We also present an expected utility maximization approach to selecting information sources that are likely to deliver better quality information to different classes of queries.

11.1 Introduction

Agent-based information gathering and recommendation systems are being reviewed with ever-increasing interest, and such systems are very likely to be the waive of the future [55, 682, 137, 146, 329, 667]. Such information agents will have to cater to a varied range of user needs. To effectively serve associated users, they need to be able to store, learn, and manipulate user preferences and changes in them. In addition, they need to flexibly react to changing environments. The latter requirement implies both the capability of agents to interact with heterogeneous information repositories, and also the capability of learning from and with other agents that have related capabilities. It is well-recognized that learning and adaptive information agents can provide several advantages over static agents whose hand-coded strategies can become outdated with changing environments or user requirements, preferences, etc.

In this chapter, we highlight some of our work on developing mechanisms that can be used by information agents to intelligently respond to changes in their environment. We will assume that such intelligent agents are embedded in open environments, i.e., they do not have significant control on either the composition of other agents they are likely to interact with or on the loads on information sources they use. The goal of adaptive information agents should include the following:

Decrease response time: Static designs can lead to significant deterioration in response time due to unforeseen changes in the environment that leads to congestion in information sources. Adaptive agents should be able to seek out alternative sources to circumvent congestion.

Improve stability: Adaptive agents need to coordinate with other agents so that system performance is predictable. For example, agents can learn to achieve a balanced load on system resources. Arrival or removal of information sources or agents can change the configuration of the environment, but a desired characteristic of the adaptive process would be to re-establish a stable configuration. Adaptive schemes that can converge to balanced and stable configurations can also improve the average throughput of a collection of distributed information sources.

Improve information quality: Static choice of information sources is not preferable when new information sources come online after an information agent has been fielded. In such cases, we would want our agents to seek out and exploit new opportunities as they surface. Also, often the quality of the same information source may vary over time. At other times, the quality of different sources can only be estimated by online exploration and different information sources may reveal different strengths or expertise. To identify such patterns, agents require the use of adaptive procedures that can balance exploration and exploitation of information source capabilities.

The above discussion highlights only some of the possible applications of intelligent information agents that we have investigated. In addition, a number of researchers report learning information agents acting as personal assistant agents [171, 407, 406]. Application areas range from learning user preferences for scheduling meetings [97], web-browsing preferences [515], recommending entertainment items like movies [406], etc. These applications have focused largely on agents learning user preferences. There has been also a growing body of literature in trying to unearth contents of information sources and learning to navigate the external information space. Our approach is closer to this second group of work in that we focus on utilizing opportunities and avoiding inefficiencies posed by the external information sources and interaction of other agents.

We should also clarify that most of the research we are going to summarize here is targeted towards developing and evaluating techniques for adaptation and how such techniques can be used in information agents. We will not be presenting details of implemented information systems, or any other system specific performance measurements.

The organization of the rest of the chapter is as follows: in Section 11.2 we provide a classification of the approaches to developing adaptive information agents that we will describe in the following sections; in Sections 11.3, 11.4, and 11.5 we detail three specific examples of different approaches to developing adaptive agents to serve the goals listed before; in Section 11.6 we summarize our main results and also identify other benefits of adaptive behavior in information agents.

11.2 A Categorization of Approaches to Developing Adaptive Information Agents

Our efforts in developing adaptive information agents have largely concentrated on making agents adaptive to environmental changes. In particular, we have investigated mechanisms to reduce response time, and increase system stability and the quality of retrieved information. Viewed another way, our work can be described as efforts to identify and utilize information sources that provide the desired level of performance in terms of throughput while providing information of a sufficient quality. The third criteria, i.e., stability, becomes relevant when our information agent is working in an environment with other adaptive information agents. In such cases, agents must coordinate their choices either by mutual modeling or by explicit communication. The goal would be to reduce imbalance in the system. This would also have the desirable side-effect of increasing the performance predictability in terms of response time.

Our approaches can be broadly classified into two classes:

Adaptive schemes to be used by multiple information agents: The main concern here is to identify lightly loaded resources. In these approaches, we assume all information sources provide the same quality information, and the throughput of a source decreases monotonically with its load. We study two different classes of solutions two this problem:

State-based: In the state-based scheme the adaptive agent bases its decision solely on the system state, or the observed load distribution on the information sources. All agents base their decision about choice of information source based on snapshots of the world at fixed intervals. The research problem that we investigate in this context is whether limiting the amount of system-wide state information available to agents can actually accelerate convergence of the system to stable configurations. We investigate the advantage gained by forming agent coalitions compared to the scenario where all agents choose their decisions independently.

Model-based: In the model-based approach, an agent considers not only the state, but also the expected behavior of other agents, in choosing an information source to query. The key research problem here is to learn the decision strategy of another agent based on observations of its past decisions. We analyze the stability of such systems when the heterogeneity of the group in terms of agent strategies and adaptive capabilities are varied.

Adaptive schemes to be used by a stand-alone information agent: The criteria to be optimized is the quality of information retrieved. In our formulation of this problem, an agent learns to choose from several information sources of varying expertise based on the context of the query. We assume different information sources have different expertise about different knowledge areas. The adaptive agent is posed the task to learn about the different expertise levels or specializations of the information sources. Using this knowledge, the agent can direct new queries to the most appropriate subset of information sources.

11.3 A State-Based Approach to Load Balancing

In this section we present our motivation for studying a state-based adaptive scheme that can be used by information agents to distribute their queries over a number of information sources without explicitly communication. Agents consider periodically observed load distributions over information sources in the system to decide on which source to use next. The basic assumption is that all loads can provide the same information, but the response time of a source increases with its workload. The goal would be to achieve a stable and balanced load distribution over the information sources (or resources, in short).

Within this context, we have studied one particular aspect of distributed decision-making in some detail: the effect of limited local knowledge on group behavior [604, 605]. Whereas intuition suggests that agents are equipped to make better local decisions with more complete and correct information, self-interested choices can at times lead to group instabilities with complete global information. We believe that reducing the amount of information available to such rational decision makers can be an effective mechanism for achieving system stability. The research question that we are asking is the following: Can limited local knowledge be a boon rather than a bane in an information system consisting of multiple agents?

To investigate this issue, we use a resource utilization problem where a number of agents are distributed between several identical resources. We assume that the cost of using any resource is directly proportional to its usage. This cost can be due to a delay in processing of the task in hand, or a reduction in the quality of the resource due to congestion. Hence, there is a justified need for agents to seek out and move to resources with lesser usage. Other researchers have shown that such systems can exhibit oscillatory or chaotic behavior where agents continually move between resources resulting in lack of system stability and ineffective utilization of system resources. The case has also been made that the introduction of asynchronous decision making or heterogeneous decision-making schemes can improve system convergence. We see our current work as providing a natural, complimentary mechanism for enabling agents in similar situations to quickly converge to the optimal system state.

We assume that there are m agents and n identical resources (in general, $m > n$). Moreover, resources are neither introduced nor eliminated during the life time of the agents. All agents remain active and they make their decisions synchronously. At any time instant, an agent uses only one resource, and over time tries to move to a resource that is less used by other agents. In this study, we show that when an agent has less knowledge about the utilization of each resource in the resource set, the contention for resources decreases and results in quicker convergence to stable resource usage.

At present we model the knowledge of an agent about the resources by using an *r-window*. An r-window is a window through which an agent can observe the load on some of its neighboring resources. At each time step, each agent has to make the following decision: whether it should continue to use the present resource or should it move to another resource in its r-window with less utilization.

It can be shown that a deterministic and greedy decision procedure of choosing the resource with the lowest utilization in the r-window will lead to system oscillations. Hence, we are motivated to use a probabilistic decision procedure. The probability that an agent will shift from the current resource to another resource is inversely proportional to the difference of the usage of these two resource. The particular procedure that we use first calculates the probability of moving to each of the resources in the r-window, and then normalizes theses values by the corresponding sum. The probability of an agent that decides to continue to use the same resource i is given by:

$$f_{ii} = \frac{1}{1 + \tau \exp^{\frac{r_i - \alpha}{\beta}}}, \tag{11.1}$$

where r_i is the number of agents currently using resource i (this is also the utilization of or load on that resource), and τ, α, and β are control parameters. On the other hand, the probability of moving to another resource $j \neq i$ is given by:

$$f_{ij} = \begin{cases} 1 - \frac{1}{1 + \tau \exp^{\frac{r_i - r_j - \alpha}{\beta}}} & \text{if } j \in W_i \ \& \ r_i > r_j, \\ 0 & \text{otherwise,} \end{cases} \tag{11.2}$$

where W_i are the resources within the r-window of an agent using resource i. Now, the probability that an agent a_k occupying a resource i will occupy a resource j in the next time step is given by normalizing the above terms:

$$Pr(i, j) = \frac{f_{ij}}{\sum_j f_{ij}}. \tag{11.3}$$

11.3.1 Results and Analysis

Using a series of experiments we have reached the following conclusions:

- If agents are allowed access to the status of smaller number of resources, the loads on different resources are balanced in less time.
- Convergence rate to stable configurations can be significantly enhanced if local groups make their decisions sequentially.

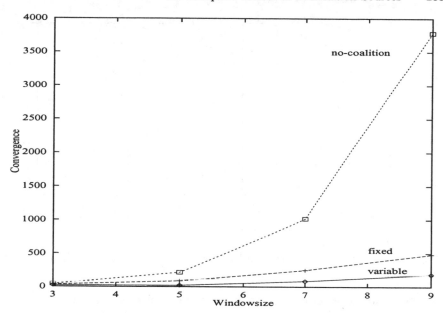

Fig. 11.1. Number of steps to convergence for different r-window sizes and with or without the use of coalitions.

We assume that the resources are arranged in a ring and each agent knows the number of agents using the resource it is using and the neighboring resources within the r-window to the left and right. Each time step consists of all agents making a decision regarding which resource to use next. In figure 11.1 we present experimental results with 27 agents using 9 resources. For now, consider the plot labeled "no-coalition" (the other plots will be discussed in Section 11.3.1). The data for these plots are averaged over 10 random initial assignments of agents to resources. Starting from r-window size of 3, as we increase the size of the window to 9, we observe that the system takes much more time on the average to stabilize. The system can only converge to the optimal state with uniform distribution of agents to resources. This is the only state for which the probabilities for any agent moving out of any resource is zero. It is clear from the figure that increasing the window size leads to considerable increase in the time taken by the system to converge to a stable state.

We conjectured that some of the convergence problems mentioned above can be alleviated by forming coalitions of agents, where agents belonging to a given coalition will cooperatively decide on their next move. For example, within any such coalition, agents may take turns in selecting which resource they are going to occupy in the next time step and then inform other agents in the coalition about that decision. Thus, agents will have more up-to date and accurate information about the likely resource usages in the next time step,

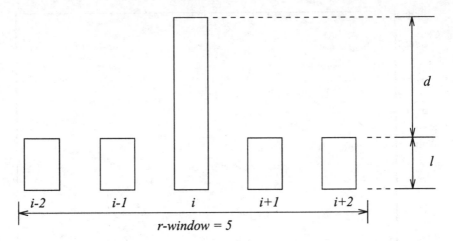

Fig. 11.2. Resource i has d agents more than every other resource in its r-window.

and hence are in a position to make a more effective movement decision. In the extreme case, if all agents form one coalition and the R-window included all resources, each agent will have a complete and correct global information at all times, and the system will immediately converge if each agent moves to the least used resource at the time it makes its movement decision.

We studied two modes of forming coalitions: in the first mode agents were randomly partitioned into equal-sized coalitions before the start of the simulation and no agents ever changed coalitions (we use a coalition size of 5); in the second mode, agents occupying the same resource at any given time formed a coalition and hence coalitions changed from one time step to the next. In both the groups, an individual agent's movement decision is not only based on the current utilization of the resources within its r-window but is also guided by the actual status of those resources after some of the other agents in its group have decided on their moves.

The results of experiments with agent coalitions are shown in the figure 11.1. Runs with coalitions converged significantly faster than runs with no coalitions. This was particularly true for larger window sizes where runs without coalition often took extremely long times to converge.

Probabilistic Analysis. We now present a probabilistic analysis of the behavior of the system to explain slower convergence of the system when agents use larger r-windows, i.e., have more information available locally to base their decisions on.

Consider a resource i which has higher load than the surrounding resources (as shown in the figure 11.2). We further assume that n agents are using that resource at a given instance of time. Let X be a random variable corresponding the number of agents who will not leave the resource in the

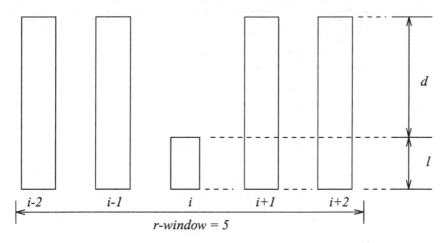

Fig. 11.3. Resource i has d agents less than every other resource in the r-window.

next time step. Therefore, values for X follow a binomial distribution with probability $Pr(i,i)$. The expected value of X is therefore given by:

$$E[X] = nPr(i,i), \tag{11.4}$$

and the variance of X is given by:

$$Var[X] = nPr(i,i)(1 - Pr(i,i)). \tag{11.5}$$

Similarly, as the figure 11.3 shows, the resource i is being less utilized when compared with its neighbors. Obviously there will be a tendency of an agent who is currently not using i to move to resource i. Let Y be the random variable corresponding to the number of agents who will move into resource i in the next time step. Therefore values for Y follow a binomial distribution with the probability $\sum_{j \neq i} Pr(j,i)$. We can also think of Y as a sum of several independent binomially distributed random variables, Y_{ji}, where Y_{ji} corresponds to the number of agents who will move into resource i from resource j in the next time step. Y_{ji} has an expected value of $nPr(j,i)$ and a variance of $nPr(j,i)(1 - Pr(j,i))$. Therefore, the expected values of Y is given by:

$$E[Y] = \sum_{j \neq i} nPr(j,i). \tag{11.6}$$

And the corresponding variance is:

$$Var[Y] = \sum_{j \neq i} nPr(j,i)(1 - Pr(j,i)). \tag{11.7}$$

Let us now analyze the implications of these analysis. Figure 11.4 plots the expressions in equations 11.4 and 11.5 for different d values and different r-window sizes. The plot for expectations of X confirms the intuition that with

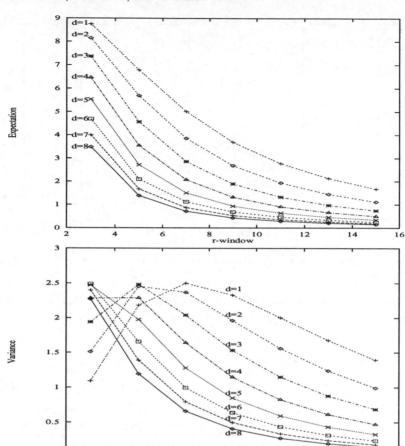

Fig. 11.4. Expectation and variance of an agent staying in the current resource, and $l + d = 10$.

larger window sizes and larger d values (difference between current resource load and the loads on the neighboring resources), a larger number of agents are expected to move out of the current resource. But figure 11.4 also reveals a very interesting phenomena. For large window sizes, the variance of the number of agents staying in the resource increases as the difference between the loads of the current and neighboring resource decreases. The two plots together can be used to draw the following conclusion: initially the agents will quickly spread out from a highly utilized resource to neighboring, less utilized resources. But when all resources have approximately the same load, high variance will probably cause some imbalance in the resource usages leading the system back towards the initial situation. This kind of behavior can go on in a cyclical manner for some time.

The situation is precisely the opposite for small window sizes: here, the variance decreases with the decreasing difference between the current and the neighboring resource loads. This means that even though there is a relatively slower convergence towards a near-uniform distribution of agents to resources (as inferred from the expectations plot), there is a continuing pressure towards a completely uniform distribution of agents to resources. This process is further helped by a greater inertia of moving out of the current resource at smaller r-window sizes as seen from expectation plot in figure 11.5 (this plot corresponds to agents moving in to a lesser loaded resources from surrounding highly loaded resources).

Figure 11.5 plots the expressions in equations 11.6 and 11.7 for different d values and different r-window sizes. The variance plot in this figure also supports a similar trend. Here, for all window sizes, the variance of the number of agents moving to the less loaded resource increases with decreasing difference between the loads of the less loaded resource and the surrounding resources. However, the increase in variance for small window sizes is much less compared to when large window sizes are used. This means that when the system comes to a near uniform agent distribution to resources, larger instabilities can be introduced when using larger window sizes. Figures 11.4 and 11.5, therefore, help us develop a more more formal explanation of the faster system convergence with smaller windows.

Adaptive Agents. The probabilistic analysis of agent movements in Section 11.3.1 suggests a possible improvement in agent behaviors over the use of fixed r-window sizes that we have seen so far. We will briefly revisit the analysis here to precisely identify the scope for improvement. From figure 11.4 we observed that for large r-windows, the variance of the number of agents staying in the resource increases as the difference between the utilization of the current resource usage and the neighboring resource usages decreases. The opposite is the case for small r-windows. Also, the expected value of the number of agents leaving the resource more loaded than its neighbors is higher for large rather than small r-windows. Hence, if the initial distribution of agents to resources had a marked imbalance and if the agents were using a large r-window, agents will quickly spread out to a near uniform distribution. At this point, the discrepancy of usage between neighboring resources will be much less than it was at the initial state. Now, from figure 11.4, agents will be better served to use a small, rather than large, r-window to reduce the variability in their movements in the next time steps (which is equivalent to a reduction in the variance in the occupancy of the associated resources). Therefore, a likely effective adaptive agent strategy would be to initially use a large r-window size, but quickly reduce this size after some initial movements.

Admittedly, our analysis is based on idealized scenarios in figures 11.2 and 11.3, where all but one resource have the same occupancy. Our conjecture is that the analysis will still apply, with some loss of accuracy, to more realistic situations where resource occupancies are more graded. To verify

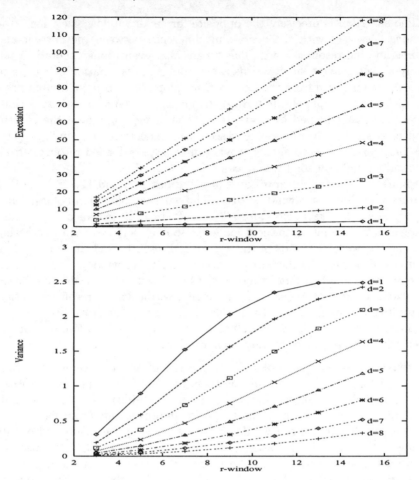

Fig. 11.5. Expectation and variance of an agent moving to the less used resource, and $l + d = 10$.

our conjecture, we ran some experiments with the following adaptive agent decision mechanism for dynamically selecting an r-window size: *agents initially start with an r-window which includes all resources; any time an agent changes resources consecutively for k time steps, it narrows its r-window size down to 3 (i.e., from thereon the agent considers only the load of the current and neighboring resource when making a movement decision).* The motivation for this strategy is that if an agent continually jumps from one resource to another, the system is unstable. Assuming that using too much global information is the cause of this instability, the agent decides to focus on its current neighborhood.

In a set of exploratory experiments we observed best results when we used $k = 1$ in the above-mentioned decision mechanism, i.e., each agent reduced the window size the first time it moves from the resource that it initially occupied. Subsequently, we ran experiments using both adaptive and static window sizes and with 27 agents and 9 resources. In our prior experiments the initial allocation of agents to resources was obtained by using a uniformly distributed random number generator. This resulted in almost uniform resource usage to begin with. However, we are more interested in evaluating agent strategies when the initial distribution is particularly skewed. We generated 10 random scenarios each for skewed and uniform initial distributions of agents to resources. For each initial distribution, experiments were run with 10 random seeds of the random number generator (the agent algorithms use random numbers to make probabilistic choices). Table 11.1 presents results from these set of experiments. The table clearly demonstrates the effectiveness of our proposed adaptive strategy for choosing r-window size over the best static-window size choice (always using a window size of 3).

Initial distribution	Window size=3	Adaptive window sizing	Improvement
Skewed	47.62	37.8	21%
Uniform	45.74	44.42	3%

Table 11.1. Average time steps taken to convergence with adaptive and static window sizes. Experiments involved 27 agents and 9 resources.

It is instructive to note that while the improvement of the adaptive scheme over the static choice is remarkable when the initial agent distribution is skewed, the corresponding improvement for uniform initial agent distribution is minimal. This observation lends further credence to the accuracy of our probabilistic analysis, which was developed with skewed distributions.

11.3.2 Summary

In this study we investigated the problem of resource utilization and global performance based on limited local information. The agents with a limited view of global scenario converged faster to optimal states. We provide a probabilistic analysis that sheds some light on this interesting phenomenon. It appears that strategic, limited usage of local knowledge may be an effective way to address stability issues in open systems containing multiple information agents.

Another important lesson from this set of experiments is that in order for agents to be flexible to changing environmental demands, it is more appropriate to provide a coalition formation and dissolution mechanism that utilizes current problem loads and inter-relationships between agents. We believe that for even larger window sizes and/or with more resources, the system may not converge if some form of coalitions is not used.

11.4 A Model-Based Approach to Load Balancing

Adaptive information agents can benefit by modeling other information agents in their environment. In particular, being able to predict decisions to be taken by other agents enables an agent to improve its own utility. We have developed a learning mechanism by which an agent can approximately model the decision function used by another agent given a collection of decisions made by that agent. We consider the case of binary decisions based on a single decision variable. We have developed a polynomial time, incremental algorithm to adjust the coefficients of a family of orthogonal functions, Chebychev polynomials [239], to develop a model of other agent's decision function. We have proved that, in the limit, this algorithm is guaranteed to produce an accurate model.

11.4.1 Modeling Agent Decision Functions Using Chebychev Polynomials

Chebychev polynomials are a family of orthogonal polynomials [239]. Any function $f(x)$ may be approximated by a weighted sum of these polynomial functions with an appropriate selection of the coefficients.

$$f(x) = \frac{a_0}{2} + \sum_{i=1}^{\infty} a_i * T_i(x)$$

where

$$T_n(x) = \cos(n * \cos^{-1}(x))$$

and

$$a_i = \frac{2}{\pi} \int_{-1}^{1} \frac{f(x) * T_i(x)}{\sqrt{1 - x^2}} dx$$

Let $f(x)$ be the target function in and $\hat{f}(x)$ be the approximation of it based on the set of samples $S = \{S_j\}$, where $S_j = \langle x_j, v_{x_j} \rangle \forall j = 1, 2, \ldots, k$ and $k =$ Number of instances. We have $v_{x_j} \in [True, False]$. We may have to change the scale for the values x_j, so that all the values are in the range $[-1 : 1]$ and we get the approximated function in the range $[-1 : 1]$, which we may need to scale back to get the desired value.

Let n be the number of Chebychev polynomials we are going to use for the purpose of learning. Let $T_i(x)$ $i \in [0..n]$ be the Chebychev polynomials. The steps of the algorithm are:

1. Initialize $C_i = 0, \quad \forall i = 0, 1, 2, \ldots, n$
2. For all j do

3. $\forall i = 0, 1, 2, \ldots, n$
   If $v_{x_j} = $T then,

$$C_i \leftarrow C_i + \frac{T_i(x)}{\sqrt{1 - x^2}}$$

4. $\forall i = 0, 1, 2, \ldots, n$
   If $v_{x_j} = $F then,

$$C_i \leftarrow C_i - \frac{T_i(x)}{\sqrt{1 - x^2}}$$

5. End for
6. Set

$$\hat{f}(x) = K * (\frac{C_0}{2} + \sum_{i=1}^{n} C_i * T_i(x))$$

   where $K = \psi(k)$, is function of number of interactions.
7. Set

$$\hat{f}(x) \leftarrow \hat{f}(x) + 0.5$$

Theorem 1 Under complete information the algorithm can approximate the probability function.
Proof: See Appendix.

Experimental Results. We applied this modeling approach to the problem of balancing the loads on resources in a distributed system. In this domain, each of a set of A agents receive JR jobs to process per unit time. There are P resources, each of which can process jobs at the rate of SR jobs per unit time. Each resource also has an unbounded input queue on which jobs can be placed. When an agent receives a job to process, it visits the resources in some random order. For each processor, it looks at the input queue length of waiting jobs, and then samples a probability function, P, with this queue length to decide whether or not to place the job on this queue. This process is repeated until the job is assigned. This decision time to select a resource is assumed to be negligible. We assume that each agent observes the load on the resource in which another agent places a job as well as the number of previous visits in which it did not place the job. The resources visited or the loads on those resources is not available to other agents. A modeling agent will use the information available about the decisions taken by other agents to find resources which are less likely to be selected by other agents. If only some of the agents in the system are modelers, this approach can produce more equitable distribution of jobs to resources. In our experiments we have used 50 agents, 5 resources, JR=1, and SR=10. The performance metric we want to minimize is the standard deviation of the queue-lengths.

The non-modeling agents are assumed to be using either a greedy strategy of choosing the minimum loaded resource after visiting all resources (these

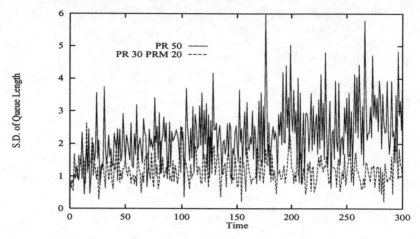

Fig. 11.6. Homogeneous P-agent group Vs. Mixed P and M-agent groups. PR n PRM m implies a group with n P-agents and m M-agents.

are called G-agents), or choosing the resource based on a probability function of the queue-length (these are called P-agents). The probability function used by P-agents to decide on submission of a job to a resource with current queue length Ql is selected to be

$$P(Ql) = -0.02 * Ql + 0.2.$$

The modeling agents (M-agents) choose the probability for submission from the probability of submission of other agents in that resource. The probability that a modeling agent i is going to submit its job to resource j is given by:

$$P_{ij} = min(1, 10 - \sum_{a \in A - \{i\}} P_{aj}).$$

Given that with equal load distribution, 10 jobs would be submitted per time period per resource, this function means that modeling agents are likely to choose resources that are expected to have lower than average submission of new jobs.

We ran experiments both homogeneous groups of P-agents and G-agents, as well as when we mix some M-agents in each of these groups. Results from homogeneous and mixed groups are shown in figures 11.6 and 11.7. We observe that in general, addition of M-agents reduces the standard deviation of loads across the resources. This implies that our modeling scheme enables agents to balance loads more effectively. The performance is particularly noticeable in the case of G-agents. We have further observed that a homogeneous group of M-agents do not produce effective performance. This is probably due to the instability produced by concurrent learning by too many agents.

In open systems, agent groups may migrate or agents can change policies over time. Hence, it is necessary for any agent to be able to adapt to new

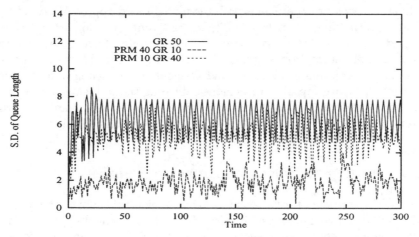

Fig. 11.7. Homogeneous G-agent group Vs. Mixed G and M-agent groups. PRM n GR m implies a group with n M-agents and m G-agents.

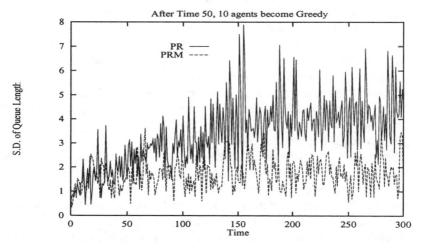

Fig. 11.8. Adaptation by modeling agents in a dynamic environment when other agents change their decision function.

environments for maintaining effective system performance. To simulate such a changing environment, we ran a farther set of experiments in which 20 P-agents are substituted with G-agents after 50 time steps. Figure 11.8 presents results comparing the situation when the rest 30 agents are P-agents and when they are M-agents. The figure clearly demonstrate that the M-agents are able to maintain system performance while the P-agents cannot. This set of experiments demonstrate that our modeling scheme is indeed incremental in nature, and is able to track changes in agent behaviors.

In summary, our experiments with the model-based approach to load balancing confirm that whereas a homogeneous group of modeling agents do not perform much better than a homogeneous group of greedy agents, the throughput of information sources are significantly enhanced when heterogeneous groups containing modeling and G-agents or modeling and P-agents are used. Also, we are able to demonstrate that the modeling mechanism can incrementally adjust to changing behaviors of other agents and maintain system performance when other agents change their decision function.

11.5 Learning to Select Information Sources

Agents that learn about other agents and can exploit this information possess a distinct advantage in competitive situations. Games provide stylized adversarial environments to study agent learning strategies. We have developed a scheme for learning opponent action probabilities and a utility maximization framework that exploits this learned opponent model. We have shown that the proposed expected utility maximization strategy generalizes the traditional maximin strategy, and allows players to benefit by taking calculated risks that are avoided by the maximin strategy [603]. To show the general applicability of the expected utility maximization framework, we have also developed an agent that learns to select one of several search engines to query depending on the nature of the query posed by the user. Assuming different search engines are good for different kinds of queries, our agent will use its experience to probabilistically model the expected utility to be obtained from these search engines given the category of a query.

Decision theoretic principles can be used by agents to make rational action choices in the face of environmental uncertainty. An agent is rational if and only if it chooses an action that yields the highest expected utility, averaged over all the possible outcomes. This is called the principle of Maximum Expected Utility. If the outcome of an action a at a state E is uncertain and can result in one of several possible outcomes $Result_i(a)$, and the function $U(S)$ measures the utility of state S to the agent, then the expected utility of taking action a in state E can be expressed as

$$EU(a|E) = \sum_i Pr(Result_i(a)|E, Do(a)) \times U(Result_i(a)),$$

where $Pr(.)$ represents probabilities, $Do(a)$ represents the proposition that action a is executed in the current state, and i ranges over different outcomes. Let A be the set of actions available to the agent. The MEU principle prescribes that the agent would choose the action that maximizes expected utility: $MEU(A, E) = argmax_{a \in A} EU(a|E)$.

We have shown that MEU agents can outperform minimax players in board game situations. To demonstrate the applicability of the MEU principle in non-game situations, we investigated the decision problem of an agent choosing one of several search engines for performing category based search on the internet so as to maximize the quality of information retrieved. The agent has the option of choosing from a finite set of search engines for its search queries on a finite set of categories. The performance of the search engines are modeled probabilistically. We have approximated the utilities of the search engines discretely by assuming the utility to be the number of quality matches returned with a corresponding probability. Our search agent learns these probabilities from experience and calculates the expected utilities for each of the search engines for different categories.

When queried for a particular category of search, the agent chooses the search engine with the maximum expected utility (MEU). We have experimented with a single search category and three simulated search engines. Each search engine is defined by a probability distribution over one of several utility values. The search engine selection agent learns an approximation of these probabilities by repeatedly querying the search engines. Once the probabilities are learned, the expected utilities of each of the search engines are calculated and the MEU strategy chooses the search engine with the maximum expected utility.

To evaluate the performance of the MEU strategy we compare it against the following heuristic strategy. For N queries, each of the three search engine is queried. The search engine that returns the highest utility result in the most number of such cases is then selected for subsequent usage (this strategy is similar to what naive users use to select a search engine based on their initial experience with search engines). This can be termed as the *most-often-liked* heuristics.

Our experiments show that the MEU strategy outperforms the most-often-liked heuristic when the probability distribution for the search engines are skewed such that one search engine returns very high utilities with relatively small probabilities. When all utilities are returned equiprobably, the MEU and most-often-liked heuristic returns identical choices. Two such situations are depicted in figure 11.9. In the figures the leaf values represent utilities of different results returned by the search engines, and the numbers on the edges connecting the leaf nodes denote the probability of returning that utility. The internal nodes represent the different search engines, and the branches from the root to these nodes are labeled with are labeled with expected utility values of choosing that search engine (M) and the number of times that search engine returned the highest quality in N samplings (H). MEU chooses the search engine with the highest M value, and most-often-liked heuristic chooses the search engine with the highest H values. Their choices are identical in the scenario represented in figure 11.9(a), but differ in the scenario represented in figure 11.9(b).

These results are quite preliminary, and we plan to further investigate the applicability of MEU strategies on multiple categories, more search engines, and on more complex queries with disjunctions and conjunctions. Special operators have to be defined for combining results for queries that span multiple categories.

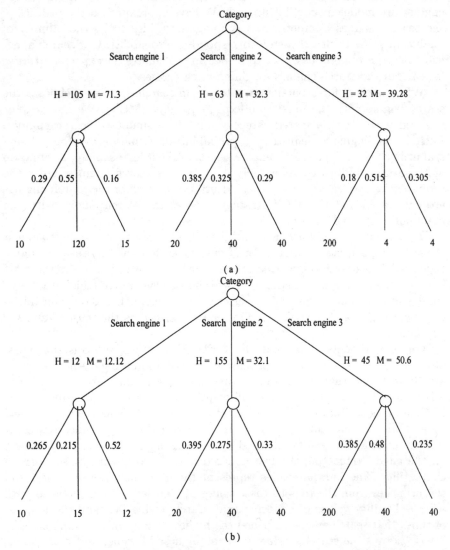

Fig. 11.9. (a) Identical choice by MEU and most-often-liked heuristics for a more uniform distribution. (b) MEU and most-often-liked heuristics select different sources for skewed distributions.

11.6 Observations

In this chapter, we have summarized the findings and highlighted important results from some of our research projects in developing computational mechanisms that can be used by information agents to adapt to their environment. In particular, we have concentrated on individual learning agents which use feedback from their environment and observations of the actions taken by other agent to adaptively choose information sources. The goal has been to improve the quality of the information obtained or reduce congestion in sources, thereby improving response time. Another concern has been to develop robust procedures for arriving at stable configuration of querying the information sources to ensure predictability of system performance.

We have investigated adaptive agents that do or do not explicitly model the behavior of other agents. Agents that do not explicitly model other agents can be made to converge faster to stable distributions by introducing asynchrony of some form. In our approach, we have used restricted, differential system view to introduce this asynchrony. Agents that do model other agent raises other interesting issues not inherent in pure state-based agent systems. For example, homogeneous groups of adaptive agent appears to be acting at cross-purposes. That is, when everyone models everyone else, circular reasoning can actually deteriorate performance. However, when we evaluate a mix of adaptive and static-strategy agents, everyone benefits.

We are also evaluating an expected utility maximizing paradigm to develop on or off-line learning agents that can learn to query different information sources based on query type. Such adaptive agents can be used to advantage in selecting one or few information sources when quality information has to be returned in real-time.

A number of other applications of adaptive information agents can be envisaged. These include:

Bargaining agents: Agents that can learn to negotiate with other agents to increase their capability. We can envisage the formation of coalitions of information agents to increase coverage by reducing overlap. Agents within a coalition agree to specialize in different areas and then share the information within the coalition as necessary.

Learning to organize information: Agents that adapt to information demands to internally organize information such that frequently asked queries are answered more promptly. Past queries can also be used to model user preferences and requirements, and this can trigger the gathering of other information that may be of interest to the user. The goal is to keep ahead of the demand by foreseeing future queries.

Acknowledgments:. These research projects have been supported, in part, by the National Science Foundation under a Research Initiation Award IRI-9410180 and a CAREER award IRI-9702672. We would also like to acknowledge the contribution of Neeraj Arora and Shounak Roychowdhury towards developing and evaluating some of the approaches referred to in this chapter.

12. Personal Assistants for the Web: An MIT Perspective

Henry Lieberman

MIT Media Laboratory, Cambridge, MA 02139, USA.
E-Mail: Lieber@media.mit.edu

Summary.

The growing complexity of sources of information and users' needs for information is fast outstripping the manual browsing and searching interfaces of the past. A long-term approach to the complexity problem is to design intelligent information agents that provide active assistance in the process of finding and organizing information. These agents differ from conventional information retrieval in how they interact with the user and the dynamic nature of the information they deal with. This article surveys some work at the MIT Media Lab in developing intelligent information agents, especially as assistants to users browsing the Web. These agents don't replace conventional browsing or direct manipulation interfaces, but work with such interfaces to learn from interaction with the user, anticipate the user's needs, and connect the user with other people who may share his or her interests.

12.1 Introduction

The sudden increase in the availability of information as a result of the World Wide Web has brought the problem of information complexity into sharp focus. Despite enormous efforts in categorizing information, linking information and search and retrieval, this complexity has not yet been tamed.

A possible approach to a solution to information management is to delegate some of the tasks of finding, retrieving, organizing, and presenting information from the human to some software that acts on behalf of the user. We term this category of software *intelligent information agents*.

By "intelligent", we don't necessarily mean that the computer is as intelligent as a human. This is a difficult goal that will remain out of range for the foreseeable future. Yet there are many kinds of intelligent behavior for which it is feasible to embed similar behavior in the computer, at least for simple cases. Simple learning, inference, user modeling and context sensitivity, does make a significant difference in the perceived competence of the system. The key is to understand when and how limited forms of inference and learning can actually be of real assistance, so that the user and the machine can form a fruitful partnership.

By an "information agent", we mean an agent that operates in the domain of some external information space, and whose task is to assist the user in accessing and managing such information. Traditionally, those information spaces resided in databases, but they are now best exemplified by the Web, and are becoming increasingly dynamic and heterogeneous all the time.

The word "agent" itself is controversial, even within the fields of artificial intelligence and human-computer interaction. It is hard to agree on a single definition, but some of the characteristics associated with agent software, besides intelligence per se, are autonomy, distributed computing, and interface agents that personify the software using an anthropomorphic character. But for the purposes of this article, the most important aspect of an agent is that the user can view it as an assistant. Today's so-called direct-manipulation software conceptualizes the computer as a box of tools, where each menu command or icon represents a single tool, specialized for a single job. Fine, but the burden is still on the user to decide which tool to use, and when. Tomorrow's agent software will perform more like a human assistant, providing help and suggestions, proactively trying to anticipate needs, and automating complex procedures.

This chapter will present some examples of intelligent information agents under development at the MIT Media Laboratory and discuss issues that arise in the development of such agents. No attempt will be made to cover this rapidly growing field comprehensively, but hopefully these examples and issues will give the reader a flavor of the era of intelligent information agents which is ahead of us.

12.2 Intelligent Information Agents Can Break the Knowledge Bottleneck

For years, artificial intelligence was plagued by the *knowledge bottleneck*. [Feigenbaum 83] It was possible for people to build systems that had sophisticated inference and learning procedures, but when knowledge had to be coded by hand in formal languages, a process called *knowledge engineering*, it was difficult to build into a system enough knowledge to actually perform significantly well on tasks of real interest to people.

Now, all that has changed. With the advent of the Web, every computer connected to the Internet has quick access to huge bodies of computer-readable information on every conceivable subject. But the problem is that the information is highly unstructured, most in the form of natural language or pictures understandable only by humans. However, many ways of partially understanding the information available on the Web exist, and so the game has shifted to how to leverage that partial understanding into effective assistance to the user.

The Web is the world's biggest semantic network. Two pages are linked on the Web only because some person thought that a person looking at one might also want to see the other. That information can be used equally by information agents. However, unlike a semantic network, there is no formalization of the semantics of the link. Therefore the agent must perform some inference to deduce the meaning of the link.

The range of possible intelligent information agents is as wide as the kinds of information that appear on the Web, and as diverse as the information needs and preferences of its users. No one kind of agent will solve everyone's information needs. But many kinds of information manipulation occur repeatedly, many users share common generic information needs, and knowledge of specific domains, users, or subject matter can be brought into play. Thus it makes sense to build agents that automate common patterns of assistance that can be helpful to users.

12.3 Intelligent Information Agents and Conventional Information Retrieval

The traditional discipline concerned with the management of information spaces is Information Retrieval (IR). Information retrieval has been traditionally concerned with information in relatively static databases, usually concentrated in a single place geographically, and organized in records, according to some form of schema or pattern. On the Web, though, data is linked in a hypertext fashion, may be distributed, is unstructured, and may contain non-textual information. Nevertheless, many techniques developed in Information Retrieval are indeed quite relevant to information agents. Search engines such as AltaVista, Lycos, Excite, Infoseek, and HotBot could be considered as a kind of simple retrieval agent, and have become an integral part of every user's interface with the Web. These engines use IR keyword-frequency analysis techniques for analyzing the subject matter of documents, and for matching documents.

As an example of such techniques, TFIDF (term frequency times inverse document frequency) is often used by both search engines and by agents as a means of heuristically approximating subject classification. It weights frequently-appearing terms that have the maximum power to distinguish the document from other documents in a corpus. An example of a clustering technique is Latent Semantic Indexing, which represents a document as a vector space of terms, and finds new basis vectors that better characterize the space in fewer dimensions. Such clustering may deal more effectively with the problem that many terms can be synonymous or have minor variations, but require more computation than simple keyword frequency analysis.

Nevertheless, it is important to understand that the task that information agents are trying to do differs significantly from the underlying assumptions of the field of Information Retrieval [Salton 89]. IR assumes a conversational paradigm, where in each interaction, the user emits a *query* and the system chooses a subset of the information space to return as *hits*. The user evaluates the hits, and may either refine the query or place a new one. This paradigm may not apply directly to information agents. Users may not know how to precisely express a query that says what it is they want. Indeed, the task of the information agent is often to figure out what kind of query is appropriate.

The conversational nature of the IR system may also not apply. Increasingly, information agents will be continuously active, proactively trying to gather information even without the user's explicit command. There may be no clear sense in which a query is ever "finished", since agents may operate over the long term. Because systems may learn over time, the same query expressed at different times or by different users may have very different results.

Technical notions that appear in the information retrieval literature need to be reconsidered. Some IR techniques, such as TFIDF, depend on computation relative to a corpus, assumed to be a traditional database. On the Web, there is no such thing as the collection of "all the documents"; the Web is not static, and any static snapshot is likely to be too large to be computationally feasible. The traditional measures of information retrieval are *precision*, which measures how likely the hits are to satisfy the query, and *recall*, which measures what fraction of the corpus satisfying the query is reflected in the hits. Both measures lose much of their sense, since both the query and the corpus may be open-ended. Further, while traditional databases and corpora are disconnected sets of entries, the Web is a highly structured network. Retrieval and search engines take no advantage of the interconnection of links, and that is precisely what information agents can do.

12.4 From Information Retrieval to Information Reconnaissance

12.4.1 Letizia

Letizia [Lieberman 95, 97], is an example of the new breed of intelligent information agents. Letizia is a new kind of agent, which might be called an *information reconnaissance* agent. In the military, a reconnaissance mission is one which surveys unknown territory before the troops are committed to entering it. On a Web page, every link is unknown territory, and clicking on a link involves a leap of faith that the page referenced by the link will in fact be of interest. That leap of faith is not always justified. If the page turns out not to be interesting, you can always return, but time is lost, and more importantly, frustration ensues.

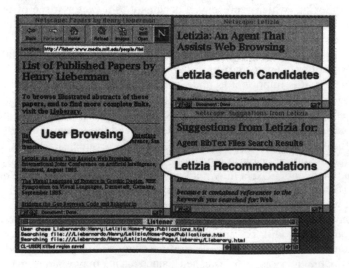

Letizia shows recommendations while the user browses

But what if an information agent could perform reconnaissance, constantly checking out links from whatever page you are on, much faster than you could yourself? It could rapidly bring the pages that are most interesting to your attention, saving time and energy. It could detect hidden traps and time-wasting junk.

Letizia is an information reconnaissance agent for the Web. It operates with a conventional Web browser, such as Netscape, in a multiple-window configuration. As you are looking at a page, Letizia does an incremental breadth-first search from the current page, previewing the links. It provides a continuous display of recommended Web pages.

But to be effective in this job, the agent has to know you, to be able to anticipate what you might think of the page. Many kinds of personalized news services on the Web, such as My Yahoo, require the user to fill out questionnaires with lengthy lists of interest keywords. And if the user's interests change, he or she must return and refill out the questionnaires, which users rarely do.

Instead, Letizia uses a machine learning approach. It observes the user's behavior, and tries to infer interest automatically. It records every choice the user makes in the browser, and reads every page the user reads. It takes the act of viewing a page as evidence of an interest in the page without asking for explicit user evaluation of the page, although it could perhaps be improved by some sort of evaluative feedback from the user. It applies a modified TFIDF analysis to each page, and adds the result to a user profile, which is essentially a list of weighted keywords. The notion of "inverse document frequency" in traditional TFIDF doesn't quite make sense for Letizia, since there is no way to compute it over all the documents in the Web. Instead the inverse document frequency is computed dynamically over the user's browsing history. This has the consequence that the IDF component itself is time-dependent, so that words that are considered important relative to the user's browsing history will be learned over time.

Letizia's approach is that search through the information space is a co-operative venture between the user and the information agent. Each contributes what it does best. The computer is good at doing fast searching. The human is good at deciding whether a page is interesting or not. So the agent uses its search capability to look at pages in advance and do a preliminary evaluation of the page. It tries to learn the evaluation function for pages incrementally from observing user behavior, without requiring explicit user interaction.

Unlike search engines, which are "big bags of pages" with no connectivity information, Letizia takes advantage of the connectivity of Web pages. Since links represent some author's judgment of the relevance of two pages, the set of pages that are connected by just a few links to a given page constitute a kind of *semantic neighborhood* of that page. Thus Letizia performs its search in that semantic neighborhood, interleaving its breadth-first search with the largely depth-first search encouraged by the control structure of browsers such as Netscape. Letizia searches "wide" while the user searches "deep".

Of course, search engines still excel over Letizia-like agents in targeting highly specific information, e.g. "Australian tree frogs", or when the user doesn't know where to start. A search engine or Yahoo-like catalog returns a list of possibilities which can then be explored by Letizia as well as manually.

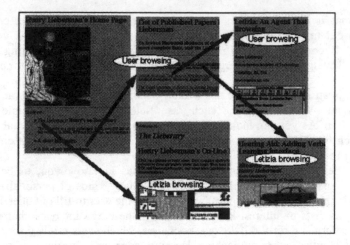

Letizia interleaves a breadth-first search with the user's depth-first search

These incremental searches within a semantic neighborhood are much more likely to return relevant results than the global search performed by search engines. If I'm looking for a place to eat lunch and I like Indian food, it's not a very good idea to type "Indian food" to a search engine -- I'm likely to get wonderful Indian restaurants, but they might be in New Delhi and Mumbai. What I want is the intersection of my interests and "what's in the neighborhood". If the idea of geographic neighborhood is replaced by the idea of semantic neighborhood on the Web, that intersection is what Letizia provides.

Letizia operates as a program that runs concurrently with Netscape, using Netscape's interface as a tool to communicate both with the Web and the user. This kind of organization will become increasingly common for information agents, which use conventional direct-manipulation applications at the same time that the user is interacting with them. However, since conventional applications are not designed to be operated concurrently by another program as well as a human user, that brings up many issues of software integration which will need to be solved for the next generation of information agents. Such issues are discussed in [Lieberman 98].

Another approach to recommending Web pages was taken by Alex Moukas [Moukas 96], and also described in the next chapter of this book. Amaltheaea establishes an ecology of agents, where agents that represent both information sources and filtering procedures based on user interest compete and evolve to improve predictions over time.

12.4.2 The Remembrance Agent

The Remembrance Agent [Rhodes 96] by Brad Rhodes and Thad Starner, is another kind of reconnaissance agent. Like Letizia, it is continuously running in parallel with the user's interaction with a conventional application, and its function is to suggest to the user information which the user might consider relevant to the information current being examined. Rather than tracing through Web links to find interesting information, The RA maintains an index of the user's personal information, taken typically from the user's electronic mail or from the set of files in the user's home directory. Text is indexed using Savant, a variant of the SMART information retrieval system. The user can use an ordinary text editor (Emacs) and the system continuously displays single lines from each of several e-mail messages or files that the agent decides are relevant to the currently viewed text.

The Remembrance Agent was especially designed for use on the new generation of wearable computers, where keeping user input to a minimum is essential, and full-blown window-oriented GUIs may be impractical. Another characteristic of wearable computers is that the user may not be fully engaged in interaction with the computer as a primary task, so that agents such as the RA serve as a kind of „peripheral information vision".

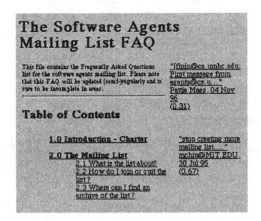

Margin Notes: Reminders of personal information

Another version, Margin Notes, allows the user to use a Web browser, and provides commentary inserted into the right margin of the page, again reminding the user of relevant files or messages. The Remembrance Agent can be considered to "remember the past" [acts as a reminder service] whereas Letizia "remembers the future" [does lookahead].

12.5 Information Agents Can Help People Find Common Interests

In addition to exploring the space of information resources, a very important function of information agents can also be to explore the space of *people*. Information is also inextricably tied up with the people who produce it and have interest in it, and sometimes it is important either to find people who share an interest, or find information of shared interest between a group of people. Agents can often be of help in automating such matching and finding unexpected connections.

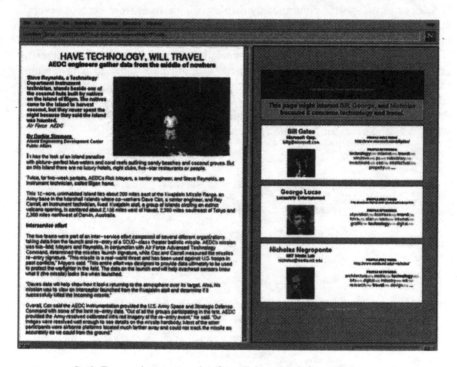

Let's Browse is an example of a collaborative information agent

12.5.1   Let's Browse

Let's Browse, currently under development by myself and students Neil Van Dyke and Adriana Vivacqua [Lieberman, Van Dyke and Vivacqua 99], is an extension to Letizia that allows a group to collaboratively browse together. Collaborative browsing might take place in situations such as a business meeting or in a family situation using home browsing services such as WebTV, which estimates the number of people using its service at once at a little over two. Even if one person has control of the browser, the success of the interaction also depends on taking the interests of the other participants into account.

Like Letizia, it works with a browser such as Netscape, and its job is to recommend pages likely to be of interest, but to the entire group rather than a single individual. The group's interests are determined by intersecting individual profiles of the users.

Unlike Letizia, where we can learn the profile by watching the user's browsing behavior, if the group is browsing together it is difficult to separate the effect of each individual's interests. Instead, in advance, we run an off-line Web crawler that performs a Letizia-like scan of a breadth-first neighborhood surrounding each user's home page, or their organization's home page if the individual one is not available.

Let's Browse also features a visualization of the recommendation process not supplied by Letizia. For each user, the terms computed for the user profile are visible, and the common terms reflected in the page currently being recommended are highlighted, to show each individual's interests and how they relate to the common interest in the chosen Web page.

Agents like Let's Browse open up a wealth of new possibilities for collaboration and sharing. People could exchange profiles, which would allow you to "browse with someone else's eyes". The agent could supply a preview of someone else's point of view that would be informative both to your informant's viewpoint as well as act as a guide to the underlying subject material.

12.6   Information Agents as Matchmakers

12.6.1   Firefly

Whereas Let's Browse has the function of helping small groups find what interests they have in common, other agents may help a user find others who have similar interests from among a large, anonymous group. Pattie Maes, Max Metral, Upendra Shardanand, and Yezdi Lashkari [Shardanand and Maes 95] developed a series of collaborative filtering agents, the latest of which, now commercialized, is *Firefly*. Firefly asks for ratings on specific musical artists, correlates each user with others who share their tastes, and recommends songs or albums which their cohorts have rated highly.

Firefly [left] collaborative filtering music recommendation and Yenta [right] matchmaker

The object of Yenta, which also uses a statistical clustering technique to match users who share similar tastes, is to introduce the users to each other, rather than to recommend specific items. Yenta indexes e-mail and personal files off-line in a manner similar to the RA rather than ask for interests explicitly. Another interesting feature of Yenta is that it does not rely on a centralized server that stores the entire database of people, like many matchmaking recommendation systems would. Instead, individual Yenta agents representing each participant interactively negotiate to see if matches are feasible. Yenta agents enter the community by referrals from other agents, and groups of agents with similar interests are clustered. Yenta also addresses issues of privacy and security, because users may be reluctant to reveal too much personal information.

In a similar vein is Nelson Minar's Friend-of-a-Friend Finder, which performs matchmaking by tracing through each person's network of friends and acquaintances. Preserving locality in an acquaintance network is an important criterion for enhancing social cohesion in a community.

12.6.2 Butterfly

Neil Van Dyke's Butterfly [Van Dyke, Lieberman and Maes 99] is a recommendation system for chat channels. There are thousands of chat channels on the Internet Relay Chat network, simultaneously-occurring real-time textual conversations. Which one should you join? Chat channels are named, ostensibly describing their subject matter, but these descriptions are frequently inaccurate, and no mechanism enforces staying on topic. Butterfly provides advice as to which channels are most likely to be of interest at any given moment. It is therefore one of the few real-time matchmaking systems, and many interesting issues come up as a consequence of its real-time nature.

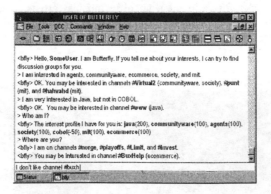

Butterfly recommends chat channels

Interestingly, Butterfly's interface metaphor is the chat interface itself. The user converses with the Butterfly "chatterbot" as if it itself were a participant in a chat. Of course, its natural language understanding repertoire is quite limited, but chat users are now quite accustomed to such limited-capability conversational "bots", so providing assistance in this manner is quite natural. The user simply tells

Butterfly of his or her interests, in the form of keywords. Butterfly periodically scans the thousands of available chat channels, sampling each only for a short time, and matches the channel content to the user's declared interests. Channel content is represented, as it is in search engines or agents such as Letizia, by vectors of keyword frequencies.

12.6.3 ExpertFinder

Expert Finder, being developed by Adriana Vivacqua, assists with the problem of finding another user who is knowledgeable to answer a question. A preliminary version of Expert Finder monitors a user's activity within desktop applications and so is able to observe what kind of experience the user is having. When a user requests help it tries to match the help request with the user who has the most appropriate experience. Users who provide help retain control of their own availability and the system load-balances requests among helpers with similar experience to avoid the phenomenon of the most knowledgeable helpers being overwhelmed with requests.

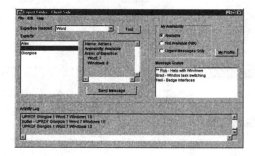

Expert Finder, a recommendation system for help between users

Another version of Expert Finder is being developed for Java programming. By observing the user's Java programming, Expert Finder can classify the user's knowledge according to an ontology of Java's facilities. Users encountering problems can then be referred to helpers who display significant experience in the area in which the trouble occurs.

12.7 Agents for Electronic Commerce

12.7.1 Tête-à-Tête

Rob Guttman's Tête-à-Tête (see Chapter 6 and [Guttman and Maes 98]) performs matchmaking between buyers and sellers in an electronic shopping context. The profusion of commercial Web sites has made buying and selling over the Web more convenient, but also exploding the number of possibilities that a consumer needs to consider, and leaving merchants with the dilemma of how to differentiate their products and services.

Tête-à-Tête uses the paradigm of *integrative negotiation*, where buyers and sellers are represented by software agents that negotiate along multiple dimensions rather than just price. The buyer's interface displays a set of product attributes, and the user can specify values of attributes and their relative importance, through a set of sliders. These preferences are transmitted to buyer's agents, which may propose product offerings. Any change to the preference variables is reflected quickly in a different set of product offerings, and the user may see how tradeoffs affect the offerings. The list of product offerings is displayed as bars which indicate how well the offering fits the user's constraints. Buyer's agents can be programmed with strategies for making offers according to the user's preferences. Merchants can differentiate themselves by offering a combination of products and services that provide a unique value according to the customer's preferences.

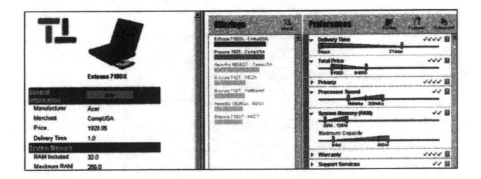

Tête-à-Tête matches buyers and sellers through integrative negotiation

Giorgios Zacharias is investigating the idea of a Reputation Server to address one of the most significant uncertainties in electronic commerce. Users who have not before interacted with a particular merchant or customer can benefit from a referral from the experience of a previous user who has had interaction with that participant. Issues in this work include whether to assume good or bad reputations for new participants, how to tell if another's experience with a given participant is relevant to the current situation, how to avoid malicious manipulation of reputations or evasion of bad reputations, and how to evolve reputations over time. An initial experiment involves using a formula similar to how chess ratings are computed by FIDE, the international chess federation.

12.7   Agents for Visualization of Information Spaces

12.8.1   The Footprints System

In addition to using agents to recommend particular pieces of information, it is sometimes useful to be able to get the "overall feel" of an information space. Agents can serve this function as well. Alan Wexelblat's *Footprints* [Wexelblat and Maes, 97] focuses on visualization of the dynamic behavior of the *use* of information rather than just its structure. Footprints builds on the notion of „history-rich" objects, objects that carry evidence of their use, just as dog-ears on a book's pages indicate pages selected by a reader. Footprints draws a graph of the structure of users' access to Web pages, with the links color-coded to indicate their level of activity. Patterns of information access, such as hot spots, dead ends, and garden paths can be discerned in the structure, and used as an aid to reorganizing the information.

Footprints attempts to capture and display the user's cognitive model of how the space *ought* to be organized, rather than just the Web site designer's model. In doing this, we treat all information accesses equivalently, whether they come from the user following links embedded in the pages by designers, or by selecting relevant bookmarks, typing in URLs, following links sent by friends in e-mail messages, etc.

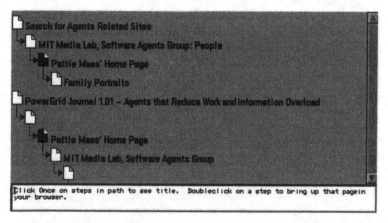

Footprints displays a dynamic graph of the pattern of use of Web pages

The use of dynamic visualizations to display the structure of the information spaces explored by agents is in fact a common theme in the user interfaces of all the agents described in this paper. If the goal of information agents is to help the user explore and understand the content of information spaces, it is essential to present the results of agent selection of information and agent computation in a manner that displays the right information and the right time and lets the user visually grasp meaningful relationships between pieces of information.

12.9 Information Agents Can Be Controversial

Not everyone thinks information agents are always a good idea. Some people worry about the potential for agents to make mistakes, and that the indirection of agents might alienate people too much from direct contact with sources of information [Maes and Shneiderman 97]. But as we have seen, information agents can operate in conjunction with conventional direct-manipulation and visualization software, giving the user the opportunity to use both approaches as the need or desire arises. Feedback between the user and the agent can prevent misunderstandings and make sure that the agent never strays too far from the user's intent. The variety of roles that an information agent can play allows for a flexibility in our relationship to information that cannot be achieved by direct-manipulation or conventional information retrieval software alone. Amid the growing information explosion, intelligent information agents can lend a helping hand.

Acknowledgments

Major support for this work comes from the grants from British Telecom, IBM, the Digital Life Consortium, the News in the Future Consortium, and other sponsors of the MIT Media Laboratory. My thanks go to all the members of the MIT Media Lab's Software Agents Group: Lenny Foner, Rob Guttman, Pattie Maes, Nelson Minar, Alex Moukas, Brad Rhodes, Neil Van Dyke, Adriana Vivacqua, Alan Wexelblat and Giorgios Zacharias. Thanks especially to Neil Van Dyke and Alan Wexelblat for comments on previous versions of this chapter.

13. Amalthaea and Histos: MultiAgent Systems for WWW Sites and Reputation Recommendations

Alexandros Moukas, Giorgos Zacharia, and Pattie Maes

Software Agents Group, MIT Media Laboratory, Cambridge,
MA 02139, USA.
E-Mail: {moux, lysi, pattie}@media.mit.edu

13.1 Introduction

As stated in the previous chapters, recommender systems have long been a favorite application area for agent and multiagent systems researchers. The recommender systems space has traditionally been divided into systems that try to analyse the contents of documents and system that use methods other than content analysis. Content-based filtering systems are using techniques like weighed keyword vectors and SVD, while collaborative filtering and pair-wise ratings are used in the second systems category. In this chapter we will introduce two systems: Amalthaea, that falls in the former category and uses weighed keyword vectors as its representation and *Histos*, a pair-wise rating system that falls in the latter category.

Amalthaea is a multiagent ecosystem that assists users in coping with information overload on the World-Wide-Web. Amalthaea tries to identify potential sites of interest to the user based on a model of his/her interests. In Amalthaea, the information is presented to the user in the form of a digest which includes new URLs that might be interesting, personalized news and notification of new material at certain sites. The user browses Amalthaea's results, is able to follow the links and gives feedback on how good or bad an item is by rating the relevance of an item or keyword etc. Amalthaea learns the user's interests and habits using machine learning techniques, maintains its competence by adapting to the user's interests which may change over time while at the same time exploring new domains that may be of interest to the user.

We implemented Amalthaea by creating an artificial ecosystem of evolving agents that cooperate and compete. Two general species of agents exist: the Information

Filtering (IF) Agents and Information Discovery (ID) Agents. The information filtering agents (augmented weighted keyword vectors) are responsible for the personalization of the system and for keeping track of (and adapting to) the interests of the user. The information discovery agents are responsible for information resources handling, adapting to those information sources, finding and fetching the actual information that the user is interested in. Each user has its own distinct populations of Information Filtering and Discovery Agents.

Evolving a multiagent solution is particularly suited to this domain since it provides a way of utilizing the best possible existing solution to the problem (in our case the best possible match to the user's interests) with the ability to quickly adapt in new situations (for instance following a new user interest or adapting to changes in the domain). The system continues to explore the search space for better solutions using evolution techniques such as mutation and crossover for refreshing and specializing the agents population. Our approach to creating an ecosystem is influenced by Belkin and Croft's (Belkin and Croft, 1992) approach to information filtering and information retrieval: filtering and retrieval are in fact two sides of the same coin.

Significant work has been done on applying artificial intelligence techniques to information filtering. In contrast, our work is inspired by the artificial life approach resulting in fully distributed learning and representation mechanisms. In order to understand the system's global behavior in filtering one has to think of each information filtering agent as a very specialized filter that is applied only in a narrow sector of the domain. When a user changes interests, the filters specialized in the old interests are eventually destroyed and new ones are created that are directed towards the new interests by evolution and natural selection. The intriguing issue in such multiagent systems is to find ways of allowing the system to reach a stable convergence point while continuously adapting to new user interests. In order to evaluate the performance of each agent we have established the notion of an ecosystem which operates on the basis a simple economic model: the agents that are useful to the user or to other agents get positive credit, while the bad performers get negative credit. The more credit an agent has the better it stands and the less chances it has of being destroyed. We address ways of integrating simple non-intelligent computational entities into a system that performs intelligent actions in assisting the user.

The second system we present, *Histos* is a transitive recommender system like FFF (Minar et al, 1998), or the sixdegrees (Sixdegrees, 1998). Unlike collaborative filtering where the recomendations are produced from the direct ratings of preferences, in transitive systems like *Histos*, the recomendations are generated from the connected paths of ratings of the human users themselves, as individual sources of recommendations. We applied *Histos* to Kasbah (Chavez 1996), where agents pro-actively seek out potential buyers or sellers and negotiate with them on their creator's behalf. Each agent's goal is to make the "best deal" possible, subject to a set of user-specified constraints, such as a desired price, a highest (or lowest) acceptable price, a date to complete the transaction and the reputation of the other party. After the transaction is completed with the exchange of payment and goods, the two parties rate each other and their reputation rating is updated.

In a sense we incorporated into the system a reputation brokering mechanism, so that a party can actually customize its pricing strategies according to the risk implied by the reputation values of the potential counterparts. Reputation is usually defined as the amount of trust inspired by the particular person in a specific setting or domain of interest (Marsh 1994). In "Trust in a Cryptographic Economy" (Reagle 1996) reputation is regarded as asset creation and it is evaluated according to its expected economic returns.

Reputation is conceived as a multidimensional value. The same individual may enjoy a very high reputation in one domain, while he/she has a low reputation in another. For example, a Unix guru will naturally have a high rank regarding Linux questions, while he may not enjoy that high a reputation for questions regarding Microsoft operating systems. These individual reputation standings are developed through social interaction among a loosely connected group that shares the same interest. We are developing methods through which we can automate the social mechanisms of reputation for the purposes of an electronic marketplace. These reputation mechanisms are implemented and tested in the Kasbah electronic marketplace. The reputation values of the individuals trying to buy or sell books or CDs are a major parameter of the behavior of the buying, selling or finding agents of the system.

The next session will give some background information and discuss algorithms, architectures related to recommender systems, including content-based and non-content-based filtering.

13.2 Background and Related Work

The domain of recommender systems for reputation has generally focused on content filtering. We can divide the related work into two major categories: the non- computational and the computational ones. The computational methods cover a broad domain of applications, from rating of newsgroup postings and webpages, to rating people and their expertise in specific areas. In this section we focus on the related computational methods and compare their major features in Table 1. One approach to building a reputation mechanism is to have a central agency that keeps records of the recent activity of the users on the system, very much like the (FairIsaac 1998). This central agency also keeps records of complaints by users in textual formats and even publishes warnings against possibly malicious users, pretty much like the local Better Business Bureaus in the US. Adopting such a solution requires a lot of overhead on the behalf of the providers of the online community.

Other proposed approaches are more distributed. For example, approaches such as Yenta (Foner 1997), Weaving a web of Trust (Khare 1997), or the Platform for Internet Content Selection (PICS) (Resnick 1996), (like the Recreational Software Advisory Council) would require that users give a rating for themselves and either have a central agency or other trusted users verify their trustworthiness. We can make the reasonable assumption that no user would ever label him/herself as a non-trustworthy person. Thus all new members would have to await the validation by other trustworthy users of the system. A user would end up evaluating their counterparts' reputation as a consequence of number and trustworthiness of the recommendations for each user.

Friend of a Friend Finder (Minar et al, 1998), Yenta and Weaving Web of Trust introduce computational methods for creating personal recommendation systems, the former two for people and the latter for WebPages. FFF and the Weaving a Web of Trust rely on the existence of a connected path between two users, while Yenta clusters people with shared interests according to the recommendations of users that know each other and can verify the assertions they make about themselves. All three systems require the a priori existence of social relationships among the users of their online community, while in the online marketplaces, deals are brokered among people who probably have never met each other.

Collaborative filtering is a technique used to detect patterns among the opinions of different users and to make recommendations to people, based on others who have shown similar taste. It essentially automates the process of "word of mouth" to produce an advanced, personalized marketing scheme. Examples of collaborative filtering systems are HOMR, Firefly (Shardanand and Maes 1995) and GroupLens (Resnick 1994). GroupLens is a collaborative filtering solution for rating the content of Usenet articles and presenting them to the user in a personalized manner. Users are clustered together according to the ratings they give to the same articles. The user sees the articles with a value equal to the average of the ratings given to the article by users in the same cluster.

Table 1 Reputation Systems: Computational, Pair-wise rating, personalization and textual comments capabilities

System	Computa-tional	Pair-wise rating	Personal.	Comments
GroupLens	Yes	rating of articles	Yes	
Elo & Glicko	Yes	result of game		
OnSale	Yes	buyers rate sellers		
FairIsaac	Yes		Yes	
Local BBB's				Yes
Web of Trust	Yes	Self rating of cost	Yes	
Kasbah	Yes	Yes	Yes	
Firefly	Yes	Rating of recommendations	Yes	
Ebay	Yes	buyers rate sellers		Yes

The most relevant computational methods to our knowledge, are the reputation mechanism of the OnSale Exchange (OnSale, 1998) and the eBay (eBay, 1998). OnSale allows its users to rate and submit textual comments about sellers and overall reputation value of a seller is the average of his/her ratings through his usage of the OnSale system. In eBay, sellers receive +1, 0 or -1 as feedback for their reliability in each auction and their reputation value is calculated as the sum of those ratings over the last six months. In OnSale , the newcomers have no reputation until someone eventually rates them, while on eBay they start with zero feedback points. However, bidders in the OnSale Exchange auction system are not rated at all. OnSale tries to ensure the bidders' integrity through a rather psychological measure: bidders are required to register with the system by submitting a credit card. OnSale believes that this requirement helps to ensure that all bids placed are legitimate, which protects the interests of all bidders and sellers. In both sites the reputation value of a seller is available with any textual comments that may exist to the potential bidders. The latest release of Kasbah (Chavez 1996) features a Better Business Bureau service that implements our reputation mechanisms.

Quite a few WWW agents were introduced in the last four years. They were mainly based on content-based filtering techniques and provided recommendations both on-the-fly, while the user is browsing (by suggesting related sites related to the ones the user is viewing) and off-line (by suggesting sites of general interest to the user.) Two of these agents is Carnegie Mellon's University Webwatcher (Armstrong et al., 1995) and MIT Media Laboratory's Letizia (Lieberman, 1995). These agents are designed to assist the user and provide personalization, while the user browses the WWW. They perform a breadth-first search on the links ahead and provide navigation recommendations. More similar to our Amalthaea work in terms of application domain and representation is Fab, a system built at Stanford (Balabanovic and Shoham, 1995). They introduced a system for WWW document filtering which also utilized the weighted keyword vector representation.

Metacrawler (Etzioni, 1995) is an agent that operates at a higher abstraction level by utilizing eight existing WWW index and search engines. Metacrawler is an example of a "parasite" agent that does not index the documents itself, but provides a common interface to a number of search engines. The user posts his/her query once, and metacrawler forwards it to all search engines, collects the results and returns a unified list. It is easy to extend this approach to a higher level of abstraction and have agents that filter information which consult agents that discover information, which in turn consult search engines that index information. By creating several processing levels between the actual information and the user, we allow for greater flexibility in utilizing other novel forms of filtering or other forms of discovery. Etzioni is referring to that as the information food chain and is advocating that Metacrawler is an information carnivore high up the information food source (Etzioni, 1996). Webcompass is a WWW product by Quarterdeck. Webcompass is directed towards off-line search and indexing. It enables the user to generate queries that will search the WWW off-line and presents the results at a later time. CMU's RETSINA project (Sycara et al., 1996, Sycara and D., 1996 , Decker et al., 1997) defines a framework for distributed intelligent agents. The MACRON multiagent system (Decker and Lesser, 1995) developed at UMass/ Amherst, is built on top of the CIG searchbots and uses a centralized planner to generate sub-goals that are pursued by a group of cooperating agents, using KQML (Labrou and Finin, 1994), a standardized language for inter-agent communication and negotiation. A comparable system is RAISE (Grosof, 1995), developed by IBM. RAISE is a rule-based system that provides a framework for knowledge reuse in different domains (like electronic mail, newsgroups e.t.c.) INFOrmer (Riordan and Sorensen, 1995), developed at University of Cork introduces the idea of using associative networks instead of keywords for information retrieval.

In terms of evolutionary recommender systems, NewT (Sheth and Maes, 1993) developed at the Media Lab, is a multiagent system that uses evolution and relevance feedback for information filtering. NewT's application domain is structured newsgroups documents (clarinet) and the system is able to adapt successfully to such a dynamic environment. The main difference between NewT and Amalthaea (apart from the application domain) is that NewT employed only one kind of agent, namely specialized information filters, while the system presented here introduces different types of agents which base their relationships on a simple market-based model. The Infospiders or ARACHNID project (Menczer et al., 1995) at the University of California at San Diego combine evolutionary techniques with the idea of endogenous fitness to create a scalable distributed information retrieval system. This system is described in detail in the following chapter. Finally analysis of text fitness in the internet in an ecological framework was done at the MIT Media Lab using LSI techniques (Best, 1997.)

13.3 Amalthaea

13.3.1 Architecture Overview and User Interface

Amalthaea's architecture assigns to each user her own Information Filtering and Information Discovery Agents and generates a closed ecosystem. More than one person can use the system but all their files are separate; no interaction between different users is taking place in the system. All the components of the system that will be discussed in this chapter operate on a single user. For handling multiple users the system just uses multiple instances of those components. Amalthaea is composed of the following parts (illustrated in Fig. 13.1):

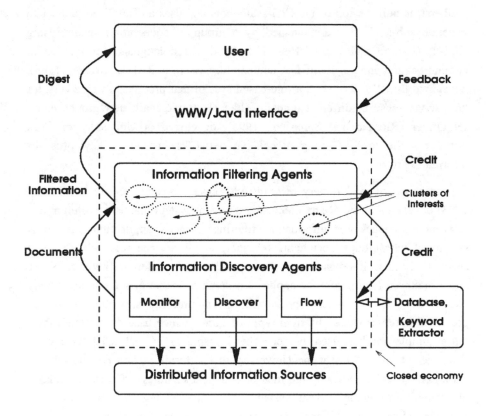

Fig 13.1 An overview of the architecture: The user is presented with a digest of sites by Amalthaea. S/he then provides feedback by rating the sites included in the digest. Based on the user's ratings, credit is assigned to the related filtering and discovery agents.

- The user interface is a Java-enabled WWW browser which enables the communication between the user and the application
- The information filtering agents which request broad categories of documents that are similar to the user profile and the information discovery agents that, given the above-mentioned requests, query various search engines to get relevant sites and then fetch the contents of those sites.
- The evolution mechanisms that are applied to the above two populations.
- The text processing and vectorization mechanisms that, given a retrieved document, produce a keyword vector.

- The credit allocation mechanisms that convert the rating that the user gives to the system's recommendations into credit. Those mechanisms distribute the credit to the filtering and discovery agents that were responsible for presenting that digest item
- The database where the URLs of all the retrieved articles are stored

Amalthaea runs on a centralized server system. The server contains the various Filtering and Discovery Agents for each user, his/her preferences and information about the sites that the user has already visited. Amalthaea is controlled via a graphical user interface (GUI) that runs on the user's own computer. The GUI is built around the Java development environment. When a user connects to the Amalthaea server, the GUI is brought up on his/her screen as a Java window (separate from the browser). This Amalthaea interface is continuously running while the user is connected to the system. Via the GUI the user can find WWW sites that are of interest to him or her, give feedback, configure and visualize the state of the system.

Fig. 13.2. shows the Amalthaea's main user interface window containing the digest. This is the part of the GUI where the system presents its suggestions to the user and the user gives feedback. The suggested URLs are structured in sections (where each section contains the documents that were retrieved by a certain cluster of information filtering agents), and are displayed along with a small part of the actual contents of the site and the confidence level that the system has about each URL. The user can click on those URLs and the GUI opens the browser to that specific URL. The user can check out the site and then select a rating for that suggestion (the GUI is always running on a separate window outside the browser.) This rating is going to be the user's feedback to the system. The user feedback is used by the system to support a credit allocation mechanism to the information filtering agents that were responsible for selecting that document. A seven-scale feedback mechanism is available to the user (7 = excellent, 1 = bad). The user can also pick a number of keywords from the document vector that best describe the given document and the weights of these keywords will be reinforced.

Amalthaea is bootstrapped by generating a number of information filtering and information discovery agents. This first generation of information filtering agents has to be somewhat relevant to the user's interests. This can be done in one of the following ways:

- The users submit a list of their favorite bookmarks or documents. Each of the sites in the list is examined and for each site an Information Filtering Agent is created
- Amalthaea checks the user's browser history file.
- Users can point Amalthaea at a specific page (while they are browsing) and request the generation of more agents that will find similar information.
- Finally users can select pre-trained "packages" of agents (each package focuses on a particular topic; for instance "European soccer", "Greece", "Agents research" etc.) This method speeds up the learning curve of the system significantly.

13.3.2 Document Representation and Evolutionary Mechanisms

Amalthaea's internal representation of documents is based on a standard information retrieval technique called weighted vector representation (Salton and Buckley, 1987). The basic representation for the Information Filtering Agents as well as for the parsed HTML files is the weighted keyword vector. When an HTML file is processed, a clear- text version is generated, the text is decomposed into its keywords, which are weighted and compose the keyword vector. Each keyword is weighted by producing its "tfidf" measure. The "tfidf" acronym stands for term frequency times inverse document frequency and it is a standard information retrieval weighting mechanism. The weight of a keyword k is given by:

$$W_k = H_C \cdot T_f \cdot \log\left(\frac{N}{df_k}\right)$$

(13.1)

where T_f is the frequency of the keyword in the current document (*term frequency*), H_c is a header constant (was this keyword part of the header?), N is the total number of documents that have already been retrieved by the system and df_k is the document frequency of keyword k. The last term is the frequency of the keyword in the whole collection of N documents (*document frequency*). In this case the collection of documents is the set of all weighted keyword vectors, which are the internal representation of the documents retrieved so far.

The evolution of the agents is controlled by two elements: their individual fitness and the overall fitness of the system. Only a variable number of the top ranked (the best performers) of the whole population is allowed to produce off-

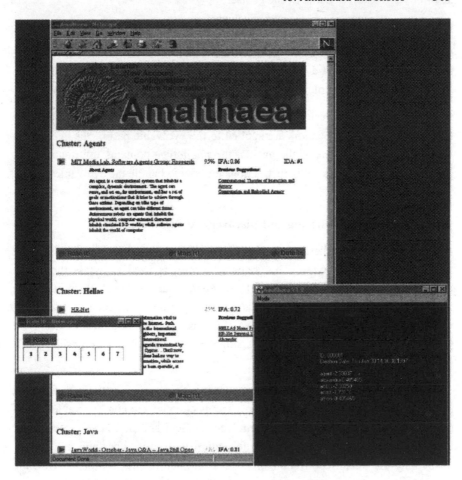

Fig 13.2: A user's digest with recommended sites. On the lower left hand side there is the rating window (the higher the number, the more interesting was the recommendation) and on the lower right hand side a visualization of the Information Filtering Agents. Each entry of the digest contains the URL of the recommended site, its title, the first 300 bytes of its contents as well as the IFA and the IDA that are suggesting this item and the confidence of the suggestion. On the right half of the browser, the system displays other sites (WWW pages) that were recommended by the same IFA at previous digests.

spring. The rank of an agent is based solely on its fitness. The number of the agents that will be allowed to produce offspring is linearly related to the number of agents that will be purged because of poor performance (low fitness). These numbers are not constant and are related to the overall fitness of the system. If the overall fitness is diminishing then the evolution rate is increased in search for quicker adaptation to the user's new interests. If the overall fitness is increasing the evolution is kept at a lower rate to allow the system to slowly explore the search space for better solutions.

New agents are created by copying (or cloning), crossover or mutation (see Mitchell, 1996). All operators are applied to the evolvable part of the agents, the *genotype*. The other part of the agents, the *phenotype* contains information that should not be evolved, usually instructions on how to handle the evolvable part.

13.3.3 Information Filtering and Discovery Agents

An information filtering agent is based on a keyword vector (which is the major part of its genotype). This keyword vector is used to assess the match between an information filtering agent and a particular document. In addition to a keyword vector, an IF agent also contains other information such as whether it was created by the user explicitly or not. If it was, then the long-term interest field (a boolean parameter) is activated indicating that the documents proposed by this agent are treated more favorably.

The genotype of the information filtering agents is essentially a weighted keyword vector. The phenotype of these agents contains the non-evolvable part of the agent like its fitness, the long-term interest field and of course the behavior that enable the agents to exchange information with each other and the system. Essentially the phenotype resembles a fixed template that is completed with the genotype information. Figure 13.3 visualizes the relation between the genotype and the phenotype of the information filtering agents.

The information filtering agents are presented some documents by the information discovery agents (described later on.) The former act as filters that allow only the documents that are close to their weighted keyword vectors to pass through. Each filtering agent selects the documents that is closest to its vector and calculates how confident it is that the specific document will interest the user. In this decentralized approach each agent believes that it is a perfect model of part of the user's interests:

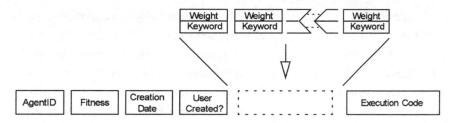

Fig 13.3 The information filtering agent genotype and phenotype

In order for an Information Filtering Agent to assess its similarity to a given WWW page, it has to compare its genotype to the vector representation of the text inside that page. As mentioned above, each document is represented by a multi-dimensional vector (each vector can have different dimensions). In order to make the document comparison and clustering feasible we project each vector in the multidimensional space of the hypervector that includes all the keywords found in the whole collection of the Information Filtering Agents. Their dimensionality is expanded by adding to them all the additional keywords of hypervector and setting their weight to zero.

When two keyword vectors are compared for similarity, we compute the cosine of the angle between the two vectors. This is done by evaluating the dot product of the two vectors and dividing it by the product of their magnitudes. The formula that returns the distance between two keyword vectors a and b is the following:

$$D_{IFA_{a,b}} = \frac{\sum_{k=1}^{j} w_{ak} \cdot w_{bk}}{\sqrt{\sum_{k=1}^{j} (w_{ak})^2 \cdot \sum_{k=1}^{j} (w_{bk})^2}} \qquad (13.2)$$

As mentioned in the previous section, not all documents introduced by filtering agents make it into the digest. The system decides if the agent is going to present something to the user by ranking the proposed documents using the following formula (confidence level):

$$C_i = D_{IFA} \cdot F_i \qquad (13.3)$$

where i is the document number, and F is the fitness of the filtering agent that proposed the document. The top n documents are selected from the ranked list, where n is a user-definable number that indicates the amount of items that the user is interested in including in the digest. Although the agents that present items are not always the same, they usually represent the top 40% of the population, fitness-wise. The rest of the population is there for diversity purposes. One would notice that if an information filtering agent doesn't present anything to the user then its credit would remain constant. In order to accelerate the destruction of non-competent agents and the evolution of new ones we introduced a linear decay function which can be seen as a type of "rent" (Baclace, 1992). In order for the agents to inhabit the ecosystem they have to pay something. If the credits they gain fall short this "rent" they are removed from the system. Finally, if two agents propose the same document then the one with the least credit receives a penalty in order to discourage its behavior and increase the diversity of the population.

The Information Filtering Agents evolution has one particularity: the whole population is not evolved together; instead, Filtering Agents compete with each other inside a given cluster. Information Filtering Agents with similar keyword vectors belong to the same cluster. For instance all the IFAs that belong to cluster "Greece" are evolved together, the "Computer Science" IFAs together, etc. This yields better performance in terms of user feedback, merely because it is in the interest of the system to create niches of agents, and inside those niches to keep the best IFAs. The size of the clusters is a result of the overall feedback that the user has given to its members.

Each information filtering agent issues "requests" to information discovery agents about the type of documents they are interested in finding. Each request includes a list of keywords and the ID of the IFA that made the request. An information discovery agent is based on a genotype that contains information on the keywords it should utilize when querying the WWW indexing engines, along with the canonical URL of the engine (or information source) that it contacts. The aim here is to create a diverse body of agents that will allow different types of documents to be discovered through different search engines. Distinct characteristics of information discovery agents include that they search alternative information sources in remote computers and that they are parasitic (in the sense that they are utilizing existing WWW search engines to find information and not dig it up on their own, a type of meta-search). The IDAs do not receive credits directly from the user but indirectly, from the information filtering agents that "employ" them

The second major category of agents in the system, the Information Discovery Agents (IDAs) are responsible for posting queries to various Internet

Search Engines, collect the results and present them to the Information Filtering Agents that requested them. The number of spiders that concurrently post and process the queries is configurable by the user. In our current implementation we are running 64 spiders at any given time.

The Information Discovery Agents select which Information Filtering Agents' requests to fulfill. From an implementation point of view this is happening in the following way: All Information Filtering Agents' requests are placed on a table. When an Information Discovery Agent selects a request, that request is erased from the table. The Information Discovery Agents refer to their history logs and check if the Information Filtering Agents which has been the most profitable for doing business with has posted any requests. If not, it proceeds to the next preferred Filtering Agent and checks again. If yes, that request is selected. Then the system proceeds to the next Information Discovery Agent, until all Information Filtering Agents' requests are fulfilled (so usually an IDA serves more than one IFA). The Information Discovery Agents use the above-mentioned method for 80% of the time. The rest of the time the selection is random in order for the system to explore its search space and identify new potentially interesting matches.

13.3.4   Evolution of the System

The interactions between filtering agents and discovery agents, as well as among themselves control the global behavior of the system. Our form of control views the system as a miniature economy. We are trying to yield desirable global behavior in a complex system on the basis of agents acting on local information. The agents that compose the ecosystem operate under a penalty/reward strategy, supported by the notion of *credit* that is assigned indirectly by the user based on the system's performance. The user gives feedback on the relevance of an item in the digest. The system relates this feedback to the filtering agent that proposed the item and the discovery agent that retrieved it and assigns the credit. Credit serves as the fitness function in both populations which are evolved separately. The higher the fitness of an agent, the more chances it gets to survive and produce offspring.

If the user feedback is positive then the information filtering agent that proposed the item is awarded an amount of credit directly proportional to its proposal's confidence level. If an agent is confident that the user would like the item it proposed, it receives positive credit, but not as much as when it would be very confident. If on the other hand it is very confident that the document would be of interest and the user's feedback is negative then it receives a lot of negative credit, which is bad for its fitness. Information filtering agents pass on some of the credit (positive as well as negative) to the information discovery agents whose outputs they used.

13.3.5 Testing and Evaluation

The experiments conducted to validate the hypotheses of this paper were developed along two axes. One group of experiments focused on testing the ability of the system to evolve and converge into stable equilibrium points and infering the optimal distribution of agents. For those experiments we used the notion of "virtual users", profiles created by real user interests that automatically tested the system. The virtual users enabled us to perform big scale lenghty experiments without the use of people (the complete results can be found in Moukas, 1998).

The second axis which we worked along is that of testing the performance of the whole system with real users. We tested if the system could actually find useful information on the WWW and present it to its users. We used a group of seven people and analyzed the data from their interaction with the system to measure quantities like the mean absolute error between an agent's suggestions and the user's feedback, its standard deviation, and the correlation coefficient between Amalthaea's predictions and actual user ratings. One important aspect of the testing phase was to select a set of metrics for evaluating the performance of the system. Those metrics combine overall user satisfaction from using the system (as reported by the users themselves at the end of the experiments) as well as system-recorded user feedback for its recommendations.

Experiments with Virtual Users

In order to provide an objective and consistent evaluation of the system's performance we had to use fixed points of reference in the two external factors that were influencing the system's performance: the user interests and the results of the queries posted to the WWW indexing engines. We compiled several different user profiles with different interests each and we also collected a fixed set of HTML pages. The user profiles had the form of a number of different keyword weighted vectors. We then compared the items created by the filtering agents in the digest with the user profiles and provided positive or negative feedback based on their similarity. The items that the agents were presenting to the user profiles were selected from the fixed collection of HTML documents arranged in different directories to resemble the different search engines. The use of those local documents provided us with a quick response time and more importantly with a constant reference frame for evaluating the convergence of the system.

The purpose of this set of experiments was to evaluate the ability of the system to converge to a stable equilibrium and adapt to slowly changing user interests. At the beginning of the experiments a random set of user interests was created. Those interests were not static, but they were changing at a rate of 5% per system iteration. At random time intervals there was a big change in the user profile. We configured the system in such a way as to alter the user's profile by a mean of 50% and a standard deviation of 15% (i.e. on the average, half of the user profile is changed). These random changes were necessary in order to test if the system would be able to adapt to abrupt changes on its equilibrium position. As Figure 13.4 a-b. shows, the system is able to converge starting from different (random) initial populations and can track changes in the user's interests and recover after a sudden decrease of its fitness (because of the negative feedback it is receiving, since a big percentage of the user interests has changed), by retrieving documents that interest the user more.

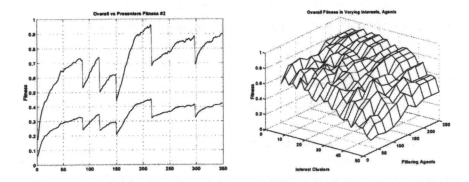

Fig 13.4 a-b (a) Results of changing the user interests suddenly: Evaluation of Amalthaea's performance for user profile two. The higher group of curves represents the average fitness of the IFAs that present digest items to the user; the bottom group represents the average fitness of all the IFAs.
(b) Overall System fitness vs. Number of User Interest Clusters vs. Number of Agents. The value displayed for each data point is the maximum of all generations (0-200). The number of User Interest vectors per cluster, totaling more than 550 vectors). It is quite unlikely that a user will have that many interests at the same time. Note that when the number of agents is small and the number of interest clusters is large (greater than 40) the results are not satisfactory. Nevertheless, when the number of agents increases above 100 the overall fitness rises significantly

The first curve in the figure (with the lower fitness) indicates the average fitness of all the agents in the system, while the second curve represents the average fitness of the agents that actually present documents in the user's digest. The two curves exhibit in general the same behavior, although (as expected) the curve that represents the fitness of all agents is smoother. The number of generations is that high because the initial user profiles used are random (regular users use their bookmark list to bootstrap the system.)

The second set of experiments examines the relation of the number of filtering agents to the number of user interests. We compiled different user profiles using data from actual users and clustered the resulting filtering agents into groups by keyword vector similarity. The definition of an "interest" varies from very narrow-focused when the radius that defines a cluster around the centroid is quite small, to very wide-spread when the radius is greater and contains a large number of agents. We set the radius equal to a value that gave us the best results in a number of preliminary test runs. Figure 13.4b illustrates an overview of all the experiments. The results demonstrate that: *i)* the more agents the better the performance of the system, although increasing the agents to very large numbers doesn't help; *ii)* the number of interest clusters does affect the overall fitness (especially in the case of many user interest clusters, that is more than 40) and *iii)* there seems to be a flattening of the performance curve above 225 agents. Probably the diversity of the population needs to be enforced in large numbers of agents.

Experiments with Real Users

After validating the assumption that the multiagent system can converge and adapt to the user interests regardless of the degree with which these were changing, we performed a set of experiments that involved a set of seven real users. Our experimentation methods closely follow those introduced by the NewT and Webhound research projects (Sheth and Maes, 1993 and Lashkari, 1995). One of the goals of this research project was to produce a useful system, utilized frequently by internet users. Experiments to assess the positive or negative feedback of the users were an important part of the evaluation process. A group of seven people were asked to test the system. The testers were given a set of instructions on how to submit their bookmark lists to the system, how to manually generate agents and a few overall instructions on how to interact with the system. Because the parameter tuning space in Amalthaea is very big (number of agents, mutation rates, crossover rates, cloning rates, etc.) all the tests were conducted using a fixed set of parameters (due to time and computational resource limitations.)

The evaluation criteria for the first set of the experiments are similar to Lashkari (1995). Assuming that the set $C = \{ c_1, c_2, c_3, \ldots, c_N \}$ represents the confidence (or rating) of the agents' recommendations and set $F = \{ f_1, f_2, f_3, \ldots, f_N \}$ the user feedback on the system's suggestions, we define the error set $E = \{ e_1, e_2, e_3, \ldots, e_N \} = \{ c_1 - f_1, c_2 - f_2, c_3 - f_3, \ldots, c_N - f_N \}$. The measured quantities are the following:

• *Mean Absolute Error*. The smaller this error, the better the performance of the system (equation 4)

• *Standard Deviation of Error*. This quantity measures the consistency of the algorithm's performance over the data set. The smaller the standard deviation, the better the algorithm. The standard deviation of the error is defined in (equation 5):

• *Correlation Coefficient*. The higher the correlation of the agent's confidence to the user rating, the better the algorithm according to Hill et al., 1995 (equation 6).

$$|\overline{E}| = \frac{\sum\limits_{i=1}^{N} |e_i|}{N}, \qquad \sigma = \sqrt{\frac{\sum\limits_{i=1}^{N} \left(E - |\overline{E}|\right)^2}{N}}$$

(13.4, 13.5)

$$r = \frac{\sum\limits_{i=1}^{N} \mathrm{cov}\,ariance(c_i, f_i)}{\sigma_c \cdot \sigma_f}$$

(13.6)

Extreme Values. Lashkari (1995) and Shardanand and Maes (1995) assert that the confidence of the agents for extreme values (that is weighted values above six or below two) "indicate very strong user preferences" and "are probably more important than other values" (i.e. the users care about the system being right about high and low ratings, but not that much about average ratings). The ability of the system to maintain a low absolute mean error, standard deviation and a high correlation coefficient both for all and especially for extreme confidence values is important.

• *Precision:* The percentage of the articles presented to the user that were relevant. Precision is a standard performance measure quantity in the Information Retrieval community.

During the testing period we logged the behavior of the system and the users' feedback in order to perform the above analysis. Fig. 13.5 a-b. shows the distribution of the user feedback over a scale of 1 (for bad) to 7 (for excellent). The x axis measures the feedback scale and the y axis the number of occurrences. In general, users gave more positive feedback to the system than negative. When users disliked a recommendation, they preferred to give the absolute negative rating (1) rather than a somewhat negative rating (3 or 2).

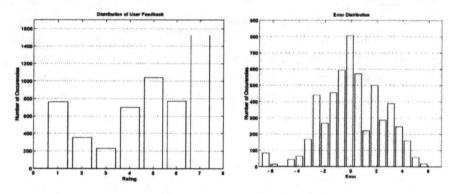

Fig 13.5 a-b **(a)** Distribution of Rating Values in the User Feedback Data Set. The y-axis denotes the number of documents the users that participated in the experiment rated, while the x-axis denotes the sum of the ratings that the user gave to those document. **(b):** Error Distribution in the whole data set. The y-axis expresses the number of occurencies of the errors in each range. The distribution has an gaussian-like form.

Figure 13.5 a-b.a shows the distribution of the error in the whole data set. The error distribution has a gaussian form centered around zero with a couple high peaks around +2 and -2. One feature of the error distribution is the usually high peak in the negative end of the x axis, around -6.5.

Figure 13.5b depicts the evolution over time of the users' feedback to the system. The x axis represents the number of times the users provided feedback to the system while the y axis represents the error. The line represents a least-squares fit on the data set. At the beginning of the experiments the absolute error was quite high, around 2.5 (or 35.71%). However, as time passed, users provided feedback and the system evolved, the error dropped to nearly 0.5 (or 7.14%). Also, at the beginning of the experiments users provided both positive and negative feedback: their response to the system's performance had a lot of variations. However, later on as the system's performance increased, the user feedback improved a lot and at the end were mostly positive.

Table 13.2 summarizes the performance of the system using the metrics introduced in Section 4.2.1. The mean absolute error of all the users throughout the experiment was roughly 1.5 on a scale of 7. So on the average, an agent's recommendation will be within 1.5 rating points from the user's actual interest; in the percentage scale this is translated to an error of 22%. The standard deviation of the absolute error is 1.4 and the correlation between the agents recommendations and the users' interests (as expressed by their feedback) is 0.57. The mean error in the extreme values ratings (1 and 7) is slightly higher (approximately 24%). The standard deviation exhibits the same increasing behavior. The correlation between the mean error and the user interests increases in the case of extreme values to 0.62.

Table 13.2 Mean Absolute Error

	All Values	**Extreme Values**
Mean Absolute Error	1.5536 (22.19%)	1.6874 (24.11%)
Standard Deviation	1.4015	1.6239
Correlation Coeff.	0.5728	0.6214

A set of standard performance measures of information retrieval system are precision and recall. Precision is defined as the percentage of the retrieved articles that is relevant and recall as the percentage of relevant articles that were retrieved. In this case, the whole World-Wide-Web constitutes our document collection so we cannot compute the recall performance of the system. In order to compute the progress of the precision rate of the system over time, we counted as relevant all the documents for which the users gave a rating of more than four. The results are displayed in Figure 13.6b and show that the precision of the system is increasing as time passes and Amalthaea is modelling the users better

Although precision is a useful measurement for comparison purposes, we cannot draw many conclusions for the system's performance because we cannot compute the recall quantity. In information retrieval systems, precision improves at the expense of recall. In this case (where the recall cannot be computed), we believe that the mean error is a better quantitative method for evaluating the ability of the system to perform better over time, since it takes into consideration the agents' confidence when proposing a document. The experiments performed with real users suggest that Amalthaea can be a useful tool that serves the everyday information needs of its users. The overall performance of the system was improving over time.

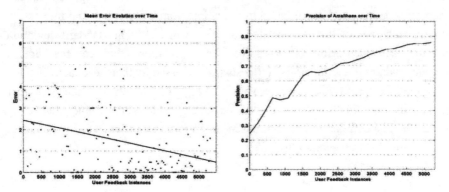

Fig 13.6 (a) Plot of the mean absolute error of predictions over time. As the total number of feedback instances from the users increases, the system is providing better recommendations. **(b)** Precision over time

13.4 Histos

13.4.1 Desiderata for Online Reputation Systems

While the reputation mechanisms discussed in Section 2 have some interesting qualities, we believe they are not perfect for maintaining reputations in online communities and especially in online marketplaces. This section describes some of the problems of online communities and their implications for reputation mechanisms.

In online communities, it is relatively easy to adopt or change one's identity. Thus, if a user ends up having a reputation value lower than the reputation of a beginner, he/she would have an incentive to discard his/her initial identity and start from the beginning. Hence, it is desirable that while a user's reputation value may decrease after a transaction, it will never fall below a beginner's value. We therefore decided for the reputation mechanisms described in the following section that a beginner cannot start with an average reputation.

We also want to make sure that even if a user starts receiving very low reputation ratings, he/she can improve his/her status later at almost the same rate as a beginwner. If the reputation value is evaluated as the arithmetic average of the ratings received since the user joined the system, users who perform relatively bad at the beginning, have an incentive to adopt a new identity so that they get rid of their bad reputation history.

Another problem is that the overhead of performing fake transactions in both Kasbah and OnSale Exchange is relatively low (OnSale does not charge any commission on its Exchange service yet). Therefore two friends might decide to perform some dozens of fake transactions, rating each other with perfect scores so as to both increase their reputation value. Even if we allow each user to rate another only once, another way to falsely increase one's reputation would be to create fake identities and have each one of those rate the user's real identity with perfect scores. A good reputation system would avoid both these problems.

We have to ensure that those ratings given by users with an established high reputation in the system are weighted more than the ratings given by beginners or users with low reputations. In addition the reputation values of the users should not be allowed to increase at infinitum like the case of eBay, where a seller may cheat 20% of the time but he/she can still maintain a monotonically increasing reputation value.

Finally we have to consider the effect of the memory of our system (Marsh 1994). The larger the number of ratings used in the evaluation of reputation values the highest the predictability of the mechanism it gets. However, since the reputation values are associated with human individuals and humans change their behavior over time it is desirable to disregard very old ratings. Thus we ensure that we the predicted reputation values are closer to the current behavior of the individuals rather their overall performance.

13.4.1   Sporas: A Reputation Mechanism for Loosely Connected Online Communities

Sporas provides a reputation service based on the following principles:

- New users start with a minimum reputation value, and they build up reputation throughout their activity on the system.
- The reputation value of a user should not fall below the reputation of a new user no matter how unreliable the user is.
- After each rating the reputation value of the user is updated based on the feedback provided by the other party to reflect his/her trustworthiness in the latest transaction.

- Two users may rate each other only once. If two users happen to interact more than once, the system keeps the most recently submitted rating.
- Users with very high reputation values experience much smaller rating changes after each update. This approach is similar to the method used in the Elo and the Glicko system for pairwise ratings.

Each user has one reputation value, which is updated as follows:

$$R_{t+1} = \frac{1}{\theta} \sum_{1}^{t} \Phi(R_i) \bullet R_{i+1}^{other} \bullet (W_{i+1} - E(R_{t+1}))$$

$$\Phi(R) = 1 - \frac{1}{1 + e^{\frac{-(R-D)}{\sigma}}}$$

$$E(R_{t+1}) = R_t / D$$

(13.7, 13.8, 13.9)

Where, t is the number of ratings the user has received so far, θ is a constant integer greater than 1, W_i represents the rating given by the user i, R^{other} is the reputation value of the user giving the rating D is the range of the reputation values, σ is the acceleration factor of the dumping function Φ. The smaller the value of σ, the steeper the dumping factor Φ(R).

New users start with reputation equal to 0 and can advance up the maximum of 3000. The reputation ratings vary from 0.1 for terrible to 1 for perfect. Since the reputation of a user in the community is the weighted average of non-negative values, it is guaranteed that no user can ever have a negative reputation value, thus no user can ever have lower than that of a beginner. Also the weighed average schema guarantees that no user exceeds the maximum reputation value of 3000. If a user has a persistent real reputation value, the iteration of the equation over a large number of ratings will give as an estimate very close to that value.

As we can see from the equation, the change in the reputation value of the user receiving a rating of W_i from user R_i^{other}, is proportional to the reputation value R_i^{other} of the rater himself. The expected rating of a user is his/her current reputation value over the maximum reputation value allowed in the system. Thus if the submitted rating is less than the expected one the rated user loses some of his reputation value.

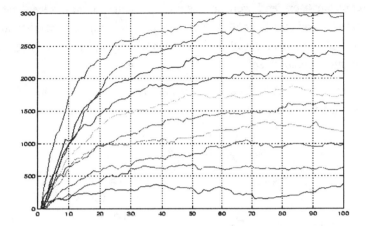

Fig 13.7 Change of reputation for 10 different users over 100 ratings with θ=10

The value of θ determines how fast the reputation value of the user changes after each rating. The larger the value of θ, the longer the memory the system. Thus, just like credit card history schemes [7], even if a user enters the system being really unreliable in the beginning, if he/she improves later, his/her reputation value will not suffer forever from the early poor behavior.

13.4.2   *Histos*: A Reputation Mechanism for Highly Connected Online Communities

The reputation mechanism described in the previous section provides a global reputation value for each member of the online community, which is associated with them as part of their identity. Besides the online agent mediated interaction, our users will eventually have to meet each other physically in order to commit the agreed transaction, or they may even know each other through other social relationships. The existing social relationships as well as the actual physical transaction process create personalized biases on the trust relationships between those users. Friend of a Friend Finder (Minar et al., 1998) and the PGP web of Trust (Garfinkel 1994) use the idea that as social beings we tend to trust a friend of a friend more than a total stranger.

Following a similar approach, we decided to a more personalized system. In Weaving a Web of Trust (Khare 1997), what matters is that there is a connected path of PGP signed webpages between two users. In our case we have to take into consideration the different reputation ratings connecting the users of our system. We can represent the pairwise ratings in the system as a directed graph, where nodes represent users and weighted edges represent the most recent reputation rating given by one user to another, with direction pointing towards the rated user. If there exists a connected path between two users, say from A to AL, we can compute a more personalized reputation value for AL.

When the user A submits a query for the *Histos* reputation value of a user AL we perform the following computation:

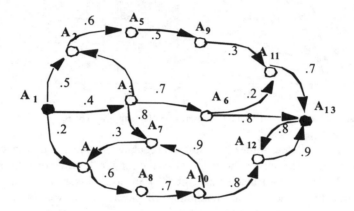

Fig 13.8 A directed graph representing the rating paths between A_1 and A_{13}

• The system uses a Breadth First Search algorithm to find all directed paths connecting A to AL that are of length less than or equal to N. As described above we only care about the chronologically θ most recent ratings given to each user. Therefore, if we find more than θ connected paths taking us to user AL, we are interested only in the most recent θ paths with respect to the chronological order of the rating events represented by the last edge of the path.
• We can evaluate the personalized reputation value of AL if we know all the personalized reputation ratings of the users at the last node of the path before AL. Thus, we create a recursive step with at most θ paths with length at most N-1.
• If the length of the path is only 1, it means that the particular user, say C, was rated by A directly. The direct rating given to user C is used as the personalized reputation value for user A. Thus, the recursion terminates at the base case of length ? and has an order of growth bounded by:

$$O(\theta \bullet N)$$

(13.10)

Note that for any length N user A may have even been among the last θ users that have rated A_L directly. However, user A has the option of getting other peoples' opinions about A_L by evaluating his personalized value for A_L in a more collaborative fashion. Also for the purpose of calculating the personalized reputation values, we use a slightly modified version of the reputation function described above. For each user A_L, with m connected paths coming towards A_L from A, we calculate the reputation of A_L as follows:

$$R_{t+1} = \frac{1}{\theta'} \sum_{t-\theta'}^{t} \Phi(R_{i+1}) \bullet \left(R_{i+1}^{other} \bullet W_{i+1}\right) \bigg/ \sum_{t-\theta'}^{t} R_{i+1}$$

$$\theta' = \min(\theta, m)$$

$$m = \deg(A_L)$$

(13.11)

Where deg (A_L) is the number of connected paths from A to AL with length less than or equal to the current value of L. In the base case where L=1, since we have a connected path it means that A has rated A_1 him/herself, the personalized value for A_1 is naturally the rating given by A.

In order to be able to apply the *Histos* mechanism we need a highly connected graph. If there does not exist a path from A to A_L with length less than or equal to N, we fall back to the simplified *Sporas* reputation mechanism.

13.4.3   Results

While we are still gathering real data from our experiment with Kasbah, we ran some simulations in order to test our system. The four figures above represent the results from some preliminary simulations we have run in order to evaluate our proposed solution for Sporas. The difference between the first three figures and the last one is that in the first three we calculated the expected change of the reputation instead of the exact one. The reason, as the graphs show, was to be able to get a smoother behavior that would make the features of the graphs more legible. Thus in the first three graphs we calculated the reputation R_t as follows:

$$R_{t+1} = \frac{1}{\theta}\Phi(R_i)R_{i+1}^{other}\left(W_{i+1} - R_t\Big/D\right) + R_t$$

(13.12)

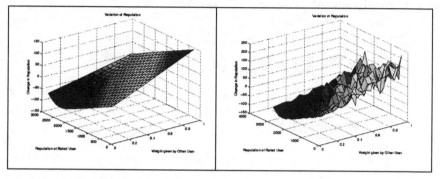

Fig 13.9 **(a)** Change of Reputation with respect to the value of the other user and the weight received **(b)** Change of Reputation with respect to the value of the other user and the weight received

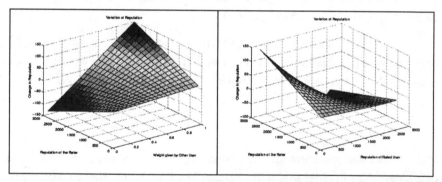

Fig 13.10(a) Change of Reputation with respect to the value of the two users **(b)** Change of Reputation with respect to the value of the user rated and the weight received

Figures 13.9 give the change of the Reputation of a user A, with average reputation (1500), rated by 20 users with reputations varying from 150 to 3000. The graph shows how much the reputation of the user would change if he/she received any rating between 0.1 and 1.

Figure 13.10a gives the change of the reputation of a user A, who receives an average rating with respect to his/her own reputation and the user B who rates A. The graph shows how the change in the reputation of A varies if the reputations of users A and B vary from 150 to 3000.

Figure 13.10b gives the change in the reputation of a user A, if A is rated by a user B with an average reputation (1500), with respect to the previous reputation of user A and the rating which user B gives to user A. Like the two previous cases the ranking of user B varies from 150 to 3000, and the weight B gives to A varies from 0.1 and 1.

These graphs demonstrate the desired behavior by satisfying all the desiderata in a pairwise reputation system for an online community. As we can see from Figures 13.9a and 13.9b, even if the user giving the feedback has a very high reputation, he/she cannot affect significantly the reputation of a user with an already very high reputation. However if the user rated has a low reputation rating, he/she occurs much more significant updates whenever he/she receives a new feedback. From Figures 13.9a and b we can also see that when the user giving the feedback has a very low reputation, the effect of the rating is very small unless the user being rated has a very low reputation value him/herself, in which case the effect is actually negative for the user being rated. In Figure 13.9b we observe exactly the same phenomena with respect to the weight given as feedback.

13.5   Conclusion and Future Work

The first part of this chapter discussed the idea of using evolving populations of agents for personalized information filtering and discovery. In particular, we introduced the idea of integrating two different populations of agents, Information Filtering Agents and Information Discovery Agents into an ecosystem. The two different populations compete and cooperate as the ecosystem evolves towards better fitness levels. We have shown that an evolving multiagent system can converge to loci useful to their users. Based on the above-described architecture, we have built a working system, Amalthaea, that provides to its users personalized information from the World-Wide- Web. In Amalthaea agents that are of service to users or other agents will run more often, reproduce, and survive while incompetent agents will be removed from the population. The experiments we conducted suggested that the ecosystem of Amalthaea can reach stable equilibria states with both varying and suddenly changing user interests. Moreover the real-users testing phase showed that the system is indeed useful to its users, that the error rate on its predictions goes down and that the precision rate of its predictions goes up after receiving user feedback.

The second part of the chapter introduced two reputation recommender mechanisms that establish reputation ratings for the users themselves. Incorporating reputation mechanisms in online communities may induce social changes in the way users participate in the community. We have discussed desiderata for reputation mechanisms for online communities and presented two systems that were implemented in Kasbah, an electronic marketplace.

A future scenario we have been considering looks for ways of combining Amalthaea, a content-based recommender system and a transitive recommender system like *Histos*. We plan to to use *Histos* evaluate the reputation of the users in the context of recommending webpages. Therefore, when a user joins the system he/she is asked to rate the active users according to how much he would trust their recomendation for a webpage. Each user will run his/her own version of Amalthaea. When a user approves of a recommended webpage proposed to him/her by the daily digest of Amalthaea, the recommendation is submitted to *Histos*. *Histos* subsequently compiles a list with the favorite webpages of each user and proposes them separately to every user on the *Histos* system. However, each user on the *Histos* system will receive the list of webpages sorted in a personalized manner according to the receiver's opinion on the reputation of each and every user on the system. Finally, the feedback loop of the *Histos* system is completed by asking the user to rate the authors of the recommendations presented to him/her.

A key issue of this combination is that each user must receive the wholelist of the recommended webpages so that he is urged to give ratings to users he did not have an opinion about them before. This way we try to increase the connectivity of the system so that the several clusters of users get interconnencted. The different users may have a wide domain of interests and their interests may not even be overlapping. Thus some of the pages recommended by *Histos* may be beyond the domain of interests of the user. The ranking of these pages tries to predict the quality of their content and not their relevance to the user's interests, which is what Amalthaea does. Therefore the user may submit a 'Don't Know' rating so that the recommender's reputation is not influenced by the incompatibility of interests or expertise of the two users.

14. Scalable Web Search by Adaptive Online Agents: An InfoSpiders Case Study

Filippo Menczer[1] and Alvaro E. Monge[2]

[1] Management Sciences Department, University of Iowa, Iowa City,
IA 52245, USA.
E-Mail: filippo-menczer@uiowa.edu

[2] Computer Science Department, University of Dayton, Dayton,
OH 45469, USA.
E-Mail: monge@cps.udayton.edu

Summary.
The trend of the recent years in distributed information environments is a good example of the *life-like* complexity that we expect to observe in most aspects of information and computational science. The explosion of the Web and electronic mail, multiplying the number of information providers and consumers many times over and bringing the Internet inside the average home, has created formidable new opportunities and challenges in almost every area of computer and information science.

In an effort to address such problems, researchers in artificial intelligence and information retrieval have already been successful in developing agent-based techniques to automate many tedious tasks and facilitate the management of the growing amounts of information flooding users. But the work has just begun. There is still much need for tools to assist users in ways that scale with the growth of the Web, and adapt to both the personal preferences of the user and the changes in user and environmental conditions.

This chapter discusses an agent-based approach to building scalable information searching algorithms. For systems designed to let users locate relevant information in highly distributed and decentralized databases, such as the Web, we argue that *scalability* is one of the main limitations of the current state of the art. Given such an ambitious goal, it probably comes as no surprise that the solution proposed here draws on many ideas and issues discussed in other parts of this book: cooperation in multi-agent systems, information chain economy in rational agents, and spawning and security in mobile agents.

14.1 Introduction

The complexities emerging in networked information environments (decentralization, noise, heterogeneity, and dynamics) are not unlike those faced by ecologies of organisms adapting in natural environments. The capabilities of such *natural* agents — local adaptation, internalization of environmental signals, distributed control, integration of externally driven and endogenous behaviors, etc. — represent desirable goals for the next generation of *artificial* agents: autonomous, intelligent, distributed, and adaptive. These considerations, along the lines of the artificial life approach, inspired us to base our model upon the metaphor of an *ecology* of agents.

In this sense, the *multi-agent* system is not composed of a few agents with distinct and clearly defined functions, but rather by a (possibly very) large number of agents collectively trying to satisfy the user request. The number of agents is determined by the environment, in turn shaped by the search task. This does not mean that all agents responding to a specific search are identical; each will adapt to both the local context set by the environment and the global context set by the user.

Cooperation results from the indirect interaction among agents, mediated by the environment. If there are sufficient resources to sustain multiple agents in a given environmental neighborhood, then new agents will spawn and collaborate with the existing ones. If resources are scarce, on the contrary, the agents will compete and some of them will be eliminated.

The ecological metaphor thus induces a rational use of the information resource chain. Computational resources (CPU time) and network resources (bandwidth) are allocated in proportion to the recently perceived success of an agent, estimated from the relevance of the consumed information resources. Ideally, each agent would browse the Web neighborhood in which it is situated like its human master would, given her finite resources — time and attention.

The approach discussed in this chapter assumes that, in exchange for improved bandwidth or payments, servers may allow trusted mobile agents to execute and possibly even spawn new agents using their hardware (CPU, memory, disk storage) in a controlled operating environment. If such an assumption holds, agents can take advantage of the distributed nature of our algorithm. They can execute in a parallel, asynchronous fashion, resulting in a great potential speedup. Security and distributed systems issues are central to the implementation of such mobile agents. If the assumption fails, however, the agents can still execute in a client-based fashion. The algorithm becomes essentially sequential (although possibly multi-threaded), and thus simpler to implement. The decrease in performance can be partially offset by the use of a central cache. While the distributed execution of our mobile agents has been simulated successfully, the case study illustrated in this chapter assumes a client-based implementation.

Structure of the Chapter

The next section provides background on the current state of the art in information gathering from networked and distributed information sources. To be sure, the field is evolving very rapidly and agent research is playing a key role in generating the technological advances that may soon allow us to tame the complexity of the Web. Therefore we have no aspiration at completeness, but merely intend to set a stage in which to identify, in the following section, the limitations of the current methodologies. We then give an overview of the *InfoSpiders* system, an implementation that embodies the approach suggested here to complement the scale limitations of search engines. InfoSpiders have been introduced and described elsewhere [426, 428, 429, 427], so our purpose is to summarize those aspects of the model that are relevant to the issue of scalability. Section 14.5 illustrates through a case study how these adaptive online search agents can complement search engines to achieve scalability. The chapter concludes with an outline of InfoSpiders' previous results and a discussion of the possible applications of the InfoSpiders approach.

14.2 Search Engines and Agents

Exploiting the proven techniques of information retrieval, search engines have followed the growth of the Web and provided users with much needed assistance in their attempts to locate and retrieve information from the Web. Search engines have continued to grow in size, efficiency, performance, and diversity of services offered. Their success is attested by both their multiplication and popularity.

The model behind search engines draws efficiency by processing the information in some collection of documents once, producing an *index*, and then amortizing the cost of such processing over a large number of queries which access the same index. The index is basically an inverted file that maps each word in the collection to the set of documents containing that word. Additional processing is normally involved by performance-improving steps such as the removal of noise words, the conflation of words via stemming and/or the use of thesauri, and the use of the word weighting schemes.

This model, which is the source of search engines' success, is also in our opinion the cause of their limitations. In fact it assumes that the collection is static, as was the case for earlier information retrieval systems. In the case of the Web, the collection is highly dynamic, with new documents being added, deleted, changed, and moved all the time. Indices are thus reduced to "snapshots" of the Web. They are continuously updated by *crawlers* that attempt to exhaustively visit and periodically revisit every Web page. At any given time an index will be somewhat inaccurate (e.g., contain stale information about recently deleted or moved documents) and somewhat incomplete (e.g., missing information about recently added or changed documents).

The above observations are quantified in sect. 14.3. The problem, compounded by the huge size of the Web, is one of scalability. As a result, search engines' capability to satisfy user queries is hindered. Users are normally faced with very large hit lists, low *recall* (fraction of relevant pages that are retrieved), even lower *precision* (fraction of retrieved pages that are relevant), and stale information. These factors make it necessary for users to invest significant time in manually browsing the neighborhoods of (some subset of) the hit list.

A way to partially address the scalability problems posed by the size and dynamic nature of the Web is by decentralizing the index-building process. Dividing the task into localized indexing, performed by a set of *gatherers,* and centralized searching, performed by a set of *brokers,* has been suggested since the early days of the Web by the Harvest project [81]. The success of this approach has been hindered by the need for cooperation between information providers and indexing crawlers.

A step toward enriching search engines with topological information about linkage to achieve better precision has been suggested by the CLEVER group at IBM Almaden Research Labs. The idea is to use hyperlinks to construct "hub" and "authority" nodes from the Web graph and it has proven effective in improving document retrieval and classification performance [116, 115].

Autonomous agents, or semi-intelligent programs making automatic decisions on behalf of the user, are viewed by many as a way of decreasing the amount of human-computer interaction necessary to manage the increasing amount of information available online [406]. Many such information agents, more or less intelligent and more or less autonomous, have been developed in the recent years. The great majority of them suffer from a common limitation: their reliance on search engines. The limited coverage and recency of search engines cannot be overcome by agents whose search process consists of submitting queries to search engines. However, many agents partially improve on the quality of any search engine's performance by submitting queries to many different engines simultaneously. This technique, originally called *metasearch* [433], has indeed proven to increase recall significantly [694].

Typical examples of agents who rely on search engines to find information on behalf of the users are homepage or paper finders. CiteSeer [74] is an autonomous Web agent for automatic retrieval and identification of publications. Ahoy [609] is a homepage finder based on metasearch engine plus some heuristic local search. WebFind [447] is a similar locator of scientific papers, but it relies on a different information repository *(netfind)* to bootstrap its heuristic search. While agents like CiteSeer, Ahoy and WebFind may perform some autonomous search from the pages returned by their initial sources, this is strongly constrained by the repositories that provided their starting points, and usually limited to servers known to them.

A different class of agents are designed to learn user interests from browsing for recommendations purposes. Syskill & Webert [515] is a system that identifies interesting Web sites from large domain-specific link lists by learning to rate them based on relevance feedback. WebWatcher [21, 315] is a tour guide agent that learns from experience of multiple users by looking over their shoulders while browsing. Then it provides users with suggestions about what links to follow next. Similarly, Letizia (see Chapter 12) is an autonomous interface agent that assists the user in browsing the Web by performing look-ahead searches and making real-time recommendations for nearby pages that might interest the user. WebMate [122] assists browsing by learning user preferences in multiple domains, and assists searching by automatic keyword extraction for query refinement. All these agents learn to predict an objective function online; they can also track time-varying user preferences. However, they need supervision from the user in order to work; no truly autonomous search is possible.

Amalthaea (see Chapter 13) and Fab [34] share many features with the model described in this chapter. They are multi-agent adaptive filtering systems inspired by genetic algorithms, artificial life, and market models. Term weighting and relevance feedback are used to adapt a matching between a set of discovery agents (typically search engine parasites) and a set of user profiles (corresponding to single- or multiple-user interests). These systems can learn to divide the problem into simpler subproblems, dealing with the heterogeneous and dynamic profiles associated with long-standing queries. However they share the weak points of other agents who perform no active autonomous search, and therefore cannot improve on the limitations of the metasearch engines they exploit.

FishSearch [82] is a search system inspired by some of the same ideas from artificial life that motivated the research in this chapter. Fish Search is based on a population of search agents who browse the Web autonomously, driven by an internally generated energy measure based on relevance estimations. The population is client-based, and uses a centralized cache for efficiency. Each agent has a fixed, nonadaptive strategy: a mixture of depth-first-, breadth-first-, and best-first-search, with user-determined depth and breadth cutoff levels. One difficulty of the Fish Search approach is in determining appropriate cutoff levels *a priori*, possibly resulting in load-unfriendly search behaviors. Therefore Fish Search suffers from limitations that are in a sense opposite to those of all the previously discussed agents; all it does is search, but it cannot adapt to user or environmental conditions.

14.3 Scalability

As was discussed in the previous section, scalability is a major issue limiting the effectiveness of search engines. The factors contributing to the problem are the large size of the Web, its rapid growth rate, and its highly dynamic nature. The scalability problem is quantified in a recent study by Lawrence and Giles [371]. Their estimates of the current size (over 320 million pages) and growth rate (1000% in a few years) of the Web attest to this environment's increasing complexity.

Lawrence and Giles also measure the *coverage* and *recency* of six among the most popular search engines. The coverage achieved by these search engines varies approximately between 3% and 34% of the Web's indexable pages. An estimate of recency was obtained by counting the fraction of returned hits

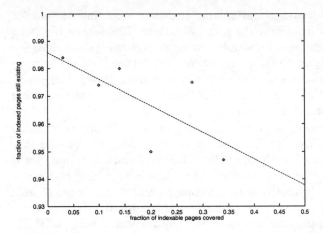

Fig. 14.1. Scatter plot of coverage versus recency in six popular search engines: Alta Vista, HotBot, Northern Lights, Excite, InfoS-eek, and Lycos. Data from [371]. Linear regression is also shown. The correlation coefficient is -0.7.

corresponding to broken URLs, i.e., pages that have been deleted or moved.[1] Among the search engines considered, the one with highest coverage also has the most broken links (5%), and vice versa — the engine with lowest coverage is the one with highest recency. Such a trade-off between coverage and recency is illustrated in Fig. 14.1. Coverage and recency are indeed anti-correlated, as expected. Increasing the coverage of an index, given some limited bandwidth resource, imposes a search engine's crawler to "spread itself thin" and update pages less frequently, thus increasing the amount of stale information in the index.

In order to keep indices as up-to-date as possible, crawlers have to revisit documents often to see if they have been changed, moved, or deleted. Further, crawlers have to try to exhaustively visit every new document to keep indices as complete as possible. Such crawler behaviors impose significant loads on the net, as documents must be examined periodically. Heuristics are used to estimate how frequently a document is changed and needs to be revisited, but the accuracy of such statistics is highly volatile. The network load scales as n/τ, where n is the number of documents in the Web and τ is the time scale of the index, i.e. the mean time between visits to the same document. The longer τ, the more stale information found in the index. If q is the number of queries answered by the search engine per unit time, then the amortized cost of a query scales as $n/q\tau$.

Agents searching the Web *online* do not have a scalability problem because they search through the *current* environment and therefore do not run into stale information. On the other hand, they are less efficient than search engines because they cannot amortize the cost of a search over many queries. Assuming that users may be willing to cope with the longer wait for certain

---

[1] URLs with changed content do not appear broken, therefore this method measures a lower bound on the amount of stale information in an index.

queries that search engines cannot answer satisfactorily, one might ask, *What is the impact of online search agents on network load?*

In our opinion, because of the scalability effect, making an index less up-to-date can free up sufficient network resources to completely absorb the impact of online searches. Consider increasing the τ of a search engine by a factor of $(1+\epsilon)$, allowing the information in the index to become correspondingly more stale. Maintaining a constant amortized cost per query, we could now refine the results of each query with an online search using an amount of network resources scaling as

$$\frac{n}{q\tau} - \frac{n}{q\tau(1+\epsilon)} \sim \frac{n}{q\tau}\frac{\epsilon}{1+\epsilon} \; .$$

As an example, imagine visiting 100 Web pages online for each query, and accepting $\epsilon = 1$ (bringing τ, say, from one to two weeks). This could be achieved without impacting network load by satisfying the condition $n/q\tau = 200$. Assuming $q\tau$ (the number of queries posed over a constant time interval) is a constant, the current growth of the Web assures that the condition will be met very soon. For Alta Vista, we recently estimated $n/q\tau \approx 5$ [9, 427]; even at a conservative growth rate of a doubling per year, the condition would be met within at most 5 years.[2] This simple argument, in our opinion, shifts the question: we should not ask what is the network impact of online search agents, but rather, *What ϵ achieves an appropriate balance between the network loads imposed by search engines' crawlers and online agents?*

We make the assumption in this chapter that as the Web continues to grow and its dynamics become even more life-like, users will increasingly rely on personalized tools in addition to global search engines. Under this assumption, we envision that the relative load of the network will shift from "dumb" crawlers to "smart" browsing agents, while users will develop a more distal relationship with the information sources by way of trusted (agent) intermediaries. But this vision can become reality only when agents will offer the capability to add the value of scalability to search engines. We must therefore prove that an agent-based solution can indeed reach beyond search engines and effectively locate information unknown to them.

14.4 InfoSpiders

Let us operationalize the ideas discussed in the previous section into an agent framework. The goal addressed in this chapter is to achieve scalable Web search by complementing search engines with an agent-based algorithm. The agent collective is endowed with a distributed adaptive representation, aiming to take advantage of both the statistical (word) and structural (link)

---

[2] If we consider the coverage factor of 3 due to the discrepancy between the n of the search engine and the actual size of the Web, the condition will be met a lot sooner.

topology of the Web. We have argued that the agents in such collective must be *autonomous, online, situated, personal browsers* [429].

Our approach is therefore based on the idea of a multi-agent system. The problem is decomposed into simpler subproblems, each addressed by one of many simple agents performing simple operations. The divide-and-conquer philosophy drives this view. Each agent will "live" browsing from document to document online, making autonomous decisions about which links to follow, and adjusting its strategy to both local context and the personal preferences of the user. Population-wide dynamics will bias the search toward more promising areas.

In this framework, both individual agents and populations must *adapt*. Individually learned solutions (e.g., by reinforcement learning) cannot capture global features about the search space or the user. They cannot "cover" heterogeneous solutions without complicated internal models of the environment; such models would make the learning problem more difficult. On the other hand, if we allowed for population-based adaptation alone (e.g., by an evolutionary algorithm), the system might be prone to premature convergence. Genetically evolved solutions would also reflect an inappropriate coarseness of scale, due to individual agents' incapability to learn during their lives. Incidentally, these are the same reasons that have motivated the hybridization of genetic algorithms with local search [274], and reflect the general problem of machine learning techniques in environments with very large feature space dimensionalities [380, 381].

The approach and methods introduced above have been applied in the construction of populations of adaptive information agents. The InfoSpiders system was implemented to test the feasibility, efficiency, and performance of adaptive, online, browsing, situated, personal agents in the Web. In this section we outline the InfoSpiders implementation and briefly describe the distributed evolutionary algorithm and agent representation used. A more detailed account can be found elsewhere [427].

14.4.1 Algorithm

Distributed search in networked environments is a multimodal problem that presents many of the characteristics making it an ideal target for *local selection* algorithms [430]. This task requires a heterogeneous cover of the search space rather than a convergence to the perceived global optimum. Indeed it can easily be cast into a graph search framework, in which local selection algorithms have proven very effective [430, 427].

InfoSpiders search online for information relevant to the user, by making autonomous decisions about what links to follow. How long should an agent live before being evaluated? What global decisions can be made about which agents should die and which should reproduce, in order to bias the search optimally? No answer to these questions would appear satisfactory.

```
InfoSpiders(query, starting_urls, MAX_PAGES, REL_FBK_FLAG) {
   for agent (1..INIT_POP) {
      initialize(agent, query);
      situate(agent, starting_urls);
      agent.energy := THETA / 2;
   }
   while (pop_size > 0 and visited < MAX_PAGES) {
      foreach agent {
         pick_outlink_from_current_document(agent);
         agent.doc := fetch_new_document(agent);
         agent.energy +=  benefit(agent.doc) - cost(agent.doc);
         apply_Q_learning(agent, benefit(agent.doc));
         if (agent.energy >= THETA) {
            offspring := mutate(recombine(clone(agent)));
            offspring.energy := agent.energy / 2;
            agent.energy -= offspring.energy;
            birth(offspring);
         }
         elseif (agent.energy <= 0) death(agent);
      }
      if (REL_FBK_FLAG) process_relevance_feedback(input);
   }
}
```

Fig. 14.2. Pseudocode of the InfoSpiders algorithm for distributed information agents. This is an instance of an evolutionary algorithm based on local selection.

Fortunately, the local selection algorithm provides us with a way to remain agnostic about these questions. Such an algorithm is shown in Fig. 14.2.

The user initially provides a list of keywords (query) and a list of starting points, in the form of a bookmark file. This list could typically be obtained by consulting a search engine. First, the population is initialized by pre-fetching the starting documents. Each agent is "positioned" at one of these document and given a random behavior (depending on the representation of agents) and an initial reservoir of energy. The user also provides a maximum number of pages that the population of agents are allowed to visit, collectively. This would depend on how long the user is willing to wait, or how much bandwidth she is willing to consume. Finally, the user may specify whether and how often she is willing to provide the population with relevance feedback, to help focus or shift the search toward relevant areas by "replenishing" the resources in those areas. This chapter does not discuss the use of relevance feedback in depth, as relevance feedback is not used in the reported case study.

In the innermost loop of Fig. 14.2, an agent "senses" its local neighborhood by analyzing the text of the document where it is currently situated. This way, the relevance of all neighboring documents — those pointed to by the hyperlinks in the current document — is estimated. Based on these link relevance estimates, the agent "moves" by choosing and following one of the links from the current document.

The agent's energy is then updated. Energy is needed in order to survive and move, i.e., continue to visit documents on behalf of the user. Agents are rewarded with energy if the visited documents appear to be relevant. The `benefit()` function is used by an agent to estimate the relevance of documents. In the absence of relevance feedback, this function return a non-zero value only if the document had not been previously visited by any agent, and according to a standard measure of similarity between the query and the document. The "marking" of visited pages models the consumption of finite information resources and is implemented via a cache, which also speeds up the process by minimizing duplicate transfers of documents.[3]

Agents are charged energy for the network load incurred by transferring documents. The `cost()` function should depend on used resources, for example transfer latency or document size. For simplicity we assume a constant cost for accessing any new document, and a smaller constant cost for accessing the cache; this way stationary behaviors, such as going back and forth between a pair of documents, are naturally discouraged.

Instantaneous changes of energy are used as reinforcement signals. This way agents adapt during their lifetime by Q-learning [700]. This adaptive process allows an agent to modify its behavior based on prior experience, by learning to predict the best links to follow.

Local selection means that an agent is selected for reproduction based on a comparison between its current energy level and a constant that is independent of the other agents in the population. Similarly, an agent is killed when it runs out of energy. At reproduction, agents may be recombined by the use of one of two types of crossover. In the case study illustrated later in the chapter, an agent may recombine with any other agent in the population, selected at random. Offspring are also mutated, providing the variation necessary for adapting agents by way of evolution. Energy is conserved at all reproduction events.

The output of the algorithm is a flux of links to documents, ranked according to estimated relevance. The algorithm stops when the population goes extinct for lack of relevant information resources, visits MAX_PAGES documents, or is terminated by the user.

14.4.2 Agent Architecture

Figure 14.3 illustrates the architecture of each InfoSpiders agent. The agent interacts with the information environment, that consists of the actual networked collection (the Web) plus data kept on local disks (e.g., relevance

---

[3] While in the current client-based implementation of InfoSpiders this poses no problem, caching is a form of communication and thus a bottleneck for the performance of distributed agents. In a distributed implementation, we imagine that agents will have local caches.

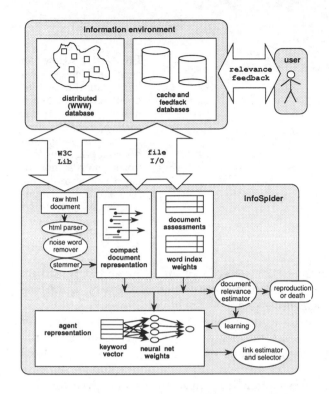

Fig. 14.3. Architecture of an InfoSpiders agent. From [429].

feedback data and cache files). The user interacts with the environment by accessing data on the local client (current status of a search) and on the Web (viewing a document suggested by agents) and by making relevance assessments that are saved locally on the client and will be accessed by agents as they subsequently report to the user/client. There is no direct interaction between the user and the agents after the initial submission of the query and starting points.

The InfoSpiders prototype runs on UNIX and MacOS platforms. The Web interface is based on the W3C library [696]. Agents employ standard information retrieval tools such as a filter for noise words [219] and a stemmer based on Porter's algorithm [220]. They store an efficient representation of visited documents in the shared cache on the client machine. Each document is represented by a list of links and stemmed keywords. If the cache reaches its size limit, the LRU (least recently used) replacement strategy is used. In the case study illustrated later in the chapter, the cache can grow arbitrarily.

14.4.3 Adaptive Representation

Figure 14.3 highlights the central dependence of the InfoSpiders system on agent representation. The adaptive representation of InfoSpiders consists of

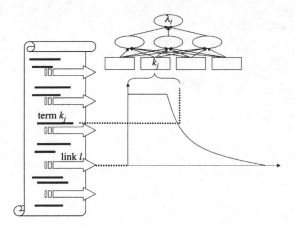

Fig. 14.4. How an agent estimates each link from the current document. For each link in the document, each input of the neural net is computed by counting the document words matching the keyword corresponding to that input, with weights that decay with distance from the link.

the genotype, that determines the behavior of an agent and is passed on to offspring at reproduction; and of the actual mechanisms by which the genotype is used for implementing search strategies.

The first component of an agent's genotype consists of the parameter $\beta \in \Re^+$. Roughly, it represents the degree to which an agent trusts the descriptions that a page contains about its outgoing links. β is initialized with β_0.

Each agent's genotype also contains a list of keywords, initialized with the query terms. Since feed-forward neural nets are a general, versatile model of adaptive functions, we use them as a standard computation device. Therefore genotypes also comprise a vector or real-valued weights, initialized randomly with uniform distribution in a small interval $[-w_0, +w_0]$. The keywords represent an agent's opinion of what terms best discriminate documents relevant to the user from the rest. The weights represent the interactions of such terms with respect to relevance. The neural net has a real-valued input for each keyword in its genotype and a single output unit. We want to allow the inputs and activation values of the network to take negative values, corresponding to the possibly negative correlations perceived between terms and relevance. For this reason the network uses the hyperbolic tangent as its squashing function, with inputs and activation values in $[-1, +1]$.

An agent performs action selection by first computing the relevance estimates for each outgoing link from the current document. This is done by feeding into the agent's neural net activity corresponding to the small set of (genetically specified) keywords to which it is sensitive. Each input unit of the neural net receives a weighted count of the frequency with which the keyword occurs in the vicinity of the link to be traversed. In the experiments reported here, we use a distance weighting function which is biased towards keyword occurrences most close to the link in question.

More specifically, for link l and for each keyword k, the neural net receives input:

$$in_{k,l} = \sum_{i:\text{dist}(k_i,l)\leq\rho} \frac{1}{\text{dist}(k_i,l)}$$

where k_i is the ith occurrence of k in D and $\text{dist}(k_i,l)$ is a simple count of other, intervening links (up to a maximum window size of $\pm\rho$ links away). The neural network then sums activity across all of its inputs; each unit j computes activation

$$\tanh(b_j + \sum_k w_{jk}in_k^l)$$

where b_j is its bias term, w_{jk} are its incoming weights, and in_k^l its inputs from the lower layer. The output of the network is the activation of the output unit, λ_l. The process is illustrated in Fig. 14.4 and is repeated for each link in the current document. Then, the agent uses a stochastic selector to pick a link with probability distribution:

$$\Pr[l] = \frac{e^{\beta\lambda_l}}{\sum_{l'\in D} e^{\beta\lambda_{l'}}} \; .$$

After a link has been chosen and the corresponding new document has been visited, the agent has to determine the corresponding energy gain. For a previously unvisited document,

$$\texttt{benefit}(D) = \tanh\left(\sum_{k\in D} \text{freq}(k,D) \cdot I_k\right)$$

where $\text{freq}(k,D)$ is the frequency of term k in document D normalized by document size, and I_k is the weight of term k. In the absence of relevance feedback, $I_k = 1$ if k is in the query and $I_k = 0$ otherwise.[4]

The agent then compares the (estimated) relevance of the current document with the estimate of the link that led to it. By using the connectionist version of Q-learning [387], the neural net can be trained online to predict values of links based on local context. After the agent visits document D, the value returned by the $\texttt{benefit}()$ function is used as an internally generated reinforcement signal to compute a teaching error:

$$\delta(D) = \texttt{benefit}(D) + \mu \cdot \max_{l\in D}\{\lambda_l\} - \lambda_D$$

where μ is a future discount factor and λ_D the prediction from the link that was followed to get to D. The neural net's weights are then updated by back-propagation of error [569]. Learned changes to the weights are "Lamarckian"

---

[4] If the user provides relevance assessments, I_k becomes an algebraic extension of the TFIDF (term frequency-inverse document frequency) index weighting scheme, allowing for negative relevance feedback and consequent energy losses.

in that they are inherited by offspring at reproduction. In the absence of relevance feedback this learning scheme is completely unsupervised, in keeping with the autonomy of InfoSpiders.

InfoSpiders adapt not only by learning neural net weights, but also by evolving all of the genotype components — β, the neural net, and the keyword representation. At reproduction, the offspring clone is recombined with another agent. Two-point crossover is applied to the keywords of the clone, so that a subset of the mate's keywords is spliced into the offspring's keyword vector.

Then mutations are applied. If a' is an offspring of a:

$$\beta_{a'} \leftarrow U[\beta_a(1 - \kappa_\beta), \beta_a(1 + \kappa_\beta)] \ .$$

The values of β are clipped to $\beta_{\max}$ to maintain some exploratory behavior. The neural net is mutated by adding random noise to a fraction ζ_w of the weights. For each of these network connections, i:

$$w_{a'}^i \leftarrow U[w_a^i(1 - \kappa_w), w_a^i(1 + \kappa_w)] \ .$$

U is the uniform distribution and $\kappa_\beta, \kappa_w \in [0, 1]$ are parameters.

The keyword vector is mutated with probability ζ_k. The least useful (discriminating) term $\arg\min_{k \in a'}(|I_k|)$ is replaced by a term expected to better justify the agent's performance with respect to the user assessments. Ties are broken randomly. In order to keep any single keyword from taking over the whole genotype, this mutation is also stochastic; a new term is selected with probability distribution

$$\Pr[k] \propto \text{freq}(k, D) \cdot \delta_{<1}(|I_k| + \chi)$$

$$\delta_{<1}(x) \equiv \begin{cases} x \text{ if } x < 1 \\ 1 \text{ otherwise} \end{cases}$$

where D is the document of birth and $\chi \in [0, 1]$ is a parameter. The first factor captures the local context by selecting a word that describes well the document that led to the energy increase resulting in the reproduction. The second factor, in the presence of relevance feedback, captures the global context set by the user by selecting a word that discriminates well the user's preferences. The parameter χ regulates the amount of supervised (small χ) versus unsupervised (large χ) keyword mutation; if $\chi = 0$, only keywords important to the user can be internalized, while if $\chi > 0$ new keywords can be internalized based on local environmental context alone. Learning will take care of adjusting the neural net weights to the new keyword.

The evolution of keyword representations via local selection, mutation and crossover implements a form of *selective query expansion*. Based on relevance feedback and local context, the query can adapt over time and across different places. The population of agents thus embodies a distributed, heterogeneous model of relevance that may comprise many different and possibly inconsistent features. But each agent focuses on a small set of features, maintaining a well-defined model that remains manageable in the face of the huge feature dimensionality of the search space.

14.5 Case Study

In this section we want to illustrate how scalability in Web search can be achieved using InfoSpiders as a front-end to a traditional search engine. We do this with a case study, corresponding to a query that search engines cannot satisfy alone.

Table 14.1. InfoSpiders parameter descriptions and values.

Parameter	Value	Description
MAX_PAGES	200	Max number of new pages visited per query
REL_FBK_FLAG	FALSE	Relevance feedback disabled
INIT_POP	10	Initial population size
THETA	2.0	Reproduction threshold
CACHE_SIZE	MAX_PAGES	Effectively unbounded cache
c_n	0.01	Energy cost per new document
c_o	0.0001	Energy cost per cached document
β_0	4.0	Initial β
κ_β	0.5	β mutation range
β_{max}	5.0	Max β
ρ	5	Half-size of link estimation sliding window
ζ_k	0.0	Keyword mutation rate
N_{layers}	2	Neural net layers (excluding inputs)
w_0	0.5	Initial neural net weight range
ζ_w	0.2	Neural net weight mutation rate
κ_w	0.25	Neural net weight mutations range
η	0.05	Neural net Q-learning rate
μ	0.5	Q-learning discounting factor

In order to keep the analysis of our case study as simple as possible, agents are disallowed to differentiate on the basis of keyword vectors; all InfoSpiders focus on the same terms over time. The neural nets are allowed to adapt by evolution and reinforcement learning, and the β gene can evolve as well. The cache size is large enough to contain all the visited documents. Table 14.1 shows the values of the main parameters discussed in sect. 14.4 and their default values used in the case study.

14.5.1 Search Engine Defeat

Pat is a prospective student in a database class offered at the University of Iowa, and has heard from a friend the name of the instructor who

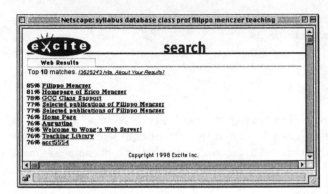

Fig. 14.5. The top ten hits returned by Excite in response to Pat's query and fed to InfoSpiders as a list of starting URLs. The HTML source file has been edited for readability.

will be teaching the course. Pat wants to find out about the class in order to make an informed decision before registering for the class. Having access to the Web, Pat submits a query to a search engine, say, Excite [195]. The query is reasonable: SYLLABUS OF DATABASE CLASS PROF FILIPPO MENCZER IS TEACHING. Unfortunately, Excite does not return any page that seems relevant.[5]

In fact, the class syllabus has been available on the Web for a couple of weeks already, and there is a pointer to it from the homepage of the department offering the course. However, because of the limited coverage and recency of search engines, the three documents with the information sought by Pat (the relevant set) have not yet been found by any crawler and therefore the pages are not indexed in any search engine. All major search engines, including MetaCrawler [433], return large hit lists with zero precision and zero recall.

14.5.2 InfoSpiders to the Rescue

For the purpose of this case study, we assume that Pat is a very busy student who cannot afford to spend much time manually surfing the net in search of class information. Before giving up, however, Pat decides to try launching a search with the InfoSpiders tool that (coincidence!) is available on the local computer. InfoSpiders need a list of starting points, in the form of a bookmark or hit list file. Pat uses the first page of hits returned by Excite, shown in Fig. 14.5.

Ten InfoSpiders are initialized, one at each of the top ten URLs returned by Excite. They all share the same keyword vector, whose components correspond to the query terms (after filtering out noise words and stemming). The log file created during the InfoSpiders search is partially shown in Fig. 14.6. It shows that some of the starting points are perceived as dead ends

---

[5] Unbeknownst to Pat, none of the other major search engines would have done any better.

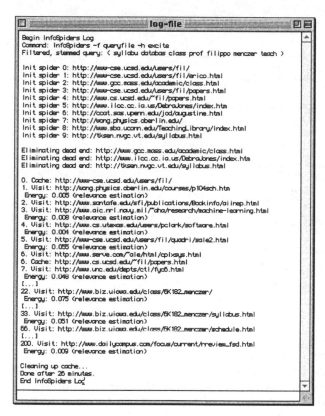

```
                         log-file
Begin InfoSpiders Log
Command: InfoSpiders -f queryfile -h excite
Filtered, stemmed query: ( syllabu databas class prof filippo menczer teach )

Init spider 0: http://www-cse.ucsd.edu/users/fil/
Init spider 1: http://www-cse.ucsd.edu/users/fil/erico.html
Init spider 2: http://www.gcc.mass.edu/academic/class.html
Init spider 3: http://www-cse.ucsd.edu/users/fil/papers.html
Init spider 4: http://www.cs.ucsd.edu/~fil/papers.html
Init spider 5: http://www.ilcc.cc.ia.us/DebraJones/index.htm
Init spider 6: http://coat.sas.upenn.edu/jod/augustine.html
Init spider 7: http://wong.physics.oberlin.edu/
Init spider 8: http://www.sba.uconn.edu/TeachingLibrary/index.html
Init spider 9: http://tksen.nvgc.vt.edu/syllabus.html

Eliminating dead end: http://www.gcc.mass.edu/academic/class.html
Eliminating dead end: http://www.ilcc.cc.ia.us/DebraJones/index.htm
Eliminating dead end: http://tksen.nvgc.vt.edu/syllabus.html

0. Cache: http://www-cse.ucsd.edu/users/fil/
1. Visit: http://wong.physics.oberlin.edu/courses/p104sch.htm
   Energy: 0.005 (relevance estimation)
2. Visit: http://www.santafe.edu/sfi/publications/Bookinfo/aiinep.html
3. Visit: http://www.aic.nrl.navy.mil/~aha/research/machine-learning.html
   Energy: 0.008 (relevance estimation)
4. Visit: http://www.cs.utexas.edu/users/pclark/software.html
   Energy: 0.004 (relevance estimation)
5. Visit: http://www-cse.ucsd.edu/users/fil/quadri/sale2.html
   Energy: 0.055 (relevance estimation)
6. Visit: http://www.serve.com/~ale/html/cplxsys.html
6. Cache: http://www.cs.ucsd.edu/~fil/papers.html
7. Visit: http://www.unc.edu/depts/ctl/fyc6.html
   Energy: 0.048 (relevance estimation)
[...]
22. Visit: http://www.biz.uiowa.edu/class/6K182_menczer/
   Energy: 0.075 (relevance estimation)
[...]
33. Visit: http://www.biz.uiowa.edu/class/6K182_menczer/syllabus.html
   Energy: 0.051 (relevance estimation)
66. Visit: http://www.biz.uiowa.edu/class/6K182_menczer/schedule.html
[...]
200. Visit: http://www.dailycampus.com/focus/current/rreview_fsd.html
   Energy: 0.009 (relevance estimation)

Cleaning up cache...
Done after 26 minutes.
End InfoSpiders Log
```

Fig. 14.6. InfoSpiders log file for the search launched by Pat. The file has been edited for brevity. The relevant URLs appear as entries 22, 33, and 66 in the log sequence.

by InfoSpiders, and discarded.[6] This happens, for example, for broken links yielding a "404 Not Found" error. Such dead ends need to be discarded only from the starting points; later on they pose no problem because InfoSpiders can always follow a special back link.

After fetching the starting URLs, InfoSpiders begin to browse autonomously. Certain pages contain the query words and yield energy used by the agents to prolong their survival in those neighborhoods. Eventually, after 66 pages have been visited, InfoSpiders locate all three relevant documents. This takes less than 9 minutes of search time. Of course InfoSpiders do not know the size of the relevant set, and continue to search as long as they live (or until, in this case, 200 pages are visited over night).

The next morning, Pat finds the report of the InfoSpiders search. The result is shown in Fig. 14.7. The visited pages are ranked by estimated relevance — in this case simply by their similarity to the query; the cosine matching score is listed next to each visited page. Two of the three relevant documents

---

[6] The crude parser in the current prototype fails to recognize relative URLs, as well as anchors with incorrect syntax.

Fig. 14.7. Report of the InfoSpiders search launched by Pat. The original HTML document created by InfoSpiders has been edited for brevity and is viewed through a browser.

(those containing query terms) are ranked in the top ten positions (3 and 7) while the third appears later in the list.

By combining the starting points provided by the search engine and the online search provided by InfoSpiders, Pat has found all of the needed information and decides to enroll in the class. This result could not have been reached through search engines alone, at the time when Pat's information need arose. It could have been achieved by manually browsing through the top pages returned by Excite, but this is a very time-consuming activity — one better delegated to intelligent information agents!

14.6 Discussion

If InfoSpiders overcome the scalability limitation of search engines, why use search engines at all? We want to briefly discuss the issue of topology, in support of our view that the two approaches are really complementary to each other, and either one alone is insufficient to achieve scalable search. In this section we also summarize some more quantitative results previously obtained by InfoSpiders, since the case study described above is merely intended as a qualitative illustration of the scalability argument. We conclude with a look at the future.

14.6.1 Links vs. Words

Indexing can be described as the process of building a *statistical topology* over a document space. A search engine will show similar documents next to each other, effectively creating on the fly a topology based on their word statistics. This is a very useful model because the user can immediately make assumptions about the contents of retrieved documents, for example about the fact that they contain certain words.

However, networked information environments contain additional structure information, which can be used to provide browsing users (or agents) with helpful cues. Here we focus on linkage information that is at the basis of hypertext markup languages such as those used in the Web. One cannot submit to search engines queries like "Give me all documents k links away from this one," because the space to store such information would scale exponentially with k.[7]

While much linkage information is lost in the construction of indices, it is there to be exploited by browsing users, who in fact navigate from document to document following links. We have argued that *linkage topology* — the spatial structure in which two documents are as far from each other as the number of links that must be traversed to go from one to the other — is indeed a very precious asset on the Web. Even in unstructured portions of the Web, authors tend to cluster documents about related topics by letting them point to each other via links, as confirmed by bibliometric studies of the Web [368]. Such linkage topology is useful inasmuch as browsers have a better-than-random expectation that following links can provide them with guidance — if this were not the case, browsing would be a waste of time!

Let us quantify the notion of value added by linkage topology. We have conjectured that such value can be captured by the extent to which linkage topology "preserves" relevance (with respect to some query) [427]. Imagine a browsing user or agent following a random walk strategy.[8] First define R as the conditional probability that following a random link from the current document will lead to a relevant document, given that the current document is relevant. We call R *relevance autocorrelation*. Then define G as the probability that any document is relevant, or equivalently the fraction of relevant documents. We call G *generality* (of the query) [574].

For the random browser, the probability of finding a relevant document is given by

$$\nu = \eta R + (1 - \eta)G ,$$

where η is the probability that the current document is relevant. If linkage topology has any value for the random browser, then browsing will lead to

---

[7] Several search engines now allow such queries for $k = 1$.

[8] We make the conservative assumption of random walk to obtain a lower bound for the value added of linkage topology.

relevant documents with higher than random frequency. In order for this to occur the inequality

$$\nu/G > 1$$

must hold, which upon simplifying for η is equivalent to

$$R/G > 1 \ .$$

This linkage topology conjecture is equivalent to the cluster hypothesis [551] under a hypertext derived definition of association. We can then express the linkage topology value added by defining the quantity

$$\Theta \equiv R/G - 1 \ .$$

As a reality check, we measured Θ for a few queries from a couple of search engines [426]. Relevance autocorrelation statistics were collected by counting the fraction of links, from documents in each relevant set, pointing back to documents in the set. Generality statistics were collected by normalizing the size of the relevant sets by the size of the collections. These were quite gross measurements, but their positive values support our conjecture about the value added by linkage topology: in Lycos [404], for example, we found $\Theta = (9 \pm 3) \times 10^3 \gg 0$.

Linkage topology also has been considered by others in the context of the Web, with different motivations. Links have been used for enhancing relevance judgments [556, 708], incorporated into query formulation to improve searching [22, 642], and exploited to determine "hub" and "authority" pages for document categorization and discovery [116, 115].

If links constitute useful cues for navigation, they can be exploited by autonomous browsing agents just as they are by browsing users — indeed, even the dumbest of agents (random walkers) can exploit linkage information. In fact, the random walk model may turn out to be more than just a lower bound for browsing behavior. Huberman *et al.* [289] argue that it is a very good predictive model of human browsing behavior. They assume that the *value* (e.g., relevance) of pages along the browsing path of a user follows a random walk of the form:

$$V_L = V_{L-1} + \xi_L$$

where L is the depth along the path and ξ_L is a random variable drawn from a normal distribution $\aleph(\mu, \sigma^2)$. This equation is stronger than our linkage conjecture, since it implies a positive correlation between V_L and V_{L-1} (equivalent to our relevance autocorrelation) for any $\mu > 0$. Huberman *et al.* find that the inverse-gaussian distribution of surfing depth (clicks per Web site) derived from the above random walk equation accurately fits experimental data on surfing behavior, and therefore they call such a distribution a universal *law of surfing*. Although our conjecture on the value of linkage topology is more modest, it finds strong support in these findings. Furthermore, the random-walk assumption implies normative models for constructing browsing agents who make optimal local decisions about when to stop surfing, in much the same way in which real options are evaluated in financial markets [403]. Thus we feel justified in our confidence that browsing is not an unreasonable task for autonomous agents.

Linkage topology is not a sufficient condition for an effective search, however. For a given query q, it seems plausible that relevance autocorrelation decays rapidly for distances greater than some correlation distance $\Delta_{R,q}$. If an agent is farther than $\Delta_{R,q}$ links away from a relevant document, the search is blind. Since $\Delta_{R,q}$ is unknown, there is no way to estimate the necessary amount of energy with which to initially endow agents at any arbitrary starting point. If such amount is underestimated, extinction will ensue before any relevant document is located. And if it is overestimated, resources will be unnecessarily wasted searching through unlikely neighborhoods.

It appears then crucial to launch InfoSpiders from "good" starting points. By this we mean that a starting point should be within a radius $\Delta_{R,q}$ of a target page. Our previous experiments (see the next subsection) quantitatively confirm this necessity. A naive way to meet this condition would be to start from pages with very high numbers of out-links. This is not a solution, however, because the probability of choosing an appropriate link from such a page decreases in proportion to its fan-out.

Search engines, on the other hand, can rely on statistical topology to provide for good starting points. Even if the index does not contain the target, it probably contains pages within a radius $\Delta_{R,q}$ of it. We are assured that the pages returned by the engine contain the query words. Linkage topology can then lead the agents in the right direction. We conclude that the information encoded by statistical and linkage topologies are complementary — search engines and browsing agents should work together to serve the user most effectively.

14.6.2 Previous Results

The InfoSpiders system was evaluated, at both the level of the population and of single agents, on a more limited and controlled subset than the whole Web. A subset of the Encyclopaedia Britannica [187] was chosen, among other methodological reasons, because of its reliable and readily available relevant sets corresponding to a large number of test queries. Each query had a *depth* describing the minimum distance between the starting points and the relevant set. Depth was roughly inverse to generality — deeper queries were more specific and their smaller relevant sets added to their difficulty.

The collective performance of InfoSpiders was assessed, and compared to other search algorithms, by a variation of the *search length* metric [142]. We measured the total number of pages visited by InfoSpiders before some fraction of the relevant set was discovered. As a sanity check, InfoSpiders were first compared against a simple non-adaptive algorithm, *breadth-first-search* [428]. In this experiment the use of the centralized cache was allowed, so that

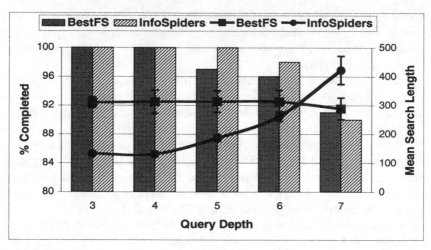

Fig. 14.8. Performance of unsupervised InfoSpiders versus best-first-search. Non-completed queries were those for which InfoSpiders ran out of time, or went extinct; and for which best-first-search ran out of time, or became engulfed in previously visited areas. Search length was averaged over same-depth queries, and error bars correspond to standard errors. The implementation used in this experiment simulated distributed execution of agents across servers. Therefore InfoSpiders had no cache and counted all (new and old) pages visited; but search length was measured concurrently, i.e., taking the maximum parallel length across all agent lineages.

only new pages counted toward the search length. Encouragingly, the search length of InfoSpiders across the whole depth spectrum was as much as an order of magnitude shorter than that achieved by breadth-first-search.

In a second series of experiments, distributed InfoSpiders were compared against a priority-queue implementation of *best-first-search* [429]. This algorithm used the InfoSpiders machinery at the agent level, combined with a globally-optimum heuristic to decide the order in which to visit the pages.[9] The results, partly reproduced in Fig. 14.8, were illuminating. For the more general queries InfoSpiders had a significant advantage over best-first-search, while for the deepest queries the situation was reversed. Furthermore, both algorithms degraded in performance with increasing depth, i.e., they succeeded less frequently at locating the required fraction of relevant documents. These results support our argument of the previous section, in favor of using search engines to provide InfoSpiders with good starting points.

Focusing our analysis at the level of single agents, we also observed individual agents in the course of single search runs to evaluate whether they were capable of internalizing spatially and temporally local features (words) from the environment into their adaptive search behaviors [429, 427]. In fact, we

---

[9] InfoSpiders can implement a search strategy similar to best-first-search by evolving high values for the β gene, but only from the local "perspective" of single agents; best-first-search is an upper bound for global search algorithms.

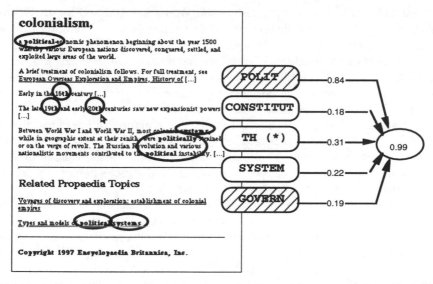

Fig. 14.9. Internalization of spatial, temporal, and experiential context. An agent's representation is shown along with its page of birth. This agent retained some of the original query words (shown as shaded input units) that were locally relevant, but eliminated others in favor of terms that better correlated locally with relevance. One of these (marked by a star) was the product of a new mutation, capturing the occurrence of this term in the page whose relevance resulted in the agent's birth. Relevance was part of the temporal context because it was determined by user feedback. The weights of the neural net (in this case a simple perceptron) will eventually encode the relative importance attributed to the keywords.

found that two agents born at the same time but in different places (pages) had adapted to the spatial context in which they had evolved. Their keyword vectors contained different words that were locally correlated with relevance, in their respective neighborhoods. Similarly, along the temporal dimension, two agents born on the same page but at a different times were subject to different user assessments; the different keywords appearing in their representations were consistent with the shifting importance associated with locally occurring terms in their respective temporal contexts. Finally, two agents born at the same time and in the same place learned during their lifetimes different neural net weights for the same keywords, reflecting the reinforcement signals provided to Q-learning by their respective life experiences. Figure 14.9 illustrates these observations.

14.6.3 The Role of Context

The results just described point to some other limitations of search engines, besides those of scalability. Adaptive information agents can further improve on search engines with their capability to deal with *context*.

All samples of language, including the Web pages indexed by search engines, depend heavily on shared context for comprehension. An author must make assumptions about the intended audience of a document, and when the latter appears in a "traditional" medium (conference proceedings, academic journal, etc.) it is likely that typical readers will understand it as intended. But the Web brings to the document a huge new audience, a good part of which will not share the author's intended context.

These vague linguistic concerns have concrete manifestation in the global word frequency statistics collected by search engines. The utility of an index term, as a discriminator of relevant from irrelevant items, can become a muddy average of its application across multiple, distinct sub-corpora within which these words have more focused meaning [646].

Situated agents, on the other hand, can rely on local coherence in keyword distributions by exploiting their linkage topology. Over time, agents may come to internalize the features that best describe the current documents and discriminate relevant pages. For example, agents browsing through pages about "rock climbing" and "rock'n'roll" should attribute different weights to the word "rock" depending on whether the query they are trying to satisfy is about music or sports. The neighborhood where an agent is situated in the environment provides it with the local context within which to analyze word meanings. Conversely, the words that surround links in a document provide an agent with valuable information to guide its path decisions.

Indices are also constructed without knowledge of the particular queries that they will answer, or of the users posing them. A universal ranking scheme may be generally good but probably will not be the best for each specific query or particular user. Conversely, personal agents may adapt to a user's interests, even if they change over time. They can internalize the user's preferences with respect to, e.g., vocabulary, word disambiguation, and relative importance of terms.

14.6.4 The Future

This chapter has discussed the scalability limitation of search engines and suggested a solution based on populations of adaptive information agents. The case study of sect. 14.5 has illustrated the potential search scalability achievable through the synergy between search engines and online browsing agents.

The viability of adaptive information agents in achieving scalable Web search, however, cannot be demonstrated with anecdotal evidence. Quantitative confirmation of the ideas discussed in this chapter must be sought through extensive testing on the Web. One experiment would have human browsers and InfoSpiders compete in locating documents not indexed by search engines. Another approach would be to create a new page and measure how long it takes, on average, until it is found by a crawler (provided it is not directly submitted to it by the author); this time can be compared to the average time it takes InfoSpiders to find the page, starting from appropriate queries and different hit lists derived from search engines.

Continued development of the InfoSpiders prototype (starting with an urgent upgrade of the HTML parser) is a precondition for such experiments and thus represents an important goal for the near future. Many aspects of the model also remain to be explored in the "real world," from unsupervised query expansion to shifting relevance feedback under long-standing queries; from parameter optimization to the role of recombination; and from the effect of cache size to differential costs under distributed implementations.

Beyond such explorations, we envision that in the growing and increasingly complex Web of information, users will have to rely heavily on adaptive personal agents. People will need to trust their agents and delegate more and more of their tedious tasks to them. This will shift the load of the network from today's bulk of human and "dumb" crawlers to more intelligent agents, possibly exchanging information autonomously on their owners' behalf. Agents will thus shift the boundary between our brain and the world; hopefully we will be able to make a better use of our precious time and cognitive skills.

Acknowledgments

The authors wish to thank their respective departments at U. Iowa and U. Dayton for support. Parts of the InfoSpiders code are ©1997 W3C (MIT, INRIA, Keio), ©1993 Free Software Foundation, Inc., and ©1992-1997 Matthias Neeracher. We thank these sources for making such software available under the GNU General Public License. Daniel Clouse contributed a software library for associative arrays. Graziano Obertelli provided for assistance with software engineering issues. The InfoSpiders project originated from a collaboration with Richard K. Belew, whose advice is behind many of the ideas discussed in this chapter. Finally, we are grateful to Charles Elkan, Gary Cottrell, Russell Impagliazzo, and all the members of the Cognitive Computer Science Research Group in the CSE Department at U. C. San Diego for helpful discussions and suggestions.

Part IV

Mobile Information Agents and Security

Introduction

An appealing feature of next-generation information agents which is attracting increasing interest is mobility. Roughly speaking, mobile agents can be transported to different sites in the Internet and provide mobile data access and processing. Contrary to popular belief, mobile agents do not really move themselves, but depend on a given mobile agent system for this purpose. A mobile agent can be seen as a continuously executing program only interrupted during the transport between several servers. Such an agent is almost written in an interpreted machine-independent language such as Java, so it can run in heterogeneous environments. It is assumed that an appropriate computation environment is accessible on any server the agent might visit.

The new paradigm of mobile agents, or remote programming, is in contrast to the paradigm of client/server computing via remote procedure calls (RPC) conceived in the 1970s. Any two computers or software agents who communicate via RPC agree in advance upon the effect of remotely accessible procedures, the kind of arguments, and the type of results. This appears to be insufficient in dynamically changing information environments. Besides, any request for procedure performance, acknowledgement, or the data resulting from remote processing must be sent via the network that interconnects the respective computers. This may generate a high level of network traffic and, depending on the network design, can be susceptible to congestion delay. In addition, mobile devices, intelligent broadband [686] and wireless data networks are becoming more powerful and affordable, leading to the growing importance of mobile data access and processing [671]. To date, a large number of mobile agent systems have been developed, and several approaches deal with the integration of these systems and RPC-based middleware such as CORBA [409].

What are the main benefits of mobile information agents? Firstly, such agents may execute their services, e.g., intensive data processing and information extraction, locally at remote database servers. This may reduce network load significantly. Especially in wireless networks it is advantageous to do work remotely, in particular when the connection is temporarily lost. The agents may even exhibit intelligent strategies for actively searching and integrating information at multiple servers (see Fig. IV.1.). Resource and service discovery is the fundamental premise of mobile information agents.

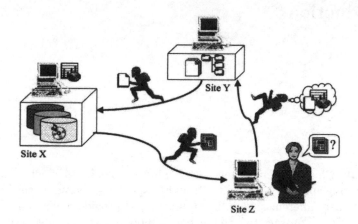

Fig. IV.1. A scenario of a mobile information agent executing tasks at multiple
  sites.

Mobile agent technology enhances distributed applications by enabling
users to access information ubiquitously - anywhere and anytime. Mobile information agents may enable migration of small application-based business
logic in corporate intranets on demand and dynamic maintenance of connected data warehouses in the Internet. In the near future, the development
of mobile agents may benefit in particular from progress on wireless, satellite-
based communication, and from mass production of wearable computers.

What can be achieved with mobile agent systems today? Actually there
are several systems available. They consist of either

- Java class libraries such as IBM Aglets [301, 367], ObjectSpace Voyager
  [695], Mitsubishi Concordia [139], and MOLE [446], or
- Scripting language systems with interpreter and runtime support, like
  D'Agents/AgentTcl (Chapter 15, [150]) and ARA [16, 518], or
- Operating system services accessible via a scripting language such as
  TACOMA [660].

Resource discovery is virtually absent in current mobile agent systems. It
is still assumed that an agent is aware of the accessible resources and services
at a site in advance. An agent might be more efficient if he can dynamically
discover the resource he needs to accomplish the tasks than if he is hardwired
to do work.

Mobile agents also require access to site resources such as CPU cycles,
disk capacities, graphics, memory, persistence service, and threads. Resource
management is hardly supported by current mobile agent systems – such as
IBM Aglets or Voyager – or not specified at all.

Mobility mechanisms include remote method invocation such as Java
RMI, agent cloning, and code on demand. Most systems use application protocols on top of TCP for transporting agent code and state.

In addition, interoperability among heterogeneous mobile agent systems is crucial for any unlimited crawling of mobile information agents through the Internet and Web. This concerns in particular the need of facilities to port and persistently store data and code of mobile agents. Portability among different mobile agent systems may be achieved either by adding features to a platform-neutral programming language such as Java to support migration via RMI, or middleware like the Internet Inter-ORB protocol (CORBA-IIOP) and the distributed component object model (DCOM). The issue of data persistence still has to be covered in most current mobile agent systems, except for, e.g., in Voyager and Concordia.

Despite the limitations of current systems, some encouraging efforts towards the standardization of an intelligent mobile agent system are under way. The most prominent efforts are the addition of a mobile agent facility (MAF [480]) to CORBA by OMG, and the proposal by the Foundation of Intelligent and Physical Agents (FIPA). These efforts even try to deal with the problem of misuse involving mobile agents.

What is the state of security when using mobile information agents? Remarkably, in most mobile agent systems the server and the computation environment are assumed to be trustworthy and not hostile to any agent. The same is assumed about the agents. There are several different types of attacks possible, in both directions: Misuse of hosting servers by mobile agents and, in turn, misuse of mobile agents by hosts and other agents.

Traditional security mechanisms rely on cryptographic methods for implementation of authentication and authorization. But there are still no satisfactory solutions to prevent an attack by a hostile server such as listening to interagent communication, refusing to execute agent code, or accessing the private data of an agent. Such misuse is hard to prevent since the server has to have access to the agent code to execute it. Even the use of a mobile agent system's own security manager implemented in Java might fail due to the fact that the Java model code was proven to be broken. Methods for protecting a server from malicious mobile agents include proof-carrying code, various schemes for access and execution control, digital signatures for authentication, and other cryptographic techniques.

To summarize, mobility may be beneficial in terms of performance, network load balancing and customization of distributed applications. However, efforts to ensure security might outweigh these benefits. The discussion of whether mobility will become an essential feature for intelligent information agents in the near future has just begun.

The Contributions

In the first chapter of this part, *Brian Brewington, Katsuhiro Moizumi, George Cybenko, Robert Gray, David Kotz* and *Daniela Rus* focus on mobile agents for distributed information retrieval. The authors survey existing mobile agent systems and examine one specific information retrieval application, searching distributed collections of technical reports, and consider how mobile agents can be used to implement this application efficiently and easily. The chapter also describes two services that allow mobile agents to deal with uncertainty in the network environment and in information resources.

Robert Tolksdorf suggests coordination patterns for mobile agents in Chapter 16. He understands mobility as a way to manage accessibility dependencies between activities. The author analyzes the entities involved in accessing information systems with regard to their mobility properties. Based on this analysis patterns of coordination amongst mobile agents are derived and sample implementations of these patterns are described. These descriptions are written in a variant of the coordination language LINDA, called Mobile Object Spaces. Finally, other approaches to coordination patterns of mobile agents are surveyed. It appears that the (re-)use of this kind of software pattern or template is certainly a valuable idea for modelling coordination mechanisms. However, it remains to be shown that more complex coordination and collaboration mechanisms such as auctions, voting, or temporary team formation may be satisfactorily described by these structures.

As mentioned above there are cases where it is more efficient for an agent to perform its activity on the remote server. One approach to deal with that situation is to spawn, i.e. to create and transport an appropriate agent to that server. In Chapter 17, *Onn Shehory* introduces the notion of agent spawning, especially what is known as agent cloning. Agent spawning is an appropriate means for resolving agent overload problems. Agents in a multi-agent system may face situations where tasks overload their computational capacities or do not fit their capabilities. Usually, this problem is solved by passing tasks to other agents or agent migration to remote hosts. Agent spawning is a more comprehensive approach to balancing local agent overloads. Agents may spawn themselves, pass tasks to others, die or merge. The author discusses the mechanisms required for deciding upon when, how and where to spawn agents in detail. Simulation results show the advantage of using the implemented agent spawning mechanism under some constraints.

The question of security in face of selfish, malicious information agents travelling among sites like 'bandits on the information highway' has become popular. In turn, an information agent itself, particularly its code and private data, could be the focus of unauthorized interest while it moves through the Internet gathering relevant informations for its users. Currently, there has been very little work on agent security other than that in the Java applet world. In the final chapter, *Christian F. Tschudin* provides the reader with a general discussion of the problem of mobile code protection and surveys current techniques that enable a mobile agent to provide some security for itself although it operates in an insecure space. Such techniques include the execution of encrypted programs, code obfuscation, deception, diffusion, and tracing of critical operations.

15. Mobile Agents for Distributed Information Retrieval

Brian Brewington, Robert Gray, Katsuhiro Moizumi, David Kotz,
George Cybenko, and Daniela Rus

Thayer School of Engineering, Department of Computer Science,
Dartmouth College, Hanover, New Hampshire 03755, USA.
E-Mail: firstname.lastname@dartmouth.edu

Summary.

  A mobile agent is an executing program that can migrate during execution from machine to machine in a heterogeneous network. On each machine, the agent interacts with stationary service agents and other resources to accomplish its task. Mobile agents are particularly attractive in distributed information-retrieval applications. By moving to the location of an information resource, the agent can search the resource locally, eliminating the transfer of intermediate results across the network and reducing end-to-end latency. In this chapter, we first discuss the strengths of mobile agents, and argue that although none of these strengths are unique to mobile agents, no competing technique shares all of them. Next, after surveying several representative mobile-agent systems, we examine one specific information-retrieval application, searching distributed collections of technical reports, and consider how mobile agents can be used to implement this application efficiently and easily. Then we spend the bulk of the chapter describing two planning services that allow mobile agents to deal with dynamic network environments and information resources: (1) planning algorithms that let an agent choose the best migration path through the network, given its current task and the current network conditions, and (2) planning algorithms that tell an agent how to observe a changing set of documents in a way that detects changes as soon as possible while minimizing overhead. Finally, we consider the types of errors that can occur when information from multiple sources is merged and filtered, and argue that the structure of a mobile-agent application determines the extent to which these errors affect the final result.

15.1 Introduction

A mobile agent is an executing program that can migrate during execution from machine to machine in a heterogeneous network. In other words, the agent can suspend its execution, migrate to another machine, and then resume execution on the new machine from the point at which it left off. On each machine, the agent interacts with stationary agents and other resources to accomplish its task.

Mobile agents have several advantages in distributed information-retrieval applications. By migrating to an information resource, an agent can invoke resource operations *locally*, eliminating the network transfer of intermediate data. By migrating to the other side of an unreliable network link, an agent can continue executing even if the network link goes down, making mobile agents particularly attractive in mobile-computing environments. Most importantly, an agent can choose different migration strategies depending on its task and the current network conditions, and then change its strategies as network conditions change. Complex, efficient and robust behaviors can be realized with surprisingly little code.

Although each of these advantages is a reasonable argument for mobile agents, none of them are unique to mobile agents, and, in fact, any specific application can be implemented just as efficiently and robustly with more traditional techniques. Different applications require *different* traditional techniques, however, and many applications require a combination of techniques. In short, the true strength of mobile agents is not that they make new distributed applications possible, but rather that they allow a wide range of distributed applications to be implemented efficiently, robustly and easily within a single, general framework.

In this chapter, we first motivate mobile agents in detail, comparing mobile agents with traditional client/server techniques and other mobile-code systems, and survey several existing mobile-agent systems. Then we consider a specific information-retrieval application, searching distributed collections of technical reports, and how this application can be implemented easily using our own mobile-agent system, D'Agents. Our mobile-agent implementation performs better than (or as well as) a more traditional RPC implementation when the query is complex or network conditions are poor, but worse when the query is simple and network conditions are good. Complex queries and slow networks allow inefficiencies in the core D'Agents and other mobile-agent systems to be amortized over a longer execution or data-transfer time. These inefficiencies, which are intrinsic to the early stages of mobile-agent development, primarily cause large migration and communication overheads.[1] Fortunately, solutions to many of the inefficiencies already exist in high-performance servers and recent mobile-agent work. Once these solutions are integrated into existing mobile-agent systems, mobile agents will perform competitively in a much wider range of network environments.

Improving the performance of the core system does not address all of an agent's needs. In particular, an effective mobile agent is one that can choose dynamically all aspects of its behavior, i.e., how many agents to send out, where to send them, whether those agents should migrate or remain stationary, whether those agents should send out children, and so on. The agent must have access to a wealth of network, machine and resource information, and a corresponding toolbox of planning algorithms, so that it can choose the most effective migration strategy for its task and the current network con-

---

[1] Migration overhead is the time on the source machine to pack up an agent's current state and send the state to the target machine, plus the time on the target machine to authenticate the incoming agent, start up an appropriate execution environment, and restore the state.

ditions. Therefore, a mobile-agent system must provide an extensive sensing and planning infrastructure.

In this chapter, we describe several simple directory and network-sensing services in the context of the technical-report application. Then we present initial work on two more complex planning services: (1) a set of planning algorithms that allow an agent or a small group of cooperating agents to identify the best migration path through a network, and (2) a set of planning algorithms that tell an agent how to observe a changing set of documents (specifically the pages available on the World Wide Web) in a way that detects changes as soon as possible while minimizing overhead. In the second case, the current planning algorithms are oriented towards a stationary agent that has moved to some attractive proxy site and is now observing the documents from across the network. We consider, however, how the algorithms can be extended to an agent that migrates continuously or sends out child agents.

Section 15.2 explores the motivation behind mobile agents in more detail. Section 15.3 surveys nine representative mobile-agent systems, and briefly mentions other mobile-agent systems. Section 15.4 describes the technical-report application and analyzes its performance. Finally, Section 15.5 discusses the two planning services.

15.2 Motivation

Mobile agents have several strengths. First, by migrating to the location of a needed resource, an agent can interact with the resource without transmitting intermediate data across the network, conserving bandwidth and reducing latencies. Similarly, by migrating to the location of a user, an agent can respond to user actions rapidly. In either case, the agent can continue its interaction with the resource or user even if network connections go down temporarily. These features make mobile agents particularly attractive in mobile-computing applications, which often must deal with low-bandwidth, high-latency, and unreliable network links.

Second, mobile agents allow traditional clients and servers to offload work to each other, and to *change* who offloads to whom according to the capabilities and current loads of the client, server and network. Similarly, mobile agents allow an application to dynamically deploy its components to arbitrary network sites, and to *re-deploy* those components in response to changing network conditions.

Finally, most distributed applications fit naturally into the mobile-agent model, since a mobile agent can migrate sequentially through a set of machines, send out a wave of child agents to visit machines in parallel, remain stationary and interact with resources remotely, or any combination of these three extremes. Complex, efficient and robust behaviors can be realized with surprisingly little code. In addition, our own experience with undergraduate programmers at Dartmouth suggests that mobile agents are easier to understand than many other distributed-computing paradigms.

Although each of these strengths is a reasonable argument for mobile agents, it is important to realize that none of these strengths are unique to mobile agents [126]. Any specific application can be implemented just as efficiently with other techniques. These other techniques include message passing, remote procedure calls (RPC) [70], remote object-method invocation (as in Java RMI [736] or CORBA [50]), queued RPC [319] (in which RPC calls are queued for later invocation if the network connection is down), remote evaluation [197, 644, 647] (which extends RPC by allowing the client to send the procedure code to the server, rather than just the parameters for an existing procedure), process migration [178, 390], stored procedures (such as [77], where SQL procedures can be uploaded into a relational database for later invocation), Java applets [102] and servlets [118] (which respectively are Java programs that are downloaded by a Web browser or uploaded into a Web server), automatic installation facilities, application-specific query languages, and application-specific proxies within the permanent network. None of these other techniques, however, share all of the strengths of mobile agents.

Messaging passing and remote invocation. In contrast to message passing and remote invocation, mobile code (including mobile agents) allows an application to conserve bandwidth and reduce latency *even if* an information resource provides low-level operations, simply because the mobile code can be sent to the network location of the resource. The mobile code can invoke as many low-level server operations as needed to perform its task without transferring any intermediate data across the network. Moreover, the mobile code can continue its task even if the network link between the client and server machines goes down. The code has been sent to the *other side* of the link, and will not need the link again until it is ready to send back a "final" result. The resource provider can implement a single high-level operation that performs each client's desired task in its entirety. Implementing these high-level operations, however, becomes an intractable programming task as the number of distinct clients increases. In addition, it discourages modern software engineering, since the server becomes a collection of complex, specialized routines, rather than simple, general primitives.

Process migration. Typically, process-migration systems do not allow the processes to choose when and where they migrate. Instead, most are designed to *transparently* move processes from one machine to another to balance load. In addition, although some process-migration systems allow the processes to migrate across heterogeneous machines [71], these facilities still are intended for "closed" environments, where security is less of a concern. Mobile agents, on the other hand, can move when and where they want, according to their own application-specific criteria. For example, although mobile agents can move solely to obtain CPU cycles, most mobile agents will move to colocate themselves with specific information resources. In addition, nearly all mobile-agent systems have been designed from the ground up to be both platform-independent and secure in open environments.

Remote evaluation, stored procedures, applets and servlets. Mobile agents are much more flexible than these other forms of mobile code. First, a mobile agent can move from a client to server or from a server to client. Most other forms of mobile code allow code transfer in a single direction only. Second, a mobile agent can move at times of its own choosing. Java applets, in particular, are downloaded onto a client machine only when a human user visits an associated Web page. Third, a mobile agent can move as many times as desired. For example, if a server is implemented as a mobile agent, it can continuously move from one network location to another to minimize the average latency between itself and its current clients [541]. Conversely, a client agent can migrate sequentially through some set of machines, accessing some resource on each. For example, if a client agent needs to query one database to determine which query it should run against a second database, it can migrate to the first database, run the first query, analyze the query results to determine the second query, throw out the analysis code to make itself smaller, migrate directly to the second database, run the second query, and carry just the final result back to its home machine. Most implementations of remote evaluation and stored procedures, along with all Web browsers and servers that support applets and servlets, do not allow the mobile code to spawn additional mobile code onto *different* machines, making any form of sequential migration impossible. Instead, the client machine must interact with each resource in turn.

Finally, a mobile agent can spawn off child agents no matter where it is in the network. For example, a mobile agent can move to a dynamically selected proxy site, send out child agents to search some distributed data collection in parallel, and then merge and filter the search results on the proxy site before carrying just the final result back to the client. As with sequential migration, most implementations of the other mobile-code techniques do not support such behavior.

Application-specific solutions. Finally, in contrast to application-specific solutions, such as specialized query languages and dedicated proxies pre-installed at specific network locations, mobile agents are distinguished by both their flexibility and their ease of implementation. An application can send its own proxy to an arbitrarily selected network location, and can move that proxy as network conditions change. In addition, a server simply can make its operations visible to visiting mobile agents, rather than implementing higher-level operations or some application-specific language to minimize network traffic.

Summary. In short, an application must use one or more of these other techniques to realize the same behavior that mobile agents allow, and different applications must use different techniques. The true strength of mobile agents is that a wide range of distributed applications can be implemented efficiently, easily and robustly within the same, general framework, and these applications can exhibit extremely flexible behavior in the face of changing network conditions. As we show in Section 15.4, mobile-agent systems are not efficient enough yet to be competitive with the other techniques in every situation. However, the potential for mobile agents is clear, and mobile-agent researchers now share a common, realizable goal: a mobile-agent system in which (1) inter-agent communication is as fast as traditional RPC, (2) migration of code is only a small factor slower than an RPC call that transfers an equivalent amount of data, (3) computation-intensive agents execute no more than twice as slowly as natively compiled code, and (4) a wide range of network-status information is available to agents for use in their decision-making process. In such a system, migration would be advantageous even if the task involved only a few operations at each information resource, and a mobile agent could use its knowledge of the task, the needed information resources and the current network conditions to decide whether to migrate or remain stationary. In other words, mobile agents would perform no worse than equivalent solutions implemented with the other techniques, and would often perform much better.

15.3 Survey of Mobile-Agent Systems

In this section, we examine nine representative mobile-agent systems, and then briefly discuss their similarities and differences.

15.3.1 Representative Mobile-Agent Systems

Multiple-Language Systems.

Ara. Ara[2] [518, 517] supports agents written in Tcl and C/C++. The C/C++ agents are compiled into an efficient interpreted bytecode called MACE; this bytecode, rather than the C/C++ code itself, is sent from machine to machine. For both Tcl and MACE, Ara provides a go instruction, which automatically captures the complete state of the agent, transfers the state to the target machine, and resumes agent execution at the exact point of the go. Ara also allows the agent to *checkpoint* its current internal state at any time during its execution. Unlike other multiple-language systems, the entire Ara system is multi-threaded; the agent server and both the Tcl and MACE interpreters run inside a single Unix process. Although this approach complicates the implementation, it has significant performance advantages, since there is little interpreter startup or communication overhead. When a new agent arrives, it simply begins execution in a new thread, and when one agent wants to communicate with another, it simply transfers the message

---

[2] http://www.uni-kl.de/AG-Nehmer/Ara/

structure to the target agent, rather than having to use inter-process communication. Nearly all Java-only systems are also multi-threaded, and see the same performance advantages.

At the time of this writing, the Ara group is adding support for Java agents, and finishing implementation work on their initial security mechanisms [517]. An agent's code is cryptographically signed by its manufacturer (programmer); its arguments and its overall resource allowance are signed by its owner (user). Each machine has one or more *virtual places*, which are created by agents and have agent-specified admission functions. A migrating agent must enter a particular place. When it enters the place, the admission function rejects the agent or assigns it a set of allowances based on its cryptographic credentials. These allowances, which include such things as file-system access and total memory, are then enforced in simple wrappers around resource-access functions.

D'Agents. D'Agents[3] [250], which was once known as Agent Tcl, supports agents written in Tcl, Java and Scheme, as well as *stationary* agents written in C and C++. Like Ara, D'Agents provides a go instruction (Tcl and Java only), and automatically captures and restores the complete state of a migrating agent. Unlike Ara, only the D'Agent server is multi-threaded; each agent is executed in a separate process, which simplifies the implementation considerably, but adds the overhead of inter-process communication. The D'Agent server uses public-key cryptography to authenticate the identity of an incoming agent's owner. Stationary *resource-manager* agents assign access rights to the agent based on this authentication and the administrator's preferences, and language-specific enforcement modules enforce the access rights, either preventing a violation from occurring (e.g., file-system access) or terminating the agent when a violation occurs (e.g., total CPU time). Each resource manager is associated with a specific resource such as the file system. The resources managers can be as complex as desired, but the default managers simply associate a list of access rights with each owner. Unlike Ara, most resource managers are not consulted when the agent arrives, but instead only when the agent (1) attempts to access the corresponding resource or (2) explicitly requests a specific access right. At that point, however, the resource manager forwards all relevant access rights to the enforcement module, and D'Agents behaves in the same way as Ara, enforcing the access rights with short wrapper functions around the resource access functions.

Current work on D'Agents falls into four broad categories: (1) scalability, (2) network-sensing and planning services, which allow an agent to choose the best migration strategy given the current network conditions; (3) market-based resource control, where agents are given a finite supply of currency from their owner's own finite supply and must spend the currency to access needed resources [87]; and (4) support for mobile-computing environments,

---

[3] http://www.cs.dartmouth.edu/~agent/

where applications must deal with low-bandwidth, high-latency and unreliable network links [355]. Some scalability issues are discussed in the next section, where we analyze the performance of a distributed retrieval application running on top of the D'Agents system. Network-sensing and planning is discussed in Section 15.5, where we examine some services necessary for a distributed information-retrieval to make efficient use of available network resources.

D'Agents has been used in several information-retrieval applications, including the technical-report searcher that is discussed in the next section, as well as 3DBase [148], a system for retrieving three-dimensional drawings (CAD drawings) of mechanical parts based on their similarity to a query drawing.

Tacoma. Tacoma[4] [316, 317] supports agents written in C, C++, ML, Perl, Python, Scheme and Visual Basic. Unlike Ara and D'Agents, Tacoma does not provide automatic state-capture facilities. Instead, when an agent wants to migrate to a new machine, it creates a *folder* into which it packs its code and any desired state information. The folder is sent to the new machine, which starts up the necessary execution environment and then calls a known entry point within the agent's code to resume agent execution. Although this approach places the burden of state capture squarely onto the *agent* programmer, it also allows the rapid integration of new languages into the Tacoma system, since existing interpreters and virtual machines can be used without modification. Tacoma is used most notably in StormCast, which is a distributed weather-monitoring system, and the Tacoma Image Server, which is a retrieval system for satellite images [317].

The public versions of Tacoma rely on the underlying operating system for security, but do provide hooks for adding a cryptographic authentication subsystem so that agents from untrusted parties can be rejected outright. In addition, the Tacoma group is exploring several interesting fault-tolerance and security mechanisms, such as (1) using cooperating agents to search replicated databases in parallel and then securely vote on a final result [441], and (2) using security automata (state machines) to specify a machine's security policy and then directly using the automata and software fault isolation to enforce the policy [593].

Java-Based Systems.

Aglets. Aglets[5] [367, 366] was one of the first Java-based systems. Like all commercial systems, including Concordia [737, 698], Jumping Beans [320], and Voyager [695], Aglets does not capture an agent's thread (or control) state during migration, since thread capture requires modifications to the standard Java virtual machine. In other words, thread capture means that the system could be used only with one specific virtual machine, significantly reducing

---

[4] http://www.tacoma.cs.uit.no:8080/TACOMA/
[5] http://www.trl.ibm.co.jp/aglets/

market acceptance.[6] Thus, rather than providing the go primitive of D'Agents and Ara, Aglets and the other commercial systems instead use variants of the Tacoma model, where agent execution is restarted from a known entry point after each migration. In particular, Aglets uses an event-driven model. When an agent wants to migrate, it calls the dispatch method. The Aglets system calls the agent's onDispatching method, which performs application-specific cleanup, kills the agent's threads, serializes the agent's code and object state, and sends the code and object state to the new machine. On the new machine, the system calls the agent's onArrival method, which performs application-specific initialization, and then calls the agent's run method to restart agent execution.

Aglets includes a simple persistence facility, which allows an agent to write its code and object state to secondary storage and temporarily "deactivate" itself; proxies, which act as representatives for Aglets, and among other things, provide location transparency; a lookup service for finding moving Aglets; and a range of message-passing facilities for inter-agent communication. The Aglet security model is similar to both the D'Agent and Ara security models, and to the security models for the other Java-based systems below. An Aglet has both an owner and a manufacturer. When the agent enters a context (i.e., a virtual place) on a particular machine, the context assigns a set of permissions to the agent based on its authenticated owner and manufacturer. These permissions are enforced with standard Java security mechanisms, such as a customized security manager.

Concordia. Concordia[7] [737, 698] is a Java-based mobile-agent system that has a strong focus on security and reliability. Like most other mobile-Java agent systems, they move the agent objects code and data, but not thread state, from one machine to another. Like many other systems, Concordia agents are bundled with an *itinerary* of places to visit, which can be adjusted by the agent while en route.[8] Agents, events, and messages can be queued, if the remote site is not currently reachable. Agents are carefully saved to a persistent store, before departing a site and after arriving at a new site, to avoid agent loss in the event of a machine crash. Agents are protected from tampering through encryption while they are in transmission or stored on disk; agent hosts are protected from malicious agents through cryptographic authentication of the agent's owner, and access control lists that guard each resource.

Jumping Beans. Jumping Beans[9] [320] is a Java-based framework for mobile agents. Computers wishing to host mobile agents run a Jumping Beans

---

[6] D'Agents, which does use a modified Java virtual machine to capture thread state, is a research system and is under no such market constraints.

[7] http://www.concordia.mea.com/

[8] Aglets calls the same method at each stop on the itinerary, while Jumping Beans, Concordia, and Voyager all allow the agent to specify a different method for each stop.

[9] http://www.JumpingBeans.com/

agency, which is associated with some Jumping Beans *domain.* Each domain has a central server, which authenticates the agencies joining the domain. Mobile agents move from agency to agency, and agents can send messages to other agents; both mechanisms are implemented by passing through the server. Thus the server becomes a central point for tracking, managing, and authenticating agents. It also becomes a central point of failure or a performance bottleneck, although they intend to develop scalable servers to run on parallel machines. Another approach to scalability is to create many small domains, each with its own server. In the current version, agents cannot migrate between domains, but they intend to support that capability in future versions. Security and reliability appear to be important concerns of their system; public-key cryptography is used to authenticate agencies to the server, and *vice versa;* access-control lists are used to control an agent's access to resources, based on the permissions given to the agent's owning user.

Although they claim to move all agent code, data, and state, it is not clear from their documentation whether they actually move thread state, as in Agent Java. They require that the agent be a serializable object, so it seems likely that they implement the weaker form of mobility common to other Java-based agent systems.

Other Systems.

Messengers. The Messenger[10] project uses mobile code to build flexible distributed systems, not specifically mobile-agent systems [673, 173, 453]. In their system, computers run a minimal Messenger Operating System (MOS), which has just a few services. MOS can send and receive *messengers,* which are small packets of data and code written in their programming language MO. MOS can interpret MO programs, which may access one of their two bulletin-board services: the *global dictionary,* which allows data exchange between messengers, and the *service dictionary,* which is a searchable listing of messengers that offer services to other messengers. Ultimately, most services, including all distributed services, are offered by static and mobile messengers. In one case, they allow the messengers to carry native UNIX code, which is installed and executed on MOS; system calls are reflected back to the interpreted MO code, allowing fast execution of critical routines, while maintaining the flexibility of mobile code [676].

Obliq. Obliq [104, 94] is an interpreted, lexically scoped, object-oriented language. An Obliq object is a collection of named fields that contain methods, aliases, and values. An object can be created at a remote site, cloned onto a remote site, or migrated with a combination of cloning and redirection. Implementing mobile agents on top of these mobile objects is straightforward. An agent consists of a user-defined procedure that takes a *briefcase* as its argument; the briefcase contains the Obliq objects that the procedure needs to perform its task. The agent migrates by sending its procedure and current

---

[10] http://www.ics.uci.edu/~bic/messengers/

briefcase to the target machine, which invokes the procedure to resume agent execution.

Visual Obliq[11] [68] builds on top of Obliq's migration capabilities. Visual Obliq is an interactive application builder that includes (1) a visual programming environment for laying out graphical user interfaces, and (2) an agent server that allows Visual Obliq applications to migrate from machine to machine. When the application migrates, the state of its graphical interface is captured automatically, and recreated exactly on the new machine. Obliq does not address security issues. Visual Obliq does provide access control, namely, user-specified access checks associated with all "dangerous" Obliq commands, but does not have authentication or encryption mechanisms. Typically, therefore, the access checks will simply ask the user whether the agent should be allowed to perform the given action.

Telescript. Telescript[12] [718, 719, 721], developed at General Magic, Inc., was the first commercial mobile-agent system, and the inspiration for many of the recent mobile-agent systems. In Telescript, each network site runs a server that maintains one or more virtual *places*. An incoming agent specifics which of the places it wants to enter. The place authenticates the identity of the agent's owner by examining the agent's cryptographic credentials, and then assigns a set of access rights or *permits* to the agent. One permit, for example, might specify a maximum agent lifetime, while another might specify a maximum amount of disk usage. An agent that attempts to violate its permits is terminated immediately [718]. In addition to maintaining the places and enforcing the security constraints, the server continuously writes the internal state of executing agents to non-volatile store, so that the agents can be restored after a node failure.

A Telescript agent is written in an imperative, object-oriented language, which is similar to both Java and C++, and is compiled into bytecodes for a virtual machine that is part of each server. As in D'Agents and Ara, a Telescript agent migrates with the go instruction. A Telescript agent can communicate with other agents in two ways: (1) it can meet with an agent that is in the same place; the two agents receive references to each other's objects and then invoke each other's methods; and (2) it can connect to an object in a different place; the two agents then pass objects along the connection. Despite the fact that Telescript remains one of the most secure, fault-tolerant and efficient mobile-agent systems, it has been withdrawn from the market, largely because it was overwhelmed by the rapid spread of Java.

15.3.2 Similarities and Differences

All mobile-agent systems have the same general architecture: a server on each machine accepts incoming agents, and for each agent, starts up an appropriate

---

[11] http://www.cc.gatech.edu/gvu/people/Phd/Krishna/VO/VOHome.html
[12] http://www.genmagic.com/technology/mobile_agent.html

execution environment, loads the agent's state information into the environment, and resumes agent execution. Some systems, such as the Java-only systems above, have multi-threaded servers and run each agent in a *thread* of the server process itself; other systems have multi-process servers and run each agent in a separate interpreter process; and the rest use some combination of these two extremes. D'Agents, for example, has a multi-threaded server to increase efficiency, but separate interpreter processes to simplify its implementation. Jumping Beans [320] is of particular note since it uses a centralized server architecture (in which agents must pass through a central server on their way from one machine to another), rather than a peer-to-peer server architecture (in which agents move directly from one machine to another). Although this centralized server easily can become a performance bottleneck, it greatly simplifies security, tracking, administration and other issues, perhaps increasing initial market acceptance.

Currently, for reasons of portability and security, nearly all mobile-agent systems either interpret their languages directly, or compile their languages into bytecodes and then interpret the bytecodes. Java, which is compiled into bytecodes for the Java virtual machine, is the most popular agent language, since (1) it is portable but reasonably efficient, (2) its existing security mechanisms allow the safe execution of untrusted code, and (3) it enjoys widespread market penetration. Java is used in all commercial systems and in several research systems. Due to the recognition that agents must execute at near-native speed to be competitive with traditional techniques in certain applications, however, several researchers are experimenting with "on-the-fly" compilation [400, 275]. The agent initially is compiled into bytecodes, but compiled into native code on each machine that it visits, either as soon as it arrives or while it is executing. The most recent Java virtual machines use on-the-fly compilation, and the Java-only mobile-agent systems, which are not tied to a specific virtual machine, can take immediate advantage of the execution speedup.

Mobile-agent systems generally provide one of two kinds of migration: (1) go, which captures an agent's object state, code, and control state, allowing it to continue execution from the exact point at which it left off; and (2) *entry point*, which captures only the agent's object state and code, and then calls a known entry point inside its code to restart the agent on the new machine. The go model is more convenient for the end programmer, but more work for the system developer since routines to capture control state must be added to existing interpreters. All commercial Java-based systems use entry-point migration, since market concerns demand that these systems run on top of unmodified Java virtual machines. Research systems use both both migration techniques.

Finally, existing mobile-agent systems focus on protecting an *individual* machine against malicious agents. Aside from encrypting an agent in transit and allowing an agent to authenticate the destination machine before migrating, most existing systems do not provide any protection for the agent or for a group of machines that is *not* under single administrative control.

Other differences exist among the mobile-agent systems, such as the granularity of their communication mechanisms, whether they are built on top of or can interact with CORBA, and whether they conform to the emerging mobile-agent standards. Despite these differences, however, all of the systems discussed above (with the exception of Messengers, which is a lighter-weight mobile-agent system) are intended for the same applications, such as workflow, network management, and automated software installation. All of the systems are suitable for distributed information retrieval, and the decision of which one to use must be based on the desired implementation language, the needed level of security, and the needed performance.

15.4 Application: The Technical-Report Searcher

Mobile agents are commonly used in distributed information-retrieval applications. By sending agents to proxy sites and to the information sources themselves, the applications can avoid the transfer of intermediate data, can continue with the retrieval task even if the network link with the client machine goes down, and can merge and filter the results from the individual document collections inside the network, rather than pulling all the results back to the client machine. In addition, many retrieval tasks require the application to simply invoke a sequence of server operations with only a modest amount of "glue" code to decide which server operation should be invoked next. Since such tasks are bound by the execution time of the server operations, rather than the execution time of the glue code, a mobile agent can perform well even when implemented in one of the interpreted languages that are found in most existing mobile-agent systems. In this section, we consider such a retrieval application, namely the retrieval of documents from a distributed collection of technical reports. This application is representative of many other distributed locating, gathering and organizing applications, and results from its study are applicable to other applications with similar structure.

15.4.1 Description

Figure 15.1 shows the structure of the technical-report application, which was implemented on top of our mobile-agent system, D'Agents. The technical reports themselves come from the Department of Computer Science at Dartmouth College. We distributed the reports across multiple Dartmouth machines, each of which is running the D'Agents system and the Smart system. The Smart system is a successful statistical information-retrieval system that uses the vector-space model to measure the textual similarity between documents [573]. The Smart system on each machine is "wrapped" inside a stationary agent, which is labeled as *Smart IR agent* in the figure. This stationary agent provides a three-function interface to the Smart system: (1) run a textual query and obtain a list of relevant documents, (2) obtain the full text of a document, and (3) obtain pair-wise similarity scores for every pair of documents in a list of documents. The pair-wise similarity scores are used to construct different graphical representations of the query results.

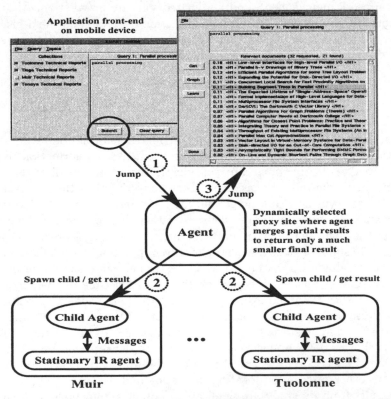

Fig. 15.1. An example application. Here a mobile agent is searching a distributed collection of technical reports. The agent first decides whether to move to a dynamically selected proxy site. Then it decides whether to spawn child agents or simply interact with the individual document collections from across the network. *muir* and *tuolomne* are two machines at Dartmouth. Note that the yellow pages, which the agent uses to discover the locations of the document collection, are not shown in this figure.

When each stationary Smart agent starts execution, it registers with a virtual *yellow pages* [571]. The yellow pages are a simple, distributed, hierarchical directory service. When the Smart agent registers with the yellow pages, it provides its location (i.e., its identifier within the D'Agents namespace) and a set of keywords that describe its service (i.e., *smart, technical-reports, text*). A client agent searches for a service by sending a keyword query to the yellow pages. The yellow pages return the locations of all services whose keyword lists match the keyword query (more specifically, all services whose keyword lists are a superset of the keyword query). A forthcoming version of the yellow pages will allow the client agents to search by interface definition as well [472].

The main application agent is a GUI that runs on the user's machine. This GUI is shown at the top of Figure 15.1. The GUI first lets the user enter a free-text query and optionally select specific document collections from a list of known document collections. Once the GUI has the query, it spawns a mobile agent onto the local machine. This mobile agent first consults one or more local network-sensing agents [571, 445], which keep track of the network connection between the user's machine and the rest of the network. These network-sensing agents know what type of network hardware is in the machine, the maximum bandwidth of that hardware, an uptime/downtime history of the network link, and the current observed latency and bandwidth of the network link. The uptime/downtime history is used to calculate an approximate *reliability factor*, i.e., the probability that the network connection will go down at some point in the next few minutes. Our reliability factor is quite simple—it is just the percentage of time that the network connection has been down during the past n hours—but is sufficient for our purposes.

After consulting the network-sensing agents, it makes its most important decision. If the network connection between the user's machine and the network is reliable and has high bandwidth, the agent stays on the user's machine. If the connection is unreliable or has low bandwidth, the agent jumps to a *proxy site* within the permanent network. This proxy site is shown in the middle of Figure 15.1. With our current reliability and bandwidth thresholds, the agent typically will remain on the user's machine if the machine is a workstation with a 10 Mbit/s Ethernet link or a laptop with a 1 Mbit/s wireless Ethernet link. The agent will jump to a proxy site if the user's machine is a laptop with a modem link. The proxy site is dynamically selected by the agent. In the current system, the selection process is quite simple—there is a designated proxy site for each laptop and for some subnetworks. The agent will go to the proxy associated with the subnetwork to which the laptop is attached, or to the laptop-specific proxy if there is no known subnetwork proxy. Currently, the proxy sites are hardcoded, but eventually, they will be listed in the yellow pages along with other services. Then an agent can search for the closest proxy site (to its current location or to the document collections), the closest proxy site owned by its owner's Internet Service Provider (ISP), the fastest proxy site, etc.

Whether or not the agent migrates to a proxy site, it consults the yellow pages to determine the locations of the document collections (assuming that the user did not select specific document collections). Once the agent has the list of document collections, it must interact with the stationary agents that serve as an interface between D'Agents and Smart. Here the agent makes its second decision. If the query requires only a few operations per document collection, the agent simply makes RPC-like calls across the network (using the D'Agent communication mechanisms as described in [472]). If the query requires several operations per document collection, or if the operations involve large amounts of intermediate data, the agent sends out child agents that travel to the document collections and perform the query operations locally, avoiding the transfer of intermediate data. In our case, the number of operations per document collection depends on whether the user wants to see a graphical representation of the query results (one additional operation per collection), whether the user wants to retrieve the document texts immediately or at a later time (one additional operation per document), and whether the user has specified alternative queries to try if the main query does not produce enough relevant documents (one additional operation per alternative query). The size of the intermediate data depends on the average size of the documents in each collection and the average number of relevant documents per query. Since the average document size and average number of relevant documents per query is nearly the same for all of our document collections, our current agent makes its decision based solely on the number and type of the required query operations. Later, once our yellow pages accept interface descriptions, we will allow each Smart agent to annotate its interface description with the expected result size for each operation (and to update those annotations based on its observations of its own behavior).

When the main agent receives the results from each child agent, it merges and filters those results, returns to the user's machine with just the final list of documents, and hands this list to the GUI. Although the behavior exhibited by this agent is complex, it is actually quite easy to implement and involves only about 50 lines of Tcl code. In particular, the decisions whether to use a proxy site and create children, although admittedly simplistic in our current implementation, involve little more than two *if* statements that check the information returned from the network sensors and the yellow pages. It is hard to imagine any other technique that would allow us to provide an equally flexible solution with the same small amount of work. More importantly, once some inefficiencies in the D'Agents implementation are addressed (and as long as the agent carefully chooses when and where to migrate), its performance should be comparable to or better than that of any other technique, regardless of the current network conditions and without any application-specific support at the collection or proxy sites. Indeed, the collection owners merely had to provide an agent wrapper that made the existing Smart operations visible to visiting agents, and the proxy site did not need to do anything at all (aside from running the agent system itself). As we will see in the next section, the critical inefficiencies involve communication and migration overhead. Due to the communication overhead, the agent performs worse than traditional client/server techniques if it chooses to remain stationary. Similarly, due to the migration overhead, the agent is better off migrating only when network conditions are poor, or when each query requires a large number of operations per collection. Fortunately, techniques to reduce these overheads already exist.

15.4.2 Analysis

A full performance analysis of the technical-report searcher is beyond the scope of the chapter. Here we consider only the case where the user's machine has a reliable, high-bandwidth network connection, specifically, a wired 10 Mb/s Ethernet link. Under these network conditions, the searcher will *not* use a proxy site, but still must decide whether to make cross-network calls or send out child agents. To understand the searcher's performance under these conditions, we ran a series of experiments, some involving traditional RPC-based clients and servers, others involving test agents. Each experiment was performed on the same two machines, two 200 MHz Pentium II laptops,[13] which were connected with a dedicated 10 Mb/s Ethernet link. The traditional clients and servers were written in C/C++, and since the technical-report searcher was written in Tcl, the test agents were written in Tcl also.

Base performance. First, we consider the base performance of the core D'Agents system. Figure 15.4.2a shows the results of three performance experiments. The first experiment, the results of which are shown as the *RPC* line in Figure 15.4.2a, measures the time needed for a client on one laptop to make a Sun RPC call into a server on the second laptop. The total size of the arguments to the RPC call was 256 bytes; the result size varied from 512 bytes to 8192 bytes. The server did no work aside from immediately responding to the client with a dummy result of the desired size. This first experiment does not involve the agent system in any way, but instead is used to place the D'Agent performance numbers in context.

The second and third experiments do involve the agent system. In the second experiment, an agent on the first laptop sent a request message to an agent on the second laptop, and the agent on the second laptop sent back a response. The *Agent (send/receive)* line in Figure 15.4.2a shows the total round trip time as a function of response size; the request size was again 256 bytes. In addition, as in the RPC experiment, the "server" agent did no work aside from immediately sending back a dummy response message. Finally, in the third experiment, an agent on the first laptop *sent a child agent* to the second laptop; the child agent then sent back a response message to its

---

[13] The laptops had 200 MHz Pentium II processors, 64 MB of main memory, 128 MB of swap space, and 1.7 GB of disk space. The operating system on each laptop was Slackware Linux, kernel version 2.0.30. All C/C++ code used in the experiments (including the D'Agent interpreters and server) was compiled with GNU gcc version 2.7.2.3 with an optimization level of 2.

parent. The *Agent (submit/receive)* line in Figure 15.4.2 shows the total time from agent submission to result reception. The size of the child agent was 256 bytes, and the child agent did no work aside from immediately sending back a dummy result.

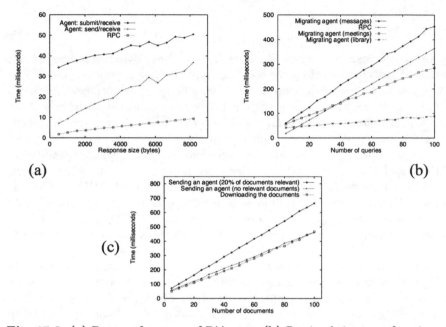

(a)   (b)

(c)

Fig. 15.2. (a) Base performance of D'Agents. **(b)** Retrieval time as a function of the number of queries per document collection. **(c)** Retrieval time as a function of the number of relevant documents per query. Each data point is the average of either 100 (agent experiments) or 1000 (RPC experiments) trials. These graphs are explained in the chapter text.

Unlike previous performance results for D'Agents [248], these agent experiments were measured with the new multi-threaded version of the D'Agents server, which eliminates significant interprocess communication. In addition, the new server maintains a pool of "hot" interpreters; it starts up a set of interpreter processes at boot time, and then hands incoming agents off to the first free interpreter in that set. In addition, an interpreter process does not die when an agent finishes, but instead stays alive to execute the next incoming agent. Although this approach still runs each agent in a separate process, it eliminates nearly all of the interpreter-startup overhead.[14] Also,

---

[14] It does not eliminate all of the overhead since each interpreter process is only allowed to handle a certain number of agents before it is killed and replaced with a new process. In addition, even though the interpreter process remains active from one agent to another, there is still some interpreter initialization and cleanup that must be done for each agent.

the agent experiments were performed with encryption turned off. The agents would perform significantly worse with encryption turned on, but so would an equivalently secure version of RPC. Turning encryption off is reasonable, since many document collections would not care about the identity of the agent's owner.

The base performance numbers illustrate two important points: (1) inter-agent communication involves significantly more overhead than RPC, and (2) migration involves even more overhead than inter-agent communication. Fortunately, this overhead comes from several clear sources. First, the agents are written in Tcl, which is a relatively slow scripting language. D'Agents, however, includes two faster languages, Java and Scheme. In addition, the newest version of the Tcl interpreter, which has not been integrated into D'Agents yet, uses on-the-fly compilation (into virtual machine bytecodes) and is more than ten times faster than previous Tcl interpreters. Second, even though the multi-threaded server uses a pool of hot interpreters, each Tcl interpreter must still execute several hundred lines of Tcl code to re-initialize itself before executing an incoming agent. This re-initialization adds nearly ten milliseconds to the migration time. Some of the re-initialization can be eliminated, and the rest can be made much faster, either by switching to the newest Tcl interpreter or re-implementing the initialization code in C.

Finally, whereas the RPC client and server use UDP, every communication between machines in the agent system involves a TCP connection. Thus, there is one TCP connection for the request message or migrating agent, and a second connection for the response. In addition, all communication goes through the agent servers, which, although necessary in the case of a migrating agent, is not necessary when one agent is simply sending a message to another. Possible implementation changes include using UDP for some agent communication, increasing the speed with which the agent server forwards incoming messages to the correct interpreter processes, allowing the agent servers to hold open connections to machines with which they are communicating heavily, and possibly even associating unique network addresses with stationary service agents so that client agents can communicate with those service agents directly. Unfortunately, this last change complicates the security implementation, since the agent server will no longer be the single point at which the system needs to authenticate incoming messages.

Performance when the searcher must perform multiple queries. With the base performance results in mind, it becomes straightforward to understand the results for the actual technical-report searcher. Figure 15.4.2b considers the case where the searcher needs to perform multiple queries against a single document collection. Perhaps, for example, the user has specified several alternative queries that should be tried if the main query does not retrieve the desired number of relevant documents. The *RPC* line shows the time needed for a traditional client (written in C) to run the queries from across the network. The query size was 256 bytes, and the result size for *each* query was 2048 bytes, which is consistent with the data volumes observed when we perform queries against our current document collections. In addition, the server did not actually perform the query, but instead sent back a dummy result. This approach allows us to run more iterations of each test. Moreover, it will not change the relative performances shown in the figure since the same query backend would be used in all four cases. In other words, we have removed exactly that portion of the code that is identical in all four cases, namely, the shared C library that actually runs the queries through the Smart system.

The remaining three cases shown in Figure 15.4.2b involve agents rather than RPC. In each case, an agent was sent to the location of the document collection, where it ran the queries locally to the collection and sent back only the final document list. The size of each test agent was $1024 + 256 + 128n$ bytes, where n is the number of queries that will be performed; the 1024 is approximately the size of the *real* agent's code, the 256 the size of the main query, and the 128 the size of the additional code and data that is needed to represent and perform the alternative queries. The final result size was 2048 bytes. In the first agent case, *Migrating agent (messages)*, the agent used D'Agent *messages* to communicate with the stationary Smart agent. In the second case, *Migrating agent (meetings)*, the agent first established a direct inter-process connection[15] or *meeting* with the stationary agent; the queries and results were sent across the meeting. Finally, in the third case, the agent loaded the Smart library itself and simply invoked the query procedures directly.

The agent that loads the Smart library itself performs quite well. As can be seen, even though the agent was written in Tcl, and the network link between the laptops was relatively fast, the agent performed better than RPC when it needed to invoke more than a dozen queries, and performed much better as the number of queries increases. Once the migration and communication overhead is reduced as discussed above, it should be competitive for even just five queries. This suggests that a useful abstraction will be services that appear to be stationary agents, but, in fact, are provided through libraries. D'Agents includes an RPC-like mechanism, which allows agents to invoke each other's procedures. This mechanism would provide a natural way of making a library appear as a stationary agent, since the client agent could make the same procedure invocations in both cases; only the hidden implementation of the stubs would be different.

On the other hand, when the client agent had to communicate with an actual stationary agent, it did worse than RPC unless it performed more than forty queries with meetings, and always did worse with messages. There are several reasons why the agent performed worse, all of which were considered

---

[15] In the current implementation, this connection is a Unix-domain Berkeley socket, which is not the most efficient connection possible, but is easy to port from one version of Unix to another.

above. Most importantly, the overhead of inter-agent communication is large
even when the agents are *on the same machine*. When an agent sends a message to another local agent, the message first is sent to the server process
(over a pipe), and then sent to the interpreter process that is executing the
recipient agent (over another pipe). The response message follows the reverse
path back to the sending agent. Thus, each message is sent twice, from agent
to server, and then from server to agent. The overhead of the double transmission is larger than the overhead of making RPC calls across the good
network link. This can be seen clearly in the *Migrating agent (messages)* line
of Figure 15.4.2b, which has a larger slope than the *RPC* line. It also comes
into play, however, when the agents are using meetings, since establishing
a meeting requires the exchange of two messages, a meeting request and a
meeting acceptance. One possible solution is to allow direct inter-process
communication between agents, even when the agents have not established
a meeting. For example, each interpreter process could have a Unix domain
socket for accepting messages from other local agents. Since the agents are
local to each other, the security concerns are significantly less than if each
process has a *network* socket for accepting messages from *remote* agents.

**Performance when the searcher must examine the document
texts.** Figure 15.4.2c shows a set of experiments where the Smart search
operations do not match the application's needs exactly. Here the application
must perform a query to get a list of potentially relevant documents, and then
examine the text of each document to decide which documents are actually
relevant. The *Downloading the documents* line shows how long it takes for a
client (written in C) to open a TCP connection to the document server (also
written in C) and send the query, plus the time needed for the server to send
back the *full text* of all potentially relevant documents. The two *Sending
an agent* lines shows how long it takes to send an agent to the document
collection, and then for that agent to perform the query locally, examine the
text of the documents, and send back all relevant documents. Each agent
was 1024 bytes, the query was 256 bytes, and each document was 4096 bytes;
the agent performed the query by loading a library and directly invoking a
procedure (i.e., the fastest case considered in the previous set of experiments);
the query procedure returned a dummy result of the appropriate size; the
agent opened the document files directly to examine their full text[16]; and the
agent decided that a document was relevant if its text contained a particular
two-word substring.

The difference between the two *Sending an agent* lines is that in the
first case, twenty percent of the examined documents are actually relevant,
while in the second case, none of the documents are actually relevant. As can
be seen, when there are no relevant documents, the agent does slightly worse
than the downloading solution, and when twenty percent of the documents are

---

[16] It is reasonable to assume that the query procedure or agent would include the
filesystem location of the document files in the result list.

relevant, the agent does significantly worse. All of the implementation issues considered above are influencing these results. Three factors, however, have the most impact. First, the time to read the document files from disk, which must be done in both the client/server and agent cases, takes nearly half of the total time (even though the document files were in the file cache for all but the first run). Second, Tcl is slow enough that it takes nearly as long to perform the substring search with a Tcl agent as to send the entire document text across our good network link. Third, and most importantly, the inefficiencies in the inter-agent communication mechanisms hurt the overall performance more and more as the number of relevant documents increases. In the worst case, 80 kilobytes of document text are sent inside an agent message. Clearly, it is necessary to implement a more efficient means of "streaming" data from an agent on one machine to an agent on another. At the same time, it is worthwhile to note that if a separate network connection must be established for each *downloaded* document (as with some Web servers), the agent solution performs far better than the document-downloading solution [571].

Summary. Taken together, these results mean that the technical-report searcher agent generally will take longer to complete its query than the corresponding client/server solution, since (1) inter-agent communication across machines is slower than RPC, (2) inter-agent communication on the same machine is also slow, making migration less useful, and (3) the searcher and all its agents are written in Tcl. At the same time, even with 10 Mb/s links and slow Tcl agents, the searcher does outperform the client/server solution in several cases, particularly when the document collections provide their search operations as a loadable library. Moreover, as network bandwidth, reliability, latency or load become worse, the technical-report searcher will have better and better performance relative to the client/server solution [248], since it transmits less data across the network and requires fewer network-communication steps.

In addition, the performance bottlenecks in the current D'Agents system are easy to identify, and several solutions exist. In fact, in some mobile-agent systems, particularly the Java-based systems where each agent executes in its own *thread*, some of the D'Agent bottlenecks have been eliminated already. For D'Agents itself, a speedup of at least two can be realized with moderate implementation effort, without abandoning Tcl as an agent language or resorting to multi-threaded interpreters. For the many applications where even the newest version of the Tcl interpreter is not fast enough, D'Agents already includes two faster execution environments, a Scheme interpreter and a Java virtual machine. Most other agent systems have similar, faster environments, and securely executing agents less than twice as slowly as the corresponding natively-compiled code (through on-the-fly compilation and other techniques) is a realizable goal [400].

In short, although current mobile-agent implementations, such as D'Agents, do not offer better performance than competing solutions in as many cases as desired, these systems are far from their maximum possible performance. As the implementations improve, mobile agents will become more and more attractive for distributed information retrieval. Finally, it is important to note that all of the experiments above involved dummy query operations, whereas the real Smart system does significant work per query. The overhead of the current D'Agents system becomes much more reasonable when considered against the Smart retrieval times, For this and other retrieval tasks, the flexibility of D'Agents makes up for the performance penalties.

15.5 Planning

15.5.1 Planning a Route

In the example of the technical-report searcher, we launched a mobile information-retrieval agent to each destination machine, and we assumed that each dispatched agent could definitely find the information it was tasked to send. A more general class of information-retrieval problem anticipates the possibility that an agent may not be able to find its desired information at a destination machine. Additionally, we may want to use less network resources by sending fewer agents than the number of possible destination machines. In this case, there is a need for planning that decides the best sequence (itinerary) of machines to be visited by each agent so that the desired information can be found in minimum time. In this section, we will discuss these planning problems, along with their solutions and some limited experimental results.

An itinerary determined by planning will be based on three things: a list of machines where an agent may be able to find its desired information, the uncertainty in the quality of the data available on those machines, and the current network conditions. The list of machines and document uncertainty are provided by a more advanced *yellow pages* service than that used in the technical report searcher. The uncertainty degree is defined to be the probability that an agent can successfully find information at each of those machines. Last, the network conditions include information regarding connectivity of links, operability of machines in the network, latency and available bandwidth of links. These statistics are collected by a *network-sensing module*.

Architecture of the Mobile Agent Planning System. The architecture of our planning system for mobile agents is depicted in Figure 15.5.1. The planning system consists of three main components: a planning module, a network-sensing module and a yellow-pages module. In our system, when a mobile agent is tasked with searching for information, it consults with the planning module first. The planning module then asks a yellow-pages module for possible locations where the mobile agent might find this desired information.

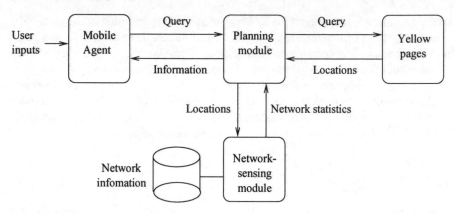

Fig. 15.3. The architecture of the planning system

Although the current implementation of the yellow-page service does not have a function to measure this probability of success, we assume that this probability is measurable. For example, the probability might be as simple as the ratio of data cached at a proxy server to the full amount of data available at the actual server.

After obtaining the list of machines and their corresponding probabilities of success, the planning module passes the list to the network-sensing module, which returns the latencies and bandwidths between the machines and their current CPU loads. The network-sensing module keeps track of these statistics by probing the network at fixed intervals.

As soon as the network statistics are returned to the planning module, the sequence in which agents are to visit machines (to minimize total expected execution time) is calculated from the network statistics and probabilities of success. The calculation is done using the algorithms and theorems described in the following subsection.

Traveling Agent Problems. The planning problem can formulated as deciding the sequence of machines to visit to minimize the total expected time until the desired information is found. We name the planning problem the *Traveling Agent Problem* (TAP) due to the analogy with the Traveling Salesman Problem [231]. Formally, the Traveling Agent Problem is defined as follows:

> *The Traveling Agent Problem* – There are $n + 1$ sites, s_i with $0 \leq i \leq n$. Each site has a known probability, $0 \leq p_i \leq 1$, of being able to successfully complete the agent's task, and a time $t_i > 0$, required for the agent to attempt the task at s_i regardless of whether it is successful. These probabilities are independent of each other. Travel times or latencies for the agent to move between sites are also known and given by $l_{ij} \geq 0$ for moving between site i and site j. When the agent's task has been successfully completed at some site, the

agent must return to the site from which it started (i.e., site 0). For site 0, $p_0 = t_0 = 0$. The *Traveling Agent Problem* is to minimize the expected time to successfully complete the task.

A solution to the Traveling Agent Problem consists of specifying the order in which to visit the sites, namely a permutation $< i_1, i_2, ..., i_n >$ of 1 through n. Such a permutation will be called a *tour* in keeping with the tradition for such problems.

The expected time to complete the task or visit all sites in failure, for a tour $T = < i_1, i_2, ..., i_n >$ is the following equation (15.0)

$$C_T = l_{0i_1} + t_{i_1} + p_{i_1} l_{i_1 0} + \sum_{k=2}^{n} \left\{ \left(\prod_{j=1}^{j=k-1} (1 - p_{i_j}) \right) \right\} (l_{i_{k-1} i_k} + t_{i_k} + p_{i_k} l_{i_k 0})$$

$$+ \prod_{j=1}^{n} (1 - p_j) l_{n0}.$$

This formula can be understood as follows. The first site, s_{i_1}, on the tour is always visited and requires travel time l_{0i_1} to be reached. Upon arrival, time t_{i_1} must be spent there regardless of success. With probability p_{i_1} the task is successfully completed in which case the agent can return to site 0 with time cost $l_{i_1 0}$. However, with probability $(1 - p_{i_1})$ there was failure and the agent proceeds to site i_2. The contribution to the expected time to moving from site i_1 to site i_2 and succeeding there is

$$(1 - p_{i_1})(l_{i_1 i_2} + t_{i_2} + p_{i_2} l_{i_2 0}).$$

Here the factor $(1 - p_{i_1})$ is the probability of failing at site i_1. Similarly, the contribution to the expected time due to moving from site i_2 to site i_3 and succeeding there is

$$(1 - p_{i_1})(1 - p_{i_2})(l_{i_2 i_3} + t_{i_3} + p_{i_3} l_{i_3 0}).$$

Here the $(1 - p_{i_1})(1 - p_{i_2})$ term is the probability of failing at both sites i_1 and i_2. In general, the contribution to the expected time due to site i_k is

(probability of failure at the first $k - 1$ sites) $\times$
(expected time for success at site i_k).

Adding all these contributions together gives us the summation in (15.0). Finally, the last term in (15.0) arises when failure occurs at all nodes and we must return to the originating site. We have used independence of the various probabilities here. Not surprisingly, this problem is NP-complete [445].

Variation of Traveling Agent Problems. Because of its NP-complete complexity, some simplifying assumptions have to be employed so as to more easily obtain optimal solutions for the Traveling Agent Problem. There are several variations of Traveling Agent Problems depending upon the assumptions employed. These assumptions are made regarding the four entities of Traveling Agent Problems, (1) the number of mobile agents, (2) the network latencies, (3) probabilities of success and (4) the task computation time at each machine. Table 15.1 shows the complexity of each of the Traveling Agent Problems when these assumptions are employed.

Case	# of agents	Latency	Probability
1	Single	Variable	Variable
2	Single	Constant	Variable
3	Single	Constant in the same subnetwork	Variable
4	Multiple	Constant	Variable
5	Multiple	Constant	Constant (0)
6	Multiple	Constant	Constant (> 0.5)
7	Multiple	Constant	Variable

Case	Computation Time	Complexity
1	Variable	NP-Complete
2	Variable	Sorting (P)
3	Variable	Dynamic Programming
4	Variable	NP-Complete
5	Variable	Partitioning (PP)
6	Variable	Sorting (P)
7	Constant	Sorting (P)

Table 15.1. Variation of Traveling Agent Problems

We present only the single-agent cases in this section. Please see [445] for a thorough discussion of the multiple-agent cases.

The complexity of the single Traveling Agent Problem can be reduced when latencies between nodes are assumed to be equal. For example, if the processing time at each node is extremely large (compared to the latency between the nodes), differences among the latencies could be ignored, or even taken to be zero. Alternately, if no information about internodal latencies is known, we might assume all of them to be constant. The constant latency assumption is reasonable in the case of a single subnetwork as well.

Theorem 1:
Under the assumption that the all the latencies are constant, the TAP can be solved in polynomial time. The optimal solution for the TAP is attained if the nodes are visited in decreasing order of $p_i/(t_i + l)$.

Refer to [445] for the proof. The proof uses an interchange argument commonly used in finance and economics [65], in which we determine the relative merit of exchanging the order of visiting two machines. The criteria for exchange is precisely that the machine with a larger value of $p_i/(t_i + l)$ be visited first. When all necessary exchanges have been made, a sorted list of $p_i/(t_i + l)$ results.

Many more complicated situations can be modeled by variable latencies that are constant within subnetworks and across subnetworks. Specifically, consider the case of two subnetworks separated by a great distance (say, one in Japan and one in the US). Latencies between any two nodes within the same subnetwork are treated as constant, as are latencies across the two subnetworks. That is, for sites in Japan, latencies are a constant, l_J, and in the USA they are l_U. Latencies between two nodes, one in Japan and one in the USA, are known to be a third constant, l_{JU}. Formally, we define the Two Subnetwork Traveling Agent Problem (TSTAP) as follows.

> *Two Subnetwork Traveling Agent Problem* — The relevant sites belong to two subnetworks, S_1 and S_2. Sites in S_i are s_{i_j} where $1 \leq j \leq n_i$. n_i is the number of sites in subnetwork S_i. There are three latencies: $L_1, L_2, L_{12} \geq 0$. For $s_{1_j} \in S_1, s_{2_k} \in S_2, l_{1_j 2_k} = l_{2_k 1_j} = L_{12}$ while for $s_{1_j}, s_{1_k} \in S_1$, we have $l_{1_j 1_k} = l_{1_k 1_j} = L_1$. Similarly, for $s_{2_j}, s_{2_k} \in S_2$, we have $l_{2_j 2_k} = l_{2_k 2_j} = L_2$. Probabilities, $p_{i_j} > 0$ are nonzero and independent as before. Computation times $t_{i_j} \geq 0$ are arbitrary but nonnegative. The home site, s_0 can be in a third sub-network. Latencies between s_0 and sites in S_i are L_{0i}. We assume that $L_{0i}, L_{12} \geq L_i$. That is, latencies within a subnetwork are smaller than latencies across networks and to the home sites.

Theorem 2:
The Two Subnetwork Traveling Agent Problem (TSTAP) can be solved in polynomial time using the algorithm in Theorem 1 and dynamic programming.

Outline of algorithm – The algorithm in theorem 2 consists of two steps. The first step is to sort machines within the same subnetwork in decreasing order of $p_i/(t_i + l)$, which can be accomplished in $n_i \log n_i$ steps. This sorted ordering is used in the second step, where a dynamic programming algorithm is used to compute the optimal solution. Actions taken in the dynamic programming are either to stay in the same subnetwork and migrate the next unvisited machine there, or to migrate the next unvisited machine in other subnetwork. Even though the problem is stochastic, it can be solved by a deterministic dynamic programming algorithm in roughly $O((n_1 + 1)(n_2 + 1))$ steps [445].

Experimental Results. Next, we show the result of an experiment where a single mobile information-retrieval agent must search for information in the network with the assistance of the planning (module) agent.

In the experiment, information-retrieval agents were launched, and the time each agent takes was measured. The task of the agent is to open a certain text file (the size is 234KB) in a text database on a machine, and parse the file to determine if the file satisfies a given query. The outcome on a machine is determined by a random number generator, so that the probability of success is the same as that given by the directory service agent. Note that the result of parsing the text while looking for a given query does not affect the success of the task, which is in fact decided by the random generator. If the search at a machine is successful, the information retrieval agent returns to the home machine where it was launched. Otherwise, it migrates to the next unvisited machine.

We ran experiments using seven laptop computers distributed in three subnetworks; one subnetwork contained the home site, and the other two subnetworks contained the document collections. We introduced artificial delays on network links so that the latencies between sub-networks were much larger than the latencies between machines within the same subnetwork. To use the TSTAP algorithm, we set the latencies both within and across subnetworks to be constant.

For the sake of comparison with our optimal planning algorithm, two greedy algorithms are employed, one of which is based on the probability of success and the other on the estimated computation time at each machine. Note that the estimated computation time at each machine is obtained based on its current CPU load, its benchmarked CPU performance, and the estimated size of a task.

The results of the experiment are shown in Figure 15.4 and Table 15.2. The top graph shows the results for the greedy algorithm that uses success probabilities, while the bottom graph shows the results for the greedy algorithm that uses estimated computation times. As we can see in the figure, the optimal planning algorithm does not always outperform the other two methods. This is due to the stochastic nature of the planning problem. For example, an agent may find the information at the first machine even if it has a small probability of success. The optimal algorithm only guarantees the minimum *expected* time until the desired information is found, not the minimum time in all cases. Thus, due to the stochastic character of the planning problem, it is more appropriate to compare algorithms based on the average values shown in Table 15.2. According to the results in the table, we can see the optimal algorithm outperforms the other algorithms.

	Optimal algorithm	Greedy algorithm (probability)	Greedy algorithm (computat. time)
First place finishes	27	15	8
Geometric mean	1	1.31	1.79
Weighted arithmetic mean	1	1.26	1.67

Table 15.2. Performance comparison: TAP. The geometric and arithmetic means are defined in the text, but essentially are normalized execution times.

The weighted arithmetic mean and the geometric means in Table 15.2 are defined as follows:

– Geometric mean: The geometric mean of the times for each method is

$$G_k = \left(\prod_{i=1}^{n} \frac{Time_{M_k}(i)}{Time_{M_{OPT}}(i)} \right)^{\frac{1}{n}}.$$

where $Time_{M_k}(i)$ stands for the execution time of method M_k on its ith run, $Time_{M_{OPT}}(i)$ stands for the execution time of the optimal algorithm on its ith run, and n is the number of runs.
– Weighted arithmetic mean: The weighted arithmetic mean of the times for each method is

$$A_k = \frac{1}{n} \left(\sum_{i=1}^{n} \frac{Time_{M_k}(i)}{\sum_{j=1}^{m} Time_{M_j}(i)} \right)$$

where $Time_{M_k}(i)$ is the execution time of method M_k on its ith run, $Time_{M_j}(i)$ is the execution time of method M_j on its ith run, n is the number of runs, and m is the number of methods.
This value is the average percentage of the combined execution time used by method M_k.

15.5.2 Observation Agents

The planning methods described in the previous section all relied upon information provided by the yellow pages service. This service provided the probability of success in a search for certain kinds of information at possible machines. As the information available on the network is in constant flux, the yellow pages must be kept up-to-date by adding new sites, removing old ones, and re-indexing sites that have changed. Our yellow pages index entire document sites; other yellow pages might index *particular* documents, such as World Wide Web pages. We consider the best ways to maintain such indices so as to catch changing content quickly. During the discussion, we will use the word *document* extensively, but the approaches apply equally well to document collections.

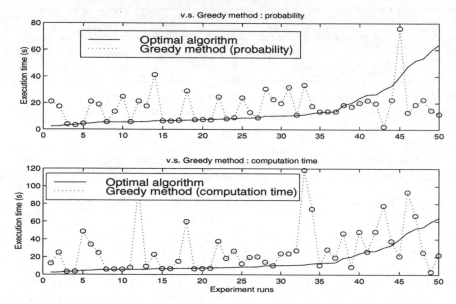

Fig. 15.4. Performance comparison: execution time. For each experimental run, we generated a new set of probabilities, and ran both the optimal and greedy algorithms with the same set. On the two graphs, the x-axis is the run number, and the run numbers are assigned in order of increasing optimal-algorithm execution time.

To solve the indexing problem, limited computational, network, and storage resources are devoted to scouring available collections for new documents, and also re-examining old documents to inspect them for changes. Whether done in sequence or in parallel, a search engine must always decide what document or documents to examine next. There are many questions to consider: when is the best time to re-examine a document, given knowledge of the document's history and the priority placed on having correct knowledge of its state? Indeed, how should we describe a document's state?

If resources were unlimited, the solution is simple: each and every document could be monitored as frequently as desired, watching for changes to appear. Of course, an observation does have obvious costs associated with it: a machine uses time (some network latency and some CPU cycle time) to retrieve and inspect a document, and disk space to store the results. In exchange for this cost, the search engine benefits from a more current index of previously explored documents, a more comprehensive collection (if new documents are discovered), and an accurate picture of the "dynamics" of the document in question.

An understanding of how documents change is necessary to maximize the recency of such an index. Knowing a document's change dynamics allows us to make fewer wasteful observations. When the engine must decide which document to examine next, some documents will be more likely to have changed since last inspection than others. If looking for changes, it makes sense to re-examine these documents more often than documents which exhibit greater stability. Algorithms for selecting which observation to make next can also account for what the collection may look like as a result of document checks yet to be run. That is, planning observations can take into account the likely outcome of making those observations. This gives rise to planning problems similar to those discussed in the context of the traveling agent problem (TAP). If the index is being used for user searches, then it has the most value for frequently-requested documents. It seems reasonable that resources should be preferentially allocated to the documents that are popular, fast-changing, or both.

Analysis and Modeling. To mathematically demonstrate how this allocation should proceed, three things are essential: a representation of the document's state, the dynamics of state evolution, and a formalization of the value of perfect state knowledge.

Time-since-modification as a Markov chain. If probability distributions on document ages can be determined, we can use the age to define the modification state of a document. This rests on the assumption that probability of modification is a strong function of the time since the previous modification, which is true for a large class of document changes [89]. Any reasonable discretization of this time will serve our purpose, such as the number of days since the last change, for example. Using this definition of state, a probability distribution of the time intervals between changes can be viewed as a Markov chain. Given a state $s = n$ days since the last change, there are only two things that can occur next: either the state will advance to $s = n + 1$, or it will reset to $s = 0$. If we model $N + 1$ states, then the state $s = N + 1$ can be treated as "N or more days since last change." In this way, we can define a matrix of transition probabilities as

$$\mathbf{M} = \begin{bmatrix} p_{reset}(0) & 1 - p_{reset}(0) & 0 & \cdots \\ p_{reset}(1) & 0 & 1 - p_{reset}(1) & \cdots \\ \cdots & \cdots & \cdots & \cdots \\ p_{reset}(N) & 0 & \cdots & 1 - p_{reset}(N) \end{bmatrix} \quad (15.1)$$

The function $p_{reset}(t)$ can be determined either from knowledge of the distribution of time intervals between changes, or from the distribution of observed ages for a particular document. Either distribution implies the conditional probability that a reset will occur in the following time interval, given that no change has occurred for t time steps. Further discussion can be found in [89].

Generally, by raising $\mathbf{M}$ to an integer power k, we can find the probability (for initial age i) that the system became age j after k time steps have elapsed since the last observation:

$$P(s_{t+k} = j | s_t = i) = \left[\mathbf{M}^k \right]_{ij} \quad (15.2)$$

Defining a cost function. Using this model, we can define an objective function that can be optimized for the collection. The objective in a real system could be fairly complex; for our discussions, more simplistic criteria are sufficient. In this section we restrict ourselves using some simplifying assumptions. First, we consider a document collection containing d documents. Second, assume that documents can be retrieved at a rate of α documents per day, and that all document fetches have identical cost. Assume the states corresponding to the rows of matrix $\mathbf{M}_r$ denote the age in days of the rth document in the collection. Any unit of time could be used, so long as it is consistent across the collection and the rate α is expressed in the same unit. For each document r, we know that it was last observed k_r days ago to have age i_r. The probability that document r has changed during this k_r-step interval is

$$P\left(change|\left\{i_r, \mathbf{M}_r, k_r\right\}\right) = \sum_{j \in [0, i_r + k_r - 1]} \left[\mathbf{M}_r^{k_r}\right]_{i_r j}$$
$$= 1 - \left[\mathbf{M}_r^{k_r}\right]_{i_r (i_r + k_r)} \tag{15.3}$$

Using this result, we can formulate a cost function for the collection. One simple cost function is the expected total number of documents that are incorrectly indexed (the indexed version is out-of-date), which is just the sum of the probabilities listed in (15.3) over the entire collection:

$$C = \sum_{r=1}^{d} \left(1 - \left[\mathbf{M}_r^{k_r}\right]_{i_r (i_r + k_r)}\right) \tag{15.4}$$

Greedy cost minimization. Using (15.4) we can find the best way to reduce the costs that we will incur in the coming day. By our assumption, we can check α documents per day. The smallest possible cost for the following day can be obtained if we fetch and re-index the α documents corresponding to the largest terms in the cost summation. These terms correspond to those documents with the largest probability of being out of date (15.4). For all of the α documents we fetch, the probability of them now being out of date is zero. If there is no single best choice for the α documents, then we can select α at random from the pool of "best choices." This situation occurs when applying (15.4) if more than α documents have probability 1 (to working precision).

"Liveness" conditions. While having the advantage of being relatively simple, greedy algorithms may force a situation in which long-term performance is not optimal. For example, in the re-indexing system, there is the possibility of never checking some subset of the documents. This is a situation the indexing system must avoid, especially if all items to be indexed are equally important. In queuing models for computer operating systems, the analogous constraint that all processes be served is termed a "liveness" condition, which would not be met if there were a subset of documents that changed so quickly that its members always contributed the largest terms in the cost function (15.4).

Liveness can be shown to hold for (15.4) under some simple constraints. The proof centers on the fact that all terms in the cost summation monotonically approach unity if the documents to which they correspond go unchecked. An unchecked document's contribution to the cost will eventually exceed any threshold value $1 - \delta, 0 < \delta < 1$. This is usually sufficient to give assurance of its inclusion in the set of largest terms. See [89] for more.

Extending the cost horizon. Having an assurance of liveness is not enough to be satisfied with the long-term performance of the indexing system. The one-step algorithm does not take into account anything other than the current probability of change for various documents. Indeed, no one-step method can take advantage of knowing the difference in change rates among documents.

Consider the following simplistic system that demonstrates how to take advantage of knowing document change rates. There are two documents, A and B, and we can check one per day. Page A changes quickly: it has a probability of 85% of having been changed today, and if unobserved, it will have a 95% chance tomorrow. If, however, we observe today, there will be a 25% chance of having been changed by the end of tomorrow. Page B changes more slowly. It has an 80% chance today, which becomes 81% tomorrow if B is unchecked today. If it is checked today, then tomorrow's probability will be 5%. Assume we can only choose one of these to observe per day, and that we wish to minimize the total number expected number of documents out-of-date over the two-day period:

$$\sum_{t=0}^{1} \kappa^t \left[Prob(A\text{changed}, t) + Prob(B\text{changed}, t) \right] \tag{15.5}$$

There are four possible strategies in this situation. We can write these as two-day sequences of observations, namely AA, AB, BA, and BB. If we observe a document, then it contributes zero cost on that day, since we consider it "up-to-date" if checked within the last day. Therefore, the cost for observing A on both days is exactly the cost of not observing B on those days, namely, $0.8 + 0.81 = 1.61$. Likewise, we can find the two-day cost for each possible sequence of observations, as shown in Table 15.3.

Sequence	Cost	Comment
AB	$0.8 + 0.25 = 1.05$	lower first day cost; one-day algorithm would pick this one
BA	$0.85 + 0.05 = 0.90$	lower total cost; two-day algorithm would pick this one
AA	$0.8 + 0.81 = 1.61$	document B ignored
BB	$0.85 + 0.95 = 1.80$	document A ignored

Table 15.3. Possible costs in example two-document, one-check system

To implement a two-day cost function in practice, we need to determine the possible costs we might see on the second day for each document. Since we are assuming that observation forces the document to contribute zero cost on the day in question, the three nonzero costs we need to be able to determine are (i) the cost of not observing on the first day (same as in previous section), (ii) the cost of not observing on the second day if we did not observe on the first day either, and (iii) the cost of not observing on the second day if we did observe on the first day. Moving through these in order, we know that the cost on the first day is of the form:

$$P_c = \sum_{j \in [0, i_r + k_r - 1]} \left[\mathbf{M}_r^{k_r} \right]_{i_r j} = 1 - \left[\mathbf{M}_r^{k_r} \right]_{i_r (i_r + k_r)} \tag{15.6}$$

After two days, the form is exactly the same, only the document has aged by one day, accounted for by incrementing the value of k_r. Therefore, if we choose not to observe on the second day, the cost for that day is:

$$\sum_{j \in [0, i_r + k_r]} \left[\mathbf{M}_r^{k_r + 1} \right]_{i_r j} = 1 - \left[\mathbf{M}_r^{k_r + 1} \right]_{i_r (i_r + k_r + 1)} \tag{15.7}$$

If we do choose to observe a document on the first day, we can calculate the expected second-day cost of not observing. The second day's costs will be calculated using the new value of $k_r^+ = 1$ (days since last observation) and the newly observed age i_r^+. Since we only know a distribution of possible values for i_r^+, second-day costs will necessarily consist of weighted values from the matrix $\mathbf{M}_r$. These correspond to one-day state transition probabilities in (15.1). If the document was observed to be in state j_r on the first day, then the probability of it being out-of-date at the end of the second day is just $p_{reset}(j_r)$, as used in (15.1). These probabilities are also the first column of the matrix $\mathbf{M}_r$. In our cost function, the values in this column vector will contribute in proportion to their probability of occurrence. These probabilities are obtained from the row over which we sum in (15.6), or the distribution of possible ages on the previous day. Therefore, the probability that the document is out-of-date at the end of the second day, given that the document was observed on the first day, is

$$\sum_{j_r = 0}^{N} \left[\mathbf{M}_r^{k_r} \right]_{i_r j_r} \mathbf{M}_{j_r 1} \tag{15.8}$$

If we choose not to observe on the second day, then (15.8) would be the cost contributed for this document. Note that this cost, being a probability, can be no greater than 1.

Even though we can now find the probabilities for a general collection, the computational situation is still rather grim. In a collection of d documents, in which we can check α per day, there are $_d C_\alpha^2$ possible strategies. A brute-force approach, in which we evaluate a cost for every strategy, is entirely infeasible for the collection sizes under consideration. Even a simple algorithm will be fairly intimidating for a collection containing literally millions of documents. Our current research [89] includes methods by which to guarantee optimal long-term performance.

Accounting for Unequal Cost of Observation. Throughout the above discussion, we have assumed that we were capable of checking α documents per day. While this may be true in the long run, there is definitely a variation in service times required for the processing of documents. Further, service times can vary dramatically even for a single document. Download and processing times are both proportional to document size, and available bandwidth depends strongly upon the time of day (e.g., one expects long service time around 4:00 PM EST). Our cost function should be modified to account for this variation both among different documents and for a single document.

Deterministic document retrieval times. We assume that all documents require some constant time to process, but that this time may not be the same for different documents. This requires us to restate our objective, since we can no longer count on a constant number of documents processed per day. Specifically, we wish to discover incorrectly indexed documents as quickly as possible.

To quantify this, we introduce some notation. We would like to determine an optimal ordering of documents to check, $S^* = \{s_1, s_2, \ldots, s_d\}$, such that the expected time t taken to find an incorrectly indexed document is minimized. Each document i has a fixed probability P_i of having been changed. In order to consider P_i constant and calculable from (15.3), we must create a new list S whenever the probabilities P_i have changed. Corresponding to each document, a time T_i is required for processing. The time t expected to find an incorrectly indexed document can be expressed by a probability-weighted sum of these times. If we assume some ordering S as listed above, then this time can be written:

$$t = P_{s_1}T_{s_1} + (1 - P_{s_1})\left[P_{s2}T_{s2} + (1 - P_{s_2})\left[P_{s_3}T_{s_3} + (1 - P_{s_3})\left[\ldots\right]\right]\right] \quad (15.9)$$

This is the same as the constant-latency TAP presented earlier as (15.0), in which the solution was to sort by decreasing order of P_i/T_i:

$$S^* = \{s_1, s_2, \ldots, s_d\}, \text{where} \frac{P_{s_1}}{T_{s_1}} \geq \frac{P_{s_2}}{T_{s_2}} \geq \cdots \geq \frac{P_{s_d}}{T_{s_d}} \quad (15.10)$$

This result is intuitively pleasant—we have moved from obtaining some fixed amount of benefit per document, to an expected benefit per unit time. In an economic context, we think of comparing salaries being offered by different employers. In order to minimize the time taken to acquire our next unit of income, we will always wish to work for the highest salary for as long as we are allowed to do so. This corresponds to the intuitive notion that a document having $T_i = 1$ second and $P_i = 0.9$ would have a payoff rate of 0.9 changed documents observed per second, and would provide the same utility as checking a sequence of two documents both having $T_i = 0.5$ seconds and $P_i = 0.45$. These two could be checked within one second, and if their changes were independent, then the expected changed documents observed per second would also be 0.9. In this formulation, we also assume that there is no reason to prefer a correct index entry for one document over that for another; the value of a correctly indexed document is independent of the document. Correspondingly, in the TAP problem presented earlier, we assumed that there was no reason to prefer one information source over another.

Nonetheless, the earlier problem (TAP) differs from this one in some important ways. First, both the probability of "success" and the processing latency are both strong functions of time. Planning by the P_i/T_i method will only be valid for time scales on which both the probability and time spent are essentially constant. While this may be an appropriate assumption for timescales on the order of a few minutes, it is certainly not correct when used for longer scales. The tradeoff for ignoring variation in the probability and the retrieval time is that we accept that some error will develop in the ordering as time elapses. That is, it is possible that by accepting lower immediate benefit, better long-term benefits might be achieved, just as was the case in the Table 15.3 example. If using single-step planning, then we must reexamine the order in which we had planned to fetch documents after either the probability or the retrieval time has changed significantly.

Problems due to variation in retrieval times. Using the methods suggested above for documents with non-constant retrieval times will result in indexing preference being given to documents that are either closer to the database or smaller in size. That is, we select between two documents with identical change probability based upon either how far away they are (if of identical size) or how large they are (if at the same location). If we truly value only the expected number of current documents or some other metric that does not account for how the entire collection is treated, then this is not a problem. Intuitively, though, an index should not assign preference based strictly upon convenience of indexing. Methods are needed for removing unwanted bias against documents that are either larger or farther away.

Reducing Observation Costs Using Mobile Agents. These two biases naturally lead into two targeted solutions whereby we might make limited use of remote sites. First, it is critical that observation time be reduced. The two sources of this time are network-related delay and document size. In this section, we discuss how these difficulties can be ameliorated by moving the observer closer to the data and using encoding schemes so as to enable more frequent observation of large documents.

In order to even consider use of a remote observation post, there must be more machines available for this limited use. We may or may not have significant privileges on these machines, but even a very narrow use, such as simply making an observation from a remote machine, could be useful. Mobile agents are a means by which such limited access might be granted. If we have this access, then we can choose to make observations from machines if it benefits us to do so. By adding mobility to the observer, we give it the freedom to observe in closer proximity to the resource and the chance to perform pre-filtering on the result.

As with the technical report searcher, mobile agents are only a good choice if the additional machines at our disposal can only be utilized through an agent server; if we have full access to a machine, there is no reason not to have a search robot permanently resident on the machine. Mobile agents enable us to take advantage of situations in which one has such limited privileges on a machine. Since relatively few permissions are necessary in order to make observations and perform simple filtering, mobile agents are a viable solution.

The simplest type of remote observer might migrate to the vicinity of a document (or collection) of interest, compress the documents and send them back to the home machine, where they would be decompressed and analyzed. If the remote machines are at a great distance, this could result in a significant time savings. More complicated agents might transmit only the changes in document state in some compressed form. This would be especially appropriate for large documents that only experienced minor changes. Being able to transmit changes in state this way is a large step towards the use of "delta encoding" (analogous to MPEG) schemes for HTTP transmissions [444]. The key to making this type of encoding work is to package the agent with knowledge of the previous state of the document. Then, when a change is observed, the agent need only transmit the change in the document's index entry, not the entire document or even the entire index entry. This scheme has the desired features of reducing network traffic as well as removing bias against large or distant documents.

As packaging agents with an index entry and a lookup mechanism might produce a rather large piece of code, a better candidate for a remote observer would probably be a simpler filter. Large routines such as compression algorithms might be made available as part of standard libraries on remote machines, preventing us from having to carry compression code from machine to machine. The proxy server agent could be modified so that it would only return requested documents if they did not match a previously hashed version of the document, carried with the agent. This agent could observe these documents more frequently (being closer to the resource of interest) and then send documents back to the server (compressed, if utilities are available to the agent) only if they had changed. A typical retrieval task would entail sending an agent with instructions to look at some set of documents and return compressed versions of those that do not match a hash carried by the agent. Alternatively, the agent could simply notify the home machine that the document had definitely changed.

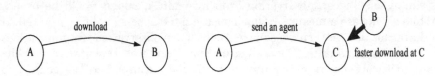

Fig. 15.5. Remote observation

While mobility may be a valuable option, we need to know the relative merit of observing locally versus using a mobile agent on a remote machine. Consider three machines, A, B, and C. Machine A contains the main document index database, machine B contains a document of interest, and machine C is available for use to a mobile agent. We emphasize that this is the only mode in which machine C can be used; for whatever reason, we are not allowed to compile and install code there on a permanent basis. We wish to determine what observation scenarios favor the use of a mobile observer in this situation. To do this, we consider a comparison of the two scenarios shown in Figure 15.5. We wish to compare the time it takes to transfer a document directly from B to A versus the time it takes to send a remote observer to C, observe the document at B and return relevant information. Making this more concrete, the document has size S_D bytes. The link from machine i to j has latency L_{ij} seconds, and an effective transfer rate of N_{ij} seconds per byte . If observed directly from machine A, the time for k observations would be:

$$t_1 = k\left(2L_{AB} + N_{AB}S_D\right) \tag{15.11}$$

The request for the document is assumed to be small enough that the time taken to transfer it is essentially the same as the link latency. Half of the latency term is due to this request, and half is due to the response. We compare t_1 with the time t_2 taken to perform the same k observations using a mobile agent of size $S_A = \beta S_D$ transferred to machine C. Further, we assume that the agent is clever enough to compress the document to a fraction η of its original size before transmitting ηS_D bytes of index information back to A. The total time is then

$$t_2 = (L_{AC} + N_{AC}\beta S_D + C_{startup}) + k((2L_{CB} + N_{CB}S_D) + \\ \gamma(L_{AC} + N_{AC}\eta S_D)) \tag{15.12}$$

To initiate the agent on the remote machine takes a time $C_{startup}$. For simple agents, this should be the only computation time on the same order as the transfer times. Other computation times, such as compression/decompression times, are assumed negligible by comparison. Also, notice that the agent's messages to the home machine are only required for the fraction γ of the observations on which a changed document is observed. It is immediately clear that the download portion of t_2, namely the term $k\,(2L_{CB} + N_{CB}S_D)$, must be strictly less than t_1 in order to even consider the use of a remote observer. If this is the case, then the sum of the outer terms in (15.12) must be less than the savings in download time in order for it to be worthwhile to observe remotely. In other words, remote observation is a good option when we save more by downloading at the alternate site than we spend in sending an agent and returning results. The two times can be estimated in advance in order to determine the relative benefit of the two modes of observation.

Multiple Tasks, Filtering, and Change Assessment. This was a relatively simple comparison, but we state it to emphasize that agents can present advantages even in simple situations. But an observation agent can be given tasks that are arbitrarily complex. For example, it need not perform observations of only a single document, and it can be free to move to a better vantage point if this saves time. In fact, the agent will multiply its efficiency if it observes many documents that might be resident on the target machine, B. Multiple observations of multiple documents will serve to amortize costs over time. Additionally, as an agent completes observations, it can "diet" by dumping code corresponding to completed tasks, whereupon it can migrate more quickly to the next observation site.

Whether observed by an remote agent, or by a robot running on the home machine, there must be a well-defined means by which to determine whether or not a document has "changed." We have been rather slippery about avoiding explanation of what might be meant by this, so as allow for more general types of observation. For example, the yellow pages index entire document sites according to the content types available at each site, rather than indexing specific documents. Our formulation above, however, is completely general, and the description we gave of document dynamics applies equally well to collection dynamics. We simply need to use a different change-detection function.

If one defines a change in the strict sense of whether or not any bytes were altered, this may be problematic, especially if we are considering changes within an entire collection. There will be situations in which the object in question has certainly changed, but the change that occurred was insignificant. For example, if the documents are Web pages, unimportant changes include the "counter" images on some web pages, randomized advertisements chosen for display, extra whitespace in the HTML source, and anything else essentially unrelated to the page's content. Furthermore, it may be simple to assess what portion of a page's content is of interest. For example, certain robots may be tasked with looking for new links. Changed pages that do not have new links are then no longer of interest. Simple filtering tasks such as this could be carried out in order to determine if a change is of interest.

15.6 Conclusion

Mobile agents have the potential to be a single, general framework in which a wide range of distributed, information-retrieval applications, such as the technical-report searcher described in this chapter, can be implemented efficiently, easily and robustly. By migrating to the location of a data repository, an agent can access the repository locally and avoid the network transfer of all intermediate data, regardless of whether the server provides low- or high-level operations. By migrating to a high-powered or lightly loaded machine, an agent can gain additional CPU cycles for its computation. By migrating to the other side of an unreliable link, the agent can continue its task even if the link goes down. By migrating to the other side of a low-bandwidth or high-latency link, an agent can avoid transferring partial results and intermediate operations across that link, reducing its total completion time. Most importantly, the agent can decide dynamically how to behave – i.e., migrate sequentially through a set of machines, send out child agents, or remain stationary – according to its task, repository characteristics, machine capabilities, and current network conditions.

To make mobile agents attractive in as wide a range of applications as possible, two key issues must be addressed. First, mobile-agent systems must become more scalable. In the short term, the main scalability problem is the raw performance of the low-level agent infrastructure. Specifically, the overhead of inter-agent communication must be reduced, so that *stationary* agents can compete with traditional client/server implementations. The overhead of agent migration must be reduced, so that an agent will find migration advantageous even in the best network environments and even if it needs to invoke only a few operations per information resource. Lastly, agent execution environments must be able to run agents nearly as fast as if they were natively compiled code; then agents could be used for load balancing tasks, and the load on a "server" machine due to an agent's presence would be only a modest amount worse than if the server implemented the agent's functionality itself. Solutions to all of these implementation problems exist in both traditional high-performance servers and the mobile-agent literature, and the main task now is to identify and combine the most suitable. In the long term, more research-oriented scalability issues revolve around higher-level services, such as agent tracking, debugging and visualization.

Second and more importantly, mobile agents require a wealth of information to make reasonable decisions about when and where to migrate. Numerous support services are needed to obtain and analyze current network, machine, and repository conditions, and then make an effective plan for accomplishing the desired task. Some of these services, such as directories and network-sensing modules, have seen extensive development within other distributed-computing contexts. Much work remains, however, to make these services work well within mobile-agent systems, where software components move rapidly and continuously from one machine to another. Other services are more unique to mobile-agent systems. Such services include planning algorithms that allow a single agent or a small group of cooperating agents to identify the best migration path through the network, as well as algorithms that allow an agent application to determine how to best "observe" a changing document collection. Promising work on both these services was described in this chapter.

Acknowledgments:

Many thanks to the Office of Naval Research (ONR), the Air Force Office of Scientific Research (AFOSR), the Department of Defense (DOD), and the Defense Advanced Research Projects Agency (DARPA) for their financial support of the D'Agents project: ONR contract N00014-95-1-1204, AFOSR/DOD contract F49620-97-1-03821, and DARPA contract F30602-98-2-0107; to the legion of graduate and undergraduate students who have worked on D'Agents, particularly Katya Pelehkov, Debbie Chyi, Pablo Stern and Ron Peterson, who implemented significant portions of the technical-report application (and associated support services) and are now implementing the next-generation version of the technical-report application.

16. On Coordinating Information Agents and Mobility

Robert Tolksdorf

Technische Universität Berlin, Fachbereich Informatik, FLP/KIT,
Sekr. FR 6–10, Franklinstr. 28/29, D-10587 Berlin, Germany.
E-Mail: tolk@cs.tu-berlin.de

16.1 Introduction

Mobile agents have gained enormous attention in recent years. In this chapter, we look at mobility as a coordination mechanism. We claim that mobility of entities in information systems serves the management of dependencies amongst activities.

The issue of coordination becomes vitally important for any system in which multiple components or agents work together. While agent technology has still not reached maturity outside of research labs, it can be predicted that the advent of systems with thousands of agents will shift the focus of attention from technology for communication and coordination towards software engineering problems.

Of central importance then will be the efficient selection and implementation of solutions to coordination amongst agents. This problem in turn, can be attacked by using techniques of reuse. In this contribution, we argue in favor of capturing knowledge about coordination mechanisms as *coordination patterns* in the spirit of recent developments within the object-oriented software engineering community.

In Section 16.2 we first discuss mobility as coordination mechanisms and mobile entities found in information systems. We point out in Section 16.3 our view on reusing coordination solutions by describing them with coordination patterns. The coordination language that we use to illustrate our coordination patterns is a variant from the Linda-family and described in Section 16.4. We exemplify our approach by some simple coordination patterns relevant for information systems in Section 16.5. We review related work and conclude in Section 16.6.

16.2 Coordination and Mobility in Information Systems

Information systems have undergone radical changes over the past years because of their growth in size and accessibility. Instead of a single answer to a single query, users are interested in integrated results from multiple information sources.

The new technologies in the area of agent research are quite promising for applications in the field of information systems. Characteristics such as autonomy and adaptability seem to match the requirements of complex information system access quite nicely. Should intelligent agents mature one day, they could be images of human users seeking for information at various places, changing the direction of the research on the fly, or probably throwing away prior results that seem to be outdated by others found later.

Because of the size and the static nature of information systems, mobile agents seem especially attractive for these tasks, as they are able to move to where the large amount of information is, filter it there according to some query and carry only relevant results to the next stop at an information source before returning to the user.

Of course, using multiple agents for performing such queries will be more efficient in time than using a single one. However, in order to have a set of agents interwork successfully, additional effort has to be put into their coordination. This is the issue we are interested in with this contribution.

16.2.1 Coordination Manages Dependencies

Coordination is a phenomenon which pervades our daily life and work. However, if we are well organized, coordination is invisible. Only its absence reveals the necessity for coordinative action. Uncoordinated situations lead to noticeable chaos and to failures of work. Coordination is embodied in human interaction, such as in a discussion where only one participant speaks at a time, in the design of organizations by prescribing workflows, or in computing systems by mechanisms in parallel and distributed computations such as scheduling, locking etc.

The currently most accepted definition of coordination is from [412]:

Coordination is managing dependencies between activities.

We use this definition in the following, as it seems most useful in that it abstracts from the actors involved and the activities they implement. As [592] points out, this definition shifts the focus from components coordinated to the relations amongst them that determine the dynamics of a system.

Information systems provide one of the target application areas for *mobile agents*. It is hoped that network load can be reduced by sending agents to information sources and performing information filtering there. Also, mobile agents could exhibit intelligent strategies for localizing and integrating information at multiple sources before delivering the result to the user. It is generally assumed that applications in the areas of data mining, electronic commerce, and system administration – especially in the field of telecommunication networks – will demonstrate the usefulness of the mobility approach [437].

Aside from exploring the technical fascination of being able to migrate live agents and objects, we believe that understanding mobility as a mechanism of coordination could provide a clearer view on possible applications. Mobility is not a unique characteristic of agents – it is a more natural characteristic of users and of information.

In [169] "*accessibility dependency*" is identified as a dependency in resource flows, that states simply that produced resources must be made accessible to users. The placement or movement of activities, and the transport of resources is identified as the basic coordination mechanisms, i.e. the alternatives to manage an accessibility dependency.

The placement of activities in a computing system means configuration, whereas the movement of activities at runtime is the coordination mechanism of central interest in the field of mobile agents and objects.

Transport of passive resources is obviously at the heart of communication based systems. In addition, this activity can also manage a second dependency as it allows for the synchronization on the availability of some data. In coordination theory, this dependency is called "*prerequisite dependency*" meaning that the start of some activity depends on the presence of some result of some other activity.

By that, mobility is an option to manage dependencies amongst activities and we conclude that *mobility is a coordination mechanism*. We believe that it can be explained as such from a coordination theory perspective.

16.2.2 Mobile Entities in Information Systems

The notion of mobility can be applied to different classes of entities in information systems. We distinguish passive but mobile information, active and mobile agents, and mobile human users.

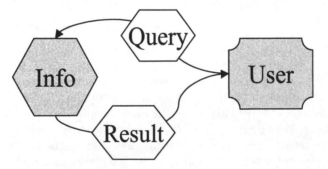

Fig. 16.1. Moving Information

Mobility of information is the very basic requirement to exchange knowledge amongst users, systems, and agents and synonymous to communication. Figure 16.1 shows this basic kind of interaction: A query is moved from the user to an information source and answered with the result information. In the case of the information source, the result moved to the agent is usually a copy of the information available at the information source.

This pattern of mobility of information is basic for distributed systems that follow a client/server style of interaction. It is the usual way that people access information systems like the Web, Gopher, or databases.

Mobile agent technology introduces the notion of moving an active entity over spatially different places. Such an agent maintains a state across movements and thereby is a sort of active container for mobile information.

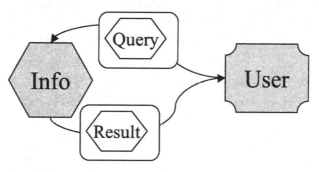

Fig. 16.2. A mobile agent

Figure 16.2 shows the classic scenario to demonstrate the benefits of mobile agent technology. Here, an agent is sent to an information source together with a query. The agent can actively interact with the information source, eg. to refine the query. The scenario exhibits a reduced communication load as the interaction occurs at the same place.

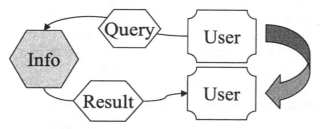

Fig. 16.3. A mobile user

The ultimate client of information access is the human user who has some information need that shall be satisfied at least in part by using an information system. Considering mobility and information systems has to include *mobility of users*.

Mobility of human users is a given fact. Currently, however, users remain rather stationary with respect to their use of information systems. They are online at some workstation or terminal. However, current technology already indicates that mobility of users will be important in the future. Examples for mobile users are usually given in terms of highly active information managers whose main activity seems to be moving between meetings etc. Two scenarios seem reasonable:

- *The user is relatively stationary towards a mobile device.* This includes all well known examples of using mobile telecommunication devices like mobile phones etc.
- *The user is mobile in relation to access devices.* This includes examples of users changing devices with different capabilities – like moving from an ASCII-terminal to a color-workstation – or different location – like moving from the office-terminal to the home.

The first category does not seem interesting in our context, as the technology of mobile devices aims centrally at masking the spatial transfer of the device.

Given that mobility is a coordination mechanism and that it applies to virtually all entities of interest in information systems, the range of solving coordination problems by using mobility at various places becomes very broad. The design of a specific coordination structure for a given coordination problem becomes a complex task as the number of agents to be coordinated scales up. Whereas the technological specifics of implementing mobile agent systems are interesting at a low scale, putting large-scale agent systems to work depends on solving a software engineering problem.

16.3 Software Engineering for Multi Agent Systems

The management of dependencies is a complex task that cannot be described by a handful of primitive coordination operations. The structure of such complex coordination activities is of interest, as they are solutions to coordination problems. We could hope to reuse such solutions in different contexts. Reuse, in turn, is a key to successful software engineering.

16.3.1 Reuse of Coordination Solutions

Coordination theory is characterized as an interdisciplinary enterprise to study how coordination can occur in different kinds of systems. Disciplines involved include computer science, organization theory, management sciences, economics, linguistics, and psychology [412]. The effort of establishing a separate field is motivated by the observation that the phenomenon *coordination* is apparent in all of these disciplines. It is hoped that the transfer of ideas on coordination amongst them leads to a better understanding of coordination fundamentals and to new ideas in the respective disciplines.

Work in coordination theory has led to a number of studies which aim at identifying categories of coordination processes and management options [145]. The sources for the detection of such processes include computer science, organization theory, management sciences, economics, linguistics, and psychology.

Proponents of coordination theory emphasize that the novelty of their approach is to look for ideas in other systems that solved coordination problems similar to a coordination problem at hand [411].

Although not specifically bound to the production of software, this approach can well be understood as a *reuse* of proven solutions to coordination problems.

16.3.2 Patterns

In object-oriented programming, the notion of *patterns* has become very popular in recent years. It has been discovered that inheritance alone is not sufficient to express the structure of object-oriented applications and their implementations. Also, it has shown that code reuse alone is not sufficient and that design reuse is even more important.

This has led to the development of generic software architectures as object-oriented *frameworks* [318] and of *design patterns* [229] describing known ways to design solutions to related problems in the implementation of software components.

The initial focus on mining patterns of program design has been successfully broadened to other domains, such as object-oriented modeling with *analysis patterns* [217]. More recently, the notion of *organizational patterns* develops as an attempt to detect reoccuring and reusable structures in the design of organizations.

The focus of patterns is to capture knowledge about a proven solution to a problem that can be applied in a certain context. As such, it describes one choice a designer has when confronted with a certain problem.

16.3.3 Coordination Patterns

We propose to take a similar approach and to target the discovery of reoccuring structures of management of dependencies. We see the notion of *coordination patterns* as an attempt to study in an interdisciplinary manner reoccuring and reusable structures of management of dependencies in organizations, economy, and computing systems, etc.

The benefit of detecting coordination patterns is their reuse in different fields. For example, the family of auction patterns has been discovered in *market-oriented programming* as solutions to resource allocation problems and for service trading in distributed systems [711].

[345] emphasizes the value of detecting dependency structures in coordinated processes and the coordination mechanisms used for making them

work. Coordination patterns could serve as a *rationale language* as demanded by Klein to document decisions taken in designing a coordination solution.

The goal within this contribution is to identify coordination patterns that use mobility mechanisms wrt. information, agents, and users. The aim is to find reoccuring structures and to collect them. The patterns could well be implemented as some higher order coordination operations, or as agents that execute them as services.

To describe patterns, we use a template as described in figure 16.4. The template is different from the ones used in object-oriented design, such as in [229] which include forces, solution, and consequences. The most important difference to design patterns is that we require a coordination pattern to state what kind of dependency it manages. We consider the ability to identify the kind of dependency as discriminating for coordination patterns.

Pattern: Name

Also Known As
Other names for the pattern.

Intent
Rationale and intended use.

Motivation
A scenario of application.

Dependency Managed
The dependency managed by the coordination pattern.

Structure
An illustration of the entities involved.

Collaborations
How the entities involved interact.

Implementation
Implementation remarks.

Sample Code
An example for implementing the pattern. We use MOS (see Section 16.4) as the implementation language here. The code only has to illustrate the idea, but does not have to be executable or complete.

Known Uses
Where the pattern can be found in application. The rule-of-three applies: There should be at least three distinct known applications to qualify as a pattern.

Related Patterns
Patterns related to the one described.

Fig. 16.4. The pattern template

In the following we will use a coordination language from the Linda family [237] to express mobility of agents and data. Coordination languages are unique wrt. the dependencies managed as they contain primitive operations that communicate and synchronize processes with data in one operation.

16.4 A Coordination Language for Mobility

Coordination languages from the Linda family are especially interesting to study the implementation and the support of coordination processes. Of specific importance for information systems is that these languages are able to support interaction with multiple information sources, whereas client/server is bound to a two-party interaction. Coordination languages demonstrated that their high level of abstraction is well suited to support mobility of information and agents, eg. in [467].

16.4.1 Mobile Object Spaces

We define the following coordination model called *Mobile Object Spaces* which is an object oriented Linda [237] variant implemented in Java.

In Mobile Object Spaces (MOS) we introduce a set of related types of objects. The types of main interest describe multiset collections of elements with different functionalities used as coordination media. These multisets are central to this kind of coordination language. The language itself is given by the definition of the coordination medium, the elements used therein and a set of operations for its manipulation [128].

As in Linda, elements in multisets are accessed associatively. That is, a *matching* relation is defined on objects and object templates. Reading from the multiset is relative to a template that describes what kind of object is sought. It results in one element that fulfills the matching relation.

The definition of the matching relation depends on the kind of object inspected. In MOS, we define a type *Matchable* that is implemented by classes that define an operation *boolean match(Entry o)*. We define a type *Entry* which is basically an empty type used to denote classes that can be stored in a multiset. Thus, tuples as in Linda are one implementation of entries and the matching relation of Linda is implemented by the *match* method in a *Template* class that implements the type *Matchable*.

Objects of type *Databag* are collections of communicable data. A Databag offers operations for adding, copying and retrieving entries. It is functional in that no notion of processes is introduced. The operations of a Databag are:

– *void out(Entry d)*: An entry is stored in the Databag, that is, the entry *d* is cloned at the Databag.

- *Entry inp(Matchable t)*: An entry matching *t* is sought in the Databag and retrieved. If none can be found, a bottom element *null* is returned instead. Retrieval means to remove the data object from the Databag and thereby move the found entry to the client.
- *Entry rdp(Matchable t)*: An entry matching *t* is sought in the Databag and a copy of it is returned. If none can be found, a bottom element *null* is returned instead. The entry found is cloned at the client.

The type *Objectbag* is a subtype of *Databag*. It introduces a notion of processes that can be blocked and resumed. It adds the following operations:

- *Entry in(Matchable t)*: An entry matching *t* is sought in the Objectbag and retrieved. If none can be found, the process executing *in* is blocked, until a matching entry is available. Its execution then is resumed with the retrieval of the matching object which moves it to the client.
- *Entry rd(Matchable t)*: An entry matching *t* is sought in the Objectbag and a copy of it is returned. The found entry thus is cloned at the client. Similar to *in*, the operation is blocking.

The type *Objectbag* is not functional, as the execution of operations for reading and writing can overlap. MOS does not define any precedence in the case of race conditions – all necessary decisions are taken nondeterministically.

Objects of type *Agentbag* are collections of agents. An Agentbag thus is an environment in which active resources execute. It subtypes *Objectbag* and introduces the notion of starting, stopping and copying a process.

In order to refer to processes and locations therein, we introduce two types. *Future* describes a process which, when evaluated, becomes an entry (see also [312]). Thus a future is the target of process creation. Within such a process, a *Continuation* represents a place of execution at which the evaluation of the future can be stopped and resumed.

With these, the Agentbag type is characterized by the following additional operations:

- *void eval(Future future)*: The Agentbag evaluates the active resource *future* to an entry. It is stored in the state of the Agentbag (see below).
- *void move(Agentbag destination, Continuation continuation)*: An agent executing the operation at the Agentbag it is executed in (see below) is stopped, moved to *destination* and continued there at *continuation*.

Depending on how they use objects of the named classes, we can classify objects. *Clients* are processes that use a Databag or an Objectbag. *Agents* are clients that implement an Objectbag as their state and can be used by clients. *Hosts* are agents that implement an Agentbag. Each agent has exactly one host. *Nodes* are hosting a host. Nodes are not hosted.

With these, we have a model which follows the agent/place distinction usually applied in mobile agent systems, but are able to understand an agent also as a place – in our terminology as a host.

16.4.2 A MOS Implementation with Java

As an experiment, we have designed a simple implementation of MOS in Java. The types of objects that are represented as Java interfaces. They are implemented by objects from certain classes. In our Java implementation we define a set of respective classes that implement the named interfaces.

– *DataSpace*: An implementation of *Databag*.
– *ObjectSpace*: An implementation of *Objectbag*. It contains a *Databag* plus information about currently blocked operations. An *ObjectSpace* is an *Agent*.
– *AgentSpace*: An implementation of an *Agentbag*. It contains an *Objectbag* and a set of processes that execute active entities.

For *Client*, *Agent*, and *Host* we provide a set of abstract classes to be implemented by application objects.

While Java includes an easy to use thread model, the grain size of referring to places within code is that of individual methods. Thus, continuations cannot be used to refer to arbitrary locations in the code. This technical detail does not change the model implemented and is open to changes in future Java versions.

Our classes do also implement the Java specific type *Remote* which allows objects at distant locations to invoke their methods by Java's Remote Method Invocation mechanism RMI. In part they implement the type *Serializable* which makes them exchangeable amongst virtual Java machines.

Each entity in MOS is at a certain location. A location can be a logical or physical locality and is denoted by a unique name such as a URL. The following rules apply. The logical location of a node equals its physical location. An agent can have a logical location within a host. The physical location of an agent is the physical location of its host. Each resource is located within another resource.

The locality of entities is embedded in *references* to clients and agents executed at some host. These references are matchable objects and thus can be stored in dataspaces. Matching is defined as substring inclusion within the name of the reference.

On each node a MOS environment runs. It includes the top level agent which is the host for all other agents on this node. Also, it includes a special agent, called the *registry* whose state is a collection of references running on that host. The registry is changed by *eval*, *move*, and the termination of an agent.

16.4.3 Coordinating Mobility in MOS

Mobility of information is embodied in the MOS coordination model as primitives. Using the operations inherited from Linda, we can move information *i* to an agent *a* with *a.out(i)*, copy information matching *j* from agent *a* by *a.rdp(j)*, and move information matching *j* from agent *a* by *a.inp(j)*. These are the operations that characterize the type *Databag* as described above.

We also find operations to coordinate with the presence of information at a certain location with the Linda primitives as follows:

- We can manage prerequisite dependencies by synchronizing with the presence of information matching *j* at an agent *a* with *a.rd(j)*.
- We can coordinate exclusively with the presence of information matching *j* at an agent *a* with *a.in(j)*.

In MOS, these primitives characterize the type *Objectbag*.

To move agents with MOS, we declare a class *Future* which instantiates to object that can be evaluated. The respective operations to transfer such a future are to move future *f* to host *a* with *a.out(f)*, to execute the evaluation of future *f* within host *a* with *a.eval(f)*, or agent *a* can move from its host *h* to host *i* continuing at *c* with *h.move(i,c)*. In MOS, *i* has to fulfill the type *Agentbag*.

To coordinate with other agents at locations, we can use the registry. Specifically, we can detect the presence of agents whose references match the partial reference *r* by *registry.rdp(r)* or coordinate with the presence of an agent whose reference matches the partial reference *r* by *registry.rd(r)*.

To coordinate with users, we have to assume that human users are represented by some agent. Such an agent then has a locality and can be referenced. Coordinating with a human user thus is similar to coordinating with agents.

With MOS we have a language which captures actions that we consider primitive wrt. mobility by primitive operations. Our interest is on how such actions are combined and how reoccuring structures of such combinations can be captured as coordination patterns. This is the topic for the next section.

We consider the migration of data or agents from a source to a destination as a primitive coordination mechanism. When aiming at real applications, the question is how to combine such primitives in a useful way. In order to facilitate easy construction of applications with mobile agents, it seems necessary to record such useful combinations as *reusable* higher order structures. These are the structures that we intend to capture as coordination patterns.

16.5 Simple Coordination Patterns

The following subsections describe some simple patterns observed in information systems. The list is not complete at all and shall demonstrate our approach. It could serve as a basis for a coordination pattern catalog, or pattern system for coordination.

16.5.1 Pulling Information from a Source

As stated in the introduction, moving information is the basic mechanism of communication in distributed systems. We describe it as a coordination pattern Pull as in figure 16.5.

Pattern: Pull

Also Known As
Query/Result, Client/Server

Intent
To transfer information from an information source to a client. The information has to be in a class described by a query.

Motivation
The information source has more information than the client.

Dependency Managed
Access dependency of client to information.

Structure

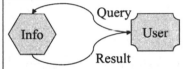

Collaborations
The client moves a query describing a class of information to an information source. The information source selects all information entities in the class and moves a copy to the client.

Sample Code
```
Id queryId=source.in(new Formal(new Id()));
source.out(queryId,query);
Result result=source.in(queryId, new Formal(new Result()));
```

Known Uses
SQL servers, Web-services, client-server interaction

Related Patterns
Push

Fig. 16.5. The pattern Pull

16.5.2 Pushing Information to the User

Pull describes mobility that is initiated by the agent that has a query. The information copied and moved is valid at the time the result was generated, but not necessarily longer. A pattern where the transfer of information is initiated at the location of the information source is Push as described in figure 16.6.

Pattern: Push

Intent

To transfer a stream of information from an information source to a client. The stream is initiated by an agent sent to the source.

Motivation

The information at the source is dynamic. It is not possible to transfer a complete result as an answer to a query.

Dependency Managed

Prerequisite dependency of client to presence of information.

Structure

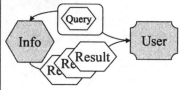

Collaborations

The client moves an agent containing a query to an information source. The agent monitors the source wrt. information entities in the class described by the query and moves copies continuously to the client.

Sample Code

```
source.eval(agent(q,self))

void agent(Query query, Reference dest) {
  do {
    Id queryId=source.in(new Formal(new Id()));
    source.out(queryId,query);
    Result result=source.in(queryId, new Formal(new Result()));
    dest.out(result);
  } while (true);
}
```

Known Uses

Databases, servlets, personalized information services, eg. URLminder, automated mailing-list systems, MBone.

Related Patterns

Pull

Fig. 16.6. The pattern Push

Pattern: Index

Also Known As

Cache

Intent

To copy information from several information sources at a central and fast place. The place may transform the information, for example by indexing it, or just store it, for example as a cache.

Motivation

The information is of higher accessibility to the user when the information is moved to a fast source before a query is posed.

Dependency Managed

Accessibility dependency of client to information. Index partially manages the dependency by making the access more efficient in terms of interactions and transfer.

Structure

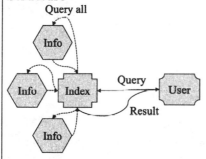

Collaborations

The index retrieves copies of information from several informations sources. It repeats it in intervals.

Sample Code

```
source1.eval(agent(q,self));
source2.eval(agent(q,self));
...
sourceN.eval(agent(q,self));
```

Known Uses

Web search engines, Web caches

Related Patterns

Push, Pull used to access the index and used to access sources.

Fig. 16.7. The pattern Index

Pattern: Traveler

Also Known As
Plan, Itinerary

Intent
To send out an autonomous agent that visits several information sources and adapts a query autonomously to the results received.

Motivation
The result is required to be of high timeliness or the query changes depending on partial results.

Dependency Managed
Access dependency for the user and prerequisite dependencies amongst partial results and refined queries.

Structure

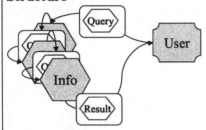

Collaborations
An agent or query is sent to an information source which passes it on to another source. The result is returned at the end to the user.

Sample Code
```
source1.eval(traveler(
 new Plan(source2, source3, self)));

void traveler(Plan plan) {
  Id queryId= in(new Formal(new Id()));
  out(queryId,query);
  result.updateWith(in(queryId, new Formal(new Result())));
  query.updateOn(result);
  move(plan.next(), traveler);
}
```

Known Uses
Meta search engines, research prototypes of mobile agent systems

Fig. 16.8. The pattern Traveler

16.5.3 Copying Information to an Index

In Push and Pull the user interacts directly with the information source. This is not necessarily an efficient solution and can be enhanced by an intermediate Index as described in figure 16.7.

16.5.4 Visiting Places

In Index copying information to the index is done asynchronously with the access of the index. This might not be appropriate when a timely result is required, or when queries have to be refined depending on intermediate results collected. In figure 16.8 we describe the pattern Traveler in which a query or an agent passes by multiple information sources.

16.6 Related Work and Conclusion

The rich set of work on mobile agents – with the ancestor Telescript [721] – has focused very much on the technology involved and on finding useful applications for mobile agent systems. For the Aglets system, a set of templates has recently been proposed [438] which capture basic collaborative behaviors of mobile agents as plans. These templates include patterns like spreading a set of agents over places where they perform activities and join later.

[224] describes a simple coordination pattern, namely Master/Worker for parallel computing. Although older, [106] is even more ambitious in describing three patterns of coordination in parallel programming, namely result-, specialist- and agenda-parallelism. [628] introduces the notion of coordination skeletons that capture the externally observable behavior of an agent as a finite state machine.

All these efforts of finding higher level coordination mechanisms as templates, patterns, skeletons etc., are similar to our notion of coordination patterns in that they focus on the structure of coordination.

With this paper we tried to explore mobility as a coordination mechanism and to experiment with the notion of coordination patterns. We conclude that understanding mobility as a mechanism that manages dependencies can lead to a uniform model of communication, synchronization and mobility. From the experiments with coordination patterns we conclude that their description leads to schemas of complex coordination activities above the level of coordination language primitives.

We take these experiments as a starting point to discover and collect solutions to coordination problems from various fields. We hope that the reuse of solutions from different systems can lead to a better understanding of coordination fundamentals and to new ideas in the respective disciplines.

17. Spawning Information Agents on the Web

Onn Shehory

The Robotics Institute, Carnegie Mellon University, Pittsburgh,
PA 15213, USA.
E-Mail: onn@cs.cmu.edu

Summary.

   Network bandwidth limitations must be considered by information
agents when retrieving information from remote sources. There are cases
where it should be more efficient (considering network constraints) that an
agent will perform its activity on the remote server. This can be performed
by spawning an agent on that server. Agent spawning is an appropriate
means for resolving agent overload problems as well. Agents in a multi-
agent system may face situations where tasks overload their computational
capacities or do not fit their capabilities. Usually, this problem is solved by
passing tasks to other agents or agent migration to remote hosts. Agent
spawning is a more comprehensive approach to balancing local agent overloads. According to our paradigm, agents may spawn, pass tasks to others,
die or merge. We discuss the mechanisms required for deciding upon and
performing agent spawning. The requirements for implementing a spawning mechanism and the advantages of using it are addressed.

17.1 Introduction

Information agents situated on the web, as other computational systems, are
subject to limitations on the use of resources. In the current setting of the
Internet, it is evident that the major bottleneck agents face is the communication bandwidth. Agents that need a large amount of remotely located
information may face a long delay before they are able to acquire the required information. Thus, overall task execution may be poor. As we show in
this chapter, creating an agent that will be sent to the information site may,
in cases, be more efficient than transferring the information itself. Yet, information needs and network bandwidth are not the only source of poor task
performance. The loads of tasks the agents have may either result in overloading their local computational resources, or simply be beyond their expertise,
thus hamper task performance. Redistribution of tasks (when possible) and
the creation of new agents with the appropriate expertise for handling excess
and incompatible tasks resolve such difficulties. These solutions are demonstrated and discussed in this chapter.

Assume a multi-agent system (MAS) situated on the web. Agents in the
system dynamically receive tasks. These tasks require gathering, filtering,
fusing and processing information. The agents are heterogeneous, that is,
agents have different *capabilities* which indicate the types of tasks they can
perform — their expertise. Also, they have different computational *capacities*

which indicate the amounts of resources (memory, cpu, communication) that the agents can access and use for task execution. Tasks are categorized by types that can be handled by agents with appropriate capabilities. In this chapter we discuss two problems which are typical in such MAS, and are usually entangled:

1. What should an agent do when it receives a task for which it does not have the right capabilities? How should an agent react to situations where the incoming tasks, although within its capabilities, overload its capacities? Task delegation may be the answer to both questions: delegation to other agents where the appropriate capabilities are available may resolve the first; when overloads are local to the agent, delegating tasks to other agents with similar capabilities may resolve the second problem. However, given the above situations, how should an agent react when other agents, that have the capabilities required for the incompatible or overloading tasks, appear overloaded as well, or are unreachable?

2. In cases where the amount of remote information to be processed for the performance of a task is large, how should an agent handle the task to reduce (and possibly optimize) the communication overhead for transferring the necessary information?

As shown in [613], several solutions may apply for the first problem, and details of these solutions will be presented later[1]. However, since the second problem is commonly present as well, a more comprehensive solution is needed. In [613], predictive agent cloning was presented. Agent cloning entails the creation and activation of identical copies of the original, creator agent. One of the advantages of cloning is in the relative simplicity of creating a new agent, given that all of the expertise necessary for it are already present in the older one (the creator), so there is no need to create new capabilities. However in this property lies also a major disadvantage of cloning: it limits the newly created agent (the clone) to handling only the same types of tasks that its creator can handle. In addition, cloning dictates the size of the new agent, thus the level of computational resources it may consume. This results in newly created agents that may be too complex (hence heavy-weight) to run on the intended clone host, thus may prevent from achieving a solution to the overload problem. At the same time, it may be the case that, for executing the tasks for which the cloning mechanism was activated, it is sufficient to have a lighter-weight agent with only part of the capabilities of its creator, or completely different ones. The cloning approach does not allow for such agent creation. We suggest an alternative to this approach that would extend it to overcome the above limitation. The agent computational problems we address, i.e., overloads and large information transfer requirements, have several characteristic patterns as deliberated below.

---

[1] In this chapter we extend the work presented in [613]. Some of the results we present are already presented there.

Overloads may occur in two major forms: an agent is overloaded, but the MAS in which it is situated as a whole has the required capabilities and capacities; the MAS as a whole is overloaded, i.e., the set of agents which are accessible and capable of performing the current tasks do not have the necessary capacities. At the same time there may be idle computational resources in the system where the agents are situated. As a result of overloads, either local to an agent or at the MAS level, the MAS will not perform all of the tasks in time, although the required computational resources may be available to it.

Information processing and transfer are inseparable from the activity of agents on the web. The common approaches to remote information processing are: transferring the information to the agent that needs it for local processing; relying on services located at the site of the information to perform the processing (as common in distributed databases); allowing the agent in need of the information to migrate to the information site, process it at the remote cite, and return with the results. Alternatively, we suggest that a new agent which has only the capabilities necessary for a specific task should be spawned on the remote site. Situations that justify such spawning are when the ratio between the amount of raw data to be transferred to an agent for its tasks' need and the amount of processed information resulting form these tasks is large, and when the agent to be remotely spawned is light weight.

The following solutions, combined, address the problems above:

1. A single overloaded agent should pass tasks to other agents which have the capabilities and capacities to perform them.
2. When all of the accessible and capable agents are overloaded, agents should create new agents to perform excess tasks and utilize unused resources. Alternatively, agents may migrate to other hosts.
3. When new tasks are created or arrive at the agents such that no accessible agent has the required *capabilities* for executing them, either users or agents should create and activate new agents which have the capabilities for performing the new tasks (but may be different from the active agents). For this, there should be some capability server available to users and agents, where they can locate the components necessary for the sought agent expertise and construct the agents using these components.
4. When the expected amount of remotely located information necessary for executing a task is very large compared to the size of the agent code and the amount of produced information, the agent that needs to perform the task should either migrate to the site of the information or spawn an agent at this site.

In this research we study the mechanisms required for *agent spawning* as a means for implementing the above solutions. In particular, we investigate agent spawning in an open environment, such as the Internet, where agents might dynamically and unpredictably appear or disappear. To study MAS issues in such an environment, we refer to the RETSINA agent infrastructure [655]. In RETSINA, there are three types of agents: *providers*, who possess certain capabilities and perform tasks that require these capabilities; *requesters*, who have tasks to be performed and who locate agents with the required capabilities to whom they delegate the tasks; *middle agents* such as matchmakers [165], by whom requester agents locate provider agents. Provider agents advertise their capabilities to middle agents and requesters ask the latter to find providers with required capabilities. Part of our spawning mechanism is applied to a simulated RETSINA infrastructure as follows. When an agent perceives a problem of the type described above, i.e., incompatible tasks, overloads or large volume of information to be transfered, it can find, through middle agents, provider agents with appropriate capabilities to whom it can consider transferring tasks. When no such providers are found, spawning a new agent is considered. Once created, the new agent advertises itself with a middle agent and becomes familiar to the multi-agent society.

In the rest of this chapter we provide guidelines and mechanisms to be used for implementing spawning. We analyze the circumstances under which agent spawning should be considered. We investigate reasoning, decision making and actions that are necessary for agents to perform spawning. Results of simulations we have performed on a subset of the spawning problem are presented. In this simulation, agent cloning (which is a specific case of agent spawning), and its effects on the performance of a MAS, were examined. The results show that using cloning protocols to address local overloading problems improves agent and system performance. The analysis of the wider problems and their solution - agent spawning - shows that, under some conditions, spawning should be highly beneficial.

17.2 Why Is Spawning Necessary?

While agent cloning is a possible response of an agent to overloads, agent spawning includes, in addition, consideration of the data transfer necessary for task execution, and it relaxes the requirement of creating an identical copy of the original agent. Thus, spawning further enhances efficiency of network utilization and reduction of communication and computation loads.

Agent overloads are due, in general, to either the agent's limited capacity to process current tasks, or machine overloads. Other approaches to overloads include task transfer and agent migration. Task transfer, where overloaded agents locate other agents which are lightly loaded and transfer tasks to them, is very similar to processor load balancing. Agent migration, which requires that overloaded agents, or agents that run on an overloaded machine[2], migrate to less loaded machines, is closely related to process migration and

---

[2] We assume some correlation between machine load and agents' loads, however these are different overloads.

to the recently emerging field of mobile agents [126]. Agent migration can be implemented by an agent creating a copy of itself (a clone) on a remote machine, transferring its tasks to it and dying. Thus, agent mobility is an instance of agent cloning, which is in turn an instance of agent spawning. A main difference between load balancing and agent cloning is that, while the first explicitly discusses machine loads and process migration, the latter, in addition, considers a different type of load — the agent load, which is unique in its reference to agent expertise (referred to as capabilities). Agent spawning further adds upon load balancing and cloning by allowing for creation of new agents different from the original and considering information transfer requirements.

While cloning is a superset of task transfer and process migration (it includes them and adds to them as well), agent spawning is even wider in its scope. One facet of spawning refers to capability and resource overloads (and was previously referred to as agent cloning [613]). Spawning does not necessarily require migration to other machines. Rather, a new agent is created either on the local or a remote machine. Note that there may be several agents running on the same machine, and having one of them overloaded does not necessarily imply that the others are overloaded. An agent overload does not imply a machine overload, and therefore local spawning (that is, on the same machine) may be possible. As shown in the load balancing literature [393], within a distributed system there is a high probability of having some of the processors idle, while others are highly loaded. This facet of spawning takes advantage of these idle processing capacities.

To perform agent spawning, an agent must reason about its tasks, referring to current and future information requirements and loads, the load of its host and capabilities and loads of other machines and agents. Accordingly, it may decide to: create a new agent; pass tasks to this agent; merge with other agents; or die. Merging of two agents and self-extinction of underutilized agents is an important mechanism to control agent proliferation which otherwise may result in overloaded network resources.

Reasoning about spawning begins with recognizing the type of problem that should be resolved:

– Capacity and capability overloads, or
– Large information transfer requirements.

In the case of overloads, the reasoning begins with considering local spawning. This will prevent the communication overhead of trying to access and reason about remote hosts. When local spawning is found infeasible or non-beneficial, the agent proceeds to reason about remote spawning. Once remote spawning is decided upon, an agent should be created and activated on a remote machine. Assuming that the agent has access and a permit to work on this machine, there may be two main methods to perform this spawning: (1) creating the new agent locally and allowing it to migrate to the remote machine or, (2) creating and activating the agent on the remote machine.

While the first method requires very little on the part of the remote machine, it requires mobilization properties. It also requires additional resource consumption on local host, where the creation and activation are performed. The second method, while avoiding mobilization and local resource consumption, requires that a copy of the agents' code be located on the remote machine. Similar requirements also hold for mobile agent applications [250, 720], since an agent server or an agent dock is required.

Since the information needs of an agent as well as its own load and the loads of other agents vary over time in a non-deterministic way, the decision of *whether and when* to spawn is non-trivial. Prior work on cloning [162] has presented a model of cloning based on prediction of missed task deadlines and idle times on the agent's schedule in the RETSINA multi-agent infrastructure [655]. In this research (Section 17.3.1), we present a stochastic model of decision making based on dynamic programming to determine the optimal timing for spawning.

In cases where the problem dealt with is of large information transfer requirements, local spawning is an inadequate solution. In addition, the only reasonable target hosts for the spawned agents are the sites of the (large volume) needed data, that have caused the need for spawning. Therefore, only remote access to these specific hosts is necessary. After acquiring the information with regards to the propreties relevant to spawning from the appropriate hosts, their consideration for spawning will be performed utilizing reasoning and decision making procedures similar to those used in the overload case.

Several questions are of interest when a new spawn is created and activated. These regard its autonomy, its tasks, its lifetime, and its access to resources. *Autonomy* refers to the independence of a spawn vs. its being subordinate. Once created and activated, an independent spawn is not controlled by its creator. Such a spawn agent will continue to exist after completion of the tasks provided by its initiator agent. Hence, a mechanism for deciding what it should do after task completion is necessary. Such a mechanism must allow the spawn to reason about the agent- and task-environment, and accordingly decide whether it should continue to work on other tasks (if necessary and if the computational resources allow), merge with others, or perform self extinction.

A *subordinate* spawn will remain under the control of its initiator. This will prevent the complications arising in the independent spawn case - i.e., it is not necessary to decide what activity it should perform after the tasks that were delegated to the spawn are accomplished. However, in order to control a subordinate agent, the initiating agent must be provided with a control mechanism for remote agents. Such a mechanism will require additional communication between the two agents, thus increasing the communication overhead. In addition, control of other agents may be a partially centralized solution and is usually undesirable in multi-agent systems. However, for the problem of large amount of remote information, an agent that creates a spawn on the site of the information would prefer having at least some loose control of its spawn, since this spawn is specifically created to serve the information needs of its creator. On the other hand, when the sole reason for spawning was overloads, it is preferable to allow for an independent spawn.

17.3 Requirements for Spawning

An agent should consider spawning in the following cases:

- Data transfer problems:
  The volume of remotely-located information it needs to process for performing its tasks is large in comparison with the volume of the agent's code used for this processing and the produced information, or
- Task and resource load balancing problems:
  - It cannot perform all of its tasks on time by itself nor can it decompose them so that they can be delegated to others, and
  - There is no lightly-loaded agent that can receive and perform its excess tasks (or sub-tasks when tasks are decomposable), and
  - There are sufficient resources for creating and activating a spawn agent (either on the same machine or on a remote one), and
  - The efficiency of the spawn agent and the original agent is expected to be greater than that of the original agent alone.

Later in this chapter we discuss the methods according to which agents reason about themselves and their environment to perceive these conditions.

The necessary information used by an agent to decide whether and when to initiate spawning comprises parameters that describe both local and remote resources. In particular, the necessary parameters are as follows:

- The expected ratio between the amount of remotely located raw data necessary for its tasks and the amount of information produced by these tasks. Both raw and produced information are measured in bytes (the ratio is a pure number).
- The CPU and memory loads, both internal to the agent (which result from planning, scheduling and task-execution activities of the agent) and external (on the agent host and possibly on remote hosts).
- The CPU performance[3], both locally and remotely.
- The load on the communication channels and their transfer rate, both locally and remotely.
- The current queue of tasks, the resources required for their execution and their deadlines.
- The future expected flow of tasks.

---

[3] We utilize standard methods (e.g., MIPS) to estimate it.

To acquire the above information an agent must be able to read the operating system variables. In addition, the agent must have self awareness on two levels—an agent internal level and a MAS level. The internal self awareness should allow the agent to verify what part of the operating system retrieved values are its own agent internal parameters. The system-wise self awareness should allow the agent to find, possibly via middle agents [165], information regarding available resources on remote machines. In some MAS models, e.g., [477, 733], the first is referred to as self-model, and the latter is called (agent) acquaintance module. Without middle agents, servers that are located on the remote hosts (as in e.g. D'Agents - see Chapter 15 and [250]) can supply such information upon request[4]. When such information is not available, an agent may compute the expected values of the attributes of remote machines relying on probability distributions either specifically by machine id (e.g. IP address) or groupwise, by machine type.

17.3.1 Optimization of Decision Making: When To Spawn?

We present the formal method used for optimizing the spawning decisions. Each agent A_i has a load tuple $l_i = < p_i, m_i, c_i >$ (processing load p_i, memory load m_i and communication load c_i). This load results from the agent's tasks' makeup. In general, an agent's load is time dependent (denoted by $l_i(t)$ where t stands for time). We assume that the time t is measured in discrete units. The distance d_{ij} between agents A_i and A_j is the network latency (measured in milliseconds) based on the communication route between the machines on which the agents are running. To assess the time a remote spawn should consume for performing its given tasks, the computational resources of the *remote* machine must be considered. These are the CPU performance (e.g., given in MIPS), the size of memory (MB) and the communication capabilities (e.g., transmission rate in bps).

To maximize benefits, an agent should decide on spawning at the optimal time. Below, we provide a method for optimizing the spawning decision making. For this, each decision regarding spawning has a value, calculated with respect to loads and distances as a function of time. Each agent A_i has a valuation function $\text{Val}_i(l_i, \overline{L_i}, d, t)$ for evaluating decision points. Here, $\overline{L_i}$ is a set of loads of agents $A_j, j \neq i$ and $d = \{d_{ij}\}, j \neq i$ a set of distances to other agents[5]. We describe the possible decisions of A_i by a decision tree $T_i = < \mathcal{V}_i, E_i, t, R_i, r_i >$, where $\mathcal{V}_i = \{v_1, v_2, \ldots, v_m\}$ is a set of decision points (which are the nodes of the tree), $E_i \subseteq \mathcal{V}_i \times \mathcal{V}_i$ is the set of tree edges, $\tau : \mathcal{V}_i \to \mathbb{N}$ function that attaches time (in natural numbers) to tree nodes (the attached number is equivalent to the level of the node in the decision

---

[4] In our simulation we have examined both of these methods as well as match-making for acquiring information with regards to remote hosts and found no significant difference in performance.

[5] Although Val_i may depend on other agents' loads, such dependency is not required.

tree T), $R_i \in \mathcal{V}_i$ the root of T, and r_i a discount rate which A_i uses in cases where it assumes that the value of a decision is discounted over time (otherwise $r_i = 0$).

Decision points in the decision tree have two types of valuation functions: (i) valuation of a decision which is made independently of other nodes in the tree, denoted by $V_I^i(v_j)$, where v_j is the evaluated node; (ii) valuation of a decision which is made dependent on other decisions in the tree denoted by $\mathrm{Value}_i(v_j)$. In case (i), if no independent decision can be made at node v_j, the independent value assigned to it is $V_I^i(v_j) = 0$. Otherwise, node v_j is assigned an independent value $V_I^i(v_j) = \mathrm{Val}_i(l_i, \overline{L}_i, d, \tau(v_j))$. In case (ii), the value of a node v_j is defined by the recursive valuation function as follows:

$$\mathrm{Value}_i(v_j) = \begin{cases} \mathrm{Val}_i(l_i, \overline{L}_i, d, \tau(v_j)) & \text{if } V_I^i(v_j) \neq 0 \\ \frac{1}{1+r_i} \sum_{k=1}^{m} p_k \cdot \mathrm{Value}_i(v_k) & \text{otherwise} \end{cases}$$

where the sum is over all of the edges (v_j, v_k) emanating from v_j and p_k is the probability of (v_j, v_k) being chosen. Note that p_k may be updated over time, based on learning from previous decisions. Given this representation, we can use standard dynamic programing methods to compute the optimal decision with respect to a given decision tree. For the spawning mechanisms this implies a spawning timing which is optimal with respect to the available information with regards to future loads and information requirements. Although this optimization is local to an agent and not global to the system, simulation results (Section 17.5) of the overload facet of spawning show a significant increase in the overall system performance.

17.4 The Algorithm

As stated previously, one aspect of spawning is the balancing of task distribution and resource usage, which we express in terms of capability and capacity loads. One may find two main approaches to load balancing [619]: (1) overloaded processors that seek other, idle (or just random other) processors to let them perform part of their processes; (2) idle (or lightly-loaded) processors that look for processes to increase their load. These approaches are sometimes merged, or combined with additional heuristics. Both approaches, (1) and (2), may be utilized when designing a spawning algorithm for agents. However, in the case of spawning in open, dynamic systems, considerable difficulties arise. Both (1) and (2) require that an agent locate other agents for task delegation. When matchmaking agents are used, a spawning mechanism that follows approach (1) only requires that underloaded agents advertise their capabilities. Thus, overloaded agents may contact the underloaded ones via matchmaking. Similarly, approach (2) requires that overloaded agents advertise their overloads and required capabilities and resources. Though, in addition, (2) requires that underloaded *machines* will be known to the overloaded agents as well. This information is not given in an open, dynamic system. It could be provided if each machine in the system runs an agent whose sole task would be supplying such information. This would lead to an undesirable overhead of communication and computation. To avoid this overhead we utilize the first approach. That is, with regards to overloads, our spawning mechanism is designed for agents who perceive or estimate self-overloads.

The other aspect to be considered is the rate between the remotely located raw data necessary for task execution and the information produced by the agent when processing this data. The raw data and the produced information can be measured by the storage space they occupy. These sizes may be characterized by the type of the task and its details. When extracting information about the information needs and sizes is not possible, it may still be possible to learn about this information from previous instances of similar tasks.

17.4.1 Overview of the Spawning Procedure

The spawning procedure consists of the following components:

- Reasoning before spawning: includes the reasoning about the (possibly dynamic) task list with respect to time restrictions and capability, resource and information requirements. The consideration of the task list as well as agent capabilities, capacities, loads, information needs and production, as well as machine loads, results in a decision to spawn or transfer tasks to already existing agents.
- Task splitting: includes reasoning that considers scarce capabilities and the time intervals in which overloads are expected, and accordingly selects tasks to be transferred, which results in task splitting.
- Spawning: includes the creation and activation of the spawn, the transfer of tasks, and the resulting inevitable updates of connections between agents via matchmaking. The following are the basic actions to be taken:
  - Create the code for the new agent by copying the generic parts of the agent and adding to them the components that enhance the specific capabilities required for the spawn to perform its prospective tasks.
  - When spawning while performing a specific task, an agent should pass to its spawn only the relevant sub-tasks and information which are necessary for the tasks passed to the spawn. Otherwise, in the case of spawning as a result of overloads, the spawn may face the same overload problem as its creator. Note that in contrast to the typical approach to agent migration [130], the spawning paradigm does not require the transfer of an agent state. The only transfer necessary is of the set of tasks to be performed by the spawn[6].

---

[6] One may distinguish two components of an agent state: machine and operating system state vs. planning and task execution state. Agent spawning does not

– Reasoning after spawning: collects information regarding the benefits of the spawning and environmental properties (such as task stream distribution), and statistically analyzes them, as a means of learning for future spawning.

While the reasoning of whether to initiate spawning is performed continually (i.e., when there are changes in the task schedule or if previous attempts to spawn have failed), the spawning itself is a one-shot procedure.

17.4.2 The Spawning Algorithm

Some details of the algorithm are provided below. Note that separate activities are performed concurrently and periodically in separate threads of control. For instance, agent self-awareness is periodically updating the information with regards to the agent self loads in an autonomous manner. Other parts of the code are implemented in the same manner, even if not explicitly expressed below.

Self-awareness activity:

– Do periodically, forever, (in a separate thread of control):
  – Retrieve the resources $R(t_0)$ available to self at current time (refer to cpu, memory, disk space, communication bandwidth, etc).
  – Retrieve the current self loads $L(t_0)$.
  – Anticipate current and expected self tasks T_s. Refer to the information needs I_n and produced I_p, capabilities and resources required and deadlines. According to the information regarding tasks, do:
    • Compute future expected self loads $L(t)$ and available self resources $R(t)$.
    • Compare $L(t)$ and $R(t)$ to locate time periods of overloads. Store information about overloads in $OV(t)$. Include in $OV(t)$ the types of overloads and the tasks T_{ov} in T_s that may have caused it.
    • For each task $T \in T_s$, compute the ratio $\rho(T)$ between the non-local information required for this task, $I_n(remote)$, and the information produced by the task, $I_p(T)$.

Reasoning for spawning to reduce information transfer:

– For each task T in T_s such that $\rho(T) \gg 1$ do:
  – Add the task to a task list T_ρ.
  – Locate the list of hosts H that hold information relevant for $I_n(T)$.
  – Retrieve $L_H(t)$, the loads of hosts in H.
  – Solve the optimization problem of spawning and allocating all tasks T in T_ρ to hosts in H. Refer to:

require the transfer of the first, however may require transfer of some parameters related to the latter. Nevertheless such parameters are passed as part of the transferred tasks, and not as a distinguished state.

- Size of a spawn agent necessary for a given task.
  - The loads $L_H(t)$ and the relevancy of information on hosts to each task.
  - Task deadlines and required capabilities and resources.
  - Computational overhead for creating and activating a spawn agent.

Reasoning for spawning to handle overloads:

- While $OV(t)$ in not empty, do:
  - Locate other agents and hosts. For each located entity E perform:
    - Retrieve current loads $L_E(t_0)$.
    - Anticipate future tasks and loads $L_E(t)$.
  - Solve the optimization problem of allocating the tasks T_{ov} to the located entities. Refer to:
    - The remote loads $L_E(t)$.
    - Task deadlines and the required capabilities and resources.
    - If an entity is not an agent - consider (in the optimization) the computational overhead for creating and activating an agent.

Results provided by the optimization processes:

- For overloads handling only:
  - A set S of agents that can execute tasks in T_{ov}.
  - For each agent $A_i \in S$, a unique timed task list T_{A_i}. For each task in T_{A_i}, an earliest and latest starting time (esl and lst) is provided.
- For handling information transfer requirements (and overloads):
  - A set H of hosts with resources available and relevant information for the tasks in T_ρ and T_{ov}.
  - A timed task list T_H for remote hosts.
  - A matching between hosts in H and tasks in T_ρ.

Spawning and task delegation activities:

- For each agent $A_i \in S$, do:
  - Delegate tasks in T_{A_i} at an appropriate time (between est and lst) to it.
- Create and activate spawns:
  While T_H and T_ρ are not empty, do:
  - Select the most appropriate host h in H.
  - Create and activate a spawn agent A_h on host h.
  - Delegate tasks form T_H or T_ρ to a_h.

Activities after spawning:

- Reason about the spawning performed and learn from it for future spawning.
- Reason about underloads. Consider the following activities:
  - Merging with under-loaded agents.
  - Self-extinction.

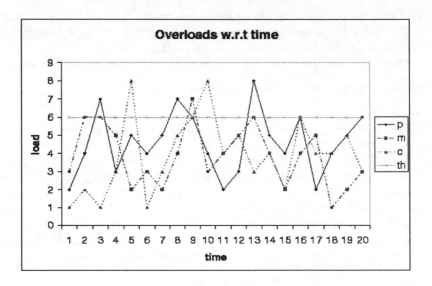

Fig. 17.1. CPU, memory and communication loads

The above algorithm sketches the guidelines of the reasoning about spawning. One issue to be considered for this reasoning it splitting the tasks in the list T_s between an agent and its spawn. We illustrate the task-split mechanism by the following example. Suppose the current and future tasks have been scheduled. At each point in time, the required resources are the sum of the resources required for all of the tasks that were scheduled to be executed at this time. Figure 17.1 brings an example of the sums of three resources: cpu(p); memory(m); communication(c), with respect to time. The maximal capacity of the agent is depicted by the threshold horizontal line (th) leveled at 6. One can observe overloads whenever any type of resource crosses this threshold. A periodic overload can be observed at times 3,8,13 with a period of 5 time units. Other overloads do not seem periodic. When attempting to prevent overloads, the agent first looks for periodical tasks with a period that fits the period of the overloads and puts them in the the list of candidate tasks for splitting. After re-computing the loads, it transfers additional one-shot tasks, if still necessary.

17.5 Simulation: The Cloning Case

To examine the properties of a subset of spawning, that is, cloning, a simulation was performed. The limitation of having cloning implies that only exact copies of the original agents may be created, whereas the general spawning approach allows for spawns which are different from their creators. Cloning

Agent type	Mem. size	CPU(1)	CPU(3)	Comm.(1)	Comm.(3)
Matchmaker	7.5 MB	43%	18-20%	94%	42%
Information	9.5-12 MB	45%	18-22%	94%	42%
Task	7 MB	44%	18-20%	94%	12%
Interface	9.6 MB	41%	18-20%	94%	15%

Fig. 17.2. Resource consumption

is simpler to implement, however since it is restricted in the type of solutions it provides for overloads and network congestion, it is expected to provide results which are inferior to an implementation of a broad spawning mechanism. Nevertheless, the results of our simulation show that (on average) cloning increases the performance of the multi-agent system. In more detail, the additional performance as a result of cloning (if any) outweighs the efforts put into cloning. Since agent spawning is a broader solution, we are confident that its implementation should provide even better results.

The method of simulation was as follows. Each agent was represented by an agent-thread that simulated the resource-consumption and the task-queue of a real agent. The simulated agent has a reasoning-for-cloning method which, according to the resource-consumption parameters and the task-queue, reasons about cloning. As a result of this reasoning, it may create a clone by activating another agent-thread (either locally or remotely). During the simulation, information is collected about the usage of CPU and the memory and communication consumption of the agents. Each agent-thread receives a stream of tasks according to a given distribution. For each task it creates a task-object that consumes time and memory and requires communication. Some of these task-objects are passed to the clone agent-thread. The simulation was performed with and without cloning, to allow comparison.

An agent-thread in the simulation must be subject to CPU, communication and memory consumption similar to those consumed by the agent it models in the MAS. Such information was collected from the real agent-system (RETSINA [167]) prior to the simulation as described below.

To properly simulate the RETSINA agents, we measured the resource consumption of the various types of its agents, when running 1 or 3 agents on each machine (in figure 17.2, when relevant, referred to by parentheses). The platforms on which these agents were examined are Sun Ultra-1s with 64MB, running Solaris. The resource consumption is summarized in Figure 17.2. As one can observe, when running alone, all types of agents consume 40% to 45% of the CPU, whereas when running 3 agents on the same machine each consumes around 20% of the CPU. Not surprisingly, this results in a slower task performance. The same effect holds for the communication consumption[7].

---

[7] Here, communication refers to the use of bandwidth.

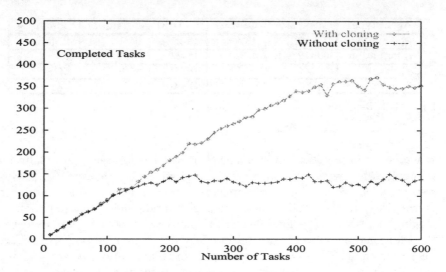

Fig. 17.3. Task execution with and without cloning

17.5.1 Simulation Parameters and Results

We simulated the agent system with and without cloning, with the following settings:

- Number of agents: 10 to 20.
- Number of clones allowed: 10.
- Number of tasks dynamically arriving at the system: up to 1000.
- Task distribution with respect to the required capabilities and resources for execution: normal distribution, where 10% of the tasks are beyond the ability of the agents to perform them within their particular deadlines.
- Agent capacity: an agent can perform 20 average[8] tasks simultaneously.

The results of the simulation are depicted in Figure 17.3. The graph shows that for small numbers of tasks (0 to 100) a system which practices cloning performs (almost) as well as a system with no cloning (although difficult to see in the graph, the performance is slightly lower due to the reasoning costs). However, when the number of tasks increases, the cloning system performs much better. Nonetheless, beyond some threshold, (around 350 tasks) even cloning cannot help. Note that in the range 150 to 350 tasks, cloning results in task performance which is close to the optimal (85% as compared to 90% which, in our setting, is the optimal since some tasks cannot be performed at all), where optimality refers to the case in which all of the available resources are efficiently used for task performance (which does not necessarily imply that all of the tasks are performed).

---

[8] An average task is one that the requires average resources (the center value of a normal distribution).

17.6 Spawning: Information Requirements Analysis

A major question to be asked with respect to information-related spawning is what the properties of the relevant information that should induce spawning are. Intuitively, when the amount of raw data to be transferred is significantly greater than the amount of the produced information and the size of the agent, spawning an agent and sending it to the information (instead of transferring the information) seems an appropriate approach. Below we address this issue analytically.

Assume a task (or a set of tasks) that requires information transfer. Assume also that the remote hosts where data is located may have some local information processing mechanisms (as common in databases). These mechanisms can be used to extract relevant information thus reduce the amount of information to be transferred. In addition, assume that agents have some unique expertise for information processing which is not provided by the remote host, where the information is located. Otherwise, there is no justification for sending the agent to the information, since all of the processing can be done at the remote site by the local information processing service. Denote the size of the remotely located raw data required for the task by I_r, the size of the information produced by the task by I_p, and the size of the prospective spawn agent by S. All sizes are measured by standard units (e.g. bytes). Denote the ratio between the size of the raw data on a remote host and the size of data extracted by its local information processing by α. Note that α may be a complicated function, however here we refer to it as a constant. For a given task T, the ratio $\rho(T)$ between the remote extracted data and the information produced by the task and the agent code size is given by

$$\rho(T) = \frac{\frac{1}{\alpha}I_r}{I_p + S}$$

Evidently, a greater ρ implies an increased advantage of sending a spawn to the information site. This is because spawning when ρ is greater results in a larger decrease in information transmission.

In figure 17.4 we demonstrate the relation between the size of the (extracted) remote data, the sum of sizes of the produced data and the spawn agent code, and the ratio between them. A high ratio ρ refers to advantageous agent spawning since it implies a vast reduction in data transfer, thus reducing network congestion. In the graph it shows that large agent code and large amount of produced information hardly justify agent spawning, since the information size ratio is small. This also applies for cases where the information to be transferred is small. The back corner of the graph, which refers to small agent size, small size of produced information, and large size of extracted remote data, shows a steep increase in the ratio. This means that when such conditions hold spawning becomes highly beneficial, when refer-

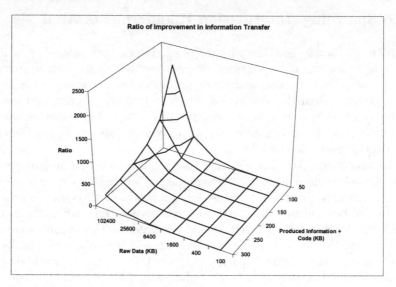

Fig. 17.4. The ratio between raw data and produced information and agent code.

ring to communication costs. One important outcome of this observation is that spawned agents must be light-weight.

17.7 Related Work

The idea of agent composition and decomposition was previously introduced in [306]. Although the ideas presented there by Ishida et al have some similarities to agent spawning and merging, there are several important differences. In [306], the issue of distributed problem solving was addressed. Our MAS is not a DPS system in the sense that it is not provided with a global goal which it must solve[9] nor is it designed for such a specific goal. Instead, we have an open system of autonomous agents, where each receives its own tasks, possibly from different sources, and they each try to satisfy its tasks, occasionally via cooperation. Our agents are heterogeneous, i.e., they have different capabilities and capacities, whereas the agent described in [306] seem to all be of a single type — rule firing agents. Therefore the only type of load discussed there is the rule firing load. This load may inaccurately represent the actual use of resources in the system. We measure operating systems' resource use directly and upon such loads carry out decisions for spawning and merging, thus balancing their use. In addition, we consider the effect of information transfer requirements on spawning, which is not addressed in that work. An-

---

[9] Yet, one may view the goal of increasing overall system performance as such a goal.

other limitation introduced in Ishida's work is the requirement to establish synchronization between agents. In contrast, our agents work asynchronously.

Methods for procedure cloning [143] and object cloning [529] were presented in the software engineering literature. The first serves as means for inter-procedural optimization, and the latter is used for eliminating parametric polymorphism and minimizing code duplication to overcome some typical inferior performance of object-oriented programs. Agent spawning (which subsumes agent cloning) is performed differently and has a different aim. Although it attempts to improve the system's performance (as other cloning paradigms do), it concentrates on balancing the work loads of agents and reduce the information transfer among them, and not on the other computational issues. In addition, it allows for agent mobility.

The issue of agent load balancing was previously studied in [590], where the authors concentrate on multi-agent reinforcement learning in the context of adaptive load balancing. The MAS dealt with in that research was dynamic in the sense that resources and tasks were given probabilistically, and the agents had to efficiently allocate resources to tasks in order to optimize the global resource usage, while ensuring fairness. The underlying load balancing of the spawning paradigm has some similarities, however is conceptually different. Spawning intends to optimize the resource usage of the whole system, and our simulation results show that to some extent this was achieved. However we do not address the issue of fairness. In addition, we discuss spawning when the only effector is the requirement for large information transfers, yet loads may be balanced. More significantly, we deal with a system in which, in addition to resource and task dynamics, agents may dynamically appear and disappear, thus increasing the complexity of the load balancing. Finally, while the agents in [590] attempt to adapt their resource selection to the behavior of other agents (using reinforcement learning), our agents attempt to either delegate tasks to other existing agents or create other agents that will perform the overloading tasks.

In [418], different approaches to agent mobility are discussed, concentrating on messengers, which are mobile threads of execution who coordinate without central control. The salient features of messengers are their mobility, the creation of new messengers at run-time and collaboration and dynamic formation of sets of messengers for this collaboration. These properties seem quite similar to our requirements for MAS with spawning. However there is a major difference — messengers use a shared memory and rely on it for their functioning. This implies a strong restriction on their autonomy, which is unacceptable in MAS. Nevertheless, the π-calculi presented for messengers may be used to describe spawning MAS as well.

Mobile agents are an approach to remote computing which, in contrast to remote procedure calls, allows for sending the procedures to be performed on the remote host [720]. The procedure as well as its state are transported, and processing on the remote host is performed under previously-given authentication constraints. Spawning supports remote computing as well (however does not require it), but does not require the transmission of a procedure (or agent) state. This property significantly simplifies the performance of remote computing (especially due to the complexity encapsulated in state transmission). In addition, the spawning mechanisms presented here provide methods for analysis and optimization of decisions to spawn.

17.8 Conclusion

Agent Spawning is the action of creating and activating a spawn agent, either locally or remotely, to perform some or all of an agent's tasks. A spawn may be either a copy of its creator or a specifically tailored agent for the performance of given tasks. Spawning is performed either when an agent perceives or predicts an overload, or when it predicts the need for a large amount of remotely located information. Spawning increases the ability of a MAS to perform tasks and reduces network congestion. In this chapter, we have provided methods for analysis and implementation and tested these methods via simulation. Our conclusions are that for large numbers of tasks, spawning significantly increases the portion of tasks performed by a MAS. In a MAS where tasks require information gathering on the web (e.g., RETSINA), the additional efforts needed for reasoning for spawning is small compared to the requirements for task execution. Hence, we are confident that agent spawning should be a useful tool for improving the performance of web-based information agent systems. The next steps to be performed in this research include an implementation of the spawning protocol in a real MAS (this step is already in process). It is also necessary to provide a better evaluation, based on experimentation, of spawning as a result of information transfer requirements. In addition, using the spawning mechanisms to achieve agent mobility should be examined. Protocols for agent merging or self-extinction are underway as well. These should increase the efficiency of garbage-collection and monitoring of the spawning activity.

Acknowledgement

This chapter is based upon previous research that was performed by the author and his colleagues Katia Sycara, Prasad Chalasani and Somesh Jha at Carnegie Mellon University. These results were published in [613, 612] and some of them are presented in this chapter, as part of a more broader research. The author wishes to thank his colleagues for their invaluable contribution to the initial work.

18. Mobile Agent Security

Christian F. Tschudin

Department of Computer Systems, Uppsala University,
Box 325, S - 751 05 Uppsala, Sweden.*
E-Mail: tschudin@docs.uu.se

18.1 Motivation

Let's get mobile! This is the Zeitgeist at the end of this century. The cold war is over and with it disappeared the literally frozen constellation of opposing power blocks. Money is flowing almost freely through a increasingly global economy, data is even more mobile, computer networks at the lowest sea levels as well as in space provide global connectivity to stationary as well as mobile end devices. But mobility is also on a triumphant march into the very core of computers: The JAVA programming language has demonstrated to everybody that software can be mobile too. Today, software mobility is studied at the application layer (Mobile Software Agents) as well as network layer (Active Networks). Indeed, we only see the beginning of a new technology. Consequently, code mobility is subject to intense research. In this chapter we look at one of these research topics that, as everybody agrees, is critical for the success of mobile agent technology: security.

18.2 Is Code Mobility Dangerous?

For decades we have built computer systems where everything was stationary and where the hardware provided the basic security anchor. Some of us may remember the university's computing center as a "closed shop" where you could type in your program on consoles in the public room and then had to wait for printer output that was put by operators in the user's box – an organizational form that is still in place for many large enterprises' IT solutions. The physical security of such computing centers provides a domain (secure premise) in which sensitive data can be manipulated and stored without further protection (see figure 18.1, adapted from [554]). The agents are humans working inside the premise and for the computing center. Their task is to write programs and to apply them to the stored data. Data items can be stored in clear form inside the premise. Only when data has to be exported (e.g., via public networks) do we need encryption and other cryptographic means for protecting it during transfer.

---

* Part of this work was done while at the Computer Science Department of the University of Zurich, Switzerland.

Such an "easy" environment where all entities can trust each other does not exist for mobile code. In a mobile code setting we observe that the owner of the hardware, the user of a program and the author of this software can be all different entities, being governed by different security policies and sharing different trust relationships. This multitude of parties leads to different security concerns, depending on which role we examine.

First, there is the execution platform that receives mobile agents. The operator wants to protect the hosting computer, its services, local data, and, indirectly, its reputation. We call this facet of mobile code security the *host security* part. Second, there is the mobile program that has to deal with unreliable communications, malicious hosts and uncooperative or other untrustworthy mobile agents. This aspect is called *mobile agent security*. Note that the views and security requirements from these two sides are not necessarily complementary: for example, mobile agents (or their owners) may wish to remain anonymous, while certain hosts will simply refuse to execute a mobile agent if it can not be linked to a human user. Both host and agent security will be discussed in this chapter.

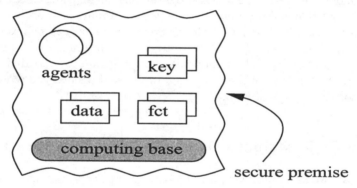

Fig. 18.1. The old "fortress" model of a trusted computing base.

Code mobility creates new security problems, for the executing host as well as the program to execute. Today we have to acknowledge that we do not have good answers for all of these security problems. However, the number of existing mobile agent systems shows that code mobility is attractive enough to start using it. The current approach is to identify special constellations with restricted mobility and explicit trust relationships that nevertheless allow for a secure operation of a mobile agent system. Also, theoretical advances in cryptography and in the design of security aware agent interaction are encouraging signs that security will become a handable issue. This is important, because the promise of code mobility is that of emancipating the software with regard to hardware: Programs should be able to decide themselves where to compute what. If we can not provide security for mobile programs, ultimately we would remain bound forever to the old world of physical security. Another reason for being optimistic is, that we have first cases where code mobility enables new security solutions that were not conceivable beforehand. Code mobility is not only a security challenge, it is also a chance.

18.3 Protecting the Host

The entity that executes an incoming mobile agent is called an *execution environment* (EE). This can be the more or less bare computer hardware with a tiny communication layer responsible for receiving and sending mobile agents. But in most of the cases it is an interpreter that executes an agent's high level instructions. The reason for using an interpreter is of course portability, because native machine instructions limit mobile agents to machines of one specific hardware architecture. However, using an interpreter is also a safety measure: the interpreter acts as a *sand-box* and can check memory bounds at arbitrarily fine granularity, can verify parameters for system service requests, and can maintain lists of access rights. JAVA is a very popular basis for building an EE: it comes with its own virtual machine (the JAVA byte code interpreter). The D'Agents system (see Chapter 15 and [250]) is based on Tcl, another interpreted language, the same interpreter principle is used for MO messengers [675] and was the basis of General Magic's Telescript cn vironment [718], interpreted Forth was used for Softnet [748], one of the very first active networks.

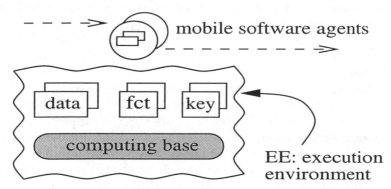

Fig. 18.2. The agent interpreter as a secure premise: The mobile agents' data, code and keys are not protected.

Figure 18.2 shows an execution environment with a fully separated interpreter. Agent programs have their own address space from where they have no direct access to a host's data items, program libraries and keying information.

Each access must be mediated by the interpreter. With respect to figure 18.1 we basically equate the secure premise with the execution environment – the mobile agent remains unsecured!

18.4 Run–Time Checks and How To Avoid (Some of) Them

An important aspect is to make the interpreter as fast as possible without compromising safety. In other words, one would like to reduce the number of checks to be made at run times. If, for example, we knew that some code never violates the boundaries of a certain array, we can simply skip this check that otherwise is necessary for every array access. Thus, we move the burden of checking memory accesses out of the critical execution path. The solution in JAVA is to start with a type safe language and to have a specially designed low–level instruction set that is suitable for deciding such questions by analyzing the code. A special code verifier checks all received code before it can be loaded into the JAVA virtual machine. This incurs an initial delay before a mobile agent is executed, but this delay can be eliminated for subsequent agents of the same type by caching the agent's verified code.

Single Virtual Machine Architecture. Reducing the number of run-time checks for (memory) access protection is but one of several possible benefits of being able to give guarantees about the behavior of a piece of code. Another optimization can be achieved by placing several mobile programs in the same memory address space (a single interpreter for multiple mobile agents is more efficient than a multi–interpreter architecture). Because the memory accesses are proven to be bound, mobile agents will not be able to tamper with other agents' memory, interaction is possible through the official method calls only. In this environment it is even possible to place parts (or all) of the EE's logic in the same address space, as is most often done with JAVA based mobile agent systems.

Proof Carrying Code. Another approach for avoiding runtime checks is to ship every piece of mobile code with a proof that it behaves according to some security policy e.g., regarding array boundaries or liveness properties. Proof carrying code aims at making the *verification* of a proof fast and to shift the major computational effort of *constructing* such a proof to the creator of a mobile program. This approach has been demonstrated to work for native machine code. Further efforts are under way to automate and generalize the construction of proofs [463].

18.5 Authentication, Authorization, Allocation

Safety of code execution comes into play at a quite late state of mobile agent processing. Beforehand, a host must agree to execute the mobile agent i.e., the host must agree to allocate part of the CPU and memory resources to the mobile agent. In reality, many hosts will be even more restrictive: First, they attempt to *authenticate* the source of the incoming agent, second they verify with this information the *authorization* for each access to local resources and third, they will *allocate* only a limited amount of the available resources to the requesting agent.

The host can try to associate an agent with either the agent's author, or the agent's sender, or the identity of the previous EE that forwarded the agent. This requires some form of *authentication*. Most commonly one will use digital signatures to this end: the author signs the code, the sender signs the code and other information like start time and initial parameters, the previous EE signs the whole agent and the send time etc. The receiving host can verify the signatures and convince itself that in fact an agent stems from the stated author, was started by the pretended sender and was sent by the previous host. An asymmetric cryptosystem can be used for the signatures: the signing party computes a hash value over the bits to sign and encrypts this hash value with its private key – the signature can be verified by everybody by decrypting the signature with the public key and comparing it with the locally computed hash value.

Once we know who vouches for a mobile agent, we can assign rights to individual mobile agents. A host can either decide on each access, or give a resource specific "capability" to the mobile agent that the agent has to show every time the access is requested. This *authorization* decision is far from being simple: Should a host grant write access rights to an agent whose sender is known but which arrived from an untrusted host? What rights should be given to an agent whose code stems from an certified SW company but whose sender used a key whose validation date expired? The answer to such questions depend on the security policy that a host's operator wants to impose. A common formalization of a security policy is an *access control list* that associates principles with their rights.

Finally, a host has to *allocate* the available resources to the competing mobile agents. For some resource types it may be possible to schedule requests in time (e.g., delay them) such that all resource requests of authorized mobile agents can be satisfied eventually. But it may also be possible that resource requests are conflictual (e.g., leading to a deadlock among a set of agents) or that available resources are far too limited in which case the host must decide on which agent to penalize. The host's allocation decisions are relevant for security, especially for denial–of–service attacks where malicious mobile agents try to force a host into a behavior that prevents legitimate agents from obtaining the requested resources. Flooding a host with memory greedy agents may be such an attack, another case being a mobile agent that errs forever from host to host, just eating up precious bandwidth. Techniques to address these issues have been and are being developed in the domain of distributed operating systems. One noteworthy approach for solving the allocation problem are market–based mechanisms. Agents would have to pay for their resource consumption – the allocation problem then becomes a problem of steering and securing the flow of money.

Mobile Agents Helping Host Security.   Introducing mobile agents doesn't solely pose security problems for a host – it can also help to simplify a security solution. Consider for example a database owner that would like to offer a more flexible interface to its database without loosing control over the amount and type of data that is exported [124]. Mobile query programs are a very generic and elegant way to realize the desired flexibility. By letting them freely browse the full database content, we can satisfy this part. To solve the restriction part, we prevent the mobile agents to leave a server and, in fact, kill them after a while. Beforehand, an agent would have to deposit its result in a standardized form (e.g., a list of 100 record numbers) which the host would transform into a query result that it sends back to the client.

18.6 Protecting the Mobile Agents

The problem is simple to state: Can a software agent defend itself against one or multiple malicious hosts? In the previous section we asked the other way round and showed that hosts can be protected against malicious agents quite effectively (except perhaps the resource allocation part). Mobile agents are in a far less advantageous situation: They consists of software only, thus have no hardware premise to which security could be anchored. Protecting mobile agents from malicious hosts is clearly a hard problem.

An already classic example that nicely illustrates the vulnerability of mobile code is a mobile agent that has to shop for an inexpensive air travel ticket. It will visit the servers of various carriers, check availability of seats and compare prices. At the end, it should also buy the ticket that it found to match best the user's requirements. A hosts can behave unfairly in several ways: it can increase prices that the agent already collected, or could erase all of them. The server can also peek at the agent's reservation price and offer a slightly lower price still higher than the official fair, or it can modify the agent's code to play havoc with the competition's server e.g., by reserving 100 seats instead of 1.

Extending the Trusted Computing Base. These are quite disturbing scenarios and not few system designers may wish themselves back in an environment with a nice security perimeter wherein one can trust all elements. Thus, the straightforward approach is to extend the fortress model to a distributed setting: All communications between execution environments are encrypted and signed by the sending host, mobile agents can only move inside this system of secured circuits. Note that this yields no additional protection for the mobile agents against those execution environments that are part of this system. But it protects the agents against external attackers. In fact, the distributed trusted computing base is a closed world where considerable care has to be applied so that no malicious host ever joints the system and no malicious mobile code is ever injected into the system that could harm an EE or other mobile agents.

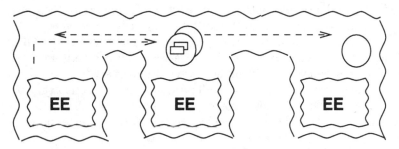

Fig. 18.3. Closed circuits: Creating a distributed secure premise.

Farther below we will see how these mutual trust requirements can be somewhat weakened by introducing means to specify and enforce trust levels. Nevertheless remain mobile agents in a weak position with respect to the executing hosts. This justifies to explore ways of detecting and preventing tampering of mobile agents.

18.7 Detecting Agent Tampering

A minimal form of shifting the asymmetric distribution of power from the execution environment to mobile agents is to set up a system that enables to *detect* tampering and incorrect execution of a mobile agent and to *identify* the culprit. Because detection always happens after the attack, detection only makes sense if the damage can be recovered in some way or if it helps to make future attacks less probable. Thus, detection is of little use if the malicious entity can not be identified, or if a server does not exist anymore once the attack is detected, or if the costs to rectify the fraud are too high when compared to the damage. But even then there may be settings were a small amount of fraud is tolerable (e.g., like in the credit card business), simply because the overhead to prevent incidents is too high.

Several sources are available to detect irregularities in the processing of a mobile agent (i.e., violation of the so called "execution integrity"). Context information may be used to judge if the results returned by an agent are faithful. Among possible checks we mention range verification or timing information. Another approach is to add dummy items and functions to an agent and to check whether these have been correctly processed [424]. These checks could also be done by the agent itself on its journey or by intermediate hosts that impose some security policy. Finally, cryptographic techniques were proposed to construct functions that watermark their result: only a correct execution of the function will produce the expected steganographic watermark [581].

What should the owner of a mobile agent do when he detects tampering? Clearly we need a parallel infrastructure where the operator of a host can be sued or otherwise threatened. A reputation system would allow to harm a service provider by publishing ratings based on incident reports. Of course, such a "social" system is vulnerable to attacks by competitors that could wrongfully pretend to be a victim. One way to protect a rating system is to use cryptographic techniques that allow all parties to prove whether they behaved correctly or not. For this, hosts would be required to trace all security relevant actions like reception of a mobile agent, access to local resources, intermediate results, hand over of the agent to a next host etc. and to digitally sign the validity of these traces [691]. Based on the log records, a judge (this means: an arbiter program) could decide whether a malicious execution happened or not. Based on such hard evidences, a victim could address the legal system or feed this information into the rating system.

18.7.1 Trusting Hosts and Agents

Traces document partial state of a mobile agent system over time – proofs are the outcome of applying some evaluation function to the traces. In the case that a maliciousness proof could be constructed as outlined above, we would rather believe that a host behaved incorrectly i.e., we trust the underlying cryptographic theory, the mechanisms to collect and evaluate the traces, the correct generation and distribution of cryptographic keys needed for the digital signatures, the compiler used for building the program etc. In fact, it turns out that trust is a compound thing that depends on many elements. Formal theories have been proposed how to compute trust [62]. At the center are "state appraisal" functions that evaluate some state of the system. These functions can be carried by the (self–checking) agent itself, but may also be provided and executed by the host; they are applied to state of the agent and/or to state found in the executing host. A host's as well as an agent's further behavior is then made conditional on the outcome of a state appraisal function which effectively enforces a desired security policy.

This model is general enough that it also covers classical authorization frameworks. An access control list, for example, is part of a host's state: The authorization procedure is the state appraisal function that takes this list as well as an agent's identifier in order to compute a trust value on which the host will decide to grant access or not.

Note that in the case of an execution environment where authorization procedure and access decision are inside the trusted premise we can *prevent* malicious actions. A mobile agent however, can usually not rely on the faithful execution of its state appraisal function or the correct branching based on the value returned and therefore, can not prevent breach of its security policy. It can, however, detect tampering once it reaches a honest host.

18.8 Preventing Agent Tampering

The interest in *detecting* attacks on mobile agents is motivated by the lack of efficient and effective means to protect them. Consisting of software only, a mobile agent seems to be at the full mercy of the executing hosts. However, this does not exclude that we can introduce asymmetries into the game in order to render some attacks by a host infeasible. This is currently a field of increased bottom up research that hopefully will lead to a spectrum of protection techniques that covers all important aspect of a mobile agent' security.

Potential for introducing asymmetries in favor of mobile agents can be identified both in computational complexity and the network's complexity. More and more these two elements are used intertwined so that a separation is somewhat artificial. In the following we nevertheless maintain this classification as it helps to organize the presentation.

18.8.1 Environmental Security

The distributedness of the execution substrate for mobile code means that there is no global state that could be assessed and, equivalently, that there is no full control over all parts of a mobile agent system. This trivially starts with the host where an agent is created and that we assume to be a secure and trusted place.

Security Through Shared Secrets and Interlocking. An asymmetric constellation is easily created by injecting two or more mobile agents per task into the network. These agents can, unlike the hosts, move and therefore configure themselves such that they always have a subset of them executing on trusted hosts [565]. In a kind of checks–and–balance approach, no agent would possess all elements required for a major action or financial commitment. Consider a negotiating agent A that finds out the best price for a product: without contacting its companion agent B it cannot proceed with buying the good because the agent B carries the e–money in encrypted form. Similarly it is not possible for agent B to spend the money (neither is this possible for the EE that hosts B) because A carries the decryption key, so they have to communicate in order to proceed. To further decrease the possibility of collusion we can introduce a third agent C to be part of the gang. It would first securely log the intended transaction before agreeing in the buy procedure: e–money could be double encrypted such that A needs C's key to decrypt the digicoin received from B. Another security approach based on distributed mobile agents can be found in [593].

A Distributed Shelter for Data. Where would you store data that should never be lost? Imagine that like in the movie Fahrenheit 451 (1967) the said information should be eradicated for political reasons and that the police, intelligence services, perhaps even the army is mobilized to "cleanse" your computer, destroy all backups, torn down your house inch by inch, examine the office you are working in, all persons you contacted in the past two years and so on, so that in fact there wouldn't remain a single spots where your precious data could survive. Things look different if we had a mobile agent system of sufficient size. You would then write a self-replicating and self-modifying agent that senses if sufficient copies are still crawling through the net and, if necessary, would spawn new copies and variants. In the Fahrenheit 451 movie, the ideas survived by being told from generation to generation instead of being carried by books. Here, mobile agents continue to tell their story over and over, complementing the approach of [11].

Clueless Agents. Another simply asymmetry in favor of mobile code can be introduced by "logical bombs" that are well known from computer viruses i.e., code sequences which trigger only when some environmental condition is met. The environmental condition can be the current date and time, but could also be the presence of another companion agent on the same host, or any information that a mobile agent may want to check. The bomb's effect does not need to be malign – our interest is in securing the trigger and protecting it from ilegitim third parties. Blending the sensing of environment data with simple cryptographic techniques it is possible to completely hide the exact condition as well as the code to be eventually executed. In fact, code portions of an agent can easily be made "clueless" for the executing hosts! This works by using the value of the condition (imagine a password) as the key for encrypted code portion [553]. The mobile agent thus consists of a loop that reads some environment data with which it tries to decode the encrypted code portion. If the decryption yields a well formated code, it is executed (execution of dynamically generated (decrypted) code is easy in interpreted languages, but with some tricks is also possible to realize it with languages like JAVA). Note however, that once the logical bomb "explodes", the agent reveals its intentions and any other information that resides in the encrypted code portion. This technique thus doesn't provide privacy for the agent's code nor can it guarantee the integrity of code execution.

Hiding in the Masses. According to a recent result, privacy does not need encryption although all bits are sent in clearform over open networks [555]. By "chaffing and winnowing" data streams it is possible to make an attacker clueless about which bits belong to which stream: Only the intended receiver is able to filter out the meaningful bits. Rivest's technique seems well suited for mobile agents. Combined with environmental key generation one could send out code fragments that recombine only on the intended hosts to full agents.

18.8.2 Cryptographic Protection

The use of cryptography is essential for creating the "distributed fortress" environment described on page 436. It allows, among others, to authenticate an incoming agent and to protect the agents' privacy while being transfered. In the following paragraphs we describe other places in a mobile agent system where cryptography is useful too. We also examine how close we can come to the ultimate *goals* of cryptographic protection of mobile code which are unconditional code privacy and execution integrity.

Encryption "à la carte". The distributed secure premise (figure 18.3) works by creating secure channels between the execution environments. With a traditional, symmetric cryptosystem each pair of neighbor nodes needs a common encryption key. Using an asymmetric cryptosystem, it is sufficient that each node has a single private key and that it knows the public key of each neighbor it is connected to. In both cases we can then encrypt all agent transfers, which effectively shields the mobile agents from external observers.

An asymmetric cryptosystem allows to shift the responsibility of encryption from the execution platform to the level of mobile agents. A mobile agent can encrypt itself (or critical parts of itself) using the destination EE's public key: The ciphertext is then put inside a clearcode wrapper that navigates the encrypted payload to the desired destination. This yields privacy for the agent while it is in transit. Furthermore it guarantees that only the destination EE can decrypt the code because it is the only instance to know the matching secret key. This is a highly desirable property because the agent does not need to trust the intermediate forwarding nodes' repeated encryption activity but can impose which EE shall be able to decrypt. A core functionality that an EE has to provide to this end is the "encrypted–execute" service: the cleartext wrapper code will request it on arrival. This is quite an old concept: It is part of the PostScript language where the function is called eexec. PostScript is in fact an early mobile code language, and the eexec's primary usage is (was) to protect font descriptions.

Untraceable and Anonymous Agents. Putting the control over encryption in the hands of the mobile agents allows to implement security services. In the previous case we described the secure end–to–end transfer of a mobile agent (the forwarding nodes do not need to be trusted). A more complex security service that can be realized with mobile agents and an asymmetric cryptosystem is untraceable communications [674]: Chaum's MIX nodes that hide the correlation between incoming and outgoing agents can be implemented by mobile agents without requiring any additional support from the EE. It makes it also possible to send out anonymous agents that can carry a reply back to its origin without letting the recipient know who sent the initial agent.

Smartcards as a Safe Haven. The feasibility of end–to–end encryption is also the basis for smartcard enhanced hosts [726] (figure 18.4). A tamper

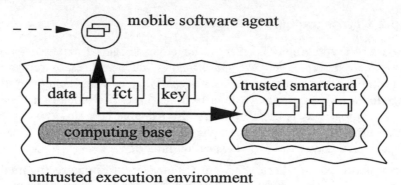

Fig. 18.4. Independent smartcards as a security anchor inside an untrusted host.

resistant smartcard with a cryptographic co–processor is locally attached to a host: Mobile agents can send security sensitive code fragments to the smartcard and request their execution. In fact, it is like a mobile agent sending mini–agents to the smartcard which becomes a security anchor and "safe haven".

The point of this configuration is that the smartcard is manufactured by an independent entity. You would trust the card manufacturer's and rely on its reputation: The card enables your agents to visit potentially untrusted hosts because the agents can "out–source" critical computations to the smartcard.

Sealing and Signing of Results. To hide information collected so far, mobile agents can encrypt the data immediately after having acquired it. They can do so by using the owner's public key. This effectively conceals the data items, but it also renders them unusable for the rest of the journey because only the respective agent owners will be able to decrypt them. And, of course, a malicious host can replace (or remove) items because it knows the public key and can apply the same encryption function.

Agents can ask the execution platform to sign new data or state and to append this information to the agent. If appropriately linked with other information, a malicious host will not be able to modify the signed data because it can not forge the signatures of other hosts.

Executable Encrypted Functions. Protecting the code's logic and preventing code diversion seemed until recently impossible to achieve because the executing host has access to the code's instructions and all memory content. However, it was shown that many computations can be effectively concealed although the executing host carries them out [580]! The approach consists in encrypting polynomials such that they are transformed into a still executable program. This program accepts input in clear form and computes an encrypted result without providing a clue about which function is computed. It is like data encryption: you can *transmit* encrypted data without knowing the cleartext. In our case you can *execute* an encrypted function without knowing the clearfunction.

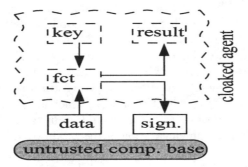

Fig. 18.5. A "cloaked" agent securely computing and signing data on an untrusted host.

The implication of this cryptographic technique is that you no longer need to trust a host for secure code execution. While this is not applicable to arbitrary programs right now, it shows a possible venue to completely "cloaking" a mobile agent (see figure 18.5). In the same way that we can create secure end–to–end communication at the mobile agent level, we would obtain a secure premise that does not need the inclusion of a (physically) secure computing base.

18.9 Secure or Open, Is This the Question?

If you want security, you must at some places restrict what the elements in a system *can* do and at some places impose what they *have to* do. This could lead to the impression that there is a more or less continuous spectrum of choices between unsecured freedom and secure jail house. The open task then would be to find an optimal point on this spectrum where mobile code yields a maximum of freedom without sacrificing too much security. However, we argue that code mobility is not an antagonist to security, as we tried to show in the previous sections: Mobile code can be used to implement i.e., enables security services rather than just requiring them. The true question that is underlying this discussion is how *open* a mobile agent system can be if it should remain secure.

What we are currently witnessing is that, because of the security concerns, system designers are in fact working their way away from openness. The prototypical system architecture for mobile agents is still the "distributed fortress" (figure 18.3): Hosts exchange encrypted mobile agents, agents have an identity, their code, owner and origin are authenticated on entry, trust systems of some form define the security policy of these systems. All these are reasonable choices considering the currently available agent protection techniques. But this creates a rather monolithic and closed system! What if some mobile agents would like to remain anonymous? They are not allowed to enter the fortress. What if a new cryptosystem or new certification methods should be introduced? It will partition the mobile code network by introducing incompatible methods and policies. Note that trust systems already tend to create partially closed worlds where it is difficult for mobile agents to escape the closed circuit in which they were placed. At best, the monolithic architecture resembles a "Borg" approach (in analogy to the science fiction TV series StarTreck New Generation) which is based on a uniform organization. Borg "evolution" is by incorporation instead of coexistence and competition – it is the implementation of the totalitarian face of security.

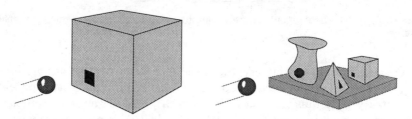

Fig. 18.6. Security as architecture: "Borg vs. Federation".

The SciFi analogy of course suggests that there is another way of organizing security. The "Federation" approach is individualistic, it aims at the peaceful coexistence of different cultures. Transposing this back into our security discussion this means that a security architecture should only provide the essential building blocks but remain open with regard to which method should be used by whom. Thus, different security architectures could be built on top of a minimal security layer of each execution platform (figure 18.6). An example how this works was already given above: Mobile agents can very well invoke encryption routines themselves and implement secure end–to-end communication channels without requiring that all intermediate nodes are part of a trusted network. The use of encrypted functions are a similar case where the mobile agent's execution integrity can be enforced even on malicious hosts.

18.10 Outlook

In this chapter we made a plea in favor of mobile agents and the possibility to find ways to unconditionally protect them. We made this at the danger of caricature the current research field and partially by drawing from results that are not available yet. Today we have to accept the limitation that major parts and moves of a mobile agent cannot be fully secured, while at the same we observe that many problems of host security are solved, although the issue of resource control remains a formidable security and operational challenge. On the other hand it is encouraging to see that novel security services are being enabled by mobile agents. What we hope is that security concerns will not lead to restrictive mobile agent systems but that these concerns will help to push the creation of a safe *and* open environment where mobile code can excel at last.

References

1. Abinavam, S., et al.: *San Francisco Concepts & Facilities*. International Technical Support Organization, IBM, February 1998. SG24-2157-00.
2. Abiteboul, S., and S. Grumbach: Col: a logic-based language for complex objects. *Proc. European Conference on Database Technology EDBT-88*, Lecture Notes in Computer Science, Vol. 303, pages 271–293, Springer, 1988.
3. Abiteboul, S., and R. Hull: IFO: A formal semantic database model. ACM Transactions on Database Systems, Vol. 12(4):525–565, 1987.
4. Abiteboul, S., and P. Kanellakis: Object identity as a query language primitive. ACM SIGMOD, pp. 159–173, ACM Press, 1989.
5. Ahmed, R., et al.: The Pegasus heterogeneous multidatabase system. IEEE Computer, Vol. 24:19-27, 1991.
6. Ahuja R., T. Magnanti T, and J. Orlin: *Network Flows: Theory, Algorithms, and Applications*. Prentice Hall, Englewood Cliffs, New Jersey, 1993.
7. Albayrak, S., U. Meyer, B. Bamberg, S. Fricke, and H. Tobben: Intelligent agents for the realization of electronic market services. *Proceedings of First International Conference on the Practical Application of Intelligent Agents and Multi Agents Technology PAAM-96*, pages 11–23, April 1996.
8. Allen, J.: *Natural Language Understanding*. Benjamin Cummings, 1987.
9. Altavista. Digital Equipment Corporation. http://altavista.digital.com.
10. Andersen, P.: A Theory of Computer Semiotics. *Semiotics Approaches to Construction and Assessment of Computer Systems*, Cambridge University Press, Cambridge, Mass., 1990
11. Anderson, R.J.: The Eternity Service. *Proceedings of PragoCrypt-96*, 1996. http://www.cl.cam.ac.uk/users/rja14/eternity/eternity.html
12. Andrade,J.M., M. Carges, T. Dwyer, and S. Felts: *The Tuxedo System*. Addison Wesley Publishing Co., Reading Mass., 1996.
13. Andre, E., J. Müller, and T. Rist: WebPersona: A LifeLike Presentation Agent for the World Wide Web. *Proc. of IJCAI-97 Workshop on Animated Interface Agents*, Nagoya, Japan, 1997.
14. Andre, E., T. Rist, and J. Müller: Guiding the User through Dynamically Generated Hypermedia Presentations with a Life-Like Presentation Agent. *Proceedings of International Conference on Intelligent User Interfaces*, pages 21-28, San Francisco (CA, USA), 1998.
15. Andreasen, A.: Attitudes and Customer Behavior: A Decision Model. L. Preston (Ed.), *New Research in Marketing*. California Institute of Business and Economics Research, University of California, 1965.
16. ARA. University of Kaiserslautern, Germany. http://www.uni-kl.de/AG-Nehmer/Projekte/Ara/
17. Arens, Y., C.Y. Chee, C.N. Hsu, and C.A. Knoblock: Retrieving and integrating data from multiple information sources. Intl. Journal of Intelligent and Cooperative Information Systems, Vol. 2(2):127-158, 1993.

18. Arens, Y., C. A. Knoblock and C. Hsu: Query Processing in the SIMS Information Mediator. Austin Tate (Ed.), *Advanced Planning Technology*, AAAI Press, CA, 1996.

19. Arens, Y., C. A. Knowblock, and W.-M. Shen: Query Reformulation for Dynamic Information Integration. Journal of Intelligent Information Systems, Vol. 6(2/3), pp. 99-130, 1996.

20. Armstrong, A., and E. Durfee: Mixing and memory: emergent cooperation in an information marketplace. *Proc. of Second International Conference on Multiagent Systems* ICMAS-98, Paris, IEEE Press, 1998.

21. Armstrong, R., D. Freitag, T. Joachims, and T. Mitchell: Webwatcher: A learning apprentice for the world wide web. *Working Notes of the AAAI Spring Symposium on Information Gathering from Heterogeneous, Distributed Environments*, 1995.

22. Arocena, G.O., A.O. Mendelzon, and G.A. Mihaila: Applications of a web query language. *Proc. 6th International World Wide Web Conference*, 1997.

23. Arrow, K.J., S. Karlin, and H. Scarf: *Studies in the Mathematical Theory of Inventory and Production*. Stanford University Press, 1958.

24. Ash, R.B.: Real Analysis and Probability. *Probability and Mathematical Statistics*, Academic Press, 1972.

25. Atkinson, M., et al.: The object-oriented database system manifesto. *Proc. 1st Intl. Conf. on Deductive and Object-Oriented Databases*, Springer, 1989.

26. ATMS. http://yoda.cis.temple.edu:8080/books/forbus/atms/

27. Atzeni, P., (Ed.): *LOGIDATA+: Deductive Databases with Complex Objects*. Springer, LNCS, Vol. 701, 1993.

28. AuctionBot. http:auction.eecs.umich.edu

29. AuctionWeb (Ebay). http://www.ebay.com/aw

30. Austin, J.: *How to do things with words*. Oxford University Press, 1962.

31. Axelrod, R.: *The Evolution of Cooperation*. Harper Collins, 1984.

32. Baclace, P.: Competitive agents for information filtering, Communications of the ACM, Vol. 35 (12):50, 1992.

33. Balabanovic, M., and Y. Shoham: Learning information retrieval agents: Experiments with automated web browsing. *Proc. of the 1995 AAAI Spring Symp., AAAI Tech. Report SS-95-08*, 1995.

34. Balabanović, M.: An adaptive web page recommendation service. *Proc. 1st International Conference on Autonomous Agents*, 1997.

35. Balabanović, M., and Y. Shoham: Learning Information Retrieval Agents: Experiments with Automated Web Browsing. *Proceedings of the 1997 AAAI Spring Symposium Series on Information Gathering from Heterogeneous, Distributed Environments*, pp. 13-18, 1997.

36. Balabonović, M., and Y. Shoham: Combining Content-Based and Collaborative Recommendation. Communications of the ACM, March, 1997.

37. Ballerini, J.P., S. Bergamaschi, and C. Sartori: The ODL-DESIGNER prototype. P. Atzeni (Ed.), *LOGIDATA+: Deductive Databases with complex objects*. Springer, 1993.

38. Barbuceanu, M., and M.S. Fox: The information agent: an infrastructure for collaboration in the integrated enterprise. *Proc. CKBS-SIG Meeting on Cooperating Knowledge-based Systems*, Keele (UK), 1994.

39. Barbuceanu, M., and M.S. Fox: The Architecture of an Agent Building Shell. M. Wooldridge et al., *Intelligent Agents II*, Springer, LNAI, Vol. 1037, 1994.

40. BargainFinder. http://bf.cstar.ac.com/bf

41. Bates, J.: The role of emotion in believable agents. ACM Communications, Vol. 37(7), 1994.

42. Batini, C., M. Lenzerini, and S.B. Navathe: A comparative analysis of methodologies for database schema integration. ACM Computing Surveys, Vol. 18(4):323-364, December 1986.

43. Bauer, M., and D. Dengler: TrIAS - An Architecture for Trainable Information Assistants. *Working Notes of the Autonomous Agents'98 Workshop on Agents in Interaction-Acquiring Competence through Imitation, 1998.*

44. Beck, H.W., S.K. Gala, and S.B. Navathe: Classification as a query processing technique in the CANDIDE data model. *Proc. 5th Intl. Conf. on Data Engineering*, Los Angeles (CA, USA), pp. 572 - 581, 1989.

45. Belew, R.: *Evolution Learning and Culture: Computational metaphors for adaptive algorithms.* University of California at San Diego Technical Report CS-89-156, 1989.

46. Belew, R.K.: Adaptive information retrieval: Using a connectionist representation to retrieve and learn about documents. *Proc SIGIR Conference*, Cambridge, MA (USA), 1989.

47. Bellman, R.: *Dynamic Programming.* Princeton University Press, 1957.

48. Belkin, N., and B. Croft: Information Filtering and Information Retrieval. Communications of the ACM, Vol. 35, No. 12:29-37, 1992.

49. Ben-Daya, M., and A. Raouf: Inventory Models Involving Lead Times as a Decision Variable. Journal of Operational Research Society, Vol. 45(5), pp.579-582, 1994.

50. Ben-Natan, R.: *CORBA: A guide to Common Object Request Broker Architrecture.* McGraw-Hill, 1995.

51. Ben-Shaul, I., and G. Kaiser: Coordinating distributed components over the Internet. IEEE Internet Computing, March/April 1998.

52. Beneventano, D., and S. Bergamaschi: Incoherence and Subsumption for cyclic queries and views in Object Oriented Databases. IEEE Transactions on Knowledge and Data Engineering, Vol. 21(3):217–252, February 1987.

53. Beneventano, D., S. Bergamaschi and C. Sartori: Semantic Query Optimization by Subsumption in OODB. *Proc. of the Int. Workshop on Flexible Query-Answering Systems (FQAS-96)*, Roskilde (Denmark), pp. 167-185, May 1996.

54. Beneventano,D., S. Bergamaschi, C. Sartori, M. Vincini: ODB-QOptimizer: a Tool for Semantic Query Optimization in OODB. *Proc. Intl. Conference on Data Engineering (ICDE-97)*, 1997.

55. Benn, W., and O. Görlitz: Semantic navigation maps for information agents. M. Klusch and G. Weiß(Eds.), *Cooperative Information Agents II*, Proc. Workshop CIA-98, Paris (France), Springer, LNAI, Vol. 1435, pp. 228–245, 1998.

56. Berg, A. van den, and P. Pottjewijd: *Work Flow: Continue verbetering door Integraal Procesmanagement.* Academic Service, Schoonhove (The Netherlands), 1997.

57. Bergamaschi, S.: Extraction of Informations from highly Heterogeneous Sources of Textual Data. P. Kandzia and M. Klusch (Eds.), *Cooperative Information Agents*, Proc. Workshop CIA-97, Kiel (Germany), Springer, LNAI, Vol. 1202, 1997.

58. Bergamaschi, S., S. Castano, S. De Capitani di Vimercati, S. Montanari, and M. Vincini. An intelligent approach to information integration. *Proc. of Formal Ontology in Information Systems (FOIS-98)*, June 1998.

59. Bergamaschi, S., S. Castano, S. De Capitani di Vimercati, S. Montanari, and M. Vincini: Exploiting schema knowledge for the integration of heterogeneous sources. *Proc. of Convegno Nazionale Sistemi Evoluti per Basi di Dati SEBD-98*, June 1998.

60. Bergamaschi, S., and B. Nebel: Acquisition and validation of complex object database schemata supporting multiple inheritance. Applied Intelligence: The International Journal of Artificial Intelligence, Neural Networks and Complex Problem Solving Technologies, 1993.

61. Bergamaschi, S., and C. Sartori: On taxonomic reasoning in conceptual design. ACM Transactions on Database Systems, Vol. 17(3):385–422, September 1992.

62. Berkovits, S., S.D. Guttmann, and V. Swarup: Authentication for Mobile Agents. In [690], April 1998.

63. Berners-Lee, T., R. Cailliau, A. Loutonen, H. F. Nielsen, and A. Secret: The World-Wide Web. Communications of the ACM, Vol. 37, pp. 76-82, 1994.

64. Bertino, E.: Integration of heterogeneous data repositories by using object-oriented views. *Proc. IEEE RIDE Workshop on Interoperability in Multi-database Systems*, Kyoto (Japan), pages 22-29, 1991.

65. Bertsekas, D.P.: *Dynamic Programming and Optimal Control.* Athena Scientific, 1995.

66. Best, M.: Corporal ecologies and population fitness on the net. Journal of Artificial Life, MIT Press, 1997.

67. Bettman, J.: *An Information Processing Theory to Consumer Choice.* Addison-Wessley, 1979.

68. Bharat, K.A., and L. Cardelli: Migratory applications. *Proceedings of the Eighth Annual ACM Symposium on User Interface Software and Technology*, November 1995.

69. Biddle, B.J., and E.J. Thomas (Eds.): *Role Theory: Concepts and Research*, John Wiley & Son, 1966.

70. Birrell, A.D., and B. J. Nelson: Implementing remote procedure calls. ACM Transactions on Computer Systems, 2(1):39–59, February 1984.

71. Bishop, M., M. Valence, and L. F. Wisniewski: *Process migration for heterogeneous distributed systems.* Technical Report PCS-TR95-264, Dept. of Computer Science, Dartmouth College, August 1995.

72. Blacker, K.: *The Basics of Electronic Data Interchange*, 2nd Edition. ISBN 1-897815-04-2, February 1994.

73. Bodin F., Seznec A.: *Cache organization influence on loop blocking.* IRISA Internal Report, PI-803, 1994.

74. Bollacker, K.D., S. Lawrence, and C.L. Giles: CiteSeer: An autonomous web agent for automatic retrieval and identification of interesting publications. *Proc. 2nd International Conference on Autonomous Agents (Agents-98)*, 1998.

75. Bond, A., and L. Gasser: An Analysis of Problems and Research in DAI. A. Bond and L. Gasser (Eds.), *Readings in Distributed Artificial Intelligence.* Morgan Kaufmann, 1988.

76. Borgida, A., R.J. Brachman, D.L. McGuinness, and L.A. Resnick: CLASSIC: A structural data model for objects. *Proc. ACM SIGMOD Conference*, Portland (Oregon, USA), pp. 58–67, 1989.

77. Borr, A.J., and F. Putzolu: High performance SQL through low-level system integration. *Proceedings of the ACM SIGMOD International Conference on Management of Data*, pages 342–349, Chicago, Illinois, 1988. ACM Press.

78. Bosak, J.: XML, Java, and the Future of the Web. March 1997.

79. BotSpot. A Collection of Bots in the Web. http://www.botspot.com/

80. Boutilier, C., Y. Shoham, and M. Wellman: Economic principles of multi-agent systems. AI Journal, Vol. 94, 1997.

81. Bowman, C.M., P.B. Danzig, U. Manber, and M.F. Schwartz: Scalable internet resource discovery: Research problems and approaches. Communications of the ACM, Vol. 37(8):98–107, 1994.

82. Bra, P.M.E. De, and R.D.J. Post: Information retrieval in the world wide web: Making client-based searching feasible. *Proc. 1st International World Wide Web Conference*, Geneva, 1994.

83. Brachman, R.J., and J.G. Schmolze: An Overview of the KL-ONE Knowledge Representation System. Cognitive Science, Vol. 9(2):171–216, 1985.

84. Bratman, M.E.: *Intention, Plans, and Practical Reason*. Harvard University Press, Cambridge, MA, 1987.

85. Bratman, M.E.: Shared cooperative activity. The Philosophical Review, Vol. 101:327–341, 1992.

86. Brauer, W., and G. Weiß: Multi-Machine Scheduling - a multiagent learning approach. *Proc. of Second International Conference on Multiagent Systems* ICMAS-98, Paris (France), IEEE Press, 1998.

87. Bredin, J., D. Kotz, and D. Rus: Market-based resource control for mobile agents. *Proceedings of the Second International Conference on Autonomous Agents*, pages 197–204. ACM Press, May 1998.

88. Breibart, Y.J., et al.: Database integration in a distributed heterogeneous database system. *Proc. 2nd Intl IEEE Conf. on Data Engineering ICDE-86*, Los Angeles (CA, USA), February 1986.

89. Brewington, B.: Ph.D. thesis proposal: Optimal observation with WWW applications. Available from http://comp-engg-www.dartmouth.edu/~brew/research/proposal.ps, 1998.

90. Bright, M.W., A.R. Hurson, and S. Pakzad: Automated Resolution of Semantic Heterogeneity in Multidatabases. ACM Transactions on Database Systems, Vol.19, No.2, pp.212-253, June 1994.

91. Brodie,M.L.: The emperor's clothes are object oriented and distributed. M.P. Papazoglou and G. Schlageter (Eds.), *Cooperative Information Systems: Trends and Directions*, pages 15–48. Academic Press, 1998.

92. Brodie,M.L., and M. Stonebraker: *Migrating Legacy Systems: Gateways, Interfaces and the Incremental Approach*. Morgan Kaufman Publishing Company, 1995.

93. Brooks, R.: Intelligence Without Representation. AI Journal, Vol. 47, 1991.

94. Brown, M.H., and M. A. Najork: Distributed active objects. Dr. Dobb's Journal, Vol. 263:34–41, March 1997.

95. Buchheit, M., M. A. Jeusfeld, W. Nutt, and M. Staudt: Subsumption between queries to object-oriented database. *Proc. European Conference on Database Theory EDBT-94*, pp. 348–353, 1994.

96. Bulinskaya, E.: Some Results Concerning Optimum Inventory Policies. International Journal on Theory of Probability and its Applications, Vol. 9(3), pp. 389 - 403, 1964.

97. Bui, H.H., D. Kieronska, and S. Venkatesh: Learning other agents' preferences in multiagent negotiation. *Proceedings of the Thirteenth National Conference on Artificial Intelligence*, Menlo Park (CA, USA), AAAI Press, pages 114–119, 1996.

98. Bunemann, P., L. Raschid, J. Ulman: Mediator Languages - a Proposal for a standard. Report of an I3/POB working group held at the University of Maryland, April 1996. (available as ftp://ftp.umiacs.umd.edu/pub/ONRrept/medmodel96.ps).

99. Buneman, P., S. Davidson, M. Fernandez and D. Suciu: Adding a Structure to Unstructured Data, *Proc. Int. Conf. on Database Theory*, Delphi (Greece), pp. 336-350, 1997.

452   References

100. Burt, A.: Modelling Motivational Behaviour in Intelligent Agents in Virtual Worlds. *Proceedings of International Conference on Virtual Worlds and Simulation*, 1998.
101. Business Object Domain Task Force. Common facilities RFP-04: Common business objects and business object facility. OMG TC document cf/96-01-04, Object Management Group (OMG), 1996.
102. Campione, M., and K. Walrath: *The Java tutorial: Object-oriented programming for the Internet*. Addison Wesley, 1997.
103. Cardelli, L.A.: Semantics of multiple inheritance. *Semantics of Data Types*, pages 51–67. Springer, LNCS, 1984.
104. Cardelli, L.: A language with distributed scope. Computing Systems, Vol. 8(1):27–59, Winter 1995.
105. Carey, M.J., et al.: *Towards heterogeneous multimedia information systems: the Garlic approach*. Technical Report RJ 9911, IBM Almaden Research Center, 1994.
106. Carriero, N., and D. Gelernter: ock How to Write Parallel Programs: A Guide to the Perplexed. ACM Computing Surveys, Vol. 21(3), pp. 323–357, 1989.
107. Cassady Jr., R. *Auctions and Auctioneering*. U. of California Press, 1967.
108. Castano, S., V. De Antonellis: Semantic Dictionary Design for Database Interoperability. *Proc. of Int. Conf. on Data Engineering (ICDE-97)*, Birmingham, UK, April 1997.
109. Castano, S., V. De Antonellis, M.G. Fugini, and B. Pernici: Conceptual Schema Analysis: Techniques and Applications. ACM Transactions on Database Systems, 1998.
110. Castelfranchi, C., and E. Werner: *Artificial Social Systems*, LNAI, Springer, 1994.
111. Catarci, T., and M. Lenzerini: Representing and using interschema knowledge in cooperative information systems. Journal of Intelligent and Cooperative Information Systems, Vol. 2(4), 375-398, 1993.
112. Cattel, R.G.G., et al.: *The Object Database Standard - ODGM93. Release 1.2.*, Morgan Kaufmann, 1996.
113. Cavanaugh, K.: Bandwidth's new bargaineers. Technology Review, Vol. 101(6), 1998.
114. Cavedon, L., and L. Sonenberg: On Social Commitment, Roles and Preferred Goals. *Proceedings of the 1998 International Conference on Multi-Agent Systems ICMAS-98*, Paris, July 1998.
115. Chakravarthy, S., B. Dom, and P. Indyk: Enhanced hypertext categorization using hyperlinks. *Proc. ACM SIGMOD Conference*, Seattle (WA, USA), 1998.
116. Chakravarthy, S., B. Dom, P. Raghavan, S. Rajagopalan, D. Gibson, and J. Kleinberg: Automatic resource compilation by analyzing hyperlink structure and associated text. *Proc. 7th International World Wide Web Conference*, 1998.
117. Chakravarthy, U.S., J. Grant, and J. Minker: Logic-based approach to semantic query optimization. ACM Transactions on Database Systems, Vol. 15(2):162–207, June 1990.
118. Chang, P.I.: Inside the Java Web Server: An overview of Java Web Server 1.0, Java Servlets, and the JavaServer architecture. Sun Microsystems White Paper, Sun Microsystems, 1996.
119. Chauhan D., and B. Baker: *JAFMAS: Java Based Framework for MultiAgent Systems Development and Implementation*. PhD Thesis, ECECS Department, University of Cincinnati, (http://www.ececs.uc.edu/ abaker/JAFMAS/), 1997.

120. Chavez, A., and Pattie Maes: Kasbah: An agent marketplace for buying and selling goods. *Proceedings of the First international conference on the practical Application of Intelligent Agents and Multi Agents Technology (PAAM-96)*, pages 75–90, April 1996.

121. Chavez, A., D. Dreilinger, R. Guttman, and P. Maes: A Real-Life Experiment in Creating an Agent Marketplace. *Proceedings of the Second International Conference on the Practical Application of Intelligent Agents and Multi-Agent Technology (PAAM-97)*. London (UK), April 1997.

122. Chen, L., and K Sycara: WebMate: A personal agent for browsing and searching. *Proc. 2nd International Conference on Autonomous Agents (Agents-98)*, 1998.

123. Cheng, J., and M. Wellman: The WALRAS algorithm: A Convergent Distributed Implementation of General Equilibrium Outcomes. Computational Economics.

124. Chess, D.M.: E-mail message for the mailing list 'agents', April 1997.

125. Chess, D.M.: Security Issues in Mobile Code Systems. In [690], April 1998.

126. Chess, D., B. Grosof, C. Harrison, D. Levine, C. Parris, and G. Tsudik: Itinerant agents for mobile computing. In [296], pages 267–282. 1997. (Reprinted from *IEEE Personal Communications, 1995*).

127. Chu, W.W., H. Yang, K. Chiang, M. Minock, G. Chow, and C. Larson: CoBase: A Scalable and Extensible Cooperative Information System. Journal of Intelligent Information Systems, vol. 6, 2/3, pp. 223-259, June 1996.

128. Ciancarini, P.: Coordination Models and Languages as Software Integrators. ACM Computing Surveys, Vol. 28(2), pp. 300–302, 1996.

129. Clark, A., and Scarf, H.: Optimal Policies for a Multi-Echelon Inventory Problem. Management Science, Vol. 6(4), pp. 475-490, 1960.

130. Clark, R., C. Grossner, and T. Radhakrishnan: CONSENSUS and COMPROMISE: Planning in cooperating expert systems. Int. Journal of Intelligent and Cooperative Information Systems, 1993.

131. Clearwater, S.: *Market-based control: A paradigm for distributed resorce allocation*. World Scientific, 1995.

132. Clearwater, S.: A comparative-developmental approach to understanding imitation. Clearwater, S. (Ed.), *Market Based Control: A paradigm for distributed resource allocation*, World Scientific, 1995.

133. Cockayne, W., and M. Zyda: *Mobile Agents*. Manning Publications Co., USA, 1998.

134. Cohen, P.R. and H.J. Levesque: Communicative Actions for Artificial Agents. *Proceedings of the First International Conference on Multi-Agent Systems*, AAAI Press, San Francisco, June 1995.

135. Collin, Z., R. Dechter, and S. Kaiz: On the Feasibility of Distributed Constraint Satisfaction. *Proceedings of the 10th International Joint Conference on Artificial Intelligence (IJCAI-91)*, 1991.

136. Collins, J., B. Youngdahl, S. Jamison, B. Mobasher and M. Gini: A market architecture for multi-agent contracting. *Proceedings of Conference on Autonomous Agents*, pp. 285–292, 1998.

137. Communications of the ACM, Special issue on Intelligent Agents, volume 37, number 7, July 1994.

138. compare.net. http://www.compare.net

139. Concordia. Mitsubishi Concordia:
http://www.meitca.com/HSL/Projects/Concordia/

140. Contact Consortium: Audio Tapes of the panel "Earth to Avatars" with the theme "Contact, Culture, and Community in Digital Space", First Annual Conference of the Contact Consortium (http://www.ccon.org), October 1996.

See also: *Proceedings of Avatars-97 (and Avatars-98) International Conference on Avatars inside Cyberspace*, http://www.ccon.org/conf97/index.html (http://www.ccon.org/conf98/index.html), 1997 (1998)

141. Contreras,J., M. Klusch, and J. Yen: Multi-Agent Coalition Formation in Power Transmission Planning. *Proc. 4th International Conference on Artificial Intelligence in Planning Systems (AIPS-98)*, Carnegie Mellon University, Pittsburgh (USA), June 1998.

142. Cooper, W.S.: Expected search length: A single measure of retrieval effectiveness based on weak ordering action of retrieval systems. *Journal of the American Society for Information Science*, 19:30–41, 1968.

143. Cooper, K., M. Hall, and K. Kennedy: Procedure cloning. *Proceedings of the International Conference on Computer Languages*, IEEE Computer Society, pp. 96 - 105, April 1992.

144. CORBA. OMG Object Management Group - Common Object Request Broker Architecture. References: http://www.cs.wustl.edu/ schmidt/corba-papers.html

145. Crowston, K.G.: *Towards a Coordination Cookbook: Recipes for Multi-Agent Action.* Ph. D. thesis, Sloan School of Management, MIT, CCS TR# 128, 1991.

146. Cunningham, P., S. Green and F. Somers: Agent mediated collaborative web page filtering. M. Klusch and G. Weiß(Eds.), *Cooperative Information Agents II*, Proc. Workshop CIA-98, Springer, LNAI, Vol. 1435, pages 195–205, 1998.

147. Curran,T., G. Keller, and A. Ladd: *SAP R/3 Business Blueprint: understanding the business process reference model.* Prentice-Hall, New Jersey (USA), 1998.

148. Cybenko, G., A. Bhasin, and K. D. Cohen: Pattern recognition of 3D CAD objects: Towards an electronic yellow pages of mechanical parts. Smart Engineering Systems Design, Vol.1:1–13, 1997.

149. Daft, R.L.: *Organization Theory and Design.* West Publishing Company, 1992.

150. D'Agents. Dartmouth College, USA. http://www.cs.dartmouth.edu/ agent

151. D'Aloisi, D., V. Giannini: The Info Agent: An Interface for Supporting Users in Intelligent Retrieval. *Proceedings of the ERCIM Workshop on Towards User Interfaces for All: Current Efforts and Future Trends*, Heraklion, 145-158, October 30-31, 1995.

152. Dao, S., and B. Perry: Information Mediation in Cyberspace: Scalable Methods for Declarative Information Networks. Journal of Intelligent Information Systems, Vol. 6, 2/3, pp. 131-150, 1996.

153. DARPA I3 Project. Intelligent Integation of Information. http://mole.dc.isx.com/I3/

154. Data Access Technologies. Business object architecture (BOA) proposal. bom/97-11-09, OMG Business Object Domain Task Force, 1997.

155. Dautenhahn, K., and C. Numaoka (Eds.), International Journal on Applied Artificial Intelligence, Special Issue on Socially Intelligent Agents, Vol. 12 (7-8), 1998.

156. Davenport,T.H.: *Process Innovation, Reengineering Work through Information Technology.* Harvard Business School, Boston, 1993.

157. Davis, R., and R. Smith: Negotiation as a Metaphor for Distributed Problem Solving. Journal on Artificial Intelligence, Vol. 20, pp. 63-109, 1983.

158. Dayal, U., and H. Hwuang: View definition and generalization for database integration in a multidatabase system. In *Proc. IEEE Workshop on Object-Oriented DBMS*, Asilomar (CA, USA), September 1986.

159. DCOM. Microsoft Distributed Component Object Model.
     http://www.microsoft.com/com/default.asp
160. Decker, K. and V. Lesser: Macron: An architecture for multi-agent cooperative
     information gathering. *Proc. CIKM-94 Workshop on Intelligent Information
     Agents*, 1994.
161. Decker, K., V. Lesser, M.V.N. Prasad, and T. Wagner: MACRON: An Archi-
     tecture for Multi-agent Cooperative Information Gathering. *Proccedings of the
     CIKM Workshop on Intelligent Information Agents*, Baltimore (Maryland,
     USA), December, 1995. (see also http://dis.cs.umass.edu/research/cig.html)
162. Decker, K., K. Sycara, and M. Williamson: Inteligent adaptive information
     agents. *Proceedings of AAAI-96 workshop on Intelligent Adaptive Agents*,
     Portland (Oregon, USA), 1996.
163. Decker, K. M. Williamson, and K. Sycara: Modeling information agents:
     Advertisements, organizational roles, and dynamic behavior. *Proceedings of
     the AAAI-96 Workshop on Agent Modeling*, 1996.
164. Decker, K., K. Sycara, and M. Williamson: Intelligent adaptive information
     agents. Journal on Intelligent Information Systems, Vol. 9:239-260, 1997.
165. Decker, K., K. Sycara, and M. Williamson: Middle-agents for the Internet.
     Proceeding of IJCAI-97 Conference, Nagoya (Japan), pp. 578 - 583, 1997.
166. Decker, K., and Victor R. Lesser: Designing a family of coordination al-
     gorithms. *Proceedings of the First International Conference on Multi-Agent
     Systems*, pages 73–80, San Francisco, June 1995. AAAI Press. Longer version
     available as UMass Technical Report CS-TR 94–14.
167. Decker, K., A. Pannu, K. Sycara, and M. Williamson: Designing behaviors
     for information agents. W. Lewis Johnson (Ed.), *Proceedings of the First In-
     ternational Conference on Autonomous Agents (Agents-97)*, New York, ACM
     Press, 1997.
168. DeKleer, J.: An Assumption-Based Truth Maintenance System. AI Journal,
     No. 28. 1986.
169. Dellarocas, C.N.: *A Coordination Perspective on Software Architecture: To-
     wards a Design Handbook for Integrating Software Components*. Ph. D. thesis,
     Massachusetts Institute of Technology, 1996.
170. Dennet, D.: *The Intentional Stance*. The MIT press, 1987.
171. Dent, L., J. Boticario, J. McDermott, T. Mitchell, and D. Zabowski: A per-
     sonal learning apprentice. *Proceedings of the Tenth National Conference on
     Artificial Intelligence*, pages 96–103, July 1992.
172. Dignum, F., and B. van Linder: Modeling social agents: Communication as
     action. J. Müller, M. Wooldridge, and N. R. Jennings (Eds.), *Intelligent
     Agents III*, Springer, LNAI, Vol. 1193, 1996.
173. Di Marzo, G., M. Muhugusa, C.F. Tschudin, and J. Harms: The Messenger
     paradigm and its implications on distributed systems. *Proceedings of the
     ICC'95 Workshop on Intelligent Computer Communication*, 1995.
174. Dio, L. Di: Do you know if you've been hacked?. Computerworld, July 1998.
175. Donini, F.M., M. Lenzerini, D. Nardi, and W. Nutt: The complexity of con-
     cept languages. *Proc. 2nd Intl. Conf on Principles of Knowledge Representa-
     tion and Reasoning (KR-91)*, Cambridge MA, pages 151–162, Morgan Kauf-
     mann, 1991.
176. Doran, J.E., S. Franklin, N.R. Jennings, and T.J. Norman: On Cooperation in
     Multi-Agent Systems. The Knowledge Engineering Review, Vol. 12(3), 1997.
177. Doorenbos, R.B., O. Etzioni, and D. Weld: A Scalable Comparison-Shopping
     Agent for the World Wide Web. *Proceedings of the First International Confer-
     ence on Autonomous Agents (Agents-97)*, Marina del Rey (CA, USA), Febru-
     ary 1997.

178. Douglis, F., and J. Ousterhout: Transparent process migration: Design alternatives and the Sprite implementation. Software: Practice and Experience, Vol. 21(8):757–785, August 1991.

179. Drummond, R., M. Jansson, and C. Shih: *Requirements for Inter-operable Internet EDI*. Internet Engineering Task Force (IETF) Working Draft, 4 December 1997. ftp://ietf.org/ internet-drafts/draft-ietf-ediint-req-04.txt

180. Durfee, E., D L. Kiskis, and W. P. Birmingham: The agent architecture of the University of Michigan Digital Library. *IEE Proceedings on Software Engineering*, Vol. 144(1):61–71, 1997.

181. Dyke, N. van, H. Lieberman, and P. Maes: Butterfly: A Conversation-Finding Agent for Internet Relay Chat. *Proc. International Conference on Intelligent User Interfaces*, Redondo Beach (CA, USA), January 1999.

182. Edmond, D., and M.P. Papazoglou: Reflection is the essence of cooperation. In M.P. Papazoglou and G. Schlageter (Eds.), *Cooperative Information Systems: Trends and Directions*, Academic Press, pp. 233- 262, 1998.

183. Eeles,P., and O. Sims: *Building Business Objects*. John Wiley & Sons, New York, 1998.

184. Elliott, C., and J. Brzezinski: Autonomous Agents as Synthetic Characters. AI Magazine, 1998.

185. Elmasri, R., and S. Navathe: *Fundamental of Database Systems*. Benjamin Cummings, Redwood City, CA, second edition, 1994.

186. Elo, A. E.: *The Rating of Chessplayers, Past and Present*. Arco Publishing Inc., New York, 1978.

187. Encyclopaedia Britannica, Inc.: http://www.eb.com.

188. Engel, J., and R. Blackwell: *Consumer Behavior*, 4th edition, CBS College Publishing, 1982.

189. Engelfriet, J., C. M. Jonker, and J. Treur: Compositional verification of multi-agent systems in temporal multi-epistemic logic. *Intelligent Agents V*, Proceedings Workshop on Agent Theories, Architectures, and Languages (ATAL-98), Springer, 1998.

190. Es, R.M. van, and H. A. Post: *Dynamic Enterprise Modeling: A Paradigm Shift in Software Implementation*. Kluwer Bedrijfsinformatie B.V., 1987.

191. Etzioni, O.: Results from using the metacrawler. F. Varela, and P. Bourgine (Eds.), *Proceedings of the Fourth WWW Conference*, MIT Press, 1995.

192. Etzioni, O. and E. Selberg: The MetaCrawler architecture for resource aggregation on the Web. IEEE Expert, 1997.
http://www.cs.washington.edu/homes/speed/papers/ieee/ieee-metacrawler.ps

193. Etzioni, O.: Moving up the information food chain: deploying softbots on the WWW. *Proceedings of the AAAI-96 Conference*, AAAI Press, 1996.

194. Etzioni, O., and D.S. Weld: A SoftBot based interface to the Internet. ACM Communications, 37(7), 1996.
and in: M. Huhns and M.P. Singh (Eds.), *Readings in Agents*, Morgan Kaufmann, 1998.

195. Excite. http://www.excite.com.

196. Extempo. http://www.extempo.com/

197. Falcone, J.R.: A programmable interface language for heterogeneous systems. ACM Transactions on Computer Systems, Vol. 5(4):330–351, November 1987.

198. Fair Isaak Co. (1998). http://www.fairisaac.com

199. FairMarket. http://auctions.fairmarket.com/ (http://www.fairmarket.com/)

200. Feigenbaum, E.A.: *The Fifth Generation : Artificial Intelligence And Japan's Computer Challenge To The World*. Reading, Mass., Addison-Wesley, 1983.

201. Fido - The Shopping Doggie. Continuum Softwar Inc.
     http://www.shopfido.com/
202. Fikes, R., R. Engelmore, A. Farquhar, and W. Pratt: Network-Based Information Brokers. *Proc. AAAI-95 Symposium on Information Gathering from Distributed, Heterogeneous Environments*, Palo Alto CA, March 1995.
203. Finin, T., R. Fritzson, D. McKay, and R. McEntire: KQML as an agent communication language. *Proceedings of the Third International Conference on Information and Knowledge Management CIKM'94*, ACM Press, November 1994.
204. Finin, T., Y. Labroux, and J. Mayfeld: KQML as an agent communication language. J. Bradshaw (Ed.), *Software Agents*, MIT Press, Menlo Park, 1995.
205. Finin, T., D. McKay, R. Fritzson, and R. McEntire: KQML: An Information and Knowledge Exchange Protocol. K. Fuchi and T. Yokoi (Ed.), *Knowledge Building and Knowledge Sharing*, Ohmsha and IOS Press, 1994.
     See also: http://www.csee.umbc.edu/pub/ARPA/kqml/papers/
206. FIPA: Foundation for Intelligent Physical Agents. http://drogo.cselt.it/fipa/ see also: L. Chiariglione: FIPA - Agent technologies achieve maturity. AgentLink Newsletter, 1, November 1999, http://www.agentlink.org
207. FIPA Agent Communication Language.
     http://www.fipa.org/spec/fipa97/FIPA97.html
208. Firefly network. http://www.firefly.com/
209. Fischer, K., and J.P. Müller: A decision-theoretic model for cooperative transportation scheduling. *Proceedings of MAAMAW-96 Workshop*, Eindhoven, Springer, LNAI, Vol. 1038, 1996.
210. Fischer, K., J. P. Müller, I. Heimig, and A.-W. Scheer: Intelligent agents in virtual enterprises. *Proceedings of The first international conference on the practical Application of Intelligent Agents and Multi Agents Technology*, pages 250–223, April 1996.
211. Fishmarket Project. http://www.iiia.csic.es/Projects/fishmarket/
212. Fishmarket Tournament.
     http://www.iiia.csic.es/Projects/fishmarket/tournament.html
213. Foltz, P.W., and S.T. Dumais: Personalized Information Delivery: An Analysis of Information Filtering Methods. Communications of the ACM, Vol. 35(12):51-60, 1992.
214. Foner, L.: Yenta: A Multi-Agent, Referral Based Matchmaking System. presented at The First International Conference on Autonomous Agents (Agents '97), Marina del Rey, California, February 1997.
215. Ford, K.M., and P.J. Hayes: On computational wings: Rethinking the goals of Artificial Intelligence. Scientific American, Vol. 9(4), 1998.
216. Forrester Research Report. Affordable intimacy strengthens online stores. September 1997.
217. Fowler, M.: *Analysis Patterns: reusable object models*. Addison-Wesley, Menlo Park, California, 1997.
218. Fowler, M.: *UML Distilled: Applying the Standard Object Modeling Language*. Addison-Wesley, Reading, MA, 1997.
219. Fox, C.: Lexical analysis and stop lists. *Information Retrieval: Data Structures and Algorithms*. Prentice-Hall, 1992.
220. Frakes, W.B.: Stemming algorithms. *Information Retrieval: Data Structures and Algorithms*. Prentice-Hall, 1992.
221. Franchitti, J.C., and R. King: Amalgame: a tool for creating interoperating persistent, heterogeneous components. *Advanced Database Systems*, Springer, LNCS, Vol. 759, 1993.

222. Franklin, S., and A. Gaesser: Is it an agent , or just a program?: A taxonomy for autonomous agents. *Proc. 3rd International Workshop on Agent Theories, Architectures and Languages (ATAL-96)*, Springer, LNAI, 1996.
223. Freedman, M.: *WILLOW: Technical overview.* Available by anonymous ftp from ftp.cac.washington.edu as the file willow/Tech-Report.ps, September 1994.
224. Freisleben, B., and T. Kielmann: Coordination patterns for parallel computing. D. Garlan and D. Le Métayer (Eds.), *Coordination Languages and Models*, Proceedings of COORDINATION-97 Conference, Springer, LNCS, Vol. 1282, pp. 414–417, 1997.
225. Frew, J., M. Freeston, R. B. Kemp, J. Simpson, T. Smith, A. Wells, and Q. Zheng: The Alexandria digital library testbed. D-Lib Magazine, July/August 1996.
226. Fukuda, Y.: Optimal Policies for the Inventory Problem with Negotiable Leadtime. Management Science, Vol. 10(4), pp. 690 - 708, 1964.
227. Gaines, B.R.: Knowledge Management in Societies of Intelligent Adaptive Agents. Journal of Intelligent Information Systems, vol. 9, pp. 277-298, 1997.
228. Gamma, E., R. Helm, R. Johnson, and J. Vlissides: *Design Patterns: Abstraction and Reuse of Object-Oriented Design.* Addison-Wesley, Reading, MA, 1994.
229. Gamma, E., R. Helm, R. Johnson, and J. Vlissides: *Design Patterns.* Addison-Wesley, 1995.
230. Garcia-Molina, H., et al.: The TSIMMIS Approach to Mediation: Data Models and Languages. *Proc. Workshop NGITS*, 1995.
(ftp://db.stanford.edu/pub/garcia/1995/tsimmis-models-languages.ps)
231. Garey, M.R., and D. S. Johnson: *Computers and Intractability: A Guide to the Theory of NP-Completeness.* W.H. Freeman and Company, 1979.
232. Garfinkel, S.L.: *PGP: Pretty Good Privacy.* O'Reilly and Associates, 1994.
233. Garfinkel, S.L.: The Web's unelected government. Technology Review, Vol. 101(6), 1998.
234. Gasser, L.: Information and Collaboration from a Social/Organizational Perspective. S.Y. Nof (Ed.), *Information and Collaboration Models of Integration*, 237-261, Kluwer Academic Publishers, 1994.
235. Gauch, S., and R.P. Futrelle: Experiments in Automatic Word Class and Word Sense Identification for Information Retrieval. *Proceedings of the Third Annual Symposium on Document Analysis and Information Retrieval.*
236. Gehmeyr,A., J. Müller, and A. Schappert: Mobile Information Agents on the Web. M. Klusch, and G. Weiß(Eds.), *Cooperative Information Agents II*, Proc. Intern. Workshop CIA-98, Springer, LNAI, Vol. 1435, 1998.
237. Gelernter, D., and N. Carriero: Coordination Languages and their Significance. Communications of the ACM, Vol. 35(2), pp. 97–107, 1992.
238. Genesereth, M.R., and S. P. Ketchpel: Software agents. Communications of the ACM, Vol. 37(7), July 1994.
239. Geronimus, L.Y.: *Orthogonal Polynomials.* Consultants Bureau, New York, NY, 1961.
240. Gimenez, E., L. Godo, and J.A. Rodriguez-Aguilar: Designing bidding strategies for trading agents in electronic commerce. *Proc. of Second International Conference on Multiagent Systems (ICMAS-98)*, Paris, IEEE Press, 1998.
241. Glickman, M.: *Paired Comparison Models with Time-Varying Parameters.* PhD Thesis, Harvard University, 1993.
242. Gmytrasiewicz, P., E. Durfee, and D. Wehe: A Decision-Theoretic Approach to Coordinating Multiagent Interactions. *Proceedings of the Eleventh International Joint Conference on Artificial Intelligence*, August 1991.

243. Goh, C., M. Siegel, and S. Madnick: Context Interchange: Overcoming the challenges of Large Scale Interoperable Database Systems in a Dynamic Environment. *Proc. of the 3rd Int'l Conf. on Knowledge Management CIKM-96*, Maryland, 1996.

244. Goldman, C.V., and J.S. Rosenschein: *Mutual Adaptation Enhanced by Social Laws*. The Hebrew University Jerusalem, Technical Report CS-98-5, 1998.

245. Goodhue, D.L., M.D. Wybo, and L.J. Kosh: The Impact of Data on the Costs and Benefits of Information Systems. MIS Quarterly, pp 293-310, September 1992.

246. Gordin, T.R., N. Puppala, and S. Sen: Evolving cooperative groups: preliminary results. *AAAI Technical Report WS-97-03, Proc. AAAI Workshop on Multiagent Learning*, 1997.

247. Graham, I.: *Migrating to Object Technology.* Addison-Wesley Publishing Company, Workingham (England), 1994.

248. Gray, R.: *Agent Tcl: A flexible and secure mobile-agent system.* PhD thesis, Dept. of Computer Science, Dartmouth College, June 1997. Available as Dartmouth Computer Science Technical Report TR98-327.

249. Gray, J., and A. Reuter: *Transaction Processing: Concepts and Techniques.* Morgan Kaufmann, San Mateo, 1993.

250. Gray, R.S., D. Kotz, G. Cybenko, and D. Rus: D'agents: Security in a multiple-language, mobile-agent system. Giovanni Vigna (Ed.), *Mobile Agent Security*, Springer, Lecture Notes in Computer Science, 1998.

251. Green, S., L. Hurst, B. Nangle, P. Cunninggham, F. Somers, and R. Evans: Software Agents: A review, 1997. available at http://www.cs.tcd.id/Brenda.Nangle/iag.html

252. Greenberg, M.S., J.C. Byington, T. Holding, and D.G. Harper: Mobile Agents and Security. IEEE Communications, Vol. 36(7), July 1998.

253. Greening, D.R.: Building Consumer Trust with Accurate Product Recommendations - A White Paper on LikeMinds WebSell 2.1. 1998. available at: http://www.likeminds.com/technology/$white_papers$/websell/

254. Grice, P.: *Studies in the way of words.* Harvard University Press, Cambridge (Mass., USA), 1989.

255. Grosof, B.: Reusable architecture for embedding rule-based intelligence. *Proc. of CIKM-95 Workshop on Intelligent Information Agents*, 1995.

256. Gruber, T.R.: *Ontolingua: A Mechanism to Support Portable Ontologies.* Stanford University, Knowledge Systems Laboratory, Technical Report KSL-91-66, March 1992.

257. Gruber, T.R.: A Translation Approach to Portable Ontology Specifications. Knowledge Acquisition, Vol. 5(2): 199-220, 1993.

258. Grosz, B.J., and S. Kraus: Collaborative plans for group activities. Ruzena Bajcsy (Ed.), *Proceedings of the 1993 International Joint Conference on Artificial Intelligence (IJCAI-93)*, San Mateo (CA, USA), pp. 367 - 373, Morgan Kaufmann Publishers, 1993.

259. Grosz, B.J., and S. Kraus: Collaborative plans for complex group action. AI Journal, Vol. 86(2):269–357, 1996.

260. Grosz, B.J., and S. Kraus: The evolution of SharedPlans. A. Rao and M. Wooldridge (Eds.), *Foundations and Theories of Rational Agency.* Kluwer Academic Publishers, 1998. (to appear).

261. Gudivada, V.N.: Information retrieval on the world wide Web. IEEE Internet Computing, Vol. 1(5), September 1997.

262. Gupta, A.: *Integration of Information Systems: Bridging heterogeneous Databases.* IEEE Press, 1989.

263. Guttman, R.: Automated Integrative Negotiation in Retail Electronic Commerce. MIT, Working paper.
264. Guttman, R., and P. Maes: Agent-mediated Integrative Negotiation for Retail Electronic Commerce. *Proceedings of the Workshop on Agent Mediated Electronic Trading (AMET'98)*, May 1998.
265. Guttman, R.H., and P. Maes: Cooperative vs. competitive multi-agent negotiations in retail electronic commerce. M. Klusch and G. Weiß(Eds.), *Cooperative Information Agents II*, Proceedings of CIA-98 Workshop, Paris (France), Springer, LNAI, Vol. 1435, July 1998.
266. Guttman, R. H., P. Maes, A. Chavez, and D. Dreilinger: Results from a multi-agent electronic marketplace experiment. *Proceedings of Workshop MAAMAW-97*, 1997.
267. Hadad, M.: *Using SharedPlan model in electronic commerce environment.* M.Sc. Thesis, Dept. of Mathematics and Computer Science, Bar-Ilan University, Ramat Gan, 1997.
268. Haddadi, A., and K. Sundermeyer: Belief-Desire-Intention Agent Architectures. G.M.P. O'Hare and N.R. Jennings (Eds.): *Foundations of Distributed Artificial Intelligence*, John Wiley and Sons, 1996.
269. Hamblin, C. L.: *Fallacies.* Methuen, 1970.
270. Hammer, M., and J. Champy: *Reengineering the Corporation: A Manifesto for Business Revolution.* Harper Collins, New York, 1993.
271. Hammer, J., and D. McLeod: An approach to resolving semantic heterogeneity in a federation of autonomous, heterogeneous database systems. Intl Journal of Intelligent and Cooperative Information Systems, Vol. 2:51-83, 1993.
272. Hammer,J., H. Garcia-Molina, K. Ireland, Y. Papakonstantinou, J. Ullman, and J. Widom: Integrating and Accessing Heterogeneous Information Sources in TSIMMIS. *In Proceedings of the AAAI Symposium on Information Gathering*, pp. 61-64, Stanford (CA, USA), March 1995.
273. Han, C., H. Fujii, and W.B. Croft: *Automatic Query Expansion for Japanese Text Retrieval.* University of Massachussets, USA, Technical Report, 1994.
274. Hart, W.E., and R.K. Belew: Optimization with genetic algorithm hybrids that use local search. In R.K. Belew and M. Mitchell (Eds.), *Adaptive Individuals in Evolving Populations: Models and Algorithms*, Santa Fe Institute Studies in the Sciences of Complexity, Addison Wesley, Reading MA, 1996.
275. Hartman, J., U. Manber, L. Peterson, and T. Pröbsting: *Liquid software: A new paradigm for networked systems.* Technical Report TR96-11, Department of Computer Science, University of Arizonia, 1996.
276. Hawkins, D., K. Coney, and R. Best: Consumer Behavior: Implications for Marketing Strategy. Business Publications Inc., 1980.
277. Hendricks, K., and H.-J. Paarsch: A survey of recent empirical auctions. Canadian Journal of Economics, Vol. 33, No.2, 1995.
278. Henschen, Fernandes, Neild and Li: Modelling Data Correspondance in Multidatabase Systems. *Proc. of the IASTED/ISMM Conf. on Intelligent Information Management Systems*, Washington D. C., pp 19-23, June 1996.
279. Hewitt, C.: Viewing Control Structures as Patterns of Passing Messages. P. Winston and R. Brown (Eds.), *Artificial Intelligence: An MIT Perspective*, MIT Press, 1979.
280. Hewitt, C.: Open Information Systems Semantic for Distributed Artificial Intelligence. AI Journal, January 1991.
281. Hill, W., L. Stead, B. Resenstein, and G. Furnas: Recommending and evaluating choices in a virtual community of use. Proceedings of Computer Human Interaction CHI 95, Denver, CO, 1995.

282. Hintikka, J.: *Models for Modalities*. D. Reidel Publishing Company, Dordrecht, Netherlands. 1969.
283. Hogg, T., and B. A. Huberman: Controlling chaos in distributed systems. IEEE Transactions on Systems, Man, and Cybernetics, Vol. 21(6):1325–1332, December 1991. (Special Issue on Distributed AI).
284. Horty, J.: Deontic Logic as founded in Nonmonotonic Logic. Annals of Mathematics and Artificial Intelligence, 1993.
285. Howard, J., and J. Sheth: *The Theory of Buyer Behavior*. John Wiley and Sons, 1969.
286. Howe, A.E., and D. Dreilinger: SavvySearch - A metasearch engine that learns which search engines to query. AI Magazine, Summer 1997.
287. Hsu, A., and D. Zeng: Finding Ordering Policies Given Multiple Leadtime Options. Graduate School of Industrial Administration, Carnegie Mellon University, Pittsburgh (PA, USA), Working Paper, 1997.
288. Huberman, B.A., and M. Kaminsky: Beehive: A System for Cooperative Filtering and Sharing of Information, 1996.
289. Huberman, B.A., P.L.T. Pirolli, J.E. Pitkow, and R.M. Lukose: Strong regularities in world wide web surfing. Science, Vol. 280(5360):95–97, 1998.
290. Huhns, M.N., and M. P. Singh: Conversational agents. IEEE Internet Computing, March/April 1997.
291. Huhns, M.N., and M. P. Singh: The agent test. IEEE Internet Computing, Vol. 1(5):78–79, October 1997. Instance of the column *Agents on the Web*.
292. Huhns, M.N., and M. P. Singh: Ontologies for agents. IEEE Internet Computing, Nov/Dec 1997.
293. Huhns, M.N., and M. P. Singh: Managing heterogeneous transaction workflows with co-operating agents. N.R. Jennings and M. Wooldridge (Eds.), *Agent Technology*, Springer, 1998.
294. Huhns, M.N., and M. P. Singh: Agents and multiagent systems: Themes, approaches, and challenges. In *[296]*, chapter 1, pages 1–23. 1998.
295. Huhns, M.N., and M. P. Singh: A multiagent treatment of agenthood. Journal of Applied Artificial Intelligence, 1998. in press.
296. Huhns, M., and M.P. Singh (Eds.): *Readings in Agents*. Morgan Kaufmann, San Francisco, 1998.
297. Huhns, M.N., U. Mukhopadhyay, L. M. Stephens, and R. D. Bonnell: DAI for document retrieval: The MINDS project. In Michael N. Huhns (Ed.), *Distributed Artificial Intelligence*, pages 249–283. Pitman/Morgan Kaufmann, London, 1987.
298. Huhns, M., et al.: *Enterprise information modeling and model integration in Carnot*. Technical Report Carnot 128-92, MCC, 1992.
299. Huhns, M.N., et al.: Integrating Enterprise Information Systems in Carnot. M. Huhns, M. Papazoglou, G. Schlageter (Eds.), *Proc. 1st Int'l Conf. on Intelligent and Cooperative Information Systems*, Rotterdam, May 1993.
300. Hull, R.: Managing Semantic Heterogeneity in Databases: A Theoretical Perspective. *Proc. ACM Symp. on Principles of Database Systems*, pp. 51-61, 1997.
301. IBM Aglets. IBM Research Center Tokyo, Japan. http://www.trl.ibm.co.jp/aglets/
302. I3Net. The European Network of Excellence on Intelligent Information Interfaces. http://www.i3net.org/
303. Imam, I., and L. Kerschberg: Adaptive Intelligent Agents. Journal of Intelligent Information Systems, vol. 9, pp. 211-214, 1997.
304. Indermaur, K.: At your service? A state-of-the art report on electronic agents in e-commerce. Magazine DBMS, Vol. 11(10), September 1998.

305. Internet Magazine. Issue November 5, 1998.
     http://www.internet-magazine.com/news/nov/05c.htm
306. Ishida, T., M. Yokoo, and L. Gasser: An organizational approach to adaptive
     production systems. *Proceedings of the National Conference on Artificial
     Intelligence*, pages 52–58, July 1990.
307. Jacobson, I., M. Christerson, and G. Overgaard: *Object-Oriented Software
     Engineering: A Use Case Driven Approach*. Addison-Wesley, 1992.
308. Jacobson, I., and M. Ericsson: *The Object Advantage: Business Process
     Reengineering with Object Technology*. ACM Press, Addison-Wesley Pub-
     lishing Company, Workingham (England), 1995.
309. Jain, A.K., and M. P. Singh: Using spheres of commitment to support vir-
     tual enterprises. *Proceedings of the 4th ISPE International Conference on
     Concurrent Engineering: Research and Applications (CE)*, pages 469–476. In-
     ternational Society for Productivity Enhancements (ISPE), August 1997.
310. Jango. Jango/Excite: http://www.jango.com
311. Jennings, N.R.: Controlling cooperative problem solving in industrial multi-
     agent systems using joint intentions. AI Journal, 75(2):1–46, 1995.
312. Jensen, K.K.: *Towards a Multiple Tuple Space Model*. Ph. D. thesis, Aalborg
     University, 1993.
313. Jeusfeld, M., and M.P. Papazoglou: Information brokering. M.P. Papazoglou
     (Ed.), *Information Systems Interoperability*, pages 265–302, Somerset, Eng-
     land, 1998. Research Studies Press, J. Wiley & Sons Inc.
314. Jha, S., P. Chalasani, O. Shehory and K. Sycara: A Formal Treatment of Dis-
     tributed Matchmaking. *Proceedings of the Second International Conference
     on Autonomous Agents (Agents-98)*, Minneapolis (MN, USA), May 1998.
315. Joachims, T., D. Freitag, and T. Mitchell: WebWatcher: A tour guide for the
     world wide web. *Proc. International Joint Conference on Artificial Intelli-
     gence*, 1997.
316. Johansen, D., F. B. Schneider, and R. van Renesse: Operating system support
     for mobile agents. D. Milojicic, F. Douglis, and R. Wheeler (Eds.), *Mobility,
     Mobile Agents and Process Migration – An Edited Collection*. Addison Wesley,
     1998. Originally appeared in the *Proceedings of the 5th IEEE Workshop on
     Hot Topics in Operating Systsems*.
317. Johansen, D., F. B. Schneider, and R. van Renesse: What TACOMA taught
     us. D. Milojicic, F. Douglis, and R. Wheeler (Eds.), *Mobility, Mobile Agents
     and Process Migration – An Edited Collection*. Addison Wesley, 1998.
318. Johnson, R.E.: Frameworks = (Components + Patterns). Communications
     of the ACM, Vol. 40(10), pp. 39–42, 1997.
319. Joseph, A.D., A. F. de Lespinasse, J. A. Tauber, D. K. Gifford, and M. F.
     Kaashoek: Rover: A toolkit for mobile information access. *Proceedings of the
     Fifteenth ACM Symposium on Operating Systems Principles*, pages 156–171,
     ACM Press, Copper Mountain, Colorado, December 1995.
320. Jumping Beans white paper. Ad Astra Engineering, Inc., September 1, 1998.
     See http://www.JumpingBeans.com/.
321. Junglee. http://www.junglee.com
322. Kahan, J.P., and Amnon Rapoport: *Theories of Coalition Formation*,
     Lawrence Erlbaum Associates, Publishers, Hillsdale, NJ, 1984.
323. Kahng, J., and D. McLeod: Dynamic Classificational Ontologies: Mediators
     for Sharing in Cooperative Federated Database. *Proceedings of International
     Conference on Cooperative Information Systems CoopIS-96*, Brussels, Bel-
     gium, June 1996.
324. Kandzia, P., and M. Klusch (Eds.): *Cooperative Information Agents*, Proc. of
     First International Workshop CIA-98, Kiel, Springer, LNAI, Vol. 1202, 1997.

325. Kaplan, R.S.: A Dynamic Inventory Model with Stochastic Lead Times. Management Science, Vol. 16(7), pp 491 - 507, 1970.
326. Kasbah. http://kasbah.media.mit.edu/
327. Kashyap, V., and A. Sheth: Schematic and Semantic Similarities between Database Objects: A Context-based Approach. VLDB Journal, Vol. 5(4), October 1996.
328. Kashyap, V., and A. Sheth: Semantic heterogenity in global information systems: the role of metadata context and ontology. M.P. Papazoglou and G. Schlageter (Eds.), *Cooperative Information Systems: Trends and Directions*, pages 139–178, Academic Press, 1998.
329. Kautz, H. (Ed.): *Proc. AAAI-98 Workshop on Recommender Systems*, 1998.
330. Kautz, H., B. Selman, and A. Milewski: Agent amplified communication. *Proceedings of the National Conference on Artificial Intelligence*, pages 3–9, 1996.
331. Kavakli, V., and P. Loucopoulos: Goal-driven business process analysis: Application in electricity deregulation. B. Pernici and C. Thanos (Eds.), *Proceedings of International Conference, CAiSE'98, Pisa, Italy*, pages 305–325, 1998.
332. Keeney, R., and H. Raiffa: *Decisions with Multiple Objectives: Preferences and Value Trade-offs*. John Wiley and Sons, 1976.
333. Kemper, A., P. C. Lockemann, G. Moerkotte, and H.-D. Walter: Autonomous Objects: A Natural Model for Complex Applications. Journal of Intelligent Information Systems, Vol. 3, pp. 113-150, 1994.
334. Kerschberg, L.: Knowledge Rovers: Cooperative Intelligent Agent Support for Enterprise Information Architectures. P. Kandzia and M. Klusch (Eds.), *Cooperative Information Agents*, Proceedings of First International Workshop CIA-97, Lecture Notes in Artificial Intelligence, Vol. 1202, Springer, 1997.
335. Kerschberg, L.: The Role of Intelligent Agents in Advanced Information Systems. C. Small, P. Douglas, R. Johnson, P. King, and N. Martin (Eds.), *Advances in Databases*, Lecture Notes in Computer Science, Vol. 1271, Springer, 1997.
336. Ketchpel, S.: Coalition Formation Among Autonomous Agents. C. Castelfranchi and J. Muller (Eds.), *From Reactions to Cognition*, Proceedings of MAAMAW'93 Workshop, Springer, LNAI, Vol. 957, 1995.
337. Ketchpel, S.: Forming coalitions in face of uncertain reward. *Proc. AAAI-94 Conference*, 1994.
338. Ketchpel, S.P., H.Garcia-Molina, and A. Paepcke: Shopping models: A flexible architecture for information commerce. *Proceedings of the Second ACM International Conference on Digital Libraries*, 1997.
339. 13-16 Khare, R., and A. Rifkin: Weaving a Web of Trust. The World Wide Web Journal, Volume 2, Number 3, pp. 77-112, 1997.
340. KIF. Knowledge Interchange Format. URL: ¡http://logic.stanford.edu/kif/¿
341. Kim, W., and F. Lochovsky (Eds.): *Object-Oriented Concepts, Databases, and Applications*. Addison-Wesley, Reading (Mass.), 1989.
342. Kim, W., et al.: On resolving schematic heterogeneity in multidatabase systems. Intl. Journal on Distributed and Parallel Databases, Vol. 1:251-279, 1993.
343. King, J.J.: Quist: a system for semantic query optimization in relational databases. *Proc. 7th Int. Conf. on Very Large Databases VLDB-81*, pp. 510–517, 1981.
344. Kinny, D., M. Ljungberg, A. S. Rao, E. Sonenberg, G. Tidhar, and E. Werner: Planned team activity. C. Castelfranchi and E. Werner (Eds.), *Artificial Social Systems*, Amsterdam, Springer, LNAI, Vol. 830, 1994.

345. Klein, M.: Coordination Science: Challenges and Directions. W. Conen and G. Neumann (Eds.), *Coordination Technology for Collaborative Applications*, Springer, LNCS, Vol. 1364, pp. 161–176, 1998.

346. Klusch, M.: Cooperative Recognition of Interdatabase Dependencies. *Proc. Intern. Workshop on Description Logics DL-95*, Rome (Italy), 1995.

347. Klusch, M., and O. Shehory: A Polynomial Kernel-Oriented Coalition Algorithm for Rational Information Agents. *Proc. 2nd International Conference on Multi-Agent Systems ICMAS-96*, Kyoto (Japan), AAAI Press, 1996.

348. Klusch, M.: *Cooperative Information Agents on the Internet*, PhD Thesis (in German), University of Kiel, Germany, Kovac, ISBN 3-86064-746-6, 1996.

349. Klusch, M., and G. Weiß(Eds.): *Cooperative Information Agents II*, Proc. 2nd Intern. Workshop CIA-98, Paris (France), Springer, LNAI, Vol. 1435, 1998.

350. Knoblock,C.A., and J.L. Ambite: Agents for information gathering. J. Bradshaw (Ed.), *Software Agents*, MIT Press, Chapter 16, 1997.

351. Knoblock, C.A., Y. Arens, and C.N. Hsu: Cooperating agents for information retrieval. *Proceedings of 2nd Int'l Conf. on Cooperative Information System*, pages 122–133, Toronto, Canada, 1994.

352. Knoblock, C.A., Y. Arens, and C-H. Nsu: Query Processing in the SIMS Information Mediator. M. Huhns, and M.P. Singh (Eds.), *Readings in Agents*, Morgan Kaufmann, 1998.

353. Kohonen, T.: *Self-Organization and Associative Memory*. Springer-Verlag, Berlin, 1989.

354. Komorowski, J., and J. Zytkow (Eds.): *Principles of Data Mining and Knowledge Discovery*. Proc. First European Symposium PKDD-97, Trondheim (Norway), 1997.

355. Kotz, D., R. Gray, S. Nog, D. Rus, S. Chawla, and G. Cybenko: Mobile agents for mobile computing. D. Milojicic, F. Douglis, and R. Wheeler (Eds.), *Mobility, Mobile Agents and Process Migration— An Edited Collection*. Addison Wesley, 1998.

356. Kraus, S.: Negotiation and cooperation in multi-agent environments. Artificial Intelligence, Vol. 94(1-2):79–98, 1997.

357. Kraus, S., J. Wilkenfeld, and G. Zlotkin: Multiagent negotiation under time constraints. AI Journal, Vol. 75(2):297–345, 1995.

358. Krause, S., and T. Magedanz: Mobile service agents enabling intelligence on demand in telecommunications. *Proc. of IEEE GLOBCOM-96 Global Communications Conference*, 1996. http://www.tinac.com

359. Kumar, V.: Algorithms for Constraint Satisfaction Problems: A Survey. AI Magazine, Vol. 13(1):32-44, 1992.

360. Kuokka, D., and L. Harrada: Supporting Information Retrieval via Matchmaking. C. Knoblock and A. Levy (Eds.), *Working Notes of the AAAI Spring Symposium Series on Information Gathering from Distributed, Heterogeneous Environments*, Stanford (CA, USA), AAAI Press, March 1995.

361. Kuokka, D., and L. Harada: Integrating Information via Matchmaking. Journal of Intelligent Information Systems, Vol. 6(2/3), pp. 261-279, 1996.

362. Kushmerick, N., D. Weld, and R. Doorenbos: Wrapper Induction for Information Extraction. *Proceedings of the 16th International Joint Conference on Artificial Intelligence (IJCAI'97)*, 1997.

363. Labrou, Y., and T. Finin: A semantics approach for KQML - a general purpose communication language for software agents. *Proceedings of Conference on Information and Knowledge Management CIKM-94*, ACM Press, 1994.

364. Laird, J.E., D. J. Pearson, and S. B. Huffman: Knowledge-Directed Adaptation in Multi-Level Agents. Journal of Intelligent Information Systems, vol. 9, pp. 261-276, 1997.

365. Lang, K.: Newsweeder. *Proceedings of the 12th International Conference on Machine Learning ML-95*, Morgan Kaufmann, 1995.
366. Lange, D.B., and D. T. Chang: IBM Aglets Workbench: Programming mobile agents in Java. IBM White Paper, 1996.
367. Lange, D.B., and M. Oshima: *Programming and deploying Java mobile agents with Aglets.* Addison Wesley, 1998.
368. Larson, R.R.: Bibliometrics of the world wide web: An exploratory analysis of the intellectual structure of cyberspace. *Proc. 1996 Annual ASIS Meeting*, 1996.
369. Lashkari, Y.: *Webhound.* Master's Thesis, MIT Media Laboratory Technical Report, 1995.
370. Lau, H.-S., and L.-G. Zhao: Optimal Ordering Policies with Two Suppliers when Lead Times and Demands Are All Stochastic. European Journal of Operational Research, Vol. 68, pp. 120 - 133, 1993.
371. Lawrence, S.R., and C.L. Giles: Searching the world wide web. *Science*, Vol. 280:98–100, 1998.
372. Lécluse, C., and P. Richard: Modelling complex structures in object-oriented databases. *Proc. ACM Symp. on Principles of Database Systems*, pp. 362–369, Philadelphia, PA, 1989.
373. Lécluse, C., and P. Richard: The O_2 data model. *Proc. Intl. Conf. On Very Large Data Bases VLDB-89*, pp. 411–422, Amsterdam, 1989.
374. Lesser, V., et al.: BIG: A Resource-Bounded Information Gathering Agent. *Proceedings of the Fifteenth National Conference on Artificial Intelligence AAAI-98.* Also available as University of Massachusetts Technical Report UMASS-CS-TR 1998-03.
375. Levesque, H., P. Cohen, and J. Nunes: On acting together. *Proceedings of The 1990 AAAI Conference*, pages 94–99, Boston (MA, USA), 1990.
376. Levy, A.Y., A. O. Mendelzon, Y. Sagiv, and D. Srivastava: Answering queries using views. *Proc. Intl. ACM Symp. on Principles of Database Systems*, pp. 95-104, 1995.
377. Levy, A.Y., A. Rajaraman, and J. J. Ordihe: Querying heterogeneous information sources using source descriptions. *Proc. of Intl. Conf. on Very Large Data Bases VLDB-96*, pp. 251-262, 1996.
378. Levy, A.Y., A. Rajaraman, and J. D. Ullman: Answering queries using limited external query processors. *Proc. ACM Symp. on Principles of Database Systems*, pp. 227-237, 1996.
379. Lewicki, L., D. Saunders, and J. Minton: *Essentials of Negotiation.* Irwin, 1997.
380. Lewis, D.D.: Information retrieval and the statistics of large data sets. *Proc. NRC Massive Data Sets Workshop*, Washington, DC, 1996.
381. Lewis, D.D.: Challenges in machine learning for text classification. *Proc. 9th Annual Conference on Computational Learning Theory*, New York (NY, USA), 1997.
382. Lewis, M.: Designing for Human-Agent Interaction. AI Magazine, Summer 1998.
383. Lieberman, H.: Letizia: An Agent That Assists Web Browsing. *Proc. 14th International Joint Conference on Artificial Intelligence*, Montreal, August 1995.
384. Lieberman, H.: Autonomous Interface Agents. *Proc. ACM Conference on Computers and Human Interfaces (CHI-97)*, Atlanta, March 1997.
385. Lieberman, H.: Integrating User Interface Agents with Conventional Applications. *Proc. ACM Conference on Intelligent User Interfaces*, San Francisco, January 1998.

386. Lieberman, H., N. Van Dyke, A. Vivacqua: Let's Browse: A Collaborative Browsing Agent. *Proc. International Conference on Intelligent User Interfaces*, Redondo Beach (CA, USA), January 1999

387. Lin, L-J.: Self-improving reactive agents based on reinforcement learning, planning, and teaching. Machine Learning, Vol. 8:293–321, 1992.

388. Linden, G., S. Hanks, and N. Lesh: Interactive Assessment of User Preference Models: The Automated Travel Assistant. *Proceedings of the Sixth International Conference on User Modeling*, 1997.

389. Litwin, W., L. Mark, and N. Roussopoulos: Interoperability of multiple autonomous databases. ACM Computing Surveys, Vol. 22(3):267-293, 1990.

390. Litzkow, M., and M. Solomon: Supporting checkpointing and process migration outside the Unix kernel. *Proceedings of the 1992 Winter USENIX Technical Conference*, pages 283–290, 1992.

391. Liu, K.: *Semiotics Applied to Information Systems Development*. Ph.D. Thesis, University of Twente, Enschede (Holland), 1993.

392. Liu, J.S., and K. Sycara: Coordination of Multiple Agents for Production Management. Annals of Operations Research, Vol. 75, pp. 235 - 289, 1997.

393. Livny, M., and M. Melman: Load balancing in homogeneous broadcast distributed systems. *Proceedings of the ACM Computer Network Performance Symposium*, April 1982.

394. Lochbaum, K.: *Using Collaborative Plans to Model the Intentional Structure of Discourse*. PhD thesis, Harvard University, Available as Tech Report TR-25-94, 1994.

395. Lochbaum, K., B.J. Grosz, and C. Sidner: Models of plans to support communication: An initial report. *Proceedings of The 1990 AAAI Conference*, pages 485–490, Boston, MA, 1990.

396. Lockier, P.C., P. Edwards, C.L. Green, and T.C. Lukins: Exploiting Learning Technologies for World Wide Web Agents. IEE Colloquium on Intelligent World Wide Web Agents, Digest No: 97/118, IEE, Savoy Place, London, 1997.

397. Loucopoulos, P., et al.: Using the ekd-approach - the modelling component. Wp/t2.1/umist/1 april 1997, UMIST, 1997.

398. Loucopoulos, P., and V. Karakostas: *System requirements engineering*. McGraw-Hill Book Company, 1995.

399. Loui, R., and J. Norman: Rationales and argument moves. Artificial Intelligence and Law Journal, Vol. 3(3), 1995.

400. Lucco, S., O. Sharp, and R. Wahbe: Omniware: A universal substrate for web programming. World Wide Web Journal, Vol. 1, December 1995.

401. Luck, K. von, and B. Nebel and C. Peltason and A. Schmiedel: *The BACK System*. Technical Report 41, Tech. University of Berlin, 1987.

402. Luke, S., L. Spector, D. Rager, and J. Hendler: Ontology-based Web agents. *Proceedings of First International Conference on Autonomous Agents (Agents-97)*, Marina del Rey, USA, 1997.

403. Lukose, R.M., and B.A. Huberman: Surfing as a real option. In *Proc. 4th International Conference on Computational Economics*, 1998.

404. Lycos. http://www.lycos.com.

405. Lynch, N.: *Distributed Algorithms*. Morgan Kaufmann, 1996.

406. Maes, P.: Agents that reduce work and information overload. Communications of the ACM, Vol. 37(7):30–40, July 1994.

407. Maes, P., and R. Kozierok: Learning interface agents. *Proc. Eleventh National Conference on Artificial Intelligence*, pages 459–464, July 1993.

408. Maes, P., and B. Shneiderman: Intelligent Software Agents vs. User-Controlled Direct Manipulation: A Debate. *Proc. ACM Conference on Computers and Human Interface (CHI-97)*, Atlanta, March 1997.

409. Magedanz, T., M. Breugst, I. Busse, and S. Covaci: Integrating mobile agent technology and CORBA middleware. AgentLink Newsletter, Issue 1, November 1998. http://www.agentlink.org (Newsletter)

410. Mahesh, K., and S. Nirenburg: A Situated Ontology for Practical NLP. *Proc. of Workshop on Basic Ontological Issues in Knowledge Sharing*, Int'l Joint Conf. on AI (IJCAI-95), Montreal, Canada, August 1995.

411. Malone, T.: Free on the Range: Tom Malone on the Implications of the Digital Age. IEEE Internet Computing, Vol. 1(3), pp. 8–20.

412. Malone, T., and K. Crowston: The Interdisciplinary Study of Coordination. ACM Computing Surveys, Vol. 26(1), pp. 87–119, 1994.

413. Malone, T., R. Fikes, K. Grant, and M. Howard: Enterprise: A Market-like Task Scheduler for Distributed Computing Environments. B.A. Huberman (Ed.), *The Ecology of Computation*, North-Holland Publishing Company, 1988.

414. Manola, F., and et al.: Supporting cooperation in enterprise scale ditributed object systems. In M.P. Papazoglou and G. Schlageter (Eds.), *Cooperative Information Systems: Trends and Directions*, Academic Press, London, 1998.

415. Marchal, B., N. Mikula, B. Peat and D. Webber: Guidelines for using XML for Electronic Data Interchange, Version 0.03. M. Bryan (Ed.), 21 October 1997. http:// www.geocities.com/WallStreet/Floor/5815/guide.htm

416. Mark, L., and N. Roussopoulos: Information interchange between self-describing databases. IEEE Data Engineering, Vol. 10:46-52,1987.

417. Marsh, S.: *Formalising Trust as a Computational Concept*. PhD Thesis, University of Stirling, April 1994.

418. Marzo, G. Di, M. Muhugusa, and C. Tschudin: Survey of theories for mobile agents. Working paper, The Computing Science Center, University of Geneva, Switzerland, November 1995.

419. Mas-Colell, A., M.D. Whinston, and J.R. Green: *Microeconomic Theory*. Oxford University Press, 1995. Specially Chp. 23. Incentives and Mechanism Design.

420. Matos, N., C. Sierra, and N. Jennings: Determining successful negotiation strategies: an evolutionary approach. *Proc. of Second International Conference on Multiagent Systems ICMAS-98*, Paris, IEEE Press, 1998.

421. McAfee, R. P., and J. McMillan: Auctions and bidding. Journal of Economic Literature, Vol. 25, 1987.

422. McGregor, R.M.: The evolving technology of classification-based knowledge representation systems. John. F. Sowa (Ed.), *Principles of Semantic Networks*, Morgan Kaufmann, pp. 385-400, 1991.

423. McKnight, L.W., and J.P. Bailey: Internet economics: when constituencies collide in Cyberspace. Internet Computing, Nov/Dec 1997.

424. Meadows, C.: Detecting Attacks on Mobile Agents. *Proceedings of the DARPA workshop on foundations for secure mobile code*, Monterey CA, March 1997.

425. Meeker, M., and S. Pearson: *The internet retailing report*. Tech. Rep., Morgan Stanley, 1997. http://www.ms.com.

426. Menczer, F.: ARACHNID: Adaptive retrieval agents choosing heuristic neighborhoods for information discovery. *Proc. 14th International Conference on Machine Learning*, 1997.

427. Menczer, F.: *Life-like agents: Internalizing local cues for reinforcement learning and evolution*. PhD thesis, University of California, San Diego, 1998.

428. Menczer, F., and R.K. Belew: Adaptive information agents in distributed textual environments. *Proc. 2nd International Conference on Autonomous Agents*, Minneapolis, MN, 1998.

429. Menczer, F., and R.K. Belew: *Adaptive retrieval agents: Internalizing local context and scaling up to the web.* Technical Report CS98–579, University of California, San Diego, 1998.

430. Menczer, F., and R.K. Belew: Local selection. *Evolutionary Programming VII*, Springer, LNCS, Vol. 1447, 1998.

431. Menczer, F., R. Belew, and W. Willuhn: Artificial life applied to adaptive information agents. *Working Notes of the AAAI Symposium on Information Gathering from Distributed, Heterogeneous Databases*, AAAI Press, 1995.

432. Mertoguno, J.S. and W. Lin: Distributed knowledge-base: adaptive multi-agents approach. *Proceedings International Joint Symposia on Intelligence and Systems*, Rockville (Maryland, USA), November 1996.

433. Metacrawler. http://www.metacrawler.com.

434. Michelis, G. De, and et al. Cooperative information systems: a manifesto. M.P. Papazoglou and G. Schlageter (Eds.), *Cooperative Information Systems: Trends and Directions*, Academic Press, 1998.

435. Mikrokosmos Ontology. http://crl.nmsu.edu/Research/Projects/mikro/ontology/onto-intro-page.html

436. Milliner, S., A. Bouguettaya, and M.P. Papazoglou: A scalable architecture for autonomous heterogenuous database interactions. *Proceedings of the 21st VLDB Conference, Zurich*, 1995.

437. Milojicic, D.S., D. Bolinger, M. E. Zurko, and M. S. Mazer: *Mobile Objects and Agents.* Technical report, The Open Group Research Institute, 1996.

438. Minami, K., and T. Suzuku: JMT (Java-Based Moderator Templates) for Multi-Agent Planning.   *Proc. OOPSLA-97 Workshop on Java-based Paradigms for Agent Facilities*, 1997.

439. Minar, N., A. Moukas, and P. Maes: Friend of a Friend Finder. Software Agents Group, MIT Media Laboratory, Working paper, 1998.

440. Minsky, M.: *Society of Mind.* Simon and Schuster, 1986.

441. Minsky, Y., R. van Renesse, F. B. Schneider, and S. D. Stoller: Cryptographic support for fault-tolerant distributed computing. *Proceedings of the Seventh ACM SIGOPS European Workshop*, pages 109–114, September 1996.

442. Mitchell, M.: *An Introduction to Genetic Algorithms.* MIT Press, 1996.

443. Mitchell, T.: *Machine Learning*, McGraw-Hill, 1997.

444. Mogul, J., F. Douglis, A. Feldmann, and B. Krishnamurthy: Potential benefits of delta-encoding and data compression for HTTP. *Proceedings of ACM SIGCOMM'97 Conference*, pages 181–194, September 1997. Available from http://www.research.digital.com/wrl/techreports/abstracts/97.4.html

445. Moizumi, K.: *The mobile agent planning problem.* PhD thesis, Thayer School of Engineering, Dartmouth College, November 1998.

446. MOLE. University of Stuttgart, Institute for Parallel and Distributed Computer Systems. http://www.informatik.uni-stuttgart.de/ipvr/vs/projekte/mole.html

447. Monge, A.E., and C.P. Elkan: The WEBFIND tool for finding scientific papers over the worldwide web. *Proceedings of the 3rd International Congress on Computer Science Research*, 1996.

448. Motro, A.: Multiplex: A Formal Model for Multidatabases and Its Implementation. ISSE Department, George Mason University, Fairfax, VA, Technical Report ISSE-TR-95-10, 1995.

449. Motro, A., and P. Smets: Uncertainty Management in Information Systems: from Needs to Solutions. Norwall, MA: Kluwer Academic Publishers, 1996.

450. Moukas, A.: Amalthaea: Information Filtering and Discovery using a Multi-Agent Evolving Ecosystem. *Proceedings of the Conference on Practical Application of Intelligent Agents and Multi-Agent Technology PAAM-96*, London, 1996. also in: Journal of Applied AI, Vol. 11, No. 5, 1997.

451. Moukas, A.: An Evolving Multi-Agent Information Filtering and Discovery Sytem for the WWW. Journal of Autonomous Agents and MultiAgent Systems, Vol. 1(1):59-88, 1998.

452. Moukas, A., K. Chandrinos, P. Maes: Trafficopter: A Distributed Collection System Traffic Information. M. Klusch and G. Weiß(Eds.), *Cooperative Information Agents II*, Proceedings of CIA-98 Workshop, Paris (France), Springer, LNAI, Vol. 1435, 1998.

453. Muhugusa, M.: Implementing distributed services with mobile code: The case of the Messenger environment. *Proceedings of the IASTED International Conference on Parallel and Distributed Systems (Euro-PDS'98)*, Austria, July 1998.

454. Mullen, T., and M.P. Wellman: A simple computational market for network information systems. *Proceedings of ICMAS-95*, 1995.

455. Mullen, T., and M.P. Wellman: Market-based negotiation for digital library services. *Proc. Second USENIX Workshop on Electronic Commerce*, 1996.

456. Mylopoulos, J., A. Borgida, M. Jarke, and M. Koubarakis: Telos: representing knowledge about information systems. ACM Transactions on Information Systems, Vol. 8(4):325–362, 1990.

457. Nagao, K., and A. Takeuchi: Social interaction: Multimodal conversation with social agents. *Proc. of AAAI-94 Conference*, Seattle, 1994.

458. Naiman, C., A. Ouksel: A Classification of Semantic Conflicts. Journal of Organizational Computing, Vol. 5(2), 167-193, 1995.

459. Nass, C.S., J. Tauber, and R. Ellen: Computers are social actors. *Proc. of CHI-94 Conference*, Boston, 1994.

460. National Research Council. *Realizing the Information Future: the Internet and Beyond.* National Academy Press, 1994.

461. Navathe S., H. Garcia Molina, J. Hammer, K.Ireland, Y. Papakostantinou, J.Ullman, J. Widom: The TSIMMIS Project: Integration of Heterogeneous Information Sources. *Proceedings of IPSJ Conference*, pp. 7–18, Tokyo, Japan, October 1994. (Also available via anonymous FTP from host db.stanford.edu, file /pub/chawathe/1994/tsimmis-overview.ps.).

462. Nebel, B.: Terminological cycles: Semantics and computational properties. J.F. Sowa (Ed.), *Principles of Semantic Networks*, Chapter 11, Morgan Kaufmann, 1991.

463. Necula, G.C. and P. Lee: The design and implementation of a certifying compiler. In ACM SIGPLAN'98 Conference on Programming Language Design and Implementation, June 1998.

464. Nestorov S., S. Abiteboul, and R. Motwani: Inferring Structure in Semistructured Data . *Proc. Workshop on Management of Semistructured Data*, Tucson (AZ, USA), May 1997.

465. NetSage Sage. http://www.netsage.com

466. Newell, A.: *Unified Theories of Cognition.* Harvard University Press, 1990.

467. Nicola, R. De, G. L. Ferrari, and R. Pugliese: Coordinating Mobile Agents via Blackboards and Access Rights. D. Garlan and D. Le Métayer (Eds.), *Coordination Languages and Models, Proceedings of COORDINATION '97*, Springer, LNCS, Vol. 1282, pp. 220–237, 1997.

468. Nicosia, F.: *Consumer Decision Processes: Marketing and Advertising Implications*. Prentice Hall, 1966.
469. Nodine, M.: The InfoSleuth Agent System. M. Klusch, and G. Weiß(Eds.), *Cooperative Information Agents II*, Proc. Intern. CIA-98 Workshop, Paris (France), Springer, LNAI, Vol. 1435, 1998.
470. Nodine, M. and J. Fowler: An overview of active information gathering in InfoSleuth. *Proceedings International Conference on Autonomous Agents (Agents-99)*, Seattle (WA, USA), 1999. submitted.
471. Nodine, M., W. Bohrer, and A.H.N. Ngu: Semantic Brokering over Dynamic Heterogeneous Data Sources in InfoSleuth. *Proc. International Conference on Data Engineering* ICDE-99, 1999.
472. Nog, S., S. Chawla, and D. Kotz: *An RPC mechanism for transportable agents*. Technical Report PCS-TR96–280, Department of Computer Science, Dartmouth College, March 1996.
473. Noriega, P.: *Elementos para una caracterización formal de los diálogos: Aspectos estructurales*. Tech. Rep. 95-N1, LANIA, Xalapa, MX, 1995.
474. Noriega, P.: *Agent-Mediated Auctions: The Fishmarket Metaphor*. PhD thesis, Universitat Autònoma de Barcelona, 1998.
475. Noriega, P., and C. Sierra: Towards layered dialogical agents. J. Müller, M. Wooldridge, and N. R. Jennings (Eds.), *Intelligent Agents III*, Springer, LNAI, Vol. 1193, 1996.
476. Noriega, P., J.A. Rodriguez-Aguilar, F.J. Martin, P. Garcia, and C. Sierra: Competitive Scenarios for Heterogeneous Trading Agents. *Proc. Second International Conference on Autonomous Agents* Agents-98, pp. 293-300, 1998.
477. Norman, T., N. Jennings, P. Faratin, and E. Mamdani: Designing and implementing a multi-agent architecture for business process management. J. Müller, N. Jennings, and M. Wooldridge (Eds.), *Intelligent Agents III*, Springer, LNAI, Vol. 1193, pages 261–275, 1996.
478. North, D. C.: *Institutions, Institutional Change and Economic Performance*. Cambridge Univ. Press, Cambridge, U.K., 1990.
479. Oates, T., M.V. Nagendra Prasad, and V. Lesser: Cooperative information gathering: A distributed problem-solving approach. *IEE Proceedings on Software Engineering*, Special Issue on Agent-based Systems, Vol. 144(1), 1997.
480. Object Management Group's (OMG) Mobile Agent Facility (MAF). http://www.omg.org/library/schedule/CF-RFP3.htm
481. Object Request Broker Task Force. The Common Object Request Broker: Architecture and Specification, December 1993. Revision 1.2, Draft 29.
482. OCDE. *Measuring electronic commerce*. Tech. Rep., OCDE Committee for Information, Computer and Communication Policy, Paris, 1997. OCDE/GD(97)185.
483. Odyssey. General Magic Odyssey: http://www.genmagic.com/html/more-odyssey.html
484. OFX. Open Financial Exchange. http://www.ofx.net
485. OMG. Web site of object management group. http://ruby.omg.org/index.html.
486. OnSale. http://www.onsale.com/
487. OnSale Exchange. http://www.onsale.com/exchange.htm
488. Ontologies. http://www.dfki.uni-kl.de/ vega/CoMem/Ontology/onto-design-gruber/subsection312.html, Plan Ontology Construction Group (POCG): KRSL 2.0.2 Ontology Hierarchy.
489. Onyshkevych, Boyan, and S. Nirenburg: Lexicon, Ontology, and Text Meaning. James Pustejovsky (Eds.), *Lexical Semantics and Knowledge Representation*, Springer.

490. Open Buying on the Internet: A Standard for Business-to-Business Internet Commerce. SupplyWorks white paper. http://www.supplyworks.com/obi/white-paper.html

491. Open Profiling Standard. http://developer.netscape.com/ops/ops.html

492. Ortiz, C.L.: Introspective and elaborative processes in rational agents. Annals of Mathematics and Artificial Intelligence, 1998. submitted.

493. Ouksel, A.: SCOPES: Technical Specifications. CISORS Lab, Working Paper 1, 1998.

494. Ouksel, A., and I. Ahmed: Plausible Inference of Context in Heterogeneous Information Systems *Proc. 5th International Workshop on Information Systems and Technology*, Amsterdam, Dec 1995.

495. Ouksel, A., and I. Ahmed: Coordinating Knowledge Elicitation to Support Context Construction in Cooperative Information Systems. *Proc. of Intern. Conference on Cooperative Information Systems CoopIS-96*, Brussels, Belgium, June 1996.

496. Ouksel, A., and I. Ahmed: Ontologies are not the Panacea in Data Integration. Journal of Distributed and Parallel Databases, Vol. 7, pp. 1-29, 1999.

497. Ouksel, A., and A. Ghazal: Subsumption in Constraint Query Languages Involving Disjunction of Range Constraints. *Proc. International Symposium on Mathematics and Artificial Intelligence*, 1994.

498. Ouksel, A., and C. Naiman: Semantic Mechanisms for Cooperation in Heterogeneous Database Systems. *Proc. International IEEE Conference on Man and Cybernetics*, October 1992.

499. Ouksel, A., and C. Naiman: Coordinating Context Building in Heterogeneous Information Systems. Journal of Intelligent Information Systems, Vol. 3, pp. 151-183, 1994.

500. Ouksel, A., and A. Sheth (Eds.), Semantic Interoperation in Global Information Systems. Special Issue of Journal ACM SIGMOD Record, 1999.

501. Padget, J., and R. Bradford: *A π-calculus model of the Spanish fish market.* Tech. rep., School of Mathematical Sciences. University of Bath, 1997.

502. Pannu, A. and K. Sycara: A Personal Text Filtering Agent. *Proceedings of the AAAI Stanford Spring Symposium on Machine Learning and Information Access*, Stanford (CA, USA), March 25-27, 1996.

503. Papakonstantinou, Y., H. Garcia-Molina, J. Ulman: MedMaker: A mediation system based on declarative specification, 1995, avaible at ftp://db.stanford.edu/pub/papakonstantinou/1995/medmaker.ps.

504. Papakonstantinou, Y., H. Garcia-Molina, J. Ulman and Ashish Gupta: A query translation scheme for rapid implementation of wrappers, 1995. ftp://db.stanford.edu/pub/papakonstantinou/1995/querytran-extended.ps.

505. Papakonstantinou, Y., H. Garcia-Molina and J. Widom: Object Exchange Across Heterogeneous Information Sources. *Proceedings of IEEE International Conference on Data Engineering*, pp. 251–260, Taipei, Taiwan, March 1995. (Also available via anonymous FTP from host db.stanford.edu file /pub/papakonstantinou/1994/object-exchange-heterogeneous-is.ps.)

506. Papazoglou, M.P., A. Delis, A. Bouguettaya, and M. Haghjoo: Class library support for workflow environments and applications. IEEE Transactions on Computer Systems, Vol. 46(6):673–686, June 1997.

507. Papazoglou, M.P., S. Laufmann, and T.K. Sellis: An organizational framework for cooperating intelligent information systems. Int'l Journal of Cooperative Information Systems, Vol. 1(1):169–202, 1992.

508. Papazoglou, M.P., and S. Milliner: Subject-based organization of the information space in multi-database networks. *Proceedings of the CAiSE'98: 10th*

Int'l Conf. on Advanced Information Systems Engineering, Pisa, pages 251–272, June 1998.

509. Papazoglou, M.P., and G. Schlageter: *Cooperative Information Systems: Trends and Directions*. Academic Press, London, 1998.

510. Park, S., E. Durfee, and W. P. Birmingham: Advantages of Strategic Thinking in Multiagent Contracts (A Mechanism and Analysis). *Proceedings of the Second International Conference on Multi-Agent Systems (ICMAS-96)*, pp. 259–266, 1996.

511. Park, S., E. Durfee, and W. P. Birmingham: Emergent properties of a market-based digital library with strategic agents. *Proceedings of the Third International Conference on Multi-Agent Systems (ICMAS-98)*, pp. 230–237, 1998.

512. Pasula, H.: *Design of a collaborative planning system*. Harvard University, Senior Honors Thesis, 1996.

513. Patil,R., et al.: The DARPA knowledge sharing effort. *Proc. of the 3rd Int'l Conference on Principles of Knowledge Representation and Reasoning*. Morgan-Kaufmann, 1992.

514. Patil, R.S., R. E. Fikes, P. F. Patel-Schneider, D. McKay, T. Finin, T. Gruber, and R. Neches: The DARPA knowledge sharing effort: Progress report. In *[296]*, pages 243–254. 1998. (Reprinted from *Proceedings of the Third International Conference on Principles of Knowledge Representation and Reasoning, 1992*).

515. Pazzani, M., J. Muramatsu, D. Billsus: Syskill & Weber: Identifying interesting web sites. *Proc. Fourteenth National Conference on Artificial Intelligence*, pages 54–61, Menlo Park, CA, 1997. AAAI Press/MIT Press.

516. Pearl,J.: *Probabilistic Reasoning in Intelligent Systems*. Morgan Kaufman, Palo Alto, CA, 1991.

517. Peine, H.: Security concepts and implementations for the Ara mobile agent system. *Proceedings of the Seventh IEEE Workshop on Enabling Technologies: Infrastructure for the Collaborative Enterprises*, Stanford University, USA, June 1998.

518. Peine, H., and T. Stolpmann: The architecture of the ARA platform for mobile agents. K. Rothermel and R. Populescu-Zeletin (Eds.), *Mobile Agents*, Proceedings of the First International Workshop on Mobile Agents MA-97, Springer, LNCS, Vol. 1219, 1997.

519. Peirce, C.: *Collected Papers of Ch.S. Pierce*. Hartshorne and Weiß(Eds.), Cambridge (MA, USA), 1990.

520. Pentland, A.P.: Wearable Intelligence. Scientific American, Vol. 9(4), 1998.

521. Personal Privacy Preferences (P3) Project Architecture Working Group. General Overview of the P3P Architecture. World Wide Web Consortium (W3C) Working Draft, 22 October 1997. http://www.w3.org/TR/WD-P3P-arch.html

522. PersonaLogic. http://www.personalogic.com/

523. Persuader. http://almond.srv.cs.cmu.edu/afs/cs/user/katia/www/persuader.html

524. Petrie, C.J.: Agent-based Engineering, the Web, and Intelligence. IEEE Expert, Vol. 11(6):24–29, December 1996.

525. Petrie, C.: Simple wins. IEEE Internet Computing, Vol. 2(4), 1998.

526. Pham, V.A., and A. Karmouch: Mobile Software agents: An overview. IEEE Communications, July 1998.

527. Picard, R.W.: *Affective Computing*, MIT Press, Cambridge, 1997. http://www-white.media.mit.edu/vismod/demos/affect/

528. Plaza, E., P. Noriega, and C. Sierra: Competing agents in agent-mediated institutions. International Journal of Human Computer Interactions, 1998. submitted.

529. Plevyak, J., and A. Chien: Type directed cloning for object-oriented programs. *Proceedings of the workshop for Languages and Compilers for Parallel Computers*, Columbus, Ohio, 1995.

530. Plu, M.: Software technologies for building agent based systems in telecommunication networks. N.R. Jennings and M. Wooldridge (Eds.), *Agent Technology*, Springer, 1998.

531. Pollack, M.E.: Plans as complex mental attitudes. P.N. Cohen, J.L. Morgan, and M.E. Pollack (Eds.), *Intentions in Communication*, Bradford Books, MIT Press, 1990.

532. Porter, M.: An algorithm for suffix stripping. Program, Vol. 14(3):130 138, 1980.

533. Praaken, H.: *Logical Tools for Modelling Legal Argument*. PhD thesis, Free University of Amsterdam, 1993.

534. Prasad, M.V.N., V. Lesser: Learning situation-specific coordinating in cooperative multi-agent systems. Journal on Autonomous Agents and Multi-Agent Systems, 1998. submitted.

535. Prasad, M.V.N., V.R. Lesser, and S.E. Lander: Learning organizational roles in a heterogeneous multi-agent system. *Proc. of Second International Conference on Multi-Agent Systems ICMAS-96*, Kyoto (Japan), AAAI Press, 1996.

536. *Premenos' Electronic Commerce Resource Guide to ANSI X12 and UN/EDIFACT Standards*, http://www.premenos.com/standards/

537. Pressman, R.S.: *Software Engineering: A Practitioner's Approach*. McGraw Hill, New York, 4th edition, 1997.

538. Prins, R.: *Developing Business Objects: A Framework driven approach*. McGraw-Hill Publishinbg Company, Berkshire (England), 1996.

539. *Proceedings of the Workshop on Management of Structured Data*, Tucson (AZ, USA), 1997.

540. *Proceedings of Workshop on Deception, fraud and trust in agent societies* at International Conference on Automous Agents (Agents-98), Minneapolis/St.Paul (USA), May 9, 1998.

541. Ranganathan, M., A. Acharya, S. Sharma, and J. Saltz: Network-aware mobile programs. *Proceedings of the 1997 USENIX Technical Conference*, pp. 91–104, 1997.

542. Rao, A.S., and M.P. Georgeff: BDI- Agents: From Theory to Practice. *Proceedings of the First International Conference on Multi-Agent Systems (ICMAS-95)*, San Fransisco (CA, USA), pp. 312-319, June 1995.

543. Reagle, J.: *Trust in a Cryptographic Economy and Digital Security Deposits: Protocols and Policies*. Master Thesis, Massachusetts Institute of Technology, May, 1996.

544. Rescher, N.: *Dialectics: A controversy-oriented approach to the theory of knowledge*. SUNY, 1977.

545. Resnick, P.: Filtering Information on the Internet. 1997. available at http://www.sciam.com/0397issue/0397resnick.html

546. Resnick, P., and J. Miller: PICS: Internet Access Controls Without Censorship. Communications of the ACM, Vol. 39(10), pp. 87-93, 1996.

547. Resnick, P., R. Zeckhauser R. and C. Avery: *Roles for Electronic Brokers*. United States, Cambridge, 1995.

548. Resnik, P., N. Iacovou, M. Sushak, P. Bergstrom, and J. Riedl: Grouplens: An Open Architecture for Collaborative Filtering of Netnews. *Proceedings of Conference on Computer Supported Cooperative Work (CSCW'94)*, 1994.

549. Rhodes, B.J.: Remembrance Agent: A continuously running automated information retrieval system. *Proceedings of The First International Conference on The Practical Application Of Intelligent Agents and Multi Agent Technology PAAM-96*, London (UK), pp. 487-495, April 1996.
550. Rich, C., and C. L. Sidner: *Adding a collaborative agent to direct-manipulation interfaces*. Technical Report 96-11, Mitsubishi Electric Research Laboratories, Cambridge, MA, May 1996.
551. Rijsbergen, C.J. van: *Information Retrieval.* 2nd edition, Butterworths, London, 1979.
552. Riordan, A. O., and H. Sorensen: An intelligent agent for high-precision information filtering. *Proceedings of the CIKM-95 Conference*, 1995.
553. Riordan, J. and B. Schneier: Environmental Key Generation Towards Clueless Agents. In [690], April 1998.
554. Rivest, R.L., L. Adleman, and L. Dertouzos: On Data Banks and Privacy Homomorphisms. DeMillo, R.A. et. al., *Foundations of Secure Computation*, Academic Press, 1978.
555. Rivest, R.L.: Chaffing and Winnowing: Confidentiality without Encryption. http://theory.lcs.mit.edu/~rivest/chaffing.txt, April 1998.
556. Rivlin, E., R. Botafogo, and B. Shneiderman: Navigating in hyperspace: designing a structure-based toolbox. Communications of the ACM, Vol. 37(2):87–96, 1994.
557. RMI and Java Distributed Computing. SunSoft white paper, 1997. http://www.javasoft.com/features/1997/nov/rmi.html
558. Rockafellar, R.T.: *Convex Analysis.* Princeton University Press, 1970.
559. Rodríguez, J. A., P. Noriega, P., C. Sierra, and J. Padget: FM96.5: A Java-based electronic auction house. *Proceedings of Second International Conference on The Practical Application of Intelligent Agents and Multi-Agent Technology (PAAM-97)*, London (UK), 1997.
560. Rodríguez-Aguilar, J. A., F. Martín, P. Noriega, P. Garcia, and C. Sierra: Towards a test-bed for trading agents in electronic auction markets. AI Communications, Vol. 11(1), 1998.
561. Röscheisen, M., M. Baldonado, K. Chang, L. Gravano, S.P. Ketchpel, and A. Päpcke: The Stanford InfoBus and its service layers. *Proc. MeDoc Dagstuhl Workshop: Electronic Publishing and Digital Libraries in Computer Science.* To appear.
562. Rogerson, D.: *Inside COM: Microsoft's Component Object Model.* Microsoft Press, 1997.
563. Rosenfeld, R.: *Adaptive Statistical Language Modeling: A Maximum Entropy Approach.* PhD Thesis, Carnegie Mellon University, Pittsburgh (PA, USA), 1994.
564. Rosenschein, J.S., and G. Zlotkin: *Rules of Encounter: Designing Conventions for Automated Negotiation among Computers.* The MIT Press, 1994.
565. Roth, V.: Secure Recording of Itineraries through Co-operating Agents. *Proceedings of 4th ECOOP Workshop on Mobile Object Systems*, Brussels, July 1998.
566. Roth, M.T., P. Scharz: Don't Scrap It, Wrap it! A Wrapper Architecture for Legacy Data Sources. *Proc. of the 23rd Int. Conf. on Very Large Databases VLDB-97*, Athens, Greece, 1997.
567. Rothermel, K., and R. Popescu-Zeletin (Eds.): *Mobile Agents.* Springer, LNCS, Vol. 1219, 1997.
568. RSAC (1998): Recreational Software Advisory Council. http://www.rsac.org

569. Rumelhart, D.E., G.E. Hinton, and R.J. Williams: Learning internal representations by error propagation. D.E. Rumelhart and J.L. McClelland (Eds.), *Parallel Distributed Processing: Explorations in the Microstructure of Cognition*, Volume 1. Bradford Books, MIT Press, Cambridge (MA, USA) 1986.

570. Runyon, K., and D. Stewart: *Consumer Behavior*. 3rd edition, Merrill Publishing Company, 1987.

571. Rus, D., R. Gray, and D. Kotz: Transportable Information Agents. M. Huhns and M.P. Singh (Eds.), *Readings in Agents*, Morgan Kaufmann, 1998.
see also *Journal of Intelligent Information Systems*, Vol. 9:215–238, 1997.

572. Salton, G.: The SMART Retrieval System. Experiments in Automatic Document Processing. 1971.

573. Salton, G.: The Smart document retrieval project. *Proceedings of the Fourteenth International ACM/SIGIR Conference on Research and Development in Information Retrieval*, 1991.

574. Salton, G.: The 'generality' effect and the retrieval evaluation for large collections. Journal of the American Society for Information Science, Vol. 23:11–22, 1972.

575. Salton, G.: *Automatic Text Processing: The Transformation, Analysis and Retrieval of Information by Computer*, Addison Wesley, 1989.

576. Salton, G., and C. Buckley: *Text Weighting Approaches in Automatic Text Retrieval*. Cornell University, Technical Report 87-881, 1987.

577. Salton, G., and C. Buckley: *Improving Retrieval Performance by Relevance Feedback*. Cornell University, Technical Report 88-898, 1988.

578. Salton, G., and M.J. McGill: *Introduction to Modern Information Retrieval*. McGraw Hill CS Series, NY, 1983.

579. Saltor,F., M. Garcia-Solaco, and M. Castellanos: Semantic heterogeneity in multidatabase systems. Bukhres,O.A., Elmagarmid,A. (Eds.), *Object-oriented multidatabase systems*, Chapter 5, Prentice Hall, 1996.

580. Sander, T., and C. Tschudin: Towards Mobile Cryptography. *Proceedings of the IEEE Symposium on Security and Privacy*, Oakland, May 1998.

581. Sander, T., and C. Tschudin: On Software Protection via Function Hiding. Aucsmith, D. (Ed.), *Information Hiding*, Proceedings Second International Workshop, Portland (OR, USA), Springer, LNCS, Vol. 1525, 1998.

582. Sandholm, T.: An Implementation of the Contract Net Protocol Based on Marginal Cost Calculations. *Proceedings of the Eleventh National Conference on Artificial Intelligence* (AAAI'93), Washington D.C., 1993.

583. Sandholm,T.: TRACONET - An implementation of the contract net protocol based on marginal cost calculations. Journal on Group Decision and Negotiation, 1996.

584. Sandholm, T.: Limitations of the Vickrey Auction in computational multiagent systems. *Proceedings of Conference ICMAS-96*, pp. 299–306, 1996.

585. Sandholm, T.: Unenforced e-commerce transcations. Internet Computing, Nov/Dec 1997.

586. Sandholm, T., and V. Lesser: Equilibrium Analysis of the Possibilities of Unenforced Exchange in Multiagent Systems. *Proc. 14th International Joint Conference on Artificial Intelligence* (IJCAI'95), Montreal, Canada, 1995.

587. Sandholm, T., and V. Lesser: Issues in Automated Negotiation and Electronic Commerce: Extending the Contract Net Framework. *Proc. First International Conference on Multiagent Systems* (ICMAS'95), San Francisco, 1995.

588. Sandholm, T., and V. Lesser: Coalition Formation among Bounded Rational Agents. *Proc. 14th International Joint Conference on Artificial Intelligence* (IJCAI), Montreal, Canada, 1995.

476   References

589. Sandholm, T., and V.R. Lesser: Coalitions among computationally bounded agents. AI Journal, Vol. 94, 1997.
590. Schaerf, A., Y. Shoham, and M. Tennenholtz: Adaptive load balancing: a study in multi-agent learning. Journal of Artificial Intelligence Research, Vol. 2:475–500, 1995.
591. Scheer, A.W.: *Business Process Engineering: Reference Models for Industrial Enterprises.* Springer, 1994.
592. Schiefloe, P.M., and T. G. Syvertsen: Coordination in Knowledge-Intensive Organizations. W. Conen and G. Neumann (Eds.), *Coordination Technology for Collaborative Applications,* Springer, LNCS, Vol. 1364, pp. 9–23, 1998.
593. Schneider, F.B.: Towards Fault-Tolerant and Secure Agentry. *Proceedings of the 11th International Workshop on Distributed Algorithms,* Sep 1997.
594. Schrooten, R.: Agent-based electronic consumer catalog. *Proceedings of The first international conference on the practical Application of Intelligent Agents and Multi Agents Technology,* pages 543–556, April 1996.
595. Schwartz, R., and S. Kraus: Bidding mechanisms for data allocation in multi-agent environments. *Proceedings of Workshop ATAL-97,* 1997.
596. Sciore, E., M. Siegel, and A. Rosenthal: Using Semantic Values to Facilitate Interoperability among Heterogeneous Information Systems. ACM Transactions on Database Systems, June 1994.
597. Sculley, J.: The Knowledge Navigator. Video, 1987.
598. Searle, J.R.: *Speech Acts.* Cambridge University Press, 1969.
599. Searle, J.R.: A taxonomy of illocutionary acts. Language, Mind and Knowledge. Minnesota Studies in the Phil of Science 11, 1975.
600. Searle, J.R.: Collective intentions and actions. *Intentions in Communication,* chapter 19. The MIT Press, 1990.
601. Searle, J. R., and D. Vanderveken: *Foundations of illocutionary logic.* Cambridge University Press, 1985.
602. Seligman, L., and L. Kerschberg: A Mediator for Approximate Consistency: Supporting "Good Enough" Materialized Views. Journal of Intelligent Information Systems, Vol. 8, pp. 203-225, 1997.
603. Sen, S., and N. Arora: Learning to take risks. *Collected papers from AAAI-97 workshop on Multiagent Learning,* AAAI Press, 1997.
604. Sen, S., N. Arora, S. Roychowdhury: Effects of local information on group behavior. *Proc. of the Second International Conference on Multiagent Systems,* Menlo Park (CA, USA), AAAI Press, pp. 322-329, 1996.
605. Sen, S., N. Arora, S. Roychowdhury: Using limited information to enhance group stability. International Journal of Human-Computer Studies, Vol. 48(1):69–82, January 1998.
606. Sen, S., and M. Sekaran: Indidvidual learning of coordination knowledge. Journal of Experimental and Theoretical AI, Special Issue on Learning in DAI Systems, 1998.
607. SET. Visa's Secure Electronic Transactions. http://www.visa.com/cgi-bin/vee/nt/ ecomm/set/main.html
608. Shafer, G.: *A Mathematical Theory of Evidence.* Princeton University Press, Princeton N.J., 1976.
609. Shakes, J., M. Langheinrich, and O. Etzioni: Dynamic reference sifting: A case study in the homepage domain. *Proc. 6th International World Wide Web Conference,* 1997.
610. Shardanand, U., and P. Maes: Social Information Filtering: Algorithms for Automating 'Word of Mouth'. *Proceedings of the CHI-95 Conference,* Denver (CO, USA), ACM Press, May 1995.

611. Shehory, O., and S. Kraus: Coalition Formation among Autonomous Agents: Strategies and Complexity. C. Castelfranchi and J. Muller (Eds.), *From Reactions to Cognition*, Proceedings of MAAMAW'93 Workshop, Springer, LNAI, Vol. 957, 1995.

612. Shehory, O., K. Sycara, P. Chalasani, and S. Jha: Agent cloning: an approach to agent mobility and resource allocation. IEEE Communications, Vol. 36(7):58–67, July 1998.

613. Shehory, O., K. Sycara, P. Chalasani, and S. Jha: Increasing resource utilization and task performance by agent cloning. *Proceeding of ATAL-98 Workshop*, Paris (France), pages 305–318, 1998.

614. Shenoy, S., and M. Ozsoyoglu: Design and implementation of a semantic query optimizer. IEEE Trans. Knowledge and Data Engineering, Vol. 1(3):344–361, September 1989.

615. Sheth, A., and J.A. Larson: Federated Database Systems. ACM Computing Surveys, Vol. 22(3), 1990.

616. Sheth, B., and P. Maes: Evolving agents for personalized information filtering. *Proceedings of the Ninth Conference on Artificial Intelligence for Applications*, IEEE Computer Press, 1993.

617. Sheth, A., E. Mena, A. Illaramendi, and V. Kashyap: OBSERVER: An approach for query processing in global information systems based on interoperation across pre-existing ontologies. *Proc. of First International Conf. on Cooperative Information Systems* CoopIS-96 , Brüssel, IEEE Computer Soc. Press, 1996.

618. Sheth, A., A. Illaramendi, V. Kashyap, and E. Mena: Managing multiple information sources through ontologies: relationship between vocabulary heterogeneity and loss of information. *Proc. of 12th European Conf. on Artificial Intelligence* ECAI-96, Budapest, 1996.

619. Shirazi, B.A., A. R. Hurson, and K. M. Kavi (Eds.): *Scheduling and Load Balancing in Parallel and Distributed Systems*. IEEE Computer Society Press, New York, 1995.

620. Shoens, K., et al.: The RUFUS system: Information organization for semistructured data. *Proc. VLDB Conference* , Dublin, Ireland, 1993.

621. Shoham, Y., and M. Tennenholtz: On social laws for artificial agent societies: Off-line design. AI Journal, 1993.

622. Shoham, Y., and M. Tennenholtz: On the emergence of social conventions: modeling, analysis, and simulations. AI Journal, Vol. 94, 1997.

623. Siegel, M., and S. Madnick: A Metadata Approach to Resolving Semantic Conflicts. *Proc. Intern. Conf. on Very Large Databases VLDB-91*, Sept 1991.

624. Sierra, C., N.R. Jennings, P. Noriega, and S. Parsons: A framework for argumentation–based negotiation. A. R. M. P. Singh and M. J. Wooldridge (Eds.), *Intelligent Agents IV*, Springer, LNAI, Vol. 1365, 1997.

625. Simon, H.A.: Bounded rationality and organizational learning. Organizational Sciences, 1991.

626. Sims, O.: *Business Objects: Delivering Cooperative Objects for Client-Server*. McGraw-Hill, 1994.

627. Singh, M. P.: A semantics for speech acts. Annals of Mathematics and Artificial Intelligence, Vol. 8, 1993.

628. Singh, M.P.: A Customizable Coordination Service for Autonomous Agents. M. P. Singh, A. Rao, and M. J. Wooldridge (Eds.), *Intelligent Agents IV (ATAL'97)*, springer, LNCS, Vol. 1365, pp. 93–106, 1997.

629. Singh, M.P.: Commitments among autonomous agents in information-rich environments. *Proceedings of the 8th European Workshop on Modelling Autonomous Agents in a Multi-Agent World (MAAMAW)*, Springer, pages 141–155, May 1997.

630. Singh, M.P.: An ontology for commitments in multiagent systems: Toward a unification of normative concepts. *Artificial Intelligence and Law*, 1998. In press.

631. Sixdegrees (1998). http://www.sixdegrees.com

632. Slee, C., and M. Slovin: Legacy asset management. Information Systems Management, pages 12–21, Winter 1997.

633. SMASH Project. Systems of Multiagents for Medical Services in Hospitals. http://www.iiia.csic.es/Projects/smash

634. SMIL (Synchronized Multimedia Integration Language). W3C recommendation status. http://www.w3.org/TR/REC-smil

635. Smith, R.: The Contract Net Protocol: A High Level Communications and Control in a Distributed Problem Solver. IEEE Transactions on Computers, 1980.

636. Smith, R. G., and R. Davis: Frameworks for cooperation in distributed problem solving. IEEE Trans on Systems, Man and Cybernetics, Vol. 11(1), 61–70, 1981.

637. Smith, V. L.: Auctions. J. Eatwell, M. Milgate and P. Newman (Eds.), *The new Palgrave: a dictionary of Economics*, McMillan (London),pp. 39–53, 1987.

638. Soley, R.M., and W. Kent: The OMG object model. W. Kim (Ed.), *Modern Database Systems: The Object Model, Interoperability, and Beyond*, Addison-Wesley, Reading MA, 1995.

639. Song, J.-S.: The Effect of Leadtime Uncertainty in a Simple Stochastic Inventory Model. Management Science, Vol. 40(5), pp.603-613, 1994.

640. Sowa, F.J.: *Conceptual Structures: Information Processing in Mind and Machine*. Addison-Wesley, Reading MA, 1984.

641. Sperber, D., and D. Wilson: *Relevance: Communication and Cognition*. 2nd edition, 1995.

642. Spertus, E.: Parasite: Mining structural information on the web. *Proc. 6th International World Wide Web Conference*, 1997.

643. Sridharan, P.: *Advanced Java Networking*. Prentice Hall, 1997.

644. Stamos, J., and D. Gifford: Remote evaluation. ACM Transactions on Programming Languages and Systems, Vol. 12(4):537–565, October 1990.

645. Steels, L.: The origins of ontologies and communication conventions in multiagent systems. Journal on Autonomous Agents and Multi-Agent Systems, Vol. 1(2), 1998.

646. Steier, A.M., and R.K. Belew: Exporting phrases: A statistical analysis of topical language. R. Casey and B. Croft (Eds.), *Proc. 2nd Symposium on Document Analysis and Information Retrieval*, 1994.

647. Stoyenko, A.D.: SUPRA-RPC: SUbprogram PaRAmeters in Remote Procedure Calls. Software–Practice and Experience, Vol. 24(1):27–49, January 1994.

648. Subrahmanian et al.: IMPACT: The Interactive Platform for Agents Collaborating Together. *Proc. of Second International Conference on Multiagent Systems* ICMAS-98, Paris, IEEE Press, 1998.

649. Subrahmanian, V.S., et al.: *Heterogeneous Agent Systems*, MIT Press, 1999. submitted. see also http://bester.cs.umd.edu/AdminPages/Events/IMPACT-07August98.html

650. Summer Institute of Linguistics XML. http://www.sil.org/sgml/xml.html

651. Sycara, K.: The PERSUADER. D. Shapiro (Ed.), *The Encyclopedia of Artificial Intelligence*, John Wiley and Sons, January 1992.
652. Sycara, K.: Levels of adaptivity in systems of coordinating information agents. M. Klusch and G. Weiß(Eds.), *Cooperative Information Agents II*, Proc. CIA-98 Workshop, Paris (France), July 1998.
653. Sycara, K., and D. Zeng: Coordination of multiple intelligent software agents. International Journal of Cooperative Information Systems, Vol. 5(2/3), pp. 181 - 211, World Scientific, 1996.
654. Sycara, K., and D. Zeng: Benefits of learning in negotiation. *Proc. AAAI-97 Conference on AI*, Providence (USA), 1997.
655. Sycara, K., K. Decker, A. Pannu, M. Williamson, and D. Zeng: Distributed intelligent agents. IEEE Expert, pages 36–45, December 1996.
656. Sycara, K., J. Lu, and M. Klusch: *Interoperability among heterogeneous software agents on the Internet*. Technical Report CMU-RI-TR-98-22, Carnegie Mellon University, Pittsburgh (USA), 1998.
657. Sycara, K., K. Decker, and D. Zeng: Intelligent agents in portfolio management. N. Jennings and M. Woolridge (Eds.), *Agent Technology: Foundations, Applications, and Markets*, chapter 14, pages 267–283, Springer, 1998.
658. Sycara, K., M. Klusch, J. Lu, and S. Widoff: Dynamic service matchmaking among agents in open information environments. A. Ouksel and A. Sheth (Eds.), Journal ACM SIGMOD Record, Special Issue on Semantic Interoperability in Global Information Systems, 1999. to appear.
659. Takahashi, K., Y. Nishibe, I. Morihara, and F. Hattori: Collecting shop and service information with software agents. *Proceedings of The first international conference on the practical Application of Intelligent Agents and Multi-Agent Technology*, pages 587–595, April 1996.
660. TACOMA. Cornell University, USA. http://www.cs.uit.no/DOS/Tacoma/index.html
661. Taligent. *Taligent's Guide to Designing Programs*. Addison-Wesley, Reading MA, 1994.
662. Tambe, M.: Toward flexible teamwork. Journal of Artificial Intelligence Research, Vol. 7:83–124, 1997.
663. Tambe, M.: Implementing Agent Teams in Dynamic Multiagent Environments. Applied AI Journal, Vol. 12, No. 2-3, 1998.
664. Tapscott, D.: *The digital economy: promise and peril in the age of networked intelligence*. McGraw-Hill, 1996.
665. Tenenbaum, J., T. Chowdhry, K. Hughes: eCo System: CommerceNet's Architectural Framework for Internet Commerce, White Paper and Prospectus. Second draft, April 1997. http://www.commerce.net/eco/index.html
666. Terpsidis, I., A. Moukas, B. Pergioudakis, G. Doukidis, and P. Maes: The Potential of Electronic Commerce in Re-Engineering Consumer-Retail Relationships through Intelligent Agents. J.-Y. Roger, B. Stanford-Smith, and P. Kidd. (Eds.), *Advances in Information Technologies: The Business Challenge*, IOS Press, 1997.
667. Theilmann, W., and K. Rothermel: Domain experts for information retrieval in the world wide web. M. Klusch, G. Weiß(Eds.), *Cooperative Information Agents II*, Proc. CIA-98 Workshop, Paris (France), Sprinvger, LNAI, Vol. 1435, pages 216–227, 1998.
668. Thomas et al.: Heterogeneous distributed database systems for production use. ACM Computing Surveys, Vol. 22(3):237-266, September 1990.
669. Thomas, J.D., and K. Sycara: Heterogeneity, stability, and efficiency in distributed systems. *Proc. of Second International Conference on Multiagent Systems ICMAS-98*, Paris, IEEE Press, 1998.

670. Tolksdorf, R. (Ed.), Journal on Autonomous Agents and Multi-Agent Systems, Special Issue on Coordination Mechanisms and Patterns for Web Agents, 1999.

671. Truman, T.E., T. Pering, R. Döring and R.W. Brodersen: The InfoPad multimedia terminal: a portable device for wireless information access. IEEE Trans. on Computers, Vol. 47(10), 1998.

672. Tsang, E.: *Foundations of Constraint Satisfaction*. Academic Press, 1993.

673. Tschudin, C.F., G. Di Marzo, M. Muhugusa, and J. Harms: Messenger-based operating systems. Technical Report 90, University of Geneva, Switzerland, July 1994. Revised September 14, 1994.

674. Tschudin, C., G. Di Marzo, M. Murhimanya, and J. Harms: Welche Sicherheit für mobilen Code?. K. Bauknecht, D. Karangiannis, and S. Teufel (Eds.), *Proceedings der Fachtagung SIS'96 Sicherheit in Informationssystemen*, Vienna, Vdf Verlag, March 1996.

675. Tschudin, C.: The Messenger Environment M0 – A Condensed Description. J. Vitek and C. Tschudin (Eds.), *Mobile Object Systems*, Springer, LNCS, Vol. 1222, April 1997.

676. Tschudin, C.F., M. Muhugusa, and G. Neuschwander: Using mobile code to control native execution of distributed UNIX. *Proceedings of the Third ECOOP Workshop on Mobile Object Systems*, Finland, June 1997.

677. TSIMMIS. The Stanford-IBM Manager of Multiple Information Sources. http://www-db.stanford.edu/tsimmis/

678. Tsvetovatyy, M., and M. Gini: Toward a Virtual Marketplace: Architectures and Strategies. *Proc. 1st International Conference on the Practical Application of Intelligent Agents and Multi-Agent Technology* (PAAM-96), pp. 597-613, 1996.

679. Turkle, S.: *Life on the Screen: Identity in the Age of the Internet*, Simon & Schuster, New York, 1995.

680. Ullman, J.D.: Information integration using logical views. *Proc. Intl. Conf on Database Theory*, pages 19-40, 1997.

681. Umar, A.: *Application (Re)Engineering: Building Web-based Applications and Dealing with Legacies*. Prentice Hall, New Jersey, 1997.

682. Ura, T., J. Delgado, and N. Ishii: Content-based collaborative information filtering: Actively learning to classify and recommend documents. M. Klusch, and G. Weiß(Eds.), *Cooperative Information Agents II*, Proc. of Second International Workshop, springer, LNAI, Vol. 1435, pages 206–215, 1998.

683. US Framework for Global Electronic Commerce. http://www.iitf.nist.gov/electronic-commerce.

684. van Eemeren, H., R. Grootendorst, and F. Henkemans: *Fundamentals of Argumentation Theory, A Handbook of Historical Backgrounds and Contemporary Developments*. Lawrence Erlbaum Associates, 1996.

685. Varian, H. R.: *Economic mechanism design for computerized agents*. Tech. Rep., School of Information Management and Systems. University of California. Berkeley, 1995.

686. Venieris, I., and H. Hussmann (Eds.): *Intelligent Broadband Networks*, Wiley, 1998.

687. Vickrey, W.: Counterspeculation, auctions and competitive sealed tenders. Journal of Finance, Vol. 16, pp. 8–37, 1961.

688. Vidal, J.M., and E. Durfee: Task planning agents in the UMDL. *Proceedings of the Fourth International Conference on Information and Knowledge Managment (CIKM) Workshop on Intelligent Information Agents*, 1995.

689. Vidal, J.M., and E. Durfee: The impact of nested agent models in an information economy. *Proceedings of the Second International Conference on Multi-Agent Systems (ICMAS-96)*, pp. 377–384, 1996.
690. Vigna, G. (Ed.): *Mobile Agents and Security*, Springer, LNCS, Vol. 1419, April 1998.
691. Vigna, G.: Cryptographic Traces for Mobile Agents. In [690], April 1998.
692. Vinowski, S.: CORBA: Integrating Diverse Applications Within Distributed Hetergeneous Environments. IEEE Communications Magazine, Vol. 14, No. 2, February 1997.
693. Vivaqua, A.: The Expert Finder: Agents to assist in finding help. Working Paper, MIT Media Laboratory.
694. Vogt, C.C., and Cottrell., G.W.: Predicting the performance of linearly combined ir systems. *Proceedings of the ACM SIGIR Conference*, 1998.
695. Voyager. ObjectSpace Voyager Inc., USA. http://www.objectspace.com/voyager/ ObjectSpace Voyager core package technical overview. ObjectSpace, Inc., December 1997. Version 1.
696. W3C Reference Library. Libwww version 5.1. http://www.w3.org/Library, 1997.
697. Wagman, M.: *The ultimate objectives of AI*, Praeger, 1998.
698. Walsh, T., N. Paciorek, and D. Wong: Security and reliability in concordia. *Proceedings of the Thirty-First Annual Hawaii International Conference on System Sciences*, Vol. VII, pp. 44–53, January 1998.
699. Walton, D. N.: *Informal Logic*. Cambridge University Press, Cambridge, UK, 1989.
700. Watkins, C.J.C.H.: *Learning from delayed rewards*. PhD thesis, King's College, Cambridge, UK, 1989.
701. Watson, M.: *Intelligent Java Applications for the Internet and Intranets*. 1997.
702. Webster, k., and K. Paul: Beyond Surfing: Tools and Techniques for Searching the Web. Information Technology, January 1996.
703. Wegner, P.: Why interaction is more powerful than algorithms. Communications of the ACM, Vol. 40(5):80–91, May 1997.
704. Weihmayer, R., and H. Velthuijsen: Intelligent agents in telecommunications. N.R. Jennings and M. Wooldridge (Eds.), *Agent Technology*, Springer, 1998.
705. Weinstein, P., and G. Alloway: Seed ontologies: growing digital libraries as distributed, intelligent systems. *Proceedings of the Second ACM International Conference on Digital Libraries*, June 1997.
706. Weiß, G. (Ed.): *Distributed Artificial Intelligence meets Machine Learning*, Selected papers from ECAI-96 Workshop LDAIS and ICMAS-96 Workshop LIOME, Springer, LNCS, Vol. 1221, 1997.
707. Weiß, G., and S. Sen (Eds.): *Adaption and Learning in Multi-Agent Systems*, Proceedings of IJCAI-95 Workshop, CA, Springer, LNCS, Vol. 1042, 1995.
708. Weiß, R., B. Velez, M. Sheldon, C. Nemprempre, P. Szilagyi, and D.K. Giffor: Hypursuit: A hierarchical network search engine that exploits content-link hypertext clustering. *Proc. Seventh ACM Conference on Hypertext*, 1996.
709. Weld, D.: Planning-Based Control of Software Agents. Proc. of *The Third International Conference on Artifical Intelligence Planning Systems* (AIPS'96), Edinburgh, Scotland, May 1996.
710. Wellman, M. P.: A market-oriented programming environment and its application to distributed multicommodity flow problems. Journal of Artificial Intelligence Research, Vol. 1, pp. 1–22, 1993.

711. Wellman, M.P.: Market-oriented Programming: Some Early Lessons. S. H. Clearwater (Ed.), *Market-Based Control: A Paradigm for Distributed Resource Allocation*, World Scientific, 1995.

712. Wellman, M., and J. Doyle: Modular utility representation for decision-theoretic planning. *Proceedings of 15th National Conference on Artificial Intelligence AAAI-92*, June 1992.

713. Wellman, M.P., P.R. Wurman, and W.E. Walsh: The Michigan Internet AuctionBot: A configurable auction server for human and software agents. *Proc. Second International Conference on Autonomous Agents*, 1998.

714. Wellman, M.P., P.R. Wurman, and W.E. Walsh: Flexible double auctions for electronic commerce: Theory and implementation. Decision Support Systems, 1998.

715. Werner, E.: Cooperating agents: A unified theory of communication and social structure. M. Huhns and L. Gasser (Eds.), *Distributed Artificial Intelligence: Volume II*, Morgan Kaufmann, 1990.

716. Wexelblatt, A., and P. Maes: Footprints: History-Rich Web Browsing, *Proc. Computer-Assisted Information Searching on Internet (RIAO-97)*, Montreal, June 1997.

717. Wexelblatt, A., and P. Maes: Experiments on Anthropomorphising Agents. ACM Interactions, ACM Press. submitted.

718. White, J.E.: Telescript technology: The foundation for the electronic marketplace. General Magic White Paper, 1994.

719. White, J.E.: Mobile agents make a network an open platform for third-party developers. IEEE Computer, Vol. 27(11):89–90, November 1994.

720. White, J.E.: Telescript technology: Mobile agents. General Magic White Paper, 1996.

721. White, J.E.: Mobile Agents. J. M. Bradshaw (Ed.), *Software Agents*, Chapter 19, MIT Press, 1997.

722. Wiederhold, G.: Mediators in the architecture of future information systems. IEEE Computer, Vol. 25:38-49, 1992.

723. Wiederhold, G.: Interoperation, mediation and ontologies. *Proc. Int'l Workshop on Heterogeneous Cooperative Knowledge-Bases, Tokyo*, 1994.

724. Wiederhold, G.: Foreword: Intelligent integration of information. Intl. Journal of Intelligent Information Systems, Vol. 6(2/3):93-97, May 1996.

725. Wiederhold, G.: Mediators in the architecture of future information systems. In [296], pages 185–196. 1998. (Reprinted from *IEEE Computer, 1992*).

726. Wilhelm, U.G., and S. Staamann: Protecting the Itinerary of Mobile Agents. *Proceedings of 4th ECOOP Workshop on Mobile Object Systems*, Brussels, July 1998.

727. Wille, R.: Concept lattices and conceptual knowledge systems. In F. Lehmann (Ed.), *Semantic Networks in Artificial Intelligence*, pages 493–515. Pergamon Press, 1992.

728. Williamson, M., K. Decker, and K. Sycara: Unified information and control flow in hierarchical task networks. *Proceedings of the AAAI-96 workshop on Theories of Planning, Action, and Control*, 1996.

729. Wilson, W. K.: Confession of a Weak Anti-Intentionalist: Exposing Myself. Journal of Aesthetics and Art Criticism, Vol. 55:3, 1997.

730. Winograd, T., and F. Flores: *Understanding Computers and Cognition: A New Foundation of Design*. Norwood, NJ.; Ablex, 1986.

731. WiseWire. http://www.wisewire.com

732. Wittgenstein, L.: *Philosophical Investigations*, Macmillan Publishing: New York, NY, 1953.

733. Wittig, T. (Ed.): *ARCHON: an architecture for multi-agent systems*. Ellis Horwood, 1992.

734. Woelk, D., and C. Tomlinson: Carnot and InfoSleuth: Database Technology and the World Wide Web. ACM SIGMOD Intl. Conf. on the Management of Data, May, 1995.

735. Wolfstetter, E.: Auctions: an introduction. Journal of Economic Surveys, Vol. 10(4), pp. 367–420, 1996.

736. Wollrath, A., R. Riggs, and J. Waldo: A distributed object model for the Java system. Computing Systems, Vol. 9(4):265–290, Fall 1996.

737. Wong, D., N. Paciorek, T. Walsh, J. DiCelie, M. Young, and B. Peet: Concordia: An infrastructure for collaborating mobile agents. *Proceedings of the First International Workshop on Mobile Agents (MA '97)*, pp. 86–97, 1997.

738. Woods, W.A., and J.G. Schmolze: The KL-ONE family. F.W. Lehman (Ed.), *Semantic Networks in Artificial Intelligence*, pp. 133–178, Special issue of *Computers & Mathematics with Applications*, Volume 23, Number 2-9, Pergamon Press, 1992.

739. Wooldridge, M., and N. R. Jennings: Intelligent Agents: Theory and Practice. Knowledge Engineering Review, Vol. 10(2), 1995.

740. Workflow management coalition (WfMC) reference model. http://www.aiai.ed.ac.uk/WfMC/, 1995.

741. Wurman, P.R., M. P. Wellman, and W. E. Walsh: The michigan internet auctionbot: A configurable auction server for human and software agents. *Proceedings of the Second International Conference on Autonomous Agents*, May 1998.

742. XML. Extensible Markup Language. World Wide Web Consortium (W3C) Working Draft, 17 November 1997. http://www.w3.org/TR/WD-xml-link.

743. Yee, B.S.: A Sanctuary for Mobile Agents. *Proceedings of the DARPA workshop on foundations for secure mobile code*, Monterey CA, March 1997.

744. Yu, E.: *Modelling Strategic Relationships for Process Engineering*. PhD thesis, University of Toronto, 1994.

745. Yu, E., P. Dubois, E. Dubois, and J. Mylopoulos: From organization models to system requirements: a cooperating agents approach. M. P. Papazoglou and G. Schlageter (Eds.), *Cooperative Information Systems: Trends and Directions*, Academic Press, 1998.

746. Yu, C., W. Sun, S. Dao, and D. Keirsey: Determining Relationships among Attributes for Inter-Operability of Multi-Database Systems. *Proc. of the 1st Int'l Workshop on Interoperability in Multidatabase Systems*, IEEE Computer Society Press, Los Alamitos (CA, USA), 1991.

747. Zamora, J., J.R. Millan and a. Murciano: Learning and stabilization of altruistic behaviors in multi-agent systems by reciprocity. Biological Cybernetics, Vol. 78, 1998

748. Zander, J., and R. Forchheimer: SOFTNET - High Level Packet Communication. Forth Dimensions, Vol. 6(5), Jan/Feb 1985.

749. Zlotkin, G., and J. Rosenchein: Coalition, Cryptography, and Stability: Mechanisms for Coalition Formation in Task Oriented Domains. *Proceedings of the National Conference on Artificial Intelligence*, Seattle, Washington, July 1994. Also appeared as a MIT Center for Coordination Science Technical Report 168 and MIT Sloan School WP 3703-94, July 1994.

About the Authors

Domenico Beneventano is a Research Associate at the Dipartimento di Scienze dell'Ingegneria, University of Modena, Italy. He received a Laurea degree in Electronic Engineering in 1990 and a Ph.D. in Computer Science and Electronic Engineering in 1994, both from the University of Bologna. His research interests include complex object data models and reasoning techniques applied to databases for knowledge representation and query optimization.

Sonia Bergamaschi is an Associate Professor at the Dipartimento di Scienze dell'Ingegneria, University of Modena, Italy, teaching courses on Database Management Systems and Knowledge Representation. She received her Laurea degree in Mathematics on 1979 from the University of Modena. From 1979 to 1983 she participated, as a member of the Emilia-Romagna region technical staff, in many research and development database projects. From 1984 to 1992 she worked as a researcher at the CIOC-CNR Research Centre of the Italian National Research Council and was involved in European and national database research projects. Her research interests are in reasoning activities in database environment with a focus on conceptual database design, query optimization, and integration of structured and semistructured information.

Anish Biswas is a graduate student in the Department of Mathematical and Computer Sciences, University of Tulsa, USA. His research interests include machine learning, multiagent systems, and application of chaos theory.

Brian Brewington received his his B.Sc. in Engineering and Applied Science, emphasizing robotics and control systems, from the California Institute of Technology in 1995. He is currently in his fourth year of Ph.D. work at the Thayer School of Engineering at Dartmouth College, USA, where he is focusing on problems of optimal allocation of observation resources. His other research interests include signal processing, data mining, and aspects of information theory.

George Cybenko is a Dorothy and Walter Gramm Professor of Engineering in the Thayer School of Engineering at Dartmouth College, USA. He received his B.Sc. in mathematics at the University of Toronto, and an M.A. in mathematics and Ph.D. in electrical engineering from Princeton. He has taught on the computer science faculty at Tufts University and was professor of electrical engineering and computer science at the University of Illinois, Champaign-Urbana. At Illinois, he was also a director of the university's Center for Supercomputing Research and Development. He has served as editor for several mathematics, computer and information-theory publications, and has published over fifty journal papers, book chapters and conference papers.

Sumit Ghosh is a graduate student in the Department of Mathematical and Computer Sciences, University of Tulsa, USA. His research interests include intelligent agent architectures and information systems.

Robert Gray is an Assistant Research Professor in the Thayer School of Engineering at Dartmouth College, USA. He is the lead researcher and programmer for the D'Agents system, one of the mobile-agent systems discussed in this book. He is primarily interested in performance, security and fault-tolerance of mobile agents. He received his Ph.D in computer science from Dartmouth College in 1997.

Robert H. Guttman studied Artificial Intelligence at the University of Michigan where he developed SoarSIM, an object-oriented simulation tool for the Soar general intelligence architecture. After receiving a BSE in Computer Engineering in 1992, Robert worked as a Software Engineer for Motorola where he helped develop expert system and natural language processing tools for writing patent applications. He is currently an S.M. candidate and a Telecom Italia Fellow in Pattie Maes' Software Agents group at MIT's Media Laboratory in Cambridge, USA. Robert is focusing on a variety of issues in Agent-mediated Electronic Commerce including agent-mediated integrative negotiation mechanisms in retail markets. He has published several papers and has given invited talks in academic and business settings on software agents and electronic commerce.

Merav Hadad is a Ph.D graduate student of Computer Science at Bar-Ilan University, Israel. She received her B.Sc. degree in mathematics and computer science and her M.Sc. degree in computer science from Bar-Ilan University, in 1995 and 1997 respectively; the title of her M.Sc. thesis is "Using SharedPlan Model in Electronic Commerce Environments". Her research interests are in distributed artificial intelligence, cooperation among automated agents, electronic commerce, real-time, and AI.

Willem-Jan van den Heuvel received a Master's degree in Information Management from Tilburg University, Tilburg, the Netherlands. After his graduation, he worked for two years as a researcher in the Information Technology section of the Economics Institute of Tilburg. During this time, he participated in a project to develop a case-tool (the Grammalizer) that supports analysts in extracting meaningful concepts out of textual representations of problem domains. Since joining the Faculty of Economics of Tilburg University in 1997, he has been developing the Binding business Applications to LEgacy Systems (BALES) methodology to support the mapping between forward engineered enterprise models, and reverse engineered legacy system models. He is also active in the fields of object-oriented (enterprise) modeling, electronic commerce and legacy systems

Michael Huhns (Ph.D., Southern California, 1975) is Director of the Center for Information Technology at the University of South Carolina. He edited the books *Distributed Artificial Intelligence*, volumes 1 and 2, and authored over 100 papers and reports. Dr. Huhns has served on numerous program committees and conference advisory boards, and is an Associate Editor for IEEE Expert, ACM Transactions on Information Systems, and the Journal of Autonomous Agents and Multiagent Systems. He serves on the editorial boards for the International Journal of Cooperative Information Systems, the Journal of Intelligent Manufacturing, and IEEE Internet Computing.

Matthias Klusch (Ph.D., University of Kiel, 1997) is an Assistant Professor in Computer Science at the Chemnitz University of Technology. He is on the organizational board of the Special Interest Group (SIG) on Distributed AI of the German Computer Society. He is also the coordinator of the SIG on Intelligent Information Agents as part of the ESPRIT Network of Excellence for Agent-Based Computing (AgentLink). He is chair of the annual international workshop series on Cooperative Information Agents (CIA), and is a program committee member for numerous international conferences in the research areas of DAI and Information Systems. He is a co/editor of four books and co/author of several papers on intelligent and collaborating information agents, and reviewer for international journals and press in related research areas. He visited the Robotics Institute at Carnegie Mellon University in Pittsburgh (USA) in 1998, during a sabbatical year taken for working in research projects on intelligent software agents. His research mainly focuses on the application of software agent technology in modern information environments, especially adaptive and rational collaborating information agents on the Internet and Web.

David Kotz is an Associate Professor of Computer Science at Dartmouth College, USA. He received the M.Sc. and Ph.D degrees in computer science from Duke University in 1989 and 1991, respectively. He received the A.B. degree in computer science and physics from Dartmouth College in 1986. He rejoined Dartmouth College in 1991 and was promoted with tenure to Associate Professor in 1997. His research interests include parallel operating systems and architecture, multiprocessor file systems, transportable agents, and parallel computing in computer-science education.

Sarit Kraus is an Associate Professor of Mathematics and Computer Science at Bar-Ilan University, Israel, and an adjunct Associate Professor at the Institute for Advanced Computer Studies, at the University of Maryland, USA. She graduated from the Hebrew University of Jerusalem with a Ph.D. in computer science in 1989; the title of the her thesis was "Planning and Communication in a Multi-Agent Environment". Subsequently, she spent two years at the University of Maryland, College Park as a postdoctoral fellow, before joining the faculty at Bar-Ilan University. Sarit has worked extensively in the following areas: automated negotiation and cooperation among automated agents, development of intelligent agents, information agents, distributed artificial intelligence, combining knowledge-based systems and maintaining security, user interfaces and decision support tools. She has published over 80 papers in leading journals, proceedings of major conferences and has received substantial grants from a various of agencies. She is on the editorial board of the Annals of Mathematics and Artificial Intelligence, the Journal of Artificial Intelligence Research, Journal of Autonomous Agents and Multi-Agent Systems, and AI Communications. In recognition of her research accomplishments on intelligent agents, Kraus was awarded the 1995 IJCAI Computers and Thought Award.

Henry Lieberman has been a Research Scientist at the MIT Media Laboratory in Cambridge, USA, since 1987. His interests are in the intersection of artificial intelligence and the human interface. He is a member of the Software Agents group, which is concerned with making intelligent software that assists users in interactive interfaces. His current projects involve intelligent agents for the Web that learn by "watching what you do". He has also built an interactive graphic editor that learns from examples, and from annotation on images and video. He worked with graphic designer Muriel Cooper in developing systems that supported intelligent visual design. Other projects involve reversible debugging and visualization for programming environments, and new graphic metaphors for information visualization and navigation. From 1972 to 1987, he was a researcher at the MIT Artificial Intelligence Laboratory. He started with Seymour Papert in the group that originally developed the educational language Logo, and wrote the first bitmap and color graphics systems for Logo. He also worked with Carl Hewitt on actors, an early object-oriented, parallel language, and developed the notion of prototypes and the first real-time garbage collection algorithm. He holds a Habilitation à Diriger des Recherches degree from the University of Paris VI Pierre et Marie Curie and was a Visiting Professor there in 1989/90.

Pattie Maes is an Associate Professor at MIT's Media Laboratory in Cambridge, USA, where she founded and directs the Software Agents Group. Her areas of expertise are Artificial Intelligence, Artificial Life, Human Computer Interaction, Computer Supported Collaborative Work, Information Filtering, and Electronic Commerce. She is a founder and board member of the Agent Society, an international industry and professional organization established to assist in the widespread development and emergence of intelligent agent technologies and markets. She edited three books and is an editorial board member for professional journals such as User Modeling, Personal Technologies and Artificial Life. Her work won several prizes: Ars Electronica 1995 award, Interactive Media Festival Award 1995, and ArcTec 1995 award. She was a founder and director of Firefly Network, Inc. in Cambridge, Massachusetts, one of the first companies to commercialize software agent technology.

Filippo Menczer is an Assistant Professor in the Department of Management Sciences at the University of Iowa, USA, where he teaches courses in Management Information Systems. In 1991, after receiving his Laurea degree in Physics from the University of Rome "La Sapienza", he was affiliated with the Institute of Psychology of the Italian National Research Council. In 1998 he graduated from the University of California at San Diego, where he received a M.Sc. in Computer Science and a Ph.D. in Computer Science and Cognitive Science. He has published 18 refereed papers and served as a reviewer for many journals and conferences. He has developed the LEE artificial life simulation tool, which is distributed with Linux and widely used in experimental and instructional settings. He has been the recipient of Fulbright, Rotary Foundation, and NATO fellowships, among others. His interdisciplinary research interests span from ecological theory to distributed information systems; they include artificial life, evolutionary computation, neural networks, machine learning, information retrieval, and adaptive intelligent agents.

Katsuhiro Moizumi is a postdoctoral researcher in the Thayer School of Engineering at Dartmouth College, USA. He received his Ph.D. degree in computer engineering from Dartmouth College in 1998. His research interests include planning, scheduling, Markov Decision processing, optimal control, machine learning, mobile computing, and agent systems.

Alvaro Monge is an Assistant Professor in the Department of Computer Science at the University of Dayton, USA. He teaches courses in Algorithms, Data Structures, and Database Management. He completed his graduate work at the University of California, San Diego where he earned a M.Sc. and Ph.D. degree in computer science. His undergraduate work at the University of California, Riverside earned him the B.Sc. degree in computer science with honors. Dr. Monge has published papers in the areas of online information retrieval over the World-Wide Web, and data mining and knowledge discovery. In addition his work experience has taken him to organizations such as AT&T Bell Labs, Los Alamos National Laboratory, and the Jet Propulsion Laboratory. As part of his Ph.D. research, he developed the WebFind tool for discovering scientific papers over the World-Wide Web. He was also the recipient of an AT&T Labs Fellowship and National Hispanic Scholarship. He is active in undergraduate education issues and has participated in the National Science Foundation Engineering Education Scholars Workshop. His research interests lie in the areas of knowledge discovery, search algorithms, information retrieval, data mining, machine learning, and intelligent software agents.

Alexandros G. Moukas holds a B.Sc. in Business Administration, Computer Information Systems (1993) from the American College of Greece, an M.Sc. in Artificial Intelligence (1995) from University of Edinburgh, Scotland and an M.Sc. from MIT Media Laboratory (1996) on intelligent agents for information discovery and dynamic resource allocation. Currently he is a Ph.D. candidate at the Software Agents Group, working on agent-mediated electronic commerce. A Media Lab AT&T Fellow, he has published more than twenty journal and conference articles, has given lectures and has served as a reviewer in a number of scientific journals and conferences. Alexandros worked as an IT consultant in Greece at Athens Children's Hospital. He is currently involved in a number of European Union-funded ESPRIT projects.

Pablo Noriega (PhD C.Sc. Univ. Aut. Barcelona, Spain) is the General Director of Informatics at the Mexican Institute for Statistics, Geography and Informatics (INEGI). He was recently a visiting researcher at the AI Research Institute in Barcelona (IIIA-CSIC) (1994-1998). His research interests are centered around agent-mediated institutions and computational dialectics. Prior to his appointment in Barcelona, he chaired the taskforce for the establishment of an Information Technologies Strategic Plan (1995–2000) in Mexico while he was Head of the Mex. Govt. IT-Policy Office (1989–1994). He has been President of the Mexican AI Society (1989–1991), Head of AI projects at IBM Mexico's Scientific Center (1986–1988) and Professor at various Universities (1983–1989). He is currently President of the Board of the Mexican National AI Lab (LANIA).

Aris M. Ouksel received the M.Sc. and the Ph.D. degrees in Computer Science in 1980 and 1985, respectively, from Northwestern University. After four years abroad, teaching and consulting in information technology strategic planning and transfer, in 1989 he joined the Department of Information and Decision Sciences at the University of Illinois at Chicago, where he is currently an associate professor. Aris Ouksel is also the director of the Management Information Systems Ph.D. program and the Director of Information

Technology at the College of Business Administration. His research interests include information technology strategic planning, organizational structure and learning, knowledge discovery and cooperative information systems, data structures and algorithm design and analysis, and query processing. Aris is a member of ACM, IEEE, INFORMS, and SIMS; he has provided consulting services in telecommunications and information technology strategic planning to private corporations such as Ameritech, AT&T, Motorola, and at several hospitals, etc., and information technology strategic planning and information reengineering services at several public entities such as the City of Chicago, the Metropolitan Water Reclamation District, and the Bureau of Land Management at US Interior Agency.

Michael Papazoglou is a full Professor and director of the Infolab at the University of Tilburg in the Netherlands. Prior to this he held the positions at the Queensland Univ. of Technology (QUT), the Australian National University Dept. of Computer Science (1989–1991) and GMD, in St. Augustin, Germany. He is the founding editor and co-editor in charge of the International Journal of Cooperative Information Systems and serves on several committees and advisory boards for international journals. He has served as general and program chair for a number of well-known international conferences. He has authored or edited eight books and approximately 100 journal articles and refereed conference papers. He has given invited lectures on Information Technology related topics in several countries around the globe. He is a Senior and Golden Core Member of the Institute of Electrical & Electronics Engineers (IEEE), and a Distinguished Visiting Lecturer for the IEEE. His scientific interests include cooperative information systems, heterogeneous database systems, object-oriented systems, distributed computing, digital libraries, electronic marketing and commerce.

Daniela Rus is an Assistant Professor in the Computer Science Department at Dartmouth College, USA. Previously, she was a research associate and director of the Information Capture and Access project at Cornell University. She holds a Ph.D. degree in computer science from Cornell University. Her research interests include distributed manipulation, three-dimensional navigation, self-reconfiguring robotics, mobile agents, and information organization. She holds an NSF Career award and a Sloan fellowship.

Sandip Sen is an Assistant Professor in the Department of Mathematical and Computer Sciences, University of Tulsa, USA. His research interests include multiagent systems, genetic algorithms, and machine learning.

Onn Shehory is a visiting assistant professor at the Robotics Institute of the Carnegie Mellon University in Pittsburgh, USA, where he is involved in the RETSINA project. Within the project, he develops theories as well as applications of multi-agent systems. He received his Ph.D. in computer science from Bar Ilan University, Israel, in 1997. The title of his thesis was "Cooperation and Coalition Formation among Distributed Inteligent Systems". His research focuses on methods for cooperation among agents, architectural and system considerations in MAS, and efficiency in resource utilization and task allocation in agent systems.

Carles Sierra has held a permanent senior research position at the Artificial Intelligence Research Institute of the Spanish Scientific Research Council (IIIA-CSIC) since 1990. He received the M.Sc. in Computer Science (1986) and the Ph.D. in Computer Science (1989) from the Technical University of Catalonia, Barcelona, Spain. His current research interests include: multi-agent systems, formal methods applied to knowledge-based systems analysis, computational reflection and applications of AI to medicine and electronic commerce. In this last topic he has published several papers on electronic auctions and on automatic negotiation models among autonomous agents.

Munindar Singh (Ph.D., Texas, 1993) is the director of the Database Laboratory at North Carolina State University. He authored the book *Multiagent Systems* and several papers and reports on agents and databases. He was the Americas program chair for the International Conference on Cooperative Information Systems (CoopIS), 1997, and the general chair and Americas program chair for the International Workshop on Agent Theories, Architectures, and Languages (ATAL), 1997. He is Associate Editor-In-Chief of IEEE Internet Computing, and a member of the editorial board of the Journal of Autonomous Agents and Multiagent Systems.

Katia Sycara is a Senior Research Scientist in the Robotics Institute in the School of Computer Science at Carnegie Mellon University, Pittsburgh, USA. She is also the Director of the Enterprise Integration Laboratory. She is directing/conducting research and developing technology for integrating organizational decision making. She holds a B.Sc. in Applied Mathematics from Brown University, M.Sc. in Electrical Engineering from the University of Wisconsin, and Ph.D. in Computer Science from the Georgia Institute of Technology. Her research has contributed to the definition of case-based reasoning and the development of computational negotiation models as a means of resolving goal conflicts and inconsistencies in assumptions and viewpoints of heterogeneous agents in distributed problem solving. She has applied her research to concurrent engineering design, crisis action planning and manufacturing scheduling. She has published extensively in these areas. Currently, she is engaged in the development of intelligent agents that interact with their users, other agents and distributed information resources in order to assist their users in the planning and execution of various tasks. Katia Sycara is Area Editor for AI and Management Science for the journal Group Decision and Negotiation and on the editorial board of IEEE Expert, AI in Engineering, and Concurrent Engineering, Research and Applications. She is a member of AAAI, ACM, Cognitive Science Society, IEEE, and the Institute of Management Science (TIMS).

Robert Tolksdorf is an Assistant Professor at the study group "Formal Models, Logic and Programming" at the Technical University of Berlin, Department for Computer Science. He received his Dr.-Ing. in Computer Science from TU Berlin in 1995. His research interests include coordination languages, open distributed systems, and Web technology. He is one of the main proponents and responsible for coordinating the TU Berlin site of the ESPRIT Open LTR project 20179 PageSpace on coordination in distributed WWW applications. He is a member of the ESPRIT Working Group Coordina "From Coordination Models to Applications".

Christian Frédéric Tschudin holds a M.Sc. degree in Mathematics and obtained his Ph.D. in Computer Science from the University of Geneva, Switzerland, in 1993. He conceived and implemented the Messenger Mobile Code System in the early 1990s, which was one of the first active network systems. Since 1998 he has been an associate professor at Uppsala University, Sweden. His main research interests are active networks, mobile code security, and open control architectures based on economic models.

Giorgos Zacharia holds a B.Sc. in Mathematics, and a B.Sc. in Computer Science and Engineering with minor in Economics, both from the Massachusetts Institute of Technology (MIT). He was a Fulbright scholar throughout his undergraduate studies. Currently he is an M.Sc. candidate in Media Technology at the Software Agents group of the MIT Media Laboratory. He is doing research on Agent Mediated Electronic Commerce (AmEC) focusing on Collaborative Reputation Mechanisms for online communities. As an undergraduate researcher at the Agents Group, he worked on the development of Amalthaea (Information Filtering) and the PDA@Shop (AmEC). Before joining the Agents Group he worked in research projects in neural networks at the Laboratory for Information and Decision Systems and in parallel processing at the Laboratory for Computer Science. During summers he has worked as a software engineer in the Cyprus Telecommunications Authority, LogosNet, and the Press and Information Office in Cyprus.

Daniel Dajun Zeng (Ph.D., 1998) is Assistant Professor in Management Information Systems at the University of Arizona, Tucson, USA. Formerly he worked in an interdisciplinary program jointly offered by the Graduate School of Industrial Administration (GSIA) and the School of Computer Science at Carnegie Mellon University. He finished his B.Sc. in Operations Research/Economics with a minor in Computer Science from the University of Science and Technology of China, Hefei, China in 1990. He completed his M.Sc. in Industrial Administration from GSIA, Carnegie Mellon University in 1994. His research and teaching interests include MIS, Electronic Commerce, Supply Chain Management, Web-based Software Agents, Expert Systems, and Automated Negotiation. He is a student member of INFORMS and AAAI.

List of Contributors

Domenico Beneventano
Dipartimento di Scienze dell'Ingegneria
University of Modena
Viale Campi 213/B
41100 Modena, Italy.

Sonia Bergamaschi
CSITE - CNR
University of Bologna
Viale Risorgimento 2
40136 Bologna, Italy.
sbergamaschi@deis.unibo.it
sonia@dsi.unimo.it

Anish Biswas
Department of Mathematical
and Computer Sciences
University of Tulsa
600 South College Avenue
Tulsa, OK 74104-3189, USA.

Brian Brewington
Thayer School of Engineering
Department of Computer Science
Dartmouth College, Hanover, New
Hampshire 03755, USA.
brian.brewington@dartmouth.edu

George Cybenko
Thayer School of Engineering
Department of Computer Science,
Dartmouth College, Hanover, New
Hampshire 03755, USA.
george.cybenko@dartmouth.edu

Edmund H. Durfee
AI Laboratory
EECS Department
University of Michigan
1101 Beal Avenue
Ann Arbor, MI 48109-2110, USA.
durfee@umich.edu

Sumit Ghosh
Department of Mathematical
and Computer Sciences
University of Tulsa
600 South College Avenue
Tulsa, OK 74104-3189, USA.

Robert Gray
Thayer School of Engineering
Department of Computer Science
Dartmouth College, Hanover, New
Hampshire 03755, USA.
Robert.Gray@dartmouth.edu

Robert Guttman
Software Agents Group
MIT Media Lab
Cambridge MA 02139, USA
guttman@mit.media.edu

Merav Hadad
Department of Mathematics
and Computer Science
Bar-Ilan University
52900 Ramat-Gan, Israel.
hadad@cs.biu.ac.il

Michael N. Huhns
Department of Electrical
and Computer Engineering
University of South Carolina
Columbia, SC 29208, USA.
huhns@sc.edu

Matthias Klusch
Department of Computer Science
Chemnitz University of Technology
Strasse der Nationen 62
09111 Chemnitz, Germany.
klusch@informatik.tu-chemnitz.de

David Kotz
Thayer School of Engineering
Department of Computer Science
Dartmouth College, Hanover, New
Hampshire 03755, USA.
David.Kotz@dartmouth.edu

Sarit Kraus
Department of Mathematics
and Computer Science
Bar-Ilan University
52900 Ramat-Gan, Israel.
sarit@cs.biu.ac.il

Henry Lieberman
Media Laboratory
Massuchesets Institute
of Technology MIT
Cambridge, MA 02139, USA.
lieber@media.mit.edu

Pattie Maes
Software Agents Group
MIT Media Laboratory
Cambridge, MA 02139, USA.
pattie@media.mit.edu

Filippo Menczer
Management Sciences Department
University of Iowa

Iowa City, IA 52245, USA.
filippo-menczer@uiowa.edu

Katsuhiro Moizumi
Thayer School of Engineering
Department of Computer Science
Dartmouth College, Hanover, New
Hampshire 03755, USA.
Katsuhiro.Moizumi@dartmouth.edu

Alvaro E. Monge
Computer Science Department
University of Dayton
Dayton, OH 45469, USA.
monge@cps.udayton.edu

Alexandros Moukas
Software Agents Group
MIT Media Laboratory
Cambridge, MA 02139, USA.
moux@media.mit.edu

Tracy Mullen
AI Laboratory
EECS Department
University of Michigan
1101 Beal Avenue
Ann Arbor, MI 48109-2110, USA.
mullen@umich.edu

Pablo Noriega
Institut d'Investigacio en
Intelligencia Artificial
CSIC-Spanish Scientific
Research Council
Campus UAB, 08193 Bellaterra
Barcelona, Catalonia, Spain.
pablo@iiia.csic.es

Aris Ouksel
University of Illinois at Chicago
Department of Information
and Decision Sciences
Chicago, IL 60607, USA.
aris@uic.edu

Mike Papazoglou
InfoLab
Tilburg University
PO Box 90153, Tilburg
The Netherlands.
M.P.Papazoglou@kub.nl

Sunju Park
AI Laboratory
EECS Department
University of Michigan
1101 Beal Avenue
Ann Arbor, MI 48109-2110, USA.
boxenju@umich.edu

Daniela Rus
Thayer School of Engineering
Department of Computer Science
Dartmouth College, Hanover, New
Hampshire 03755, USA.
Daniela.Rus@dartmouth.edu

Sandip Sen
Department of Mathematical
and Computer Sciences
University of Tulsa
600 South College Avenue
Tulsa, OK 74104-3189, USA.
sandip@kolkata.mcs.utulsa.edu

Onn Shehory
The Robotics Institute
Carnegie Mellon University
5000 Forbes Ave, DH 3311
Pittsburgh, PA 15213, USA.
onn@cs.cmu.edu

Carles Sierra
Institut d'Investigacio en
Intelligencia Artificial
CSIC-Spanish Scientific
Research Council
Campus UAB, 08193 Bellaterra
Barcelona, Catalonia, Spain.
sierra@iiia.csic.es

Munindar P. Singh
Department of Computer Science
North Carolina State University
Raleigh, NC 27695-7534, USA.
singh@ncsu.edu

Katia Sycara
The Robotics Institute
Carnegie Mellon University
5000 Forbes Avenue, DH 3315
Pittsburgh, PA 15213, USA.
katia@cs.cmu.edu

Robert Tolksdorf
Technische Universität Berlin
Fachbereich Informatik, FLP/KIT
Sekr. FR 6–10, Franklinstr. 28/29
D-10587 Berlin, Germany.
tolk@cs.tu-berlin.de

Christian F. Tschudin
Department of Computer Systems
Uppsala University
Box 325, S-751 05 Uppsala, Sweden.
tschudin@docs.uu.se

Willem-Jan van den Heuvel
InfoLab
Tilburg University
PO Box 90153, Tilburg
The Netherlands.
wjheuvel@kub.nl

José M. Vidal
AI Laboratory
EECS Department
University of Michigan
1101 Beal Avenue
Ann Arbor, MI 48109-2110, USA.
jmvidal@umich.edu

Peter Weinstein
AI Laboratory
EECS Department
University of Michigan

1101 Beal Avenue
Ann Arbor, MI 48109-2110, USA.
peterw@umich.edu

Giorgos Zacharia
Software Agents Group
MIT Media Laboratory
Cambridge, MA 02139, USA.
lysi@media.mit.edu

Daniel Dajun Zeng
Graduate School of Industrial
Administration
Carnegie Mellon University
Pittsburgh, PA 15213, USA.
dz25@andrew.cmu.edu

Springer
and the
environment

At Springer we firmly believe that an
international science publisher has a
special obligation to the environment,
and our corporate policies consistently
reflect this conviction.

We also expect our business partners –
paper mills, printers, packaging
manufacturers, etc. – to commit
themselves to using materials and
production processes that do not harm
the environment. The paper in this
book is made from low- or no-chlorine
pulp and is acid free, in conformance
with international standards for paper
permanency.

Springer

Printing: Saladruck, Berlin
Binding: Buchbinderei Lüderitz & Bauer, Berlin